New Directions in Philosophy and Literature

New Directions in Philosophy and Literature

Edited by David Rudrum, Ridvan Askin, and Frida Beckman

EDINBURGH
University Press

Edinburgh University Press is one of the leading university presses in the UK. We publish academic books and journals in our selected subject areas across the humanities and social sciences, combining cutting-edge scholarship with high editorial and production values to produce academic works of lasting importance. For more information visit our website: edinburghuniversitypress.com

© editorial matter and organisation David Rudrum, Ridvan Askin, and Frida Beckman, 2019, 2024
© the chapters their several authors, 2019, 2024

Edinburgh University Press Ltd
13 Infirmary Street, Edinburgh, EH1 1LT

First published in hardback by Edinburgh University Press 2019

Typeset in 11/13 Bembo by
IDSUK (DataConnection) Ltd

A CIP record for this book is available from the British Library

ISBN 978 1 4744 4914 4 (hardback)
ISBN 978 1 4744 4915 1 (paperback)
ISBN 978 1 4744 4916 8 (webready PDF)
ISBN 978 1 4744 4917 5 (epub)

The right of the contributors to be identified as the authors of this work has been asserted in accordance with the Copyright, Designs and Patents Act 1988, and the Copyright and Related Rights Regulations 2003 (SI No. 2498).

Contents

Acknowledgements   viii
Editors' Preface   ix
David Rudrum, Ridvan Askin, and Frida Beckman

General Introduction: Opposition of the Faculties, Philosophy's Literary Impossibility   1
Claire Colebrook

Part I Beyond the Postmodern: Literature, Philosophy, and the Question of the Contemporary

    Editor's Introduction   19
    David Rudrum

1. The Polymodern Condition: A Report on Cluelessness   22
David Rudrum

2. Metamodernism: Period, Structure of Feeling, and Cultural Logic – A Case Study of Contemporary Autofiction   41
Robin van den Akker, Alison Gibbons, and Timotheus Vermeulen

3. The Ends of Metafiction, or, The Romantic Time of Egan's *Goon Squad*   55
Josh Toth

4. Virtually Human: Posthumanism and (Post-)Postmodern Cyberspace in Gary Shteyngart's *Super Sad True Love Story*   74
Nicky Gardiner

Part II Beyond the Subject: Posthuman and Nonhuman Literary Criticism

    Editor's Introduction   99
    Ridvan Askin

5. Hélène Cixous's *So Close*; or, Moving Matters on the Subject   102
Birgit Mara Kaiser

6. Meillassoux, the Critique of Correlationism, and British Romanticism 122
   Evan Gottlieb

7. Fictional Objects Fictional Subjects 138
   Graham Priest

8. On the Death of Meaning 152
   R. Scott Bakker

Part III Beyond the Object: Reading Literature through Actor-Network Theory, Object-Oriented Philosophy, and the New Materialisms

   Editor's Introduction 175
   Ridvan Askin

9. Neither Billiard Ball nor Planet B: Latour's Gaia, Literary Agency, and the Challenge of Writing Geohistory in the Anthropocene Moment 179
   Babette B. Tischleder

10. Three Problems of Formalism: An Object-Oriented View 198
    Graham Harman

11. A Field of Heteronyms and Homonyms: New Materialism, Speculative Fabulation, and Wor(l)ding 215
    Helen Palmer

12. Emerson's Speculative Pragmatism 234
    Ridvan Askin

Part IV Ordinary Language Criticism: Reading Literature through Anglo-American Philosophy

   Editor's Introduction 255
   David Rudrum

13. Two Examples of Ordinary Language Criticism: Reading Conant Reading Rorty Reading Orwell – Interpretation at the Intersection of Philosophy and Literature 258
    Ingeborg Löfgren

14. Stanley Cavell and the Politics of Modernism 279
    R. M. Berry

15. Inferentialist Semantics, Intimationist Aesthetics, and *Walden* 297
    Bryan Vescio

Part V Embodiment as Ethics: Literature and Life in the Anthropocene

   Editor's Introduction 317
   Frida Beckman

16. Living to Tell the Story: Characterisation, Narrative Perspective, and Ethics in Climate Crisis Flood Novels 321
    Astrid Bracke

17. Contemporary Anthropocene Novels: Ian McEwan's *Solar*, Jeanette Winterson's *The Stone Gods*, Margaret Atwood's *Oryx and Crake* and *The Year of the Flood* 338
    Robert P. Marzec

18. The Day of the Dark Precursor: Philosophy, Fiction, and Fabulation at the End of the World – A Fictocritical Guide 361
    Charlie Blake

19. So to Speak 382
    Adrian Parr

Part VI Politics after Discipline: Literature, Life, Control

Editor's Introduction 391
Frida Beckman

20. Literary Study's Biopolitics 394
    Rey Chow

21. We Have Been Paranoid Too Long to Stop Now 410
    Frida Beckman and Charlie Blake

22. Securing Neoliberalism: The Contingencies of Contemporary US Fiction 429
    David Watson

23. Automatic Art, Automated Trading: Finance, Fiction, and Philosophy 450
    Arne De Boever

Notes on Contributors 466
Index 471

Acknowledgements

The editors would like to thank all contributors for their patience, hard work, and commitment to the project. We would also like to thank the Universities of Huddersfield, Basel, and Stockholm for financial support towards the publication of this volume. For her diligent proofreading, our thanks are due to Alexandra Grasso. They are also due to Fiona Sewell, who provided expert copy-editing services. Finally, we would like to thank Carol Macdonald and her team at Edinburgh University Press for their forthcoming and professional guidance and support.

Editors' Preface

David Rudrum, Ridvan Askin, and Frida Beckman

The relationship between literature and philosophy has always been stormy, and has taken on many different forms and inflections over the centuries. But the early years of the twenty-first century have seen it flourish in surprising new ways. The desire to conceptualise what comes 'after' postmodernity has drawn upon the resources of philosophy and literary study alike. Debates around what it is to be posthuman and nonhuman have asked probing questions of the traditional conception of human subjectivity that cannot be answered by either philosophy or literature alone. The return of speculative metaphysics to continental philosophy after an absence of about a century and a half has brought about a range of new ways to think materiality and the nature of the real, as in speculative realism and object-oriented philosophy – a tendency paralleled by developments in literary studies and other fields in the humanities with the emergence of the new materialisms and a renewed focus on objects and things. The necessity for a truly planetary consciousness has transformed the sphere of ethics as it wrestles with conceptions beyond the reach of anthropocentric humanism, epitomised in the concept of the Anthropocene, which has been no less influential on the formation of contemporary ecophilosophy. The intensification of a culture of surveillance and control has given added urgency to biopolitical philosophy, and its salience has been every bit as noteworthy in the study of literature as in that of philosophy. More traditional forms of analytic thought have been enriched as the insights of ordinary language philosophy have engaged in a dialogue with literary criticism, to the benefit of both disciplines. All in all, then, the interface between literature and philosophy has seldom been more varied, more dynamic, more exciting, and more important for our culture.

This collection accordingly surveys a different ambit from any other. Most guides to work on the intersection of philosophy and literature confine themselves to the familiar methods of analytic philosophy, while the kinds of interdisciplinarity surveyed in guides to contemporary literary theory tend to focus on cognitive theory and affect theory, on the politics of gender, sexuality, and race, on popular culture, and on narrative theory. This is the first attempt to map out the many exciting ways in which new developments in twenty-first-century philosophy are entering into dialogue with the study of literature, and the profound consequences of this interaction for questions of ethics, politics, subjectivity, materiality, reality, and the nature of the contemporary itself.

In order to do so, we have divided the book into six sections, preceded by a general and orientational introduction written by Claire Colebrook, one of the world's foremost authorities in the field. Part of our intention in designing the volume in this way was to break down the term 'philosophy' – arguably a 'catch-all' term so broad as to risk becoming unwieldy – into more focused areas of discussion, which draw on, but do not just replicate, the traditional formations of philosophy's conventional sub-disciplines. Following Colebrook's introduction, which clears the ground by surveying the parallel but fraught development of philosophy and literature in the twentieth century from the vantage point of the twenty-first, the first section deals with the question of the aftermath of postmodernity; the second with challenges to subjectivity posed by posthuman and speculative thought, in both their continental and analytic guises; the third with reconceiving the nature of the (literary) object in the light of actor-network theory, object-oriented philosophy, and the new materialisms; the fourth with the different approach to the linguistic called for in ordinary language criticism; the fifth with the task of thinking of alternative models of ethics to the anthropocentric; and the sixth with new developments in political and biopolitical philosophy. To provide further guidance, each section is prefaced by a short editorial introduction.

Overall, the editors hope that the collection succeeds in both acknowledging and encouraging new ways of configuring the relationships between literature and philosophy, broadly conceived.

Huddersfield, Basel, and Stockholm, December 2018

General Introduction: Opposition of the Faculties, Philosophy's Literary Impossibility

Claire Colebrook

On or about 1919 something happened to the relationship between literature and philosophy. T. S. Eliot published 'Literature and the Individual Talent', and at one and the same time added to the long debate about literary value and how poetry works – a conversation going back at least as far as Aristotle's *Poetics* – and brought to the fore the theoretical problem of philosophy and literature. Eliot insisted that the value of a work lay in the extent to which it transformed 'tradition', where tradition was something like a virtual whole of all literary works, and where these literary works in turn took personal feelings and somehow rendered them impersonal, setting them apart – within time – for all time (Eliot 1930). Eliot's conception of poetry as a distinct mode of generating a dynamic, virtual, and trans-temporal whole emerged alongside a whole series of literary and philosophical endeavours that sought to establish a certain purity of thought, by distinguishing philosophical from literary formality. The year 1910 saw the publication of the first volume of Bertrand Russell and Alfred North Whitehead's *Principia Mathematica*, setting itself the task of providing a logical foundation for mathematics, and – however problematically – marking out a new mode of philosophy in which questions would be formal and analytic, rather than metaphysical. Edmund Husserl would also try to provide a ground for logic, shifting this foundation from a psychological to a transcendental basis in his second edition of the two-volume *Logical Investigations* published in 1913 and 1921. As analytic philosophy was being forged by steering away from grand metaphysical and speculative accounts of existence towards philosophy as a rigorous science; literary criticism was moving away from questions of taste and biography towards its own criteria of timelessness. In both cases an attention to the text itself would open out to a question of the truth that precedes and exceeds the formal system of inscription. Despite this convergence on questions of rigour, two quite different and divergent conceptions of transcendental criteria were at work. Philosophy would focus on logical purity, to the point where Gottlob Frege would refer to a 'third realm' of truth for mathematics (Dummett 1993: 24). Husserl would seek to provide a transcendental foundation for philosophy irreducible to the psyche or history, while literary ideals would require capturing the singularity of the moment. In 'Philosophy as a Rigorous Science', Husserl insists on a revolution in philosophical thought that would nevertheless draw on centuries of the ideal of philosophy:

> the highest interests of human culture demand the development of a rigorously scientific philosophy; consequently, if a philosophical revolution in our times is to be justified, it must without fail be animated by the purpose of laying a new foundation for philosophy in the sense of a strict science. (Husserl 1965: 78)

Virginia Woolf, in turn, writing on E. M. Forster, described the passage from the particular to the infinite in the following words: 'A room is to him a room, a writing table a writing table, and a waste-paper basket a waste-paper basket. At the same time, the paraphernalia of reality have at certain moments to become the veil through which we see infinity' (Woolf 1994a: 495). In so doing she anticipated the way Gilles Deleuze and Félix Guattari would come to talk about art in general:

> the artist turns his or her attention to the microscopic, to crystals, molecules, atoms, and particles, not for scientific conformity, but for movement, for nothing but immanent movement; the artist tells him- or herself that this world has had different aspects, will have still others, and that there are already others on other planets; finally, the artist opens up to the Cosmos in order to harness forces in a 'work' (without which the opening on to the Cosmos would only be a reverie incapable of enlarging the limits of the earth); this work requires very simple, pure, almost childish means, but also the forces of a people, which is what is still lacking. (Deleuze and Guattari 1987: 337)

While analytic philosophy strove to be purely formal, with mathematics and logic providing the ideals for proper inquiry, continental philosophy took a different path towards truth and rigour, while nevertheless insisting that logic should not simply be accepted but should have a secure foundation. Grounding not only turned attention away from systems towards their genesis, it also had a critical effect of marking out differences. As Henri Bergson, and Deleuze after him, would note: what we experience may always be a mixture – never a pure concept or a simple sensation – but we can nevertheless intuit or think about the pure forces or potentials from which systems are composed (Deleuze 1991: 112). Mathematics may always require some inscriptive and material condition, but the truths of math transcend conditions of genesis. Analytic philosophy would think of science as a stripping away of metaphysical assumptions, relying on systemic or pragmatic analysis, while continental philosophy would increasingly turn to the texts from which norms, assumptions, and structures had emerged; in either case philosophy took the form of re-grounding. Husserl's *Cartesian Meditations* argued that Descartes had not been radical enough in his doubt, still allowing the assumption of the cogito to act as an unexamined presupposition, 'rescuing a little *tag-end* of the world' (Husserl 1973: 24). Woolf, like Husserl, had criticised the naturalism that would begin with a part of the world and not intuit the genesis of the world:

Look within and life, it seems, is very far from being 'like this'. Examine for a moment an ordinary mind on an ordinary day. The mind receives a myriad impressions – trivial, fantastic, evanescent, or engraved with the sharpness of steel. From all sides they come, an incessant shower of innumerable atoms; and as they fall, as they shape themselves into the life of Monday or Tuesday, the accent falls differently from of old; the moment of importance came not here but there; so that, if a writer were a free man and not a slave, if he could write what he chose, not what he must, if he could base his work upon his own feeling and not upon convention, there would be no plot, no comedy, no tragedy, no love interest or catastrophe in the accepted style, and perhaps not a single button sewn on as the Bond Street tailors would have it. Life is not a series of gig lamps symmetrically arranged; life is a luminous halo, a semi-transparent envelope surrounding us from the beginning of consciousness to the end. (Woolf 1994b: 160)

For Woolf, it was the ordinary and everyday that would open out to the eternal, and in different ways it was the turn back to everydayness – away from grand assumptions and speculations – that opened both philosophy and literature to a new or untimely timelessness. Husserl also insisted that if one examined the natural attitude – our simple experience of everyday 'thereness' – we would be compelled to acknowledge a new realm of transcendental subjectivity. In a quite different manner, Ludwig Wittgenstein would turn to everyday language practices and discover a complexity and wondrous dexterity that could not be captured by the rigid schemes of metaphysics. This trend would continue into the twentieth century with writers like Stanley Cavell noticing the ways in which the turn back to everyday simplicity was ultimately a liberation of thought, was both a liberation from the generality of concepts and an intuition of commonality:

And when Wittgenstein finds the task of philosophy to be the bringing of our words back to (everyday) life, he in effect discerns two grades of quotation, imitation, repetition. In one we imitatively declare our uniqueness (the theme of skepticism); in the other, we originally declare our commonness (the theme of acknowledgment). (Individuality, always to be found, is always at the risk of loss.) What you might call philosophy can be in service of either possibility; hence philosophy is never at peace with itself. (Cavell 1988: 132)

Not only is philosophy never at peace with itself, philosophy's ongoing internal tension is bound up with its ongoing difference and complicity with literature. This is primarily because both literature and philosophy are bound up with a system of language that both enterprises seek to save from everyday banality for the sake of everyday richness.

For both literature and philosophy, foundations are secured through some process of retrieval, away from sedimented and accepted systems towards things themselves, from which a genuine (rather than received) wisdom would emerge. Martin

Heidegger's 'destruction' would find truth not in the way statements matched the world but rather in the very genesis of language (Heidegger 2010: 19). It was this problem of genesis (Derrida 2011), or the coming into being of the transcendent from the immanent, that would mark modernism, modern theory, philosophy, and deconstruction. Heidegger was the most philosophical of thinkers in demanding that the question of being be renewed but without the usual language of ontology and metaphysics, at the same time as he also raised the stakes for literature by arguing that it is the emerging moment of language that unfolds a world that can then be the subject of metaphysical inquiry. It was by heightening the demands of philosophical truth that literature not only acquired its own unique domain, but also seemed to haunt philosophy as its hidden or repressed condition.

At the most extreme, one might think of late twentieth-century French thought's radical separation of philosophy and literature, either with Derrida's insistence on metaphysics' demand for presence that is haunted by the letter, or Deleuze and Guattari's distinction between philosophy's concepts and art's affects and percepts, or Alain Badiou's distinction between the event of the poem and philosophy, as the discourse that negotiates such events. It is true that there are many thinkers for whom this event of diremption either did not happen or was spectacularly disastrous. Jürgen Habermas diagnosed the current crisis of master thinkers by looking back to Nietzsche, for whom truth was more aesthetic than communicative, and saw all those who followed in his wake as missing the extent to which philosophical reflection worked alongside literature's capacity to disclose the world (Habermas 1990). Martha Nussbaum felt that philosophical strictness and rigour could be tempered by the sympathy entrepreneurs of literature (Nussbaum 2001). There are journals, university courses, and networks devoted to philosophy and literature, as though the two could be coupled without altering the integrity of either discipline. If one is not too strict with one's definitions, literature and philosophy can be paired and compared like any other two disciplines. Yet it is precisely at the moments of seemingly maximal harmony that one might also lose sight of any sense of what might be generated from discord. It is almost certainly the case when one is dealing with philosophy and literature that – to quote William Blake – 'opposition ... is true friendship'. (Has *Huckleberry Finn* been enriched as a result of all the analytic philosophy articles using Huck's apparent 'freeing' of Jim as a moral case study? Has philosophy benefited from taking scenes in novels and treating them as exercises in character analysis?) If, for example, we take on Richard Rorty's suggestion of thinking of philosophy as a 'kind of writing' (Rorty 1982), we fail to understand why some of the most difficult and resistant philosophical and literary writing takes the form that it does, especially the writing of the twentieth and twenty-first centuries. If all philosophical and literary texts do is engage in conversation, each trying to reconfigure the possibilities of conversation, then why have the conflicts regarding the border between philosophy and literature been so provocative and impassioned? I would suggest that rather than philosophy and literature being collapsed into a common domain of conversation, it is their intense, impossible, but problematic division that explains and enriches today's terrain of literature and philosophy, and the odd hybrid that is 'theory', as well as today's current state of post-theory.

What was much later to become known as 'theory' emerged from a conflict among faculties that it may have been possible to trace back to Plato's dismissal of poetic simulacra, but which only came to the fore once the genealogy of literature's distinction from philosophy enabled a new way of thinking about life and language. If philosophy and literature had been in constant tension, it was only with those anti-philosophers (such as Nietzsche) that the relation between philosophical truth and literary simulation became scandalous. Michel Foucault follows Nietzsche in seeing Plato's 'routing of the Sophists' as an inaugural moment in which something like truth as such is set apart from the force of language, generating an ideal of pure formality that will exceed and transcend the force of any speech act:

> The day dawned when truth moved over from the ritualised act – potent and just – of enunciation to settle on what was enunciated itself: its meaning, its form, its object and its relation to what it referred to. A division emerged between Hesiod and Plato, separating true discourse from false; it was a new division for, henceforth, true discourse was no longer considered precious and desirable, since it had ceased to be discourse linked to the exercise of power. And so the Sophists were routed. (Foucault 1972: 218)

It is Nietzsche's and Foucault's insistence on this historically distant separation, rather than anything in Plato as such, that becomes significant for the impossible relation between literature and philosophy in the twentieth century. It is only with claims like Nietzsche's and Foucault's – that truth is an army of metaphors, or that language bears its own 'shining' – that the relation between philosophy and literature is no longer that of two disciplines but instead a problem internal to philosophy and to the possibility of thought. This is as true of Badiou's notion of the poem as a truth procedure (Badiou 2008: 23) as it is of Derrida's conception of literature as the right to 'say anything' (Derrida 1992: 34), and of Julia Kristeva's definition of 'poetic language' as that which frees thought from the logical conditions of the symbolic order (Kristeva 1984). In all these cases, what is meant by 'poetry' is not what is contained in the *Norton Anthology*, but a potential for thinking that resides within and alongside philosophical thought. It is this conception of the poetic – going back to Heidegger's *poiesis* as a creation that stands apart – that is at the heart of those philosophical-literary hybrid texts of 'theory', which are only possible because philosophy and literature are no longer so easily coupled.

One might chart a quick, provisional, and largely heuristic genealogy: literature as a discipline begins in the early twentieth century (Baldick 1983), differing from both the literary criticism that had been found in magazine culture going back to the eighteenth century, and the uses and references to literature that philosophers had made when discussing poetry, rhetoric, the imagination, or the sublime. If Joseph Addison and Richard Steele had discussed John Milton in *The Spectator*, and claimed that his sublimity was comparable to the ancients, they did not yet establish criticism, judgement, and taste as a distinct discipline. Discussing the value of literature was not yet something distinct from philosophy; it was either an occasional strand of conversation in the emerging modern public sphere, or took the form of an occasional aside within the discourses of philosophy. Like Plato and Cicero before him, Immanuel Kant would mention the poets, but merely as one of philosophy's many sources of examples. If Kant also, like Plato and the philosophical tradition before him, had reason to distrust the simulacra of the poets, he still presented philosophy as the necessary arbiter of the proper place or function of the imagination. Despite Kant's typically eighteenth-century assumption that the works of the imagination were philosophy's objects of study, rather than equal or competing partners, he nevertheless established a mode of philosophy – a uniquely modern mode – that would make something like literature as such possible. When Kant writes his *Critique of Pure Reason*, he at one and the same time establishes the rigour and foundation of philosophy and also reins in philosophy's possible objects of knowledge. Being critical of pure reason was possible and necessary to the task of enlightenment and rigour: while reason in its pure mode is capable of thinking of the infinite, of God, and of freedom, no such 'objects' could ever be experienced or known:

> Here I content myself with defining theoretical cognition as that through which I cognize **what exists**, and practical cognition as that through which I represent **what ought to exist**. According to this, the theoretical use of reason is that through which I cognize *a priori* (as necessary) that something is; but the practical use is that through which it is cognized *a priori* what ought to happen. (Kant 1998: A633/B661)

Kant marks a distinction between theoretical and practical tasks of reason: theoretical uses of reason concern what we know, or what can be given to us through experience. One could not, therefore, have a legitimate dispute regarding the nature of God, or the reality of human freedom; these ideas can be thought but not known. (At around the same time Blake is making a similar argument: God is not an object of knowledge, and what can be imagined is not reducible to a variant of what can be known (Blake 1988: 33).) For many writers of the Enlightenment, philosophy needs to be marked off from poetic or mystical flights of imagination that would claim to intuit God or the absolute. For Kant, what is important is not simply limiting theoretical knowledge to that which can be known and experienced through concepts, but also then allowing reason's other capacities of desire and reflection to operate practically. The ideas of freedom, God, and the infinite to which pure reason is naturally drawn cannot be the objects of theoretical knowledge. Theory, in this Kantian moment of delimiting and elevating philosophical reason, has explicitly to do with what we can legitimately claim about the world that we experience. The world can only be known insofar as it is given; what can be thought, however, has practical but not theoretical legitimacy. Theoretical knowledge is achieved when we are able to conceptualise the world; without the content that experience offers, the forms of thought on their own cannot offer knowledge. Once we recognise this limit of theoretical knowledge – and it is philosophy's task to do so – this opens up the possibility of practical reason. Even if we cannot have knowledge of God, the infinite, or freedom, the possibility to think and act as if we were free members of the kingdom of ends generates an elevated subjectivity. Once philosophy is no longer – as it had been prior to the eighteenth century – a broad domain that would include what today we think of as the natural sciences, poetics, theology, mysticism, and history, it becomes feasible to form a conception of humanity in which quite distinct modes of thought become possible, and necessary. *Theoretical* knowledge is confined to what we can experience. *Practically* we can act as if we were not bound by the natural laws that govern the causal order. *Reflectively*, both in our considerations of how science is possible and in terms of how we think about art, we can concede that we never experience anything like the causal order of nature, or the progress of morality, or anything objectively beautiful, but we can (and must) perceive nature *as if* it were in accord with laws that others would also be able to discern, just as we must view art objects and the beauty of nature as if they were also perceivable as harmonious for any subject whatsoever.

This demarcation of various modes of reason, with theoretical knowledge being confined to what can be experienced, is – though Kantian – not confined to Kant's thought alone. Instead, we might think of Kant as articulating a problem of theory, philosophy, and the imagination that is broadly explored in the eighteenth century and that allows for the convergence and radical separation of literature and philosophy.

Historians of philosophy have often lamented the extent to which this supposedly modern distinction between what we can experience (or the way the world is) and what we can desire (or what ought to be the case) has created a legitimation crisis, or an impossibility for ethical thought. Alasdair MacIntyre blames the Enlightenment for separating moral judgements from the lived world, insisting that the world we live in and our own personhood come into being through imagining ourselves in terms of an ongoing narrative (MacIntyre 1981). Rorty also sees the elevation of philosophy and its distinction from the arts of narration as a catastrophe that lingered well into the late twentieth century (Rorty 1979). Habermas, who decades ago lamented the fact that master thinkers had fallen on hard times, traces today's paralysing state of philosophy to the fact that claims for reason were separated from the domain of lived practice, allowing reason to be emptied of its grounding in the lifeworld (Habermas 1976). Nussbaum, aiming to repair the divide, asks that philosophers look to literature to recognise the sympathy entrepreneurs who enable the exploration of affect in our moral reasoning (Nussbaum 2001: 314). Bruno Latour does not so much lament the separation of reason from the lifeworld as deny that such a divorce ever took place; the most detached, objective, and pure modes of thinking were the outcomes of complex compositions among people, things, and forces (Latour 1993).

This separation of reason from desire, of philosophy from the imagination, or pure thought and abstraction from the domain of narrative and poetics, though most apparent in Kant, marks an entire field of what increasingly comes to be known as literature. When Milton wrote *Paradise Lost* his task as an epic poet sat alongside his writings on government, history, censorship, and divorce. Even a writer as late as Jean-Jacques Rousseau produced novels, philosophy, and an opera. But it is not long after Rousseau that poets start to claim a special place for the imagination that will heal the poverty of reason, while philosophers will increasingly seek to set philosophy on a rigorous or scientific footing. The separation of reason from the imagination can be at one and the same time lamented, demanded, deemed to be impossible yet desirable, and impossible but necessary. It is this last imperative – that the separation of reason is necessary but impossible – that characterises what comes to be known as theory, and which emerges from the modern non-relation between philosophy and literature. To make sense of this, it is perhaps best to think of the two thinkers in the twentieth century who were philosophers while also shifting the domain of philosophy towards 'theory'.

Both Derrida and Deleuze, despite claims from anti-theory theorists that they had killed truth and rigour, actually heightened the stakes for philosophy. In his debate with John Searle, Derrida had insisted that one cannot reduce the meaning of concepts to their contextual use (Derrida 1977), just as in his earlier work he had insisted that inscriptive systems such as geometry and mathematics cannot be explained away by referring to their cultural or historical emergence (Derrida 1978b). It is by insisting on the idea of pure truth – that we cannot will away the demand for a truth that insists and persists across contexts – that Derrida forges deconstruction:

> pure truth is missed in its meaning as soon as one attempts . . . to account for it from within a determined historical totality, that is, from within a factual totality, a finite totality all of whose manifestations and cultural productions are structurally solidary and coherent, and are all regulated by the same function, by the same finite unity of a total subjectivity. This meaning of truth, or of the pretension to truth, is the requirement of an absolute, infinite omni-temporality and universality, without limits of any kind. (Derrida 1978b: 200)

It is only by taking the philosophical requirement for pure reason so seriously that deconstruction also generates the impossibility of anything that might reach the purity and abstraction of metaphysics. In a quite different manner Deleuze will devote his corpus to the difference between philosophical and literary modes of thought, where the philosopher creates concepts that reorient the plane of possible problems, while the great writers forge a minor literature that is no longer at home in the communicative ease of language. In so doing, the coupling of philosophy and literature is no longer the encounter between two disciplines – in the way that one might have a philosophy of sport, food, race, or climate change, or in the way one might look at literature's engagement with history, medicine, and oceanography. Rather, philosophy harbours within its very possibility something like the expulsion or internal difference of literature. Literature, in turn, can never be reduced to the simply fictive: it cannot be reduced to an expression of ideas or even a thought experiment that might then be available for philosophical reflection. For Deleuze and Guattari, there is a 'becoming' that only literature and art bring to the fore, but that is a virtual potential of all life. There are only the stable beings that texts and persons can know and describe because there has already been a composition, inscription, and tracing out of relatively stable forms: 'A matter-content having only degrees of intensity, resistance, conductivity, heating, stretching, speed, or tardiness; and a function-expression having only "tensors", as in a system of mathematical, or musical, writing. Writing now functions on the same level as the real, and the real materially writes' (Deleuze and Guattari 1987: 141). As with Derrida, but in different ways, the tracings and inscriptive processes that we tend to consign to literature alone are, for Deleuze and Guattari, conditions for life as such. What literary texts do is take that inscriptive process beyond the closed forms it has enabled, freeing inscription from the human, such that all writing is a 'becoming-animal'. In *A Thousand Plateaus* Deleuze and Guattari will describe the ways in which stable bodies emerge through the repetition and variation of traits, as though life itself were theme and variation, with life becoming ever more complex through the taking up of traits that are not of one's own kind. Philosophy, for Deleuze, takes a quite different path in its creation of problems and concepts; but in both art and philosophy, an inscription that is embedded in all life achieves a distinction that allows for the detachment of affects and perceptions from the lived (Deleuze and Guattari 1994). For Derrida, the inscription of voices within the literary text allows for meaning to be articulated without attribution, such that literature is the right to say anything; the literary text is not an allegory or double of philosophical sense but something like a scene of writing, a confrontation with the tracings, markings, and figures that make sense possible. Rather than collapsing literature into philosophy or vice versa, Derrida insists that both possibilities haunt each other.

The literary text at its height – in modernist writers like James Joyce and Stéphane Mallarmé – seeks to capture writing as such, as though it might be freed from the empty abstractions of philosophy and be the pure materiality of the word; but this very attempt to be text as such relies upon some general concept or idea of inscription, such that the great modernist work would encompass all the voices of the world. Deleuze and Guattari express this thought in their take on what one might call modernism's idea of unity regained:

> The abortionists of unity are indeed angel makers, *doctores angelici*, because they affirm a properly angelic and superior unity. Joyce's words, accurately described as having 'multiple roots', shatter the linear unity of the word, even of language, only to posit a cyclic unity of the sentence, text, or knowledge. (Deleuze and Guattari 1987: 6)

Derrida, in turn, captures it in terms of relativity:

> Husserl's project, as the transcendental 'parallel' to Joyce's, knows the same relativity. Joyce's project, which also proceeded from a certain anti-historicism and a will 'to awake' from the 'nightmare' of 'history', a will to master that nightmare in a total and present resumption, could only succeed by allotting its share to univocity, whether it might draw from a given univocity or try to produce another. Otherwise, the very text of its repetition would have been unintelligible; at least it would have remained so forever and for everyone. Likewise, Husserl had to admit an irreducible, enriching, and always renascent equivocity into pure historicity. (Derrida 1978a: 103)

Derrida's philosophy is a philosophy of impossibility: it insists that we cannot abandon the philosophical ideals and ideas of justice, truth, democracy, friendship, and forgiveness, but also notes that any articulation of those concepts is bound up with a singular inscriptive dimension that precludes any true purity or universality. But reducing the world to so many texts or voices has its own unavoidably transcendental dimensions; meaning and truth emerge from inscription but cannot be reduced to inscription. There is no such thing as pure reason, for philosophy cannot reduce the inscriptive, figural, and material means through which it expresses itself. Nor is there such a thing as pure text: whatever is inscribed can be read as the sign of an intention, event, or sense.

What is left, then, is the predicament of *theory*: on the one hand concepts have a force that allows them to operate beyond any particular intention, context, or text; on the other hand, concepts are never articulated in general, but are always given in singular texts. Philosophy and literature are two sides of the predicament of theory. When Kant aimed to ground philosophy by insisting on the rigours of theoretical knowledge – that we can only have legitimate disputes about what we experience and conceptualise – he precluded flights into mysticism, theological dogmatism, and the tyranny of any single individual claiming moral privilege or expertise, but he also exemplified the modern condition of what has come to be known as 'theory' or what Paul de Man referred to as the problem of aesthetic ideology (de Man 1996). A text is, ultimately, a series of material traces, and yet is nevertheless read as a sign of a meaning or sense. A purely literary reading would be radically material, but also impossible: there is no such thing as a pure text, for even our encounter with a handwritten manuscript prompts us to see the marks as repetitions of letters, words, and concepts. There is no such thing as pure sense, for even the texts of logic rely on inscriptive systems – despite constituting a sense and truth that would remain in the imagined absence of inscription. This theoretical predicament is confined neither to Derrida's post-Kantianism, nor to twentieth-century French thought.

One unremarkable way of thinking about romanticism in general is to see it as a similarly dynamic oscillation between the problem of the purity and ideality of universals and the claim of what Blake referred to as 'minute particulars' – the same

Blake who insisted on seeing eternity in a grain of sand. Modernism also recognises that the only escape from the same dull round of an increasingly mechanised existence is the claim of the universal, and yet universality is only given when one breaks through the rigidity of conceptual thinking. One might think here of Woolf's attempt to capture the moment, to saturate every atom, to liberate language from communication in order to follow the flow of consciousness, and yet at the same time find something like the purity of colour as such, light as such, or line as such. Indeed, it is perhaps not surprising that literature after Kant becomes ever more theoretical – hovering between breaking through conceptual formations to capture singularity and rejecting the banality of day-to-day particulars to forge a universal. This is perhaps why Deleuze and Guattari trace their account of modern art in just these terms. In one of the later plateaus of *A Thousand Plateaus*, '1837: Of the Refrain', they do not chart a straight line from the intensive difference of chaos, where one might intuit ever smaller and more acute distinctions, to the grasp of universals in modern art. Rather, all life follows the problem that reaches its clearest articulation in modernism. All life is formed through the creation of refrains, where qualities form repeatable and variable patterns. The ongoing repetition, with variation, is what allows the difference of intensities to be felt, along with the universality of forms. Deleuze and Guattari see in the refrains of life the capacity at one and the same time to be utterly singular and yet – in that very singularity – to reach a cosmic level such that one might hear the forces from which the cosmos is composed:

> At infinity, these refrains must rejoin the songs of the Molecules, the newborn wailing of the fundamental Elements, as Millikan put it. They cease to be terrestrial, becoming cosmic: when the religious Nome blooms and dissolves in a molecular pantheist Cosmos, when the singing of the birds is replaced by combinations of water, wind, clouds, and fog. (Deleuze and Guattari 1987: 327)

The history of life as it is recounted in *A Thousand Plateaus* might be thought of as a universal history written from the threshold point or problem of modern theory. The problem articulated in Kant (and in classicism and romanticism) comes to the fore in the relation between philosophy's striving for concepts and modern literature's striving for what Foucault will refer to as language's own shining (Foucault 1970). But this problem, once recognised and intensified in a high modernism that will try to capture something like colour as such, light as such, line as such – and thereby open up to the cosmos – is a problem not of art, but of life. How does each aspect of life at one and the same time have some grasp of the infinite, while also remaining the minute particular that it is? Deleuze describes this in terms of Gottfried Wilhelm Leibniz's monadology: every aspect of the world expresses the infinite, and therefore is nothing more than its point of view on the whole; and the whole is nothing more than all the perspectives that express the infinite in their own way (Deleuze 1993). The history of art in modernity is therefore the history of the problem of theory, of the universality of philosophy, and the grasp of singularities in art.

We do not have to confine ourselves to Kant to recognise that pure reason, or a reason that is not subject to the vagaries of affect, becomes increasingly problematic in the history of philosophy, literature, and politics. How else might one read Theodor Adorno's *Aesthetic Theory*, in which modernism is not simply another movement in art but the result of a history of philosophy where the demand for conceptual rigour sits alongside the silencing of the world's complexity and suffering? The modern artwork is not an object that can be explained in terms of aesthetic delight, authorial intention, or historical context, but requires theory. Artworks are attempts to capture the universal that has been covered over by day-to-day banality, while also articulating the singular differences that have been negated in the conceptual formalisation of the world. Adorno's work is typical of the broader problem of theory that marks the twentieth century. Either one confines philosophy to purely formal problems of logic, or one starts to negotiate the relation between the formality of concepts and the differential intensity of existence. Well before Derrida's deconstruction, Luce Irigaray's 'sensible transcendental', and Deleuze and Guattari's rhizomatics, philosophers like Bergson defined the problem of philosophy's relation to the world not as a disciplinary problem but as a problem of life and art. To live is to negotiate some ongoing sameness, some sense of the form of the world that allows for day-to-day recognition, but that same enabling power of sameness is also an ongoing deadening of life. Formalism is anything but a purely academic problem, and might be thought of more broadly as the relation between the forms we possess to make sense of the world, and then life's and experience's ongoing challenge to those forms. In stark disciplinary terms one might think of this in two ways, either through philosophy's attempt to capture form as such – the truth of form – or through literature's ongoing deformation or estrangement of forms. It is in the early twentieth century that the modern rift between literature and philosophy reaches its zenith and is also placed under maximum duress. Part philosophy, part universal history, part literary analysis, Max Horkheimer and Adorno's *Dialectic of Enlightenment* paves the way for a series of works that will insist that modern philosophy's claim of rational purity is utopian in its demand for something more than the demands of life, and yet violent in its occlusion of the singular differences of existence. In very different and incompatible ways one might think of Derrida's deconstruction, Irigaray's sensible transcendental, Deleuze and Guattari's claim for expressive matters, or Frantz Fanon's dialectic of recognition as insisting upon the force of that which transcends the contingency of particulars, while nevertheless recognising the blindness and violence of conceptual generality. The problem of philosophy as the task of the universal cannot repress the force of the literary, or the inscriptive condition for the emergence of any concept.

The twentieth century increasingly becomes the century of theory, which will grant poetry a power to express the eternal but only by giving force to what begins as the singularity of affect. Where romanticism had already worked through the problem of the sublime, or the infinite's withdrawal given through the experience of finitude, modernism would add to this an even stronger sense of the inscriptive, archival, and material condition in which this impossibility is played out. Thus, alongside Eliot's work in literature we get Husserl's call to take philosophy back to the 'things themselves' of experience, to chart the genesis of truth and universality. Not surprisingly, those later texts of high theory – Derrida's deconstruction, and Deleuze and Guattari's distinction between philosophy's creation of concepts and art's creation of affects – will be a reprise of these early twentieth-century literary-philosophical problems. Like Husserl, but in a more radical manner, Derrida recognised that truth could not be reduced to historical or cultural contexts, even if truth necessarily has its genesis and maintenance in some inscriptive system. Like T. S. Eliot and European modernists, Deleuze saw every artwork as capturing a fragment of the eternal, within time, but for all time. The problem of theory that for Kant had required the strict partition of reason into its distinct faculties, allowing for a theoretical knowledge of the world, and a practical imperative to act as if one's reason could legislate for all, becomes the twentieth century's defining problem. Philosophy either takes the form it does in continental philosophy, constantly negotiating its relation to inscription, or it pares itself down – as in analytic philosophy – focusing less on meaning and more on the formal problems of logic.

Twentieth-century philosophy in the Kantian tradition forms what comes to be known as theory, a part-philosophical, part-literary enterprise that takes seriously Kant's distinction between pure and practical reason. For Kant, what we can think about but not know allows us to act as if we were members of the kingdom of ends, as if we were not bound up with the causality and mechanism of the world. Here it is desire or what can be imagined as brought into being that is essential for morality, allowing our practical world – or status as human subjects rather than objects – to be tied directly to the power to imagine what is not actual. It is the negation of the world as it is, or desire's capacity to imagine oneself as other than the same dull round of the world, that at once ties Kant's thought to modern liberalism's conception of literature as the creative sphere of imaginative exploration, to Derrida's notion that literature is the right to say anything, to Rorty's ideal of philosophy as a kind of writing, and to Badiou's insistence on the subject, not as a part of the world but as a break with the world. Literature, in this tradition, is not the reflection of the world, but a positive capacity to generate something other than the world. The desire of the literary text is not a wish fulfilment, but a marking out of a space, voice, or figure that is not of this world.

From Kant to the present, in different and divergent ways, philosophy and literature become inextricably intertwined precisely through their radical separation. If philosophy concerns itself with the formal conditions for thought, literature becomes a medium not simply – as it was for Kant – for a reflective judgement that allows us to feel the harmony of our forming powers, but for a more radical power to deform and recreate the world. For Kant, the very means through which we know the world – the ways in which we experience a causal and coherent world – allow us to imagine first causes, or objects without a cause, such as God or freedom. The ordering, communicative, and theoretical power of reason can (and, for Kant, must) extend beyond this world. For Kant, the power to think but not know ideas of freedom and the infinite allowed for morality, with art forming merely the means through which we recognise our capacity as subjects. For Kant one could solve the problem of theory by creating strict tasks for reason – separating what we can know from a moral world that we can imagine. But this separation ultimately generated an ongoing series of crossings, contaminations, traversals, and cross-fertilisations. As Derrida's debate with Searle would prove, the more insistent one is about the rigours and heights of philosophy, the more one is forced to confront the problem of literature. Searle had argued that one can use concepts and be confident of their meaning because of the context in which they are used. Derrida replied that a concept only works if it can be employed across contexts. Derrida's strict sense of the concept is therefore more stringently philosophical than Searle's reliance on day-to-day usage. This commitment to concepts places ever more inscriptive pressure on the limits of philosophy, its purity and universality always disturbed by the singularity of its articulations. As I have already noted, Deleuze and Guattari also mark out the in-principle difference between philosophy (as creation of concepts) and art (as the creation of affects and percepts). A concept is not what is given through opinion or day-to-day communication, but is an orientation formed in relation to other concepts, allowing for new formations of thought to emerge. The affects and percepts of art are not the effects of the reception of artworks (not feelings or how the artwork is lived) but rather what can be felt or can be seen by any subject whatever. One might think of concepts, then, as having a quite different temporality, so that all the philosophical texts written about justice, democracy, or virtue occur in time but nevertheless discuss something irreducible to any one time. Each philosopher who creates a genuine concept recreates the entire plane of possible philosophical events. Similarly, the affects and percepts of art occur when 'expressive matters' appear as if for all time, as though one could see the red on the canvas, the melancholy captured by the tone of the cello, or the claustrophobia marked out by the description of an office space, as taking a fragment in time in order to open to a cosmos from which all these singularities entered into composition to generate the whole. For both Derrida and Deleuze, in very different ways, it is the difference between philosophy and literature that demands their constant encounter. One cannot avoid the universal strivings of thought, but any attempt to articulate universals requires some specific and singular inscription. Philosophy is inevitably caught up with the force of literature.

Bibliography

Adorno, Theodor (2004), *Aesthetic Theory*, Robert Hullot-Kentor (trans.), London: Continuum.
Badiou, Alain (2008), *Conditions*, Steven Corcoran (trans.), London: Continuum.
Baldick, Chris (1983), *The Social Mission of English Criticism, 1848–1932*, Oxford: Clarendon Press.
Blake, William (1988), 'The Marriage of Heaven and Hell', in David Erdman (ed.), *The Complete Poetry and Prose of William Blake*, New York: Anchor, pp. 33–44.

Cavell, Stanley (1988), *In Quest of the Ordinary: Lines of Skepticism and Romanticism*, Chicago: University of Chicago Press.
de Man, Paul (1996), *Aesthetic Ideology*, Andrzej Warminski (ed.), Minneapolis: University of Minnesota Press.
Deleuze, Gilles (1991), *Bergsonism*, Hugh Tomlinson and Barbara Habberjam (trans.), New York: Zone Books.
Deleuze, Gilles (1993), *The Fold: Leibniz and the Baroque*, Tom Conley (trans.), Minneapolis: University of Minnesota Press.
Deleuze, Gilles and Félix Guattari (1987), *A Thousand Plateaus: Capitalism and Schizophrenia*, Brian Massumi (trans.), Minneapolis: University of Minnesota Press.
Deleuze, Gilles and Félix Guattari (1994), *What Is Philosophy?*, Hugh Tomlinson and Graham Burchell (trans.), London: Verso.Derrida, Jacques (1977), *Limited Inc: Abc . . .*, Samuel Weber (trans.), Baltimore: Johns Hopkins University Press.
Derrida, Jacques (1978a), *Edmund Husserl's Origin of Geometry: An Introduction*, John P. Leavey Jr. (trans.), Lincoln: University of Nebraska Press.
Derrida, Jacques (1978b), *Writing and Difference*, Alan Bass (trans.), London: Routledge.
Derrida, Jacques (1992), *Acts of Literature*, Derek Attridge (ed.), London: Routledge.
Derrida, Jacques (2011), *The Problem of Genesis in Husserl's Philosophy*, Marian Hobson (trans.), Chicago: University of Chicago Press.
Dummett, Michael (1993), *Origins of Analytical Philosophy*, London: Duckworth.
Eliot, T. S. (1930), *The Sacred Wood: Essays on Poetry and Criticism*, New York: Knopf.
Foucault, Michel (1970), *Order of Things: An Archaeology of the Human Sciences*, London: Tavistock.
Foucault, Michel (1972), *The Archaeology of Knowledge and the Discourse on Language*, A. M. Sheridan Smith (trans.), London: Tavistock.
Frege, Gottlob (1950), *The Foundations of Arithmetic*, J.L. Austin (trans.), New York: Harper and Row.
Habermas, Jürgen (1976), *Legitimation Crisis*, Thomas McCarthy (trans.), Cambridge: Polity.
Habermas, Jürgen (1990), *The Philosophical Discourse of Modernity: Twelve Lectures*, Frederick G. Lawrence (trans.), Cambridge, MA: MIT Press.
Heidegger, Martin (2010), *Being and Time*, Joan Stambaugh (trans.), Albany: SUNY Press.
Horkheimer, Max and Theodor W. Adorno (2002), *Dialectic of Enlightenment: Philosophical Fragments*, Gunzelin Schmid Noerr (ed.), Edmund Jephcott (trans.), Stanford: Stanford University Press.
Husserl, Edmund (1965), 'Philosophy as a Rigorous Science', in Edmund Husserl, *Phenomenology and the Crisis of Philosophy*, Quentin Lauer (trans.), New York: Harper and Row, pp. 71–147.
Husserl, Edmund (1973), *Cartesian Meditations: An Introduction to Phenomenology*, Dorian Cairns (trans.), The Hague: Martinus Nijhoff.
Kant, Immanuel (1998), *Critique of Pure Reason*, Paul Guyer and Allen W. Wood (eds and trans.), Cambridge: Cambridge University Press.
Kristeva, Julia (1984), *Revolution in Poetic Language*, Leon Roudiez (trans.), New York: Columbia University Press.
Latour, Bruno (1993), *We Have Never Been Modern*, Catherine Porter (trans.), Cambridge, MA: Harvard University Press.
MacIntyre, Alasdair C. (1981), *After Virtue: A Study in Moral Theory*, Notre Dame: University of Notre Dame Press.

Nussbaum, Martha (2001), *Upheavals of Thought*, Cambridge: Cambridge University Press.
Rorty, Richard (1979), *Philosophy and the Mirror of Nature*, Princeton: Princeton University Press.
Rorty, Richard (1982), 'Philosophy as a Kind of Writing', in Richard Rorty, *Consequences of Pragmatism*, Minneapolis: University of Minnesota Press, pp. 89–109.
Russell, Bertrand and Alfred North Whitehead (1910), *Principia Mathematic: Volume 1*, Cambridge: Cambridge University Press.
Woolf, Virginia (1994a), 'The Novels of E. M. Forster', in Virginia Woolf, *The Essays of Virginia Woolf, Vol. 4: 1925–1928*, Andrew McNeillie (ed.), London: Hogarth Press, pp. 491–501.
Woolf, Virginia (1994b), 'Modern Fiction', in Virginia Woolf, *The Essays of Virginia Woolf, Vol. 4: 1925–1928*, Andrew McNeillie (ed.), London: Hogarth Press, pp. 157–65.

PART I

Beyond the Postmodern: Literature, Philosophy, and the Question of the Contemporary

Editor's Introduction

David Rudrum

The intersection between literature and philosophy entered a particularly synergistic phase in the mid-to-late twentieth century, thanks to the hotly contested issue of the postmodern. Philosophers like Jean-François Lyotard and Jürgen Habermas were weighing up the aftermath of modernity, while critics like Fredric Jameson and Linda Hutcheon were pondering the demise of literary and cultural modernism, with the ideas discussed in both sets of arguments frequently crossing between the two disciplines in mutually informative ways.

In the early twenty-first century, however, debates around modernity, postmodernity, and postmodernism have subsided, and there seems to be a pervasive acceptance that the postmodern moment has come to an end. Even some of the most authoritative commentators on postmodernism – for example, Linda Hutcheon and Ihab Hassan, both of whom helped coin the term and propagate its widespread usage – have openly stated that its usefulness has passed.

Concurrently with these developments, the last decade or two have seen an intriguing (if bewildering) array of exciting new terms coined to describe the 'post-postmodern' culture of the early twenty-first century. Such neologisms as 'altermodernism' and 'automodernism', 'digimodernism' and 'hypermodernism', 'remodernism' and 'metamodernism', 'performatism' and 'renewalism' have all been mooted recently, giving rise to much debate as to how to characterise and label our contemporaneity.

What does all this mean for the relationship between literature and philosophy? Does it mean the end of an era of particularly close interdisciplinary dialogue, or the opportunity to take that dialogue in a range of new directions? And now that the debates around postmodern themes lie in the past, how might we go about weighing up their legacy? Is it possible that, having worked so closely in tandem for so long, the lines between literary and philosophical approaches to these issues can no longer be so readily drawn?

This section seeks to bring both philosophical and literary perspectives to bear on the task of evaluating the characteristics of the contemporary, in the aftermath of postmodernism. It aims to reflect on the literary, philosophical, and broader cultural trends behind the aesthetic questions of the present day, and on the task of finding a new name for designating the now.

Opening the section, David Rudrum's chapter surveys the range of newly prefixed '-modernisms' which claim to supplant the postmodern. Searching for similar characteristics and common denominators between these new coinages, he argues that there are in fact none, and that indeed most of the designations like 'metamodernism' and 'automodernism' contain ambivalence or even self-contradiction. This he takes as evidence that there is an expanding number of different and diverse ways of experiencing and exploring our modernity. That being so, asking which of the new coinages describes it best is simply asking the wrong question. Instead, Rudrum diagnoses a 'polymodern condition', in which the modern is an ongoing experience with an increasing array of insubsumably different inflections. The upshot of this diagnosis, however, is that it is no longer possible to enumerate or characterise the nature of the contemporary accurately. Surveying a range of novels, films, and digital literature, he argues that the polymodern condition is characterised not by the relativism of the postmodern condition, but by a general cluelessness.

The second chapter, by Robin van den Akker, Alison Gibbons, and Timotheus Vermeulen, outlines and argues the case for 'metamodernism', a term the authors coined back in 2010, and have elaborated and expanded upon in the years since. One of the most influential of the terms used to designate what follows postmodernism, metamodernism is a periodising term, in that it seeks to describe both a cultural logic (in the Jamesonian sense) and a structure of feeling (in Raymond Williams's sense). It is, however, of more than historical significance: it entails a philosophical dimension too, encapsulated by the notion of metaxy as found in Plato's writings. Designating a sense of in-betweenness, of both affirming and negating contradictory positions, metaxy is suggestive of how the metamodernist subject oscillates between a modernist and a postmodernist sensibility, without ever fully belonging to either. The authors contrast brief readings of classic modernist (Woolf's *Mrs Dalloway*) and postmodernist (Barth's *Lost in the Funhouse*) fiction with detailed readings of more recent, twenty-first-century autofiction by Ben Lerner (*10:04*) and Adam Thirlwell (*Kapow!*), so as to demonstrate how metamodernism is distinctive from the postmodernism that preceded it.

Josh Toth, who coined the term 'renewalism' in his earlier work, argues in the next chapter that the evolving nature of metafiction reveals much about what lies beyond postmodernism. Moving on from what Linda Hutcheon influentially labelled 'historiographic metafiction' – taken at the time to be one of the most prominent genres of postmodern literature – Toth claims that although metafiction is still a thriving, vibrant tendency in the fiction of the twenty-first century, it now tends towards a historioplastic rather than a historiographic character. His notion of plasticity comes from Hegel, and in particular from recent reinterpretations of Hegel's thought in the writings of Slavoj Žižek and Catherine Malabou, where plasticity means the infinite potential of the real (or, in Hegel's terms, of spirit) to exceed the shapes and forms into which it is moulded. Historioplastic metafiction, Toth contends, involves a form of what Hegel calls 'sublation' – it both negates and renews the structures and strategies of postmodern fiction, holding onto them through a process of letting go. He illustrates his argument through a reading of Jennifer Egan's *A Visit from the Goon Squad* (2010), a metafictional novel in which authenticity has become a marketing gimmick and handheld digital technology has debased language and expression to the point of infantilism, and yet the extreme and obvious nature of this debasement allows its narrators and characters to move beyond the recursive, nihilistic tropes of postmodernism, towards the reality and authenticity they are said to have lost. Thus, in a manner that recalls the 'romantic art' Hegel privileges in his *Lectures on Aesthetics*, novels like Egan's work to sublate the more corrosive tendencies of postmodernism.

Continuing the theme of digital technology and its impact on our thought and culture, Nicky Gardiner's chapter closes the section with a reflection on Robert Samuels's notion of 'automodernism' – a portmanteau term coupling the automation of new media and digital technologies with the new forms of autonomy they are said to enable, and which, Samuels claims, characterises what lies beyond postmodernism. Gardiner analyses Samuels's ideas to reveal what he calls a 'virtual humanism' implicit in the way we think about cyberspace and its potential. The subject of virtual humanism paradoxically finds their autonomy and agency enhanced at the same time as technological prosthetics mean they are no longer exactly human. Gardiner thus brings the idea of automodernism into dialogue with contemporary philosophical debates around the posthuman, as explored by N. Katherine Hayles and many others. Where postmodern novels like William Gibson's classic *Neuromancer* once depicted cyberspace as an edgy new frontier where selfhood could be abstracted, deconstructed, and displaced, a contemporary novel like Gary Shteyngart's *Super Sad True Love Story* depicts humans as reduced to data, enslaved by the very technology that is said to set them free. (Incidentally, this novel, published the very same year as Egan's, also resembles the final chapter in *A Visit from the Goon Squad* as discussed by Josh Toth: both Shteyngart's novel and the final chapter of Egan's are set in a near-future New York City, in which everyday life and everyday language have undergone dystopian transformation thanks to handheld technological devices.) Thus, Gardiner's concept of 'virtual humanism' connects the debates surrounding the aftermath of postmodernism with those around the challenges to traditional subjectivity in the next section.

1

The Polymodern Condition: A Report on Cluelessness

David Rudrum

Modernity is back; the mid-twentieth-century thesis of a postmodern era turns out to have been a false alarm. In the social sciences, erstwhile commentators on the postmodern like Ulrich Beck and Antony Giddens now talk of an era of 'reflexive modernity', and Zygmunt Bauman of a 'liquid modernity'. Fredric Jameson, whose writings on the postmodern surely did more than anyone else's to shape our understanding of the term, has floated the idea of 'singular modernity'.[1] Meanwhile, the arts of the early twenty-first century, and their attendant criticisms and theories, are awash with coinages such as 'remodernism', 'hypermodernism', 'automodernism', 'digimodernism', 'altermodernism', and 'metamodernism'.[2] This list is by no means exhaustive: 'neomodernism', 'geomodernism', and 'cosmodernism' have also been mooted. In each case, what is being proposed is a neologism meeting the need for a term to describe what emerges from the aftershocks of a now defunct postmodernism. And in each case, a new prefix is bolted on to the supposedly outworn term 'modernism'. The modern is back on the twenty-first-century scene with a vengeance. Rumours of its death, as spread by the philosophical wing of postmodernism, must have been greatly exaggerated.

Let me take a few moments at the outset to indicate what I mean by this claim. At stake here is, and always was, something more than a style or school or movement in the arts: postmodernism was never just the vanquisher of modernism, much less a successor to it. It may once have been possible to distinguish, as Steven Connor did in his influential work *Postmodernist Culture*, between a postmodern*ism* that constituted something approximating a late twentieth-century aesthetic, and a postmodern*ity* which amounted to a transformation in the way the West conceived – or, more importantly, experienced – the modern world it had built around itself. Looking back at this debate, it is small wonder that Jameson has reflected on the inadequacies of its terminology. In those days, Connor later wrote, 'How one capitalized or hyphenated the word – "post-modern", "Post-Modern", "postmodern", or "Postmodern" – seemed to many to matter a great deal, along with whether one chose to refer to "postmodernism", "postmodernity" or simply "the postmodern"' (Connor 2015: 36).

But this, as the saying goes, was merely a stage we were going through. The distinction became untenable because, as Connor neatly puts it, 'postmodernity had itself become postmodernist' (Connor 2015: 36). That is, where politics was once judged by social change and economics by the production of goods and capital, both had come to operate in the realms of signs and symbols, narratives and spectacles, and, latterly, data. In other words, the material conditions of the postmodern world had somehow entered the circus that was postmodernism. But something like the opposite was simultaneously true. Debates about postmodernist culture, even in its minutiae, had become indissociable from debates about huge issues raised by the idea of the end of modernity. That is, aesthetic discussions about anything from the gnomic fiction of Lydia Davis to risible Hollywood blockbusters like *Last Action Hero* could no longer be held without being drawn into much broader philosophical debates about some of the most deeply cherished assumptions of Western thought.

This was because, within a short period of about fifteen years, Roland Barthes had mooted the death of the author, Michel Foucault the disappearance of man, Jacques Derrida the non-existence of the *hors-texte*, Jean Baudrillard the loss of the real, and Jean-François Lyotard the demise of grand narratives. Each of these dramatic pronouncements had called into question one of the intellectual pillars of modern thought, taking 'modern' here to mean the liberal values born of humanism and of the Enlightenment that are integral to the West's self-image as progenitor and guardian of modernity. Thus, criticism of culture and of the arts had become the barometer for assessing our verdict on the modern itself – a verdict on its health that often turned into a coroner's report on its death. As John McGowan put it:

> Nothing less than the West's soul hung in the balance. The postmodernism debate was about the Western tradition's crimes and accomplishments.... Specifically, was Western philosophy – its traditional canons of thought, knowledge production, and rationality – and Western political commitments – to rights, equality, and popular sovereignty under the banner of a universalist humanism – root causes of these crimes or a potential source for protesting against or even remedying them? The Enlightenment, especially, came in for criticism. In retrospect, the European attempt to replace divinely ordained hierarchies with polities grounded on popular sovereignty, the rule of law, and universal rights (all justified and underwritten by reason) seemed a disaster. Specific battles were waged over the terms 'reason', 'truth', 'human' and others. But the main battle was clear: what, if anything, of the tradition could be salvaged, could be justified? How fully and completely had the West gone off the rails? (McGowan 2007: 93)

There was no shortage of commentators – philosophers and critics alike – for whom the period of modernity itself had finally come to an inglorious end, followed by a triumphal entry into postmodernity.

McGowan is no doubt right that at times, it seemed that the debate that was raging in those days was about nothing less than the troubled soul of the West. But it can hardly seem contentious to assert that, half a century on from the landmark year of 1968, the soul of the West is being troubled by new things. Consider, for example,

Foucault's devastatingly blunt prophecy, at the end of *The Order of Things*, of the disappearance of man – that dependable subject of Enlightenment thought – from our philosophical constitution. Notwithstanding the recent turn towards the 'inhuman' or the 'posthuman' in certain quarters of contemporary philosophy, the fact remains that plenty of the hallmarks of the modern philosophical subject that Foucault calls 'man' have become more rather than less central to twenty-first-century culture. Thus, according to Robert Samuels, the importance of (a sense of) autonomy has undergone a resurgence, fuelled by the admittedly questionable perception that digital technologies enable new forms of freedom, self-expression, political agency, and self-determination – an unexpected and somewhat ambivalent alliance between automation and autonomy that Samuels terms 'automodernism' (see Samuels 2007, 2009). Equally, Gilles Lipovetsky points out that the subject of early twenty-first-century life inhabits a culture characterised by a hyperindividualism – we live in hypermodern times, where the emphasis on a personal identity has not diminished one drop as a result of the postmodern assertion that all such identities are constructs (see Lipovetsky 2005). On the contrary, this seems merely to fuel a desire to construct them and yet, bizarrely and paradoxically, to regard them simultaneously as grounded, even sacrosanct. (The wave of nationalisms and regionalisms that have swept Europe since 1989, and the DIY religions that cherry-pick and then 'fuse' Eastern and Western faiths, are Lipovetsky's key examples.) *Pace* Foucault, then, it does not seem as if anthropocentric patterns of thought are going to disappear from our lives any time soon. Indeed, perhaps it is worth asking whether the philosophical anthropocentrism of modernity was ever really abrogated by a postmodern rupture with it in the first place.

The question seems all the more pressing when one evaluates the uptake of other canonical postmodern ideas in the culture of the early twenty-first century. Consider Barthes's much-vaunted 'death of the author' thesis. Certainly, the digital revolution might seem to have brought this prophecy to fruition, with its proliferation of anonymously, multiply, or socially authored texts. The form of the mashup, in particular, would seem to offer hard evidence of Barthes's description of the author as 'forever anterior, never original; his only power is to combine the different kinds of writing' into 'a tissue of citations, resulting from the thousand sources of culture' (Barthes 1977: 146). But at the same time, the phenomenon of blogging would seem to suggest that the author is alive and well and living in cyberspace. Bloggers often write under their own names, and even when they do not, they tend to choose a descriptive alias intended to characterise their bloggings accurately. The genre brings expectations of truthfulness and honesty – blogging things you do not believe in or know to be incorrect is not blogging, it is trolling. Blogging thus depends on a facile notion of authorship, in which the author means (and is) exactly what they say. Its popularity – the sheer scale of the blogosphere – might give us pause here: if authorship is so readily available to everyone, no doubt it ceases to be authorship, thereby vindicating Barthes in ways he could not have anticipated. But is this a safe conclusion to draw? Certainly, the networked era has not stopped us wanting to be authors. On the contrary, the digital revolution has enabled a massive surge in the phenomenon of self-publishing. The Author-God derided by Barthes still remains an aspirational figure, with a status and kudos that plenty of writers clearly desire and seek, even without the backing of the publishing industry. It is unsurprising, then, that many of the qualities traditionally attributed to the modern author figure have made a resurgence in the wake of the postmodern: in particular, remodernism, as formulated by Billy Childish and Charles Thomson, champions the modernist emphasis on spirituality, sincerity, and authenticity as against the postmodern valorisation of irony, and so does metamodernism, as articulated by Timotheus Vermeulen and Robin van den Akker, albeit with a knowing scepticism as to whether these, in their view, neo-romantic notions can actually be recuperated from the longstanding postmodern debunking of them.[3]

Much the same pattern can be seen in the fate of other quintessentially postmodern ideas. Think of Baudrillard, whose cryptic pronouncements that a precession of simulacra had triumphed over reality itself, replacing it with a hyperreality of depthless images and banishing referentiality to 'the desert of the real', were once taken seriously enough to position him at the forefront of France's philosophers. In the culture of the early twenty-first century, though, the real, far from being banished, plays a more central role than ever, thanks to what Alan Kirby has called 'the rise of the apparently real' (see Kirby 2009: 139–50). Reality TV, docusoaps, selfies, vlogging, and even some cult movies like *Jackass* or *Borat* all trade to some considerable degree on the claim that what they purvey is real – genuine and authentic, unposed and unstaged. Kirby claims that the aesthetic of the apparently real is driven by the digital revolution: the explosion in reality TV coincided with the advent of the technology that made it possible for viewers to vote; the ubiquity of the smartphone is responsible for the cult of the apparently spontaneous selfie; the availability of affordable digital movie cameras has accustomed us to the handheld shots and clumsy editing of the docusoap, and so forth. The postmodern, according to Kirby, has been outmoded by technological changes, and replaced by what he calls 'digimodernism':

> The apparently real, one of digimodernism's recurrent aesthetic traits, is so diametrically opposed to the 'real' of postmodernism that at first glance it can be mistaken for a simple and violent reaction against it. Postmodernism's real is a subtle, sophisticated quantity; that of digimodernism is so straightforward it almost defies description.... For postmodernism, there is no given reality 'out there'.... The real is, at best, a social construct, a convention agreed in a certain way in a certain culture at a certain time, varying historically with no version able to claim a privileged status.... The aesthetic of the apparently real seems to present no such predicament. It proffers what seems to be real – and that is all there is to it. The apparently real comes without self-consciousness, without irony or self-interrogation, and without signaling itself to the reader or viewer. (Kirby 2009: 139–40)

From this perspective, the cameo role played by Baudrillard's ideas in the celebrated movie *The Matrix* seems philosophically anachronistic: it was once widely assumed that the digital world would lead to an era of seamless virtual reality, bringing about simulation of a technological sophistication and scale that Baudrillard could not possibly have dreamed of when he wrote his key texts in the early 1980s. In fact, the digimodern condition is as likely to default to an unthinking, uncritical conception of reality, where contesting the real through philosophical debate has been replaced by taking a selfie in front of it.

Probably the most influential claim of postmodern philosophy was Lyotard's assertion that 'We no longer have recourse to the grand narratives' (Lyotard 1984: 60). I will deal with his formulations around *petits récits* in due course, but would point out for now that the early twenty-first century has seen the dramatic and violent spread of a grand narrative capable of inspiring a loyalty so fanatical as to inspire people both to kill and to die for it, sometimes simultaneously. Extremist (mis)interpretations of Islam are clearly capable of attracting followers around the world, from Syria, Iraq, and Afghanistan, to Nigeria, Libya, and Somalia, to Madrid, London, and Paris. The West's response to the challenge from this grand narrative has not been a postmodern one, based on cultural relativism or on parodic irony: recall George W. Bush's description of the perpetrators of the 9/11 attacks as 'evildoers', and his pledge to 'go forward to defend freedom and all that is good and just in our world' (Bush 2001). Since then, both the idealism invoked in Obama's 2008 calls for 'Hope' and 'Change' and the jingoism inherent in Trump's 2016 boasts to 'Make America Great Again' have depended on an underlying appeal to a metanarrative that is in both cases time-honoured and traditional. No longer can one claim that there is no longer a recourse to grand narratives.

Next to Lyotard, the best-known theorist of postmodernity was Fredric Jameson. As Jameson saw it, postmodernism was the cultural logic of late capitalism. 'Late for what?', Jeffrey Nealon wittily asks in his study of twenty-first-century post-postmodernism (Nealon 2012: 15). It is a fair question. Where Jameson saw the fate of the modern as bound up with the fate of capitalism, it is apparently far easier nowadays to conceive an end to modernity itself than an end to capitalism. As Slavoj Žižek observed, when addressing the Occupy Wall Street movement in 2011, 'It's easy to imagine the end of the world. An asteroid destroying all life and so on. But you cannot imagine the end of capitalism.'[4] Nealon demonstrates how the economic forces driving Jameson's analysis have mutated and intensified in the three decades since its publication. In the 1980s, capitalism was simply the system of commerce underpinning the way of life in the West; in the twenty-first century, global capital sweeps all before it, and there can be few corners of the world left that have not been transformed by the impact of a rampant globalisation. Thus, it is not surprising that Nicolas Bourriaud equates the globalised world with the surmounting of the postmodern condition. For Bourriaud, the twenty-first-century subject is a *homo viator*, navigating ever diverging paths through a cultural landscape that is thoroughly 'creolised' in space and time. This networked, globalised subject inhabits a mobile, multiple world that Bourriaud terms 'altermodern', suggesting that 'we are experiencing the emergence of a global altermodernity' (Bourriaud 2009).

It is important to note that Bourriaud conceives this experience as 'the recomposition of a modernity in the present' (Bourriaud 2009). The trouble with such a view is that it sets out a narrative in which modernity, which is often said to have begun in the seventeenth or eighteenth century, died a death in the postmodern years of the late twentieth century, only to come back to life just a generation or two later. If the advent of a philosophical modernity in the Enlightenment was among the most prolonged, painstaking, and provocative chapters in the intellectual history of the West, it is not easy to see how such a hard-won achievement could simply come and go like this, disappearing and then reappearing in sudden fits and starts, well within the lifetime of the average adult. Surely a better conclusion to draw from this remarkable wave of new '-modernisms' and '-modernities' is that the postmodern did not in fact supplant the modern to begin with: the world we live in remains a modern world. The fact that it remains necessary to prefix a word like 'modern', 'modernity', or 'modernism' in order to describe it ought to evidence this – and perhaps lead us to question whether the diagnosis of *post*modernity was not perhaps somewhat premature.

So: which of these newly prefixed '-modernisms' describes the culture of the early twenty-first-century world best? That question, I want to argue, is the wrong one to ask. Instead, a better response to the multiplicity of new modernisms and modernities is to recognise that their collective significance is greater than that of their individual claims. As I have sketched them here, some of these new '-modernisms' and '-modernities' share a few salient features. For example, the early twenty-first century differs from the late twentieth most clearly in its embrace of digital technology, as highlighted in the formulations of digimodernism and automodernism, and in its entry into an era of globalisation, as emphasised in the idea of altermodernism. Aesthetically, remodernism and, more persuasively, metamodernism have argued the importance of a resurgent sense of authenticity or sincerity, but perhaps this is better understood as just one aspect of a broader shift in the nature of individualism in contemporary culture – certainly, hypermodernism, automodernism, and altermodernism, albeit from somewhat different coordinates, would seem to corroborate the idea of such a shift. However, what strikes me as more important about these new '-modernisms' is not that they have a common vision of what it is to be modern in the twenty-first century, but rather that they lack one.

For example, Bourriaud's altermodernist artist is a semionaut, traversing pathways between different networks of signs and forms of expression; the remodernist artist envisaged by Childish and Thomson is a painter, seeking a return to spirituality and sincerity by rejecting conceptualism in art. It seems doubtful whether either would recognise the other as an artist, let alone a fellow traveller responding to the aftermath of postmodernity. The subject of Samuels's automodernist world and the subject of Kirby's digimodernist world are both technologically driven individuals, but the former regards social networks, chatrooms, and blogs – whether misguidedly or not – as means of enhancing their freedom to self-expression, whereas the latter is enslaved by the very same technology to the forces of populism and consumerism, with all the dumbing down this entails. Lipovetsky's hypermodern individual is similarly envisioned as inhabiting a world saturated by consumerism, in which a 24-hour culture promises to free our lives from the constraints of time, in the same breath that it makes our time constantly available for new forms of exploitation that curtail this very freedom. The metamodern individual described by Vermeulen and van den Akker has a basically romantic outlook on our culture, but one that is tempered with a postmodern irony that cannot quite be left behind. Though both the hypermodern and the metamodern condition can be characterised by a certain ambivalence, the former is an ambivalence in response to the economics of our society, and the latter an ambivalence in the aesthetic of contemporary culture. Thus, to suggest, as I did a moment ago, that there has been a broad shift in the nature of individualism in contemporary culture is to say little of any real use when it comes to characterising the present — perhaps it is apt to say nothing at all. In point of fact, there are few common denominators, whether low or high, amongst these successors to the postmodern. Yet rather than a Lyotardian archipelago of multiple language games or micronarratives, each incommensurable with one another, these new '-modernisms', as we are about to see, are scarcely consistent even within themselves. Nor is it desirable, let alone likely, that any one of them, or even any one grouping of them, should encapsulate all of what it is to be post-postmodern (if we are prepared to accept that such a thing exists). Together, they show instead that the modern is an ongoing experience with an increasing array of insubsumably different inflections. Rather than looking for what Jameson would call a 'cultural dominant', then, we would do better to accept that there is an expanding number of different and diverse ways of experiencing and exploring our modernity. This I propose to designate the 'polymodern condition'.

The polymodern condition is a term with which to encapsulate the two most fundamental contentions I am trying to make here: first, the idea that modernity died a postmodern death is a myth,[5] and second, that contemporary modernity has so many different inflections that it is impossible to characterise. Modernity, then, is still with us not because it is the 'unfinished project' of Jürgen Habermas, but rather because it is no longer possible to say what would count as having finished it. As Simon Critchley puts it, 'We have ... no clue when it might end' (Critchley and McCarthy 2009: 171). This cluelessness is no glib turn of phrase. It is rather the destination to which any attempt at making philosophical sense of twenty-first-century culture is propelled.

Consider the following assertions: according to Lipovetsky, in these hypermodern times 'cyberspace is making communication virtual, while individuals are voting overwhelmingly for live performances' (Lipovetsky 2005: 54); according to Kirby, in the digimodernist era 'advanced technology is used to medieval ends: the uploading to the Internet of films showing the innocent being beheaded; the recording and dissemination by cell phone of images of torture at Abu Ghraib' (Kirby 2009: 237); according to Samuels, in an automodern world, 'new media technologies ... simultaneously erase and produce individual freedom' (Samuels 2007: 236); according to Childish and Thomson, a remodernist art 'embraces all that it denounces' (Childish and Thomson 2000a: 10); according to Vermeulen and van den Akker:

> Metamodernism ... seeks forever for a truth that it never expects to find. If you will forgive us for the banality of the metaphor for a moment, the metamodern thus willfully adopts a kind of donkey-and-carrot double-bind. Like a donkey it chases a carrot that it never manages to eat because the carrot is always just beyond its reach. But precisely because it never manages to eat the carrot, it never ends its chase, setting foot in moral realms the modern donkey (having eaten its carrot elsewhere) will never encounter, entering political domains the postmodern donkey (having abandoned the chase) will never come across. (Vermeulen and van den Akker 2010: n.p.)

The point I am trying to make here is that practically all of these would-be descriptors of the present end up resorting to formulations that involve ambivalence, paradox, or even flat self-contradiction. To one degree or another, they are predicated on a polymodern cluelessness – an inability to make sense of the many bafflingly different ways in which the contemporary is experienced. Importantly, these moments of internal conflict function differently from the kind of aporetic moments once familiar from deconstruction – that is, a moment of impasse which is nonetheless productive, and which somehow both cannot yet must be negotiated. If Derrida's were postmodern aporias, they were based on deep-seated quirks and inconsistencies in the metaphysical basis of modern Western thought, and above all they were the product of detailed and thorough study of the philosophical legacies of modernity. The polymodern aporia, by contrast, comes from an inability to make sense of the tangled web of life in the modern world.

But what is new? After all, there has probably never been a time in which human beings have felt comfortable making sense of the culture of the world around them – and if there has, it has certainly been the exception rather than the norm. Those living a hundred years ago had to make sense of the unprecedented scale of human slaughter in the trenches, the mechanisation of everyday life through electricity, and the biggest sea-change in gender norms there has probably ever been; those living the century before that had to confront the unforeseen consequences of industrialisation, incomprehensibly rapid urbanisation, the birth of a proletariat, and the death of God. Before that, the rights of man and the social contract stood for many years in direct opposition to the principles of absolute monarchy, just as Luther's 95 theses remained at loggerheads with Catholic dogma for centuries until Europeans found other things to fight about instead. Earlier still, Columbus's discovery of a continent unknown to Christendom in the West went against all that was known of theology, geography, and cosmography at the time. What age has lacked its St Paul, repudiating the old laws? What society has ever been free from gadflies like Socrates, showing us either that we do not understand the world around us, or that what we understand around us is not actually the world?

If I am right, then what is new is that the question as to how the polymodern world differs from what came before it cannot be answered. The radical modernists of the early twentieth century had a clear sense of what differentiated them from the Victorians, and though there were many avant-garde movements to pick and choose between, with aims and ideas that were often at variance, there was nevertheless a discernible underlying commonality: a background of convention and taste they were rebelling against. The *Lumières* of the Enlightenment, deep-seated though the disagreements between them often were (one thinks of how scandalised Kant was by Hume, for instance), could nevertheless have found common cause in the need for a crusade against the irrationality and ignorance of dogmatism and superstition, just as the Renaissance men before them shared a focus on antiquity as preferable to the orthodoxies of the medieval world. But our time, precisely inasmuch as it is a polymodern time, has no such focus.

Such is the upshot of Tom McCarthy's 2015 novel *Satin Island*, in which a young anthropologist named U. is commissioned by a bafflingly large corporation to write the Great Report, a document which will '*name* what's taking place right now'. The head of the corporation, Peyman, gives him a rather vague set of orders:

> U., write the Great Report. The Great Report? I asked, my hand still clenched in his; what's that? The Document, he said; the Book. The First and Last Word on our age.... Not just *a* book: *the* fucking *Book*.... What do you want this Great Report to look like? I asked. What form should it take? To whom should it be addressed? These are secondary questions, he said. I leave it to you to work them out. It will find its shape. (McCarthy 2015: 56–8)

And so U. expends a great deal of time, if not much effort, contemplating the contemporary. His directionless meditations take in the beauty of oil slicks, speculations on the existence of a global suicide cult among sky-divers, and recollections of police brutality at the notorious G8 summit in Genoa. At one point, he muses that the flow of traffic circling a roundabout traces the same pattern as the buffering symbol on his computer screen, which traces the same pattern as the never-ending ouroboros. This is not a bad metaphor for the novel itself.

Charged with summing up contemporaneity, U. finds the task impossible, for two reasons: first, no anthropologist or philosopher, no artist or writer, can achieve an overview of the complexity of the present. Second, the Great Report on the contemporary is already being written – but in a form that is completely illegible. To quote the novel at some length:

> Write Everything Down, said Malinowski. But the thing is, now, it *is* all written down. There's hardly an instant of our lives that isn't documented. Walk down any stretch of street and you're being filmed by three cameras at once – and even if you aren't, the phone you carry in your pocket pinpoints and logs your location at each given moment. Each website that you visit, every click-through, every keystroke is archived: even if you've hit *delete, wipe, empty trash*, it's still lodged somewhere, in some fold or enclave, some occluded avenue of circuitry. Nothing ever goes away. And as for the structures of kinship, the networks of exchange within whose web we're held, cradled, created – networks whose mapping is the task, the very *raison d'être*, of someone like me: well, those networks are being mapped, that task performed, by the software that tabulates and cross-indexes what we buy with who

we know, and what they buy, or like, and with the other objects that are bought or liked by others who we don't know but with whom we cohabit a shared buying- or liking-pattern. Pondering these facts, a new spectre, an even more grotesque realisation, presented itself to me: the truly terrifying thought wasn't that the Great Report might be unwritable, but – quite the opposite – that it had *already been written*. Not by a person, nor even by some nefarious cabal, but simply by a neutral and indifferent binary system that had given rise to itself, moved by itself and would perpetuate itself: some auto-alphaing and auto-omegating script – that's what it *was*. And that we, far from being its authors, or its operators, or even its slaves (for slaves are agents who can harbour hopes, however faint, that one day a Moses or a Spartacus will set them free), were no more than actions and commands within its key-chains. This Great Report, once it came into being, would, from that point onwards, have existed always, since time immemorial, and nothing else would really matter. But who could read it? From what angle, vantage-point or platform, accessed through what jetty leading to what study (since all studies and all jetties were already written into it), could it be viewed, surveyed, interpreted? None, of course: none and no one. Only another piece of software could do that. (McCarthy 2015: 123–5)

The vocabulary of U.'s boss Peyman strongly implies that the report U. is expected to write will supersede Lyotard's *The Postmodern Condition*, the erstwhile great report on its age which named the era that was taking place around it. However, unlike Lyotard's, U.'s Great Report is not a report on knowledge, but a report on cluelessness.

What I am calling the polymodern condition in fact embraces cluelessness to a further extent even than U. realises in this passage. Consider, as evidence of this, a project called 'You Are Not Your Browser History', a collaboration between data artist Jer Thorp of the Office for Creative Research, and ten anonymous creative writers. I quote from the project's website:

> I'm a 26 year-old from Montreal, a 27 year-old in Vegas, and a retiree with a penchant for photography. Mostly I'm unemployed. I'm a gamer, a fashionista, an occasional beer drinker, and a dog owner. I graduated from a community college, I like to travel, and I wear glasses. Also, I might be Jewish.
>
> Last week, I paid ten strangers five dollars to write character studies of me based on the advertisements that show up in my web browser. I told them nothing about my age, gender, location, lifestyle or career – instead they were asked to stitch a biography together from banner ads for bicycles, underwear, software, books and movies. While no one managed to Sherlock out my life story from 2,000 advertisements, the results offer an interesting look at a kind of second self that we all carry around with us: our browser history doppelgängers. (Thorp 2014: n.p.)

What the writers made of this raw material is instructive. For example, one deduced that 'The random individual who viewed web-based ads over a two week period is most likely an unemployed man in his early thirties', while another observed 'he seems to be fun, exciting and kind with a bit of an extravagant lifestyle . . . just a little lonely is all' (Thorp 2014). If being extravagant is rarely compatible with being unemployed, at least the loneliness was picked up on by another writer, albeit for rather different reasons: 'Some of the advertisements look like pornography so it is probably safe to assume that he lives alone' (Thorp 2014). The generalisations drawn here may or may not be the same conclusions reached by those in the web marketing departments who determine who sees which ads, based on what. We will never know. That in itself is instructive. As Thorp puts it, 'We know for a fact that people are being shown different ads depending on demographics like age, gender, perceived income level and geographic location. Does this constitute discrimination? What kind of impact do these practices have on marginalized groups?' (Thorp 2014). The fact is that since much of this demographic information is arrived at through dubious inference, we simply do not know, and the 'You Are Not Your Browser History' project seeks to draw attention to this cluelessness. It suggests that, *pace* McCarthy, even software cannot produce a comprehensible Great Report on our age.

In fairness, the conclusion I have just drawn is somewhat less nuanced than the one drawn by Thorp. He observes:

> Although many of the assumptions that were made about me based on my ad history were wrong, few were groundless. I'm not Jewish. However, we've been working on a project for the Museum of Jewish History so I've been visiting a lot of websites for Jewish cultural organisations. I don't live in Los Angeles, but I was there for a conference, and did do a lot of local LA browsing. I'm not a big gamer, but I've been following the politics of the gaming community fairly closely over the last few months. . . . They can also be reminders of the long memory of our ad identities – that brief dalliance with a jewelry site 18 months ago means I'm still seeing ads for watches every day. The aggregated portrait is not so much an image of me as it is an image of what advertisers see of me. It is an identity assembled from fleeting glimpses, long-expired actions, and, more than anything, guesswork. (Thorp 2014)

Thus, there remain grains of fact scattered throughout our browser histories. Certainly, they are not pure simulacra. But the relationship of these rare nuggets of fact to truth is not a classically postmodern one – say, one of social construction or of legitimation or of relativism: their relationship to truth is more haphazard, more conjectured, more supposed, presumed, or hypothesised. Moreover, it is not distinguishable from the reams of data that are false. Our browser histories, I contend, are perfect metaphors for the cluelessness of the polymodern condition.

Who, today, could enumerate the big questions facing our time? How would we recognise what would count as answers to them? In the name of what ideology, or principle, or faith, would such answers be legitimated? It is probable – or so I would like to think – that many people reading this chapter would feel that climate change, linked to human behaviour, and to the irresponsible consumption of fossil fuels in particular, constitutes the biggest threat to humankind at the present time.

Yet certain governments elected democratically in the twenty-first century have disputed its very existence, let alone the link to carbon emissions, while many others who acknowledge the threat have continued to build motorways, airports, and coal-fired power stations regardless, often at the same time as agreeing to limit their CO_2 output. Some of them square this circle by turning to nuclear power. For this they must build waste storage facilities that will contain radioactive material with a half-life of 24,000 years, which, in some cases, will remain hazardous to life for up to 100,000 years. As Michael Madsen's 2010 film *Into Eternity* points out, no human-built structure has remained watertight and airtight for a fraction of this time, nor has any human language remained intelligible for this long, begging the question as to how appropriate warning signs, telling future generations to keep away, could ever be written. It is not so much that these governments have been elected by people who do not care about the environment, or by people who do not believe the science behind global warming, or by people who have faith in nuclear power. They have been elected by people who lack the means to weigh competing truth claims against each other, because even where the evidence points almost unequivocally to an answer, as in the case of climate change, there are always other questions from which this answer cannot be disentangled, such as the pros and cons of the nuclear alternative, and a general framework within which the future of energy policies cannot be divorced from broader economic questions (how our actually existing economy might transition to a carbon-neutral status is hardly clear) and geostrategic ones (the thirst for petroleum in the West cannot be held apart from violence in the Middle East, and elsewhere).

Bruno Latour has discussed the complexities involved in such matters very eloquently. When reading a daily newspaper that deals with them, he observes:

> The same article mixes together chemical reactions and political reactions. A single thread links the most esoteric sciences and the most sordid politics, the most distant sky and some factory in the Lyon suburbs, dangers on a global scale and the impending local elections or the next board meeting. The horizons, the stakes, the time frames, the actors – none of these is commensurable, yet there they are, caught up in the same story. (Latour 1993: 1)

For Latour, postmodern thought was ill-equipped to grapple with such a story, because its rejection of empiricism meant its 'disappointed rationalists' have recourse only to 'groundless denunciations' (Latour 1993: 46). Thus, Latour says, the postmodern world was a 'polytemporal' one, in which:

> No one knows any longer whether the reintroduction of the bear in the Pyrenees, kolkhozes, aerosols, the Green Revolution, the anti-smallpox vaccine, Star Wars, the Muslim religion, partridge hunting, the French Revolution, service industries, labour unions, cold fusion, Bolshevism, relativity, Slovak nationalism, commercial sailboats, and so on, are outmoded, up to date, futuristic, atemporal, nonexistent, or permanent. (Latour 1993: 74)

At the time he wrote the above paragraph, Latour quipped that it was impossible to imagine a step beyond postmodern thought, because in order to do so, 'we have to imagine some super-hyper-incommensurability' (Latour 1993: 62). Twenty-five years later, we no longer have to imagine such a thing, because we live in a world in which a man best known as a reality TV star can be elected to the White House on the basis of statements that are obviously lies and pledges that are manifestly undeliverable – elected, seemingly, precisely *because* those lies and bogus promises flew in the face of received wisdom (they were said to defy 'the establishment', the 'elite', the 'system', to 'challenge political correctness', and so forth). This is unashamedly a politics of cluelessness. Or take the European refugee crisis that began in 2015. The United Nations currently tells us that there are more international migrants on the move than ever before in human history. Some experts point out that reliable figures are impossible to verify, while some demagogues point out that since the UN takes money for its humanitarian work with refugees, its numbers must be biased. Some politicians believe the best response is to build walls; others believe a better response is to welcome as many refugees as will benefit the economy. Some, ranging in their outlooks from fascists to philanthropists, feel that migration ought to be tackled at source, by addressing its root causes in the countries of origin, while for others, often no less philanthropic, this is neo-imperialism. The attitude currently prevailing in Western culture towards such intractably complicated issues has been characterised by filmmaker Adam Curtis as 'Oh dearism' – an attitude which fosters political quietism while simultaneously absolving us of any guilt arising from its consequences, and which consists of a desperate wringing of Western hands in the face of events that seem dreadful yet impossible to understand, let alone control. 'Oh dearism', then, is what happens to ethics under conditions of a polymodern cluelessness (see *Oh Dearism* 2009).

In Latour's terms, such 'Oh dearism' could be regarded as the ethical and political posture to which postmodern thought inevitably leads, because the latter's emphasis on knowledge as something constructed and legitimated was a dead end, failing adequately to grasp the nuances that differentiate matters of fact from what he calls matters of concern (see Latour 2004). Yet I wish to refute this: what I am terming our polymodern moment is characterised not by its recognition of the constructed or legitimated nature of knowledge or reality, but by its submitting to the embrace of cluelessness. In other words, in a polymodern world, it is not so much truth that is socially constructed, but a special kind of ignorance, born of a helpless ambivalence in the face of complexity – in short, cluelessness.

For some brief examples of what is at stake, let us start by considering Lyotard, the prophet of postmodernism, for whom the multiplicity of language games and micronarratives meant we were in what he called a pagan position, having to judge between multiple incommensurable positions without criteria, and then legitimate these groundless judgements as somehow grounded on some sort of foundation. In the polymodern world, there is no such 'and then'. Not only are judgements made without criteria, but they can be made on the basis of information that is known to be false, and legitimation of any kind is superfluous. Consider the difference between the lies told about weapons of mass destruction to justify the invasion of

Iraq in 2003, and the claim made during the UK's so-called Brexit referendum by Eurosceptic politician Nigel Farage that the EU costs Britain £350 million per week, or the erratic claims made by Donald Trump (the 'alternative facts' that his inauguration attracted the biggest crowd in history, or that millions of people voted against him illegally). In 2003, an infamous 'dodgy dossier' of prefabricated half-truths and conjectures was released to justify military action, but for far-fetched claims made in 2016, no evidence of any kind was offered, and in the former case, Farage himself would go on to deny that he ever said these things in the first place – and to continue to do so in the face of clear video evidence that he did.[6]

This, I want to argue, is something qualitatively different from a postmodern politics. Lyotard's micronarratives, and perhaps Rorty's pragmatism, shared a vision of a proliferation of multiple truth claims which, though in competition with one another, lack any objective yardstick by which to measure their success other than their uptake – a model unsurprisingly similar to the neoliberal capitalism inspired by Friedrich August von Hayek.[7] The polymodern condition might seem to carry the pluralistic, anti-foundational zeitgeist of the postmodern through to its most extreme logical conclusion, but actually, it does no such thing: its pluralistic, anti-foundational mindset is not (as postmodernism purported to be) a challenge to a *sensus communis*, or a rebuke to Enlightenment values like the good, the true, or the beautiful – these intellectual frameworks have in large measure already been dismantled by postmodern philosophy. Indeed, rather than falling into the same repetitive narrative of modern–postmodern–some-form-of-post-postmodern, a loosely synonymous way of designating what I am calling the polymodern condition might be to borrow another phrase from Adam Curtis: 'the post-truth world'.[8] The polymodern condition is reached when our culture remains so fragmented and so protean that it is strikingly modern, while being so fragmented and so protean that its modernity is impossible adequately to characterise. Hence, we find ourselves in a position of cluelessness.

Perhaps, at this point, my argument might seem to fall apart in at least two ways: I both admit the existence of a postmodern moment I have occasionally tried to call into question, and assert its distinctiveness from a polymodern moment that succeeds it, despite asserting that the latter is impossible to define. Such a conclusion seems unavoidable in the claim that a transition was made from a postmodern relativism to a polymodern cluelessness. In order to address this problem, let me turn once again to contemporary fiction. Ali Smith's 2016 novel *Autumn* was marketed as a state-of-the-nation novel, inasmuch as it presented British literary fiction's response to the shock wave of the Brexit vote, which had taken place just a few months before. The passage that captures this response most vividly and evocatively reads like this:

All across the country, there was misery and rejoicing ...

All across the country, people felt it was the wrong thing. All across the country, people felt it was the right thing. All across the country, people felt they'd really lost. All across the country, people felt they'd really won. All across the country, people felt they'd done the right thing and other people had done the wrong thing. All across the country, people looked up Google: *what is EU?* All across the country, people looked up Google: *move to Scotland.* All across the country, people looked up Google: *Irish passport applications.* All across the country, people called each other cunts. All across the country, people felt unsafe. All across the country, people were laughing their heads off. All across the country, people felt legitimized. All across the country, people felt bereaved and shocked. All across the country, people felt righteous. All across the country, people felt sick. All across the country, people felt history at their shoulder. All across the country, people felt history meant nothing. All across the country, people felt like they counted for nothing. All across the country, people had pinned their hopes on it. All across the country, people waved flags in the rain. All across the country, people drew swastika graffiti. All across the country, people threatened other people. All across the country, people told people to leave. All across the country, the media was insane. All across the country, politicians lied.... All across the country, social media did the job. All across the country, things got nasty. All across the country, nobody spoke about it. All across the country, nobody spoke about anything else. All across the country, racist bile was general. All across the country, people said it wasn't that they didn't like immigrants. All across the country, people said it was about control. All across the country, everything changed overnight. All across the country, the haves and the have nots stayed the same. All across the country, the usual tiny per cent of the people made their money out of the usual huge per cent of the people. All across the country, money money money money. All across the country, no money no money no money no money.

All across the country, the country split into pieces. (Smith 2016: 59–61)

Perhaps the most striking thing about this passage is the unashamedly self-contradictory cluelessness it describes. In a state-of-the-nation novel, the state of the nation is irreducibly and irreconcilably plural. There is no state of the nation – there are states, certainly, but none of these states are states of the nation. Indeed, the very idea of that nation itself has been split into pieces. It is not that the idea of the nation is shown to be ungrounded or socially constructed à la postmodernism: it is blindly at odds with itself, clueless.

The next most striking thing about this extract is its explicit debt to Charles Dickens's *A Tale of Two Cities* – a presence echoed elsewhere throughout Smith's novel. Smith's repetitive, anaphoric list of antinomies clearly recalls Dickens's celebrated opening paragraph in enumerating the contradictory ways of accounting for a sense of crisis, and is hence a very significant choice of intertext. Dickens famously undercuts his own bold assertions: not only is it somehow the best of times *and* the worst of times, but these hyperboles are belied at the end of the passage with a glib and disconcerting summary – 'in short, the period was so far like the present period, that some of its noisiest authorities insisted on its being received, for good or for evil, in the superlative degree of comparison only' – which strongly suggests it was neither the best nor the worst of times, since those superlatives might just as well be applied to the present period. It probably does not make sense to suggest that Dickens was a polymodernist novelist. Yet he shows us the key to our problem: if the period under discussion can be described in such contradictory ways, how could a definition of it ever be agreed, and how can its similarity to or difference from the present be gauged? Smith's remediation of Dickens's problem adds a twist to it in saying that 'everything changed overnight' while, at almost all levels, pretty much everything stayed exactly the same. It is no wonder that her characters struggle to make sense of this:

> It has become a time of people saying stuff to each other and none of it actually ever becoming dialogue.
> It is the end of dialogue.
> She tries to think when exactly it changed, how long it's been like this without her noticing. (Smith 2016: 112)

Smith's novel evokes the polymodern, post-truth epoch nowhere more clearly than in this extract, and that because of the difficulty of saying when it might have begun. Simplistically: if we could say with certainty how and when the post-truth world came about, then it would not make sense to call it a post-truth world.

Unlike commentators on postmodernism – unlike, say, Lyotard or Jameson – commentators on the polymodern are in the position of the Cretan liar: if what I say is true, my thesis must be false. That this difference can be drawn in turn makes sense of my suggestion that the postmodern and the polymodern are quite distinct despite the impossibility of defining the latter. But it also helps underscore my suggestion that there might not have been a 'postmodern era' in the first place. Truth and its groundings have always been hard to separate from the notion of modernity, probably because of modernity's origin in the age of reason and science that was the Enlightenment. The idea of polymodernism, then, is meant to challenge the received assumption that modernity came to a postmodern end. The post-truth world is a modern world, but it is a *poly*modern one – simultaneously hypermodern and altermodern, digimodernist and remodernist. It is a world in which, for example, we are not our browser histories, but the fictions our browser histories spin about us will have the final say nonetheless.

Notes

1. See Bauman 2000; Beck, Giddens, and Lash 1994; Jameson 2002.
2. For a selection of the key writings involved in these new '-modernisms', and a discussion of the issues they raise, see Rudrum and Stavris 2015.
3. On remodernism, see Childish and Thomson 2000a, 2000b. On metamodernism, see Vermeulen and van den Akker 2010, as well as their contribution, with Alison Gibbons, to the present volume (Chapter 2).
4. The definitive exploration of this problem is Mark Fisher's magnificent *Capitalist Realism* (Fisher 2009).

5. For more on this, see Rudrum 2015.
6. Despite having campaigned from a bus with the pledge that Brexit would deliver £350 million a week to the National Health Service written all over it in huge letters, and despite having repeated this pledge for weeks, Farage famously disowned it, Orwell-style, the very morning after the referendum, on live television. For the relevant footage, see https://www.independent.co.uk/news/uk/politics/eu-referendum-result-nigel-farage-nhs-pledge-disowns-350-million-pounds-a7099906.html. For footage of him making the claim, see https://www.independent.co.uk/news/uk/politics/brexit-eu-referendum-nigel-farage-nhs-350-million-pounds-live-health-service-u-turn-a7102831.html.
7. It could be argued that what I am calling the polymodern condition is simply the cultural logic of neoliberalism. Several of the papers in the special issue of *Social Text* 'Genres of Neoliberalism' (Elliott and Harkins 2013) would endorse such a view. Or recall, for example, Fisher's brilliant analysis of the structure of today's call centres:

   > The closest that most of us come to a direct experience of the centerlessness of capitalism is an encounter with ... the crazed Kafkaesque labyrinth of call centers, a world without memory, where cause and effect connect together in mysterious, unfathomable ways, where it is a miracle that anything ever happens ... What exemplifies the failure of the neoliberal world to live up to its own PR better than the call center? Even so, the universality of bad experiences with call centers does nothing to unsettle the operating assumption that capitalism is inherently efficient, as if the problem with call centers weren't the systemic consequences of a logic of Capital which means organizations are so fixated on making profits that they can't actually sell you anything ... [T]he repeating of the same dreary details many times to different poorly trained and badly informed operatives, the building rage that must remain impotent because it can have no legitimate object, since – as is very quickly clear to the caller – there is no-one who knows, and no-one who could do anything even if they could. Anger can only be a matter of venting ... directed at someone who is a fellow victim of the system but with whom there is no possibility of communality. Just as the anger has no proper object, it will have no effect. In this experience of a system that is unresponsive, impersonal, centreless, abstract, and fragmentary, you are as close as you can be to confronting the artificial stupidity of Capital in itself. (Fisher 2009: 63–4)

   This 'artificial stupidity' is more or less what I mean by a polymodern cluelessness. But I would not want to link it too directly to the logic of neoliberalism. With President Trump imposing tariffs on imports, with Britain voting to leave the EU, and with populist leaders across Europe re-erecting border fences to keep migrants out, it is debatable at best whether neoliberalism and decentred globalisation have a future. But, as I have suggested in this paragraph, our polymodern cluelessness appears to have intensified, not waned, in their immediate aftermath. It is to Fisher's credit that he predicted some of these developments: 'while neoliberalism was necessarily capitalist realism, capitalist realism need not be neoliberal' (Fisher 2009: 78).
8. Admittedly, this phrase might sound rather glib, simplistic, perhaps even melodramatic. And it might not even be entirely accurate. But that is partly the point (see *HyperNormalisation* 2016).

Bibliography

Barthes, Roland (1977), 'The Death of the Author', in Roland Barthes, *Image-Music-Text*, Stephen Heath (ed. and trans.), London: Fontana, pp. 142–8.

Bauman, Zygmunt (2000), *Liquid Modernity*, Cambridge: Polity.

Beck, Ulrich, Anthony Giddens, and Scott Lash (1994), *Reflexive Modernization: Politics, Tradition and Aesthetics in the Modern Social Order*, Cambridge: Polity.

Bourriaud, Nicolas (2009), *Altermodern Manifesto*, Tate, <http://www.tate.org.uk/whats-on/tate-britain/exhibition/altermodern/explain-altermodern/altermodern-explainedmanifesto> (last accessed 23 December 2018).

Bush, George W. (2001), 'A Day of Terror; Bush's Remarks to the Nation on the Terrorist Attacks', *New York Times*, 12 September, <https://www.nytimes.com/2001/09/12/us/a-day-of-terror-bush-s-remarks-to-the-nation-on-the-terrorist-attacks.html> (last accessed 23 December 2018).

Childish, Billy and Charles Thomson (2000a), 'The Stuckist Manifesto', in Katherine Evans (ed.), *The Stuckists: The First Remodernist Art Group*, London: Victoria Press, pp. 8–10.

Childish, Billy and Charles Thomson (2000b), 'Remodernism', in Katherine Evans (ed.), *The Stuckists: The First Remodernist Art Group*, London: Victoria Press, pp. 10–11.

Connor, Steven (2015), 'Postmodernism Grown Old', in David Rudrum and Nicholas Stavris (eds), *Supplanting the Postmodern: An Anthology of Writings on the Art and Culture of the Early 21st Century*, New York: Bloomsbury, pp. 33–48.

Critchley, Simon and Tom McCarthy (2009), 'International Necronautical Society: Tate Declaration on Inauthenticity', in Nicolas Bourriaud (ed.), *Altermodern*, London: Tate, pp. 171–81.

Elliott, Jane and Gillian Harkins (eds) (2013), 'Genres of Neoliberalism', special issue of *Social Text*.

Fisher, Mark (2009), *Capitalist Realism: Is There No Alternative?*, Winchester: Zero.

HyperNormalisation (2016), written and directed by Adam Curtis. UK: BBC.

Into Eternity, written and directed by Michael Madsen. Denmark: Films Transit International, 2010.

Jameson, Fredric (2002), *A Singular Modernity: Essay on the Ontology of the Present*, London: Verso.

Kirby, Alan (2009), *Digimodernism: How New Technologies Dismantle the Postmodern and Reconfigure our Culture*, London: Continuum.

Latour, Bruno (1993), *We Have Never Been Modern*, Catherine Porter (trans.), Cambridge, MA: Harvard University Press.

Latour, Bruno (2004), 'Why Has Critique Run out of Steam? From Matters of Fact to Matters of Concern', *Critical Inquiry*, 30:2, pp. 225–48.

Lipovetsky, Gilles (2005), *Hypermodern Times*, Cambridge: Polity.

Lyotard, Jean-François (1984), *The Postmodern Condition: A Report on Knowledge*, Geoffrey Bennington and Brian Massumi (trans.), Minneapolis: University of Minnesota Press.

McCarthy, Tom (2015), *Satin Island*, London: Jonathan Cape.

McGowan, John (2007), 'They Might Have Been Giants', in Pelagia Goulimari (ed.), *Postmodernism: What Moment?*, Manchester: Manchester University Press, pp. 92–101.

Nealon, Jeffrey T. (2012), *Post-Postmodernism: or, The Cultural Logic of Just-In-Time Capitalism*, Stanford: Stanford University Press.

Oh Dearism (2009), written and directed by Adam Curtis. UK: BBC.

Rudrum, David (2015), 'Note on the Supplanting of "Post–"', in David Rudrum and Nicholas Stavris (eds), *Supplanting the Postmodern: An Anthology of Writings on the Art and Culture of the Early 21st Century*, New York: Bloomsbury, pp. 333–48.

Rudrum, David and Nicholas Stavris (eds) (2015), *Supplanting the Postmodern: An Anthology of Writings on the Art and Culture of the Early 21st Century*, New York: Bloomsbury.

Samuels, Robert (2007), 'Auto-Modernity after Postmodernism: Autonomy and Automation in Culture, Technology, and Education', in Tara McPherson (ed.), *Digital Youth, Innovation, and the Unexpected*, Cambridge, MA: MIT Press, pp. 219–40.

Samuels, Robert (2009), *New Media, Cultural Studies, and Critical Theory after Postmodernism: Automodernity from Žižek to Laclau*, New York: Palgrave.

Smith, Ali (2016), *Autumn*, Harmondsworth: Penguin.

Thorp, Jer (2014), 'You Are Not Your Browser History', *Wired*, 10 July, <https://www.wired.com/story/you-are-not-your-browser-history/> (last accessed 23 December 2018).

Vermeulen, Timotheus and Robin van den Akker (2010), 'Notes on Metamodernism', *Journal of Aesthetics and Culture*, 2.1, <http://www.tandfonline.com/doi/full/10.3402/jac.v2i0.5677> (last accessed 15 March 2019).

Žižek, Slavoj (2011), 'Zizek at Occupy Wall Street', 9 October, <https://zizek.uk/zizek-at-occupy-wall-street-transcript/> (last accessed 23 December 2018).

2

Metamodernism: Period, Structure of Feeling, and Cultural Logic – A Case Study of Contemporary Autofiction

Robin van den Akker, Alison Gibbons, and Timotheus Vermeulen

In this chapter, we further explore the overall argument advanced by *Metamodernism: Historicity, Affect, and Depth after Postmodernism* (van den Akker, Gibbons, and Vermeulen 2017) that metamodernism is a newly dominant cultural logic that can be conceptualised along the axes of historicity, affect, and depth, by applying its findings to a reading of autofictional literature. As such, we first revisit our notion of metamodernism along these axes. We then provide a brief overview of Fredric Jameson's conceptualisation of the cultural logic of postmodernism. Finally, we discuss Ben Lerner's *10:04* (2014) and Adam Thirlwell's *Kapow!* (2012) in order to demonstrate the way in which metamodernism manifests in literature and differs from previous postmodernist fictions.

By Way of Introduction: The Emergence of Metamodernism

Since 2009, we have sought to develop – in teams and individually – the notion of metamodernism as a period, structure of feeling, and cultural logic. In doing so, our thinking revived and revisioned the designation of metamodernism that had itself been around since the 1970s (Abramson 2015; van den Akker and Vermeulen 2017). Throughout, our critical operationalisation of the concept of metamodernism focused on charting an emergent cultural logic related to a dominant structure of feeling situated within the fourth reconfiguration of Western capitalist societies (Vermeulen and van den Akker 2010). What this means is that we have sought to understand cultural practices as expressions of what Raymond Williams has described as 'a particular quality of social experience', one that is 'historically distinct from other particular qualities, which gives the sense of a generation or of a period' (Williams 1977: 131), a zeitgeist, if you will.

Our understanding of metamodernism was conceived, originally, on the back of a double intuition (Vermeulen and van den Akker 2010). On the one hand, we perceived a gap between the many postmodern theories circulating in various studies across the arts and culture and the actual material conditions and dominant artistic and cultural phenomena of the 2000s. Our aim has always been to bring theory to bear more closely on contemporary culture by following its trajectory. On the other hand, we felt that the debate about post-postmodernism was in need of an intervention that differed from the single authorial voice publishing monographs, manifestos, or position papers based on the proposition of an idiosyncratic '-ism', including but not limited to 'performatism' (Eshelman 2008), 'digimodernism' (Kirby 2009), 'hypermodernism' (Lipovetsky 2005), and 'altermodernism' (Bourriaud 2009a, 2009b; see also Gibbons 2012 on 'altermodernist fiction'). Rather, our research on metamodernism has – from the outset – been collaborative, interdisciplinary, and open(-ended).

It is in this spirit that we published our first article, 'Notes on Metamodernism' (Vermeulen and van den Akker 2010), in an open-access journal and as an essayistic invitation to reset the debate. It is in this spirit, too, that we used this article as the point of departure when founding and editing the collaborative research platform with the same (admittedly unimaginative) name.[1] As a collaborative research platform, *Notes on Metamodernism* aimed to provide a space for upcoming and established art critics, literary critics, and cultural theorists interested in mapping and conceptualising the artistic and cultural landscape of the twenty-first century (and contrasting this twenty-first-century landscape with the dominant aesthetic forms of the postmodern years, including in terms of wider material conditions). We maintained this platform for about six to seven years (roughly spanning 2009–16) and it now serves predominantly as an archive containing the various research materials relevant to our inquiry. The platform was not a success by all standards but it succeeded on its own terms in gathering a critical mass of people willing to figure out the 'sticky mess' (Heiser 2017: 56) that is the contemporary by means of the 'dogged attention to detail' (MacDowell 2017: 27) that is the work of any serious critique of arts and culture. For a number of years, then, the platform formed the heart of a research project that spawned countless blog posts, online essays, and peer-reviewed articles as well as numerous expert meetings, symposia, and conferences in which we, alongside and with many, many others, were committed to the critical and scholarly analysis of the present.

Ours has been and still is today a research project in which we – alongside others – seek to: (1) map today's dominant cultural developments by way of the arts; (2) develop an adequate language to discuss these dominant ways of feeling, doing, and thinking; and (3) relate these contemporary concepts, percepts, and affects to recent reconfigurations of Western capitalist societies. There are at least two things that need to be explained here. First (and related to (1) and (2)), these exercises in mapping, translating, and situating are necessary to be able to discuss the ground tones in contemporary culture and, by extension, its undertones and overtones. The notion of a cultural dominant and shared language are not pointing to totalising concepts, to theories of everything. Rather, they allow for both the 'presence and coexistence of a range of very different, yet subordinate, features', as Jameson put it (Jameson 1991: 4), as well as a series of linked dialects and vernaculars (and, by extension, unrelated lingo). Second (and related to (3)), our research is firmly situated within the critical and materialist tradition. It is for this reason that we insist that artistic, cultural, and aesthetic changes must be contextualised by, and situated in, the material conditions of contemporary Western capitalist societies (or rather, the Global North). This points to a form of determination – but it is not determinism. It is, more precisely, not the determinism of an orthodox Marxism that starts from and inevitably leads back to vulgar economism (which is a rather boring procedure since the answer you seek is already implied by the question you raised). Rather it is a 'Marxism without guarantees', as Stuart Hall once put it (Hall 1996). Culture, in this sense, has relative autonomy and is co-determining as much as it must be analysed alongside the economic (Hall 1996). For us, determination then is, following Williams, 'in the *whole* social process *itself* and nowhere else' (Williams 1977: 87, our emphasis).

In our edited collection *Metamodernism: Historicity, Affect, and Depth after Postmodernism* (van den Akker, Gibbons, and Vermeulen 2017), we outlined the central lines of inquiry and key findings of research into metamodernism to date. To summarise our central argument within the confines of the present chapter, we argue that the shift from postmodernism to metamodernism should be situated in the '2000s' – that is: a historical period, roughly lasting from 1999 to 2011 rather than a temporal decade. We attribute, in other words, a similar historical importance to the '2000s' (as a transitional period) when it comes to the emergence of metamodernism as Jameson attributed to the '1960s' (as a transitional period) in relation to the emergence of postmodernism (Jameson 1984). A period, Jameson once wrote, should be understood as 'a common objective condition to which a whole range of varied responses and creative innovations is then possible, but always within that situation's structural limits' (Jameson 1984: 178). Elsewhere, we have outlined in detail the preconditions that emerged, converged, and coagulated to constitute the '2000s' (van den Akker and Vermeulen 2017: 11–17). We do not have the space to repeat this detailed outline, since it ranges from, say, the forces and relations of production to political economy and geopolitics (amongst other preconditioning elements), which, each in its own way, coalesced to form the objective or material conditions in which the metamodern structure of feeling could become dominant. Yet it suffices, perhaps, in lieu of a full-blown analysis, to point to the new cycle of struggles, as some kind of shortcut or privileged entry point into any discussion about periodisation, which characterises the '2000s' as a period. We are referring, here, to the various 'networked social movements' (Castells 2012) around economic and social inequalities and democratic deficits that neatly bookend the '2000s' – from Seattle (1999) and Genoa (2001) to Syntagma Square (Greece, 2010), the Indignados (Spain, 2011), and Occupy (US, EU, and many other countries, 2011–12).

First in 1989 and then in 1992, social theorist Francis Fukuyama declared 'The End of History', meaning that humankind had reached the zenith of its intellectual and evolutionary progress by settling 'all the really big questions' (Fukuyama 1992: xii). Yet, in response to the changed material conditions of the twenty-first century, political commentators – from across the political spectrum – have revisited Fukuyama's claim in order to argue that various world historical crises – along ecological, economic, and (geo)political dimensions – have kick-started History (with a capital 'H'). John Arquilla perhaps most aptly summarises the current historical moment with his notion of a 'bend of History' (Arquilla 2011), which implies that History is forced into a different direction or shape as well as caused to deflect from the more or less straight line of teleological narrative. The notion also captures the increasing awareness across culture that there is something at stake, yet we are still very much unsure what this something – hidden around the bend, as it were – might be (and we will only really know in hindsight).

It is for these reasons that we have described the metamodern structure of feeling as a 'sense of a bend' (playing on Arquilla's notion of the bend of History as well as Jameson's description of the postmodern structure of feeling as so many 'senses of the end of this or that' (Jameson 1991: 1)) (van den Akker and Vermeulen 2017: 2). A 'structure of feeling', as Williams argued, is 'a particular quality of social experience ... historically distinct from other particular qualities, which gives the sense of a generation or of a period' (Williams 1977: 131). The metamodern sense of a bend is most clearly articulated, in arts and culture as well as aesthetics and politics, as a constant oscillation that corresponds to the sense that the dialectic of History is no longer at a standstill, and as such, given its unstable nature, is continuously overcoming and undermining hitherto fixed and seemingly consolidated positions. We have likened this constant oscillation (and this is one of the reasons why we have chosen 'meta-' as a prefix to denote the contemporary cultural logic of Western capitalist societies) to the Platonic notion of metaxy (μεταξύ), which connotes, following Eric Voegelin's interpretation of Plato's use of metaxy in the *Symposium* (Voegelin 1989), a sense of in-betweenness, or, rather, a dialectical movement that identifies with and negates – and hence, overcomes and undermines – conflicting positions (Vermeulen and van den Akker 2010; van den Akker and Vermeulen 2017).

Jameson's Cultural Logic of Postmodernism: The Ends of Historicity, Depth, and Affect

Jameson identifies three 'constitutive features' of postmodernism, which he terms the 'weakening of historicity', 'a new depthlessness', and 'the waning of affect'; in other words, the senses of the end of historicity, depth, and affect. In terms of historicity, the postmodern is characterised by its 'a-historicity' or 'presentism' in which the temporal horizon tends not to extend beyond an immediate euphoric moment (see also Hartog 2016). The postmodern social situation – of a mass-mediatised, credit-driven consumer bubble on a local level as much as the incorporation of hitherto non-capitalist regions on a global level – results, for Jameson, in the subject's loss of their 'capacity actively to extend its pro-tensions and re-tensions across the temporal manifold, and to organize its past and future into a coherent experience' (Jameson 1991: 25). Capital had reached its spatial limits; History had seemingly reached its End. This euphoric, a-historical present has as its corollary a new depthlessness, a catch-all term for the repudiation of a variety of 'depth models' promulgated and/or popularised by modernism and modern thought more generally: the dialectic schemas of appearance and essence (including those of 'false consciousness' vs material conditions); semiotic codes distinguishing between the signifier and the signified (not to mention the referent); the psychoanalytic obsession with the manifest and the latent; and the existentialist politics of the authentic and the inauthentic. In turn, depthlessness is intimately linked with how and what we (can) feel: the waning of affect. To quote Jameson, this 'is not to say that the cultural products of the postmodern era are utterly devoid of feeling', but rather that the waning of affect points to 'a whole new type of emotional ground tone' 1991: 6) that is experienced as 'free-floating and impersonal' sensory 'intensities' and induces 'euphoria' (1991: 15–16).

Jameson argues that postmodernism – or in any case the output of thinkers and artists that we have, fairly or unjustly, come to associate with postmodernism – questions each of these hermeneutic presuppositions. Why assume that an appearance reflects or secretes an essence? Who is to say whether every sign refers to a concept? Are there urges that are latent? How can we be sure there is a soul at all? Each of these presuppositions is especially problematic, moreover, in a globalising, mass-mediated society in which the continuous circulation of capital rounds up anything in its course – like a hurricane roving across the continents, sweeping up trees and houses and people – reducing everything and everyone to the same rule of law: it's all objects for sale, every value is ultimately a market value. To be sure, Jameson sees the repudiation of the depth model as evidence of an imploding culture, where critique, for one, can no longer be differentiated from what it critiques. Yet we might equally perceive it as a critical reorientation so as to come to terms with that collapse. This is exactly what Jameson appears to have in mind when talking about the need for new 'cognitive maps' (Jameson 1990): new models are needed to make sense of new realities, especially if those realities no longer appear to bear any resemblance to what we designated as a 'reality', as something belonging to the category of the 'real', in the past. Jean Baudrillard famously termed this postmodern replacement of reality with 'hyperreality' – where the image or representation no longer stood for a referential real world – a 'simulacrum' (Baudrillard 1993, 1983).

Edvard Munch's *The Scream* (1893) is, for Jameson, a prototype of modernist cultural logic. The ghostly, tormented figure is placed at the heart of *The Scream*, both visually and psychologically: the shapes and swirls of the painted world draw the viewer's eyes towards the figure and, in an inverse movement, are emblematic of the figure's – and we assume also the artist's – tormented experience. The depth that this painting expresses creates its affect for viewers. For contrast, Jameson cites Andy Warhol's work as a model of postmodernist affect. Warhol's stripped-back images – such as the flat, oversaturated colours of *Marilyn* (1967) or the 'photographic negative' and 'X-ray elegance' (Jameson 1991: 9) of *Diamond Dust Shoes* (1980) – are superficial, and resultantly present a 'kind of death of the world of appearance' (1991: 9). The lack of depth, the viewer's inability to form an interpretative reality in order to comprehend the image, leads directly to the waning of affect. It is worth noting here that the depth model is not the exclusive property of modernism. Different depth models emerge in different eras and places. One could similarly ask how Warhol's work fits in with later postmodern practices such as those of Cindy Sherman or Jeff Koons. By and large, though, Munch and Warhol provide expressions of distinctly different structures of feelings, sentiments about what it feels like to be alive in our world at any given time.

Jameson's examples are taken from the visual arts and architecture more than literature; and cultural theory rather than literary studies. Thus, we now provide two brief examples to show how modernist and postmodernist structures of feeling work in literary contexts. This is the beginning of Virginia Woolf's modernist novel *Mrs Dalloway*:

> Mrs Dalloway said she would buy the flowers herself.
>
> For Lucy had her work cut out for her. The doors would be taken off their hinges; Rumplemayer's men were coming. And then, thought Clarissa Dalloway, what a morning – fresh as if issued to children on a beach.
>
> What a lark! What a plunge! For so it had always seemed to her when, with a little squeak of the hinges, which she could hear now, she had burst open the French windows and plunged at Bourton into the open air. How fresh, how calm, stiller than this of course, the air was in the early morning; like the flap of a wave; the kiss of the wave; chill and sharp and yet (for a girl of eighteen as she then was) solemn, feeling as she did, standing there at the open window, that something awful was about to happen. (Woolf 2000: 3)

This opening extract is predominantly written in free indirect discourse, a defining feature of the modernist rendering of stream of consciousness. The only exceptions are the indirect speech of the first sentence ('Mrs Dalloway said'), which introduces the character, and the indirect thought of the fourth sentence ('thought Clarissa Dalloway'). Like Munch's *The Scream*, Woolf's stream-of-consciousness rendering in *Mrs Dalloway* presents the events of the morning through a subjective worldview (Clarissa's). This includes the subjective distortion of time, seen in the way Clarissa's memories – in this instance, her 18-year-old self's experience of Bourton beach in the morning – occupy her thoughts.

Postmodernist fiction, like postmodernist art, rejects psychological realism, flattening representation, and offers a fragmented form of subjectivity. Indeed, Jameson acknowledges 'the "death" of the subject itself' (Jameson 1991: 14–15) and, in doing so, he is undoubtedly gesturing towards the poststructuralist pronouncement of the death of the author (Barthes 1977; Foucault 1977). Roland Barthes argued that the textuality of the late twentieth century 'is henceforth made and read in such a way that at all its levels the author is absent' (Barthes 1977: 145). In fact, in postmodernist fictions, authors themselves are often reduced to textual commodities by appearing as characters in their own fictions. Aleid Fokkema even goes so far as to call the author 'postmodernism's stock character' (Fokkema 1999). In John Barth's short story 'Autobiography', for instance, the first-person narrative voice speaks directly to a second-person reader, 'You who   listen   give me life', and confesses 'I'm a fiction without hope' (Barth 1969a: 35); at the end of the title story, 'Lost in the Funhouse', the character Ambrose 'wishes he has never entered the funhouse. But he has. Then he wishes he was dead. But he's not. Therefore he will construct funhouses for others' (Barth 1969b: 97). In both stories, fictionality is emphasised: the narrator of 'Autobiography' is a textual construct ('a fiction') who does not exist without the reader bringing him into being, whilst Ambrose stands in for an author ('construct[ing] funhouses' as a metaphor for writing fiction) in an ironic quip about the postmodern author's obsolescence.

Literary Metamodernism

The arts of the twenty-first century no longer sustain the postmodern senses of endings. What has been seen as the contemporary affective turn provides support for this shift in cultural sensibilities in response to the metamodern structure of feeling (see also Brinkema 2014: xi–xii; Gibbons 2017a, 2017b). In literary studies, it has become increasingly commonplace to note tendencies that move the dominant sensibility of the contemporary novel beyond the postmodern. Linda Hutcheon, in the now oft-quoted epilogue to the 2002 edition of *The Politics of Postmodernism*, suggested that 'the postmodern may well be a twentieth-century phenomenon, that is, a thing of the past' (Hutcheon 2002: 164).

In 2004, both Robert L. McLaughlin and Timothy S. Murphy petitioned for the supplanting of postmodernism with a more ethical, socially conscious framework. Murphy begins with the metatextual admission that his article

> is not really an objective argument for the abandonment of postmodernism as the privileged interpretive framework for analysis of the present, so much as it is a plea for another perspective to begin systematically contesting the stranglehold that postmodernism has too long exerted over study of contemporary culture. (Murphy 2004: 20)

Correspondingly, McLaughlin turns to writers Jonathan Franzen and David Foster Wallace (he also mentions Rick Moody, Lydia Davis, Bradford Morrow, Richard Powers, Cris Mazza, and A. M. Homes as post-postmodern writers), arguing that because TV culture has 'co-opted postmodernism's bag of tricks to deleterious effect, writers of fiction, especially those who see themselves as the heirs of postmodernism, need to find a way beyond self-referential irony to offer the possibility of construction' (McLaughlin 2004: 65). Ultimately, for McLaughlin, post-postmodernist fiction

> seeks not to reify the cynicism, the disconnect, the atomized privacy of our society nor to escape or mask it (as much art, serious and pop, does), but, by engaging the language-based nature of its operations, to make us newly aware of the reality that has been made for us and to remind us – because we live in a culture where we're encouraged to forget – that other realities are possible. (2004: 67; see also McLaughlin 2012)

Since these early millennial intuitions and appeals for postmodernism's demise, metamodernism has gathered critical traction as a descriptor for the sensibility of contemporary literature. In his introduction to *American Book Review*'s focus issue on metamodernism, Christian Moraru suggests its value as a 'primarily formal (stylistics-generic) and secondarily thematic-philosophical model best describing the textual-discursive level and especially in the West, postmodernism's passing by and into the "next big thing"' (Moraru 2013: 4).

Two distinct theorisations of metamodernism in literature have subsequently emerged. For David James and Urmila Seshagiri, the metamodern is a lens through which to 'reassess and remobilize narratives of modernism' (James and Seshagiri 2014: 89). The aim of this kind of work is, therefore, to unearth and foreground the stylistic features and themes of modernism within contemporary fiction. Contrastingly, in our work, metamodernism is a structure of feeling that manifests in literary works (and cultural and aesthetic forms more generally) through a mix of or oscillation between pre-modernist, modernist, and postmodernist tropes and devices (see, for instance, Vermeulen and van den Akker 2010). Thus, whilst we too perceive modernist tendencies, we also see the propensities of other movements – such as romanticism, realism, and postmodernism – as operative in metamodernist forms of cultural expression. In this sense, our thinking accords with Hutcheon's when she concludes that the 'postmodern moment has passed, even if its discursive strategies and ideological critique continue to live on – as do those of modernism – in our contemporary twenty-first-century world' (Hutcheon 2002: 181). Thus, pre-modern, modern, and postmodern devices are – in varying combinations – put to new use, engaging with, and responding to, the social, ethical, political, economic, and environment material circumstances of the twenty-first century (see Gibbons 2015, 2018; Gibbons, Vermeulen, and van den Akker forthcoming 2019).

We illustrate this herein through a concise discussion of two contemporary fictions that feature autofictional tendencies. Autofiction, as a genre, has become an ever more dominant literary form from the turn of the millennium onwards (see Mortimer 2009: 22; Gibbons 2017b). Narrowly defined, autofictional texts identify as fiction to a greater or lesser extent, and the central character or narrator bears the name of the author. Broadly defined, autofiction is a genre containing novels that conform to this narrow definition, but also other forms in which the protagonist does not take the author's name (or takes a variation of the author's name, or remains nameless), such as the related modes of fictional autobiography and fictional memoir as well as autobiographical fiction. Examples of contemporary autofiction in the strict sense are Dave Eggers's *A Heartbreaking Work of Staggering Genius* (2001), Damon Galgut's *In a Strange Room* (2010), Will Self's *Walking to Hollywood* (2010), Sheila Heti's *How Should a Person Be* (2013), Ruth Ozeki's *A Tale for the Time Being* (2013), Ben Lerner's *10:04* (2014), and Karl Ove Knausgaard's *My Struggle* series (2013 [2009]–). Broader examples of autofiction are *Every Day Is for the Thief* by Teju Cole (2007), *Shanghai Dancing* by Brian Castro (2008), *Jeff in Venice, Death in Varanasi* by Geoff Dyer (2009), *Leaving the Atocha Station* by Ben Lerner (2011), *Kapow!* by Adam Thirlwell (2012), and *The Wallcreeper* by Nell Zink (2014). By 'autofictional tendencies', we therefore mean that the novels adopt stylistic strategies central to the literary genre of autofiction, namely the blending of autobiographical and memoiristic writing with fiction proper and the presence of the author figure as an autobiographical/autofictional subject within the novel. In doing so, crucially, contemporary autofiction incorporates stylistic tropes and formal traits of what may be considered typical postmodern novels, while nevertheless redirecting, and departing from, their postmodern logic.

Take Lerner's novel *10:04* (for additional discussion of the novel as metamodernist, see Gibbons 2017c). From its opening pages, the first-person narrator is identified as a novelist who informs readers, 'the agent had emailed me that she believed I could get a "strong six-figure" advance based on a story of mine that appeared in the New Yorker; all I had to do was promise to turn it into a novel' (Lerner 2014: 4). Additionally, throughout the novel, information about the narrator's literary career bolsters an interpretation of the narrator as a representation of Lerner, as does the named address 'Ben' in letters the narrator writes to himself (2014: 127, 210). *10:04* is divided into four parts, uneven in length. Significantly, the second part is, in fact, a republication of a short story that the real Ben Lerner originally published in *The New Yorker* called 'The Golden Vanity' (Lerner 2012). Just before they encounter the reprinted story, the narrator tells readers that it 'would involve a series of transpositions' including changing characters names: 'the protagonist – a version of myself; I'd call him "the author" – would be approached by a university about selling his papers' (Lerner 2014: 55). These linguistic and ontological games (see Gibbons 2018 for an analysis of *10:04*'s style) are rather postmodernist, in the sense that they offer explicit commentary on the process of writing and that the third-person 'author' in part two of *10:04* reduces the author figure to a textual construct. However, this recursive structure – what Brian McHale identifies as the 'Chinese-box worlds' (McHale 1987: 112–30) of postmodernist fiction (the fiction within the fiction) – serves a different function in Lerner's contemporary autofiction from that it would have in a postmodernist text. This is precisely because 'The Golden Vanity' is a real story that does exist in the real world, and readers can verify this through a Google search. The story's referential existence encourages readers to interpret the first-person narrator as Lerner – though only to a certain degree, since the novel offers biographical details that both conflate and differentiate the narrator and the real author, and *10:04* includes tropes and devices that are obviously fictionalising. Even so, the story of *10:04* – in which an anxious novelist worries about his own health, climate change, and the nature of contemporary artistic and literary production – appeals to readers to enter into a depthy relationship with a reality partially existing, perhaps performatively, beyond the pages of that book, and into an affective relationship with the narrator as a version of the novelist. Whilst Ambrose in Barth's 'Lost in the Funhouse' is a flat, page-bound character, Ben in *10:04* flickers between being an inhabitant of a constructed novel and that of a seemingly depthy real world. As Lerner writes, 'the book you're reading now, [is] a work that, like a poem, is neither fiction nor nonfiction, but a flickering between them . . . an actual present alive with multiple futures' (Lerner 2014: 194).

Vermeulen has described this return of the possibility of the hermeneutic gesture, but not its actualisation, as 'depthiness':

> When I refer to the 'new depthiness', I am thinking of a snorkeler intuiting depth, imagining it – perceiving it without encountering it. If Jameson's term 'new depthlessness' points to the logical and/or empirical repudiation of ideological, historical, hermeneutic, existentialist, psychoanalytic, affective, and semiotic depth, then the phrase 'new depthiness' indicates the performative reappraisal of these depths. (Vermeulen 2015: n.p.; see also Vermeulen 2017)

Vermeulen continues: 'Depth, at least post-Jameson, will always be a "depthing" – a making, actual or virtual, of depth. In this sense, depthiness combines the epistemological reality of depthlessness with the performative possibility of depth' 2015). What Lerner's back-and-forth between biography and fiction achieves is the performance of depth where there may be one, but where there might as well not be. In *10:04*, there is a subject and a lifeworld; it is just not entirely obvious where that subject and its world begin and end (it 'flickers' at the borderlines of fiction and reality), like a body emerging from the mist, or, in Lerner's metaphors in *10:04*, a hand – of *Joan of Arc* in Jules Bastien-Lepage's painting of the same name (1879), of Marty McFly in *Back to the Future* (1985) – fading in and out between multiple spatio-temporal continuums. Indeed, Lerner stresses throughout the novel that the narrator may or may not die at any moment (but especially, perhaps, when he finds himself in Marfa) of Marfan syndrome, a disorder of the connective tissue which means his 'aorta may or may not be proportional' and rupture as a consequence (Lerner 2014: 15).

Thirlwell's *Kapow!* (2012; see Gibbons 2015 for extended discussion of *Kapow!* as metamodernist) also encourages readers to identify the narrator as a textual proxy for the real author through references to Thirlwell's own literary production: 'In my first book I'd played with space, then in my second I had the same kind of fun with time' (Thirlwell 2012: 10). The autofictional framing of the narrators in both *10:04* and *Kapow!* is at the heart of their affective gestures: readers are encouraged to experience the narrators and the storyworlds in which they exist as performatively real. Direct address between narrator and an apostrophic addressed reader ('you') is part of this gesture. The narrator of *Kapow!*, for instance, says, 'It's always been about you, dear reader' (Thirlwell 2012: 71). Similarly, in *10:04*, the narrator asks readers to believe in the referential possibility of the narrator (in this instance, walking with his friend Alex) so that they may experience an emotional rapport – rather than depthless intensities that cannot be translated into feeling – with a subject that is both/neither fictional and/nor nonfictional: 'You might have seen us walking on Atlantic, tears streaming down her face, my arm around her shoulder, but our gazes straight ahead' (Lerner 2014: 8).

Like *10:04*, *Kapow!* also adopts a recursive narrative structure, wherein the events of Cairo's Tahrir Square uprisings are told to the privileged hipster narrator (as author figure) by his London-based Arabic taxi driver Faryaq. Although Thirlwell has constructed a fictional vision of the Egyptian revolution experienced by fictional characters, the 2011 Arab Spring nevertheless is a real-world historical event and therefore offers depth through referential grounding as well as being emblematic of the return of historicity in metamodernism. The narrator of *Kapow!* is continually wondering what the outcome of the 2011 protests will be:

> I realised that for the first time I was imagining a story when the backstories were basically invisible, and so was the ending – because it was happening right in front of me. But this didn't mean, of course, that the backstories didn't exist. They existed as always. Just as the ending existed, somewhere, in an absent future. (Thirlwell 2012: 31)

Whereas the postmodern subject ultimately lost its capacity to orient itself in time on an existential level and to narrate the relation between past, present, and future on a historical level, the metamodern subject appears to be actively searching for, and cobbling together, this lost sense of temporal and historical orientation, in a mostly haphazard, helter-skelter, and makeshift manner. One obvious reason seems to be the sense of a bend creeping into the everyday experiential realm of Western capitalist societies. In *10:04*, the world is off balance, out of sync. New York is, for instance, experiencing 'unseasonable warmth' (Lerner 2014: 3) whilst the narrative arc of the book spans from superstorm Irene to superstorm Sandy, via Occupy Wall Street. This, and other more personal, conflicted moments, forces various characters to adjust their personal narratives – their auto-biographies, as it were – to the extent that they repeatedly have the experience of the 'fiction of the world rearranging itself', as the novel's refrain goes. This points to a shift in our sense of temporal orientation and our regime of historicity. James Pulford, for instance, has noted that time 'is not sequential in *10:04*'; rather 'time is on the slide, the past shunted into the present, the future hurtling backwards' (Pulford n.d.: n.p.). As van den Akker argued, it is precisely this 'multi-tensed' nature of our temporal orientation that characterises the metamodern regime of historicity (van den Akker 2017: 22).

Conclusion

Metamodernist fiction, seen through the lens of the contemporary and dominant genre of autofiction, articulates the sense of bend by means of revisiting, and reviving, in its own historically specific manner, modalities of depth and surface, registers of affect, and regimes of historicity. Authors appear as narrators and characters within the storyworld, but the effect of their appearance runs counter to the ironic play of postmodernist fictions wherein author characters serve a flattening function, foregrounding the constructed textual surface of the fiction. The appearance of author characters in twenty-first-century literature is performative (while foregrounding the real author as the creator of the work) as it applies depth and depthiness and invokes affect and affectedness by foregrounding a contemporary world that the real author and readers share. We can observe, here, a metamodern subject desperately attempting to regain a coherent and meaningful sense of self after realising that it has for too long been indulging in, and succumbing to, postmodern euphoria in the credit-driven, mediatised comfort zone at the End of History. Additionally, by frantically attempting to reorganise the temporal horizon and rearrange the fiction of the world – on a personal and world-historical level – the metamodern subject attempts to reforge the coherence between past, present, and future, albeit not necessarily in this order. Metamodern fiction, then, expresses, as Gibbons argued, an 'aesth-ethical commitment: a refusal to accept the current state of the world, asking readers instead to think critically and defiantly about the ways in which world events are connected and how their own involvement figures in such a world' (Gibbons 2015: 41).

Note

1. It has been our good fortune that 'Notes on Metamodernism' had many flaws (see also MacDowell 2017 for a description of what the article set out to do and consequently failed to do). As any scholar of Wikipedia knows, the most successful stubs are those that fail the most comprehensively. The more flaws in the stub, the more editors it attracts.

Bibliography

Abramson, Seth (2015), 'Metamodern Literature and the Metaverse', *Huffington Post*, 15 April, <http://www.huffingtonpost.com/ seth-abramson/metamodern-literature-and_b_7067708.html> (last accessed 28 December 2018).

Arquilla, John (2011), 'The (B)end of History', *Foreign Policy*, 27 December, <http://www.foreignpolicy.com/articles/2011/12/27/the_bend_of_history> (last accessed 28 December 2018).

Barth, John (1969a), 'Autobiography', in John Barth, *Lost in the Funhouse: Fiction for Print, Tape, Live Voice*, London: Secker and Warburg, pp. 35–9.

Barth, John (1969b), 'Lost in the Funhouse', in John Barth, *Lost in the Funhouse: Fiction for Print, Tape, Live Voice*, London: Secker and Warburg, pp. 72–97.

Barthes, Roland (1977), 'The Death of the Author', in Roland Barthes, *Image-Music-Text*, Stephen Heath (ed. and trans.), London: Fontana Press, pp. 142–8.

Baudrillard, Jean (1983), *Simulations*, Phil Beitchman, Paul Foss, and Paul Patton (trans.), Cambridge, MA: MIT Press.

Baudrillard, Jean (1993), *Symbolic Exchange and Death*, Iain Hamilton Grant (trans.), London: Sage.

Bourriaud, Nicolas (2009a), 'Altermodern', in Nicolas Bourriaud (ed.), *Altermodern: Tate Triennial*, London: Tate, pp. 11–23.

Bourriaud, Nicolas (2009b), *The Radicant*, New York: Lucas and Sternberg.

Brinkema, Eugenie (2014), *The Forms of the Affects*, Durham, NC: Duke University Press.

Castells, Manuel (2012), *Networks of Outrage and Hope: Social Movements in the Internet Age*, Cambridge: Polity.

Eshelman, Raoul (2008), *Performatism, or the End of Postmodernism*, Aurora: Davies Group.

Fokkema, Aleid (1999), 'Postmodernism's Stock Character', in Paul Franssen and Ton Hoenselaars (eds), *The Author as Character: Representing Historical Writers in Western Literature*, Madison: Farleigh Dickinson University Press, pp. 39–51.

Foucault, Michel (1977), 'What Is an Author?', in Donald F. Bouchard (ed.), *Language, Counter-Memory, Practice: Selected Essays and Interviews*, Donald F. Bouchard and Sherry Simon (trans.), Ithaca: Cornell University Press, pp. 113–38.
Fukuyama, Francis (1989), 'The End of History?', *The National Interest*, 16, pp. 3–18.
Fukuyama, Francis (1992), *The End of History and the Last Man*, London: Penguin.
Gibbons, Alison (2012), 'Altermodernist Fiction', in Joe Bray, Alison Gibbons, and Brian McHale (eds), *The Routledge Companion to Experimental Literature*, London: Routledge, pp. 238–52.
Gibbons, Alison (2015), '"Take that you intellectuals" and "KaPOW!": Adam Thirlwell and the Metamodernist Future of Style', *Studia Neophilologica*, 87 (Supp. 1), pp. 29–43.
Gibbons, Alison (2017a), 'Metamodern Affect', in Robin van den Akker, Alison Gibbons, and Timotheus Vermeulen (eds), *Metamodernism: Historicity, Affect, and Depth after Postmodernism*, London: Rowman and Littlefield, pp. 83–6.
Gibbons, Alison (2017b), 'Contemporary Autofiction and Metamodern Affect', in Robin van den Akker, Alison Gibbons, and Timotheus Vermeulen (eds), *Metamodernism: Historicity, Affect, and Depth after Postmodernism*, London: Rowman and Littlefield, pp. 117–30.
Gibbons, Alison (2017c), 'Postmodernism Is Dead: What Comes Next?', *Times Literary Supplement (TLS online)*, 12 June, <https://www.the-tls.co.uk/articles/public/postmodernism-dead-comes-next/> (last accessed 27 December 2018).
Gibbons, Alison (2018), 'Autonarration, "I", and Odd Address in Ben Lerner's Autofictional Novel *10.04*', in Alison Gibbons and Andrea Macrae (eds), *Pronouns in Literature: Positions and Perspectives in Language*, London: Palgrave Macmillan, pp. 75–96.
Gibbons, Alison, Timotheus Vermeulen, and Robin van den Akker (forthcoming 2019), 'Reality Beckons: Metamodernist Depthiness Beyond Panfictionality', *European Journal of English Studies* 23(2).
Hall, Stuart (1996), 'The Problem of Ideology: Marxism without Guarantees', in David Morley and Kuan-Hsing Chen (eds), *Stuart Hall: Critical Dialogues in Cultural Studies*, Routledge: New York, pp. 24–45.
Hartog, François (2016), *Regimes of Historicity: Presentism and Experiences of Time*, New York: Columbia University Press.
Heiser, Jörg (2017), 'Super-Hybridity: Non-Simultaneity, Myth-Making and Multipolar Conflict', in Robin van den Akker, Alison Gibbons, and Timotheus Vermeulen (eds), *Metamodernism: Historicity, Affect, and Depth after Postmodernism*, London: Rowman and Littlefield, pp. 55–68.
Hutcheon, Linda (2002), *The Politics of Postmodernism*, 2nd edn, London: Routledge.
James, David and Urmila Seshagiri (2014), 'Metamodernism: Narratives of Continuity and Revolution', *PMLA*, 129:1, pp. 87–100.
Jameson, Fredric (1984), 'Periodizing the 60s', *Social Text*, 9:10, pp. 178–209.
Jameson, Fredric (1990), 'Cognitive Mapping', in Cary Nelson and Lawrence Grossberg (eds), *Marxism and the Interpretation of Culture*, Chicago: University of Illinois Press, pp. 347–60.
Jameson, Fredric (1991), *Postmodernism, or, The Cultural Logic of Late Capitalism*, London: Verso.
Kirby, Alan (2009), *Digimodernism: How New Technologies Dismantle the Postmodern and Reconfigure our Culture*, New York: Continuum.
Lerner, Ben (2012), 'The Golden Vanity', *The New Yorker*, 18 June, <https://www.newyorker.com/magazine/2012/06/18/the-golden-vanity> (last accessed 27 December 2018).
Lerner, Ben (2014), *10:04*, London: Granta.

Lipovetsky, Gilles (2005), *Hypermodern Times*, Cambridge: Polity.
MacDowell, James (2017), 'The Metamodern, the Quirky and Film Criticism', in Robin van den Akker, Alison Gibbons, and Timotheus Vermeulen (eds), *Metamodernism: Historicity, Affect, and Depth after Postmodernism*, London: Rowman and Littlefield, pp. 25–40.
McHale, Brian (1987), *Postmodernist Fiction*, London: Routledge.
McLaughlin, Robert L. (2004), 'Post-Postmodern Discontent: Contemporary Fiction and the Social World', *Symploke*, 12:1–2, pp. 53–68.
McLaughlin, Robert L. (2012), 'Post-Postmodernism', in Joe Bray, Alison Gibbons, and Brian McHale (eds), *The Routledge Companion to Experimental Literature*, London: Routledge, pp. 212–23.
Moraru, Christian (2013), 'Thirteen Ways of Passing Postmodernism', *American Book Review*, 34:4, pp. 3–4.
Mortimer, Armine Kotin (2009), 'Autofiction as Allofiction: Doubrovsky's *L'Après-vivre*', *L'Esprit Créateur*, 49:3, pp. 22–35.
Murphy, Timothy S. (2004), 'To Have Done with Postmodernism: A Plea (or Provocation) for Globalization Studies', *Symploke*, 12:1–2, pp. 20–34.
Pulford, James (n.d.), 'A Flickering Presence', *Review 31*, <http://review31.co.uk/article/view/303/a-flickering-presence> (last accessed 5 October 2018).
Thirlwell, Adam (2012), *Kapow!*, London: Visual Editions.
van den Akker, Robin (2017), 'Metamodern Historicity', in Robin van den Akker, Alison Gibbons, and Timotheus Vermeulen (eds), *Metamodernism: Historicity, Affect, and Depth after Postmodernism*, London: Rowman and Littlefield, pp. 21–3.
van den Akker, Robin and Timotheus Vermeulen (2017), 'Periodising the 2000s, or, the Emergence of Metamodernism', in Robin van den Akker, Alison Gibbons, and Timotheus Vermeulen (eds), *Metamodernism: Historicity, Affect, and Depth after Postmodernism*, London: Rowman and Littlefield, pp. 1–19.
van den Akker, Robin, Alison Gibbons, and Timotheus Vermeulen (eds) (2017), *Metamodernism: Historicity, Affect, and Depth after Postmodernism*, London: Rowman and Littlefield.
Vermeulen, Timotheus (2015), 'The New "Depthiness"', *e-flux*, 61:1, <http://www.e-flux.com/journal/the-new-depthiness/> (last accessed 27 December 2018).
Vermeulen, Timotheus (2017), 'Metamodern Depth, or "Depthiness"', in Robin van den Akker, Alison Gibbons, and Timotheus Vermeulen (eds), *Metamodernism: Historicity, Affect, and Depth after Postmodernism*, London: Rowman and Littlefield, pp. 147–50.
Vermeulen, Timotheus and Robin van den Akker (2010) 'Notes on Metamodernism', *Journal of Aesthetics and Culture*, 2:1, <http://www.tandfonline.com/doi/full/10.3402/jac.v2i0.5677> (last accessed 27 December 2018).
Voegelin, Eric (1989), 'Equivalences of Experience and Symbolization in History', in Eric Voegelin, *The Collected Works of Eric Voegelin, Vol. 12: Published Essays 1966–1985*, Ellis Sandoz (ed.), Baton Rouge: Louisiana State University Press, pp. 115–33.
Williams, Raymond (1977), *Marxism and Literature*, Oxford: Oxford University Press.
Woolf, Virginia (2000), *Mrs Dalloway*, London: Penguin.

3

The Ends of Metafiction, or, The Romantic Time of Egan's *Goon Squad*

Josh Toth

> But the other side of the phenomenon is as important – that through intentions our presence in the world is across a distance, that we are separated from objects by a distance, which can indeed be traversed, but remains a distance.
>
> (Levinas 1978: 39)

The Time of EA

Jennifer Egan's *A Visit from the Goon Squad* concludes in a relatively dystopian (and seemingly 'post-postmodern') New York. After a series of non-linear chapters marked by discordant voices and styles – a self-reflexive and fake entertainment article (chapter 9), a second-person account focalised through a character who eventually drowns (chapter 10), a PowerPoint presentation (chapter 12), etc. – the novel culminates in the mid-2020s. Handheld devices and social media are even more ubiquitous than they are today; helicopters offer round-the-clock surveillance; and most infants are equipped with 'Starfish' devices that aid their efforts to walk (via an included GPS system) while allowing them to download music with the point of a finger. Significantly (if not flagrantly) titled 'Pure Language', this final chapter details a meeting between Lulu, a young millennial publicist (who works for the once-famous music producer Bennie Salazar), and Alex, an 'ageing music freak who [can't] earn his keep' (Egan 2011: 323). Alex has agreed to help Bennie promote his newest discovery – Scotty Hausmann, a guitarist who once fronted Bennie's high school punk band (The Flaming Dildos). For the past forty or so years, Scotty has lived on the margins of society. Having abandoned his musical aspirations, he has been content to work as an elementary school janitor and (when not working) fish in the 'East River near Williamsburg Bridge' (2011: 93). However, Bennie has now pulled Scotty back onto the music scene, hoping that his palpable 'authenticity' will translate into major sales and the revival of Bennie's career. And in an effort to assist the man he once idolised, Alex has somewhat begrudgingly agreed to supply Lulu with a list of people who might be willing to work as 'authentic' fans (or 'parrots'), using their social media accounts to 'sincerely' praise Scotty and generate interest in his upcoming free concert. When Lulu describes him as the anonymous 'Captain' of a 'blind team' (2011: 318), Alex wonders if Bennie had used those terms himself. Lulu laughs and tells him, in an ostensibly condescending manner, that those are 'marketing terms'. Alex, though, informs Lulu that they are, in fact, 'sports terms. From … sports' (2011: 318). Alex's disgust – with Lulu (whose millennial and market-driven indifference to linguistic usage and stable meaning clearly signals the moral vacuity of this future moment) and himself (for partaking in and enabling what is effectively a sincerity scam) – seems to echo a potential response to the novel's own overt tendency to approach the possibility of meaning and authenticity via a self-reflexive and rhizomatic (and therefore postmodern) form. After all, and even if the novel is 'our reward for living through the self-conscious gimmicks and ironic claptrap of postmodernism' (Charles 2010), its overtly fragmented and disparate perspectives and styles signal the very apotheosis of a postmodern aesthetic – an aesthetic governed by an almost perverse[1] need to 'question notions of closure, totalisation, and universality' (Hutcheon 2002: 67).

And yet the novel presents Lulu as a parody, a career-driven millennial who has discovered the marketing power of such questioning. We are, in other words, given to sympathise with Alex's almost nostalgic disgust – especially once Lulu starts to define (bombastically) a number of marketing terms and concepts, all of which have been reduced to initialisms, the meanings of which are ostentatiously dependent upon a fleeting and utterly restricted field of discourse. 'BTs' are 'blind teams' that 'work especially well with older people' – people who (Alex surmises) 'can't be bought' (Egan 2011: 319). 'DMs' are 'disingenuous metaphor[s]' (like 'being bought') that function 'like descriptions, but [are] really judgements' (2011: 319). And 'AP' stands for 'atavistic purism … [which] implies the existence of an ethically perfect state, which not only doesn't exist and never existed, but it is usually used to shore up the prejudices of whoever's making the judgements' (2011: 319). Faced with Alex's despair and bewilderment, Lulu concludes by mocking his 'calcified morality' and championing 'Ethical ambivalence – we call it EA – in the face of a strong marketing action' (2011: 320). For Lulu, Alex's insistence that some things can be 'inherently wrong' is simply judgemental and colonial: 'if I believe, I believe. Who are you to judge my reasons?' (2011: 320). The conversation thus echoes and anticipates recent political appropriations and reductions of poststructural and/or postmodern conceits: mercurial and self-serving repudiations of 'fake news', appeals to 'alternative facts', anti-intellectual rejections of climate science, neoliberal claims that all perspectives are equal, etc. Of course, this transmutation of truth into a mere matter of belief or political affiliation (and wholly unfettered by any grounding in moral absolutism) is nowhere more evident or distilled than in the rise of Donald Trump – who rode a wave of anti-intellectual nationalism while manipulating the incoherence (or cacophony) of popular media to become the forty-fifth president of the USA.

As Egan suggests, such manipulations cannot be dissociated from the rising necessity of (what Alex's academic wife, Rebecca, calls) 'word casings': 'a term she'd invented for words that no longer had meaning outside quotation marks. English was full of these empty words – "friend" and "real" and "story" and "change" – words that had been shucked of their meanings and reduced to husks' (2011: 324).

We need no longer take responsibility for what we claim because any claim is always already removed from our intended meaning. I may have said it; but it is not what I 'meant'. One imagines that Rebecca's study of word casings involves, also, a look at the contemporary overuse of the word 'like' (as everything is a mere metaphor) and the concurrent necessity of imposing 'literally' before statements of 'real' truth. The grand irony, of course, is that the tools Lulu (like Trump's 'team') employs are the bastardised tools of a postmodern intelligentsia. As Lulu asserts, in an overt parroting of poststructuralist thinking, 'All we've got are metaphors; and they're never exactly right. You can't ever just *Say. The. Thing*' (2011: 321). Moreover, Lulu's DMs and APs clearly echo Jean-François Lyotard's various efforts to champion (in his seminal *The Postmodern Condition*) 'a theory of games which accepts agnostics as its founding principle' (Lyotard 1984: 16).[2] Everything is, in this sense (and certainly for Lulu), a matter of 'arranging the data in a new way' (Lyotard 1984: 51). In other words, Lulu confirms and wantonly revels in Jürgen Habermas's 'legitimation crisis', the interruption of cultural modernity's 'project', the contemporary indifference to or impossibility of (what Fredric Jameson describes as) the Habermasian 'vision of a "noisefree," transparent, fully communicational society' (Jameson 1979: vii).[3] Such a project – which Lyotard carefully undermines in *The Postmodern Condition* – has become a liability for the consumer-oriented mandates of societal modernism, which Habermas long ago opposed to the avant-garde spirit of cultural, or aesthetic, modernism.

In this sense, the final chapter of Egan's book (which, in playing with its own series of 'little narratives',[4] delegitimises any superficial appeals to certainty, authenticity, or moral certitude) – and especially via the parody that is Lulu – stresses what Jeffrey Nealon describes as the intensification of postmodernism (in the form of post-postmodernism[5]), or what Gilles Lipovetsky calls 'hypermodernism'. As Lipovetsky puts it, 'The heroic will to create a "radiant future" has been replaced by managerial activism: a vast enthusiasm for change, reform and adaptation that is deprived of any confident horizon or grand historical vision' (Lipovetsky 2005: 34). In Lulu, we get the sense that postmodernism has won – and, in winning, lost whatever efficacy it once had as an aesthetic movement. Its once radical appeals to fragmentation, moral relativity and endless narrative play now seem 'vaguely old-fashioned' (Lipovetsky 2005: 30). But let's be careful here. Or rather, let's not forget Habermas's careful effort to maintain a line between the social and the cultural, a line neither Nealon nor Lipovetsky seems particularly interested in recovering. Such a line allows us to make sense of the seemingly contrary approaches to postmodernism's end, or apparent transmutation. How, after all, might we square Nealon and Lipovetsky's sense of societal (post)modernity gone rampant with the claim that we are now seeing (in Raoul Eshelman's terms) an aesthetic return to 'monism' – as in a renewed faith in a 'unified concept of sign and strategies of closure' (Eshelman 2008: 1)? Given these apparently opposed claims, we surely must concede that postmodernism's (aesthetic) death is paradoxically tied to its (societal) victory, to its omnipresence as contemporary society's ideological backdrop. We no longer need a Kurt Vonnegut or a John Barth (or, for that matter, a Derrida or a Michel Foucault) because the notion that identity is merely an arbitrary discursive effect,[6] or that one truth claim is just as contingent as any other, is simply ubiquitous (and endlessly confirmed every time we engage with a world that is now unapproachable except via unstable databases, anticipatory search engines, and digital profiles). On YouTube, Twitter, Facebook, or the most recent reality TV competition, we endlessly remake ourselves. For (our) truth is always only a matter of perspective.

The Goal of Plasticity

This is not to suggest that society (en masse) finally 'gets' postmodernism, that concepts like deconstruction, discursive power, performativity, schizoanalysis, *objet petit a*, the death of the author, etc., are being employed in popular culture and politics with nuance and care; it is to suggest, rather, that the more corrosive implications of postmodernism have come to buttress a societal trend towards irresponsibility, hyperindividualism, and market-empowering uncertainty. The victory *as* death of postmodernism has come at the cost of its subtler implications – its ethical efficacy, its effort to 'politicise [the historical and the factual] through [a] metafictional rethinking of the epistemological and ontological relations between history and fiction' (Hutcheon 1988: 121). At their most nuanced, the metafictional strategies of postmodernism were never about endorsing perverse and unfettered play. For confirmation, we need only re-read with care the works of Vonnegut, Barth, Philip K. Dick, Kathy Acker, or even Thomas Pynchon (in terms of literature) and Derrida, Foucault, Lyotard, Julia Kristeva, and Richard Rorty, etc. (in terms of theory). For writers and theorists of the period, the emphasis is most certainly on the instability between reference and referent, signifier and signified – and, therefore, the impossibility of articulating or sustaining a universal claim about the past or the Real; yet the purpose of such an emphasis was almost invariably political, always tied to 'dedoxification' (as Hutcheon would say) and the destabilisation of those narrative constructs that functioned to restrict possibility and 'play' in the name of hegemonic and oppressive systems of control. As Derrida assures us, '*Deconstruction is justice*' (Derrida 2002: 243); for, even in his earliest works (i.e., in his earliest efforts to expose the inescapable nature of supplementarity, the paradoxical strain of corruption that buttresses – while endlessly undoing – every effort towards coherence and closure), a certain responsibility is mandated. Were we in our constructions of the self, in our interpretations of the other, in our representations of the past, to simply 'add any old thing... the seam would not hold' (Derrida 1981: 64). The potential of play for the postmodernist at her or his most rigorous is infinite, but only within a fixed horizon of possibility. The Real, plastic-like, can yield (to) an infinite number of symbolic formulations; but some formulations are simply incorrect, simply irresponsible, self-serving. The representation of the Real (of the self, of the past, of meaning) must always entail responsibility for two interrelated tasks: (1) it must remain true to the outside limits of what cannot be denied and (2) it must signal, in a finite and always contingent construction, that the Thing represented necessarily exceeds the formative moment of its expression. It must signal, as Levinas would suggest, that the infinite is only ever accessible *in* the finite, that the infinite is always *in*finite.[7] Without fiction, as Žižek reminds us, 'reality itself dissolves' (Žižek 1993: 91). But this does not mean that we can simply deny or ignore the Real. Instead, the very experience, or trauma, of an epistemological failure signals a form of contact, a mode of knowing: 'what at first appeared to be an epistemological obstacle turns out to be the very index of the fact that we have "touched the Truth," we are in the heart of the Thing-in-itself *by the very trait which appeared to bar access to it*' (Žižek 1993: 177). What is lost on (or wilfully overlooked by) a (post-)postmodernist like Lulu is the fact that there *is* an end to interpretative play, a point at which the Real cannot be denied, or symbolically evaded – even if it must always be in excess of the frame that momentarily relates it. To counter the intensification of postmodernism (and thus the exhaustion of its aesthetic efficacy) we must then shift the emphasis from the utter inescapability of the symbolic (as stressed by Jacques Lacan and others) to the inescapability of a certain ontological gravity – that which necessarily governs, even as it is effected by, our endless failures to grasp it.

This is not a matter of simply going back, as even someone like Eshelman seems willing to admit. We now understand the danger of assuming the possibility of a universally applicable and (thus) 'radiant future', or a '"noisefree," transparent, fully communicational society' (to recall Jameson's phrasing). But does this mean, to counter the intensification of postmodernism (as a social trend) – and thus to avoid or ameliorate a future of morally vacuous Lulus – that our only recourse is to 'pretend'? A game of pretend is certainly what critics like Eshelman seem to see and advocate on the horizon. While considering a recent wave of what he terms 'performatist' works, Eshelman uncovers an apparent 'revi[val] of theist myths' and a concurrent refusal to endlessly 'track[] signs in their feminine formlessness' (Eshelman 2008: 13). This odd appeal to a type of tongue-in-cheek phallogocentrism suggests that art now counters postmodern excess by 'forc[ing] readers or viewers to make a choice between the untrue beauty of the closed work or the open, banal truth of its endless contextualisation' (2008: 37). In doing so, 'performatist' works shut down or close off the infinite regresses of postmodernism (what Eshelman somewhat reductively associates with Derridean 'undecidability'[8]), effecting something akin to a simple suspension of disbelief. We know it is not real, but we believe it anyway (at least within the restricted conceptual 'frame' of the given work). That is, we are given to pretend, in the moment, that a sense of closure or unity or harmony (or whatever) is true.

Eshelman's reading of contemporary aesthetics aligns neatly with the concept of 'metamodernism' Timotheus Vermeulen and Robin van den Akker have been developing since 2010. For Vermeulen and van den Akker, metamodernism overcomes postmodernism through pervasive and unrelenting acts of oscillation;[9] that is, metamodern works 'oscillate ... between a modern enthusiasm and a postmodern irony' (Vermeulen and van den Akker 2010: n.p.). In doing so, they rejuvenate what Vermeulen and van den Akker understand as Immanuel Kant's '"negative" idealism', which exposes us to the fact that humans are 'not really going toward a natural but unknown goal, but they [must] *pretend* they do so that they progress morally as well as politically' (Vermeulen and van den Akker 2010: n.p., my emphasis). Likewise, as Eshelman puts it, 'Performatist works of art attempt to make readers *believe* rather than convince them with cognitive judgements. This, in turn, may enable them to assume moral or ideological positions that they otherwise might not have' (Eshelman 2008: 37). But surely we must ask what this 'progress' or what these 'judgements' might (or should) look like? If this is all just a matter of belief, if this is all just a matter of pretend – of contingent truth claims that are always about to oscillate (back) into irony – then what could possibly distinguish good progress and good judgements from bad? As Lulu puts it, 'if I believe, I believe. Who are you to judge my reasons?'

Still: there are good reasons for the arguments Eshelman and Vermeulen and van den Akker advance. The post-postmodern and/as the hypermodern is undoubtedly marked by acts of oscillation and wilful moments of pretend. Take the examples (above) of social media and reality TV. Twitter, like the televised 'reality' of a 'Real Housewife' or a Hollywood family, is filled with moments of abject authenticity, and yet these moments are utterly stripped of any long-term implications or consistency; they are endlessly undermined in or forgotten by the next (always new) authentic moment. The ostensible transparency of either medium is perpetually offered even as we are perpetually reminded that there is nothing 'permanent' to see. We all know everything is scripted, staged, or spun anyway. Trump's campaign and presidency are again instructive – especially the role of Twitter in both. Even though he frequently claims that he uses Twitter because the media is not 'spreading [his] word accurately' (Trump 2017), Trump clearly understands that he can tweet or say anything. Whatever is said only matters in the moment. The complete opposite will easily outweigh a previous claim a few weeks (or even a few moments) later. Claims about the crowd size at his inauguration or the wiretapping of his offices in Trump Tower can be forced into the realm of (a type of) truth while other claims – such as the claim that 'The concept of global warming was created by and for the Chinese in order to make U.S. manufacturing non-competitive' (Trump 2012) – can simply be ignored or denied (even as they are left to linger, in some social circles, as 'fact'). The obvious point is that such oscillations are not the modus operandi of a new and viable aesthetic movement – at least not insofar as such a movement functions to resist the intensifications both Nealon and Lipovetsky identify.

Instead, the post-postmodern aesthetic – which, I think, Egan's novel (like various other works of metafiction that have appeared in the wake of postmodernism) finally exemplifies – counters the perilous intensification of postmodernism by re-engaging a type of Hegelian dialectics. But such a 'return to Hegel' (Žižek 1989: 7) is not a return to the '"positive" idealism' Vermeulen and van den Akker associate with the 'notion of history dialectically progressing toward some predetermined Telos' (Vermeulen and van den Akker 2010: n.p.). As Žižek has shown repeatedly over the course of three decades, Hegel's is not a closed system – even if it can allow us to escape a number of '"post-modernist" traps' (Žižek 1989: 7). Hegel's is a system that compels us to 'tarry[] with the negative' (Hegel 1977: 19), to perpetually endure the 'strenuous effort of the Notion' (1977: 35) – the notion, that is, of a divine or *infinite* reality (what Hegel calls 'spirit'). What allows us in Hegel to apprehend this *infinite*

Real is, paradoxically, the willingness to endure the failure to do so. It is the experience of such a failure that, finally, signals the ethical sustainment of what cannot – not with justice, at least – be contained in the finite, in the coherence of a momentary and contingent form of representation. The dialectical movement of spirit does not end, for Hegel, in closure; it is sublated the moment its paradoxically *infinite* end is signalled and sustained in a coherent expression or experience – for 'The *being* of Spirit cannot in any case be taken as something fixed and immovable' (1977: 204). As a logical consequence of this mobility or plasticity (which we might understand as endless potential within a limited field), 'the *being* of Spirit' can only know or express itself in what it is not. Only in 'utter dismemberment . . . [does spirit, or the Real] find[ ] itself' (1977: 19). In other words, and for Hegel, the 'evanescent itself must . . . be regarded as essential, not as something fixed, cut off from the True, and left lying who knows where outside it, any more than the True is to be regarded as something on the other side, positive and dead' (1977: 27). The 'strenuous effort of the Notion' entails grasping, by simultaneously remaining open to the impossibility of ossifying, the infinite plasticity of the Real – 'plasticity' being (as Catherine Malabou has demonstrated[10]) the central concept that haunts Hegel's entire project. In no way is this a matter of pretending, sustaining unjustifiable beliefs, or engaging in impulsive oscillations. It is not about ignoring or suppressing dialectical tension or swinging about between two poles. The impossible is made possible because its necessary negation (in the finite limitation of sensory experience or expression) is itself negated.

More specifically, the ethical potential of a certain 'return to Hegel' can be seen in a shift from the historiographic metafiction of postmodernism to (what I have called elsewhere) the historio*plastic* metafiction of post-postmodernism.[11] While the former maintains an often perverse emphasis on the instability and contingency of the graphic/symbolic, the latter (even as it sustains many of the conceits of its predecessor) shifts our attention to the *infinite* Real that perpetually escapes its symbolisation. Such works – Toni Morrison's *Beloved* (1987), Tim O'Brien's *The Things They Carried* (1990) and *In the Lake of the Woods* (1994), Mark Z. Danielewski's *House of Leaves* (2000), Mark Leyner's *The Tetherballs of Bougainville* (1997) and *The Sugar Frosted Nutsack* (2012), Egan's *Goon Squad*, etc. – inflict a type of metafictional diremption (which negates the possibility of mimetic closure) while simultaneously exposing such diremptions as the very condition of mimetic efficacy. Certainly, this is a very deconstructive move (and certainly tied to what I call in *The Passing of Postmodernism* an 'ethics of indecision'[12]), but one that is far more overt in returning deconstruction to its often-suppressed Hegelian origins. It is, in this sense, post-deconstructive – as Malabou might understand the phrase. Nevertheless, this negation of what is negated *sublates* (that is, holds to by letting go of) what is lost. The antithetical relation of a 'universal symbolic network' (Žižek 1993: 217) to the traumatic Real it negates is itself negated, emerging as the very condition of knowledge. What remains absent is paradoxically sustained as *infinitely* plastic, as *infinitely* mutable within the absolute limitations of a fixed horizon of possibility, a true end. We are encouraged to respect and endure the very Thing that historiography cannot help but efface through the deployment of mimetic forms. The metafiction of post-postmodernism is, therefore, neo-romantic (as Vermeulen and van den Akker suggest) – but only in the most Hegelian of senses. As such, it must be understood in relation to what Hegel (in his *Aesthetics* (1975)) defines as the 'symbolic' and the 'classical'. Or rather, the persistence of metafiction (like Egan's) in the post-postmodern era begins to make sense if we associate both modernism and postmodernism with the 'symbolic' tendency to preserve reality through acts of representational distortion, and the social realism of the nineteenth century with those works of 'classicism' that fully negate the difference between a given form and the notion it embodies. 'Historio*plastic* metafiction' functions – or moves us beyond the failures of cultural postmodernism (while simultaneously challenging its social hegemony) – by 'romantically' renewing a classical mode via the redeployment of a symbolic one. The result is what David James has recently called an 'occasion for consolidating the integrity of content and form' (James 2011: 502). But let's reapproach Hegel's aesthetic categories via a return to Egan's *Goon Squad*.

Post-Postmodern Intrusions

Not surprisingly, Lulu oscillates. After exposing his 'calcified morality', Lulu (whose generation, we are told, paradoxically shuns the corruption of tattoos and refuses to swear) suddenly asks Alex if she can 'just T [him]... Now' (Egan 2011: 321) – 'T-ing' being, in the future, a form of (hyper)texting. Before Alex can respond, Lulu begins 'working her handset'. The result is a vibration in Alex's pocket which forces him to jostle his daughter (Cara-Ann), whom he has brought to the meeting and whom he and his wife have adamantly refused to introduce to social media. Via 'T', Lulu short-circuits Alex's moral unease, asking (directly) if he has some names for her: '*U hav sum nAms 4 me?*' Alex quickly and impulsively T's a reply: '*hEr thA r*'. '*GrAt*', Lulu tells him: '*Il gt 2 wrk*' (2011: 321). The meeting, to Alex's surprise, is suddenly brought to a successful conclusion:

> They looked up at each other. 'That was easy', Alex said.
> 'I know', Lulu said. She looked almost sleepy with relief. 'It's pure – no philosophy, no metaphors, no judgements.'
> 'Unt dat', Cara-Ann said. She was pointing at Alex's handset, which he had been using, unthinkingly, mere inches from her face. (2011: 321)

The apparent irony of the scene – Lulu's sudden appeal to transparency and authentic communication (via a mode of communication that is almost too truncated and garbled to follow) – is oddly undermined by Cara-Ann's intrusion of some 'baby talk'. Her 'unt dat' clearly mimics (or parodies) the T-ing to which Lulu and Alex have just resorted, marking the very process as infantile. But it marks it, also, as something prelinguistic or trans-linguistic – as if to suggest that Lulu is actually correct: T-ing does somehow short-circuit the ideological, the inevitable bias of common usage. Indeed, Egan's depiction of T-ing – especially its overt association with Cara-Ann and that which borders on the prelinguistic – recalls, or can be easily read alongside, Kristeva's claim that a certain inexpressible truth is intimated whenever an otherwise coherent (and rule-abiding) 'phenotext' is disrupted by a troublingly and unpredictable 'genotext'. Consequently, T-ing suggests the possibility of grasping something real in the moment of its most overt distortion. Let me clarify.

For Kristeva, 'phenotext' denotes a field of symbolic coherence, that which 'obeys rules of communication and presupposes a subject of enunciation and an addressee' (Kristeva 1985: 87). 'Genotext', on the other hand, refers to those (non-symbolic) elements which 'disturb the transparency of the signifying chain ... and move ... [us] toward the instinctual, material, and social process [a] text covers' (1985: 101). The genotext functions as a type of portal through which we might glean the *chora* – the prelinguistic and 'agitated body' that coherent textuality must necessarily obscure, or utterly efface. In those texts that engage in intrusive genotextual disruptions, we experience an 'explosion of the semiotic [*chora*] in the symbolic' (1985: 69).[13] In T-ing – in abandoning the illusion of phenotextual transparence – Lulu and Alex paradoxically yield to the impossibility of full, or 'noisefree', communication. And yet, in its radically fragmented, ungrammatical, and simplified expression, the ineffable contours of Alex's desire to give Lulu his list of names (like the purely intuitive, or 'agitated', desire of a baby to touch and manipulate a parent's phone) is seemingly registered. It is registered via its profound absence, the utter impossibility of its coherent communication.

This is not to suggest that Egan is offering T-ing as a finally ethical mode of communication. Especially for Lulu, its illusion of simplicity (as well as its paradoxically concurrent tendency towards cacophonous distortion) can be a tool for manipulation, an excuse for forgoing responsibility. We should not forget that Kristeva locates the best semiotic explosions in works of modernist experimentation – works by James Joyce or Stéphane Mallarmé. This is because the effort towards revolutionary acts of authentic expression must risk eviscerating the very possibility of communication. Such modernist experimentation therefore perpetually risks (and typically succumbs to) the evasive and ethically fraught uncertainties that largely define, for Hegel, works of symbolic pre-art. As the first of art's three stages, symbolic art functions primarily to express the utter incompatibility of an idea and its expression, or objectification, in form. In its more advanced stages, the symbolic form simply confirms the sublimity of what cannot be expressed: 'For both sides [content and form, meaning and shape], although bound into an identity, still coincide neither with one another nor with the true nature of art, and therefore they struggle none the less to escape from this defective unification' (Hegel 1975: 317). Consequently, symbolic art is marked by 'confusion, [by] fermentation and wild medley, [a] staggering hither and thither' (1975: 319). Such incoherent forms, such distortions, function to express its 'inkling of the inadequacy of its pictures and shapes' (1975: 319). But it cannot get beyond this mere 'inkling'; it 'can call in aid nothing but the distortion of shapes to the point of the boundlessness of a purely quantitative sublimity .... At this stage, therefore, we live in a world full of blatant contrivances, incredibilities, and miracles' (1975: 319). Such descriptions of 'symbolic' art (with its fixation on 'defective unification') can be applied, perhaps obviously, to Egan's depiction of T-ing – just as, of course, they can be applied to the most overtly alienating works of high modernism. What, after all, marks modernism more than anything is the absence of the Thing – or as Lacan (via Kant) calls it, *das Ding*. The problem with postmodernism (as Egan suggests via her parodic depiction of Lulu) is that it simply replicated (and, at its worst, irresponsibly revelled in) this fixation on absence. This is precisely what Žižek means to show when he inverts our typical understanding of the distinction between modernism and postmodernism. Lulu's appeal to the false purity of T-ing can, therefore, help us to trace modernism's resonance in postmodernism – even if, at the same time, T-ing (like Egan's seemingly postmodern novel) finally indicates (also) the possibility of aesthetically overcoming the fecklessness of a now intensified postmodernism.

For Žižek, modernism's radical 'illegibility' – exemplified most obviously in Joyce's *Finnegans Wake* – 'functions precisely as an invitation to an unending process of reading, of interpretation' (Žižek 1991: 151). But postmodernism's distortions are no less identifiable as symbolic; they're merely the 'obverse' of modernism's engagement with sublime absence. Instead of a profound and irretrievable absence, a void around which the text organises itself (while always risking unification through increasingly incredible forms of obscurity), the absent Thing in postmodernism becomes utterly banal, nothing but a signifier that has come to occupy the place of the Thing. We are forced to confront the nauseating truth that 'there is nothing behind this mask of simulation' (Žižek 1991: 149). Divine reality, the *in*finite, is presented (merely) as finite, arbitrary, garish simulacrum. We find ourselves face to face with the horrific hollowness and inconsistency of what should be whole, coherent, absolute. While modernism presents us with an absence that may yet be discovered in a finally adequate form, postmodernism offers a nauseating presence that is horrifically contingent and fractured. Either way we get a form of the Hegelian symbolic, 'For the idea [remains] still more or less indeterminate and unshapable' (Hegel 1975: 76). One alternative, if we follow Hegel, is a classical mode – the form which originally formed out of, and finally negated, the symbolic. Exemplified in Greek statuary, the classical 'puts a stop to the purely symbolising and sublime preliminary experiments of art, because spiritual individuality now has its shape, its adequate shape, in itself, just as the self-determining Concept generates out of itself the particular existence adequate to it' (Hegel 1975: 317). The classical marks, if we can redeploy Kristeva's summation of the entire Hegelian project, a type of 'pre-symbolic immediacy' (Kristeva 1985: 69). But this immediacy is false; it simply negates the feckless incoherence of the symbolic by ossifying the idea, blinding us to any sense that the Real is *in*finitely plastic and always in excess of the form in which it is expressed or experienced. Its ability to communicate is perfect – as we see in nineteenth-century social realism or traditional forms of biography and autobiography, or the more beguiling techniques of contemporary documentaries – but such pure communication merely shifts our attention away from that which we fail to grasp. For this very reason, a work like Egan's does not (or, perhaps, cannot) simply return us to classical 'monism' – which was, from the very beginning, a mode of pretend. Instead, Egan's novel works to sublate the symbolic tendencies that long since paralysed postmodernism.

Or rather, T-ing – which seems so very like (or can be easily deployed by Lulu as) a 'symbolic' form – can be said to exemplify the goal of Egan's novel (and contemporary metafiction more generally). This is because T-ing exposes us to the risk and the necessity of traversing the delicate line that connects modern and postmodern (symbolic) forms. It points to the possibility of romantically satisfying and overcoming a desire for mimetic hegemony (and stifling closure) by carefully reinvesting in, or sublatively renewing, the symbolic. This sublation of the symbolic (mediated by the impulse towards closure that defined the classical, that defines realism) marks, for Hegel, the triumph of romantic art. In this very specific sense, we might think of contemporary metafiction, at its most efficacious, as a distinctly romantic form – or as, rather, neo-romantic. I return more fully to this possibility in the next section. For now, my point is this: Egan's depiction of T-ing opens us to the possibility of (and the dangers involved in) sublating a distinctly postmodern (symbolic) form. The full significance of this possibility becomes overt when Alex, Rebecca, and Cara-Ann finally find themselves at Scotty's concert and Egan encourages us to parallel the oddly revelatory aspects of Alex's infantile T-ing with the shared moment of authentic communion Scotty's performance effects.

Located somewhere near the reflecting pools that now mark 'the footprint' (and therefore the traumatic absence) of the World Trade Center, Scotty's venue is (by the time Alex and his family arrive) a 'sea of slings and sacs and babypacks, older children carrying younger ones' (Egan 2011: 330). It is filled, as Alex notes to himself, with an 'army of children: the incarnation of faith in those who weren't aware of having any left' (2011: 330). In an effort to capture this thought in its essence and to make some sense of it, he reconceives it in T: 'if thr r children, thr mst b a fUtr, rt?' (2011: 331). The mass of children is, as we are told earlier, the result of a recent baby boom, the response to a recent and prolonged war. They signal a form of renewal, as do 'the new buildings [that] spiral[] gorgeously against the sky, so much nicer than the old ones (which Alex had only seen in pictures)' (2011: 331). Such renewal, though, is (for Alex) only articulable in T, in the failure to apprehend it. And, when Scotty finally appears on stage – after Alex is called away from his family to help Bennie and Lulu coerce the reticent musician (who 'has a hard time with conversation' (2011: 326), never mind performance) – it is the most infantile of responses that takes hold of the audience and legitimises the false parroting that generated the crowd in the first place: 'the pointers, who already knew [Scotty's kid-oriented] songs, clapped and screeched their approval, and the adults seemed intrigued, attuned to the double meanings and hidden layers, which were easy to find' (2011: 335). In a moment that soon 'enter[s] the realm of myth' (2011: 336), the audience discovers 'the embodiment of their own unease in *the form* of a lone, unsteady man on a slide guitar' (2011: 335, my emphasis). Scotty's is, in other words, the intrusive expression of an 'agitated body'. He moves the audience (filled with 'the rapt, sometimes tear-stained faces of adults [and] the elated, scant-toothed grins of toddlers' (2011: 336)), infant-like, 'toward the instinctual, material, and social process[es]' (Kristeva 1985: 101) which invariably exceed their expression. While the moment is 'registered as pure' (Egan 2010: 336), its authenticity survives only in the vagaries of 'myth' (2011: 336). A profound distance is left open even as it is (or so that it can be) momentarily traversed – a fact that is stressed when Alex uses the zoom function on his handset to recover Rebecca and Cara-Ann in the crowd. Feeling a profound sense of separation, he T's Rebecca: '*pls wAt 4 me, my bUtiful wyf*' (2011: 336). The result is an overcoming and yet a sustainment of physical and emotional distance: she 'pause[s] in her dancing' (2011: 337) so as to reach for her handset. In this moment, the *in*finite potential of an authentic connection is experienced through its preservation, and we are again reminded that the anti-mimetic and epistemologically corrosive elements of technology can paradoxically effect eruptions of the authentic within the inertial frame of coherent and market-regulated discourse.

New Romantic Ends

In terms of the novel as a whole, the concert functions as a *mise en abyme*, metonymically echoing the way in which the various chapters effect experiences of the ungraspable. As Funk puts it, 'such moments of unstructured revelation, where the formless abyss of experience and memory encroaches on the fabricated narrative of the self, present instances of an intrusion of the authentic' (Funk 2015: 174). Given the primacy of his concert, though – as well as the details he provides in chapter 6 (that is, 'X's and O's') – Scotty is the most overt architect of such intrusions, or genotextual disruptions. For instance, Scotty tells of how, sometime in the late 1990s or early 2000s, he made the impromptu decision to reconnect with the then famous Bennie and bring to his swank, high-rise office a freshly caught bass. As with his decision to stand outside 'the public library at Fifth Avenue and Forty-Second Street during a gala benefit for heart disease' (Egan 2010: 96) – so as, that is, to prove to himself that the experience of exclusion is merely a matter of how information is processed – he makes his 'choice randomly' (2011: 96). Scotty therefore presents himself as a quintessential outsider, what Jean-Luc Nancy might call an '*intrus*' – a stranger who can never be '"naturalised"', whose 'coming will not cease; nor will it cease being in some respect an intrusion: . . . that is to say, being without right, familiarity, accustomedness, or habit' (Nancy 2002: 1–2). *L'intrus* undermines the very possibility of sustaining the difference between inside and outside, the very possibility of intrusion. Thus, in bringing his fish to Bennie's office – and especially by 'slap[ping] [it]. . . on the marble reception desk' (Egan 2011: 95) – Scotty manages to effect 'a disturbance and perturbation of intimacy' (Nancy 2002: 2). His goal, which he only realises in retrospect (and which is tied to his conviction that reality and lived experience is simply a matter of processing the available 'X's and O's' (Egan 2011: 97)), is to force Bennie to reject him, to exclude him: 'It was the reason I had come to see him' (2011: 101). Such a response, we are given to assume, would be a true affect, like the sound of the fish's 'hard wet *thwack*. . . [which] sounded like nothing so much as a fish' (2011: 95). It would entail an experience of that which a system of X's and O's functions to obscure: the unstructured Real of human connection. Or rather, this radical encounter, this *thwack* of an interruption, disrupts Bennie's inertia as an '*information processing machine*[ ]' (2011: 96); it induces revelatory 'fear', fear that (like the fish) is visceral and 'smell[s]' (2011: 103). The consequences of this moment are far reaching, as Bennie eventually decides to sabotage his career by 'serving his corporate controllers a boardroom lunch of cow pies' (2011: 312). Since they were asking him 'to feed the people shit' he decides to show them 'how it tastes' (2011: 312). Undoubtedly, he 'made this choice randomly'.

A similar appeal to intrusiveness occurs in Alison Blake's PowerPoint (that is, chapter 12). The daughter of Sasha (Bennie's one-time assistant and a recovered kleptomaniac) and Drew Blake (who was, in years past, unable to prevent the drowning of Sasha's 'fake' boyfriend, Robert Freeman, Jr), Alison spends her spare time writing a 'slide journal' (Egan 2011: 253). In the entry we are provided with – titled 'Great Rock and Roll Pauses' – Alison details her family dynamics and the way in which Robert's death continues to haunt them. Concurrently, she explains and justifies her socially awkward brother's obsession with songs that are marked by moments of silence. These pauses, Alison explains (by quoting her brother), interrupt the flow or inertia of a song, provoking a type of momentary dread, a fear that the end has arrived: 'The pause makes you think the song will end. And then the song isn't really over, so you're relieved. But then the song does end, because every song ends, obviously, and THAT. TIME. THE. END. IS. FOR. REAL' (2011: 281). Likewise, Alison works 'to make people uncomfortable' (2011: 262) – as does the PowerPoint itself. The PowerPoint chapter functions, after all, as a type of uncomfortable pause in the narrative, an abrupt and somewhat disconcerting shift. Yet Egan is careful to make the PowerPoint one of the most affective moments in the book.[14] As with T-ing, the strikingly reductive (yet potentially evocative) digital format offers the possibility of expressing what it must fail to contain: the emotional consequences of Robert's death, Alison's strained (yet loving) relationship with her mother, her touching yet problematic idolisation of her father, and her father's inability to understand his son (especially his obsession with musical pauses). Alison's PowerPoint thus functions to negotiate (while highlighting) the promise and terror of a Real and ungraspable end, a promise and terror that largely haunt the entire novel. The space between every chapter is, after all, a type of pause, another reminder that the novel itself must end, that (as Žižek puts it) '[every] story has to end at some point' (Žižek 2000: 37). This recurrent sense of an end, which is the effect of each chapter's relative discreteness and stylistic distinctiveness, forces us to acknowledge the limits of narrative play as well as the fact that (in Funk's terms) '*only death* can collapse the crevasse between experience and its aesthetic representation' (Funk 2015: 176, my emphasis). In other words, the drive towards mimetic closure is nothing other than the death drive, as attractive as it is repulsive. In Egan's novel, we are given (again and again) this terrifyingly attractive experience of an end, of true connection, of closure, of that which is perpetually antithetical to its momentary forms (in time) – but we are given it, paradoxically, through its refusal, or delay. Precisely like Hegel's spirit, the mimetic 'end' in Egan's novel 'necessarily appears in Time, and it appears in Time just so long as it has not grasped its pure Notion, i.e. has not annulled Time' (Hegel 1977: 487). Presumably for this very reason, the novel ends in a manner that echoes (while shifting the function of) postmodernism at its most recursive – by bringing us back to its beginning. In doing so, the novel once again evokes the possibility – as dangerous as it is potentially effective/affective – of sublating the postmodern. After Scotty's concert, Bennie and Alex find themselves walking past Sasha's old apartment, and Alex finally remembers an ill-fated date (long ago), one which was detailed from Sasha's perspective in chapter 1.

But this almost postmodern loop does not end up functioning as a perverse effort to deny 'our finitude', the inevitability of death, the outside limits of narrative possibility. Instead, it exposes us to the gravity of the Thing by leaving us open to its *in*finite capacity to effect and to be effected by forms of apprehension. We are immersed (à la postmodernism) within a rhizomatic and confusing 'complexity of multiple referrals and connections' (Žižek 2000: 37), but this *in*finite complexity remains consistent. This is the central difference between the perversity and fecklessness of the postmodern hypertext (which, as Žižek notes, comes to infect social responsibility in the digital era of video-game immortality) and the romantic renewal of the metafictional form – which, I am arguing, has the potential to counter postmodernism's (social) intensification. In this new metafiction, the emphasis falls on what cannot be changed or denied: the hard facts, the Real. At the same time, that which cannot be denied is given (only) as that which, in its fullness, remains outside its momentary form, its moment in time. The clear, or pure, communication of the classical is reconfigured so as to sustain the limiting, yet ungraspable, absence upon which symbolic forms fixate.

Nowhere is this sublation of the symbolic negotiation of a sublime end more evident than in chapter 4 (that is, 'Safari'), which tells a story of Bennie's womanising mentor, Lou. While relating the specifics of a family vacation Lou once took with his two children (Rolph and Charlene) and grad-school lover (Mindy), the omniscient narrator frequently interrupts – or intrudes upon – the dialogue and free indirect discourse of the characters. These interruptions tend to confirm or deny a given claim or assumption while also providing 'glimpses' of the future. At one point, for instance, the narrator intrudes upon a conversation between 'Charlie' and Rolph:

> '[Mindy's] not so bad', Charlie says.
> 'I don't like her. And why are you the world's expert?'
> Charlie shrugs. 'I know Dad.'
> Charlie doesn't know herself. Four years from now, at eighteen, she'll join a cult across the Mexican border whose charismatic leader promotes a diet of raw eggs; she'll nearly die from salmonella poisoning before Lou rescues her. A cocaine habit will require partial reconstruction of her nose, changing her appearance, and a series of feckless, domineering men will leave her solitary in her late twenties, trying to broker peace between Rolph and Lou, who will have stopped speaking.
> But Charlie *does* know her father. (Egan 2011: 80)

On the one hand, such narrative intrusions have the very postmodern function of confirming the textual and temporal prison in which the characters find themselves. Reality is only ever a discursive effect, our scripts are always already written. We are always caught up in what Lacan calls 'symbolic inertia' (Lacan 1991: 190), our innate tendency to yield to a dominant (if always arbitrary) network of perception and intersubjective relations. On the other hand, Egan's specific intrusions (especially within the context of the novel as a whole) expose the mutability of such scripts as no less limited. We are thus faced with an outside limit to the forms experience might take, with the fact that a certain inertial flow is for real and essential. Charlene's cocaine habit, like Rolph's eventual suicide (which we learn about in subsequent chapters), can be endlessly, coherently, and responsibly apprehended – as the notion of either can never be fixed – but both events mark the limit of narrative possibility: Charlene's cocaine habit, like Rolph's suicide, is simply undeniable, real. To treat them with responsibility is to endure the strenuous effort of the notion, to negate a certain postmodern negation of experiential finitude. The full field of a Thing's potential (in this case, suicide or the experience of addiction) can never be grasped in time, but the *in*finite nature of such a field is necessarily governed by an end. For this very reason they are always apprehendable in a moment of sincere expression, a moment of true communication.

What is negotiated is the unresolvable tension between the Thing and the infinite potential of its apprehension in form (and time). As, then, an exemplar of the type of work most capable of reflecting upon and countering a post-postmodern moment, a neo-metafictional work like Egan's largely returns us to something like the Hegelian romantic – that which sublates the sublimity of symbolic obscurity and confusion by refining or reapproaching the naïve unity (monism, or pure communicability) of the classical. In *Goon Squad*, as in Hegel's romantic art, the 'content, thus won, is on this account not tied to [its] sensuous presentation, as if that corresponded to it, but is freed from this immediate existence which must be set down as negative, overcome, and reflected into the spiritual unity' (Hegel 1975: 80). Or rather,

> although neither side is there without the other, both sides preserve in this loose connection their individual and mutual independence; or at least, if a deeper unification is actually achieved, the spirit becomes a centre essentially shining out as the inner life transcending its fusion with what is objective and external. (1975: 794)

The effect is always double: (1) the given representations resist becoming an ossified truth or concept, for 'such concepts and their moments are taken in a determination that stamps them as finite and makes them unfit to hold the truth which is in itself infinite' (Hegel 2010: 18); and (2) representation (like Hegel's very specific sense of the 'notion') is approached as a 'strenuous effort', one that actively resists the 'rhetoric of trivial truths', or 'ultimate truths to which no exception can be taken' (Hegel 1977: 42). Such an effort has, I am suggesting (if only tentatively in this brief space), the potential to forestall the social intensification of postmodernism (outlined above) – even as it renews its aesthetic, or cultural, potential. To escape (or recover) from our current descent into a post-truth world, we cannot simply return to hegemonic and all-encompassing truth claims. Something of postmodernism (or of the symbolic) must be retained – even as we resist exploiting 'common vagueness [or] the inadequacy of ordinary common sense' (Hegel 1977: 43). The romantic sublation of postmodernism – the possibility of which is exploited in the neo-metafictional form of a work like Egan's – entails, as Levinas might say, a radical and always intrusive 'placing of the Infinite in thought, but wholly other than thought' (Levinas 1998: 63). And indeed, contemporary works of metafiction (like Egan's) insist upon aesthetic responsibility; they reveal the manner in which the opaque or infinite Thingness of experience is only expressible in or as the mediating point that differentiates its finite form from its always *in*finite truth. To merely oscillate (between unjustified belief and the utter impossibility of a truth claim) is, surely, to evade (shuttle-like) the profound effort of grasping this diremptive point of mediation, this always vanishing point of mediation. Calcified morality is, after all, hardly any better than ethical ambivalence. Or vice versa.

Notes

1. 'Perverse', that is, in the sense Slavoj Žižek tends to employ the term. I discuss this specific usage more fully in the following sections.
2. Of course, they echo, also, Roland Barthes's efforts to privilege 'text' over 'work' (in *Image-Music-Text*), Jean Baudrillard's insistence that we have lost the real to the vagaries of simulacra (in *Simulacra and Simulation*), Gilles Deleuze and Félix Guattari's appeals to schizoanalysis and rhizomatic structures (in *Anti-Oedipus* and *A Thousand Plateaus*), and so on. And yet, at the same time, Lulu's parroting is just that: a superficial and dangerous appropriation of complex and nuanced theory. Hers is not postmodernism so much as it is an extreme canonisation and vulgarisation of postmodernism. Consider, in this sense, the hyperubiquity of 'deconstruction' in today's popular discourse. From first-year undergraduates to right-wing media stars, 'deconstruction' has become the go-to word for describing destruction or disassembly. Steve Bannon, for instance, stated at a political conference that Trump is vehemently invested in a 'deconstruction of the administrative state' (Bannon 2017). Presumably this means something akin to preparing 'deconstructed rabbit'. Regardless, the 'real' of Jacques Derrida's concept – which itself, as Derrida suggests in both 'Force of Law' (Derrida 2002: 243) and *Specters of Marx* (Derrida 1994: 59), is undeconstructible – has been lost to market-driven simulacra.
3. Habermas develops his concept of a legitimation crisis in a number of works – see, especially, *Legitimation Crisis* and 'Modernity – An Incomplete Project' (Habermas 1975, 2002).
4. Lyotard famously champions endlessly contingent 'little narratives' (that is, '*petit récits*') over the restrictive and illusionary closure of 'grand narratives'.
5. Nealon outlines his theory of intensification (of both postmodernism and late capitalism) in *Post-Postmodernism: Or, The Cultural Logic of Just-In-Time Capitalism* (2012). According to Nealon, 'post-postmodernism' is a particularly apt name for our contemporary state, since its awkward nature suggests a 'stammering inability to begin in any way other than intensifying the thing it's supposed to supersede' (Nealon 2012: x).
6. Consider, in this sense, Judith Butler reminiscing about how, one sleepless night, she found herself watching Elizabeth Fox-Genovese on C-Span. Fox-Genovese, Butler recalls, was explaining the problem with 'certain radical strains of feminist thinking ... [including] the view that no stable distinction between the sexes could be drawn or known, a view that suggests the difference between the sexes is itself culturally variable,

or, worse, discursively fabricated, as if it is all a matter of language' (Butler 2015: 17). Butler's sleeplessness is thus exacerbated, as she begins to feel that she is being accused, 'at least obliquely, with having made the body less, rather than more relevant' (2015: 17). The point here, however, is that Butler is only 'obliquely' connected to this obvious oversimplification; her earlier work (while certainly focused on the problem of discursive fabrications) never simply denied the limits of our real bodies. Nevertheless, Butler's more recent interest in ethics and self-narration surely speaks to her sense that a certain theoretical shift in emphasis is now necessary – if, that is, we are to counter the problematic pervasiveness of the thinking Fox-Genovese laments.

7. For Levinas's most accessible take on the *infinite* see 'God and Philosophy' – in which he suggests that 'the *in* of the Infinite signifie[s] at once the *non-* and the *within*' (Levinas 1998: 63).
8. It's worth noting that Eshelman's performatism often seems indistinguishable from a certain ethics of undecidability. While Eshelman works to demonstrate how performativist works leave us 'no choice' (Eshelman 2008: 2), he often finds himself negotiating significant moments of uncertainty. In the introductory pages, 'no choice' quickly mutates into 'little choice' (2008: 3) and then a 'specific choice' (2008: 4). Such shifts in phrasing are perhaps indicative of the fact that post-postmodern aesthetics are less interested in revitalising 'monism' or absolutism (pretend or not) than in shifting the emphasis of postmodernism (via a redeployment of its most striking aesthetic strategies).
9. To a certain extent, 'oscillation' has become the sine qua non (explicitly or implicitly) of post-postmodern discussions. It comes up in Eshelman (see, especially, Eshelman 2008: 222) and again in Wolfgang Funk's more recent *The Literature of Reconstruction* (see, for instance, Funk 2015: 172).
10. See, especially, *The Future of Hegel: Plasticity, Temporality and Dialectic* (Malabou 2005).
11. Indeed, the argument I forward here repeats and extends claims I make in 'Toni Morrison's *Beloved* and the Rise of Historioplastic Metafiction' and 'Historioplastic Metafiction: Tarantino, Nolan, and the "Return to Hegel"' (Toth 2017, 2018).
12. See Toth 2010: 89–106. While I do not employ the concept of historioplastic metafiction in this earlier monograph, the argument remains largely the same. What I associate here with a type of metafictional plasticity can be included in the range of texts I call 'neo-realist' or 'renewalist'. As I use it, the term 'neo-realist' in no way excludes the metafictional or the fantastic; it indicates, instead, a renewed willingness (inflected by the lessons of postmodernism) to endure the trauma of the Real, to negotiate and sustain its inherent spectrality (aka plasticity).
13. Kristeva, of course, assumes that Hegel's 'negation of the negation' is opposed to the type of revolutionary discourse she advocates, that it ultimately functions to 'suppress the contradiction generated by the thetic [or identificatory separation] and establish in its place an ideal positivity, the restorer of pre-symbolic immediacy' (Kristeva 1985: 69). If, though, we look beyond the standardised reading of Hegel (as the philosopher of 'positive idealism' par excellence) then it is possible to see that the *Aufhebung* ends (and maintains itself) in the very moment of explosion Kristeva celebrates – even if Hegel's sense of an 'explosion' is somewhat subtler, less overt, and more sustainable in coherent forms.
14. For a sustained discussion of affectivity in Egan's novel, see James P. Zappen's 'Affective Identification in Jennifer Egan's *A Visit from the Goon Squad*' (Zappen 2016). Zappen also stresses the fact that the intrusive 'pauses' discussed in Alison's PowerPoint are echoed in 'Silent pauses ... throughout the novel'. As Zappen demonstrates, such pauses 'appear at critical moments' (Zappen 2016: 300).

Bibliography

Bannon, Steve (2017), Discussion at Conservative Political Action Conference, MGM National Harbor, MD, 23 February.
Butler, Judith (2015), *Senses of the Subject*, New York: Fordham University Press.
Charles, Ron (2010), 'Jennifer Egan's "A Visit from the Goon Squad," Reviewed by Ron Charles', *Washington Post*, 16 June.
Derrida, Jacques (1981), 'Plato's Pharmacy', in Jacques Derrida, *Dissemination*, Barbara Johnson (trans.), Chicago: University of Chicago Press, pp. 61–171.
Derrida, Jacques (1994), *Specters of Marx: The State of Debt, the Work of Mourning, and the New International*, New York: Routledge.
Derrida, Jacques (2002), 'Force of Law: The "Mystical Foundation of Authority"', in Jacques Derrida, *Acts of Religion*, Gil Anidjar (ed.) and Mary Quaintance (trans.), New York: Routledge, pp. 228–98.
Egan, Jennifer (2011), *A Visit from the Goon Squad*, New York: Anchor.
Eshelman, Raoul (2008), *Performatism, or the End of Postmodernism*, Aurora: Davies Group.
Funk, Wolfgang (2015), *The Literature of Reconstruction: Authentic Fiction in the New Millennium*, New York: Bloomsbury.
Habermas, Jürgen (1975), *Legitimation Crisis*, Thomas McCarthy (trans.), Boston: Beacon Press.
Habermas, Jürgen (2002), 'Modernity – An Incomplete Project', in Hal Foster (ed.), *The Anti-Aesthetic: Essays on Postmodern Culture*, New York: New Press, pp. 1–16.
Hegel, G. W. F. (1975), *Aesthetics: Lectures on Fine Art*, 2 vols, T. M. Knox (trans.), Oxford: Clarendon Press.
Hegel, G. W. F. (1977), *Phenomenology of Spirit*, A. V. Miller (trans.), Oxford: Oxford University Press.
Hegel, G. W. F. (2010), *The Science of Logic*, George di Giovanni (ed. and trans.), Cambridge: Cambridge University Press.
Hutcheon, Linda (1988), *A Poetics of Postmodernism: History, Theory, Fiction*, New York: Routledge.
Hutcheon, Linda (2002), *The Politics of Postmodernism*, 2nd edn, New York: Routledge.
James, David (2011), 'Integrity After Metafiction', *Twentieth-Century Literature*, 57:3–4, pp. 492–515.
Jameson, Fredric (1979), 'Preface', in Jean-François Lyotard, *The Postmodern Condition: A Report on Knowledge*, Geoffrey Bennington and Brian Massumi (trans.), Minneapolis: University of Minnesota Press, pp. vii–xxi.
Kristeva, Julia (1985), *Revolution in Poetic Language*, Margaret Waller (trans.), New York: Columbia University Press.
Lacan, Jacques (1991), *The Seminar of Jacques Lacan, Book II: The Ego in Freud's Theory and in the Technique of Psychoanalysis 1954–1955*, Jacques-Alain Miller (ed.), Sylvana Tomaselli (trans.), New York: W. W. Norton.
Levinas, Emmanuel (1978), *Existence and Existents*, Alphonso Lingis (trans.), Dordrecht: Kluwer.
Levinas, Emmanuel (1998), 'God and Philosophy', in Emmanuel Levinas, *Of God Who Comes to Mind*, Bettina Bergo (trans.), Stanford: Stanford University Press.
Lipovetsky, Gilles (2005), *Hypermodern Times*, Andrew Brown (trans.), Cambridge: Polity.
Lyotard, Jean-François (1984), *The Postmodern Condition: A Report on Knowledge*, Geoffrey Bennington and Brian Massumi (trans.), Minneapolis: University of Minnesota Press.

Malabou, Catherine (2005), *The Future of Hegel: Plasticity, Temporality and Dialectic*, Lisbeth During (trans.), New York: Routledge.
Nancy, Jean-Luc (2002), 'L'Intrus', Susan Hanson (trans.), *The New Centennial Review*, 2:3, pp. 1–14.
Nealon, Jeffrey T. (2012), *Post-Postmodernism: Or, The Cultural Logic of Just-in-Time Capitalism*, Stanford: Stanford University Press.
Toth, Josh (2010), *The Passing of Postmodernism: A Spectroanalysis of the Contemporary*, New York: SUNY Press.
Toth, Josh (2017), 'Toni Morrison's *Beloved* and the Rise of Historioplastic Metafiction', in Robin van den Akker, Alison Gibbons, and Timotheus Vermeulen (eds), *Metamodernism: Historicity, Affect, and Depth after Postmodernism*, London: Rowman and Littlefield, pp. 40–53.
Toth, Josh (2018), 'Historioplastic Metafiction: Tarantino, Nolan, and the "Return to Hegel"', *Cultural Critique*, 99, pp. 1–30.
Trump, Donald J. (@realDonaldTrump) (2012), 'The concept of global warming was created by and for the Chinese in order to make U.S. manufacturing non-competitive', *Twitter*, 6 November, 11:15 a.m., <https://twitter.com/realDonaldTrump/status/265895292191248385> (last accessed 24 December 2018).
Trump, Donald J. (2017), Interview with Tucker Carlson, *Fox News*, 15 March.
Vermeulen, Timotheus and Robin van den Akker (2010), 'Notes on Metamodernism', *Journal of Aesthetics and Culture*, 2:1, <http://www.tandfonline.com/doi/full/10.3402/jac.v2i0.5677> (last accessed 15 March 2019).
Zappen, James P. (2016), 'Affective Identification in Jennifer Egan's *A Visit from the Goon Squad*', *Lit: Literature Interpretation Theory*, 27:4, pp. 294–309.
Žižek, Slavoj (1989), *The Sublime Object of Ideology*, London: Verso.
Žižek, Slavoj (1991), 'The Obscene Object of Postmodernity', in Slavoj Žižek, *Looking Awry: An Introduction to Jacques Lacan Through Popular Culture*, Cambridge, MA: MIT University Press, pp. 141–53.
Žižek, Slavoj (1993), *Tarrying with the Negative: Kant, Hegel, and the Critique of Ideology*, Durham, NC: Duke University Press.
Žižek, Slavoj (2000), *The Art of the Ridiculous Sublime: On David Lynch's Lost Highway*, Seattle: University of Washington Press.

4

Virtually Human: Posthumanism and (Post-)Postmodern Cyberspace in Gary Shteyngart's *Super Sad True Love Story*

Nicky Gardiner

Introduction: Posthumanism, Knowledge, and Cyberspace

Since the end of the twentieth century, the birth of digital technologies and rise of 'New Media' have radically transformed the means by which 'knowledge' is legitimated, distributed, and consumed in the so-called developed world. Alongside the ever-increasing centrality of digital platforms such as Twitter, Facebook, and Google News to the circulation and dissemination of information, anxieties surrounding the mediated status of knowledge re-emerge in a new context.

Consequently, cyberspace might be seen as a site which restages postmodern concerns regarding the possibility of obtaining truth, the 'internal erosion of the legitimacy principle of knowledge' (Lyotard 1984: 39), and the presumptions and practices through which such legitimation operates. Whilst the circulation of knowledge, its accessibility, intelligibility, and legitimacy, are of profound social and political importance, such concerns also have far-reaching implications for the construction of human subjectivity. The Cartesian foundations of humanism traditionally predicate human exceptionalism on the ability of a defined and delimited human subject to rationally interpret objectively perceivable information (Descartes 2008: 39). Of course, ever since its original formulation, the Cartesian subject has received numerous criticisms, but the recent digital revolution poses a set of new and specific challenges. As 'Old Media' gives way to New Media, as print journalism and televised information are subsumed by decentralised modes of informational exchange, the types of challenges posed to the rational human subject shift accordingly. If humanism is indeed 'the effect of a change in the fundamental arrangements of knowledge' (Foucault 2005: 422), by reconstituting the dynamics through which information is legitimated, cyberspace's technological mediation of knowledge also constitutes a crucial, yet underappreciated, factor for the burgeoning field of Posthuman Studies.

Since its coinage by Ihab Hassan in 1977 (Hassan 1977), the concept of posthumanism has developed into a key feature of contemporary philosophical, literary, and cultural studies, subsequently developing into one of the fundamental movements associated with what might vaguely be termed 'post-postmodernity'. Sparking debate across a range of philosophical fields such as ethics (MacCormack 2012), ontology

(Haraway 2016), and speculative philosophy (Roden 2015), posthumanism informs a variety of contemporary theoretical revaluations of what it means to be human alongside trenchant renegotiations of humanity's place in the world. The particular branch of posthuman philosophy that will be explored in this chapter is that of 'critical posthumanism', a strand of posthuman thought that aims to provide a 'philosophical corrective to humanism' (Roden 2015: 9). Varyingly articulated by figures such as Neil Badmington (2000, 2004), Cary Wolfe (2010), Rosi Braidotti (2013), Stefan Herbrechter (2013), and N. Katherine Hayles (2010), critical posthumanism denounces humanist anthropocentrism as neither applicable nor desirable in a contemporary context and attempts to think through 'the decentering of the human by its imbrication in technical, medical, informatics, and economic networks' (Wolfe 2010: xv).

Although the aforementioned figures all provide interesting variations of critical posthumanism, this chapter will concentrate on the figuration put forward by Hayles in her seminal text *How We Became Posthuman* (hereafter *HWBP*) (Hayles 2010). Although Hayles's text does not constitute a sustained philosophical investigation but rather focuses on how informational technologies renegotiate the limits of human subjectivity, its fundamental critique of ontological dualism distinguishes it as a keystone text for critical posthumanism. Hayles's persistent assault on the transhumanist fantasy of disembodiment, as one that perpetuates, rather than overturns, the Cartesian metaphysical dualisms through which the liberal humanist subject has traditionally been defined, establishes *HWBP* 'not just as an intervention in transhumanist techno-eutopian debates, but rather as one of the inaugural works that initiated a shift in theory towards an understanding of posthumanism as a form of critical discourse' (Schmeink 2016: 40).

Whilst, on the one hand, theorists such as Erik Cofer (2018), Braidotti (2013), and Ivan Callus and Stefan Herbrechter (2012) agree that 'the posthuman subject is not postmodern' (Braidotti 2013: 51) but rather one which goes beyond postmodernism, critical posthumanism's insistent deconstructive 'decentring' of the human subject conspicuously announces a continuation of postmodern practices.[1] Although the complex range of intersections and disjunctures which characterise posthumanism's troubled relationship with the postmodern have received some critical attention, such evaluations have often been cursory and conflicting. Rather than focusing on how postmodern characteristics are framed, incorporated, and reconfigured within posthumanism, such comparisons appear more intent on noting the ambiguity of their shared prefix ('post') to rehearse Jean-François Lyotard's observation that 'neither modernity nor so-called postmodernity can be identified and defined as clearly circumscribed historical entities of which the latter would always come "after" the former' (Lyotard 1996: 35), and indicate how 'the "post-" of posthumanism does not – and, moreover, cannot – mark or make an absolute break from the legacy of humanism' (Badmington 2004: 119–20).[2] Though such observations are crucial for a consideration of the posthuman, they nevertheless tend to waylay theoretical examinations of the correlations between the posthuman and the postmodern beyond cursory observations of lexical similarities. Consequently, as

Callus and Herbrechter note, 'the attempt at intersections between poststructuralism and posthumanism is not as common as one might think' (Callus and Herbrechter 2012: 252). It is with the hope of fleshing out this under-examined strand of critical genealogy that this chapter will consider the entangled nexus of issues surrounding postmodernity and (post)human subjectivity within contemporary cyberspace. In particular, it will investigate how competing formulations of posthuman subjectivity are predicated upon divergent constructions of postmodernity and their consequences for thinking cyberspace as an environment which might be considered at once 'postmodern' and 'post-postmodern'.

This will be approached through a reconsideration of the model of postmodernism fashioned in Hayles's *HWBP*, a text that influentially accentuates conventional constructions of cyberspace as an expression of postmodernism and subsequently conceptualises both cyberspace and postmodernism as superficial surfaces which, whilst potentially liberating and emancipatory, remain of little pragmatic consequence. Hayles's narrow understanding of 'postmodern cyberspace' might be seen as a primary example of the 'philosophical limitations of critical posthumanism' (Roden 2015: 29), which, according to Roden, fails to adequately nuance the varied forms of humanism and transhumanism it critiques (2015: 25).

Keeping Roden's observation in mind, this chapter also considers an alternative conception of post-postmodern cyberspace to introduce for critical consideration a further subcategory of posthuman subjectivity that will be provisionally referred to as 'virtual humanism'. This subcategory is derived from Robert Samuels's concept of 'automodernism', a 'paradoxical combination of autonomy and automation' (Samuels 2010: 45) in which technological mediation produces an illusory sense of rational autonomy by 'transcending' social and geopolitical barriers to knowledge acquisition that its presence tacitly re-enforces (2010: 13). Similarly, 'virtual humanism' denotes a paradoxical form of subjectivity in which materially embedded technological apparatuses are conceptualised as a means of salvaging the 'human' subject status that their very integration effaces. It will be argued that, where transhumanism looks to augment and enhance an already existent human subject, virtual humanism conceptualises technological prostheses as tools through which human status is paradoxically acquired. Specifically, this chapter will explore how virtual humanism's paradoxical subject position is derived from an alternative construction of cyberspace as a post-postmodern corrective to a socioculturally deterministic model of postmodernism. By bringing Hayles and Samuels into contact, I hope to illuminate how these models of posthuman subjectivity are shaped by contrasting articulations of postmodernity.

As such, this chapter has three interrelated aims. At its most general level, it aspires to contribute towards an updated understanding of cyberspace appropriate to its contemporary practices, politics, and significations; second, to explore the relationship between postmodernism and emergent forms of posthumanism; and finally, it hopes to nuance the object of critical posthumanist analysis by introducing a new variant of paradoxical posthuman subjectivity that will be referred to as 'virtual humanism'.

It is worth noting that the rhetoric of historical progression used here is purely adopted for discursive convenience. I do not want to imply a linear transition between two discrete perspectives on cyberspace but rather to suggest a coinciding and intersecting relationship. Haylesian and automodern notions of cyberspace are very much entangled and each holds a place in the contemporary imagination. Yet it is important that these two models of cyberspace are not thought to harmoniously coexist either. Rather they constantly overlap and compete with one another. It is with this duality in mind that I have decided to refer to cyberspace as a (post-)postmodern environment.

It is, I feel, this very tension which makes contemporary cyberspace such a productive site of inquiry, as it has the curious task of simultaneously enacting an expression of postmodernism and a remedy to postmodernism. 'Both remedy and poison', contemporary cyberspace is a 'pharmakon' of human exceptionalism and epistemological possibility, 'alternatively or simultaneously ... beneficent or maleficent' (Derrida 1981: 70) for the prospect of knowledge attainment and the construction of human subjectivity.

By way of illustration the chapter will analyse Gary Shteyngart's 2010 novel *Super Sad True Love Story* (hereafter *SSTLS*), a text exemplary in its depiction of contemporary anxieties surrounding posthuman subjectivity, the digital mediation of knowledge, and competing conceptions of cyberspace. Depicting a digitally saturated near-future society that culturally privileges informational abstraction yet continues to be haunted by the socio-material impacts of corporeal and economic decay, Shteyngart's novel expresses the intermingled and contradictory nature of (post-)postmodern cyberspace by manifesting a Haylesian perspective at a thematic and ideological level, whilst harbouring an automodern perspective at a narrational and diegetic level. Through its depiction of the protagonist's virtual humanism, *SSTLS* demonstrates how the seams within this contradictory logic manifest in the embodiment of 'digital grotesques', explicit images of corporeality that signify the non-delineated porosity of the 'human subject' through exaggerations of the body's apertures and orifices.

Digital Frontiers: Cyberspace as (Post-)Postmodern Environment

Functioning as a spatialising metaphor for a non-spatial phenomenon, the term 'cyberspace' was popularly introduced in 1984 by William Gibson in *Neuromancer* (Gibson 1995). Given the word's coinage in a pre-eminent postmodern text, it is unsurprising that there is a longstanding tradition which reads 'cyberspace as an attempt at a postmodern cartography' (Myers 2001: 888). A virtual landscape of floating signification that lacks direct physical correspondence to, yet nevertheless replaces, material 'reality' in the fashion of a simulacrum (Baudrillard 2007: 166), cyberspace is often positioned as the quintessential postmodern environment (McHale 1992: 252–3). A hyperspace whose abstractions and distortions of traditionally defined topographies provide a conceptual counterpart to 'the discontinuous spatial experience and confusions of the postmodern' (Jameson 1991: 154), cyberspace can also be thought to epitomise a dissolution of subjectivity in which 'the self can be called into question, decentered, split apart, and rendered unknowable' (Fair 2005: 92). Its deployment as an anarchic space within the cyberpunk genre has similarly rendered it a site that subverts traditional authoritarian structures and provides an alternative social landscape, re-empowering select marginalised communities and 'establishing new communities unhampered by traditional prejudices' (Cavallaro 2000: 26).

The prevalence of this conceptual pairing creates a mutually constitutive dynamic between cyberspace and postmodernism. That is to say that not only do perceptions of postmodernism influence the way that cyberspace is conceptualised, but it is also possible for particular understandings of cyberspace to retroactively construct different models of the aims, objectives, and practices of postmodernism.[3] After all, even though cyberspace demonstrates some important postmodern characteristics, the degree to which it metaphorically encapsulates the heterogeneous strands of postmodernism is far from comprehensive.

This false equivalence also presumes a direct correspondence between postmodernity and 'the electronic age' despite the fact that the former has waned (Hoberek 2007: 233) and the latter is far from over. Due to the uncommonly swift rate at which technology advances, it is without doubt that the practices and politics of operating within cyberspace have changed drastically since the 1980s, when such theoretical associations between cyberspace and postmodernism could be considered accurate. Alongside such changes come inevitable revisions in how networked technologies function and feature in the contemporary imagination, their significance and signification, their practical operations and symbolic associations. As such, it becomes necessary to reconsider these traditional assumptions of postmodern cyberspace and carefully avoid easy associations.

As an illustrative example, in 1983, the year before *Neuromancer*'s publication and the introduction of 'cyberspace' into the popular lexicon, the ARPANET (the Internet's forebear) switched from NCP protocols to TCP/IP, diversifying central control to a multiplicity of smaller localised networks in a move that has generally been considered the 'birth of the modern internet' (Lee 2014). The number of ARPANET users at that time can be roughly estimated at 4,000 (Roberts 1995; Office of Technology Assessment 1995) with smaller BSS messaging boards such as FIDONET accruing similarly humble figures of about 1,000 users (Bush 1992; Rheingold 1994).[4] This provides an understandable context for the prevalent theme of radical alterity within the cyberpunk genre. The cutting-edge and sparsely populated cyberspace of the 1980s was truly an undiscovered frontier that could conceivably harbour pioneering, subversive digital 'cowboys' (Gibson 1995: 11), a sentiment which is essentially embodied in FIDONET's 'itinerant hacker' (Ryan 2013: 69) founder, Tom Jennings. Within such a context, cyberspace as a manifestation of radical postmodernism, as a space in which alterity can flourish in its cyberpunk mode, seems credible and appropriate.

Jump forward to 2019 and the percentage of the population with access to cyberspace has skyrocketed to over 4.3 billion users worldwide (Digital Population

Worldwide 2019). If cyberspace was once an open, sprawling frontier, it has since become an overcrowded shopping mall, colonised by tech giants such as Google, Facebook, and Amazon (Lynn 2010). As cyber-monopolies grow in strength, so does cyberspace's capacity to re-empower the marginalised dwindle, as the ability to funnel and disseminate information is consolidated by a select commercial elite. Therefore, cyberspace's emancipatory status which was once understandably glorified in the golden age of cyberpunk seems increasingly difficult to maintain. More and more, cyberspace starts to replicate rather than subvert existent socio-economic hierarchies by providing them with new avenues of exploitation. The contemporary corporate colonisation of cyberspace might be seen to contribute to a digitally inflected return to liberal humanism (a theme which will be picked up later in the chapter) by replicating the same humanist dynamics through which corporate enterprise has traditionally enjoyed capital domination, that is, the myth of the autonomous individual.

To better understand the presumptions and inadequacies inherent in the concept of cyberspace as expressive of postmodernism, I will now turn to an examination of Hayles's *HWBP*, a text which neatly articulates the rationale of such readings. Through a critique of Hayles's use of disembodied metaphor and interpretation of postmodern constructivism, I will explore the limitations of customary claims for cyberspace as an archetypical postmodern environment.

Going Viral: Hayles, Dis/Embodiment, and Cyberspace as Postmodern Sickness

In *HWBP*, Hayles considers the majority of cybernetic posthumanist thought[5] as circulating around a desire to transcend the limitations of human corporeality through technological integration and enhancement. She identifies a 'common theme' (Hayles 2010: 2), exemplified by figures such as Hans Moravec and Marvin Minsky (2010: 22), amongst most articulations of posthumanism that theorise an equivalence between human and digital information patterns, culminating in the desire to upload human consciousness into computer processors. However, she notes that the fantasy of the human subject as a transferrable information pattern is predicated upon the humanist logic of substance dualism, which forgoes the role of the material body in determining the nature of that pattern. That is to say, Hayles demonstrates that the idea of disembodied information, of the human as information patterns that can be transferred between mediums without compromise or alteration, is dependent on an untenable separation between information and matter. This leads Hayles to conclude that 'to the extent that the posthuman constructs embodiment as the instantiation of thought/information, it continues the liberal tradition rather than disrupts it' (2010: 5).

Despite Hayles's perspective of postmodernism being appropriately ambivalent rather than artificially cohesive, she nevertheless appears emphatically dismissive of the movement as one which 'stupefy[ingly]' (2010: 192) perpetuates this aforementioned material disembodiment. That is, she subscribes to a reading of postmodernism that emphasises the 'postmodern orthodoxy that the body is primarily, if not entirely, a linguistic and discursive construction ... creating the postmodern ideology that the body's materiality is secondary to the logical or semiotic structures it encodes' (2010: 192). In contrast, critical posthumanism provides a re-embodied remedy for this perceived postmodern-inflected disembodiment. Rather than considering their commononalities, Hayles lays out her project of distancing and distinguishing post-humanism from postmodernism along the lines quoted above. Consequently, she manufactures a problematic association between postmodernism and cyberspace which foregrounds their abstract qualities whilst dismissing their more materialist aspects.

Describing cyberspace as an environment in which the binary of presence/absence is usurped by pattern/randomness, Hayles claims that 'cyberspace defines a regime of representation within which pattern is the essential reality, presence an optical illusion' (2010: 36). She goes on to claim that the most serious implication of an 'emphasis on information technologies [that] foregrounds pattern/randomness and pushes presence/absence into the background ... is the *systematic devaluation of materiality and embodiment*' (2010: 48). In her explanation and exploration of this process, Hayles insistently links the prevalence of pattern/randomness with postmodernity, citing classics of postmodern theory such as Lyotard, Fredric Jameson, Roland Barthes, and David Harvey, and literary works like *Naked Lunch, Neuromancer, Crash, White Noise*, and *If on A Winter's Night a Traveller*. In the case of *Naked Lunch*, Hayles further implicates postmodernism as an ideology of patterned disembodiment by claiming that 'the junkie's body is a harbinger of the postmodern mutant, for it demonstrates how presence yields to assembly and disassembly' (2010: 43). For Hayles, the causal chain is clear: postmodernism entails an emphasis on pattern/randomness and an emphasis on pattern/randomness leads to conceptual dematerialisation.

However, I want to resist Hayles's insinuation that postmodernism 'devalues materiality', and instead posit that the abstraction she identifies is less a feature of postmodernism than the result of an internal tension arising from her overextension of the conceptual metaphor of 'dis/embodiment'. In *HWBP* Hayles identifies and critiques two types of material disembodiment integral to cybernetic posthumanism: the disembodiment of the human subject as pure consciousness and the disembodiment of information, 'regardless of the contexts in which it is embedded' (2010: 54). Referring to the cybernetic theories of Norbert Wiener, the relationship that Hayles observes between these two modes of dematerialisation is primarily one of analogy (2010: 98) in which the general logic of informatics is extended to the human subject through neuronal biology (2010: 57). I would like to suggest that in charting the development of the cybernetic logic which allows for informational disembodiment, or perhaps more appropriately 'decontextualisation' (for human bodies and socio-historical context are very different things indeed), to be mapped onto corporeal dematerialisation, Hayles ends up partially internalising the very logic she critiques. Ultimately overextending the conceptual metaphor of disembodiment, Hayles unwittingly constructs a 'frictionless' relationship between material disembodiment and informational decontextualisation. In doing so, Hayles falls foul of her own metaphor and problematically conflates socio-historical context and materiality. Disembodiment as a concept becomes disembodied itself, a free-floating meta-concept that can be non-problematically applied to consciousness and information alike.

By allowing the concept of embodiment to signify both corporeal specificity and socio-historical contextual specificity, Hayles inappropriately identifies a successive relationship between the two in which one necessarily leads to the other. For her, material disembodiment is a natural result of informational decontextualisation. Whilst there is certainly a large degree of interconnection between material and social factors, any disparity or tension between the two is effaced within Hayles's metaphor of embodiment. However, the dematerialisation of the body can also be seen as the effect of an excessive contextualisation of information in the form of sociocultural determinism. That is to say, humans and information lose their 'bodies' in very different ways and one does not necessarily entail the other. On the contrary, informational contextualisation can also lead to material disembodiment and vice versa, a tension explored in recent studies in new materialisms (Coole and Frost 2010: 3). So whilst disembodiment remains a rich metaphor for the simultaneous dematerialisation of the biological body and the decontextualisation of information, it is one which problematically eclipses the differences and tensions between the two in Hayles's application.

This overdetermined equivalence of disembodiment and decontextualisation leads Hayles to consider postmodern explorations of discursive construction as a means of decontextualising the human subject, rather than of more accurately contextualising them in terms of their social, historical, and cultural specificity. Whereas it is possible to consider an exploration of the discursive construction of the subject as a method that entails disembodiment, though this is by no means necessarily the case, it is much harder to justify it as a decontextualisation. After all, the presumptions of universal knowledge obtained through socio-historical decontextualisation is one of postmodernism's primary targets, as its 'preferred legitimation process of knowledge becomes plural, localized and contingent' (Houliang 2014: 285).

Arguably, the perception of digital disembodiment is not so much the casualty of a postmodern logic of abstraction, but rather the cause. Hayles's perception of postmodernism as a decontextualising practice is actually an effect of the same cybernetic logic that reinscribes substance dualism within cyberspace. Although her analysis undoes this logic to reveal the embodied dimension of virtuality, she does not, unfortunately, extend this same courtesy to postmodernism. As mentioned earlier, the relationship between cyberspace and postmodernism might be meaningfully considered as mutually constitutive and, in this instance, Hayles's definition of postmodernism appears to have been retroactively constructed through the model of cyberspace established by cybernetic posthumanism. Considering postmodernism as a mode of decontextualisation, she purely associates it with the abstracted, dematerialising qualities of cyberspace. Rather than embracing postmodernism's capacity to contextualise how these simulations facilitate new forms of material re-embodiment which recalibrate the boundaries between the human and the technological, Hayles saves the task of 'problemati[sing] thinking of the body as a self-evident physicality' (Hayles 2010: 27) for her own brand of 'critical posthumanism' as a post-postmodern project.

Having considered some of the problems with Hayles's extension of embodied metaphor and its resultant misreading of an abstract, expressive cyberspace, we will move on to observe how these tensions manifest within Shteyngart's novel.

Digital Grotesques: *Super Sad True Love Story,* Explicit Acronyms, and the Limits of Embodied Metaphor

First published in 2010, *SSTLS* depicts the angst-ridden courtship of a blossoming intergenerational romance between its two protagonists, Lenny Abramov (an ageing bibliophile equipped with an inferiority complex and a romantic streak) and Eunice Park (a technologically literate but emotionally immature recent college graduate). Set against the backdrop of a quasi-dystopic, near-future New York on the brink of economic collapse, Shteyngart's critically acclaimed novel charts the development of its central relationship as it encounters the tribulations of a new cultural epoch in which data, images, and youth are privileged whilst materiality, text, and death itself are quickly receding into the past. Shteyngart's satirical vision is one of digital immediacy, a future in which all that is solid melts into images and code, in which biometrics make the man and 'äppäräti' (wearable technology that might be considered a close cousin of the iPhone or Fitbit) dictate the conditions of social interaction. As such, *SSTLS*'s New York is one in which a cultural logic of dematerialisation is encouraged within both the material and the informational/linguistic spheres. Despite this logic, however, both of these spheres ultimately reassert themselves as emphatically material entities displaying the shortcomings within the culture's ideology of dis/embodiment.

Within the text, an ideology of informational decontextualisation is exerted through the prioritisation of data as a neutral conveyor of ontological fact. This cultural naturalisation is indicated through the constant contrast between text and images and the subsequent coupling of images with the digital world. As Barthes notes, the perceptual immediacy of iconographic depiction 'naturalises the symbolic message [and] innocents the semantic artifice of connotation' (Barthes 2009: 45). In *SSTLS* this is true of both images and digitised information. Lai Tze Fang observes that the text's citizens 'rely on images to communicate because digital media are highly visual and have integrated the representational methods of visual culture as a more efficient way to organize and receive information' (Fang 2016: 43), and Raymond Malewitz identifies particular instances of this phenomenon (Malewitz 2015: 119). In depicting Eunice's technologically engulfed cohort as 'a generation reared on images' (Shteyngart 2011: 325), a correlation is established that encourages the reader to extend the cultural perception of visual immediacy to a digital immediacy. Within the novel, this comparison between the perceived naturalness of the visual image and the identifiable mediation of written text often functions to highlight the tension between digital and analogue modes of communication. Like visual images, the 'raw data' (2011: 156) which circulates in the novel is generally considered to be less thoroughly mediated than its textual counterpart, enforcing a digitised form of Derridean 'logocentrism'. Lacking a readily perceived material receptacle, data is considered to be more 'present to itself' and less compromised than material text.

Due to this popular perception, *SSTLS*'s largely illiterate society renegotiates books in an apparent attempt to alleviate their material shortcomings. Rather than reading, the dominant mode of interacting with books is 'text-scanning for data' (Shteyngart 2011: 156), an approach which inhibits critical reflection upon the linguistic, textual, and narratorial specifics of how information is related and its subsequent influence on the meaning. In the ideology of Shteyngart's New York, 'language' becomes a 'scannable' surface, a transparent medium that can non-problematically be mined for data. Collapsing materiality and mediation, this application of cyber-rhetoric pursues a logic which associates digitisation with objectivity and effaces an appreciation of how language and the written word transform content in the particularity of their material expression.

The conceptual renegotiation of material entities as decontextualised data also extends to the physical bodies of *SSTLS*'s digital denizens, as corporeality is itself reconstituted and reconceptualised as biological information. This biometric data is continuously monitored and projected by the 'äppärät', an all-purpose multi-media device that simultaneously harvests and transmits the wearer's data. This already hyperbolic situation is exaggerated further at Lenny's workplace, where employees jostle for social status based on biological statistics such as fatty acid and hormone levels.

Lenny's job at 'Post-Human Services' revolves around attempting to materialise this cultural logic. A 'Life Lovers Outreach Co-Ordinator' (Shteyngart 2011: 3), Lenny markets experimental procedures that incrementally replace the individual components of the human body with augmented and self-repairing technological counterparts, indefinitely prolonging the components' lifespan. In an embodied twist on Moravec's original concept of uploaded consciousness, Shteyngart's cynical reimagining of the posthuman draws clear inspiration from transhumanist sources – he explicitly cites the influences of prominent transhumanist Ray Kurzweil in the book's acknowledgement section (2011: 330) – in its ambitions to gradually graft a technological body onto the human subject.

However, the fact that Shteyngart's novel takes place at a time when this process of life extension is still experimental, when 'the technology is *almost* here' (Shteyngart 2011: 2, my emphasis) but ultimately debunked, indicates a crucial tension between the society's cultural logic and its material capabilities. Whilst the New York of *SSTLS* operates as if humans are data, it is notable that this is a text in which the body continues to emphatically reassert itself. The constant, anxious denigration of the body in fact enforces an adverse reassertion of the bodily presence which is supposedly mitigated. In one incident, Lenny encounters a 'fat man' who lacks an äppärät, rendering him socially and bureaucratically invisible. Paradoxically asserting 'he wasn't there' (2011: 32), Lenny recounts this incident as follows:

> He looked like a nothing. The way people don't really look anymore. Not just imperfect, but awful. A fat man with deeply recessed eyes, a collapsed chin, limp and dusty hair, a T-shirt that all but exposed his large breasts, and a gross tent of air atop where one imagined his genital would be. (2011: 33)

Ostensibly this scene demonstrates the absolute digitisation of the body in a sociopolitical context, yet the vivid description of his material appearance undermines such a conclusion. The text's deployment of a first-person epistolary structure necessitates that any events depicted are consciously witnessed by the character narrating, in this case Lenny. Therefore, the vivid description of this scene testifies to the fact that Lenny does see the fat man. Furthermore, the fact that it is relayed with such explicit detail paid to his corporeal condition implies just how omnipresent bodily materiality remains in a world that attempts to deny it. Lenny does not actually not see the man or his subsequent abduction by government forces, he simply 'd[oes] what everyone eventually did: looked away' (2011: 318). Despite his best intentions, Lenny cannot deny his material senses. Rather than truly being a 'nothing', his failure to sufficiently interact with technology renders the fat man a Derridean 'absent presence'. The insistent dematerialisation of the body into informational patterns announces its continued presence within Shteyngart's vision. Lenny witnesses this individual and his treatment whether he wants to or not. It is only at a conceptual level that he does not witness the event, whereas at a perceptual level it is all too immediate.

Similarly, although the ubiquity of virtual environments within *SSTLS* perpetuates a disembodied mindset within its citizenry (Malewitz 2015: 120), these same environments are rife with explicit acronyms and graphic corporeal content of a scatological and pornographic nature (Shteyngart 2011: 25–6, 145, 153). These acronyms, such as 'JBF (Just-Butt-Fucking)' (2011: 20), 'DO (Dick Odour)' (2011: 90), and 'TIMATOV (Think I'm About To Openly Vomit)' (2011: 76) provide a curious mixture of coy crudeness, of conservatism and excess, that neatly encapsulates the narrative's paradoxical depiction of embodiment. At the same time as providing extreme imagery of bodily porosity in long form, the abbreviated versions attempt to inoculate their offensive nature, to linguistically and typographically enclose the very images of open corporeality they conjure, just as their full, explanatory textual articulations are enclosed within parentheses. However, rather than dulling their signification, the streamlining of these signs allows them to circulate throughout *SSTLS*'s society with greater abundance, and the increased ubiquity of these acronyms perpetuates such extreme corporeal imagery all the more.

Whilst these acronyms circulate freely and fluidly within the diegetic world, Lenny's narration constantly inscribes them in long form, which counterproductively disrupts the narrative flow. From the perspective of the reader, then, rather than dematerialising language, the abbreviations end up materialising it all the more obtrusively. This is true typographically as well as rhythmically, as the visual immediacy of the capitalisations naturally draws the reader's eye, inhibiting a linear progression across the page. This acronymic re-embodiment is symptomatic of the text's wider representations of materiality. Rather than streamlining and disembodying discourse, the digital mediation of language re-embodies it all the more explosively.

This explicit 're-embodiment' that takes place within *SSTLS*'s virtual landscapes, the refusal of the human body to be abstracted, is more than a symbol of the corrupt debasement of Shteyngart's depicted society, but in fact plays a key role in signifying the mediation that operates within the realms of data. Such images of grotesque, virtual corporeality signify that, contrary to *SSTLS*'s cultural logic of informatic abstraction, data is also embodied. These 'digital grotesques', which revolve around bodily secretions and ruptures, consistently reassert explicit corporeal content, testifying to the ways in which information continues to be mediated within a digital format. Such viscerally striking exaggerations of material embodiment provide a graphically immediate metaphor for the computational revisions of cyberspace. It draws the readers' attention to the fact that data is similarly a 'language' which alters its content, albeit one that has the appearance of objectivity through a combination of perceptual immediacy and technocultural legitimation.

As such, the cultural logic that attempts to decontextualise information is explicitly framed through a corporeal register as texts become disembodied into data. This 'corporealisation' of texts is foregrounded by consistent disparaging references to their 'smell' (Shteyngart 2011: 50), a quality which the text elsewhere links to the 'vitality' (2011: 57) of bodily existence, to 'a hint of something alive and corporeal' (2011: 107). In such a way, the novel literalises Hayles's comparison that 'like the human body, the book is a form of information transmission and storage, and like the human body, the book incorporates its encodings in a durable material substrate' (Hayles 2010: 28).

What becomes apparent then, is that in the same way that Hayles overextends her metaphor of disembodiment to apply to informational decontextualisation in general, so too does Shteyngart's text operate through a primarily bodily register, yet does so in such a way that the tensions between material and informational modes of abstraction rise to the surface. One way in which this manifests is the text's frequent application of mixed metaphors that seem to fuse social and material registers. For example, Lenny elaborately states that

> nothing will cure my main genetic defect:
> My father is a janitor from a poor country. (Shteyngart 2011: 58)

On a surface level, Lenny's evocation of biogenetics to frame an emphatically socio-economic shortcoming conjures socio-material sentiments that subsume cultural values within an overriding biological discourse. However, this fusion is notably undercut by a grammatical and typographic separation. Lenny's social inadequacy is disclosed in a single sentence paragraph that isolates and demarcates it with empty space. Similarly, the colon creates a semi-permeable border, a fluid frontier that acts as the punctured boundary between the material and the social. This colon, this grammatical orifice, heralds a bodily porosity that both draws in powerful associative connections, yet simultaneously threatens to engulf and digest all that it holds itself in relation to. An overextension of metaphoric embodiment like Hayles's permeates the text stylistically and thematically, but is resisted grammatically and diegetically, generating a contradictory surface that parallels the tension between disembodied and decontextualised readings of postmodern cyberspace.

Therefore, although on a diegetic level there is a notable disjuncture between the cultural perceptions of *SSTLS*'s populace and their socio-material reality, at a thematic level a parallel emerges between these corporeal and informational spheres. Ironically, it is their analogic resistance, their insistent mediation, and their refusal to neatly translate between contexts that forges this thematic unity. Whilst coming into tension at many points, it is their mutually resolute embodiment that resists a cultural logic of abstraction which places them in uneasy accord. In this way the tension within Hayles's conceptual metaphor of embodiment infuses the novel, manifesting as a tension between its thematic and diegetic structure.

Debugging the System: Samuels, Automodernism, and Cyberspace as Post-Postmodern Remedy

Having examined the problematic nature of Hayles's expressive model of cyberspace as postmodern abstraction and its particular depiction within *SSTLS*, we will now turn to a more recent consideration of digital landscapes, Samuels's 'automodernism', which provides an altogether different perspective on the informational decontextualisation which, for Hayles, leads to disembodiment.

In the first line of *New Media, Cultural Studies, and Critical Theory after Postmodernism* Samuels states that 'we have entered a new era of cultural history, which is dominated by the paradoxical combination of social automation and individual autonomy' (Samuels 2010: 3), a concept that he refers to as 'automodernism'. Specifically applied to contemporary digital environments, this phenomenon can be understood as 'the power of automated technologies to give us a heightened *sense* of individual control [whilst] often function[ing] to undermine the awareness of social and cultural mediation' (2010: 12) by deploying 'the power of automation ... to render social and material factors invisible' (2010: 13). The starting point of automodernism, then, is a recognition that postmodernism's 'destabilized conception of knowledge and truth' (2010: 10) undermines the legitimacy of information as well as the ability of the individual to process that information.

Already a difference emerges between the constructions of postmodernism against which Hayles and Samuels respectively define their models of cyberspace.[6] For Hayles, the postmodern emphasis on discourse speaks to a wider logic of material disembodiment which manifests through cyberspace. For Samuels, the postmodern recognition of both the subject and information's socio-discursive constitution results in a post-postmodern conception of cyberspace, one that attempts to reconcile these problems by restoring the fantasy of a humanist subject capable of navigating objective fact. Automodernism frames the socio-historical contextualisation of the body as a process which effaces its agency and reverts to technological dematerialisation to reassert the possibility of the autonomous subject. Haylesian postmodernism is characterised by a primary abstraction both of materiality and of socio-historical specificity (or context). Samuels's postmodernism, on the other hand, is characterised by a comprehensive embedding of socio-historical determinants, although this does not necessarily extend to the concept of materiality itself.

The key difference in these perspectives can be seen to originate from a fundamental division in how postmodern constructivism is interpreted. For the Haylesian model, socio-discursive construction is a means by which materiality is abstracted and information is decontextualised. Within such an account, the material disembodiment of cyberspace operates as the ultimate realisation (or perhaps de-realisation) of postmodern constructivism's abstracted logic. The automodern account, however, frames socio-historical construction as an overbearing mode of informational contextualisation, which is alleviated by cyberspace's automated sensation of dematerialisation. As Samuels states,

> the automodern experience of the Web challenges the postmodern idea that we are constrained by time and space and our relationships are defined by our cultural and social differences and relations ... [since] in cyberspace, temporal and spatial restrains do not seem to matter. (2010: 17)

In short, according to Hayles's conceptual framework, cyberspace expresses postmodernism, whereas according to Samuels, cyberspace remedies postmodernism's ills.

Samuels's aim, however, is not to advocate an automodern ideology, but rather to critique it. His key project is to expose the contradiction at work within the automodern perspective; that is, the autonomy it seeks to generate is compromised through a dependency on the technologies that produce its effects (Samuels 2010: 15–16, 45). It is this fundamental paradox that defines the automodern condition and, I would like to argue, the 'virtual humanist' subjectivity it induces. Whilst Samuels does not explicitly frame his critique of contemporary cyberculture in terms of (post)humanism, it is certainly productive to do so, and his concept of automodernism provides a strong foundation upon which to consider this emergent form of subjectivity. Therefore, the model of 'virtual humanism' offered here essentially constitutes an extension of Samuels's critical insights towards a consideration of competing posthuman subjectivities.

Requiring both an autonomous perceiving subject and a distinctly sensible object of perception, the possibility of a traditional liberal humanist subjectivity becomes unsettled by postmodernism's revelation of both knowledge's and the self's socio-discursive constitution. Due to postmodernism's disruptive influence, 'virtual humanism' perceives such an autonomy to be achievable only by means of technological 'supplements', in this case the automated access to information provided by cyberspace. However, this technological dependency inescapably resituates the human subject as a biomechanical amalgamation, thereby compromising the possibility of the liberal humanist subject which it supposedly resurrects. Such a perspective considers digital technologies as a constructive apparatus by which the values and ideologies of humanism are not only preserved, but generated. In doing so, virtual humanism reconstitutes the contours of the very subject that it is evoked to defend. It is this fundamental tension between the autonomous associations of material disembodiment, both corporeal and informational, and the methods and mechanisms by which they are produced and maintained that forms the contradictory contours of this new, digitally informed, post-postmodern subjectivity that I want to call the 'virtual humanist subject'.

Of course, there is no shortage of perspectives that look to reconcile technological advancements with a humanist tradition. Such a sentiment might be said to apply to a vast number of transhumanisms, whose 'Enlightenment philosophical heritage and ascription to narratives of scientific objectivism, and historical and evolutionary progress' (Thweatt-Bates 2012: 135) is often considered 'an *intensification* of humanism' (Wolfe 2010: xv), though with varying degrees of generosity regarding the original capabilities of the human subject. However, as Hayles makes clear, cybernetic posthumanism/transhumanism operates through a logic of enhancement that aims to augment an already assumed human subject, whereas virtual humanism – I contend – operates through a logic of compensation that aims to technologically remedy that which (to rephrase Bruno Latour) has 'never been human'.

Drawing on the theories of Wiener, Hayles demonstrates that cybernetic posthumanism draws a parallel between 'perception, mathematics, and information [which] all concentrate on pattern' (Hayles 2010: 98), thereby retaining the possibility of accurate human knowledge and looking to enhance this knowledge, as a 'means to *extend* liberal humanism' (2010: 6, my emphasis). The virtual humanist subject, on the other hand, is one which is dependent upon technology to reach the status of 'human' and perform the attributed functions of rational selection and control.[7] Rather than operate through a logic of enhancement, the disruptive legacy of postmodernity compels virtual humanism to operate through a logic of compensation, in which a liberal humanist subject is paradoxically constructed through the technological production of its 'originary' traits.

Autonomy Ruptured: *Super Sad True Love Story*, Virtual Humanism, and Social Mediation

The paradoxes of a virtual humanist subjectivity can be seen articulated in Lenny's attempts to generate a sense of humanist autonomy and selfhood via digital technologies throughout *SSTLS*. An ageing bibliophile of limited social standing but some financial means, Lenny is depicted as a reluctant virtual humanist, intuitively averse to technological development yet ambivalently enthralled by its potential to compensate for his perceived inadequacies (Shteyngart 2011: 76). For all of his ambivalence, Lenny is just as fixated on digital technologies as his peers, although this is a fixation primarily motivated by fear of 'obsolescence' (2011: 62) rather than ambition or excitement. For Lenny, digital engagement is not so much an opportunity for enhancement as a matter of survival, a motivator that is literalised in his 'obsess[ion] with death' (2011: 266) and his fixation on achieving technologically induced immortality. That is to say, the primary distinction between Lenny and his peers is one between a virtual humanist ideology and a transhumanist ideology. Lenny attempts to compensate for his deficiencies via technology, whereas the social logic in operation is one of advancement through technology. It is through this framework that we can start to gain a better understanding of Lenny's complex relationship with the wider culture in which he is enmeshed.

Due to his social background and lack of technological mastery, Lenny often expresses feelings of inadequacy, 'inferiority' (2011: 7), and a heart-breaking familiarity with dehumanisation as his peers '[give] me that old familiar look that denoted I was not a human being' (2011: 317).[8] It is partially in response to his social disempowerment and perceived absence of autonomy that Lenny attempts to reassert his agency via a technologically oriented mode of humanist self-expression. Throughout the novel, it is one of Lenny's central preoccupations to utilise social media as a means of both expressing and constructing this individualised humanist self in pursuit of social and economic advancement.

And yet Lenny's pursuit of these goals through social media is not purely mercenary or cynical, but rather a sincere attempt at establishing what he considers to be a true 'human' connection, to allow his 'words to be *processed* into love' (Shteyngart 2011: 273, my emphasis). The tragedy of Lenny's situation is that his desire, both for interpersonal connection and social mobility, is prevented by the very means by which he attempts to attain them. That is, the depersonalisation of cyberspace renders the type of connections that he craves, connections between individual humanist subjects, all but impossible. Lenny's digitally mediated romantic pursuits characterise a frustrated attempt for traditional sentiments of love and connection to be translated into a digital environment which redefines these very concepts.

Splitting the narrative between two narrators, *SSTLS* deploys Eunice's distinctively sporadic techno-slang to offset the sumptuous yet sentimental prose of Lenny's diary. Emulating the nineteenth-century realist style of his literary heroes, Lenny's 'self-conscious chronicles' reveal his continued investment in a 'quaint liberal humanism ... still structured by ... a print culture that generates and sustains a solitary, introspective "individual ego"' (Malewitz 2015: 110), which is distinct and separable from external factors. Yet despite his best efforts, Lenny's diary is not a hermetically sealed interiority, but rather a permeable, fragile individuality which requires a technological supplement.

Lenny's 'undeserving diary' (Shteyngart 2011: 2) proves insufficient to sustain his fantasies of autonomous self-definition and, in fact, primarily functions as a material witness to his true ambition, attaining eternal life through cybernetic 'Life

Extension' (2011: 7) surgery. Rather than a means of attaining artistic immortality, Lenny's diary begins as a means of documenting his journey into a technologically enabled immortality and correspondingly ends once he realises its impossibility. This desire to conquer death and achieve material transcendence comprises the ultimate expression of the dominance of the human will over material factors, cultivated and intensified by technological imperatives. Yet it is crucially through an array of invasive technological interventions which recalibrate the contours of 'humanness' itself that Lenny paradoxically attempts to assert his human autonomy. For instance, Lenny's appreciation of the humanist sentiments symbolically associated with the 'heart' (2011: 188) is eventually superseded by the Life Extension processes' necessitation of jettisoning 'that useless muscle' (2011: 293).

It is, perhaps, in its depiction of social relations that *SSTLS* provides its most damning critique of Lenny's doomed efforts to acquire humanist autonomy via technological mediation. Shteyngart's use of farcical exaggeration renders the continued mediatory function of cyberspace both absurdly obtrusive and insidiously subtle by making it apparent to the reader but almost invisible to its characters. For example, social interaction in *SSTLS* primarily occurs through the FAC (Form-A-Community) interface, which provides members of the public with quantified rankings based on a combination of browsing history, biometric readouts, and accumulated capital. The simplified categories against which the population are ranked clearly re-enforce gender divides, as women are divided into 'Fuckability', 'Personality', and 'Anal/Oral/Vaginal Preference' whereas 'masculine data' (Shteyngart 2011: 90) is ranked in terms of 'Male Hotness', 'Personality', and 'Sustainability' (2011: 88–9). The discrepancy in terms of social expectation where men are expected to provide and women are reduced to the role of fragmented sex objects goes apparently unnoticed, despite the text's comparatively sensitive narrator, yet the vulgarity with which these gendered terms are relayed deliberately provokes the reader into acknowledging this institutionalised sexism. By combining explicit vocabulary with an 'in passing' referential recitation, the text simultaneously emphasises media technologies' determination of these characters' social expectations and the desensitised manner in which it is passively received. Whilst superficially allowing its users a greater degree of social autonomy by providing accessible information regarding who they are most likely to 'compute' with, the FAC system actually enforces a rigid social hierarchy dictating the possibilities and conditions of social interactions. Rather than reflecting the shallow values of a corrupted and superficial society, the FAC system and the digital environment it engenders in fact create this society.

Instead of levelling social determinants, then, *SSTLS*'s social media simply enacts a technologically oriented redeployment of these same determining factors. Although Lenny turns to technology in an attempt to mitigate any prejudice he may face as a second-generation immigrant, his technological inadequacy simply provides a new model for prejudice and victimisation (Shteyngart 2011: 67). Shteyngart's overlapping of these modes of discrimination playfully literalises the metaphor of 'digital immigrants' and 'techno-natives' and exposes how digital environments do not so much erase cultural discrimination as replace and reconstitute its manifestation as technological discrimination.

These various forms of social mediation eventually surface at the material level when, in the novel's third movement, a traumatic social disturbance referred to as 'The Rupture' propels the text from satirical speculative fiction into a more recognisable dystopic mode. Though its causes are purposefully convoluted and uncertain, the Rupture's main narrative function is to express the 'covert' social dominance that underpins the supposed freedom of Shteyngart's New York. As its name suggests, the rupture is a moment of fruition, an eruption of underlying socio-economic oppression which materially manifests the class structure that has been in technological operation throughout the novel. The Rupture is a fracturing, a secular rapture, an anti-Singularity devolving New York's eutopic transhuman dreams into an all too familiar dystopianism that brutally manifests the extent to which the text's digital environment has engrained, rather than displaced, social inequalities. Perhaps the clearest indication of this comes in Lenny's encounter with a 'five-jiao man'. A bastardised reimagining of the figure of the 'six-million-dollar man' that Hayles originally identifies as 'a paradigmatic citizen of the posthuman regime' (Hayles 2010: 3), the 'five-jiao man' is here reduced to post-Rupture New York's new slave class that materialises the inequalities of Shteyngart's dystopic posthuman vision.

The pivot of Lenny's character development is his eventual recognition of the paradoxes and limitations of virtual humanism's technologically induced autonomy. Characteristic of the text's aforementioned thematic extension of embodied metaphor, Lenny's eventual recognition of his own autonomous contradiction occurs in a manner that combines his acceptance of embodied existence with a recognition of the mediated, contextualised nature of data. Both data and self are revealed to be unshakably bound by their materiality.

As mentioned previously, the novel is bookended by extracts from Lenny's diary that contrast a stubborn defiance of mortality, his 'decision' (Shteyngart 2011: 1) never to die, with its eventual acceptance. Interestingly, however, Lenny initially expresses the fear that if he were to die 'I would disappear from the earth. And all these emotions, all these yearnings, all these *data*, if that helps to clinch the enormity of what I'm talking about, would be gone' (2011: 68). At this moment, Lenny's desire for immortality appears to be predicated on a direct equivalence between his subject status and the quantifiable data by which it is technologically legitimated within his culture. In his desire for self-preservation, he succumbs to a fundamental reconstitution of what that 'self' is. However, in the novel's closing chapter he expresses a different relationship with data, stating:

> I am going to die. Nothing of my personality will remain. The light switch will be turned off. My life, my entirety, will be lost forever. I will be nullified. And what will be left? ... my data, the soupy base of my existence uptexted to a GlobalTeens account. Words, words, words. You, dear diary. (Shteyngart 2011: 302)

This transition indicates that by the end of the novel, Lenny has started to locate his subjectivity, the 'I' of his statement, outside of data and within his own emphatically mortal and transient body. In denouncing his autonomy as defined by the conquest of mind over body, he simultaneously reclaims an aspect of that same humanist self-governance in the form of a non-quantified self. At the same time, he also acknowledges the materiality of data itself as he pairs it with the written word. Data moves from essence to byproduct, and just as physical texts are labelled throughout the novel as a problematic external object that necessarily compromises the message it transmits, so too is data's status as external mediator recognised. As the novel draws to a close, Lenny accepts that media, both material and digital, cannot ultimately provide him with the agency he craves. In doing so, he moves from a sense of omnipotence to a realisation of the limits of his agency.

Conclusion: Technological Supplements and Unattainable Prospects

As mentioned at the start of this chapter, contemporary cyberspace is a space which entangles both traditional configurations of postmodern expressivity and emergent configurations of post-postmodern remedy. It is through this layering of perspectives that we can start to appreciate the narrative tension that lies at the heart of *SSTLS*. Put another way, Shteyngart's text simultaneously reveals the contradictions of both abstracted postmodernism and its curative counterpart, and it is through the layering of these contradictions that *SSTLS* constructs Lenny's cultural estrangement. By placing an examination of the paradoxes inherent in Lenny's virtual humanist ideology within an environment that explores the limitations of embodied metaphor, the text's formal, thematic, and narrative elements coalesce to articulate the contradictions of contemporary cyberspace and its repercussions for subjectivity. This paradoxical orientation is expressed in the exposure of both information and subjectivity as socially mediated phenomena.

By positioning a character who attempts to escape socio-discursive determination through an effacement of corporeal materiality within a world which exerts its cultural logic and social stratification through material disembodiment, the text exposes the contradictory determination – the rendering of information as both abstracted and mediated, both detached and socially constructed – that subtends contemporary concepts of cyberspace. Lenny's attempts to vacate the site of his social overdetermination – his aged, immigrant body – offer no respite in a world where disembodied cyberspace itself becomes an environment punctuated by tenacious social hierarchies. Whilst fleeing the body *as* society, Lenny is equally fleeing the body *into* society. Attempting to resist the socio-discursive inscriptions enforced upon his material form, he unwittingly replicates his society's yearning for corporeal transcendence. It is this fundamental ambivalence regarding the extent to which Lenny resists or embraces his society and its cultural logic of disembodiment that forms the narrative engine of Shteyngart's novel.

As we have seen, this ambivalence has important implications for constructions of 'the human', which *SSTLS* also explores. On the one hand, the text's cultural logic of disembodiment is defied by insistent eruptions of materiality which signal the general populace's inability to reach a fully post/transhuman condition, ultimately rendering them as merely human. On the other hand, Lenny's virtual humanist logic encodes his failure to achieve disembodiment as indicative that he is less than human, a pure product of socio-discursive determinism. This creates a fundamental instability and ambivalence regarding Lenny's final designation as a non/human subject, in that his subject status is both legitimated and denied through social determination.

This paradoxical relation is emphasised during Lenny's recitation of Life Extension procedures, which include 'extracting nutrients, supplementing, delivering, playing with the building blocks, copying, manipulating, reprogramming, replacing blood, destroying harmful bacteria' (Shteyngart 2011: 122). The use of the term 'supplement', here, is not incidental but rather to be interpreted in its Derridean substantiation as a 'weaving together [of] the two significations of supplementarity – substitution and accretion' (Derrida 1998: 200). The barrage of present continuous verbs signifies the interweaving of these meanings by simultaneously evoking creation (manipulating, playing) and recreation (replacing, copying). The radical new technologies and surgeries that Lenny pursues form the 'supplement' to his humanity, simultaneously constructing and augmenting it. Just as cyberspace expresses and remedies postmodernism, technological intervention is perceived by Lenny to both express and remedy his humanity.

This 'double orientation' signals cyberspace as a site of simultaneous hope and despair for both the possibility of objective knowledge and the integrity of the human subject: hope for the possibility of recapturing a lost human essence, despair in the consistent deferment of this possibility. Both the expression of and cure for postmodernism, cyberspace is a site in which contemporary culture attempts to simultaneously construct and transcend human subjectivity. Just as Lenny's virtual humanist conflict with *SSTLS*'s transhuman culture reveals humanism's internal disidency, so too does the double orientation of cyberspace reveal the paradoxes at the heart of technologically oriented attempts to extend humanism.

Notes

1. See Roden 2015: 26; Haraway 2016: 33; Halberstam and Livingston 1995: 4.
2. See also MacCormack 2012: 7–8 and Wolfe 2010: xv.
3. As we shall see, it is precisely this latter process masquerading as the former which occurs in Hayles's *HWBP*.
4. Due to a lack of available information, these approximated figures have been compiled by cross-referencing reports detailing average number of users per messaging board with those indicating number of messaging boards active. Though this is far from ideal, paucity of available data on the subject further demonstrates the obscurity of early cyberspace and the unexpected nature of its explosion.

5. Although Hayles resists using the term 'transhumanism', her concept of cybernetic posthumanism largely refers to the same constellation of thinkers, philosophies, and outlooks that are associated with the former term.
6. We should note, however, that Samuels himself does not actively subscribe to the automodern perception of postmodernism and has an altogether more nuanced view of the term (Samuels 2010: 117). That is, Samuels's relationship with automodernism is descriptive rather than prescriptive.
7. I am grateful to Ridvan Askin for pointing out that this philosophical position bears some similarity to Bernard Stiegler's 'epiphylogenetic' model of the human subject as laid out in *Technics and Time*. However, I would contend that the primary distinction between these concepts is that Stiegler's position self-reflexively renegotiates modernist presumptions of what it means to be human by 'radically challenging the border between the animal and the human' (Stiegler 1998: 136), as well as that between human and machine. As such, Stiegler's philosophy more succinctly aligns with that of critical posthumanism. In contrast, virtual humanism, like automodernism, is a system in which such renegotiations 'are constantly being employed and then rendered invisible' (Samuels 2010: 45), producing an artificial sense of 'individual autonomy' (Samuels 2010: 15) fundamental to liberal humanism.
8. Notably, this debilitating sense of inferiority is derived from an excessive social determination due to his Jewish-Russian migrant heritage and upbringing, as Lenny is often on the receiving end of anti-Semitic remarks (Shteyngart 2011: 18, 89).

Bibliography

Badmington, Neil (ed.) (2000), *Posthumanism*, Houndmills: Macmillan.
Badmington, Neil (2004), *Alien Chic: Posthumanism and the Other Within*, London: Routledge.
Barthes, Roland (2009), *Image-Music-Text*, Stephen Heath (ed. and trans.), New York: Hill and Wang.
Baudrillard, Jean (2007), *Jean Baudrillard: Selected Writings*, Mark Poster (ed.), Stanford: Stanford University Press.
Braidotti, Rosi (2013), *The Posthuman*, Cambridge: Polity.
Bush, Randy (1992), *FidoNet: Technology, Use, Tools, and History*, Fidonet.org, <https://www.fidonet.org/inet92_Randy_Bush.txt> (last accessed 6 November 2017).
Callus, Ivan and Stefan Herbrechter (2012), 'Introduction: Posthumanist Subjectivities, or, Coming after the Subject', *Subjectivity*, 5:3, pp. 241–64.
Cavallaro, Dani (2000), *Cyberpunk and Cyberculture: The Virtual Subject in Postmodern Science Fiction*, New Brunswick: Athlone Press.
Cofer, Erik (2018), 'Owning the End of the World: Zero K and DeLillo's Post-Postmodern Mutation', *Critique: Studies in Contemporary Fiction*, 59:4, pp. 459–70.
Coole, Diana and Samantha Frost (eds) (2010), *New Materialisms: Ontology, Agency and Politics*, Durham, NC: Duke University Press.
Derrida, Jacques (1981), *Dissemination*, Barbara Johnson (trans.), Chicago: University of Chicago Press.
Derrida, Jacques (1998), *Of Grammatology*, Baltimore: Johns Hopkins University Press.
Descartes, René (2008), *Discourse on the Method and the Meditations*, John Veitch (trans.), New York: Cosimo.
Digital Population Worldwide (2019), Statista: The Statistics Portal, <https://www.statista.com/statistics/617136/digital-population-worldwide/> (last accessed 20 March 2019).

Fair, Benjamin (2005), 'Stepping Razor in Orbit: Postmodern Identity and Political Alternatives in William Gibson's *Neuromancer*', *Critique: Studies in Contemporary Fiction*, 46:2, pp. 92–103.
Fang, Lai Tze (2016), 'The Digital Intensification of Postmodern Poetics', in Tim Lanzendörfer (ed.), *The Poetics of Genre in the Contemporary Novel*, Lanham,: Lexington Books, pp. 33–55.
Foucault, Michel (2005), *The Order of Things*, London: Routledge.
Gibson, William (1995), *Neuromancer*, London: HarperCollins.
Halberstam, Judith and Ira Livingston (eds) (1995), *Posthuman Bodies*, Bloomington: Indiana University Press.
Haraway, Donna J. (2016), 'A Cyborg Manifesto: Science, Technology, and Socialist-Feminism in the Late Twentieth Century', in Donna Haraway, *Manifestly Haraway*, Minneapolis: University of Minnesota Press, pp. 3–90.
Hassan, Ihab (1977), 'Prometheus as Performer: Toward a Posthumanist Culture?', *The Georgia Review*, 31:4, pp. 830–50.
Hayles, N. Katherine (2010), *How We Became Posthuman: Virtual Bodies in Cybernetics, Literature, and Informatics*, Chicago: University of Chicago Press.
Herbrechter, Stefan (2013), *Posthumanism: A Critical Analysis*, London: Bloomsbury.
Hoberek, Andrew (2007), 'Introduction: After Postmodernism', *Twentieth-Century Literature*, 53:3, pp. 233–47.
Houliang, Chen (2014), 'Constructing Postmodernism with Incredulity to Metanarrative: A Comparative Perspective on McHale's and Hutcheon's Postmodern Poetics', *Neohelicon*, 42:1, pp. 283–95.
Jameson, Fredric (1991), *Postmodernism, or, The Cultural Logic of Late Capitalism*, London: Verso.
Lee, Timothy B. (2014), '40 Maps that Explain the Internet', *vox.com*, 2 June, <https://www.vox.com/a/internet-maps> (last accessed 6 November 2017).
Lynn, Barry C. (2010), 'Corporate Giants Have Too Much Power', *CNN*, 16 February, <http://edition.cnn.com/2010/OPINION/02/16/lynn.amazon.power/> (last accessed 6 November 2017).
Lyotard, Jean-François (1984), *The Postmodern Condition: A Report on Knowledge*, Geoffrey Bennington and Brian Massumi (trans.), Minneapolis: University of Minnesota Press.
Lyotard, Jean-François (1996), *The Inhuman: Reflections on Time*, Geoffrey Bennington and Rachel Bowlby (trans.), Stanford: Stanford University Press.
MacCormack, Patricia (2012), *Posthuman Ethics: Embodiment and Cultural Theory*, Farnham: Ashgate.
McHale, Brian (1992), *Constructing Postmodernism*, London: Routledge.
Malewitz, Raymond (2015), '"Some new dimension devoid of hip and bone": Remediated Bodies and Digital Posthumanism in Gary Shteyngart's *Super Sad True Love Story*', *Arizona Quarterly: A Journal of American Literature, Culture, and Theory*, 71:4, pp. 107–27.
Myers, Tony (2001), 'The Postmodern Imaginary in William Gibson's *Neuromancer*', *Modern Fiction Studies*, 47:4, pp. 887–909.
Office of Technology Assessment (1995), *Telecommunications Technology and Native Americans: Opportunities and Challenges*, Washington, DC: U.S. Government Printing Office.
Rheingold, Howard (1994), *The Virtual Community*, London: Secker and Warburg.
Roberts, Lawrence G. (1995), *The ARPANET and Computer Networks*, *NetExpress Inc.*, May, <http://www.packet.cc/files/arpanet-computernet.html> (last accessed 6 November 2017).
Roden, David (2015), *Posthuman Life: Philosophy at the Edge of the Human*, London: Routledge.
Ryan, Johnny (2013), *A History of the Internet and the Digital Future*, London: Reaktion Books.

Samuels, Robert (2010), *New Media, Cultural Studies, and Critical Theory after Postmodernism*, New York: Palgrave Macmillan.

Schmeink, Lars (2016), *Biopunk Dystopias: Genetic Engineering, Society, and Science Fiction*, Liverpool: Liverpool University Press.

Shteyngart, Gary (2011), *Super Sad True Love Story*, London: Granta.

Stiegler, Bernard (1998), *Technics and Time 1: The Fault of Epimetheus*, Richard Beardsworth and George Collins (trans.), Stanford: Stanford University Press.

Thweatt-Bates, Jeanine (2012), *Cyborg Selves: A Theological Anthropology of the Posthuman*, Farnham: Ashgate.

Wolfe, Cary (2010), *What is Posthumanism?*, Minneapolis: University of Minnesota Press.

PART II

Beyond the Subject: Posthuman and Nonhuman Literary Criticism

Editor's Introduction

Ridvan Askin

The emergence and consolidation of three particular and rather diverse strands of thought since, roughly, the late 1980s are pivotal for the chapters in this section: (1) a specific uptake and continuation of central poststructuralist concerns about plurality, difference, and relationality combined with a renewed emphasis on embodiment and the corporeal (in contrast to poststructuralism's predominant linguistic framework); (2) the forceful resurgence of speculative metaphysics, in both its continental and analytic guises, after what could well be called the century of antimetaphysics; and (3), an interest in the limits and limitations of the human, including its utter dissolution in some strands of cognitivist and analytic thought. These seemingly unrelated trends can well be subsumed under the headings of the post- and nonhuman, even though not everyone participating in these discussions would willingly subscribe to these designations. But the terms have the virtue of signalling what is at stake in these debates, namely the interest and urge to reconceptualise what it means to be human while at the same time eradicating all and any anthropocentrism. What is at stake, then, is to rethink and to go beyond the human subject.

Those thinkers harking back to poststructuralism pick up the poststructuralists' emphases on decentring, differentiation, and proliferation while tying these processes firmly to the realm of the material and corporeal. Where the poststructuralists were predominantly concerned with the incessant circulation and differentiation of signs, signifiers, and signification constitutive of human subjectivity, a more recent generation sees the differential process of subject formation already at work in matter itself. Or, more precisely, matter itself *is* this very process of differentiation and circulation generative of human subjectivity. While such a framework already constitutes a speculative gesture beyond the confines of the human subject and towards its generative matrix, sustained attempts to systematise (the possibility of) such a ground or grounding are the mark of a return to practising full-blown speculative metaphysics. What all these attempts share, regardless of the philosophical tradition they pertain to, is to think beyond the limits of thought (to co-opt the title of a book by one of the contributors to this section) in order to excavate or recover a terrain or territory that, according to most thinkers of the twentieth century, had been lost for good. Depending on the system in question, this terrain can turn out to be the realm of pure ideal potentiality, of absolute nothingness, or, indeed, just plain physical matter, to name but three possibilities.

The concern with the limits and limitations of the human is of course by definition at the heart of any speculative metaphysics since the speculative gesture is by default a gesture beyond the limits of human subjectivity. The project of critique as inaugurated by Immanuel Kant was, after all, precisely devised to rein in what it considered to be the illegitimate excess of thought, that is, its speculative use. Indeed, much of the current debate about the post- and nonhuman can be understood as, in one way or another, a renewed and prolonged reappraisal, negotiation, and working through of this Kantian legacy.

These developments have not left the study of literature unscathed. On the contrary, often enough they are propelled by means of discussions of literature and of literary works or even by the very works of literature themselves, as the four contributions to this section amply testify. The first chapter, in which Birgit Mara Kaiser considers Hélène Cixous's literary as well as theoretical work, constitutes a prime example in this regard as it traces the philosophical quality of Cixous's fiction and, conversely, the poetical quality of her more ostensibly philosophical texts. More importantly for the focus of this section, Kaiser does so with respect to what she singles out as Cixous's main thrust, whether in her more literary or her more philosophical works, namely precisely the question of subject formation. According to Kaiser, the poststructuralist Cixous in many ways already prefigures the later turn to the material and corporeal by emphasising human sensibility and affectivity as the very preconditions of subjectivity, always in relation to and in encounter with others, particularly nonhuman others such as animals and plants.

In the second contribution to this section, Evan Gottlieb takes up Quentin Meillassoux's influential coinage of 'correlationism', a term designed to capture the posited necessary 'correlation' of subject and object, a posit Meillassoux traces precisely to Kant's critical project. Gottlieb revisits the first immediate reaction to Kant's criticism, namely romanticism, in his chapter. Discussing English romantic poetry, particularly that of William Wordsworth and Percy Bysshe Shelley, Gottlieb showcases how the romantics grappled with the supposedly inescapable correlation between subject and object in their struggle to express the creative work of both nature and the human subject without reducing the one to the other.

With the third chapter, we move into decidedly more analytic territory. In his contribution, Graham Priest first presents his account of fictional objects, availing himself of his trademark notion of non-existent objects to push back against rival attempts to theorise fictionality. He then proceeds to use his elaboration of fictional objects – enlisting help from Buddhist philosophy along the way – to show how the human subject is nothing but precisely such a fictional object. Priest's account is the first of two eliminative accounts of subjectivity in this section, that is, accounts that eliminate, do away with, the notion of the subject as they reduce it to something else – to a mere biological organism in Priest's case.

If that were not unsettling enough for scholars of the humanities, the second eliminative account and the final contribution to this section goes yet a step further in what can only be called a provocation: R. Scott Bakker, himself a writer, draws on recent cognitive science to urge us to entertain the possibility not only that the human subject is nothing but an illusion, but that there is not even a remnant of what analytic philosophers call intentionality anywhere in the universe. Bakker suggests that pure automated mechanism is all there is, and that 'intention' and 'meaning' are phenomena to be explained away as useful evolutionary illusions produced by the human brain in order to facilitate human survival – 'meaning' and 'intention' have only practical but no theoretical import. Literature can serve to illustrate this, almost literally, mind-boggling situation – something that Bakker has indeed taken upon himself to do in his fantasy and science fiction novels.

What unites the four contributions to this section, then, is that, in one way or another, they all theorise the beyond of human subjectivity, whether in terms of a pre-subjective, generative matrix of affectivity, as the romantics' continuous struggle to escape correlationism, as nothing but biology once one ceases to buy into the fiction of the subject, or as mere meaningless mechanism that emerges as the only viable ground after the illusion of a human self has finally been shed.

5

Hélène Cixous's *So Close*; or, Moving Matters on the Subject

Birgit Mara Kaiser

For a great writer must be a poet-thinker, very much a poet and a very thinking poet.

(Jacques Derrida about Hélène Cixous, quoted in Hanrahan 2004: 8)

For a volume on literature and contemporary philosophy, I could hardly imagine texts better suited than those by – to quote Jacques Derrida from the epigraph above – feminist poet-thinker Hélène Cixous. On the one hand, Cixous's texts are 'literature' par excellence. They move, often within one text alone, between the dramatic, the narrative, the poetic, and the essayistic, thus encompassing the classical genres of drama, prose, and poetry that are usually said to constitute 'literature', while at the same time testing the borders of the literary. Moving across and between genres, Cixous's texts exceed conventional limits and resist being pinned down as this or that type of text. Touching on 'all' of literature including its border zones (for example, autobiography, autofiction, or essay) in this way, her texts put into play the very denominator of 'literature' and demonstrate how fluid the boundaries and classifications of literature are, how ultimately uncertain it is what exactly is encompassed by 'literature'.[1] Cixous's texts thus embody the question of the limits of 'literature' that this volume poses by coupling it with philosophy. On the other hand, Cixous's texts are deeply intertextual, intersecting with works of other thinkers and poet-thinkers such as St Augustine, Walter Benjamin, Jacques Derrida, René Descartes, Sigmund Freud, Heinrich von Kleist, Jacques Lacan, Clarice Lispector, Michel de Montaigne, James Joyce, and Marcel Proust. In conversation with these interlocutors, her texts touch on philosophical questions such as those of time, meaning, God, (sexual) difference, death, the subject, corporeality, the unconscious, and memory, to name but a few. Partly due to these intertextual conversations that her texts entertain, and partly due to their specific thematic and rhetorical (re)compositions of philosophical questions, her poetic fictions can be said to be philosophical in their own right. In literary form, they pose and investigate philosophical questions. Cixous, one might say, writes literature that is philosophy and does philosophy as literature.[2]

The closeness of these two fields has been a central concern of deconstruction and poststructuralism, of which Cixous herself is a prominent voice. In fact, the key point that Derrida makes on the relation of 'literature' and 'philosophy' is, as Derek Attridge notes in *Acts of Literature*, the following: the common assertion of the relation between literature and philosophy as oppositional – with philosophy being the expression of analytic thought about reality, metaphysical and of universal reach, and literature the rhetorical composition of fiction, for the ends of sensual pleasure – is itself a philosophical one 'by means of which philosophy produces, and thus constitutes itself against, its other' (Attridge 1992: 13). This oppositional way of sketching their relation attempts to delineate 'philosophy' and safeguard it from those practices of writing (rhetorical, textual, poetic) that are deemed foreign to it, expelling them to (or containing them within) the field of literature, which is consequently said to be able to permit itself, and in fact live off, textual and linguistic free play and rhetorical persuasion.[3] This insight is a key feature of deconstruction and poststructuralism. Yet, from among the many different voices of poststructuralist thought – we could think here, next to Derrida, of Gilles Deleuze, Michel Foucault, Jean-François Lyotard, Jean-Luc Nancy, Avital Ronell, and many others – Cixous is of particular interest; for one, because her texts engage this peculiar relation of literature and philosophy most directly on the grounds of the poetic and the literary, while other writings labelled as poststructuralist mostly do so on the grounds of what is more readily perceived as philosophy or theory. Engaging with Cixous's work will thus make it very difficult for us to treat the two as straightforwardly separate fields, but it will also prevent us from merely applying philosophical thought to her poetic work as if from the outside; rather, as we will see in what follows, her work demands that we read the poetic as philosophical in its own right without forsaking its singularity, its very poeticity or literariness. But even more importantly perhaps – and suitable for the issues raised in this section of the book, which invites us to reflect on formations of the subject otherwise than within humanist confines – Cixous's work permits pursuing the question of the subject in unique ways.[4]

From her earliest texts in the late 1960s onward, Cixous's writing has challenged psychoanalytic (particularly Freudian-Lacanian) and phenomenological (particularly Hegelian) notions of the subject, which, to her, start from the fundamental assumption of lack (Lacan) and a binary dialectic (Hegel). In one way or another, all her texts, stretching from *Le Prénom de Dieu* (Cixous 1967) to at present *Défions l'Augure* (Cixous 2018), have explored what it means to be human, that is, modes of 'doing subjectivity' in ways that question the two basic presuppositions of lack and a self/other dialectic. Cixous has criticised these presuppositions especially because they both operate through negativity, which makes of difference a dualism, and her work has instead stressed heterogeneous and multiple differences that exceed duality as the condition of any enunciation of subjectivity. Perhaps decisively for considerations of the posthuman and nonhuman as formations 'beyond the subject' (as the section title has it), Cixous's engagement with subjectivity – precisely by starting from heterogeneous differences as alternative grounds of its formation – has also moved along posthuman and nonhuman vectors. Her texts sound out the voices of the living and the dead, of human and nonhuman animal others, of ways of existing with/in ecologies without which no 'doing subjectivity' is feasible.[5] Pursuing human subjectivity in these ways, her texts clearly debunk and move away from the humanist Subject. To that extent, engaging with Cixous cannot but move us 'beyond the subject'. Importantly, however, while the responses she gives to the shortcomings of phallogocentric and humanist notions of subjectivity indeed leave these latter notions behind, her responses do not go beyond the subject *tout court*. Rather, they amount to revisions of its figuration. What Cixous proposes and exercises throughout her work is by no means a turn away from the concern for the subject, or a move onto new posthuman or nonhuman grounds in the sense of forsaking human subjectivity for good – as tempting as such turns may be (I am thinking here of the recent turn to objects, for example).[6] Instead, Cixous's texts critique and decisively undo any subject/object or human/animal binary, and they do so by rethinking what being human and forming subjectivity might mean. In that vein, in *Rootprints* she notes that '[f]irst of all, we are *sentient* beings' (Cixous and Calle-Gruber 1997: 18, my emphasis). Taking sensuality, affectivity, and corporeality as starting points necessarily means that human life and formations of subjectivity are fundamentally entangled with heterogeneous otherness, and if that is the case, then subjectivity will have to be otherwise than the humanist Subject.

Paying close attention to some of her key 'theoretical' texts and to *So Close* (2009a), one of her more recent fictions, this chapter will trace how exactly Cixous's figuration of subjectivity takes into account the affective, the im/material, and the nonhuman, which the idea of the humanist Subject relegates to the status of mere objects, bodies, and animality, mere inert matter foreign to thought and overcome in figurations of the self. Instead, insisting on these dimensions, *So Close* unravels the eponymous closeness as the narrator's deep proximity to and co-emergence with multiple others, in what the narrator calls 'a separation without separation' (Cixous 2009a: 82) that encompasses her dead father, her living mother, figures called J.D., Zohra Drif, and Fips, the family dog, as well as 'Algeria' itself, and – as the text's French title *Si Près* (Cixous 2007) immediately suggests – also trees. *Si Près* ('so close') is homonymous with *cyprès* ('cypress'), the trees that have kept vigil for her father in the cemetery in Algiers, as the narrator realises at the end of the book.[7] Exploring these resonances and entanglements means moving beyond the Subject, but not beyond questions of subjectivity.[8] The question of subjectivity is not surpassed, but remains relevant as a formation within meaning-mattering ecologies of difference; that is, the subject does not *enter into* relations to others or objects, but rather *co-emerges with* these multiple others and intimate echoes, never self-present and yet gaining consistency. The narrative voice in Cixous, as we will see, is such a figure of meaning-mattering multiplicity. In what follows, I will first consider how Cixous's engagement with subjectivity debunks traditional Western humanist conceptions of the Subject that are based on human exceptionalism and rationality as its anchor-points, and how she draws on entanglements of the affective, the im/material, and the nonhuman to chart different grounds instead. In a second step, the chapter then pursues how these grounds concretely come alive in *So Close*, featuring the separation-in-in/separability and continuous co-emergence that form something for which we have not yet really coined a term other than 'subject'.

Human, Subject

> We must absolutely not let go of the word 'human'. It is so important.
> (Cixous and Calle-Gruber 1997: 31)

The material and the affective are Cixous's starting points; being human means being a corporeal and sentient living being. In a conversation with Mireille Calle-Gruber, published in *Rootprints* (Cixous and Calle-Gruber 1997), Cixous qualifies human sentience as her point of departure, noting that the 'most impassioned, the most passionate in us is the quantity, the flood of extremely fine and subtle affects that take our body as a place of manifestation' (1997: 18). It is this stream of minute, yet consequential affects that her writings pay attention to, as we will see when we scrutinise *So Close* later on. In the conversation with Calle-Gruber, Cixous more than once explicitly addresses her understanding of the human (1997: 18–23, 30–8, 109–15), and it is a helpful point of entry here.

Affects, as Cixous engages with them, are common not only to all humans across cultural, social, and sexual categorisation, but also to nonhuman animals. In the conversation with Calle-Gruber, Cixous suggests that corporeal existence and affectivity demand and enable us to be with-and-of a wider universe. Due to the capacity to affect and be affected (in a Spinozian sense), humans exceed the narrow enclosures of 'one's small duration, . . . one's small house, . . . one's small sex' (Cixous and Calle-Gruber 1997: 32) and can realise that they are 'part of a whole that is worth the trip' (1997: 32). To grasp the import of the affective for Cixous's proposition of corporeality and human subjectivity, we can think of her famous exploration of writing as a bodily practice – as the very *écriture féminine* she famously sketched in 'The Laugh of the Medusa' (Cixous 1976), where writing is done with the body, as a material-symbolic (or corporeal-linguistic) invention of modes of living and desiring other than those pre-scribed by the phallogocentric libidinal economy and its Symbolic order; an invention made possible precisely because the affective exceeds the prescriptions of the symbolic.[9] Cixous's work – most explicitly during the mid-1970s in texts such as 'The Laugh of the Medusa', *The Newly Born Woman* (Cixous and Clément 1986), 'Castration or Decapitation' (Cixous 1981), and her play *Portrait of Dora* (Cixous 1983) – critically engages especially Freudian and Lacanian psychoanalysis in that regard. Psychoanalysis offered one of the most influential theories of the subject at the time of her coming to writing in the late 1960s, and alongside other feminist thinkers, most prominently Luce Irigaray and Julia Kristeva, Cixous set out to critique the psychoanalytic understanding of the subject precisely for its phallogocentric limitations.[10]

Most immediately in response to Lacan, Cixous joined the feminist critique of Freud's capitulation before feminine desire and countered Lacan's presupposition of lack as the condition of desire and motor of subject formation. In *The Question of Lay Analysis*, Freud had posited feminine sexuality as unintelligible, confessing to psychoanalysis's ignorance about 'the sexual life of adult women', which he accepted as 'a "dark continent" for psychology' (Freud 1959: 211). In *The Newly Born Woman*, Cixous argues that by culturally-symbolically deadening feminine desire between unintelligible physicality and the myth of a castrating Medusa, both Freud and Lacan pulled what she calls the '"dark continent" trick' (Cixous and Clément 1986: 68) on feminine desire and alternative modes of subject formation.[11] Alternative modes of subject formation are not unintelligible, she insists; they have merely been obfuscated, denied, and left unexplored due to the hegemonic order of knowledge and its 'monuments to Lack' (Cixous 1976: 885). What she terms the 'masculine-conjugal subjective economy' (1976: 888) has pictured desire within social parameters of bourgeois conjugality and conceptual bounds of dualism and negativity: desire as arising from that which it is lacking, seeking to overcome the subject's foundational split; a split, however, that is said to constitute the subject with the resolution of the Oedipal conflict and the subject's entry into the Symbolic order. Henceforth, the foundational split remains forever irresolvable (at best, it can be sublimated).[12] Cixous contests that these basic presuppositions are inevitable – the 'false theater of phallocentric representationalism' (1976: 884) might have very real effects, but it is neither universal nor inescapable. Feminine desire, as Cixous explores and evokes it especially in these earlier writings of the 1970s and 1980s, lives off a 'thousand and one thresholds of ardor' (1976: 885) instead of lack. Consequently, she writes, we are 'in no way obliged to . . . consider the constitution of the subject in terms of *a drama manglingly restaged* . . . to pledge allegiance to the *negative*' (1976: 884, my emphasis). Starting from the multiple, the overflow of affect and 'the erotogeneity of the heterogeneous' (1976: 889), the constitution of the subject *can* be reimagined; its fixation as a 'sequence of struggle and expulsion or some form of death' (1976: 883) – a struggle that Hegel famously theorised as the master/slave dialectic and which resonates here in Cixous's imagery of struggle and death (and the 'drama manglingly restaged' quoted above) – *can* be unworked. Whereas the dialectic divides the Subject not only internally, as Lacanian psychoanalysis reactivates the Hegelian dialectic with its foundation upon a logic of lack, but also splits it from the Other and the object side, the fundamental entwinement with otherness and present/absent others *can* be taken as alternative ground, if one starts thinking subjectivity from heterogeneous difference – a difference other than that of dialectics, something that Cixous in particular and feminist thinkers in general tirelessly insist on and demonstrate.[13] Thus, a feminine mode of subjectivity is possible; a different thinking of the constitution of subjectivity, which is by no means exclusive to those identifying as 'woman' or reducible to the biological traits of certain bodies.

Striving to overturn a notion of subjectivity based on lack and sublimation, Cixous's affective conceptualisation invites us to imagine such a feminine mode as a dynamic and ceaseless process of different subjects knowing one another and beginning one another anew only from *the living boundaries of the other*: a multiple and inexhaustible course with millions of encounters and transformations of the same into the other and into the in-between. (1976: 883, my emphasis)

We are asked to picture a formational negotiation here that runs not from subject to object, constituted upon the (ultimately) dead other, but importantly from subject to subject, from living other to living other, each with differentiated degrees of agency and within asymmetrical power-relations, which must be accounted for and criticised. That is, when beginning from the affirmation that affect and material existence are shared, we also start to see that any 'I' is always already also another subject's other; or put differently, that the other is also always a subject, mutually affecting and being affected.[14] It is important to stress that acknowledging subjects as in this sense co-emergent does not amount to the mere recognition of the other as subject, in the sense of the humanist notion of a Subject who knows himself or recognises the other as same; nor does such an acknowledgment remain with the split Subject of psychoanalysis. What emerges is rather a mode of 'doing subjectivity' that – by way of incessantly inscribing itself 'from *the living boundaries of the other*' – is textured with, through, and thanks to multiple others, and as such is always 'a multi-voiced phenomenon' (Derrida 2006b: 6).[15] The articulation of each body, as/in each continuous subjectivation, is thus irreducibly heterogenetic and polyphonic and as such also *hors de soi* in the sense of beside or outside itself, not at home, and also always other to itself, trans/formed through encounters and through 'writing' itself in a feminine mode.[16]

Importantly, for Cixous, writing as *écriture féminine* is the practice that inscribes and materialises this continuous process of co-generative negotiation from subject to subject. She understands writing – in the narrow sense of making notations on a material substance – as 'working (in) the in-between, inspecting the process of the same and of the other without which nothing can live' (Cixous 1976: 883), as pursuing and listening to the minute movements, encounters, and transformations that occur in this in-between. At the same time and in close alliance with Derrida, Cixous's notion of writing sidesteps the binaries of speech/writing, masculine/feminine, or mind/body. Her proposition of writing as *écriture féminine* from and with the body, touched on above, is closely aligned with Derrida's 'primary writing' (Derrida 1976: 7) or writing in general, which designates 'not only the physical gestures of literal pictographic or ideographic inscription' (Derrida 1976: 9), that is writing in the narrow sense, but also 'the totality of what makes it possible; and also, beyond the signifying face, the signified face itself' (Derrida 1976: 9). In view of writing as such an originary operation (Derrida 1976: 19), Kirby has argued that – far from being the secondary notation or 'image' of primary speech/thought indebted to phono- and logocentrism – with Derrida we can understand writing as expressing the 'processual work of individuate-*ing*' (Kirby 2014: 64); that writing can be taken as a name for nothing less than a 'bodying forth' (Kirby 1997: 80) of the world, including the bodying forth of subjects. However, these 'subjects' can no longer be thought according to a metaphysics of presence and the subject/object split. Cixous's texts perform writing in this double sense and thereby also make palpable subject formation as such a bodying forth with/in ecologies of multiplicity and difference.

Furthermore, Cixous's fictive-poetic work makes clear that there is no reason to reserve the transformations and resonances that constitute such 'multi-voiced phenomena' – which become *thinkable* by starting from affective-material existence and *perceptible* by listening to the millions of minute affects in each encounter as closely as possible – to human others only. Undoubtedly, nonhuman animals and plant life play significant roles in her texts, and her 'significant others' are often also nonhuman.[17] In *Rootprints*, Cixous describes these resonances that her writing explores as a 'further-than-myself in myself' (Cixous and Calle-Gruber 1997: 56) and she affirms that they exist 'in all beings' (1997: 56). Hence, the self echoes with a multiplicity of (human and nonhuman) others, is constituted relationally and within ceaselessly transforming constellations. Accordingly, Cixous notes that 'I is not I, of course, because it is I with the others, coming from the others, putting me in the other's place, giving me the other's eyes' (Cixous and Calle-Gruber 1997: 87). This returns us once again to the affective, which enables and facilitates alternative grounds for the subject. Whereas classical humanism took reason as the presupposed common ground of humanity (yet restricting it to only certain groups of humans (see, for example, Wynter and McKittrick 2015)) and as a line of demarcation of the human from the nonhuman, by contrast, affectivity is a quality that pertains to human and nonhuman animals alike. For Cixous, this implies that humans 'echo . . . with what constitutes the universe' (Cixous and Calle-Gruber 1997: 32) – even if an awareness of such echoing requires attunement and practice. If we start from this assertion, the anthropocentric delimitation of human from animal becomes untenable, and importantly for our context this is also the locus from which subjectivity can be reconfigured. Somewhat playfully, with Cixous's texts the 'I' in the famous Cartesian formula for modern subjectivity – 'I think, therefore I am' – can be morphed into something like this: 'Affected and affecting, echoing with many others, "I" therefore incessantly becomes with many others.'

Before moving on to *So Close* to flesh out this transmuted formula, it is important to remember that Cixous's emphasis on affects and corporeality does not do away with language. For Cixous, language itself is material and corporeal. The operations of *écriture féminine* have been sufficiently explored in that respect (see, for example, Blyth and Sellers 2004; Conley 1991) so I will use this reminder of language as material-affective to concentrate on its immediate purchase for the declination of the formula 'I think, therefore I am', the formula of the modern Subject. While emphasising the affective, as we saw, in the conversation with Calle-Gruber, Cixous also notes that the term 'human' designates for her 'this thing that speaks, that thinks, that loves, that desires and that one day is extinguished' (Cixous and Calle-Gruber 1997: 32). Speaking and thinking – alongside loving, desiring, and dying – remain crucial human actions and passions for Cixous. In other words, her turn to body writing does not leave thinking and speaking behind (nor, as we saw, does she turn to language – as is often claimed in the wake of the so-called 'linguistic turn' – at the expense of corporeality or materiality). Rather, she affirms thinking and speaking, yet otherwise than classical humanism, which took reason and language as markers of human exceptionalism. Already in the phrase of this 'thing that speaks, that thinks, that loves, that desires and that one day is extinguished' we find more than thinking and speaking alone; loving, desiring, and dying are actions and passions of equal weight here, underlined by the anaphoric repetition of 'that', which paratactically places the listed actions and passions side by side, without any indication of hierarchy or causality. Being human means the superposition of these different strata, and the series speaks–thinks–loves–desires–dies as a whole decries the Cartesian 'I think, therefore I am' as a reduction of the subject to the cogito, to mere thinking. As we will see when turning to *So Close*, Cixous instead proposes thinking, speaking, affecting, and being affected as irreducibly entangled, and we can explore how human subjectivity is brought to life on quite other grounds than those of classical humanism. The formation of a decision – a process traditionally pitched as reason at work and as a marker of self-transparent human agency – will play a crucial role in this conundrum.

So Close

> Nothing is ever homogeneous.
>
> (Derrida 1992: 53)

> Heterogeneous, yes.
>
> (Cixous 1976: 889)

So Close is part of a series of autobiographical texts by Cixous that pursue the echoes of Algeria in the narrator's life.[18] Present as a conglomerate of formative memories and childhood experiences from the early fiction *Inside* (Cixous 1986) onwards, Algeria surfaces more explicitly in Cixous's texts from the mid-1990s to the late 2000s, such as *OR: Les Lettres de Mon Père* (1997); 'My Algeriance' (1998b), together with the other texts gathered in the English collection *Stigmata*; *Reveries of the Wild Woman* (2006a) and its 'sister-book' *The Day I Wasn't There* (2006b); *So Close* (2009a); and *Philippines* (2011). I have selected *So Close* here, because it lends itself particularly well to fleshing out the separation-without-separation with multiple others that Cixous's take on subjectivity posits as fundamental. Specifically, this text pays very close attention to the formation of a decision – the narrator's declaration towards the beginning of the text that she will perhaps visit Algeria. Despite calling this declaration a 'decision' (Cixous 2009a: 14), as we will see Cixous muddles the conventional assumption of a speaking subject who precedes and then articulates their decisions; in *So Close*, the idea that a subject is first formed (from affects that are said to precede it, if we take this starting point) and then takes decisions is contested. Quite to the contrary, *So Close* revolves around the overflow of 'extremely fine and subtle affects' that contribute to the formation of this particular decision made by the narrator to visit Algeria. However, by intricately staging this 'decision's' temporal, affective, and contingent ramifications and pursuing its gestation, the text makes evident that the (continuously forming) 'subject' does not precede its decisions but is rather instantiated as 'subject' at the very moment of articulating its 'decision'; that what we call affects, decision, and subject are all con-temporaneous. There is no linear spatio-temporal order in which one of these precedes the others. Speaking, thinking, loving, desiring, and dying – to evoke again the series of passions mentioned above – all factor into such instantiations and none precedes or is preceded by a subject, yet all come to weigh and matter in an articulation ('decision') as a subject-at-that-instance. As readers of *So Close*, we can closely observe how the narrator's utterance arises from within contingent constellations, minute movements, and intimate entanglements with others, only to surface as the decision that 'I will perhaps go to Algiers' (Cixous 2009a: 6) – a decision that is neither the result of rational reflection, which we conventionally take decisions to be, nor a result of a drama of self vs other. Rather, the text dissects the decision to visit Algeria as emerging from within a multi-voiced negotiation of the living and the dead, present and absent voices, human and nonhuman others. Most prominently in *So Close*, these others are the narrator's mother; her long-lost classmate from her *lycée* years in Algiers in the 1950s, Zohra Drif; her deceased friend J.D.; her dead father; and, as a permanent echo throughout the text, the *cyprès* ('cypress') trees that are *si près* ('so close'). These different and in turn multilayered companions are, as the book's title evokes, *so close* to the narrator and her gestation, including the gestation of a 'decision'.

Another reason for the choice of *So Close* warrants mention, as it makes the text especially fitting for our concern here. Cixous's critique of Cartesian, humanist, and Lacanian notions of the Subject, and the proposition of another mode of subjectivity that emerges from her texts, are, as she notes, fundamentally indebted to 'Algeria'. In *The Newly Born Woman*, Cixous notes that her entire way of thinking took shape from the experience of colonial violence in Algeria and the denigrations of otherness enacted by white Western Man (Cixous and Clément 1986: 70; see also Young 1990). Witnessing the French colonial oppression of her Arab neighbours from a position of multifaceted non/belonging, she remarks frequently that she lived the experience of in-between-ness and came to understand corporeally the multi-sided and multi-sited heterogeneity inherent in the Algerian colonial situation – one that is insufficiently grasped in the colonial couple French/Algerian, or the post-independence one of Arab/Berber.[19] In much of Cixous's work, 'Algeria' functions as an allegory of these multi-sited, power-relational, dynamic in/exclusions of otherness in which any 'I' takes form. In *So Close*, this necessarily more-than-two of the Algerian scene takes form from at least five 'sides' of, or perspectives on, 'Algeria', at least five ways of living 'Algeria'. First, Algeria is the mother's accidental safe haven, after she fled Nazi Germany as an Ashkenazi Jewish woman in the early 1930s; it became her land of marriage and family life, and the centre of her professional life as midwife until her expulsion from the workplace and forced migration to France in 1971, and a country to which the mother in *So Close* will absolutely refuse to return. Second, it is the father's native land, where he was born into a Sephardic Jewish family, held French citizenship and served its army in World War II, worked as a doctor until the anti-Semitic legislation of Vichy, and where he was buried after his premature death from tuberculosis in 1948. Third, it is her friend J.D.'s country of birth, where he grew up in a Sephardic Jewish family in one of 'the more reputable neighbourhoods, El Biar' (Cixous 1998b: 160) and experienced a different Algiers from that of *So Close*'s narrator in the poorer neighbourhood of Clos Salambier. Fourth, it is also the native country of her classmate Z.D., who later became a key figure in the FLN (National Liberation Front) struggle for Algerian independence and who went, as one of only three Muslim girls in the early 1950s, to the same Catholic Lycée Fromentin as the narrator, an experience that unites and separates them simultaneously, as they experience French Algeria from differently marginalised sides. And, finally, it is the narrator's native country, where she never felt at home and which she left in 1955 to study in France.[20] 'Algeria' is all these differently shared historical contingencies, so that '[n]aturally ... there are millions of Algerias' (Cixous 2009a: 45). In its multiplicity, 'Algeria' not only exceeds the logic of binary oppositions (of self/other, coloniser/colonised, subject/object). Its heterogeneous, perspectival, and multilayered appearance also highlights a different mode of subjectivity required 'within' it, that is, within an entangled, contested site, to which multiple otherness, situated in different structural positions of power, is fundamental, constituting 'an incessant process of exchange *from one subject to another*' (Cixous 1976: 883, my emphasis). And in these perspectival ramifications, actualised in the text as at least the five sides of 'Algeria' according to the mother, the father, J.D., Z.D., and the narrator, this colonial constellation of 'Algeria' comes to inform the narrator's decision to 'perhaps' pay it a visit again.[21]

Keeping this in mind, we can zoom in on how *So Close* stages the narrator's profound proximity to her multiple others – a proximity across decades of silence in the cases of the narrator's father and Z.D. – and how the text pays closest attention to the overflow of extremely subtle affects that generate the narrator's decision to visit her family's former home town of Algiers for the first time in thirty-five years. The text opens with a scene, dated 'August 14, 2005' (Cixous 2009a: 1), in which the narrator, sitting at home in an unspecified location in France, observes her ageing mother wearing a bathing suit and ponders how she admires the 'life instinct' (2009a: 1) her mother still possesses despite her old age. Her mother had put on the bathing suit, which she had possessed for thirty years and had not worn in over a decade, in response to 'the appalling heat rising through the windows' (2009a: 1), in line with her usual sense of practicality ('her *throw-nothing-away* principle' (2009a: 1)) and despite her progressing skin disease, which covered her skin 'with large ochre patches of various sizes and shapes' (2009a: 1). After this initial scene, triggered by the contingencies of the weather and the mother's character, the reader moves through an opening of six pages (sixteen in the French original), before the narrator utters the tentative decision that she 'would *perhaps be going to Algiers*' (2009a: 6). Let us focus on the scenes and reflections of these first pages, which perform the gestation of that decision – its slow maturation and yet premature articulation (as we will see:

announced before it was taken, taken long before it was articulated, by a 'subject' forming alongside it), its ramifications, and its affective and circumstantial conditions of enunciation. We could continue to trace this kind of minute operation throughout the rest of the text – but already the first six pages contain *in nuce* the entangled formation of this utterance and can thus serve as a perfect example for a reimagining of subjectivity along the lines specified above.

During this opening scene – before the decision is uttered for the first time – the narrator observes her mother in the bathing suit, then ruminates about taking the scene in fully, 'mentally photographing' (2009a: 2) the image of '*mother-with-bathing-suit*' (2009a: 1); the swimwear intensifies the image – as it is incongruous with the mother's ageing body, it highlights her advanced age, while at the same time making her look impish and childlike – so that 'a vast zone' of affects, memories, and 'silhouettes of long ago' (2009a: 1) begins to arise from this image.[22] As much as the mother responds to the contingencies of the heat, the narrator's observations are sparked by this condensed image. Given that Cixous is a passionate reader of Kleist, it is not far-fetched to see the intertextual resonances of this opening passage with how Kleist opens his poetic (and ironic) reflection on 'The gradual formation of thoughts while speaking': it is not intentionality or premeditated thought, Kleist suggests in his eponymous text, that makes us form arguments or decisions, but our interlocutors' (in)voluntary movements and the affects they arouse – in Kleist's text a gesture by the narrator's sister and the vibes (Kleist speaks of bodily twitches signalling hesitation or disagreement) that several protagonists in his text perceive from others around them trigger the articulation of a thought or an intention (see Kleist 1997; also Cixous 1991). In a similar fashion, in *So Close* the mother's image moves the narrator to reflect on writing as a practice – a practice that can explore the 'vast zones' of memories and affects that arise in scenes such as the described '*mother-with-bathing-suit*', if sufficient time is allowed; a practice that works with a 'mental camera' (Cixous 2009a: 3), yet is entirely different from photography, as the narrator explains at length, setting the tone for the efforts of this book and preparing the ground for the presentation of the decision to come. Writing, we read, observes as closely as possible and 'dreams of not stopping what is in the process of being lost, nothing more powerless and desperate, thus nothing more faithful to the infidelities of life' (2009a: 3).[23] Unlike photography, where one captures a scene but remains external to what one has captured, writing pursues 'the intimate surfaces that, like spider's webs, are spread out by our hearts ... the innumerable palpitations, hesitations, those twists of thought, those ripples of mood, that versatility of the interior climate' (2009a: 3). Correspondingly, *So Close* explores these interior and invisible emerging complications, which are always responsive and corporeally, un/intentionally, affectively entangled and to which the Telephone rather than the camera is allied, as the narrator continues to suggest.[24]

At this point in the opening scene, the narrator has moved into the kitchen to make tea and fetch 'macaroons for my mother' (2009a: 4), which she anticipates correctly will meet with her mother's refusal. We learn that she bought them 'for her teeth' (2009a: 6) – neither mother nor daughter likes macaroons much, yet these are fresh and soft, and given her mother's 'gaping mouth' (2009a: 6) with only three teeth left, her 'losing physical density' (2009a: 4), the macaroons are an attempt to feed her. While preparing the tea, a host of invisible complications and intensities of this scene arise before the narrator's inner eye: memories of the beaches of Algiers resurface, sparked by the bathing suit; the mother's gestures of defying and thus underlining age ('all the movements, this movementing of my mother' (2009a: 2)), anticipating and challenging a death that is clearly on the horizon; the narrator's friend (who appears here for the first time, yet whom we can infer to be J.D. from later appearances in the text (see 2009a: 24–30)), who is recently deceased and with whom the narrator is now on the mental Telephone, where he encourages her to force her mother to eat something, an attempt that in turn is met with her mother's stark refusal of the macaroon. Her mother's refusal both results from these 'innumerable palpitations ... and ripples of mood' (2009a: 3; see above) and in turn prompts the utterance of the decisive sentence: '**That's when** I said I would *perhaps be going to Algiers*' (2009a: 6, my emphasis). This utterance of a potential future action – or what the narrator calls a 'decision' (2009a: 14) – sets in motion the text, which from this moment onwards slowly unravels the stakes of such a decision, the implications of the possible trip, as well as the secret inclinations and affective entanglement of a subject who might embark on it.[25] We will learn of the wish to visit the father's grave in Algiers, of the narrator's complicated proximity to her native country, to her classmate Zohra Drif, and of her striving to account for the divide between the Jewish-German-and-French-speaking girl H.C. and the Muslim-Arab-and-French-speaking girl Z.D. who went to the same class for a few years, being spatially so close, yet in the midst of politico-historical constellations that thwarted personal closeness.

Once the decision has been uttered, after the complications of the first six pages, we learn immediately that it was said without intention, hesitatingly, as a 'weakened form of a consent to external circumstances' (2009a: 6).

> That's when I said I would *perhaps be going to Algiers*. There was no urgent reason to say this, that I know of. If there was one, it was hidden from me. I said, in a distracted, colorless voice: I will perhaps go to Algiers. I cannot even be sure that I said it myself. It's more like the other voice uttered these words as if to try them out. There was no tone of authority. Myself I heard the hesitation. (2009a: 6)

We immediately realise that the sentence 'I said I would *perhaps be going to Algiers*' is not uttered by a subject who premeditated this to reach a rational decision. Rather, it is presented as a *response*, a response to everything that went before and everything that looms to come: the bathing suit, the beach in Algiers that the narrator frequently visited during the summer vacations with her mother until 1971, the fact of (the mother's, her own) ageing, the mental conversations with absent friends, the always present death of the father that here recalls the narrator to Algeria. And finally, in the moment of utterance, it is said almost as if also to defy a little the mother's refusal to eat the macaroon: 'I don't know why I advanced this sentence toward my mother at that moment' (2009a: 6). The narrator confesses her ignorance of the reasons for pronouncing this declaration of a potential future action, saying that it also may have been only to hear herself say it, 'to test its resistance to reality' (2009a: 7). Or, as she later conjectures, it may simply have been the urge to counter her mother: since she 'didn't want me to go to Algiers . . . I was attempting my chances' (2009a: 52). When, further on in the text, the narrator draws up a list with reasons for and against the journey, to come to a more clear-headed decision, she ends up with the reasons on either side 'covered in fog' (2009a: 44), with '[m]illions of complicated thoughts, an enormous quantity of memories for many screens' (2009a: 45). Uttering the decision to perhaps visit Algeria, she realises, has meant to venture 'into one of those hypersensitive regions' (2009a: 41) in which everyone involved in the scenes of the book – mother, father, J.D., Z.D., the narrator, and ultimately also the cypresses – has stakes; impulses and partialities with which the narrator has to reckon, from which her decision cannot be detached, with which it (and she) emerge(s). Finally uttering the decision produces strong effects: her mother responds with explosive cries of refusal, saying that she would never go and that '[t]here's not afffucking thing for me there' (2009a: 32), hammering down the profanity 'with the small satisfaction of feeling the word fuck around between her lips' (2009a: 32), a word she has not used in her entire life.

We might say that, triggered by '*mother-with-bathing-suit*', the decision has been articulated, suddenly and tentatively, as a response to circumstance and in affective resonance with (present and absent) others. The narrator seems to confirm this by noting a little later:

> I saw that I had thought perhaps of going to Algiers without knowing or seeing or calculating but moved by a reflex contraction of the soul, I had even said 'Algiers' without attributing any precise and excluding value to the word, I had said: Algiers, the way one says threshold or Prague or yesterday, or the part for the whole. (2009a: 36)

Being on the one hand a response to circumstance, on the other hand the gestation of this sentence has had a very long latency phase and is after all not quite as contingent as merely saying 'threshold' or 'Prague' or 'yesterday' (words thrown in here as allegedly contingent, yet which might in their own ramifications just as well be synecdoches for 'Algeria').[26] It is indebted to all the 'Algerias' and minute movements that resulted from these 'Algerias' for the narrator, in her coming to being and coming to utter this decision at that point. Although seemingly sudden, the decision has been growing for almost half a century, unbeknownst to the narrator herself, ever since she first left Algeria in 1955 and dwelled on the distant thought to write a letter to Zohra Drif, back 'in 1960, perhaps it was in 1958' (2009a: 12), trying to respond to her own implications in 'Algeria' and the asymmetries between H.C.'s and Z.D.'s respective experiences – a long incubation for a decision that erupts when offering a macaroon to her mother in 2005.[27]

The idea occurs to me at this moment, August 15, 2006, that perhaps the decision to go to Algiers was made already with this letter [to Zohra Drif] and by all the innumerable, imperceptible circumstances, gestures, consequences contained in this sheet of paper, under the name of Z.D., perhaps this letter that has stayed with me has mingled itself with me, its totally invisible phantom atoms have spread into those regions about which we know nothing where our future events foment, so much so that the decision taking shape slowly, being secreted for decades, will naturally have the slow irresistible force of an accumulated seism that has been brewing for a thousand years. (2009a: 14)

Proposing to go to Algeria builds on everything in this complicated scene: an 'Algeria' that meant colonial violence and oppression for over 130 years; childhood bliss in Oran and the tragedy of the premature loss of a parent in 1948; Jewish life in Algiers in the 1940s, cut across the communities of El-Biar and Clos Salambier; foreclosed friendship between a Jewish and a Muslim girl in a French Catholic colonial *lycée* in the early 1950s; post-independence programmes of Arabisation, resulting in her mother losing her position as midwife in 1971; a kitchen on a hot day, with her mother's advanced age in 2005; and the refusal to eat the macaroon. Within all of this, the narrator's decision gestates; out of all of this, an 'I' articulates itself in profound, formative resonance with many present and absent others. This 'I' echoes with distant and close others, past and present circumstances, so that it comes to do what it does, comes to say what it says, in separation-in-in/separability with these multiple others, including Algiers, the mother, the swimsuit, the macaroon, memories of J.D. and Z.D., death, the father, the cypresses, the family dog. In this sense, our decisions take shape slowly and in the blink of an eye at the same time, they gestate for decades and are taken in an instant, driven 'by all the innumerable, imperceptible circumstances, gestures, consequences' (2009a: 14) that articulate us as subjects, in relation to each other, and well beyond and otherwise than the Subject of traditional humanisms.

Notes

1. On Cixous's writing as questioning and putting into play the delimitations of genre, see Hanrahan 2004; Derrida 2006a.
2. This is not to suggest that Cixous's texts are philosophy strictly speaking. She has expressed her dissatisfaction with the label of a 'theorist' and with the fact that her 'theoretical' essays of the mid-1970s are more widely read and cited than her more straightforwardly poetic texts (Cixous 2010).
3. My point here is not to declare these different practices to be the same, but to understand their emergence as distinct fields that continually determine and continuously invade each other. Recently, Barbara Cassin has reminded us again of the fact that language is a shared mode of expression for both, making this dynamic possible (Cassin 2004).
4. 'Humanist' is used throughout in reference to the classical, Western, Enlightenment tradition of humanism and its idea of the subject, based on reason (Descartes) and the

master/slave dialectic and self-consciousness (Hegel). In order to distinguish broader discussions of subjectivity from this humanist idea, I use at times the capitalised Subject to refer to the latter.

5. See exemplarily for living/dead: *Or: Les Lettres de Mon Père* (Cixous 1997), *Hyperdream* (Cixous 2009b), *Death Shall Be Dethroned* (Cixous 2016); for animal/human: *Messie* (Cixous 1996), *Reveries of the Wild Woman* (Cixous 2006a), and 'Stigmata, or Job the Dog' (Cixous 1998a); for existence with/in ecologies of difference: *Rootprints* (Cixous and Calle-Gruber 1997).
6. For an example of such object-centred thought, see Graham Harman's contribution to this volume (Chapter 10). To me, Vicki Kirby's *Telling Flesh* (Kirby 1997) presents the most convincing argument on why such a reversal is insufficient; see also Kirby 2014.
7. Cixous explores what we might call a separation-in-in/separability also in *Reveries*, a text that traces the narrator's being 'separunited' (Cixous 2006a: 87) from/with her multiple others, among them prominently her brother, their dog Fips, and the narrator's classmate Zohra Drif in Algiers during the late 1940s and early to mid-1950s.
8. The term 'entanglement' is used here in Karen Barad's sense as expounded in *Meeting the Universe Halfway*, where it expresses the co-dependent and differential formation of matter and meaning (Barad 2007: 247–352; see also Kirby 2011: 76; Thiele 2017). From this angle, Barad also discusses what she calls the intra-action of human and nonhuman agents and stresses that

> [l]earning how to intra-act responsibly within and as part of the world means understanding that we are not the only active beings – though this is never justification for deflecting that responsibility onto other entities. The acknowledgement of 'nonhuman agency' does not lessen human accountability; on the contrary, it means that accountability requires that much more attentiveness to existing power asymmetries. (Barad 2007: 218–19)

9. See Cixous 1976. Cixous here devises *écriture féminine* as a response to Lacanian lack and the Hegelian dialectic of self/other, ending the text on the famous note that '[i]n one another we will never be lacking' (Cixous 1976: 893). The text stresses that writing is not a question of representation and itself not representable by means of a definition, but that, as a practice, it sets out to undo phallocentric representations of desire, subjectivity, and sexual difference, and manifests itself as 'the invention of a new insurgent writing which ... will allow [woman] to carry out the indispensable ruptures and transformations in her history' (1976: 880). For the link of feminine writing to the body, see Blyth and Sellers 2004: 18–34; see also the interviews collected in Cixous 2008: esp. 51–94.
10. For feminist responses to psychoanalysis in the 1960s and 1970s in France, see Duchen 1986.
11. See also Freud 1963; for more on Cixous's response by means of devising a laughing Medusa, see Kaiser 2017.
12. For a much more detailed reading of Lacanian psychoanalysis in this regard, see Grosz 1990; Irigaray 1985: esp. 11–147. Cixous insists at various moments in *Rootprints* that what she does is not psychology, which she calls 'a bizarre invention' (Cixous and Calle-Gruber 1997: 18). For her understanding of drives 'in terms of viscerality', see Cixous and Calle-Gruber 1997: 63ff.

13. For the stress of feminist philosophy, especially in its continental and new materialist traditions, on a different difference, see Thiele 2013, 2014.
14. It would require much more work to unravel this point adequately. For the time being, I would only like to point to Déborah Danowski and Eduardo Viveiros de Castro's discussion of originary humanicity and radical perspectivalism in *The Ends of the World* (2017: esp. 61–78), as well as Kirby's 'Originary Humanicity: Locating Anthropos' (Kirby 2018).
15. For example, in *OR: Les Lettres de Mon Père* – a text written with the many voices of the dead father, who, as the text explores, is alive to the narrator in powerful ways – Cixous notes that every being is a dissonance (*désaccord*) or cacophony (Cixous 1997: 168). For more on the polyphonic in Cixous, also beyond *OR*, see Derrida 2006b.
16. For the reasons to continue using 'feminine' while insisting on it otherwise than within a binary of masculine/feminine and the refusal to reserve 'feminine' for those identifying as woman, see Cixous and Conley 1984: 52–7. There, Cixous also notes:

    > As soon as there is appropriation in a rigid mode, you may be sure that there is going to be incorporation. It destroys the possibility of being other. It is the arrest of freedom of the other and that is enormous. A feminine libidinal economy, one which tolerates the movements of the other, is very rare. One that tolerates the comings and goings, the movements, the *écart* (space, interval, gap). (Cixous and Conley 1984: 57)

17. The pivotal role of animals and animality in Cixous's texts has been widely noted; see for example Segarra 2006; Turner 2013. The figures of the lion and the dog Fips especially are relevant in the context of Algeria, which provides the setting in which *So Close* (among many others of Cixous's texts) explores the question of the subject. Fips appears most prominently in *Reveries* and 'Stigmata, or Job the Dog'. And while only being 'salute[d] vaguely' (Cixous 2009a: 110) in *So Close*, the narrative voice, which recurs across texts in Cixous's work, is profoundly marked by the physical and spiritual closeness to animals in general, and to the narrator's cats and the dog Fips in particular (for more detail, see Kaiser 2013). Lions are equally prominent in Cixous's work (see Garnier 2013), including *So Close* (Cixous 2009a: 39ff., 87ff., 150).
18. Cixous was born in Oran in western Algeria in 1937, when it was still a colony of France, to an Ashkenazi Jewish German mother, Eva Cixous, née Klein, and a Sephardic Jewish father, Georges Cixous, a native of Oran. The recurring narrator in Cixous's texts almost collapses the distinction between authorial and narrative voice. While the extreme proximity of narrator and author (what Derrida calls Cixous's hyperrealism (Derrida 2006b: 38)) is confounding, it is precisely Cixous's point of writing: 'I am not separate from my writing. I only began to become myself in writing' (Cixous and Calle-Gruber 1997: 93). In practically all her texts we find the same narrative voice, and her narrators operate with memories that are very close to those known to belong to the living Hélène Cixous. On Cixous and autobiography, see, for example, Hanrahan 2000.
19. Cixous describes herself and her family as being, in several different regards, in liminal positions in colonial Algeria, that is, in specific ways in- and excluded at the same time. There was her family's particular non/belonging as Jews in French Algeria, with French citizenship, yet treated by their French neighbours as second-class citizens, by their Arab neighbours as too French; their non/belonging to the Jewish community in Algeria as

an Ashkenazi-Sephardic family; her liminal position as a 'frenchified' girl in the Arab neighbourhood *Clos Salambier*; and her equally liminal position as a Jewish girl in a Catholic Vichy-inclined school (see Cixous 1998b, 2006a).

20. This merely hints at the depths and ramifications of these (at least) five different perspectives on Algeria by figures that are key interlocutors in *So Close* and which return frequently in other of Cixous's texts. Their different experiences feature prominently in *Reveries*; for more on the mother's perspective, see also Cixous 1999, 2006b; for the father's, Cixous 1997; for Z.D., Cixous 2003.

21. The purchase of 'Algeria' for Cixous's alternative rendering of subjectivity is crucial because the wager of the possibility of subjectivity otherwise than via lack and a self/other binary is deeply indebted to this Algerian, colonial experience. Cixous's rearticulating of subject formation is, thus, also a move towards a postcolonial understanding of the subject. For more on this question and Cixous's and Derrida's deconstructions of the colonial, see Kaiser 2015.

22. The vast zone is what the narrator later describes as 'the life beyond life, . . . the different lives that surround the one we call ordinary Life and that is life in common, measurable by the clock' (Cixous 2009a: 4).

23. In *Rootprints*, Cixous holds that 'we have been fabricated, molded, written by millions of elements and authors ending in a different chapter' (Cixous and Calle-Gruber 1997: 14) and that writing means to draw out and make audible these minute elements, 'life itself, which is always in the process of seething, of emitting, of transmitting itself' (Cixous and Calle-Gruber 1997: 4).

24. The Telephone (capitalised) is a ubiquitous figure in Cixous's texts, an allegory for mental and intimate journeys to the voice of distant, absent, often dead others (see, for example, Cixous 2009b).

25. It is the first overt moment at which the utterance appears in the text, yet in several senses it is already a repetition, as it has been subterraneously gestating on a textual level: first, the very opening line of the text notes that 'On August 14, 2005, I dealt my mother a blow, naturally it was unintended' (Cixous 2009a: 1). Although the blow is not explained at this point, and its unintentionality underlined, we learn after the passage on page 6 that this blow is the intention of visiting Algiers, which is met with the mother's stark opposition. Second, a little later in the text, the narrator muses that 'the decision to go to Algiers' (2009a: 14) had already been taken many years before, when she intended to write a letter to her former classmate Zohra Drif, 'in 1960, perhaps it was 1958' (2009a: 14). And third, the articulation of the decision on page 6 is the first instance only in the English translation. In the French original, on the contrary, we find it already on the leaf-insertion (a *prière d'insérer*, which is missing in the English translation), whose opening sentence is 'Hier j'ai dit que *j'irais peut-être à Alger.*' The *prière d'insérer* prefigures what the passage on page 6 will say, introducing the reader already to the looped temporality that the gestation of the narrator's decision/utterance will display: uttered prematurely, while still to be articulated. Thus, before this 'first' time, it has textually (l. 1, *prière d'insérer*) and temporally in narrative time (forty-five years earlier) already occurred.

26. 'Prague', for example, almost begs to be read as such a synecdoche (a part for the whole, as the text itself insinuates), recalling the city of Kafka's Jewish-German diasporic life, then a multilingual urban space housing different religions and cultures, whose erasure during World War II is marked among other things by the city's famous Jewish cemetery, and as such quite easily standing in for Cixous's 'Algeria'.

27. On the extreme proximity of the narrator and the author, see n. 18. Because of this proximity, I say here that the narrator left Algeria in 1955, even if *So Close* does not explicitly mention this fact; other texts have explored this departure, which Cixous notes is not a departure, because she had never safely arrived in Algeria, always remaining in-between (see Cixous 1998b). In that sense, she had always already left, but was also frequently to return for the summer until her mother's expulsion in 1971.

Bibliography

Attridge, Derek (1992), 'Introduction: Derrida and the Questioning of Literature', in Jacques Derrida, *Acts of Literature*, Derek Attridge (ed.), London: Routledge, pp. 1–30.
Barad, Karen (2007), *Meeting the Universe Halfway: Quantum Physics and the Entanglement of Matter and Meaning*, Durham, NC: Duke University Press.
Blyth, Ian and Susan Sellers (2004), *Hélène Cixous: Live Theory*, London: Continuum.
Cassin, Barbara (2004), *Vocabulaire Européen des Philosophies: Dictionnarie des Intraduisibles*, Paris: Le Seuil.
Cixous, Hélène (1967), *Le Prénom de Dieu*, Paris: B. Grasset.
Cixous, Hélène (1976), 'The Laugh of the Medusa', *Signs*, 1:4, pp. 875–93.
Cixous, Hélène (1981), 'Castration or Decapitation?', *Signs*, 7:1, pp. 41–55.
Cixous, Hélène (1983), *Portrait of Dora*, *Diacritics*, 13:1, pp. 2–32.
Cixous, Hélène (1986), *Inside*, New York: Schocken.
Cixous, Hélène (1991), *Readings: The Poetics of Blanchot, Joyce, Kafka, Kleist, Lispector and Tsvetajeva*, Minneapolis: University of Minnesota Press.
Cixous, Hélène (1996), *Messie*, Paris: Des Femmes.
Cixous, Hélène (1997), *OR: Les Lettres de Mon Père*, Paris: Des Femmes.
Cixous, Hélène (1998a), 'Stigmata, or Job the Dog', in Hélène Cixous, *Stigmata: Escaping Texts*, London: Routledge, pp. 243–61.
Cixous, Hélène (1998b), 'My Algeriance, in Other Words: To Depart Not to Arrive from Algeria', in Hélène Cixous, *Stigmata: Escaping Texts*, London: Routledge, pp. 204–31.
Cixous, Hélène (1999), *Osnabrück*, Paris: Des Femmes.
Cixous, Hélène (2003), 'Letter to Zohra Drif', *College Literature*, 30:1, pp. 82–90.
Cixous, Hélène (2006a), *Reveries of the Wild Woman: Primal Scenes*, Chicago: Northwestern University Press.
Cixous, Hélène (2006b), *The Day I Wasn't There*, Chicago: Northwestern University Press.
Cixous, Hélène (2007), *Si Près*, Paris: Galilée.
Cixous, Hélène (2008), *White Ink: Interviews of Sex, Text and Politics*, Susan Sellers (ed.), Stockfield: Acumen.
Cixous, Hélène (2009a), *So Close*, Cambridge: Polity.
Cixous, Hélène (2009b), *Hyperdream*, Cambridge: Polity.
Cixous, Hélène (2010), 'Un Effet d'Épine Rose', in Hélène Cixous, *Le Rire de la Méduse et Autres Ironies*, Paris: Galilée, pp. 23–33.
Cixous, Hélène (2011), *Philippines*, Cambridge: Polity.
Cixous, Hélène (2016), *Death Shall Be Dethroned: Los, a Chapter, the Journal*, Cambridge: Polity.
Cixous, Hélène (2018), *Défions l'Augure*, Paris: Galilée.
Cixous, Hélène and Mireille Calle-Gruber (1997), *Rootprints: Memory and Life Writing*, London: Routledge.

Cixous, Hélène and Catherine Clément (1986), *The Newly Born Woman*, Minneapolis: University of Minnesota Press.
Cixous, Hélène and Verena Andermatt Conley (1984), 'Voice I . . .', *boundary 2*, 2:12, pp. 50–67.
Conley, Verena Andermatt (1991), *Hélène Cixous: Writing the Feminine*, Lincoln: University of Nebraska Press.
Danowski, Déborah and Eduardo Viveiros de Castro (2017), *The Ends of the World*, Cambridge: Polity.
Derrida, Jacques (1976), *Of Grammatology*, Baltimore: Johns Hopkins University Press.
Derrida, Jacques (1992), *Acts of Literature*, Derek Attridge (ed.), London: Routledge.
Derrida, Jacques (2006a), *Geneses, Genealogies, Genres and Genius: The Secrets of the Archive*, New York: Columbia University Press.
Derrida, Jacques (2006b), *H. C. for Life, That Is to Say . . .*, Stanford: Stanford University Press.
Duchen, Claire (1986), *Feminism in France: From May '68 to Mitterrand*, London: Routledge and Kegan Paul.
Freud, Sigmund (1959), *The Standard Edition of the Complete Psychological Works of Sigmund Freud, Vol. XX: (1925–1926), The Question of Lay Analysis*, , London: Hogarth Press, pp. 177–258.
Freud, Sigmund (1963), 'Medusa's Head', in Sigmund Freud, *Sexuality and the Psychology of Love*, New York: Simon and Schuster, pp. 202–3.
Garnier, Marie-Dominique (2013), 'Love of the Löwe', in Lynn Turner (ed.), *The Animal Question in Deconstruction*, Edinburgh: Edinburgh University Press, pp. 34–53.
Grosz, Elizabeth (1990), *Jacques Lacan: A Feminist Introduction*, London: Routledge.
Hanrahan, Mairead (2000), 'Of Altobiography', *Paragraph*, 23:3, pp. 282–95.
Hanrahan, Mairead (2004), *Cixous's Semi-Fictions: Thinking at the Borders of Fiction*, Edinburgh: Edinburgh University Press.
Irigaray, Luce (1985), *Speculum of the Other Woman*, Ithaca: Cornell University Press.
Kaiser, Birgit Mara (2013), '(Un-)Grounding the Human: Affective Entanglements and Subjectivity in Hélène Cixous's Algerian Reveries', *International Journal of Francophone Studies*, 3/4, pp. 477–96.
Kaiser, Birgit Mara (2015), 'Algerian Disorders: On Deconstructive Postcolonialism in Cixous and Derrida', *The Cambridge Journal of Postcolonial Literary Inquiry*, 2:2, pp. 191–211.
Kaiser, Birgit Mara (2017), 'The Laugh of the Medusa', in Bettina Papenburg (ed.), *Gender: Laughter*, Farmington Hills: Macmillan, pp. 149–63.
Kaiser, Birgit Mara (2018), 'So Many Tongues: Cixous and the Matter of Writing', *Comparative Literature*, 70:3, pp. 278–94.
Kirby, Vicki (1997), *Telling Flesh: The Substance of the Corporeal*, London: Routledge.
Kirby, Vicki (2011), *Quantum Anthropologies: Life at Large*, Durham, NC: Duke University Press.
Kirby, Vicki (2014), 'Human Exceptionalism on the Line', *SubStance*, 43:2, pp. 50–67.
Kirby, Vicki (2018), 'Originary Humanicity: Locating *Anthropos*', *PhiloSOPHIA: A Journal of Continental Feminism*, 8:1, pp. 43–60.
Kleist, Heinrich von (1997), 'On the Gradual Production of Thoughts Whilst Speaking', in Heinrich von Kleist, *Selected Writings*, David Constantine (ed. and trans.), London: Dent, pp. 405–9.
Segarra, Marta (2006), 'Hélène Cixous's Other Animal: The Half-Sunken Dog', *New Literary History*, 37, pp. 119–34.

Thiele, Kathrin (2013), 'Pushing Dualisms and Differences: From "Equality versus Difference" to "Nonmimetic Sharing and Staying with the Trouble"', *Women: A Cultural Review*, 25:1, pp. 9–26.

Thiele, Kathrin (2014), 'Ethos of Diffraction: New Paradigms for a (Post)Humanist Ethics', *Parallax*, 20:3, pp. 202–16.

Thiele, Kathrin (2017), 'Entanglement', in Mercedes Bunz, Birgit M. Kaiser, and Kathrin Thiele (eds), *Symptoms of the Planetary Condition: A Critical Vocabulary*, Lüneburg: Meson Press.

Turner, Lynn (ed.) (2013), *The Animal Question in Deconstruction*, Edinburgh: Edinburgh University Press.

Wynter, Sylvia and Katherine McKittrick (2015), 'Unparalleled Catastrophe for Our Species? Or, to Give Humanness a Different Future: Conversations', in Katherine McKittrick (ed.), *Sylvia Wynter: On Being Human as Praxis*, Durham, NC: Duke University Press, pp. 9–89.

Young, Robert (1990), *White Mythologies: Writing History and the West*, London: Routledge.

6

Meillassoux, the Critique of Correlationism, and British Romanticism

Evan Gottlieb

Written in a spare, quasi-analytical style, Quentin Meillassoux's *After Finitude: An Essay on the Necessity of Contingency* has earned widespread attention for defining 'correlationism' as the doctrine that has dominated philosophy since at least Immanuel Kant. By so denominating a variety of philosophical worldviews – including not only Kant's critical philosophy but also Berkeley's radical idealism, Wittgenstein's language games, Foucauldian historicism, and Derridean deconstruction – Meillassoux effectively identified what they all have in common: a singular denial that humans can have any definitive or positive knowledge of what lies outside thought. *After Finitude*'s logical demonstrations of the absoluteness of contingency – that contingency is the only necessity – also allowed Meillassoux to put a new twist on what he calls 'Hume's problem': the sceptical position, which famously galvanised Kant's development of his critical philosophy, that we rely on habit, not knowledge or reason, when making probabilistic predictions. This interest in Hume and Kant signals Meillassoux's intellectual engagement with the same philosophers who profoundly influenced the British romantics several centuries earlier. As I have argued at length elsewhere, many of the most influential British romantic poets were writing at a moment when Kant's philosophy was beginning to become known in the Anglophone world, but was not yet hegemonic (Gottlieb 2016; see also Ellermann 2015; Washington 2015). They also share with Meillassoux an intense interest in what the latter calls 'the great outdoors', understood both literally – in the romantics' well-known commitment to nature writing – and in the absolute sense that Meillassoux intends. Additionally, some of the romantics' most ambitious texts share the utopian horizon of Meillassoux's 'multiple worlds' ontology – a logical, albeit unusual, extension of his determination of the contingency of all things, worked out most fully in his *L'Inexistence Divine*, of which only portions have been officially translated and published.

My goal in this chapter, then, is twofold. First, I will explore Meillassoux's basic ideas, especially his formulation and critique of varieties of correlationism, his reasoning with regard to the necessity of contingency, and the most significant metaphysical claims of *After Finitude* and *L'Inexistence Divine*. Second, I want to outline a number of connections between Meillassoux's positions and those of the British romantics, focusing on key works by William Wordsworth and Percy Shelley. Here, my goal is to illuminate how some of their best-known poetry and prose is invested in addressing the same questions that engage Meillassoux, even as their approaches necessarily reflect their historical position at the opening of 'the Era of the Correlate' (Meillassoux 2016: 121) – an era that Meillassoux himself has done much to bring to a close.

After Finitude's signal contribution to philosophy is its identification of 'correlationism' as the dogma that has constrained Western thought ever since Kant's transcendental schema divided reality into phenomena or qualities that can be perceived and noumena or essences that cannot, and then restricted human thought to the former. (In subsequent publications, Meillassoux has identified Berkeley's radical idealism as a slightly earlier origin of this rejection of realism.) As a result, mainstream Western philosophy gave up trying to make definitive statements about reality and limited itself to thinking about the narrow corridor – the correlate – that mediates between thought and reality. Meillassoux's initial definition minces no words:

> By 'correlation' we mean the idea according to which we only ever have access to the correlation between thinking and being, and never to either term apart from the other. We will henceforth call *correlationism* any current of thought which maintains the unsurpassable character of the correlation so defined. (Meillassoux 2009: 6)

The effects of correlationism have been simultaneously widespread and underacknowledged, Meillassoux maintains, but they underpin influential twentieth-century philosophical movements like phenomenology and existentialism, both of which restrict thought to the circumference of our human perspective. The same is true of twentieth-century methodologies indebted to the linguistic turn, including structuralism, deconstruction, and various historicisms; each, again, presumes that we have no access to the world 'as it is always already there' (Gaston 2013: x), to borrow Sean Gaston's apt phrase, but only and always to the world for us (Meillassoux 2009: 6).[1] Elsewhere, in a purposeful redeployment of a phrase pioneered by Foucault, Meillassoux refers to correlationism as another version of 'the great confinement': just as the seventeenth century saw a push to institutionalise so-called madmen in asylums, so too philosophy after Kant willingly confined itself to the narrow correlate between human and the world as it is given to us (Meillassoux 2012a: 77). Furthermore, by turning its back on 'the *great outdoors*', as Meillassoux puts it in *After Finitude* (Meillassoux 2009: 7), philosophy simultaneously abrogated its traditional mission of explaining the world, understood as what exists regardless of whether we are present to experience it, thus inviting a host of fundamentalisms to fill the space of meaning. This, in short, is the 'Kantian catastrophe': '*by forbidding reason any claim to the absolute, the end of metaphysics has taken the form of an exacerbated return of the religious*' (Meillassoux 2009: 124, 45). Accordingly, the stakes of Meillassoux's identification of correlationism could not be higher: to restore to philosophy the power to attempt to understand reality itself, not merely to help navigate our representations of it, and subsequently to restore reason, rather than dogma of either the correlationist or religious varieties, to the centre of human life.

To be sure, not everyone agrees with Meillassoux on these basic points. Some scholars have taken issue with his identification of correlationism as a dominant feature of modern philosophy; others have defended the correlation and questioned the effectiveness of Meillassoux's critique.[2] Further, his broad condemnation of the role of religion in contemporary life is open to debate or at least nuance.[3] Nevertheless, for heuristic purposes, in what follows I assume that Meillassoux's diagnoses of both correlationism and fundamentalism are essentially correct: the former has indeed been a significant trend in modern philosophy, even if its reach has not been quite as extensive as Meillassoux frequently suggests, and the deleterious effects of the latter are plain to see in our contemporary geopolitical situation, even if the causes of fundamentalism's resurgence clearly have many material as well as cognitive determinations.

Meillassoux's best-known 'proof' of correlationism's limitations is his example of the 'arche-fossil' delineated in *After Finitude*'s first chapter. Given the various dating techniques available to modern scientists, it is possible to verify that certain traces of organic material in the earth's crust – arche-fossils – definitively predate the first appearance of recognisably 'conscious' life on earth. For the correlationist, Meillassoux observes, this provokes a dilemma, because accepting scientific evidence of life before consciousness contradicts correlationism's basic presupposition that we can have no knowledge of reality independent from our mind. Denying such evidence, however, lands the correlationist in the same camp as the religious fundamentalists. As a result, Meillassoux notes, most correlationists try to thread this tricky needle by adding a corrective 'for us' (or its equivalent) to the end of scientific assertions – which Meillassoux calls 'ancestral statements' – that appear to violate the correlation (e.g., 'According to the latest dating techniques, this fossil is 150 million years old – for us'). The result, however, is both chronologically and logically incoherent, since it not only makes what happened in the past dependent on what we can know in the present, but also forces the correlationist to adopt the nonsensical position that the ancestral statement is objectively true, in the sense that it is universally available to science, even though the object of its truth, the arche-fossil itself, supposedly could never have existed in and by itself (Meillassoux 2009: 16–18).

In these ways, the example of the arche-fossil shows how correlationism is at odds with contemporary scientific knowledge; it does not, however, disprove the existence of the former.[4] Interestingly, for some philosophers associated with new varieties of realism, correlationism is not even the main obstacle to knowledge of reality; Graham Harman's object-oriented philosophy, for example, takes as its 'main target ... the taxonomical dualism of subject and object', and by doing away with this distinction claims to render correlationism irrelevant, since all entities, not just humans, enjoy only partial relations with each other (Harman 2016a: 233).[5] By contrast, Meillassoux's commitment (shared with Kant) to the difference in kind of human consciousness means that he cannot take this route; instead, he must address correlationism head-on, in an undertaking that forms the burden of *After Finitude*'s main chapters. In fact, part of this work is begun before the introduction of the arche-fossil, in the opening discussion of Locke's distinction between primary and secondary qualities – a distinction Meillassoux believes can be genuinely rehabilitated once thought's ability to think the absolute is re-established.

To accomplish this, Meillassoux makes an important distinction between two kinds of correlationism: weak and strong.[6] The former, exemplified by Kant's philosophy, denies that we can ever gain absolute knowledge of reality but allows that it still must exist, since an appearance (phenomenon) without an essence (noumenon) is a logical impossibility. By contrast, the strong version of correlationism – which Meillassoux judges to be the dominant one today, even though it frequently goes unannounced (Meillassoux 2009: 30) – holds that nothing whatsoever can be known or even thought outside the human–world correlate. Strong correlationism thus rejects Kant's supposition of the existence of things-in-themselves: since we can never get outside of our own thoughts, we cannot know that things-in-themselves actually exist, only that they exist as they are given *to us*. Thus, whether it takes the form of a de-absolutisation of thought *or* of an idealism that treats thought as inextricably linked with a particular stratum of existence (a form of correlationism Meillassoux has recently taken to calling 'subjectalism', a term he feels encompasses both idealism and vitalism),[7] strong correlationism locks us firmly into the correlationist circle.

Not coincidentally, both strong and weak correlationism are well represented in the poetry of the British romantics, who not only were highly interested in exploring a range of relations between humanity and nonhuman nature, but also were writing at a time when Kantianism and then German idealism were beginning to be disseminated widely. By his own account, in the 'Preface to Lyrical Ballads', Wordsworth was committed to bringing himself – and, by extension, his readers – as close as possible to his subject matter, especially when writing about his cherished bond with the natural world (Wordsworth and Coleridge 2008: 171–87). Consider, for example, the following well-known stanzas from 'Lines Written in Early Spring':

> To her fair works did nature link
> The human soul that through me ran;
> And much it griev'd my heart to think
> What man has made of man.
>
> Through primrose tufts, in that sweet bower,
> The periwinkle trail'd its wreathes;
> And 'tis my faith that every flower
> Enjoys the air it breathes.
>
> (Wordsworth and Coleridge 2008: 231, ll. 5–12)

Unlike many of his predecessors, Wordsworth treads lightly when personifying nonhuman entities here, declining to capitalise 'nature' according to poetic convention and only granting the periwinkle an agency (trailing its wreathes) that remains well within its organic capabilities; he thus minimises his use of common poetic tropes of anthropomorphism and, by extension, anthropocentrism. He even seems to endorse a form of panpsychism when he speculates that 'every flower / Enjoys the air it breathes', crediting each blossom with an affective relationship to its surroundings that potentially surpasses the average human experience. Nevertheless, the correlationist circle is still clearly at work via the 'link' Wordsworth intuits between 'nature' and his 'human soul' – a correlate that allows the poet a certain access not to nature 'itself', but to nature as it presents itself to him. This is why, despite his obvious desire to draw as close as possible to springtime's natural phenomena, spiritually as well as physically, Wordsworth can only have 'faith' that flowers experience a kind of vital enjoyment when they respire; to *know* this as an absolute truth would be to violate the correlate's terms, which do not allow for such knowledge. Seen in this light, his subsequent reflection that musing on nature ultimately leads him to mourn 'what man has made of man' sounds less like an assertion of the ethical imperative embodied in the natural world than like a straightforward example of the logic of weak correlationism, in which every attempt to think the world *in itself* is inevitably turned back into a reflection on humanity's *relation to* the world.

Further evidence of Wordsworth's subscription to weak correlationism can be seen in the revisions he eventually made to the final stanza of 'Lines Written in Early Spring'. In every version, the lines 'And much it griev'd my heart to think / What man has made of man' make a modified return in the poem's final stanza, which appears in all editions of *Lyrical Ballads* (1798, 1800, 1802, 1805) as follows:

> If I these thoughts may not prevent,
> If such be of my creed the plan,
> Have I not reason to lament
> What man has made of man?
> (Wordsworth and Coleridge 2008: 231, ll. 21–4)

Whereas 'my creed' has traditionally been interpreted as referring to what Jerome McGann once called Wordsworth's 'Romantic ideology' (McGann 1983), Meillassoux makes it possible to be read as yet another declaration of correlationism: it is Wordsworth's adherence to weak correlationism that forces him back on 'what man has made of man' when he tries to imagine 'the great outdoors' on its own terms. Even this limited declaration of human epistemological agency seems to have felt insufficiently orthodox to the increasingly conservative poet, however, for in 1820 Wordsworth revised its final stanza for publication in his collected poems:

> If this belief from heaven be sent,
> If such be Nature's holy plan,
> Have I not reason to lament
> What man has made of man?
> (Wordsworth 1977: 312, ll. 21–4)[8]

With its explicitly pious vocabulary, baldly personified 'Nature', and speculation on knowledge derived from a transcendent source, this revised version testifies to the truth of Meillassoux's observation that, by denying thought can ever know anything definite about what lies beyond itself, weak correlationism effectively invites religious dogma to fill the void left by the retreat of reason.

This logic is especially apparent in Wordsworth's crowning achievement of *Lyrical Ballads*, 'Lines Written a Few Miles above Tintern Abbey'. Fortunately for posterity Wordsworth never altered this poem, instead keeping it intact from its first appearance at the conclusion of *Lyrical Ballads* in 1798 (although this version contains one extra line noted in the volume's errata) to its prominent position in every collected edition of his works. Even when Wordsworth was later attacked for 'not distinguishing between nature as the work of God and God himself', as he put it in an 1815 letter, he refused to alter the offending description of himself as 'A worshipper of Nature'.[9] On ontological grounds, however, there was arguably never any need for revisions, since the poem everywhere displays the two primary hallmarks of weak correlationism: a conviction that *something* real exists outside human consciousness, and an equally strong conviction that we *cannot know* anything definite about it. The primary shift described in the poem's retrospective middle stanzas tracks Wordsworth's maturation from a boyish immersion in nature – 'when like a roe / I bounded o'er these mountains' – to a less immediate, more intellectual relation to the natural world, one characterised by 'the joy / of elevated thoughts; a sense sublime / Of something far more deeply interfused' than what his younger self could appreciate (Wordsworth and Coleridge 2008: 144, ll. 68–9, 95–7). In neither case, however, does Wordsworth ever claim that his experiences of nature are of nature *itself*, as a set of slightly earlier lines makes clear:

> For I have learned
> To look on nature, not as in the hour
> Of thoughtless youth, but hearing oftentimes
> The still, sad music of humanity,
> Not harsh nor grating, though of ample power
> To chasten and subdue.
> (Wordsworth and Coleridge 2008: 144, ll. 89–94)

Traditionally, this passage has been read as an expanded version of the 'what man has made of man' lines in 'Lines Written in Early Spring', that is, as evidence of Wordsworth's faith in the moral power of the natural world and, relatedly, his awareness of the many shortcomings of humanity. From a Meillassouxian perspective, however, they index Wordsworth's devotion to correlationism. As a boy, his immersion in the natural world was so thoughtless as to be vacuous; now, when he tries to 'look on nature', he knows that what he is really observing is *himself observing nature*. Characterised as music that is 'still' and 'sad', such knowledge – the only kind that weak correlationism permits us – cannot help but 'chasten' Wordsworth inasmuch as it forbids him from exiting the correlationist circle while nonetheless maintaining the shadowy existence of 'something far more deeply interfused' that he cannot name with certainty even as he intuits that it partially inheres in everything, including 'the mind of man'. Indeed, at moments like this Wordsworth comes close to rejecting correlationism altogether, in favour of something that (as I have argued elsewhere) more closely resembles Harman's object-oriented philosophy; yet as befits the ebb-and-flow rhythm of 'Tintern Abbey', this moment of potential insight is quickly washed back into the stanza's more conventional ending, where Wordsworth concedes that his perception of 'all the mighty world' is ultimately conditioned by 'eye and ear, both what they half-create / And what perceive' (Wordsworth and Coleridge 2008: 144, ll. 100–12).

Because weak correlationism maintains a belief that *something* definitely exists outside the correlate, one might expect it to be Meillassoux's focus in order to demonstrate that we do, in fact, have access to the noumenal realm. But this is precisely what Meillassoux does *not* argue, primarily on the grounds that weak correlationism is already the object of strong correlationism's critique. As he shows in the second chapter of *After Finitude*, which imagines an encounter between these two positions, the latter invariably challenges the former's claim that we can assume the existence of a reality about which we can know nothing for certain. In doing so, strong correlationism reveals the real weakness at the heart of weak correlationism: it relies on the logic of non-contradiction – since for Kant it would be contradictory for there to be appearances without essences – while simultaneously being entirely unable to account for the necessity of that logic (Meillassoux 2009: 38–9). Combined with the fact that Meillassoux sees strong correlationism (especially its subjectalist varieties) as more dominant today than pure Kantianism, he takes it to be the ultimate position with which any speculative realism or materialism worth its name must grapple.

Before seeing how he does this, however, let us see what strong correlationism looks like in British romantic poetic practice. According to Meillassoux, the two forms that strong correlationism most frequently takes are idealism – wherein everything we see, perceive, and think is understood as a product of our minds – and vitalism, in which all of human experience is correlated with a particular substratum of existence. Although varieties of both idealism and vitalism were available to the British romantics, a still-powerful Christian monotheism dominated them all; not surprisingly, no romantic poet entirely embodies a strong correlationist position. In some of his poetry and prose, however, Percy Shelley arguably comes close. Although he is often described as a Neo-Platonist, it is more accurate to see Shelley as someone whose belief in the power of the human imagination is tempered by his sense that its limitations enforce a necessary degree of mystery beyond the mind's ken. Thus, in his 'Hymn to Intellectual Beauty', for example, Shelley begins by invoking 'some unseen Power' that 'Floats though unseen among us' (Shelley 2002: 93, ll. 1–2), only to spend the rest of the poem outlining all the ways in which that Power is unavailable to us except through earthly mediations and comparisons that inevitably fail to represent it accurately, much less to apprehend its essence. This is made especially clear in the fourth stanza where, addressing that Power directly, Shelley suggests that our lack of access to the absolute is a constituent component of being human: 'Man were immortal, and omnipotent, / Didst thou, unknown and awful as thou art, / Keep with thy glorious train firm state within his heart' 2002: 93, ll. 39–41). Although such lines appear to suggest that positive knowledge of the absolute might be possible, the poem ultimately upholds strong correlationism's basic shift 'from the unknowability of the thing-in-itself to its unthinkability' (Meillassoux 2009: 44). Much as Shelley strives to articulate any positive attributes of the 'awful LOVELINESS' that he asserts lies just beyond the circumference of human awareness, the poem's penultimate stanza admits that 'words cannot express' anything definite about it (2002: 93, ll. 71–2). Accordingly, even as it asserts Shelley's youthful devotion to a 'Spirit of Beauty' that transcends human finitude (2002: 93, l. 13), 'Hymn to Intellectual Beauty' supports strong correlationism insofar as it (perhaps unintentionally) confirms that the existence of anything outside the correlation remains a matter of faith rather than rational knowledge.

Shelley's most sustained version of this theme can be found in his 1817 poem 'Mont Blanc', which has already become something of a touchstone for literary theorists using various speculative realist lenses (Ellermann 2015; McCarthy 2015; Morton 2012; Shaviro 2014). To the extent that it conforms to a strong correlationist position, 'Mont Blanc' does so by originally affirming a materialist version of the absolute correlate, one in which the human mind is intrinsically part of 'The everlasting universe of things', as the poem's first line famously asserts (Shelley 2002: 97, l. 1). As the extended metaphor of merging waters plays out in the rest of the stanza, however, it becomes clear that, in Shelley's view, the 'feeble brook' of 'human thought' is hugely outmatched by the 'vast river' of the universe, which 'ceaselessly bursts and raves' as it absorbs the 'tribute' of humanity's offerings (2002: 97, ll. 5–11). To put this in the terms of Levi Bryant's 'flat ontology', although human thought and the universe of things may equally exist, they do not exist equally (Bryant 2011: 19; see also Bogost 2012).

Furthermore, if the first stanza of 'Mont Blanc' appears to subscribe to a one-world materialism, subsequent stanzas complicate this position via repeated metaphysical gestures. In the second stanza, for example, Shelley initially declares that what appears merely to be a mountain river is in fact 'Power in likeness of the Arve' descending Mont Blanc (Shelley 2002: 97, l. 16); then he muses that an 'etherial waterfall' creates a 'veil' that potentially 'Robes some unsculptured image' (2002: 97, ll. 26–7); finally, the second stanza ends with visions of the 'still cave of the witch Poesy' (2002: 98, l. 44), a Neo-Platonic image that seemingly confirms the ongoing presence of an authentic metaphysics in Shelley's worldview. This idea of another, non-material realm – 'gleams of a remoter world' (2002: 98, l. 49) – is raised again at the start of the third stanza, and then transformed into reveries of a mythic past in which 'the old Earthquake-daemon taught her young / Ruin' (2002: 99, ll. 72–3), before the fourth stanza reverts to a materialist vision of natural cycles: 'The fields, the lakes, the forests, and the streams, / Ocean, and all the living things that dwell / Within the daedal earth ... All things that move and breathe with toil and sound / Are born and die: revolve, subside and swell' (2002: 99, ll. 84–6, 94–5). Yet as Meillassoux argues, it is precisely strong correlationism's insistence that we cannot know anything about what lies (or does not lie) outside the correlation – indeed, we cannot even think about an 'outside' to the correlation, since whatever we think about is immediately brought within thought and thus within the correlation – that allows unreasonable faiths to proliferate and assume authority over everything that falls outside the correlation's purview. This is one way to explain Shelley's sudden swerve in the first part of the fourth stanza from a purely materialist vision of life to the bald assertion that 'Power dwells apart in its tranquility / Remote, serene, and inaccessible' 2002: 99, ll. 96–7). This poetic switchback leads Shelley to attempt yet another imaginative scaling of the mountain, first up to its 'precipice[s]' (2002: 100, l. 102), then down into the 'vast caves' (2002: 100, l. 120) that he imagines lie within Mont Blanc, and then back up to the final section's opening description of a peak that no human has ever seen, but which 'yet gleams on high' (2002: 100, l. 127). It is precisely this peak's inaccessibility to humanity that allows Shelley to imagine whatever he wants there, and although he keeps his vision naturalistic in the final stanza – avoiding the Neo-Platonic and mythical imagery of previous sections – it is nonetheless posited as the habitation above all of 'The secret strength of things' (2002: 100, l. 139), which invokes the Power first mentioned in the poem's second stanza. Having (nearly) definitively established that nothing definitive can be known about Mont Blanc, especially its almost literally unthinkable summit, Shelley then concludes the poem with his famous question addressed to the mountain: 'And what were thou, and earth, and stars, and sea / If to the human mind's imaginings / Silence and solitude were vacancy?' (2002: 101, ll. 142–4).

Traditionally, Shelley's final query has been taken to have an implied answer of 'Nothing'; thanks to the imagination's power, silence and solitude are *not* mere vacancies, which is why we can find meaning in the material (earth, stars, sea) as well as the immaterial aspects of our existence. Elsewhere, I have argued that these summative questions must be understood as authentically open-ended despite their rhetorical ring (Gottlieb 2016: 168–70); in that reading, the core insight of Shelley's question is simply that *we cannot know* what earth, stars, and sea might be without us, because we can never fully separate them from our thoughts of them. As Meillassoux puts it in one of his more recent definitive statements, 'correlationism posits . . . that thought can never *escape from itself* so as to accede to a world not yet affected by our subject modes of apprehension' (Meillassoux 2016: 118). That reading assumes the implicit synonymity of Shelley's usage of 'imaginings' – the noun used at the end of 'Mont Blanc' to describe what the human mind produces when it encounters 'silence and solitude' – and 'knowledge', which is of course what Meillassoux says strong correlationism forbids us to have of the world outside the correlate. It now strikes me, however, that it is also worth reading these final lines against the opening of Shelley's slightly later *Defence of Poetry*. Here, included in a series of longstanding conceptual distinctions, we find the following: 'Reason is the enumeration of quantities already known; Imagination the perception of the value of those quantities, both separately and as whole' (Shelley 2002: 510). In this, even if we agree with the concluding lines of 'Mont Blanc' that the imagination is capable of making something out of 'silence and solitude' beyond sheer 'vacancy', we are still left with the problem of how value can be attributed to quantities which themselves cannot be determined.

On the one hand, this problem is precisely what Meillassoux identifies as the real danger of strong correlationism: because we can know nothing outside the correlation, we can fill that void with whatever we want – and religion has done precisely this, to mostly bad effect in Meillassoux's unstinting estimation. On the other hand, the problem limned by the ending of 'Mont Blanc' – what kind of knowledge can be generated about what is by definition inaccessible to thought? – is also what Meillassoux sets out to solve in the later chapters of *After Finitude*. To do this, he leans heavily on two terms introduced in the second chapter: facticity and contingency. The latter, which is more familiar, designates more or less what it does colloquially, inasmuch as Meillassoux uses it to indicate the opposite of what is necessary; contingency is described as 'the fact that physical laws remain indifferent as to whether an event occurs or not – they allow an entity to emerge, to subsist, or to perish' (Meillassoux 2009: 39). Facticity, by contrast, refers to the givenness of the conditions that allow contingency to flourish: it 'pertains to those structural invariants that supposedly govern the world ... invariants which may differ from one variant of correlationism to another, but whose function in every case is to provide the minimal organization of representation' (2009: 39). In chapter 2 of *After Finitude*, these terms serve primarily to mark the difference between 'intra-worldly' possibilities – the contingent – and the sheer facticity of existence itself, including the correlate – which is what allows the illogic of belief (which Meillassoux calls 'fideism') to claim a monopoly on what lies beyond the supposed bounds of human knowledge. Unlike facticity, then, contingency holds out the promise of a kind of positive knowledge about the world, for when we know that something is not necessary, we have grasped 'the possibility of its not-being' (2009: 54), or of being something other than what it is now.

So how does contingency emerge as absolute – that is, how does its necessity become positive knowledge? Certainly, at first the argument for the necessity of contingency looks as though it can be defeated by the strong correlationist in the usual way, by arguing that this knowledge is only valid 'for us'. To do so, however, she effectively must re-absolutise the subject to whose thoughts everything is correlated. As Meillassoux points out, however, the strong correlationist is already committed against this idealist position on the grounds that it *is* possible to think one's own death, one's capacity not-to-be, without damaging the correlate's facticity (2009: 56–8). Accordingly, the strong correlationist can use the facticity of the correlation to defeat the idealist *or* use the absoluteness of the correlation to defeat the speculative philosopher, but she cannot logically do both at once, which would make the correlate simultaneously contingent and necessary. But because this is precisely what the strong correlationist does in practice, her position implicitly endorses the following positive knowledge: the only necessity *is* contingency. This, says Meillassoux, is 'the aperture which we have opened up onto the absolute' (2009: 64): everything – including the correlate itself – not only could be different, but *must* retain the possibility of being different to exist at all.[10]

Returning to the romantics, something of this insight is captured in Shelley's 'Mutability', which predates 'Mont Blanc' by two years. Although this earlier poem is nominally concerned with depicting humanity's changeability, Shelley's repeated use of comparisons to ephemeral natural phenomena paints a picture that encompasses all of reality:

> We are as clouds that veil the midnight moon;
> How restlessly they speed, and gleam, and quiver,
>   ... yet soon
> Night closes round, and they are lost for ever.
>
> (Shelley 2002: 91–2, ll. 1–4)

If there is one law to existence, says Shelley, it is that everything could be different from what it is. In fact, from Meillassoux's standpoint, Shelley arguably takes contingency farther than it should go when he proclaims that 'Man's yesterday may ne'er be like his morrow' (2002: 92, l. 15), since the necessity of contingency means that, contra vitalists like Bergson and process philosophers like Whitehead, we cannot assign any kind of necessity even to principles of flux or change. Accordingly, Meillassoux would probably only partially agree with Shelley's conclusion that 'Nought may endure but Mutability' (2002: 92, l. 16), since even the principle of mutability must be seen as contingent; reality is as capable 'of producing a universe that remains motionless down to its ultimate recesses' as it is 'of engendering random and frenetic transformations' (Meillassoux 2009: 64). This is why Meillassoux gives the name 'hyper-Chaos' to the state of affairs in which we find ourselves after thought's supposed finitude has given way to the knowledge that contingency is an absolute feature of the world-in-itself.

It bears repeating, however, that what defines hyper-Chaos is the lack of reason for anything to either be or not be, to change or to remain the same (as long as it is not both at once, since that would make it a necessary being). As Meillassoux puts it succinctly, it is 'the absolute absence of reason for any reality, in other words, the effective ability for every determined entity, whether it is an event, a thing, or a law, to appear and disappear with no reason for its being or non-being' (Meillassoux 2014: 23). The fact that natural laws in particular do not appear to change randomly is no obstacle, for as Meillassoux is at pains to show in the fourth chapter of *After Finitude* and elsewhere, probabilistic reasoning – the logic whereby we make predictions – incorrectly assumes the boundedness of a universe that modern mathematics has demonstrated is in fact untotalisable (Meillassoux 2009: 101–7). *After Finitude* thus concludes with a chapter that proposes that mathematics is the only mode capable of thinking reality, even in the absence of subjectivity, 'without lapsing back into any sort of metaphysical necessity' (2009: 126).

To be sure, there are forceful critiques of both Meillassoux's methods and his conclusions, including his understanding of the law of sufficient reason and his use of set theory; by the same token, most of Meillassoux's publications following *After Finitude* have sought either to clarify some of its positions or explore some of its applications.[11] His most radical extensions of the ramifications of hyper-Chaos, however, are to be found in *L'Inexistence Divine*, which was originally written before *After Finitude*, and has still neither been officially published nor been fully translated into English. Here, Meillassoux pursues the ramifications of hyper-Chaos by noting that it allows for the emergence *ex nihilo* of entirely new worlds, three of which have already come to pass via the unprecedented advents of matter, life, and thought in the known universe (Meillassoux 2015b: esp. 238–42). There is also a 'fourth World' predicted by Meillassoux: a 'World of justice' in which the righteous dead will live once more, overseen by a God-to-come in whom we have an ethical imperative to believe precisely because he does not yet exist. Not surprisingly, these messianic musings have seemed highly improbable to some critics, with Meillassoux's apparent turn towards a kind of rational messianism coming in for particular criticism.[12] As Harman notes, however, Meillassoux's theses regarding the advent of a 'World of justice' may not be as outlandish as they initially appear, especially once 'we remove all necessity from the laws of nature' and 'surf along the contours of the logically possible, treat all such possibilities as equally likely, and then focus ... on those that would be ontologically the most important' (Harman 2015: 141). For Meillassoux, the risk of sounding odd is far outweighed by the potential gains to be made by 'humans qua humans, as those who think *hope* by refusing the injustice done to their fellow humans, whether they are still alive now or not' (Meillassoux 2015b: 241).

Moreover, the emphasis in *L'Inexistence Divine* on the emergence of new Worlds – especially a World of justice towards which we must work in *this* world, even though we cannot force its emergence – seems less odd when we recognise its strong precedents in Shelley's own work. Rebirth is not an uncommon theme in romantic-era poetry, of course, but in Shelley's case there is a more specific and notable trend: a repeated theme of entirely new worlds becoming imaginable once the parameters of the present are revealed as utterly contingent. Consider, for example, his sonnet 'England in 1819', which was deemed too incendiary to publish until well after Shelley's death:

> An old, mad, blind, despised and dying King;
> Princes, the dregs of their dull race, who flow
> Through public scorn – mud from a muddy spring;
> Rulers who neither see nor feel nor know,
> But leechlike to their fainting country cling
> Till they drop, blind in blood, without a blow.
>
> (Shelley 2002: 326, ll. 1–6)

Following this opening sestet, the litany of England's woes continues for another six lines. Quite unexpectedly, however – as every advent *ex nihilo* is always unexpected, even when it is actively desired and worked towards – the sonnet offers a final couplet of surprising hopefulness: all the things previously listed, Shelley exclaims, 'Are graves from which a glorious Phantom may / Burst, to illumine our tempestuous day' (2002: 326, ll. 13–14). As James Chandler has observed, these lines neither merely sum up nor reverse the calamities that precede them; instead, 'all of the public ills catalogued in the first dozen lines are suddenly presented in a new light', thereby demonstrating that 'the present dark moment . . . holds out the possibility of a millenarian illumination that will mark its general rebirth' (Chandler 1998: 27). What appears to be stasis is in fact awaiting and perhaps even preparing for a new dispensation.

Similar situations – in which a present moment of hopelessness or paralysis suddenly gives way to a radically different future – can be found in Shelley's longer political poem 'The Mask of Anarchy', as well as in his epic verse drama *Prometheus Unbound*. In the former, the triumphal march of Murder, Fraud, Hypocrisy, and the other malevolent forces of English political life is suddenly disrupted by the appearance of 'A mist, a light, an image' which protects Hope, destroys the evil personifications, and summons all 'Men of England' to 'Shake your chains to Earth like dew . . . Ye are many – they are few' (Shelley 2002: 319–20, ll. 103, 147, 153). In the latter, which I have analysed at greater length elsewhere, the unexpected defeat of the tyrannical Jupiter by Demogorgon leads to a renovated planet, as the Ocean itself makes clear in an ecstatic speech: 'Henceforth the fields of Heaven-reflecting sea / Which are my realm, will heave, unstain'd with blood / Beneath the uplifting winds – . . . my streams will flow / Round many-peopled continents and round / Fortunate isles' (2002: 258, III.2, ll. 18–20).[13] In both works, the possibilities for new worlds to become new realities are realised when some avatar of the human spirit – which Meillassoux calls 'the existence *in us* of the idea of justice[,] since nothing corresponds to it in actual reality' (Meillassoux 2015b: 254) – refuses to give in to despair long enough for this world's conditions to give way to something novel and unprecedented.

Meillassoux's identification of correlationism as the defining feature of post-Kantian Western philosophy has been of signal importance, not only to other philosophers but also to a host of thinkers, writers, artists, and even activists eager to take up the tasks of thinking about and acting upon 'the great outdoors' that lies outside the correlationist circle.[14] His arguments in *After Finitude* that the logic of the correlate itself opens the way for us to think 'the absolute absence of reason for any reality' (Meillassoux 2014 24) continue to stimulate no small amount of discussion and debate. Among the participants in these debates, it remains for literary critics and theorists to become more fully engaged in working out the radical implications of Meillassoux's thought, for example in the general domain of narrative probability as well as in the more restricted oeuvres of individual writers. That a number of romantic-era authors, including William Wordsworth and Percy Shelley, anticipated

Meillassoux's interests and concepts to varying degrees should serve as additional motivation as well as an archive of ongoing interest in this pursuit.

Notes

1. For a more detailed investigation and reconstruction of the linguistic turn, see Birns 2017.
2. On the question of whether Meillassoux's identification and definition of correlationism are legitimate, especially with regard to Kant's thought and legacy, see, for example, Gironi 2015; Golumbia 2016; and Hallward 2011: esp. 137–8. See also Slavoj Žižek, 'Interlude 5: Correlationism and its Discontents', in his *Less Than Nothing* (Žižek 2012: esp. 641–7) and the articles in the special issue, 'New Realism and Phenomenology', of *META: Research in Hermeneutics, Phenomenology, and Practical Philosophy* (D'Angelo and Mirković 2014).
3. For a monumental account of the interpenetration of the secular and religious in contemporary life, see Taylor 2007.
4. Meillassoux makes this point clearly in a talk given at Middlesex University in May 2008, reprinted in *Time without Becoming* (Meillassoux 2014: 16).
5. On the homology between Harman's notion of 'withdrawal' and Kant's concept of the noumenal, see Harman 2016b: 27–9.
6. Harman argues that Meillassoux's position actually creates a 'spectrum' of correlationist positions (see Harman 2015: 14–18, 180–2).
7. See Meillassoux 2016: 120–6; see also Sacilotto 2015: 161–3.
8. This volume conforms to Wordsworth's own final edition of his collected poems as produced in 1849–50.
9. See Nicholas Halmi's note to 'Lines Written a Few Miles above Tintern Abbey' in Wordsworth 2014: 70n.5.
10. For another explanation of Meillassoux's logic culminating in the assertion that contingency is the only necessity, see Jackson 2015: 69–70.
11. On Meillassoux's supposed misunderstanding of the nature of mathematics, see, e.g., Wark 2017: esp. 287–90; on his alleged misuse of the principle of sufficient reason see Harman 2013: esp. 240–8; on his supposed misrepresentation of correlationism in particular and Western philosophy in general, see Golumbia 2016; Thorne 2012. Meillassoux's own most substantial follow-ups to *After Finitude* are the long essay 'Iteration, Reiteration, Repetition', in *Genealogies of Speculation* (Meillassoux 2016), and two books: *The Number and the Siren: A Decipherment of Mallarmé's* Coup des Dés, which extends his thoughts on the limitations of probabilistic reasoning and the mathematisation of reality (Meillassoux 2012b); and *Science Fiction and Extro-Science Fiction*, a short book that considers the generic differences between speculative works of fiction that fully embrace the ramifications of hyper-Chaos and those that do not (Meillassoux 2015a).
12. See, e.g., Johnston 2013. There are also plenty of accounts of the emergence of life and thought that do not necessitate the invocation of an *ex nihilo* model; see, e.g., Thacker 2010; Dennett 2017.
13. For a fuller reading of Shelley's play in light of Meillassoux's *Divine Inexistence*, see Gottlieb 2016: 176–81.
14. On the political implications of Meillassoux's philosophy see, e.g., Viriasova 2017.

Bibliography

Birns, Nicholas (2017), 'The Three Phases of the Linguistic Turn and their Literary Manifestations', *Partial Answers*, 15:2, pp. 291–313.

Bogost, Ian (2012), *Alien Phenomenology, or What It's Like to Be a Thing*, Minneapolis: University of Minnesota Press.

Bryant, Levi (2011), *The Democracy of Things*, Ann Arbor: Open Humanities Press.

Chandler, James (1998), *England in 1819: The Politics of Literary Culture and the Case of Romantic Historicism*, Chicago: University of Chicago Press.

D'Angelo, Diego and Nikola Mirković (eds) (2014), 'New Realism and Phenomenology', special issue of *META: Research in Hermeneutics, Phenomenology, and Practical Philosophy*.

Dennett, Daniel C. (2017), *From Bacteria to Bach and Back: The Evolution of Mind*, New York: W.W. Norton.

Ellermann, Gregg (2015), 'Speculative Romanticism', *SubStance*, 44:1, pp. 154–74.

Gaston, Sean (2013), *The Concept of World from Kant to Derrida*, London: Rowman and Littlefield.

Gironi, Fabio (2015), 'What Has Kant Ever Done for Us? Speculative Realism and Dynamic Kantianism', in Sarah de Sanctis and Anna Longo (eds), *Breaking the Spell: Contemporary Realism Under Discussion*, Fano: Mimesis International, pp. 89–113.

Golumbia, David (2016), '"Correlationism": The Dogma that Never Was', *boundary 2*, 43:2, pp. 1–25.

Gottlieb, Evan (2016), *Romantic Realities: Speculative Realism and British Romanticism*, Edinburgh: Edinburgh University Press.

Hallward, Peter (2011), 'Anything is Possible: A Reading of Quentin Meillassoux's *After Finitude*', in Levi Bryant, Nick Srnicek, and Graham Harman (eds), *The Speculative Turn: Continental Materialism and Realism*, Melbourne: Re.press, pp. 130–41.

Harman, Graham (2013), 'A New Look at Identity and Sufficient Reason', in Graham Harman, *Bells and Whistles: More Speculative Realism*, Winchester: Zero Books, pp. 227–56.

Harman, Graham (2015), *Quentin Meillassoux: Philosophy in the Making*, 2nd edn, Edinburgh: Edinburgh University Press.

Harman, Graham (2016a), *Dante's Broken Hammer*, London: Repeater Books.

Harman, Graham (2016b), *Immaterialism: Objects and Social Theory*, Cambridge: Polity.

Jackson, Robert (2015), 'Factiality', in Peter Gratton and Paul Ennis (eds), *The Meillassoux Dictionary*, Edinburgh: Edinburgh University Press, pp. 69–70.

Johnston, Adrian (2013), 'Pseudo-Emergence: Against Meillassoux's Duo-Theism', *Umbr(a): A Journal of the Unconscious*, pp. 51–70.

McCarthy, Anne C. (2015), 'The Aesthetic of Contingency in the Shelleyan "Universe of Things", or "Mont Blanc" without Mont Blanc', *Studies in Romanticism*, 54:3, pp. 355–75.

McGann, Jerome J. (1983), *The Romantic Ideology: A Critical Investigation*, Chicago: University of Chicago Press.

Meillassoux, Quentin (2009), *After Finitude: An Essay on the Necessity of Contingency*, Ray Brassier (trans.), London: Continuum.

Meillassoux, Quentin (2012a), 'Interview with Quentin Meillassoux', in Rick Dolphjin and Iris van der Tuin (eds), *New Materialism: Interviews and Cartographies*, Ann Arbor: Open Humanities Press, pp. 71–81.

Meillassoux, Quentin (2012b), *The Number and the Siren: A Decipherment of Mallarmé's* Coup des Dés, Robin Mackay (trans.), Falmouth: Urbanomic.

Meillassoux, Quentin (2014), *Time without Becoming*, Fano: Mimesis International.

Meillassoux, Quentin (2015a), *Science Fiction and Extro-Science Fiction*, Alyosha Edlebi (trans.), Minneapolis: Univocal.

Meillassoux, Quentin (2015b), 'Appendix: Excerpts from *L'Inexistence Divine*', Graham Harman (trans.), in Graham Harman, *Quentin Meillassoux: Philosophy in the Making*, 2nd edn, Edinburgh: Edinburgh University Press, pp. 224–87.

Meillassoux, Quentin (2016), 'Iteration, Reiteration, Repetition: A Speculative Analysis of the Sign Devoid of Meaning', Robin Mackay and Moritz Gansen (trans.), in Armen Avanessian and Suhail Malik (eds), *Genealogies of Speculation: Materialism and Subjectivity since Structuralism*, London: Bloomsbury, pp. 117–98.

Morton, Timothy (2012), 'An Object-Oriented Defense of Poetry', *New Literary History*, 43:2, pp. 205–24.

Sacilotto, Daniel (2015), 'Subjectalism', in Peter Gratton and Paul Ennis (eds), *The Meillassoux Dictionary*, Edinburgh: Edinburgh University Press, pp. 161–3.

Shaviro, Steven (2014), *The Universe of Things: On Speculative Realism*, Minneapolis: University of Minnesota Press.

Shelley, Percy (2002), *Shelley's Poetry and Prose*, 2nd edn, Donald Raiman and Neil Freistat (eds), New York: W. W. Norton.

Taylor, Charles (2007), *A Secular Age*, Cambridge, MA: Belknap.

Thacker, Eugene (2010), *After Life*, Chicago: University of Chicago Press.

Thorne, Christian (2012), 'Outward Bound: On Quentin Meillassoux's *After Finitude*', *Speculations*, 3, pp. 273–89.

Viriasova, Inna (2017), 'Speculative Political Theory: Quentin Meillassoux and "the Great Outdoors" of Politics', *Theory and Event*, 20:3, pp. 629–52.

Wark, McKenzie (2017), *General Intellects: Twenty-One Thinkers for the Twenty-First Century*, London: Verso.

Washington, Chris (2015), 'Romanticism and Speculative Realism', *Literature Compass*, 12:9, pp. 448–60.

Wordsworth, William (1977), *Poems, Vol. One*, John O. Hayden (ed.), London: Penguin.

Wordsworth, William (2014), *Wordsworth's Poetry and Prose*, Nicholas Halmi (ed.), New York: W. W. Norton.

Wordsworth, William and Samuel Taylor Coleridge (2008), *Lyrical Ballads: 1798 and 1800*, Michael Gamer and Dahlia Porter (eds), Peterborough: Broadview Press.

Žižek, Slavoj (2012), *Less Than Nothing: Hegel and the Shadow of Dialectical Materialism*, London: Verso.

7

Fictional Objects Fictional Subjects

Graham Priest

Introduction

At a visit to the local bookshop, you pick up a new book. It happens to be the stories of Sherlock Holmes by Arthur Conan Doyle. Over a coffee, you start to read. You read about things that do not really exist: objects such as Holmes and Watson, and states of affairs such as a cocaine-using detective living in 221B Baker Street, London. When you arrive home, you turn on some music to listen to. It is Giacomo Puccini's opera *Madame Butterfly*. Again, you hear of things that do not really exist, such as the unfortunate Cio Cio San, and a visit to Nagasaki by a US naval officer by the name of B. F. Pinkerton.

Well, to be precise, you read the words on the pages of the book, and you hear the words of the sung libretto. But do these words *really* refer to non-existent objects or states of affairs? Are there really such things?

And what about you – the subject reading the stories or listening to the opera? Whatever one says about Holmes and Butterfly, this subject would seem to be much more real than either of these. But is this so? Certainly there are visual or auditory experiences taking place. But is there really a subject – an entity which underlies these experiences, constituting them as a unity? Or is this just as much a mere appearance as a woman committing suicide at the end of a performance of Puccini's opera?

We might summarise these questions in a simple way. In some quite banal sense, fiction generates a relationship between a subject and objects. But what kinds of things, exactly, is that a relationship between?

Fictional Objects

Names in Fiction

Let us start with the object pole of the relationship, and get one thing clear straight away. Some names that occur in fictions, such as 'Holmes' and 'Butterfly', refer, if they refer to anything at all, to things that do not seem to exist. But some names that occur in fiction *do* refer to existent entities, such as 'Baker Street' and 'Nagasaki'. It might be thought that such names do not refer to the places in question, but to different objects — some fictional Baker Street or Nagasaki, quite distinct from the real locations. After all, a detective with the name 'Holmes' lived in Doyle's Baker Street, and no such detective ever lived in the real Baker Street. So these must be different Baker Streets, since different things are true of them (the principle of the difference of discernibles).

But this is just a confusion. It is certainly true of Baker Street that no detective with the name 'Holmes' ever lived in it. But it is not *really* true that such a detective did live in Baker Street. What *is* true is that *in Doyle's stories* a certain detective lived in Baker Street — something quite different. So one cannot apply the principle of the difference of discernibles to obtain the conclusion that they are different Baker Streets.

Moreover, both of these things are true of one and the same Baker Street. Otherwise we could not say things like: there is a place in London such that, in Doyle's stories, a certain detective lived *there*, but no such detective actually lived in *it*.[1] Similarly, when the librettists for Puccini wrote the text for his opera, although the woman they wrote about may be purely fictional,[2] the Nagasaki they wrote about was the actual Japanese city, intimidated by the US navy's Commander Perry in 1853, and later incinerated by a US atomic bomb. When the librettists wrote the words of the opera, they did not, after all, change the meaning of the word 'Nagasaki': they used it in exactly the same way that anyone else would: to refer to the city in question.

A final example: there is a story entitled 'Sylvan's Box' (see Priest 1997). It is about an old friend of mine, Richard Sylvan, and is set just after his untimely death. Many of the things in the story are actually true (and not just true-in-the-story). But it is a work of fiction: the central event recounted never really took place. The story is about Richard himself, however. How do I know? Because I wrote the story, and when I used his name in the story, I was referring to him.[3]

So a name employed in a fiction may well refer to an existent object. But of course, many names in fiction do not seem to. Let us say that a name is *fictional* if it is used in some work of fiction. If a fictional name does not seem to refer to an object which exists, let us call it *purely* fictional.

Reference Failure

Now, purely fictional names either refer or they do not. And if they refer, they refer to something that either exists or does not. So we have three possibilities. Let us consider each of these in turn.[4]

The first is that purely fictional names do not refer at all.[5] Some philosophers, for example, say that, when engaging in acts of fiction, the storyteller, and maybe the story-hearer, merely *pretend* that such names refer.[6] Now, of course, there may well be an act of pretence in fiction. The woman playing Butterfly does pretend to die at the end of Puccini's opera. But when the actress sings of Nagasaki, she is not pretending to use a name: she is using it. In that context, nothing different seems to be going on with her use of 'Pinkerton'. Indeed, the actress may be entirely unaware of whether 'Nagasaki' and 'Pinkerton' are purely fictional names – or even mistaken about matters.

Worse, we now accept that the Homeric stories are mythical: 'Zeus', 'the Minotaur', and their like are purely fictional. But in the Homeric period of ancient Greece, the stories were believed to be true. Those who recounted the tales were not pretending anything.

Even setting the notion of pretence aside, a greater problem looms. If a purely fictional name does not refer to anything, how are we to account for the truth of some things we say employing the name? We may discount things like 'Holmes lived in Baker Street.' This is not really true, as observed. We may even discount things such as 'Holmes does not exist.' Given a certain understanding of reference failure, we may take 'Holmes exists' simply to be false, and so its negation to be true.[7] These are not the problems.

Problems arise when we consider reports of what happens within works of fiction, such as:

- In Doyle's stories, Holmes lived in Baker Street.
- In Greek mythology, Zeus lived on Mount Olympus.

True, the names occur within the scope of the operator 'In such and such a story/myth', but they are still purely fictional names, and the claims made employing them are true. One might suggest that in such contexts, 'Holmes', for example, refers to an object, one that exists at the worlds that realise Doyle's narratives, but not at the actual world. But then when I make this claim, I am referring to said Holmes. So this is just to say that in my mouth 'Holmes' does refer to an object – one that does not actually exist.

Even worse is discourse of a second-order nature, such as:

(★1) Holmes is a purely fictional detective

or 'Doyle created Holmes (in some sense)', or 'Holmes was smarter than Inspector Clouseau', or 'The Homeric Greeks worshipped Zeus' – all of which are plainly true.

One might always invoke the noble art of paraphrase. Thus one might suggest that (★1), for example, means:

(★2) In some work of fiction, Holmes is a detective, but 'Holmes' does not actually refer to anything.

This throws us back to the first kind of context, of course; but now there are new problems. (★1) would seem to entail that:

(★3) *Something* is a fictional detective (namely, the referent of 'Holmes').

But (★2) cannot imply this, since, according to it, 'Holmes' has no referent. So (★1) and (★2) cannot mean the same thing.

Philosophers being the ingenious creatures they are, they will undoubtedly delight in suggesting other paraphrases. Such jugglings should, of course, be treated on their merits. But it is clear that a desperate rearguard action is being fought — and a quite unnecessary one if there are other options that work. Are there?

Existent Objects

This brings us to the second option. Purely fictional names refer to objects, but these are existent objects. Of course, no one really wants to say that Sherlock Holmes or Zeus really existed. So the names must refer to some sort of surrogate. What?

There are a couple of possibilities. One is that the name, for example 'Holmes', refers not to Holmes, but to a mental representation of Holmes. Let us call this representation *Holmes★*. What, exactly, such a representation is, one might debate; but it is, at any rate, something in the mind (however that relates to the brain).

The most obvious objection to this is that when we say that Holmes does not exist, if we are referring to *Holmes★*, this is just false. We have, then, to reinterpret the notion of existence. Perhaps when we say that Holmes does not exist, we mean something like: he does not exist outside the mind. But this seems all wrong. Suppose I say (truly) that Plato existed but, in contrast, Zeus does not. It would appear that it is exactly what I am saying of Plato that I am denying of Zeus. That is, it would seem to follow that for some property P, Plato has the property P, and Zeus does not. Clearly, this does not follow from 'Plato exists, but Zeus does not exist outside the mind.' This attributes different properties to each.

Worse is to come. Suppose I tell a story about some state of the mind. (Maybe in the story I discover it.) Call this state s. I wonder whether s really exists. I then discover that it does not. In that case I must have been talking about some mental representation of s, $s★$, and I have just discovered that it does not exist outside the mind. But this is no discovery: I never thought it did.

Or worse again, Holmes was smarter than any actual detective, we may suppose. When we do so, we are not supposing that a mental representation is smarter than any actual detective. Mental representations are not the *kind* of thing that can be smart. Similarly, Nagasaki and the concept of Nagasaki are quite different. When I say that Nagasaki is in Japan, I am talking about the place; I know that I am not talking about a mental concept. Again, when I say Butterfly is a tragic woman in a Puccini opera, I am not talking about a concept. Concepts are not the *kind* of thing that can be tragic women.

What other existent objects might purely fictional names be referring to? Some have suggested that they refer to abstract entities, like numbers — except that, unlike numbers, they can be brought into existence by human creation (maybe like social institutions).[8] The view shares many of the same problems.

First, when we say that Holmes does not exist, we have to reinterpret the notion of existence. This time, one might suggest that when we say that Holmes does not exist, we mean that he does not exist as a concrete object. But this seems all wrong. When I say that Plato existed but, in contrast, Zeus does not, it would appear that it is exactly what I am saying of Plato that I am denying of Zeus. And again: suppose I tell a story about some hypothetical number. (Maybe in this story I discover it.) Call this number n. I wonder whether n really exists. I then discover that it does not. In that case 'n' must have been referring to some abstract object, and I have just discovered that it is not a concrete object. But this is no discovery: I never thought it was.[9] Finally, once more, many of the claims we make about purely fictional objects (such as being smarter than any actual detective) cannot be true of abstract objects: they are just the wrong *kind* of thing. To say that an abstract object, such as the number 3, is smarter than any actual detective is simply a category mistake.[10]

Non-Existent Objects

This brings us to the third possibility. Purely fictional names refer to non-existent objects. This is a perfectly common-sense view. We can say that Sherlock Holmes does not exist, and mean this in a perfectly straightforward way. And how it is that we can say other true things about such objects is also clear: the objects simply have the properties being attributed to them. So why not say the obvious?

The answer will itself be obvious to anyone who knows the history of twentieth-century English-speaking philosophy — though not, perhaps, to anyone else.[11] Non-existent objects had a really bad philosophical press in the twentieth century (unlike in the other great periods in Western logic and metaphysics).

In 1948, the American philosopher Willard Quine published a paper, 'On What There Is' (Quine 1948), in which he argued that the only way to express existence is by using the word 'some'. 'Some' means 'some existent'. To say, then, that some fictional objects do not exist is a contradiction in terms.

Quine's view seems most implausible. Can we not say — truly — things such as 'Some things don't exist, like Father Christmas, Zeus, Butterfly' or 'I wanted to buy you something for Christmas, but I found out that it doesn't exist' (for example, something owned by Sherlock Holmes, whom I had mistakenly believed to be real)? But Quine's paper was enormously influential. Quine's view is now under serious — and quite justified — attack. But it is still a very common one — it is perhaps still the orthodox view: in many places in the English-speaking philosophical world, to say that you think that some things do not exist is taken to be just a shade short of insanity.

In his paper, Quine argues for his thesis by elimination. There is nothing else with which one can express existence, so it has to be the quantifier 'some'. Perhaps the most obvious thing that strikes someone who now reads the essay, and who has not taken Philosophy of Language 100 — other than its hugely rhetorical content — is this: Quine does not even mention, let alone consider, the most obvious candidate to express existence, namely the verb 'exists', as in 'Nagasaki exists; Lilliput does not.'

This odd omission is perhaps explained by the influence of Bertrand Russell on Quine. In his lectures of 1918 on logical atomism, Russell argued that 'exists', construed as a predicate, is meaningless (Russell 2010: 61–77). To say of an object that it exists (or does not exist) is literally nonsense. Existence is a notion that applies only to groups of things, and to say that they exist is to say that some things are in that group. Russell's view appears to be even more incredible than Quine's.[12] When I was a child, I believed that Sherlock Holmes existed. Later on, I learned that he did not. What I learned was nonsense? Russell defends his view with a battery of arguments, which are, frankly, frightful. Yes, I know that that is a very strong claim, and I do not intend to defend it here.[13]

There is a defensive move that may be made here. A name, n, is really a covert description, and so is really something of the form: the thing satisfying condition C.[14] To say that n exists is then to say that something — or, for Russell, some unique thing — satisfies condition C. The view that names are really covert descriptions has now been widely discredited, however.[15] The reasons are many. Here is just one. Descriptions display an ambiguity in modal contexts (such as those produced by words like 'might' and 'must'); names do not. Thus, consider, 'The 44th president of the United States might not have been a man.' This may mean 'Barack Obama might not have been a man.' Or it might mean 'The person who won the election for the 44th presidency might not have been a man.' (Hillary Clinton might have won the election.) These mean quite different things. There is no similar ambiguity in 'Barack Obama might not have been a man.'

Russell's view, to the effect that existence is not a monadic predicate, is often foisted on Kant in some of his remarks in the *Critique of Pure Reason*. The attribution is mistaken, as it must be: existence (reality) is one of Kant's categories — distinct, I note, from particularity (some) (Kant 1998: A80/B106). What Kant actually says in his discussion of the Ontological Argument (1998: A592/B620–A603/B631) is that existence is not a *determining* (*bestimmendes*) predicate. And what that means is that to say that something is an X is the same as to say that it is an existent X. The view is itself mistaken. For some sorts of Xs, existent Xs are the same as Xs. Chairs, for example, are things in space and time, and so existent. So all chairs are existent chairs. But this is not true for all Xs. Some fictional characters (that is, characters that occur in a work of fiction) exist, such as Nagasaki and Sylvan; some do not, such as Lilliput and Pinkerton. So a fictional character need not be an existent fictional character. Be that as it may, Kant's view was not Russell's. For Kant, to say that an object exists is not at all meaningless. Indeed, since the existence of something is a synthetic matter (1998: A598/B626), the discovery that something exists (or does not) can be very significant.

In sum, there seems to be no real philosophical bar to accepting the commonsense view that some names denote non-existent objects.[16] The names used in fiction, then, denote. Some denote perfectly existent objects, like Nagasaki and Sylvan; some (the purely fictional names) denote non-existent objects, such as Lilliput and Butterfly. Let us call such objects themselves purely fictional.

Properties of Non-Existent Objects

What properties, though, do purely fictional objects have? Primarily two kinds. The first comprises those which they possess in virtue of the fiction in which they occur. Thus, it is not true that Holmes has the property of living in Baker Street, but it is true that Holmes has the property of [living in Baker Street in Doyle's novels]. Similarly, Cio Cio San has the property of [committing suicide in Puccini's opera].

To determine what properties something has in a fictional context is not always straightforward. Normally, if the author of a fiction says or shows explicitly that a character is or does something, then that is, indeed, a property of the character in the fiction. But not always. Sometimes it may become clear that a character in a fiction lies or is unreliable in some other way, even the narrator[17] — think merely of Baron Munchausen. Perhaps more importantly, many things may be true in a work of fiction though the author does not say or show so explicitly. Thus, in the Holmes stories, large doses of arsenic kill people, you cannot get from London to Edinburgh in an hour, guns are not made of butter. Doyle says none of these things. It is simply assumed that facts from the real world (or the facts of the world of London *circa* the second half of the nineteenth century, as Doyle took them to be) are imported — and so may be true *simpliciter*, as well as true in the fiction. What, in general, determines what is and what is not imported is a tough question; but it is not one, fortunately, which we need to tackle here. Intuitively, the notion of truth in a work of fiction is clear enough for present purposes.

I note that, in a fiction, an object may have impossible properties. Thus, in 'Sylvan's Box', the box in question — call it b — has the property of being empty and occupied by something at the same time.[18] This in no way threatens the Principle of Non-Contradiction. The statements 'in "Sylvan's Box" b is empty' and 'in "Sylvan's Box" b is not empty' are not contradictories. What would contradict the claim 'in "Sylvan's Box" b is empty' is the claim 'it is not the case that in "Sylvan's Box" b is empty' — a quite different matter.

So much for one kind of property of non-existent objects. The other kind comprises those properties that may be attributed, but which do not employ operators of the kind 'In fiction F ...'. These are things such as: Holmes is a fictional detective, Holmes does not exist, Holmes was invented (at least in some sense) by Doyle, Holmes is more famous than many real detectives, Holmes is a possible object, Sylvan's box is an impossible object, I am now thinking of Sylvan's box; and so on.

Roughly speaking, the most obvious such properties fall into two kinds. First, there are status properties (*exists*, *is possible*, *is impossible*, and so on). Second, there are properties that hold in virtue of the intentional state of some agent directed towards the object (*is being thought about*, *has been heard of by*, *is admired by*, and so on). Whether there are other sorts of properties may be moot. But one thing we can be sure about is that non-existent objects do not — by definition — have any properties that entail existence. Thus, to exert a gravitation effect on the moon is to be involved in causal processes, and so existent. Hence, no non-existent object exerts a gravitational effect on the moon. How, exactly, to determine whether a property is existence-entailing may also be a matter of some dispute. But, again, it is not one we need to go into here. It is time to move to the second half of this chapter.

Fictional Subjects

The Sense of Self

So let us consider the subject pole of the relation. Let me start with a word of clarification. In what follows, I will often use the word 'I' and its cognates. What I am referring to is the biological organism Graham Priest. (Similarly for 'you', 'we', and so on, and their cognates.)

When I read a novel or listen to an opera, there certainly seems to be a conscious subject into which the thoughts are entering. We all of us seem to have a sense of self. When one wakes up in the morning after a deep sleep, it is as though a little voice says 'Hello, back again'. Or as Kant put it in more Teutonic terms in the *Critique of Pure Reason* (Kant 1998: B131–2), every mental act is accompanied by the thought 'I think', which constitutes the unity of my thoughts.

So we have a *sense* of self. But do we really have a self? We know that the mind – or the brain whose functioning delivers it – plays tricks. At the back of the eyeball there is a place where the optic nerve joins it. There are no rods or cones there, so the joint produces a blind spot in the field of vision. Normally, though, we are quite unaware of this, since the brain 'fills in the visual gap'. In a similar way, there is a familiar illusion known as the *Phi Phenomenon* (made use of in the production of movies). Suppose there is a sequence of lights such that from left to right, say, each light flashes momentarily after the one before it. When one looks at this, one actually sees something moving from left to right. The brain 'fills in the gaps'. Maybe the self of which one has a sense is just the brain filling in the gaps between mental events, as it were, to create the illusion of something that does not really exist.

Buddhism and Modern Science

That this is so is, in fact, a very ancient view. It is the theory of mind developed over 2,000 years ago in Buddhist philosophy. According to this, the mind is nothing more than an aggregate of mental events, causally connected in certain ways to each other and to the body. There is no self over and above – or under and beneath – them. For obvious reasons, the view is called no-self (*anātman*) (see Siderits 2007: 32–68).

The view is also a very modern one, receiving support from developments in cognitive science. Daniel Dennett describes the situation as follows:

> There is no single, definitive 'stream of consciousness', because there is no central Headquarters, no Cartesian Theater where 'it all comes together' for the perusal of a Central Meaner. Instead of such a single stream (however wide), there are multiple channels in which specialised circuits try, in parallel pandemoniums, to do their various things, creating Multiple Drafts [of a narrative of the self] as

they go. Most of these fragmentary drafts of 'narrative' play short-lived roles in the modulation of current activity but some get promoted to further functional roles, in swift succession, by the activity of a virtual machine in the brain. The seriality of this machine (its 'von Neumannesque' character) is not a 'hard-wired' design feature, but rather the upshot of a coalition of these specialists. (Dennett 1993: 253–4)[19]

This view of the mind, then, has both an ancient pedigree and contemporary scientific credentials.

Look for Yourself

The current science of the mind is, however, in a rapidly developing state. So perhaps it is wise not to put too much weight on current scientific considerations. Why else might one suppose this view of the mind to be correct? A reason was provided by David Hume (who is often held to have a view about the self akin to the Buddhist view). As he puts it in the *Treatise on Human Nature* (I, IV, 6):

> There are some philosophers who imagine that we are every moment intimately conscious of what we call our SELF; that we feel its existence and its continuance in existence; and are certain, beyond the evidence of a demonstration, both of its perfect identity and simplicity. The strongest sensation, the most violent passion, say they, instead of distracting us from this view, only fix it the more intensely, and make us consider their influence on *self* either by their pain or pleasure …
>
> For my part, when I enter most intimately into what I call *myself*, I always stumble on some particular perception or other, of heat or cold, light or shade, love or hatred, pain or pleasure. I never can catch *myself* at any time without a perception, and never can observe anything but the perception … If anyone, upon serious and unprejudiced reflection, thinks he has a different notion of *himself*, I must confess, I can reason no longer with him. All I can allow him is, that he may be in the right as well as I, and that we are essentially different in this particular. He may, perhaps, perceive something simple and continued, which he calls *himself*; though I am certain there is no such principle in me.
>
> But setting aside some metaphysician of this kind, I may venture to affirm of the rest of mankind, that they are nothing but a bundle or collection of different perceptions which succeed each other with an inconceivable rapidity and are in perpetual flux and movement. (Hume 1978: 251–2)

I am told by people who practise a certain kind of Buddhist meditation that it is exactly an exercise in simply experiencing the constant arising and ceasing of mental states.

Given his empiricism, Hume inferred from the fact that we cannot perceive the self that there is no such thing – or at least, that we have no reason to suppose that there is. That is too fast. It is true that direct experience may give us no reason to believe in the self. But there are now many things which we take to exist which we cannot perceive, such as electrons and dark matter. What it does mean is that the self has to be considered as a theoretical posit, like the scientific entities just mentioned. And to be legitimate, it therefore has to earn its theoretical keep.[20] How?

Causation and Unity

There is a methodological principle termed *Ockham's Razor*. One should not believe that something exists unless there is good reason to do so. And in the case of all theoretical posits, this means that the posit must have explanatory value. If everything can be explained without it, one should not believe in it. So what might the existence of a self explain that cannot be explained by other things that we are already committed to?

The obvious thought is the Kantian one, that it is the self — whatever that is — which accounts for the unity of experience. Some mental events hang together in a way that others do not. It is precisely the self that is, supposedly, responsible for this.

Let us pass over the somewhat awkward question of how, exactly, the self might turn this trick; but look directly at the question of whether there are other possible explanations for this unity. The unity has both a synchronic aspect and a diachronic aspect. Let us consider each of these in turn.[21]

Synchronic: A motor bike drives past. I see it and hear it. Though one sensation is visual, and the other is auditory, they work together to produce a unitary experience. By contrast: you also see the bike go past, so we both have visual experiences of the bike, but there is no sense in which they are unified in the same way.

This distinction can, however, be explained in simple causal terms. There are causal relations between my auditory and visual sensations which do not hold between your visual sensations and mine. Specifically, the visual and auditory inputs of my brain are processed by different areas of my brain (the visual and auditory cortexes), but these two cortexes communicate with each other in a process of multisensory integration to deliver the resulting mental experience. By contrast, there is no similar causal integration between your visual sensation and mine.[22]

Diachronic: This can be past-oriented or future-oriented. *Past oriented:* Yesterday I saw a road accident. Today I have a visual memory of it. For me, the visual and memory events are integrated, in a way that any of your visual events are not related to my memory. But again, there is a perfectly natural causal explanation of this integration. When I saw the accident, the results from the visual cortex were encoded in the part of the brain responsible for episodic memory (the limbic system). These can be stimulated to generate the visual memory. Obviously there is no similar connection between your visual experience and my memory.

Future oriented: Tonight I have a drink. Because of its pleasant effect, I drink too much. Tomorrow I have a hangover, with its painful mental symptoms. This evening's desire, and tomorrow's headache, go together. However, if you desire to drink, and drink too much, your hangover is not part of my experience. Again, however, there is a perfectly causal explanation of this. I desire to drink, so I drink. The alcohol enters my body, and the overdose gives me a mild case of alcohol poisoning, which my brain monitors the next day, giving rise to the headache. There is no similar causal chain between your drinking, and any headache I might have the next day.

For similar reasons, it makes sense for me not to drink too much tonight if I do not want to have a hangover tomorrow – in a way that it makes no sense for me to try to stop *you* drinking so that *I* do not get a hangover. Thus, the causal relations also make sense of agency without a self.

The Illusion of Self

Given all this, it would indeed appear that the experience of self is an illusion: there is no such thing. Of course, illusions can be useful. If you look in a mirror, what is behind you appears to be in front of you. This is an illusion; but it may be a useful one, since it lets you know what is behind you.[23] And one can well imagine that an illusion of self is useful in evolutionary terms (which might, therefore, explain why certain kinds of biological organisms have it). Plausibly, a creature with the illusion of self is more likely to survive and pass on its genes.

However, at least in Buddhist terms, the illusion is pernicious. It generates a spurious attachment at the root of much unhappiness. And once one comes to understand that the object of the attachment is non-existent, it makes no sense to maintain the attachment – any more than it makes any sense to be attached to Butterfly and her well-being, if one knows her to be non-existent. With this disappearance of attachment, the unhappiness it causes will also disappear.

Well, that is the theory. What truth there is in it is not germane to the present matter.[24] The important point here is that, given that these considerations are correct, the self is an illusion.

Conclusion

The fact that the self is an illusion does not mean that it is not an object. In an illusion, we are phenomenologically aware of something, such as the moving object in the case of the Phi Phenomenon. But the object in question is non-existent. That is part of what is involved in the experience being an illusion.

Indeed, the illusory self is a purely fictional object. It is just a character in a fiction that the brain weaves, part of a fictional narrative that the brain fashions, in much the same way that Doyle's brain also fashioned fictional narratives about a non-existent detective.[25]

And of course, this means that the self does not have the properties one may take it to have, such as existence, constancy, unifying power, and so on, any more than Holmes has the property of actually having lived in Baker Street or Butterfly has the property of actually having lived in Nagasaki. It is in Doyle's stories that Holmes lives in Baker Street, and in Puccini's opera that Butterfly lived in Nagasaki. In the same way, it is in the fiction created by the brain that the self has the properties in question.

But the fact that the self is an illusion tells us more. We are unlikely to suppose that things are as they are said to be in the Doyle stories – unless we mistakenly take the stories to be history rather than fiction. But it is a feature of illusions that we precisely *do* have a tendency to suppose that things are as the illusion shows us – especially if we do not know that matters are illusory; and even when we do, the illusion may be very hard to shake off. We naïvely take it to be the case that the self exists, is constant, has unifying power, and so on, not realising that it is only in the fiction created by the brain that these things are true.

And – to return to where we started – the fiction delivers a relation which holds between a subject pole and an object pole. The objects of the object pole may exist; more normally, they do not. The subject pole does not exist at all. It is a non-existent object of a very peculiar kind: an illusory object which, in the illusion, can grasp other non-existent objects. In the fictional narrative created by the brain, it is a purely fictional object which, in that narrative, can grasp other purely fictional objects.

Notes

For very helpful comments on earlier drafts of this chapter, thanks go to the volume editors, Franz Berto, and Amber Carpenter.

1. One might hold that this claim begs the question. But if reference in a work of fiction is *ipso facto* to a different person, then the same is true of reference to: properties (like *detective*), substances (like *cocaine*), numbers (like *three*). These words clearly have the standard meaning (and so reference) when Doyle uses them in his stories – or we could not understand his stories.
2. Actually, one might contest this. The libretto is based on a story by J. L. Long, which is, in turn, based on a semi-autobiographical novel by P. Loti. This raises the thorny question of the identity conditions of characters across works of fiction. Fortunately, we do not need to go into this here.
3. One might reply here: yes, you were referring to Richard, but the name in the text refers to someone else. In reply, one can only ask how the words magically changed their meaning when written on the page. Suppose I write a salacious story about you, and you sue me. The claim that your name did not refer to you simply because it was written down would be laughed out of court.
4. There is a substantial history of discussion about the topic, with its corresponding literature. For a survey, see Kroon and Voltolini 2011. It is impossible to do justice to it all in a chapter of this kind, so I shall not try. Apologies to anyone whose favourite theory does not get mentioned.
5. Perhaps the earliest version of this view is to be found in Frege 1892.
6. Versions of such a theory can be found in Walton 1990; Recanati 2000; and Kripke 2013: 3–28.
7. This is the view deployed in so-called negative free logics. See Priest 2008: 293–5.
8. Versions of this view are to be found in Thomasson 1999, 2003; and Kripke 2013: 79–102.
9. Or – Le Verrier postulated the existence of a sub-Mercurial planet, Vulcan. His theory turned out to be false. It seems somewhat bizarre to say that he postulated the existence of an abstract object, which, on this account, he did.

10. Some thinkers (e.g., Kripke 2013) combine the view that fictional names do not refer in the discourse of the fiction with the view that they refer to abstract objects in discourses about the fiction. This would seem to be an unstable position. Given it, it is hard to make sense of the following sort of scenario. A tourist to London asks a local policeman, 'Where is the house in Baker Street in which Sherlock Holmes lived?' The policeman replies that Baker Street is just around the corner, but no Holmes ever lived there: Holmes was just a fictional character. According to the view in question, the tourist is making a claim that is true in a fiction; so in their mouth 'Sherlock Holmes' has no referent. But the policeman is talking about the work of fiction; so in his mouth, 'Holmes' refers to an abstract object. Tourist and policeman would then seem to be talking at cross purposes.
11. For a longer discussion of the following matters, see Priest 2016: 323–42.
12. Quine is not committed to the view that a monadic existence predicate is meaningless. 'There is y such that $y = x$' is such a predicate, and it is perfectly meaningful. For him, it is just vacuously true of any x.
13. I put my intellectual money where my mouth is in chapter 18 of the second edition of *Towards Non-Being* (Priest 2016: 323–42).
14. This is essentially Russell's 1905 theory of definite descriptions. Russell's theory was indeed appealed to by Quine, to argue that names themselves have no existential import.
15. Largely due to Kripke 1972.
16. For a full defence of the view, see Priest 2016.
17. These are sometimes known as unreliable narrators.
18. If, therefore, one understands the notion of truth in a fiction in terms of what is true at those worlds that realise the fiction, the worlds in question may be impossible worlds. One may suggest that it is not the case that in 'Sylvan's Box' the box is both empty and not empty. The narrator is just unreliable. (See Nolan 2007.) Of course, there are such interpretations of the story. The story could, in fact, be interpreted in many different ways. It remains the case that there is a natural and straightforward interpretation, according to which, in the fiction, the box is empty and not empty. That is the interpretation I intended, and the one I am talking about here.
19. Dennett 1993 reviews the evidence and mounts the case for the view. See, especially, part II of the book.
20. The point is perfectly orthodox in Buddhist philosophy of mind. Thus, Vasubandhu (fl. fourth or fifth century CE), in his discussion of *anātman*, notes that if there is reason to believe in a self, it must either be perceived or inferred. See Duerlinger 2003: 73–4.
21. The most sophisticated Buddhist discussion of the matter I know is by Vasubandhu in his 'Refutation of the Theory of Self' (chapter 9 of his *Abhidharmakośa-Bhāṣya*). See Duerlinger 2003: 71–110. For further discussion, see Carpenter 2014: 117–36.
22. Of course there are also causal connections between your perception and mine; but they are just of the wrong *kind* to produce the unity in question. A similar point can be made for the examples that follow.
23. Note that an illusion does not have to be a delusion. Delusion involves a false belief.
24. See, e.g., Carpenter 2014: 1–47.
25. I am not suggesting that all purely fictional objects are illusions. I do not think that, for normal adults, the Sherlock Holmes tales deliver an illusion. ('Illusion: a deceptive appearance or impression' (*OED*).) As one of the editors noted, however, a case might be made for this.

Bibliography

Carpenter, Amber (2014), *Indian Buddhist Philosophy*, Durham: Acumen.
Dennett, Daniel C. (1993), *Consciousness Explained*, London: Penguin.
Duerlinger, James (ed. and trans.) (2003), *Indian Buddhist Theories of Persons: Vasubandhu's 'Refutation of the Theory of a Self'*, London: Routledge.
Frege, Gottlob (1892), 'Über Sinn und Bedeutung', *Zeitschrift für Philosophie und philosophische Kritik*, 100, pp. 25–50.
Hume, David (1978), *A Treatise on Human Nature*, 2nd edn, Lewis Amherst Selby-Bigge and P. H. Nidditch (eds), Oxford: Oxford University Press.
Kant, Immanuel (1998), *Critique of Pure Reason*, Paul Guyer and Allen W. Wood (eds and trans.), Cambridge: Cambridge University Press.
Kripke, Saul (1972), 'Naming and Necessity', in Donald Davidson and Gilbert Harman (eds), *Semantics of Natural Language*, Dordrecht: Reidel, pp. 253–355.
Kripke, Saul (2013), *Reference and Existence: The John Locke Lectures*, Oxford: Oxford University Press.
Kroon, Fred and Alberto Voltolini (2011), 'Fiction', in Edward N. Zalta (ed.), *Stanford Encyclopedia of Philosophy*, <https://plato.stanford.edu/entries/fiction> (last accessed 18 October 2018).
Nolan, Daniel (2007), 'A Consistent Reading of "Sylvan's Box"', *Philosophical Quarterly*, 57, pp. 667–732.
Priest, Graham (1997), 'Sylvan's Box', *Notre Dame Journal of Formal Logic*, 38, pp. 573–82; reprinted as section 6.6 in Priest (2016).
Priest, Graham (2008), *An Introduction to Non-Classical Logic: From If to Is*, 2nd edn, Cambridge: Cambridge University Press.
Priest, Graham (2016), *Towards Non-Being*, 2nd edn, Oxford: Oxford University Press.
Quine, Willard Van Orman (1948), 'On What There Is', *Review of Metaphysics*, 48, pp. 21–38.
Recanati, François (2000), *Oratio Obliqua, Oratio Recta*, Cambridge, MA: MIT Press.
Russell, Bertrand (1905), 'On Denoting', *Mind*, 14, pp. 479–93.
Russell, Bertrand (2010), *The Philosophy of Logical Atomism*, Abingdon: Routledge.
Siderits, Mark (2007), *Buddhism as Philosophy: An Introduction*, Aldershot: Ashgate.
Thomasson, Amie L. (1999), *Fiction and Metaphysics*, Cambridge: Cambridge University Press.
Thomasson, Amie L. (2003), 'Speaking of Fictional Characters', *Dialectica*, 57, pp. 205–23.
Walton, Kendall Lewis (1990), *Mimesis as Make-Believe: On the Foundations of the Representational Arts*, Cambridge, MA: Harvard University Press.

8

On the Death of Meaning

R. Scott Bakker

> The most important questions seem, therefore, to be: 'Is it possible that a man should actually know anything transcending his sensual perception unless it is told to him by some supposed authority? Can the power of intuition be developed to such an extent as to become actual knowledge without any possibility of error, or shall we always be doomed to depend on hearsay and opinions? Can any individual man possess powers transcending those which are admitted to exist by modern science, and how can such transcendental powers be acquired?
>
> (Hartmann 1890: 15–16)

What We Know of the Soul

You remain a mystery insofar as the human soul remains a mystery. The question – the one underwriting every chapter in this section of the volume, in fact – is how long this will remain the case. In the past six fiscal years, from 2012 to 2017, the National Institute of Health will have spent more than $113 billion funding research bent on solving some corner of the human soul.[1] And this is just one public institution in one nation involving health-related research. If you include the cognitive sciences more generally – research into everything from consumer behaviour to artificial intelligence (AI) – you could say that solving the human soul presently commands more resources than any domain in history.

We are a civilisation at war against our ignorance of ourselves. The question is what will come of it. Will we solve our souls? And if so, what will we find? Will it confirm our cherished prescientific images, or will it, as science typically does, surprise, shock, and dismay? Will it empower us, or will it ruin?

These are the questions that have obsessed me for over two decades now, both as a theorist and as a novelist.[2] This war commands the resources it does precisely because the information mined is utterly inaccessible otherwise. Knowledge of our nature is, from an evolutionary standpoint, quite unnatural. A tsunami lies on the horizon, a swell of knowledge unlike anything our ancestors could have dreamed.

As artefacts born in the absence of this information, the academic traditions of the human soul, I think, are about to be swept away.

The traditions, of course, disagree. But then they always do.

Aristotle's Darkness

'Books', Virginia Woolf opines in *Between the Acts*, 'are mirrors of the soul' (Woolf 1941: 16), an observation she frames as more ornamental than profound, thus implicating her reader in the very cult of representational exhaustion she represents. Whether vital or decadent, literature is generally taken to be paradigmatically human, an exemplary way to communicate the 'human condition'. And as the wild range of opinions found in this collection indicates, it remains every bit as mysterious as the humanity it reflects. More than 2,400 years have passed since Aristotle first penned *Peri Poietikes*, and in all that time no one has been able to decisively explain literature. Everything is controversial. Nothing has been resolved. The chapters here, my own included, all turn on different theoretical opinions on the nature of literature.

We wander the same darkness as Aristotle, more bruised by sharp corners and surprise encounters, wiser as to the vacant spaces perhaps, but every bit as baffled as to the space containing our ruminations. Nothing has been settled when it comes to the fundamental questions of literature. This fact is crucial because humans are so prone to mistake speculation – their own, namely – for knowledge.[3] Openness is all the more important in this instance because the question is both old enough and important enough to be institutionalised. Aristotle's successors did not simply inherit the question of literature, but the history of prior attempts to answer it as well. The competencies comprising 'literary expertise' inevitably derive from sustained engagement with this history, both ancient and modern. This means all the mistakes made, all the conceits and faulty assumptions, find themselves baked into each new generation of literary scholars.

And of course, given the radical disagreements between them, each implicitly acknowledges this is the case. One can look at various positions in literary theory (once again, my own included) as occupying different twigs on a great guesswork tree, philosophical claims forking in dispute again and again, riddled with creepers to be sure, but always ending in some theorist-specific collection of leaves. Why should we think this tree will survive the cognitive scientific tsunami described above? Why should we believe mere speculation will somehow trump scientific cognition regarding the nature of human subjectivity?

Historically at least, the cognitive legitimacy of a traditional discourse quickly evaporates once science has colonised its domain. Even if one finds the prospect of a scientific humanities logically incoherent or morally risible or intellectually impoverishing or what have you, common sense, let alone intellectual integrity, requires an honest consideration of the worst-case scenario. This is what I hope to provide.

Back in the Day

So why is the human soul so mysterious?

Back in Aristotle's day everything but everything was mysterious. The systematic interrogation of the soul was no more or less speculative than the systematic interrogation of the heavens or any other phenomena. But with the institutionalisation of science, ancient speculation gave way to empirical investigation (of speculative hypotheses), and the domains confronting the ancient philosopher found themselves sorted in some rather remarkable ways. Traditional speculation on natural phenomena gave way to genuine theoretical knowledge, claims unlocking the technological marvels that continue, for good or ill, to revolutionise our lives. Traditional speculation on various social and psychological phenomena, on the other hand, remained largely untouched, to the point where Aristotle's *On Poetics* continues to be, for many literary theorists, a legitimate source of 'insight', while cosmologists regard his *On the Heavens* as little more than a historical curiosity.

Now we find ourselves knowing what happened in the first second of creation, yet mystified by what this knowledge consists in.[4] We can explain the origin and nature of countless species, while the origin and nature of explanation itself remains, well, inexplicable, the topic of speculation merely. Certainly, a great number of these phenomena have been empirically operationalised – they are the grist of psychology and sociology, after all – but no matter what the context, experimental or theoretical, they remain 'inexplicable explainers', ways to understand processes that themselves resist formulation as explananda, let alone explanation. For whatever reason, intentional phenomena – processes and products involving meaning – remain as much the topic of speculation today as they did back in Aristotle's day.[5]

This is an extraordinary fact: science has systematically delegitimised all prescientific discourses save those involving meaning and experience (Bakker 2014). But why? Why should *On Poetics* represent an ongoing concern, while *On the Heavens* has become a diverting footnote? Why should modernity enshrine the relevance of the one, while murdering the credibility of the other?

How one answers this question determines just where a theorist finds themselves on the literary guesswork tree. The majority of thinkers will claim that intentional phenomena, unlike natural phenomena, are somehow 'irreducible'. These thinkers endorse various forms of what might be called intentional exceptionalism, the speculative conviction that the order of meaning is somehow fundamentally different from the order of nature – at least as we presently conceive it. For them, the extraordinary fact of Aristotle's continuing relevance says less about their discourse than it does about their domain.

The position taken here, however, endorses what might be called intentional mediocrity, the thesis that meaning requires no drastic renovations of the physical universe as we presently conceive it. Meaning and experience have only resisted naturalisation because the complexity of the systems responsible has – historically at least – rendered them scientifically intractable. The apparently inexplicable properties attributed to intentional phenomena (like literature), on this account, are wholly perspectival artefacts, peculiarities due to our heuristic relation to ourselves and one another. As a system adapted to solving systems without physical information, intentional cognition can only conceive meaning as something sourceless – something somehow exempt from the nature that drives all things otherwise.[6] Meaning only appears magical, paradoxical, irreducible, fundamental, and so on for the want of sensitivity to the lack of information – an incapacity, I think, that follows on any plausible evolutionary account of human reflection.

Both theoretical outlooks turn on guesswork, of course, but the latter is distinctive in a number of ways worth keeping in 'mind' as you read. First, in terms of implicature, intentional mediocrity branches from a point below Aristotle on the literary guesswork tree, insofar as Aristotle assumes the reality of intentional phenomena.[7] Second, the consequences of intentional mediocrity are out-and-out radical. Where cosmological mediocrity denied us our exceptional position, and biological mediocrity denied us our exceptional origins, intentional mediocrity denies us our exceptional being. Third, and most important, the latter stakes out a resolutely empirical position. My view, unlike any other in this collection, can and will be sorted by the science of the future. As bleak as it is, it actually offers a way to move beyond the mire of perpetual intentional speculation.

This is why I am more concerned with demonstrating the possibility, as opposed to the actuality, of intentional mediocrity. Once intentional mediocrity becomes possible, then blind faith in the cognitive autonomy of the traditional humanities becomes impossible, and the sciences of the human can no longer be ignored on the strength of catechism alone. Given a mediocre alternative, the conceits underwriting exceptionalist approaches become impossible to overlook, let alone obscure. This includes what might be called the Master Conceit, the presumption that we possess the information access and cognitive capacity required to intuit our fundamental nature (one that just happens to contravene what we know about the physical world) even though humans are arguably the most complicated systems in the known universe, and evolution relies on quick and dirty strategies to solve all such systems everywhere.

Intentional mediocrity presumes quick and dirty capacities are all we possess, that we cannot find any fundamental nature corresponding to those capacities because no such nature exists. There is no doubt that humans evolved myriad tools – the processes comprising 'intentional cognition' – to solve themselves and one another practically; the question is whether those practical problem-solving tools possess any real theoretical power. Why should we think that intentional cognition stands among the things that intentional cognition can solve? Certainly, twenty-five centuries of disputation suggest that something has gone wrong somewhere. What would the systematic misapplication of intentional cognition to the problem of intentional cognition look like, if not intentional philosophy as we know it?

Intentional mediocrity is a live alternative. The cognitive scientific deluge is real. Traditional literary discourses are speculative, and history has not been kind to any such discourses once scientific findings become relevant to their field. At the very least, we need to think the unthinkable, to dare imagine the humbling and the horrifying, and to ponder the possibility of literature without meaning.

Institutional Reflexes

'Proof of concept' is all I require, a mediocre alternative at least as plausible as any exceptional alternative. The mere existence of such an alternative forces exceptionalists to warrant their more complicated and exotic ontologies. If history is any guide, however, my account will cue at least three different intellectual reflexes typically used to immunise the humanities against the dissemination of mediocre views. As a one-time adherent of the tradition (my PhD dissertation was on fundamental ontology, no less), I know these reflexes all too well. I myself once regularly dismissed assertions of mediocrity in the humanities as scientistic, self-contradictory, and reductive. Since these reflexes tend to short-circuit the possibility of any genuine engagement with intentional mediocrity, let me say a few words about each.

Am I scientistic? Am I privileging scientific theoretical cognition to the exclusion of all other forms of theoretical cognition? Not at all. I just think it's hard to find examples of theoretical cognition (as opposed to opinion) outside of the sciences. Practical cognition, of course, abounds, but it is pretty much all just philosophy otherwise, is it not? And if it is more than philosophy, then what is it? Provide examples of extra-scientific theoretical cognition regarding the nature of meaning and I will happily count it among the things we know. But – and this is the crucial point – even if you manage to do so, science would still remain our collective paradigm for reliable theoretical knowledge. I do not think this is a good thing – in fact, I am convinced science is poised to cut our throats – but I do not see how denying the theoretical hegemony of science (on purely speculative grounds, no less) does anything but facilitate that hegemony. One's guesses regarding the transcendental conditions of this or that do nothing to blunt the monstrous efficacy of the sciences. The threat to intentional exceptionalism lies in what science is doing and what it will do.[8] Speculation regarding its 'presuppositions' are quite beside the point, particularly when they only devolve into more disputation.

Am I self-contradictory? After all, if there is no such thing as meaning, how could I be saying anything meaningful? This question seems damning, that is, until one asks what kind of problems 'meaning-talk' is capable of solving.[9] Meaning-talk is not only real, but enormously effective given felicitous, practical ecologies. Clarifying who meant what in a quarrel with your significant other has some hope of resolving disagreements (though slim, given the stubbornness of significant others). Using meaning-talk to explain the nature of something like literature, on the other hand, has yet to resolve any disagreement whatsoever. So yes, my argument can at once be meaningful (cue practical context) and inveigh against the reality of meaning (cue theoretical context). As readers and writers of literature well know, fictions can accomplish tremendous things given the proper circumstances.

Am I reductive? Yes, but methodologically, not metaphysically, and then hopefully more like Darwin than Skinner. In-principle arguments against explaining more with less simply leave me mystified – science is raised upon traditional a priori rubble – but I do appreciate the problem of explaining less with less. 'More with less' is precisely what the theory of evolution provides: a way to understand biology on nature's dime alone. 'More with less' is also what behaviourism ultimately failed to provide: since Skinner could neither explain nor explain away meaning, he could only hold it beneath cognitive contempt, despite all the practical problems it so obviously solved (Chomsky 1959: 26–58). Though mechanistic, my approach is Darwinian in that it genuinely explains intentional phenomena on nature's dime alone, rather than simply making vague gestures or ignoring them altogether.

Once again, the stakes of the worst-case scenario are such that the above considerations need only be plausible to possess dialectical significance. A great many scholars find the urge to dismiss intentional mediocrity as incoherent to be well-nigh irresistible. As a former exceptionalist, I appreciate the sentiment. All I request is charity, a willingness to genuinely understand the path that leads from you to me. Even if you remain unconvinced, you will at least be spared the futility of arguing against straw men.

And keep in mind the one point upon which all theorists of meaning agree: that everyone else has made some fundamental wrong turn somewhere. The perpetual underdetermination of theories of meaning is itself a quite remarkable social and intellectual phenomenon, one requiring explanation. For all we know, the institutional reflexes listed above, the ease with which 'Absurd!' pops from our lips, could be the cause of our predicament.

As I hope to show, our traditional difficulties with mediocrity, our perennial inability to conceive meaning in biological terms, arise as an inevitable consequence of that biology (Bakker 2017c: 31–52). We no more evolved the ability to intuit the mediocrity of our being than we evolved the ability to intuit the mediocrity of our place in the universe or the origin of our species.

The Illustrated Apple (Or How to Understand Meaning in a Different Light)

How can the same apple appear waxy or glossy? This is a phenomenon we have witnessed countless times – so much so as to seem trivial, I am sure – but like so many things apparently unremarkable it raises a profound mystery. Since the physical reflectance of an apple remains the same, why do we visually cognise that reflectance as waxy in some instances, and glossy in others? The answer is that human visual cognition relies on concatenations of heuristic devices. The visual cortex, rather than going through the trouble of assessing the apple's actual reflectance given the information available, relies on cues, information statistically correlated to the reflectance of the apple. This is why an apple that looks waxy when the curtains are drawn will suddenly look glossy when they are opened: visual cognition uses the detection of reflected highlights to decide whether an apple is glossy or waxy (Fleming 2012).

Illustration fascinated me as a child, and I have keen memories of drawing small reflected windows on various things to generate the illusion of glossiness in my creations. As it happens, the heuristic cue triggering the visual cognition of glossiness is so lean that it maps from actual apples to illustrated ones. Scrawl a highlight across whatever it is you are sketching, and glossiness will be cued where no glossiness actually exists simply because visual cognition solves environments by exploiting correlations between those environments and the visual information available. Why evolve the extravagant capacity to assess glossiness come what may when highlighting does the trick more often than not?

The first crucial feature of heuristics, then, lies in selective consumption, the way they solve computationally expensive problems on the basis of specialised bits of information, or cues possessing some reliable correlation to the actual systems requiring solution.

Thus, the second, equally crucial feature: because the information consumed is selective, dependent on hidden regularities, heuristic systems are also selective solvers. Their felicitous application turns on circumstantial prerequisites, or what Gerd Gigerenzer terms 'problem ecologies'.[10] Change the circumstances and application becomes misapplication. The illustrated apple, in fact, provides an excellent example of how the perception of apples, let alone glossy ones, can be cued 'out of school'. As our ancestors discovered, visual cognition of any number of environmental items can be triggered without the correlations underwriting our ancestral visual capacities. Imagery saturates our present-day lives, making it easy to forget the incredulity that must have occasioned the ancestral development of art, the miraculous ability to conjure the cognition of bison and horses and humans and so on by using cave walls and rudimentary pigments to cue our visual systems out of school.

This highlights a third crucial characteristic of heuristic cognition: automaticity of application. Cues cue, regardless of the media involved. The prehistoric artisans of Chauvet did not choose to see horses instead of charcoal scratched across limestone: the horses were just there, somehow in or on or across the stone. We are so accustomed to visual 'representations' that we are inclined to forget the sense in which they constitute optical illusions. Imagine never seeing a picture in your life, then suddenly encountering charcoal scratched across stone in such a way as to cue cognition of a horse. You would be no less astounded for recognising the figure – perhaps more.

A fourth important feature is that heuristic breakdowns are generally systematic (Wimsatt 2007: 79–80). Miscues, in other words, tend to have predictable effects when applied in comparable circumstances. This is precisely what allowed our ancestors to instrumentalise, or exapt, those breakdowns, as well as our own astonishing ability – think augmented or virtual reality – to play sensory cues to magical effect. With writing, we learned to gerrymander our environments in ways that allowed us to replace transient, auditory cues with more durable, visual cues, and so record linguistic activity. From a heuristic perspective, the whole of 'symbolic culture' is raised upon a series of auspicious mistakes, the deliberative exploitation of the systematic consequences of heuristic misapplication. But if the systematic nature of putative misapplications has the advantage of allowing novel uses, it has the disadvantage of concealing those misapplications as well, given our tendency to confuse cognitive systematicity with cognitive adequacy. This, as we shall see, explains much of the conviction one finds in speculative guesswork regarding experience and meaning.

Meaning Naturalised

So, what do illustrated apples have to do with the problem of meaning? The answer has already been alluded to above: 'meaning-talk' is heuristic through and through. In fact, it would be difficult to find cognitive systems more heuristic than those comprising human social cognition, insofar as they troubleshoot/manage the most computationally intractable systems known: namely, you and me, both individually and collectively. Nothing in the known universe is as complicated as the human brain, and yet we continually (and often effortlessly) solve one another all the time (Zadwidzki 2009: 149–54). I look at you, surmise that you are growing impatient, suggest that we leave for the dinner party early. You shrug and demur, understanding that I desire to continue my story, which you consider boring, yes, but perhaps important as well. Despite the 38,000 trillion-plus calculations per second underwriting this exchange,[11] despite the radically impoverished communicative channel (roughly seven to fifteen bits per second) available to manage this complexity (Baranauskas 2014), we find coordinating our evening activities effortless.

A boggling gulf lies between what we do – solve ourselves and others – and our ability to communicate what we are doing. Somehow, we are able to deftly manage what are, by any account, computationally intractable natural systems. This miraculous achievement is only possible because we have evolved specialised sensitivities keyed to specialised problem-solving mechanisms. Gesture. Expression. Posture. Vocalisation. We are (as a matter of empirical fact) walking, talking social cues, evolved and trained to coordinate behaviour via the transmission and consumption of specialised socio-cognitive information.[12] We solve one another, in other words, without any sensitivity to the actual, biological mechanisms involved, fastening instead on information reliably correlated to those biological mechanisms. A look. An exhalation. A word or two. Nothing more is needed. So long as the vast system of correlations underwriting the socio-cognitive reliability of the information available remains intact, we can ignore it entirely. Cue-based, correlative cognition, in other words, lets us out-and-out neglect everything between an available precursor and the phenomena it tracks.[13]

Since gestures, expressions, vocalisations, and so on are the purported vehicles of meaning, characterising them as heuristic amounts to sketching a heuristic theory of meaning. And it seems a promising sketch. If meaning were heuristic, we should expect it would exhibit the properties belonging to heuristic cognition: that it be cheap, situational, automatic, and inclined to systematically break down. To the extent that meaning is likewise cheap, situational (contextual), automatic (unconscious), and inclined to systematically break down, heuristics provide what, by any discursive measure, counts as a powerful explanatory head start. Add to this the way this approach potentially explains the origins of culture – as the exaptation of the systematic consequences of various miscues – and that head start becomes impressive indeed.

As any exceptionalist would be sure to object, however, the glaring problem with such a theory is that it trades exclusively in 'vehicles', and so threatens to wish away the very semantic/conscious domain at issue. What does meaning consist of, if not the lived experience of human actors? The standard complaint against mediocrity in philosophy of mind and cognitive science debates is that it 'changes the subject', or 'throws the baby out with the bathwater'. And, unlike the institutional reflexes considered above, this criticism possesses real bite. This is why any convincing, biologically informed, heuristic theory of meaning also has to be a theory of content, or intentionality in the narrow sense. The so-called vehicles of meaning, the exceptionalist will insist, only tell half the story.

Content – whether considered under the cognitivist rubric of aboutness/representation or the post-cognitivist rubrics of experience/interaction – is the fly in the empirical ointment, a problem every bit as 'hard' as the hard problem of consciousness.[14] The fundamental warrant for exceptionalism, apart, perhaps, from raw metacognitive intuition, lies in our continued inability to make naturalistic sense of content. So long as mediocrity serves only to moot this apparently self-evident domain of meaning, then it has no hope of providing any basis for understanding *any* human artefact or activity, let alone one so mediated as literature. Intentional phenomena require explanation. So long as things like rules and representations seem to so obviously exist, only the exceptionalist can aspire to explanatory authority. And so long as this remains the case, human cognition will never be prised from the tradition, at least not entirely, and *On Poetics* will remain a going theoretical (as opposed to merely descriptive) concern. Traditional authority will be preserved, securing countless pay cheques, and trapping us in Aristotle's darkness forever.

The Meaning Delusion

Usually this is where exceptionalism and mediocrity part ways. The meaning sceptic can inveigh against the speculative and supernatural excesses of intentionalism all they want, but so long as they can only deny the existence of intentional phenomena, they effectively have nothing to say regarding the nature and function of those phenomena. Historically speaking, the literary theorist has had no choice but to embrace some form of exceptionalism. They quite simply possessed no other way of exploring and explaining their domain.

But the heuristic approach possesses deep explanatory pockets – every bit as deep as a general theory of human meaning should. For instance, it elegantly explains not only the extraordinary fact of our self-ignorance, but the shape of that ignorance. Human central nervous systems are computationally intractable, period, which means they pose the same dilemma to themselves as they do to other brains. As in the case of socio-cognition, human metacognition has to be both fractionate and heuristic. Given that what moves your neighbour also moves you, you can rely on some (but not all) of the same kind of public cues to predict your own behaviour. Research is rife with examples of the inferential nature of our self-understanding, the way we interpret ourselves much the same way we interpret others.[15] Otherwise you possess the suite of hardwired (and therefore private) channels available to you now as you read. Silent vocalisations of these very words. Thoughts of your own.

An amorphous awareness of potential objections. A sense of indignation, perhaps. Curiosity. Boredom. These channels, like the machinery consuming them, are the product of countless generations of evolutionary filtration. And this is just to say the information and capacity they make available is specific to the practical metacognitive needs of Palaeolithic humans, not post-industrial theoreticians.

Small wonder the ancient Greeks were so astounded![16] Re-tasking this special-purpose information to answer general questions, the way they did, systematically revealed the profundity of human self-ignorance. Lacking any inkling of information insufficiency, the Greeks ran foul of WYSIATI, the 'what-you-see-is-all-there-is' phenomenon found widely throughout cognitive psychology.[17] Since veracity is assumed, built into the system via evolution, philosophical reflection assumes sufficiency: our ancestors need only recognise the appropriate cues, not that they are cues, components in a specialised problem-solving regime. When it comes to metacognitive channels, we quite simply lack the meta-metacognitive capacity required to distinguish goat paths from motorways. As a result, the ancient Greeks found themselves reflexively misapplying special-purpose metacognitive resources to general problems without realising as much.[18] Despite the ensuing, interminable controversy, they remained convinced, much as humanistic theoreticians remain convinced today, that they could definitively solve the conundrum they posed to themselves given endogenous inputs alone.[19]

A heuristic theory of meaning, in other words, provides a naturalistic explanation of why humanity finds meaning so difficult to understand. Experience only gives metacognition – deliberative reflection – the channels it needs to reliably solve ancestral problems. This is every bit as much the case with cognition in general – we are blind to things like infrared and gamma rays for a reason. But where environmental experience is behaviourally contingent, allowing us to amass more and more communally available information (via innovative technique and instrumentation) and so test and refine our investigations, our endogenous channels are fixed, chaining us, like Plato's prisoners in the Allegory of the Cave, to the dance of special-purpose shadows we call soul or mind or subject or what have you.[20]

So what does this have to do with content? In all signalling, information needs to synchronise receivers with environmental features, even where deception is concerned. Gross insensitivity to the enabling axis of cognition (metacognitive neglect), however, renders our actual connection to our environments (and ourselves) inscrutable. You embody, as some theorists like to say, the sum of your past and ongoing relations to your environment (and yourself), but you cognise and communicate that embodied connection in terms that cannot but neglect that embodied connection.[21] First and foremost, about-talk provides a remarkably cheap way of communicating/troubleshooting this otherwise intractable connection. We apply it automatically, resolving countless everyday communicative situations with very little, if any, deliberation. It comes to us, and we move on.

So what is 'content' on a heuristic theory of meaning? Physically speaking, content is nothing at all, though content-talk – like meaning-talk more generally – can be tremendously useful. Conversations can be followed, expectations and intentions guessed. Communicative artefacts can be condensed, filtered, and analysed. Behavioural responses can be predicted. Given formal regimentation and implementation protocols, computational devices can be engineered. Talking content allows us to fetishise strategic nodes in systems otherwise too vast and/or too intricate to be economically apprehended (Cimpian and Salomon 2014). As a theoretical entity, however, content is an inevitable cognitive illusion arising from the heuristic nature of intentional cognition and the neglect-structure of human metacognition. From an evolutionary standpoint, it would be miraculous to suppose we simply developed the metacognitive channels required to apprehend the deep nature of about-talk and the systems employing it. We should expect to find ourselves in the dark, a darkness, moreover, that we cannot cognise as dark. And lo, strip away the mountain of speculative disputation and you find 'aboutness' is nothing if not an intuitively inexplicable correlation – which is to say, all that our ancestors required to pursue and repair communication as far as their lives and deaths were concerned.

Much as heuristic misfires possess systematic consequences (optical illusions) in visual cognition, they possess systematic consequences in intentional cognition as well, deliberative counterparts. But where optical illusions can be readily recognised by visual cognition, such is not the case with deliberative cognition. Having never ancestrally encountered the kinds of deliberative 'bugs' arising from philosophical reflection, we had no decisive way of recognising them as such. Without such recognition, the manifest structure of the resulting illusions betokened profound, abstract truths. This means humanity was doomed to suffer automatic, systematic self-deception the instant it began tasking reflection with the solution of theoretical problems.

Once again, it's worth noting here that *every* theory of meaning, insofar as it contradicts every other theory, agrees with me so far as 'systematic self-deception' is concerned.[22] The difference is that I have a naturalistic explanation why, one allowing for a more empirically informed, and therefore more judicious, application of our theoretically picayune metacognitive capacities.

On the Death of Meaning

To say that meaning-talk is ecological is to say that it, like all biological phenomena, depends on certain kinds of environments. Degrade the ecology of meaning-talk, and you compromise the efficacy of that talk. In this sense, the heuristic account of meaning allows us to overcome what has to be the most pernicious illusion falling out of exceptionalism: the assurance that thought somehow stands outside the possibility of global environmental collapse. We grant the impact of changing ecologies on our ability to eat and breathe, but not on our ability to talk or think. And as a result, we are only beginning to appreciate the ways deep environmental cognition, let alone cognitive technologies, are systematically undermining the reliability of human social cognition. If the foregoing account is correct, then it is likely we stand upon the brink of what might be called a 'semantic apocalypse' (Bakker 2016).

Intentional cognition turns on shallow information environments basically structured by the ancestral success of the cooperation engendered. Not only does it ignore 'deep information', it ignores this ignorance, sealing it all away for science to plumb. This makes shallow information environments impossible to intuit as shallow or specialised. As a result, we presume the applicability of intentional cognition to the theoretical problem of intentional cognition, we presume that shallow information environments can provide deep, as opposed to merely correlational, answers. We think that a system adapted to avoid what is going on can tell us what is going on. And despite millennia of perpetual underdetermination, we persist.

'Meaning' is a shallow information device, a way to cognise and coordinate behaviour without any inkling of the natures responsible. There is, quite literally, no such thing. When we go to a poetry reading, we have no access to the vast systems, historical and ongoing, distal and proximal, underwriting our ability to understand what is being said. We just 'get it'. Since poetry typically tests the boundaries of 'getting it', we periodically lean into our companion's shoulder and ask, 'What did she mean by that?' Our companion either shrugs or offers a less challenging iteration of what she said, something we are more likely to 'get'. Despite having no access to the actual systems responsible, in other words, we can nevertheless troubleshoot those systems via meaning-talk.

And since poetry is a systematic behaviour, we can likewise ask our companion to describe the systematicity experienced, to break the performance down into manifest (shallow) features, or to plug it into various manifest backgrounds. She can describe the form and the provenance of the poetic performance. Despite the superficiality of our access, regularities abound, insofar as that access remains anchored to the biological systems churning behind the scenes. Literary experience may be shallow, radically ecological, but, as Aristotle demonstrates, it admits systematic description nonetheless.

Once curiosity prompts us to ask deep information questions regarding the nature of these manifest regularities, however, all we have is our experience, which is to say, channels and capacities adapted to the practical resolution of communicative problems. We can sort out certain confusions, but what are we sorting? We can identify patterns readily enough, but patterns of what? When it comes to our interpretations and taxonomies, just what are we 'getting'? Since the limited nature of those channels and capacities appears nowhere in that experience, we remain oblivious to their misapplication. Presuming their sufficiency, we undertake grand attempts to explain communicative cognition using woefully inadequate resources. Literary theory is born. And so our answers begin to proliferate, each as radically underdetermined as the other. No matter how hard we try, our apparently self-evident phenomenon, meaning, frustrates our every attempt at formulation, let alone explanation – to the point where we embrace deflationary and differential theorisations.[23] Our poetry reading suddenly begins to seem essentially mysterious (rather than astronomically complex), or even worse, ontologically exceptional, something antithetical to empirical investigation.

We can draw a distinction, then, between meaning-talk as a shallow information device, which is very real, very efficacious (despite the absence of any stable referent for 'meaning'), and 'meaning' as a shallow information artefact, the impenetrable figment of philosophical imagination. In this sense one can speak of meaning dying two deaths, both profound, but by no means equal. We can speak of an apocalypse of our second-order speculative traditions regarding the fundamental nature of meaning, and an apocalypse of meaning-talk itself, the collapse of our ability to solve social problems using the heuristic machinery of intentional cognition. Where the first, theoretical death amounts to a cultural upheaval on a par with, say, Darwin's theory of evolution, the second death amounts to a profound biological upheaval, a transformation of cognitive habitat more catastrophic, I think, than humanity has ever experienced.

'Theoretical meaning', then, simply refers to the endless theories of intentionality humanity has heaped on the question of the human – pretty much the sum of traditional philosophical thought on the nature of humanity. And this form of meaning, I think, is pretty clearly doomed. We began by taking stock of the out-and-out industrial scale of the cognitive scientific enterprise. People forget that every single cognitive scientific fact revealed amounts to a feature of human nature that human nature is prone to neglect. We are, once again, intuitively blind to what we are and what we do. Like traditional theoretical claims belonging to other domains, all traditional theoretical claims regarding the human neglect the deep information driving scientific interpretations. The question is one of what this deep, naturally neglected information means. What, for instance, does the mere existence of a chapter like this in a volume like this portend?[24]

If one grants that the sum of cognitive scientific discovery is relevant to all senses of the human, you could safely say the traditional humanities are already dwelling in a twilight of denial. As we saw above, the traditionalist's strategy is to subdivide the domain, to adduce a priori arguments (often transcendental) and examples that seem to circumscribe the humanistic relevance of deep information. As a way of solving one another without deep information, intentional cognition, not surprisingly, is consistently 'crashed' by the provision of deep information.[25] Mechanical cognition is unable to solve intentional problem ecologies for much the same reason: not only did we evolve to solve one another via intentional cognition, we also evolved to be so solved (Zadwidzki 2013). Characterising this difference in heuristic applicability in a priori terms, as the tradition does, transforms what are mere ecological incompatibilities into formal and ontological chasms, licensing faulty intuitions of fundamental 'irreducibility', 'autonomy', and so forth. Heuristic neglect renders such discursive extravagances superfluous.

But the larger problem with this subdivision strategy is that it completely misconstrues the challenge posed by mediocrity. The traditional humanities, as cognitive disciplines, fall under the purview of the cognitive sciences. One can concede that various aspects of humanity need not account for deep information, yet still insist that all our theoretical cognition of those aspects does.

And quite obviously so. The question, 'To what degree should we trust reflection upon experience?' is a scientific question. Just for example, what kind of metacognitive capacities would be required to abstract 'conditions of possibility' from experience? Likewise, what kind of metacognitive capacities would be required to generate veridical descriptions of phenomenal experience? Answers to these kinds of questions bear powerfully on the viability of traditional semantic modes of theorising the human. On the worst-case scenario, the answers to these and other related questions will systematically discredit all forms of 'philosophical reflection' that fail to take account of the heuristic nature of human metacognition, as well as the resulting forms of neglect. The mounting deluge of deep, naturally neglected information, in other words, almost certainly means that traditional theoretical meaning is dead.[26]

'Practical meaning', on the other hand, refers to the everyday functionality of our intentional idioms, the ways we use terms like 'means' to solve a wide variety of practical, communicative problems. This form of meaning lives on, and will continue to do so, only with ever-diminishing degrees of efficacy. Our everyday intentional idioms function effortlessly and reliably in a wide variety of socio-communicative contexts despite systematically neglecting everything cognitive science has revealed. As shallow information devices, they provide solutions despite the scarcity of data.

They are heuristic, part of a cognitive system that relies on certain environmental invariants to solve what would otherwise be intractable problems. They possess adaptive ecologies. At present, we quite simply could not cope if we were to rely on deep information, say, to navigate social environments. Luckily, we do not have to, at least when it comes to a wide variety of social problems. So long as human brains possess the same structure and capacities, the brain can quite literally ignore the brain when solving problems involving other brains. It can leap to conclusions without any natural information regarding what actually happens to be going on.

But once again, with great problem-solving economy comes great problem-making potential. Heuristics are ecological: they require that different environmental features remain invariant. Some insects, most famously moths, use 'transverse orientation', flying at a fixed angle to the moon to navigate. Veranda lights famously miscue this heuristic mechanism, causing the insect to chase the angle into the light. The transformation of environments, in other words, has cognitive consequences, depending on the kind of short cut at issue. Heuristic efficiency means dynamic vulnerability.

And this means not only that heuristics can be short-circuited, but that they can also be hacked. Think of the once omnipresent electronic insect killer. Or consider reed warblers, which provide one of the most dramatic examples of heuristic vulnerability nature has to offer. The system they use to recognise eggs and offspring is so low resolution (and therefore economical) that cuckoos regularly parasitise their nests, leaving what are, to human eyes, obviously oversized eggs and (brood-killing) chicks that the warbler dutifully nurses to adulthood.

All heuristic systems, insofar as they are bounded, possess what might be called a 'crash space' describing all the possible ways they are prone to break down (as in the case of veranda lights and moths), as well as an overlapping 'cheat space' describing all the possible ways they can be exploited by competitors (as in the case of reed warblers and cuckoos, or moths and insect killers). The death of practical meaning refers to the growing incapacity of intentional idioms to reliably solve various social problems in radically transformed socio-cognitive habitats. Even as we speak, our environments are becoming more 'intelligent', more prone to cue intentional intuitions in circumstances that quite obviously do not warrant them. We will, very shortly, be surrounded by countless 'pseudo-agents', systems devoted to hacking our behaviour – exploiting the cheat space corresponding to our heuristic limits – via, you guessed it, deep, naturally neglected information. Combined with intelligent technologies, the informational dividends of cognitive science have transformed consumer hacking into a vast research programme. Our social environments are transforming, our native communicative habitat is being destroyed, stranding us with tools that will increasingly let us down.

Where the provision of deep, naturally neglected information itself delegitimises traditional theoretical accounts of meaning (by revealing the limits of reflection), it renders practical problem-solving via intentional idioms (practical meaning) progressively more ineffective by enabling the industrial-commercial exploitation of cheat space. Given the open-ended, hegemonic nature of both science and capitalism, this means that meaning is very probably doomed, both as a second-order research programme and, more alarmingly, as a first-order practical problem-solver. Only by seeing through the ancient illusions of meaning can we glimpse the present and future peril confronting intentional cognition. This – this is the world that the reader, the consumer of meaning, now finds themselves writing in as well as writing *to*. What does it mean to produce 'content' in such a world? What does it mean to read literature after the death of meaning?[27]

The Abductive Challenge

Necessary conditions. This is how the old, exceptionalist me would have responded to the explanatory gestalt sketched here. Wearing my old hermeneutic hat, I would have insisted on the ontological priority of lived life over the merely ontic sciences, conveniently overlooking my utter inability to make any of my ontological interpretations stick. Wearing my old deconstructive hat, I would have gamed theoretical underdetermination to 'demonstrate' how every attempt to overcome representationalism finds itself necessarily reinscribed within representationalism. Wearing my pragmatic hat, I would have ceded ontological priority to the sciences while insisting on the conceptual priority of the normative, conveniently overlooking my utter inability to make any of my normative interpretations stick. If these problems were raised, I would have shrugged, insisting that they were features, not bugs, evincing the exceptional nature of human meaning.

But the warrant here is abductive. A general theory of meaning should explain – or conversely, explain away – the manifest properties of meaning. It should also make plain the natural origins of meaning, how human culture arose from biological nature. And in the course of illuminating the ecological conditions of meaning, a general theory should provide ways to understand the future of meaning, given the systematic transformation of those ecologies.

Using only the explanatory resources of biology, heuristic neglect provides a plausible explanatory framework for the features, provenance, and potential fate of human meaning. Exceptionalism, on the other hand, brackets biology, insisting on intentional orders and ontologies somehow independent of and/or prior to nature. Since meaning amounts to an exception to nature, exceptionalism has no way of explaining how meaning belongs to nature, how it turns on brain function, let alone how it arose in the course of human evolution. It strands us, moreover, with the countless conundrums and dichotomies freighting our intellectual past. And since exceptionalism cannot tell us what meaning is, it cannot tell us the future of meaning, save fostering the illusion that it is somehow fundamentally exempt from the mad transformations presently embroiling us all.

I think almost everyone recognises that something profound is afoot, something that makes hash of traditional assumptions. For all we know, the semantic vertigo occasioning terms like 'post-truth' betokens a more fundamental collapse. Cognitive scientific knowledge floods our ancestral cognitive ecologies, cuing our intuitions in unprecedented ways, generating unprecedented outcomes. The AI revolution is well under way, and with it the proliferation of counterfeit agencies, machines designed to game our social reflexes. Biology has become technology. The accelerating overthrow of cognitive habitats has already begun. Should we just trust in ancient disputation?

Or do we take a long, hard look at the worst-case scenario?

Notes

1. According to US Department of Health and Human Services 2018, this includes, in addition to the neurosciences proper, research into Basic Behavioural and Social Science ($8.597 billion), Behavioural and Social Science ($22.515 billion), Brain Disorders (£23.702 billion), Mental Health ($13.699 billion), and Neurodegenerative ($10.183 billion).
2. *Neuropath* (Bakker 2009) is the novel that most obviously tracks the issues here, but my fantasy novels are also structured about the problem of meaning.
3. The University of Chicago's Idealism Project 2017, which attempts to legitimate the cognitive status of humanistic inquiry, epitomises the straits of traditional approaches to meaning and value, 'wagering', as they do, that idealist philosophies actually secure certain strands of humanistic discourse 'as a distinct and autonomous form of knowledge'. The presumption that heaping more guesswork upon existing guesswork somehow transforms that guesswork into something more akin to knowledge is as old as philosophy, and every bit as futile.
4. Thus, the infamous 'demarcation problem', the perpetual controversy surrounding attempts to distinguish genuine scientific cognition from other kinds of theoretical claims. The presumption here is that there is a striking cognitive difference between scientific claims and extra-scientific theoretical claims. But even if one denies this presumption (at the cost of understanding the boggling power of the former), the question of whether traditional humanistic discourses have any hope of surviving the cognitive scientific tsunami remains.
5. The distinction between intentional and natural cognition is not merely a philosophical assertion, but a matter of established scientific fact. Developmental research shows that infants begin exhibiting distinct physical versus psychological cognitive capacities within the first year of life. Research into Asperger Syndrome and Autism Spectrum

Disorder (Binnie and Williams 2003) consistently reveals a cleavage between intuitive social cognitive capacities, 'theory-of-mind' or 'folk psychology', and intuitive mechanical cognitive capacities, or 'folk physics'. Intuitive social cognitive capacities demonstrate significant heritability (Ebstein et al. 2010; Scourfield et al. 1999) in twin and family studies. Adults suffering Williams Syndrome (a genetic developmental disorder affecting spatial cognition) demonstrate profound impairments on intuitive physics tasks, but not intuitive psychology tasks (Kamps et al. 2017).

6. A priori speculative assertions of the identity of the intentional and the natural in no way obviate the problem of explaining the nature of experience and cognition. The only monism that offers proof against the claims of mediocrity is a monism that is mediocre, which is to say, explains away what cannot be naturalised. Spinozisms, normativisms, and so on offer the tradition no refuge, as I think the development of cognitive science will amply demonstrate. So far as they use intentional terms as basic, unexplained explainers, they are exceptionalisms.

7. Even if my position denies the existence of intentional phenomena, it does not deny the ability of intentional cognition to usefully organise our understanding of literature. It is entirely possible to adopt Aristotelian analyses of compositional and receptive structures, for instance, without committing to any intentional metaphysics. Giving up on meaning does not mean giving up on plot, metaphor, irony, tension, etc., only on the endless parade of intentional theorisations attached to them. The quickest way to beg the question against mediocrity is presume that applications of intentional cognition entail at least one of the thousands of intentional explications given of them. This way we can come to see the abiding technical relevance of *On Poetics* in a light similar to the abiding relevance of, say, Euclid's *Elements*. We can preserve the tools of intentional cognition, apply them where they do real work, while jettisoning our endless intentional explanations of those tools.

8. This is a theme I explore in the novel *Neuropath* (Bakker 2009), the way the technological transformations of our environments are settling/obviating any number of ancient, abstract disputes in real life.

9. See William Ramsey's account of the incoherence charge (Ramsey 2013), or Stephen Turner's account of the 'tu quoque' strategy (Turner 2010). Despite the superficial appeal of such strategies, there can be little doubt that they beg the question, presuming, as they do, that any instance of meaning talk presupposes intentionalism.

10. See Gigerenzer, Todd, and the ABC Research Group 1999, or more concisely, Todd and Gigerenzer 2012: 3–30.

11. According to Greenemeier 2009. All estimates regarding the processing power of the brain are hypothetical – the computational analogy itself is suspect – and it is worth noting that the historical trend has been to continually revise these numbers upward. One finds it widely reported that the human brain operates at the 'exascale' (see Gillespie 2017), or around a billion billion operations per second. But recent evidence of dendritic computation has led some experts to suggest the human brain could be a hundred times more powerful than this – while consuming about the same amount of energy as your refrigerator lightbulb, no less. See Gordon 2017.

12. As one might expect, the question of semantic information is every bit as confounding as the question of meaning more generally. In the present context, 'information' is always understood in the non-semantic sense, namely as systematic difference making differences, which is to say, mechanically. Causality, of course, remains an unexplained

13. This is why we often find breakdowns in human communicative cognition so perplexing, if not outright threatening: the resulting behaviours represent instances where only mechanical cognition applies. In 'Mechanism and Responsibility', Dennett speaks of this process as one wherein the effectiveness of the intentional stance is progressively degraded as the reach of the physical stance extends into more and more domains of human interaction (Dennett 1978: 233–55). He also discusses it under the rubric of 'creeping exculpation' in *Freedom Evolves* (Dennett 2004: 288–308). Despite the residual traditionalism intrinsic in his notion of the intentional stance, he is one of few thinkers to engage this profoundly important topic – especially now, in the age of AI.
14. Though the problem of intentionality has been widely recognised as part and parcel of the so-called hard problem of consciousness, the 'hard problem of content' has only recently found currency, largely due to Dan Hutto and Erik Myin (Hutto and Myin 2013).
15. See Carruthers 2009: 1–65 for a comprehensive (if now somewhat dated) review of the research.
16. The classic expression of this is found in Plato's *Theaetetus*: 'By the gods, Socrates, I am lost in wonder when I think of all these things, and sometimes when I regard them it really makes my head swim' (Plato 1921: 155d).
17. Acronym coined by Nobel Laureate Daniel Kahneman (Kahneman 2011). See Bakker 2017b.
18. As Aristotle himself was aware, philosophy begins where practical concerns end. Discussing the pursuit of philosophy as the pursuit of knowledge for its own sake, he writes, 'The actual course of events bears witness to this; for speculation of this kind began with a view to recreation and pastime, at a time when practically all the necessities of life were already supplied' (Aristotle 1989: 928b).
19. Not entirely, of course, as ancient Academic and Pyrrhonian scepticism attest.
20. Although Plato gets things backwards, confusing, as he does, the metacognitive neglect described here with the lack of 'chains and fetters'.
21. Embodiment, of course, is central to post-cognitivist approaches to cognition and meaning. The cardinal mistake these approaches make, on the Heuristic Neglect Theory, is presuming that a subset of intentional tools, namely those specifically involved in normative cognition, can somehow achieve what traditional semantic tools cannot. The fact that the field suffers all the same problems of underdetermination as the semantic tradition strongly suggests that it inherits the same basic shortcomings. Far from circumventing traditional conundrums, it simply repeats them in novel guises.
22. The eclecticism of many literary theorists cuts against this point, I realise. But the fact that a theorist may apply, say, pragmatic, deconstructive, hermeneutic, structuralist, and psychoanalytic approaches in the course of reading a text does nothing to allay the profound theoretical disagreements between those approaches.
23. As I have myself over the years, deconstruction most notably. See Bakker 2017b for a naturalistic appraisal of Derridean approaches to the problem of meaning.
24. As a synthetic theory, like evolution, my position's warrant is crucially abductive, turning on the degree to which it unifies complicated sets of phenomena as a 'best explanation'. In more substantive empirical terms, it suggests that certain 'neglect effects' will occur in

predictable ways. It also predicts that human metacognitive capacities will turn out to be fractionate and heuristically specialised.

25. This problem applies to all the myriad varieties of intentional cognition but is nowhere more obvious than in the intractable problem of free will. My short story 'Crash Space' (Bakker 2015: 186–204) explores the way in which deep information, and the kinds of technological interventions it enables, absolutely scuttles our ability to make sense of 'freedom'.

26. To gain a sense of what this entails, one need only consider Jerry Fodor:

> if commonsense intentional psychology really were to collapse, that would be, beyond comparison, the greatest intellectual catastrophe in the history of our species; if we're that wrong about the mind, then that's the wrongest we've ever been about anything. The collapse of the supernatural, for example, didn't compare; theism never came close to being as intimately involved in our thought and practice – especially our practice – as belief/desire explanation is. (Fodor 1987: vii)

27. See Bakker 2017d: 21–5 for a speculative look at the forms future literatures might take.

Bibliography

Aristotle (1989), *Metaphysics*, 2 vols, Hugh Tredennick (trans.), Cambridge, MA: Harvard University Press.

Bakker, R. Scott (2009), *Neuropath*, New York: Tor.

Bakker, R. Scott (2014), 'Back to Square One: Toward a Post-Intentional Future', *Scientia Salon*, 5 November, <https://scientiasalon.wordpress.com/2014/11/05/back-to-square-one-toward-a-post-intentional-future/> (last accessed 30 September 2017).

Bakker, R. Scott (2015), 'Crash Space', *Midwest Studies in Philosophy*, 39, pp. 186–204.

Bakker, R. Scott (2016), 'Visions of the Semantic Apocalypse: A Critical Review of Yuval Noah Harari's *Homo Deus*', *Three Pound Brain*, 20 October, <https://rsbakker.wordpress.com/2016/10/20/visions-of-the-semantic-apocalypse-a-critical-review-of-yuval-noah-hararis-homo-deus/> (last accessed 20 September 2017).

Bakker, R. Scott (2017a), 'From Scripture to Fantasy: Adrian Johnston and the Problem of Continental Fundamentalism', *Cosmos and History: The Journal of Natural and Social Philosophy*, 13:1, pp. 522–51.

Bakker, R. Scott (2017b), 'Reactionary Atheism: Hagglund, Derrida, and Nooconservatism', *Three Pound Brain*, 25 January, <https://rsbakker.wordpress.com/2017/01/25/reactionary-atheism-hagglund-derrida-and-nooconservatism/> (last accessed 21 September 2017).

Bakker, R. Scott (2017c), 'On Alien Philosophy', *The Journal of Consciousness Studies*, 24:1/2, pp. 31–52.

Bakker, R. Scott (2017d), 'A Bestiary of Future Literatures', *The Liar*, 18, pp. 21–5.

Baranauskas, Gytas (2014), 'What Limits the Performance of Current Invasive Brain Machine Interfaces?', *Frontiers in Systems Neuroscience*, 29 April, <https://doi.org/10.3389/fnsys.2014.00068> (last accessed 18 September 2017).

Binnie, Lynne and Joanne Williams (2003), 'Intuitive Psychology and Physics Among Children with Autism and Typically Developing Children', *Autism*, 7:2, pp. 173–93.

Carruthers, Peter (2009), 'How We Know Our Own Minds: The Relationship Between Mind-Reading and Meta-Cognition', *Behavioral and Brain Sciences*, 32:2, pp. 1–65.

Chomsky, Noam (1959), 'A Review of B. F. Skinner's Verbal Behavior', *Language*, 35:1, pp. 26–58.

Cimpian, Andrei and Erika Salomon (2014), 'The Inherence Heuristic: An Intuitive Means of Making Sense of The World and a Potential Precursor to Psychological Essentialism', *Behavioral and Brain Sciences*, 37:5, pp. 461–2.

Dennett, Daniel (1978), 'Mechanism and Responsibility', in Daniel Dennett, *Brainstorms: Philosophical Essays on Mind and Psychology*, New York: Bradford, pp. 233–55.

Dennett, Daniel (2004), *Freedom Evolves*, New York: Penguin.

Ebstein, Richard P., Salomon Israel, Soo Hong Chew, Songfa Zhong, and Ariel Knafo (2010), 'Genetics of Human Social Behaviour', *Neuron*, 65, pp. 831–44.

Fleming, Roland W. (2012), 'Human Perception: Visual Heuristics in the Perception of Glossiness', *Current Biology*, 22:20, <http://www.cell.com/current-biology/fulltext/S0960-9822(12)00995-5> (last accessed 18 September 2017).

Fodor, Jerry (1987), *Psychosemantics: The Problem of Meaning in the Philosophy of Mind*, Cambridge, MA: MIT Press.

Gigerenzer, Gerd, Peter M. Todd, and the ABC Research Group (1999), *Simple Heuristics that Make Us Smart*, Oxford: Oxford University Press.

Gillespie, Matt (2017), 'Exascale Leaders on Next Horizons in Supercomputing', *The Next Platform*, 23 February, <https://www.nextplatform.com/2017/02/23/exascale-leaders-look-next-horizons-supercomputing/> (last accessed 18 September 2017).

Gordon, Dan (2017), 'Brain Is 10 Times More Active Than Previously Measured, UCLA Researchers Find', *UCLA Newsroom*, 9 March, <http://newsroom.ucla.edu/releases/ucla-research-upend-long-held-belief-about-how-neurons-communicate> (last accessed 18 September 2017).

Greenemeier, Larry (2009), 'Computers Have a Lot to Learn from the Human Brain, Engineers Say', *scientificamerican.com*, 10 March, <http://www.scientificamerican.com/blog/post.cfm?id=computers-have-a-lot-to-learn-from-2009-03-10> (last accessed 18 September 2017).

Hartmann, Franz (1890), *Magic, White and Black, or The Science of Finate and Infinite Life, Containing Practical Hints for Students of Occultism*, 4th (American) edn, New York: John W. Lovell.

Hutto, Daniel D. and Erik Myin (2013), *Radicalizing Enactivism: Basic Minds without Content*, Cambridge, MA: MIT Press.

Idealism Project (2017), <http://neubauercollegium.uchicago.edu/faculty/idealism_project/> (last accessed 28 April 2018).

Kahneman, Daniel (2011), *Thinking, Fast and Slow*, Toronto: Doubleday Canada.

Kamps, Frederik S., Joshua B. Julian, Peter Battaglia, Barbara Landau, Nancy Kanwisher, and Daniel D. Dilks (2017), 'Dissociating Intuitive Physics from Intuitive Psychology: Evidence from Williams Syndrome', *Cognition*, 168, pp. 146–53.

Plato (1921), *Theaetetus, Sophist*, Harold North Fowler (trans.), Cambridge, MA: Harvard University Press.

Ramsey, William (2013), 'Eliminative Materialism', in Edward N. Zalta (ed.), *The Stanford Encyclopedia of Philosophy*, 16 April, <https://plato.stanford.edu/entries/materialism-eliminative/> (last accessed 28 April 2018).

Scourfield, Jane, Neilson Martin, Glyn Lewis, and Peter McGuffin (1999), 'Heritability of Social Cognitive Skills in Children and Adolescents', *British Journal of Psychiatry*, 175:6, pp. 559–64.

Todd, Peter M. and Gerd Gigerenzer (2012), 'What Is Ecological Rationality?', in Peter M. Todd and Gerd Gigerenzer (eds), *Ecological Rationality: Intelligence in the World*, Oxford: Oxford University Press, pp. 3–30.

Turner, Stephen (2010), *Explaining the Normative*, Cambridge: Polity.

US Department of Health and Human Services (2018), 'Estimates of Funding for Various Research, Condition, and Disease Categories', 18 May, <https://report.nih.gov/categorical_spending.aspx> (last accessed 28 November 2018).

Wimsatt, William C. (2007), *Re-Engineering Philosophy for Limited Beings: Piecewise Approximations to Reality*, Cambridge, MA: Harvard University Press.

Woolf, Virginia (1941), *Between the Acts*, New York: Harcourt, Brace.

Zawidzki, Tad (2009), 'Theory of Mind, Computational Intractability, and Mind Shaping', in *Proceedings of the 9th Workshop on Performance Metrics for Intelligent Systems*, New York: ACM, pp. 149–54.

Zawidzki, Tad (2013), *Mindshaping: A New Framework for Understanding Human Social Cognition*, Cambridge, MA: MIT Press.

PART III

Beyond the Object: Reading Literature through Actor-Network Theory, Object-Oriented Philosophy, and the New Materialisms

Editor's Introduction

Ridvan Askin

In some respect, this section constitutes the counterpart to the previous section. Where the last four chapters were concerned with ways of theorising the human subject in relation to or even as the post- or outright nonhuman, the chapters in this section zoom further in on the nonhuman aspect of the equation. Where the chapters of the previous section aimed, in different ways, to go beyond the subject, the chapters of this section correspondingly explore various ways of capturing the beyond of its correlate, the object. Importantly, and as in the previous section, such exploration includes the very questioning of the supposed correlation of subject and object itself.

A number of approaches to this effect have been proposed over the last couple of decades with actor-network theory, object-oriented philosophy, and the new materialisms not just gaining traction in but often even being developed in tandem with literary studies. Thus, Bruno Latour has had recourse both to literary texts and to literary theory in devising his actor-network theory, particularly in constructing some of his most important concepts such as, indeed, actor and network. This might explain to some extent why Latour has been a favourite of theoretically inclined literary scholars in recent times. As to object-oriented philosophy, one of its most vocal practitioners, Timothy Morton, is actually a literary scholar by profession, and its originator, Graham Harman, has repeatedly discussed a variety of literary works and devices such as metaphor in elucidating his programme, devoting book-length studies to Dante's *Divine Comedy* and H. P. Lovecraft's weird fiction. Similarly, though the new materialisms originate in the context of feminist political theory, several well-known new materialists, such as Jane Bennett, Stacy Alaimo, and Elizabeth Grosz, time and again engage with and build on works of literature in their theorisations and are appointed or cross-appointed at literature departments.

While all these approaches share the general impetus of going beyond traditional understandings of the object, they differ significantly in their specifics. Originally devised as a means better to describe social relations, Latour's actor-network theory, which signals its break with the tradition already in its name – instead of subjects and objects, we have actors forming networks – provides us with a fully fledged de-hierarchised relational ontology. In this ontology everything from ideas to electrons to planets to affects to human individuals to nonhuman animals to literary works is located on the same level, actors entering, forming, changing, and dissolving ever-mutating situational networks.

In contrast, Harman's object-oriented philosophy gives us a radically non-relational ontology of a multiplicity of individual entities for which Harman retains the notion of object. But Harmanian objects no longer correlate with human subjects as they are emphatically not the subject's intentional vis-à-vis. On the contrary, the human subject simply becomes another object next to myriad others. What Harman shares with Latour is a non-materialist ontology insofar as matter does not provide the ultimate ground to which everything else can be reduced. All the entities listed above as examples of Latourian actors would suit equally well as instances of Harmanian objects. The crucial difference concerns what Latour terms 'network'. Where for Latour actors are only actors insofar as they form and partake of networks – that is, for Latour, actors are always in relation to other actors – for Harman networks or relations are just another type of object. Harmanian objects may or may not enter into relations. The related objects would then only be related to the extent that they formed parts of a third object, the very relation in question. Latourian actors are fundamentally relational, Harmanian objects are self-contained, sealed-off entities.

The new materialisms, in turn, as the very term itself suggests, insist on a material substratum. One would be wrong to think that they are thus akin to analytic philosophy's eliminative materialism or physicalism, however, as they all posit what one might call a materialism with remainder. For the new materialisms, far from reducing subjectivity to nothing but inert matter, transpose it into matter itself: for the new materialists, matter is replete with a form of subjectivity or proto-subjectivity. Matter is animate, in the traditional sense of the word: endowed with life, breath, spirit. Everything that is shares in this life at the heart of matter. This is the sense in which Bennett speaks of thing-power and the vibrancy of matter, in which Karen Barad emphasises the very entanglement of matter and meaning, and in which Rosi Braidotti tirelessly insists on what she calls nomadic subjectivity. Instead of the traditional subject–object dyad, the new materialisms all posit a kind of living matter. And as the usage of terms like 'power', 'entanglement', and 'nomadic' suggests, this ontology of living matter is a relational ontology in which living matter constitutes the all-connecting matrix from which everything springs. Essentially, the new materialisms are twenty-first-century vitalisms.

The chapters in this section all elucidate ways in which these fundamental theories are taken up fruitfully for the study of literature or, conversely, how the study of literature might help understand or even elaborate on the very theories in question. The section begins with Babette B. Tischleder's chapter, in which she traces Latour's indebtedness to literary studies. Focusing on Latour's revision of his actor-network theory in light of his recent turn to the figure of Gaia, Tischleder first elucidates Latour's reliance on semiotics and narratology for his conceptual toolbox in order to then elaborate a proper notion of what she terms literary agency, enlisting insightful close readings of passages from Mark Twain's *Life on the Mississippi* and William Faulkner's essay 'Mississippi' along the way. Like Latour in his turn to Gaia, Tischleder is particularly interested in the Anthropocene moment. What kind of agency, she asks, is literature able to assume in the Anthropocene? In doing so, she both gives us a robust account of the (possible) intersections of Latourian actor-network theory and literature and foreshadows the discussions of literature in the Anthropocene in Part V.

In the second chapter of this section, Graham Harman shows us what an object-oriented literary formalism looks like. Given the brief account of object-oriented philosophy above, it should not come as a surprise that Harman favours some kind of formalism: literary formalisms, after all, usually insist on the autonomy of literary works; that is, they take literary works to be self-contained forms. This, indeed, seems to chime well with the ontology of self-contained entities that object-oriented philosophy posits. It might thus surprise some readers to see that Harman rejects any strong account of the autonomy of the work of art. For Harman, a work of art is only a work of art in relation to the human. The form that an object-oriented literary formalism has to scrutinise, then, is the form this relation takes. The object of scrutiny is the work of art plus its reception, not just the work considered in a vacuum. In the parlance of literary studies, one could say that Harman's object-oriented formalism is a formalism with a built-in reader response theory. Harman uses the varied reception of Harriet Beecher Stowe's *Uncle Tom's Cabin*, zooming in on the contrasting views of James Baldwin and Jane P. Tompkins, to make his point.

Helen Palmer's wide-ranging and playful third chapter gives us a new materialist reading of speculative fiction, particularly recent Afrofuturist literature. Palmer first establishes what, with recourse to Martin Heidegger, Donna Haraway, and Karen Barad, she calls literature's power of wor(l)ding. Like Tischleder, Palmer is interested in the shaping powers of literature. Where Tischleder draws on Latour's own borrowings from literary studies to make her case, Palmer enlists Haraway's and Barad's insistence on the fundamental entanglement of the material and the discursive or semiotic. In addition, Palmer sees literature's shaping powers most fully on display in speculative forms of storytelling with their futural projections of worlds yet to come. Moreover, the most creative – in every sense of the word – projections, she insists, are often to be found in communities that lack a proper world of their own, that is, communities of the oppressed and disenfranchised – hence Palmer's combination of feminist onto-epistemologies and Afrofuturist literary texts. Importantly, this combination is not just a matter of applying a particular theory to a particular body of literary works. Rather, Palmer is keen on emphasising the theoretical quality of Afrofuturist art and literature and, conversely, the literary-artistic, creative quality embodied in the speculative gesture of the theories she enlists. Ultimately, both kinds of writings can be seen as forms of fictocriticism or fictophilosophy.

In the final chapter of this section, Ridvan Askin revisits Ralph Waldo Emerson's literary essays in order to showcase the contiguity of the recent speculative and new materialist turns with the romanticism of Emerson's transcendentalism. Indeed,

Askin holds that the current materialisms with remainder and large swathes of speculative realism are but reformulations of the romantics' attempt to fuse the ideal with the real and material. In this vein, Askin maintains that twenty-first-century speculative realism is but a continuation of nineteenth-century speculative idealism and that the new materialisms might just as well have been termed the new idealisms.

All chapters in this section explore alternatives to the object side of the traditional subject–object dyad, whether in terms of actors and networks, objects all the way down, or meaning-imbued and vibrant matter; and they all scrutinise how these alternatives play out in, as, or in tandem with the many forms of literature.

9

Neither Billiard Ball nor Planet B: Latour's Gaia, Literary Agency, and the Challenge of Writing Geohistory in the Anthropocene Moment

Babette B. Tischleder

In 'On Not Joining the Dots', a lecture given at Harvard in 2016, Bruno Latour talked about his concern with Gaia, the figure that has become central to his current engagement with political ecology and what he considers the collective task of responding to the challenges of global warming and climate change. Introducing his own take on planet earth, Latour invokes the modern image of the globe seen from space, only to cast it aside as an impossible view from 'nowhere'. Forming a globe's round shape with his hands, he points out that it has the size of a pumpkin, thus mocking the concepts of the globe and 'the global' as figures of thought: the place we earthbound inhabit 'is not a pumpkin' (Latour 2016a). The way we have imagined our terrestrial planet since Galileo is turned into an object of ridicule, and this mockery constitutes a typical Latourian strategy of challenging this long-standing 'scientific' conviction: 'If the Inquisition was shocked by the announcement that the Earth was nothing more than a billiard ball turning endlessly in the vast universe', he writes in his latest book, 'the new Inquisition (henceforth economic rather than religious) is shocked to learn that the Earth has become – has become again! – an active, local, limited, sensitive, fragile, trembling, and easily irritated envelope' (Latour 2017b: 60). Gaia, then, is Latour's proposal for imagining, in self-consciously mythological fashion, the 'sublunary' place we share with many other living beings.

As a major proponent of actor-network theory (ANT), Latour has inspired us to see both people and things as parts of larger networks of human and nonhuman actants; and the range of agencies that interact with one another have included everything from public transport systems to maritime habitats, from the bacteria active in our bodies to the growing levels of carbon dioxide in the atmosphere. In recent years, though, Latour has moved away from ANT 'proper', with its equal (or symmetrical) treatment of heterogeneous agencies, both human and nonhuman, inanimate objects and living creatures, to focus on the figure of Gaia. This current interest was the topic of the Gifford lectures he delivered at the University of Edinburgh in 2013, which were published in expanded form as *Facing Gaia: Eight Lectures on the New Climatic Regime* in 2017. Latour has shifted his attention from different kinds of networked assemblages to the particularities of the sublunary place that animate and inanimate beings share. The Gaia project, like his previous work, is dedicated to challenging modern worldviews, particularly our anthropocentric concepts of human agency, as they continue to inform our common epistemologies and ill-equipped 'strategies' of facing, much less dealing with, the far-reaching consequences of anthropogenic activities that have left none of the earth's ecosystems untouched.

In this chapter, I trace Latour's revision of ANT through this planetary figure, a figure that is secular rather than theological, and that serves him to think through our present moment of environmental crisis. The critical terms Latour brings to the cross-disciplinary debates on global warming, the 'new climate regime', and the Anthropocene still rely, as I will argue, on an approach informed by semiotic and narratological models. These models are helpful in conceptualising his notion of distributed agency, but they are rather limited in their ability to grasp the ways in which literary texts themselves may become 'agents of worlding' and can convey worldly experiences in registers that extend beyond description (Citton 2016: 321). What I perceive as *literary agency* is constituted by the multiple modes in which novels, poetry, and nonfiction enlist readers in projecting and inhabiting the world in new ways, and they do so by organising our attentions, puzzling our perceptions, and inciting our affections. Literary agency, then, is a key concept for my understanding of the cultural work that literature affords, and it always keeps the reader in mind – the way readers actualise texts through their aesthetic sensibility and imaginative practice.[1]

How, then, do literary texts become agents of worlding? And how do they affect their readers by staging nonhuman agency? Let us consider a passage from William Faulkner's essay 'Mississippi', published in the literary magazine *Encounter* in 1954. In the introductory note, the editor writes that Faulkner's text constitutes an account of 'his home state' that is true in both a historical and an imaginary sense: he is

> writing about a Mississippi which exists in art as well as in fact. It is *his* Mississippi which he here describes, and if it is not quite identical with the geographer's or the historian's, it is certainly no less real, and is perhaps more so. (Faulkner 1954: 3)

It is difficult indeed, if not impossible, to distinguish the historian, the geographer, and the novelist in this essay, and 'realness' is conveyed less through a descriptive mode than by aesthetic means, particularly a syntactic style that marginalises the human, while, at the same time, relying on the reader's ability to fathom the mighty powers of the Mississippi River in times of flooding. Here's the situation living creatures found themselves in after the river had been 'piling up the waters' for days and 'removing', one by one, levees, sandbags, and other tools and machinery with which people tried in vain to keep the waters at bay, with the cotton fields and roads and 'towns themselves' having finally vanished in the flood:

> Vanished, gone beneath one vast yellow motionless expanse, out of which projected only the tops of trees and telephone poles and the decapitations of human dwelling-places like enigmatic objects placed by inscrutable and impenetrable design on a dirty mirror; and the mounds of the predecessors on which, among a tangle of moccasins, bear and horses and deer and mules and wild turkeys and cows and domestic chickens waited patient in mutual armistice; and the levees themselves, where among a jumble of uxorious flotsam the young continued to be born and the old to die, not from exposure but from simple and normal time and decay, as if man and his destiny were in the end stronger even than the river which had dispossessed him, inviolable by and invincible to alteration. (Faulkner 1954: 9)

Faulkner's narrative does not reference a specific date or place; but it is safe to assume that it was inspired by the Mississippi flood of 1927, when the levees gave way to the century's most devastating 'natural' disaster, and an area of 27,000 square miles was inundated, turning vast stretches of the Mississippi Delta into a sea.[2] Footage of this flood has captured the sight of a no-longer-discernible river that had swollen into a vast muddy expanse, covering human and natural habitats, rendering them unrecognisable. On film, too, roofs and steeples and other signs of the built environment peeking out of the dirty waters were, for nearly four months, the only visible remnants of the man-made landscape.[3]

Faulkner's rendering of the flood at its peak is significant for the way in which the past participles – 'vanished, gone' – at the outset of the long sentence organise all that follows: gone with the broken levees is a recognisable order of things: the excess of water has turned the landscape with its feeble tokens of human civilisation unreadable ('enigmatic', 'inscrutable'); the river no longer reflects human design, but has become a 'dirty mirror' expressive of ungovernable physical forces. But 'vanished' relates not only to the loss of the solid structures that once constituted a manufactured landscape; it is the subject of the sentence itself that has gone astray, lost somewhere in the preceding one. It leaves the reader with a convoluted, yet incomplete, subclause; its final period only marks, yet does not reach, closure. And the sentence arrays ('and ... and ... and'), yet does not organise, the haphazardly assembled sociality of wild and domestic animals in a snake-infested environment, making us wonder how they might negotiate their coexistence on the deserted mounds of a long-gone indigenous population. The scene, in spite of all the detail given, leaves much room for our imagination; moreover, it is easy to overlook that the sentence, which stretches over eighteen lines on the original magazine page, indeed has no subject. Much like the signs and strongholds of civilisation that have been swallowed by the water, the syntax itself seems to have dissolved in the run-on sentence, thus reflecting the state of limbo in the flooded landscape through a disoriented reading experience. The sentence comes to a halt in an upbeat fashion, suggesting that the cycle of life continues even under the direst circumstances, albeit adhering to a natural ('normal') course of affairs rather than to divine or human will. Hence the flood is not the Flood; it is neither punishment nor redemption, as Faulkner makes clear in the following passage, where 'the Old Man' recedes on his own accord, leaving the soil particularly fertile in its wake, as though it was saying, 'I do what I want to, when I want to. But I pay my way' (Faulkner 1954: 10). The river comes and goes, if so inclined, following neither scheme nor purpose other than its whims, thus making human agency utterly meaningless in a world turned topsy-turvy by perpetual rain.

Literary agency speaks to us through style, diction, and syntax. Focusing merely on narrative action, as Latour tends to do, risks overlooking what is expressed in the interstices of a text. Yet it is not my intention to suggest that subject matter and narrative (should) have no say in literary and philosophical worlding. The Mississippi River, and particularly the so-called Delta region of the American South, constitute the setting of Faulkner's fictional Yoknapatawpha County, a destination much travelled in the imagination of his readers, a region that, for Latour, also serves to exemplify the Anthropocene, a concept that reflects the measurable anthropogenic impact on the ecosystems and geological formations of planet earth more generally. The Mississippi allows Latour to focus on a particularly interesting 'geohistory'. The mighty river and an equally mighty human 'footprint' have characterised the Mississippi Delta ever since European settlers started exploiting its lumber, wildlife, and fertile alluvial soil in the eighteenth century, even before it became the centre of a plantation economy that relied on slave labour and was turned into a major infrastructure of the US American economy.

In the following pages, rather than asking how literary studies can benefit from a Latourian approach, I suggest that Latour's conceptualising of nonhuman agency and his project of rewriting our geohistory may benefit from literary practices that render the agency of writing and reading palpable and go beyond his rather technical approach to storytelling. Latour is an avid reader and never claimed authority as a literary scholar; yet he regularly enlists literary authors and characters for his reasoning, and he has dedicated an entire chapter of *An Inquiry into Modes of Existence* (2013) to the beings of fiction. These beings that are not restricted to fictional worlds, and their modes of existence allow us to generate creative ways of imagining the world, modes that prompt aesthetic registers for envisioning our coexistence with other beings in imaginative and 'alien' ways.[4]

Gaia as Worldly Figure: Lovelock and Beyond

Before engaging with some specific geo-agents that Latour brings into play, I will give an account of how Gaia has become the key figure around which his critical thinking on political ecology and 'the new climatic regime' revolves.[5] Latour has always called upon scholars in the social sciences and the humanities to reconsider the centrality of the human; he has challenged our cherished beliefs in human characters as movers and shakers of politics, technological 'progress', local and global economies. Despite a growing interest in the posthuman in critical theory and popular culture, and despite a perceptible apprehension of human obsolescence in various arenas of culture,[6] most cultural and historical narratives still cast human figures in the leading roles; their actions propel the stories forward, whether we consider novels, memoirs, films, serial television, or social media. Latour has never become tired of pointing out that agency does not originate in the competences, interests, or intentions of human beings alone, but that it is widely distributed across hybrid networks of human and nonhuman agencies. Accordingly, common distinctions such as those between nature and culture, the animate and the inanimate, subject and object, cannot hold, if we take seriously the multitude of actors and actants that partake in dynamic entanglements. If we follow Latour, bacteria and algae, rivers and storms, speed bumps and hydraulic brakes have powerful tendencies of their own.[7]

Literary scholars such as Rita Felski have turned to Latour and emphasised the usefulness of actor-network theory and his notion of attachment for literary inquiry, considering the ways in which these concepts can help rethink practices of interpretation and critique. While, in my own work, I have drawn on Latour's notion of nonhuman agency and the active participation of inanimate objects in the organisation of social and intimate relations, including the ways we fashion and imagine ourselves, this chapter offers a somewhat different angle in that it critically reflects the premises of Latour's thinking. I show how his recent focus on diverse modes of existence still retains some of the restrictions of a structuralist worldview due to its reliance on semiotic coordinates of analysis. Moreover, engaging with Latour's current work on Gaia, I will consider how the latter has come to serve him as a conceptual figure for apprehending the threat of imminent ecological collapse. For Latour, Gaia constitutes the critical matrix for reconfiguring our Anthropocene moment, a moment in which he urges us to see the abstractions of modern science for what they are – abstractions that keep us from facing the multiple troubles of a damaged planet. To Latour, the modern view of the earth from outer space, as Galileo had first imagined it in the seventeenth century, long before NASA provided the image of the blue planet, no longer constitutes an adequate way of imagining life on earth. A dead celestial body that keeps moving in its destined orbit, no matter what, is based on a 'cartographic' imagination – 'Cartesian coordinates' that map the planet in scalable mathematical fashion (Latour 2017b: 135), independent of the ways in which different forms of organic life and the planet's geochemical constitution have co-evolved and reciprocally sustain each other. This is why Latour, who draws on the writings of, among others, James Lovelock, Lynn Margulis, and Isabelle Stengers, considers our moment in geohistory a new challenge to much-cherished convictions: our habitat on earth, perceived as Gaia, has become an agent to be reckoned with, an envelope that is 'ticklish' and sensitive, no longer willing to abide indifferently the ways that humankind keeps messing with it.

Gaia and the Anthropocene Moment

But what kind of figure is Gaia exactly? Latour has approached this question from a number of different angles, and, as is often done with conceptual figures, by defining first what it is not: 'Gaia is not a God of Totality' (Latour 2017a), and Gaia is not Mother Earth: 'What is certain is that she is not a figure of harmony. There is nothing maternal about her' (Latour 2017b: 82). Moreover, Latour is critical of how 'the figure of a Globe' is invoked 'without paying the slightest attention to the way in which that Globe might be built, tended, maintained, and inhabited' (Latour 2017b: 123). Rather, he proposes a more 'earthbound' approach: 'the Earthbound [the term Latour prefers to Human] have to be able to map the territories on which they depend for their existence' – territories that are increasingly sensitive to our doings (Latour 2017b: 248, 38). In his view of Gaia, which he wants to be understood as a decidedly secular figure, Latour follows the lead of Lovelock's Gaia hypothesis, and engages with the criticisms the latter confronted. He does not simply adopt Lovelock's theory, which conceptualises our planet as a self-regulating system in which biological organisms and inorganic matter mutually sustain each other and thus generate the conditions that enable the continued existence of life on earth. Latour is critical of the notion that Gaia has a 'natural' tendency to maintain a balanced biosphere that makes the planet habitable, but he embraces the way Lovelock redirects our attention from the Galilean 'view from nowhere' to the 'sublunary world':

> While Galileo, raising his eyes from the horizon to the sky, reinforced the similarity between the Earth and all other bodies in free fall, Lovelock, lowering his eyes from Mars in our direction, in effect *diminished* the similarity between all the other planets and this so peculiar Earth that is ours. (Latour 2017b: 78)

Latour contrasts Lovelock's focus on the sublunary region with the Galilean view of physical bodies in space: the earth

> seems capable of actively maintaining a difference between its inside and its outside. It has something like a skin, an envelope. More oddly still, the blue planet suddenly looks like a long string of historical *events*, random, specific, and contingent events, as though it were the temporary, fragile result of a geohistory. It is as though, three and a half centuries later, Lovelock had taken into account certain features of that same Earth that Galileo *could not* take into account ... its color, its odor, its surface, its texture, its genesis, its aging, perhaps its death, this thin film within which we live, in short, its behavior, in addition to its movement ... Serres was right: to complete Galileo's Earth, which *moves*, it was necessary to add Lovelock's Earth, which *is moved*. (Latour 2017b: 78–9)

Lovelock's Gaia, then, is seen as a welcome shift away from the modernist abstraction of the globe in order to allow into view the mutable materiality of the sphere in which we actually live. 'To discover the new Earth', Latour writes, 'climatologists are again conjuring up the climate, and bringing back the animated Earth to a thin film whose fragility recalls the old feeling of living in what was once called the *sublunary zone*' (2017b: 60).[8] While latitudes and longitudes represent the 'objective' scalability of the globe, the envelope we inhabit can best be accounted for by its responsiveness to disturbances, its 'being corruptible' (2017b: 78). Latour's understanding of Gaia is, as Bruce Clarke suggests, analogous to

> the definition of an autopoietic system. In an autopoietic conception Gaia's planetary envelope results from the active maintenance of an operational boundary separating 'inside and outside', separating its sheer immunitary sphere of inhabitability and material viability from the abiotic complexities of its cosmic environment. (Clarke 2017: 11)

Clarke's assessment may sound as though Latour follows a Lovelockian conceptualisation of Gaia as a realm in which inorganic matter and living organisms sustain each other. Yet it is important to note that the autopoietic character is defined not by any kind of equilibrium maintained between inside and outside but by the very boundaries that circumscribe the animate world as sublunary. For its continued existence, life depends on the earth's atmosphere and the biophysical interactions and processes within this sphere. What Latour takes issue with, then, is the objectification and de-animation of our earth perpetuated by the image of the blue planet, a view that does not distinguish between its animate and abiotic 'spheres'.

The view from nowhere, which renders invisible the animate aspect of the terrestrial world, invites us to imagine earth as a solid stage for human action as well as nonhuman life forms, seemingly immune to manipulation.[9] But such a stability has always been an illusion: the 'physical framework that the Moderns have taken for granted' is crumbling in our Anthropocene moment, it has 'become unstable' (Latour 2017b: 3). As the earth's ticklishness – its susceptibility to human activity – becomes ever more apparent, we can no longer uphold the notion of its incorruptibility; and its actual responsiveness challenges the conventional narratives we tell about terrestrial life, as Latour points out.

> As if the décor had gotten up on stage to share the drama with the actors. From this moment on, everything changes in the way stories are told, so much so that the political order now includes everything that previously belonged to nature – a figure that, in an ongoing backlash effect, becomes an ever more undecipherable enigma. (2017b: 3)

The metaphors of stage and drama are taken up again in the third lecture, dedicated to defining Gaia as a sensitive, yet by no means holistic figure.[10] Aligning his own argument with Lovelock's, Latour identifies the conundrum of defining earth without the premise of '*an already composed whole*' and 'without adding to it a coherence that it lacks, and yet without deanimating it by representing the organisms that keep the thin film of the critical zones alive as mere inert and passive passengers on a physio-chemical system' (2017b: 86). Latour's work on Pasteur provides an analogy that helps counter the epistemological de-animation based on the traditional distinction of biological organisms, on the one hand, and inert matter, on the other:

> The humblest accessories henceforth play a role, as if there were no more distinctions between the main characters and the extras. Everything that was a simple *intermediary* serving to transport a slim concatenation of causes and consequences becomes a *mediator* adding its own grain of salt to the story. For Lovelock, everything that is located between the top of the upper atmosphere and the bottom of the sedimentary rock formations – what biochemists aptly call the critical zone – turns out to be caught in the same seething broth. The Earth's behavior is inexplicable without the addition of the work accomplished by living organisms, just as fermentation, for Pasteur, cannot be started without yeast. Just as the action of micro-organisms, in the nineteenth century, agitated beer, wine, vinegar, milk, and epidemics, from now on the incessant action of organisms succeeds in setting in motion air, water, soil, and, proceeding from one thing to another, the entire climate. (2017b: 93)

What is at stake, then, is how we tell the story of the earth in a way that can account for the great variety of life forms. The dramatic arts and literary imagination are invoked to illustrate an animated world in which people and things, the stage and the props, are equally active. The world of bacteria, the activity of yeast, and the metabolic action of microorganisms give us a sense of the complex reciprocity of vital processes that characterise the *critical zone*, whether we are thinking of our own bodies or those of other species, whether we consider wind and water, monsoons or manure, dividing cells or rotting flesh. Latour has always relied on literary examples to dramatise our contemporary moment; he makes constant reference to 'great authors' and 'great novels', the greatness of which is characterised by the narrative capacity to transcend stereotypical storytelling by going beyond 'repertories of predictable actions' and by recruiting human as well as nonhuman actors, thus affording a 'multiplicity of modes of action that are capable of intermingling' (2017b: 50). It is formulations like these that land us back on familiar ANT turf: the focus on the semiotic workings of narrative inform Latour's sense of literary greatness. The Gaia project still rests at least with one of its feet on the firm sediment of semiotic theory. Responding to this approach, I propose a notion of literary agency that is less focused on modes of action – the actions *represented* in narrative – than on the manifold resonances that literary texts themselves are able to incite.

Before turning to Latour's literary examples, it is relevant to situate his project in the larger discursive field of scientific and humanistic discourse in order to recognise that his critique aims, above all, at the harmful epistemological division of labour that has relegated nature to the sciences, and leaves politics, philosophy, and literature to the humanities. The goal of Latour's struggle of many years has been to shake the 'certainties of those who continued to imagine a social world without objects set off against a natural world without humans – and without scientists seeking to know that world' (2017b: 3). What is lacking on either side of this artificial divide is the imagination necessary to understand the dramatic entanglement of the heterogeneous agencies that together constitute Gaia.

> We were still discussing possible links between humans and nonhumans, while in the meantime scientists were inventing a multitude of ways to talk about the same thing, but on a completely different scale: the 'Anthropocene', the 'great acceleration', 'planetary limits', 'geohistory', 'tipping points', 'critical zones', all these astonishing... terms that scientists had to invent in their attempt to understand this Earth that seems to react to our actions. (2017b: 3)

What poses the greatest challenge to imaginative storytelling, then, is the scale and complexity of the problem – the inability of the separate parties to get a grip on the processes that are threatening to veer towards a total ecological collapse, as the above list of new scientific terms suggests: we are no longer dealing just with the limits of what certain species habitats or ecosystems can bear, but with the limits of ecological sustainability – of the extraction of fossil fuels and other 'resources', of relentlessly expanding agricultural and livestock industries – that have become *planetary*. Moreover, the acceleration is *great* in terms of both the pace and the variety of phenomena subsumed: global warming, melting ice caps, the acidification of oceans, and the desertification of ever larger areas of land; population growth paralleled by an increasing number of species that are on the verge of extinction or have already vanished. There are, moreover, the unprecedented levels and quantities of plastic, carbon dioxide, methane, dioxin, nitrogen, and radioactive materials in the ground, in the oceans, and in the atmosphere. Anyone not in total denial of the alarming news that reaches us every day cannot help but see that points are already tipping, that the zone circumscribing the space we share with other living beings on earth is in critical condition indeed. Hence the vengeance with which the longstanding divisions between nature and culture, climate and capitalism, organic life and geophysical inertness come tumbling down upon us.

Even if our planet is not alive – here I follow Latour – we cannot comfortably assume that it is dead or unresponsive to anthropogenic action. The need to confront the question of where we actually reside and where we are headed urges us to gain some traction regarding our historical role in the Anthropocene, and it calls upon our foresight and creativity – not just a task to be undertaken by the sciences, but a responsibility we all share. Latour has made quite clear that neither the image of the globe nor the idea of a self-stabilising superorganism can provide us with useful concepts for understanding our sublunary existence and entanglement with other living organisms and nonorganic materiality. In this sense, then, Gaia is neither a scientific nor a quasi-religious concept, but rather a set of metaphors that Latour invokes to offer a mythology – an image for the thin skin that is home to the chaotic collectivity of overlapping and interpenetrating beings, humans among them. What has changed with the realisation of our present moment as situated in the age of the Anthropocene has to do with the enormous disparity of temporal scales – one geological, the other historical – a scalar difference so vast that it is virtually unthinkable, as Dipesh Chakrabarty has shown.[11] Yet it is an undeniable fact that humanity, despite its brief existence on the planet, has burdened itself unwittingly with an 'an unprecedented *geological power*' (Latour 2017b: 44). And this is not good news. The measurable geological impact that human activities are having on the planet has nothing to do with being in control of these effects. Quite the opposite: this legacy constitutes a heavy burden on 'humanity's shoulders', as Latour states.

> And it's not over: after turning the tiny creatures that we thought we were into a giant Atlas, they tell us very calmly at the same time that we are hurtling toward our doom if we do nothing – but that it's probably too late to do anything about it in any case. (2017b: 45)

Narratological Spheres of Action

But how, then, does Latour suggest telling Gaia's story? Diagnosing Lovelock's problem of relating the different agencies in his model of Gaia serves Latour as a stepping stone to present, once again, his own notion of distributed agencies, thereby enlisting some well-known terms from ANT and narratology. Here is how he describes the theoretical task:

> Like Pasteur, Lovelock *had to invent* a new way of *fine-tuning* the agencies that populate the world: ... he had to *find a way of creating a composition* that encompassed – without unifying them in advance – all living entities within the limits of the fragile envelope that he called Gaia. (2017b: 98, my emphasis)

The terms used to define the problem – quite remarkable to the ears of literary scholars – make clear that theorising relies on many creative faculties: rather than detecting, diagnosing, or identifying one's object of study, as one would assume, the task outlined by Latour consists of composing and detailing, even inventing, a viable description of our sublunary modes of existence. In the second lecture, entitled 'How not to (de-)animate nature', Latour presents excerpts from three different texts – a novel, a nonfiction book, and a scientific article – in order to chart the workings of narrative, thereby proposing a terminology that owes much to ANT and its semiotic predecessor, narratology.

The range of narratological terms employed and discussed throughout *Facing Gaia*, and in the second lecture in particular, includes 'action', 'actor', 'actant', 'actantial roles', 'competences', 'performances', 'the relations between causes and consequences', even 'modes of existence'.[12] Latour freely admits the significant role these categories have played in his own theoretical explication of distributed agency, as he references Greimas's work in various instances.[13] In his 2016 essay 'Life Among Conceptual Characters', Latour points out that Greimas was so 'important' to him because he 'never allowed ideas to leave narration' (Latour 2016b: 468). Narrative semiotics have served as a model for his thinking more generally: 'Just like exegesis', Latour writes, 'semiotics grounds thought in figures that can be described and studied step by step. The continuity of agency is no longer obscured by the multiplicity of its figurations' (2016b: 468). Semiotics thus informs his belief that thought takes on a narrative form and that narrative figures can ultimately be traced back to actants and their actions. 'I never took (Greimassian) semiotics as being limited to texts, but as a formidable toolbox for providing a handle on ontology' (Latour 2016b: 468). While semiotics is traditionally restricted to the field of signs and language, it takes on a much wider scope in Latour's thought; he considers it a hermeneutics 'that could move out of texts, to things, to knowledge, to technology, and, finally, to the world' (2016b: 468).

As I have related elsewhere in greater detail, Latour has always relied on narratological categories — categories that stress the functional nature of actors and actants within syntactic and narrative structures.[14] Greimas also speaks of actantial roles, which are defined by their relations and interactions in the narrative grammar of a story. Replacing Vladimir Propp's dramatis personae with actants, Greimas shifted the focus from characters, defined by a set of specific traits, to functions — 'the participatory slot[s] in the syntagmatic unfolding of a narrative' — which, taken together, constitute a '"sphere of action"' (Herman 2000: 965). 'The concept of actant has the advantage of replacing, especially in literary semiotics, the term of character', Greimas and Courtés state, 'since it applies not only to human beings but also to animals, objects, or concepts'. Moreover, considering that actant 'designates a type of syntactic unit, properly formal in character, which precedes any semantic and/or ideological investment' (Greimas and Courtés 1982: 5–6), it becomes apparent that narratology has not just provided a useful vocabulary for ANT, but laid a solid foundation for Latour's conceptualisation of nonhuman agency. The argument he proceeds to make in his second chapter once again draws on this semiotic stock. In a discussion of cause and effect, Latour reverses common notions about the relation between competences and performances; he prioritises the latter in order to locate action in the particular narrative (con)figurations rather than in individual human or nonhuman figures.

How to Tell the Stories of Interacting Geo-Agents

Telling the story of Gaia from a planetary perspective is a difficult task, which is why Latour, in 'How not to (de-)animate nature', zooms in on some specific forms of agency distributed between human, technological, and natural agents. The actants he considers more closely in a reading of a nonfictional account by John McPhee of 'heroic humans' pitted against 'invincible natural agents' are the Mississippi and Atchafalaya Rivers and a 'collective character' — the US Army Corps of Engineers that works under the supervision of the River Commission (Latour 2017b: 52). Latour gives an account of the 'battle' between the Mississippi and the smaller Atchafalaya (whose riverbed is situated much lower than the Mississippi's) and the

Army Corps over the direction of the river's flow. The odds are that the Mississippi might leave its man-made course, secured only by a 'rather small and quite fragile work of craftsmanship constructed upstream in a bend in the river', and follow its 'natural' inclination of joining the lower Atchafalaya, 'com[ing] out, through a short-cut of several hundred kilometers, to the *west* of New Orleans [rather than the east], causing massive flooding and destroying a major part of the huge Mississippi delta toward which a quarter of the American economy flows' (2017b: 52). Latour tracks the various agents in order to show how each participates in the battle – the two rivers that threaten to breach the levees, the lower Atchafalaya that might 'capture' the bigger Mississippi, the engineers that 'feed' the smaller river some of the larger stream's water because they do not have the means to 'kill' it (2017b: 53). Latour delivers a syntactic analysis, sorting out how agency is distributed between the different agents and how human technologies are employed to uphold the tenuous equilibrium and to keep the Mississippi from interfering with one of the United States' major economic infrastructures.[15]

> The agents we are dealing with here are so *mixed* that the extent of the technical and legal responsibility of the Corps is a *function* of both *the power of the Mississippi* and *the level of the Atchafalaya*, which stubbornly *continues to dig down*. The whole business is *ultimately concentrated* on the *little artisanal construction* that a *slightly stronger than anticipated surge could carry away*. And what is the consequence of these exchanges of capacities? A situation of negotiation – almost a contractual relation between anthropomorphic beings (the Corps of Engineers in particular) and others, which can logically be called *hydromorphs*. (Latour 2017b: 53, my emphases)

'Really?' one is tempted to ask. Latour clearly abandons Greimas's strategy of a narratological segmentation, which identifies action and actors by their respective syntactic functions in a narrative. In this analysis we are dealing not only with a wild mix but with a total mix-up of behaviours and competences. Only two actants in Latour's reading are deduced by their performances: the Atchafalaya by its incessant 'digging down' and the possible surge by what it might 'carry away'. The rest of the 'agents' are in fact defined by their forms or properties, thus resembling actors rather than actants according to Greimas's logic: the 'hydromorphic' rivers, the 'anthropomorphic' Corps, and their artisanal construction. One might even say they are actors endowed with some qualities that are usually reserved for characters, as the many specific traits suggest: the feeble technology, the powerful Mississippi, the low-level Atchafalaya, the unexpected strength of the anticipated surge (which produces an interesting virtuality of anticipating the unanticipated). Moreover, Latour, also in violation of narratological principles of 'neutral' syntactic analysis, isolates and even pins down some 'ultimate' attractors, which seem to coordinate the vectors of other agents: 'the whole business' that is 'concentrated' on fragile human technology, and 'a situation of negotiation' that all the exchanges between the participants are seen to boil down to.

What may appear like an overly finicky dissection of Latour's analysis on my part is not meant to question the rationality of Latour's analytic endeavour. Rather, I mean to demonstrate that even an avid proponent of Greimassian narratology may have a hard time abiding by an exclusively functional analysis of narrative structure, which would dictate singling out all the forces at play by looking exclusively for the action hiding in predicates. Unravelling narrative syntax and defining actants by their 'performances', which alone can justify saying something about their 'competences', is much less fun than indulging in a little anthropomorphising. And I see this tendency in Latour as well. In the given context, he seems to attribute 'human' motivation to nonhuman agents: his claim, for instance, that the 'competing rivers' have a 'will', or that *tension makes the actor* – a tension that results from the different levels of the riverbeds, bestowing the rivers each with their own 'goals' and 'vectors' (2017b: 53).

Latour's love of storytelling appears much more 'substantial' when he suggests that, with the Mississippi, 'we are truly facing a *natural* actor' (2017b: 52). This is a rather remarkable statement, quite out of sync with his general line of reasoning that meticulously tries to determine agency by following the action, no matter whether he is attending to fictional characters or to pharmaceutical substances. But in the given context he throws overboard all the principles of functional analysis in order to embrace the river wholeheartedly: 'whoever *has felt* the presence of a stream, a tributary, a river, and especially a river like the Mississippi, *will react* like Mark Twain did' (2017b: 52, my emphasis):

> One who knows the Mississippi will promptly aver – not aloud, but to himself – that ten thousand *River Commissions*, with the mines of the world at their back, cannot tame that lawless stream, cannot curb it or confine it, cannot say to it, 'Go here', or 'Go there', and make it obey ... the Commission might as well *bully* the comets in their courses and undertake to *make* them behave, as try to *bully* the Mississippi into right and reasonable conduct. (Twain 1944: 168, quoted in Latour 2017b: 52)

Latour's own expression of awe in the presence of a mighty river (if not the Mississippi, at least one 'like' it!) resonates nicely with Twain's whimsical ridicule of human hubris. The latter's account entails the double irony of claiming that he will keep his 'secret' expertise to himself while at the same time sharing it with the reader. Mocking the efforts of the River Commission and declaring them utterly pointless is his way of aligning his disobedience (not sharing his better knowledge) with the river's – its lawlessness and total immunity to bullying. In his comment on Twain, Latour voices his awe for the Mississippi directly:

> A force of nature is obviously just the opposite of an inert actor; every novelist and poet knows this as well as every expert in hydraulics or geomorphology. If the Mississippi possesses anything at all, it is *agency* – such powerful agency that it imposes itself on the agency of all the bureaucrats. (Latour 2017b: 67)

In the case of the Mississippi, agency is not something Latour has to carefully tease out of the narrative syntax; no, he bestows it directly on the powerful actor, who, in this account at least, appears more like a fully fledged character than an actant. Willingly or not, Latour's text seems to reverberate with the literary agency of Twain's: even if he does not say so, he must have taken great pleasure in the fact that Twain equates the Mississippi with the comets – an image that invokes, albeit in inverted form, his own ironic likening of the globe to billiard balls and pumpkins. It is the humour of hyperbole that brings another kind of agency to the fore: the ability of the literary text to make us laugh – a kind of laughter that can be seen as an aesthetic response to an overblown image of nonhuman power, with the comic effect of scaling down, at least for a moment, all claims to human importance.

What is remarkable about Latour's inclusion of the Twain quotation is also the fact that it has no function in his narrative of Gaia – it does not further his argument; it much rather seems to stand in the way of the point he is trying to make. But if the quotation lacks purpose for Latour's argument, why is it there at all? I could say it comes in handy for my own argument, and indeed it does. But that is no answer to the question. Rather the point is that the trajectory of Latour's theoretical argument allows for – in fact calls for – this kind of affective disruption. Much like the image of the globe that Latour, in front of an actual audience, likes to draw on the blackboard, only to wipe it out again and replace it with that of a ticklish envelope, so the Twain quote lifts the burden of trying, in theory, to find purely narrative models of representation. Theory, I fear, will never wholly succeed in delivering models that could live up to the complexity of the world(s) it tries to represent, no matter how intricate the textile metaphors that are proposed – network, entanglement, mesh, or Latour's more recent '*metamorphic zone*' (Latour 2017b: 58).[16] Literature, in turn, has the advantage of appealing to its readers through different – imaginative and aesthetic – registers. The scales of Gaia – her size, her age – will not become more fathomable through narrative or theoretical representation. But literary agency echoes through Latour's thinking and has left its traces, for instance when we read and understand – intuitively rather than by dint of his argument – that 'every novelist and poet knows that [a force of nature is just the opposite of an inert actor] as well as every expert in hydraulics or geomorphology'. Just like Twain, creative writers and scientific 'experts' share the secret knowledge of the Mississippi's powerful agency.

Literary agency is a power hard to capture because it floats through us rather than settling down on the page. And Latour, in his struggle to reanimate Gaia, suggests that one way in which we may begin to take responsibility is to remain responsive to the other bodies with which we share our earth. 'Instead of looking for what we know', writes Yves Citton in an article on Latour, 'we must learn to listen to the noise, in order to let the soundscape reshape our minds – Earthbound rather than task-oriented' (Citton 2016: 322). So let us not lean back. Sharing with Latour the motivation as well as the goal of attending to what we do, have done, and will do to our planet, I want to re-echo his concern with humanity's role in times of globalisation:

> Whereas we ought to have as many definitions of humanity as there are ways of belonging to the world, this is the very moment when we have finally succeeded in universalizing over the whole surface of the Earth the same economizing and calculating humanoid. Under the name of *globalization*, the culture of this strange GMO – whose Latin name is *Homo oeconomicus* – has spread everywhere. At the very moment when we have a desperate need for other forms of homodiversity! (Latour 2017b: 107)

While literary agency may grant us some imaginary space beyond calculating humanoids, Latour's own theory helps us grasp, even if only in metonymic figurations, the effects of the stuff we set in motion for profit. The products of economic calculation, consumed or not, will stick around, seeping into soil and ground water, floating and disintegrating in the ocean, stranding on the beaches of 'remote' islands, forming soups and clouds of toxic waste, and getting into the food chains of all living creatures. In their extended afterlives these substances enter all kinds of unforeseen and unforeseeable assemblages, will fall apart and reunite, toxins attaching themselves to ever-tinier plastic particles, so that no place in the critical zone of our planet will be spared these new and strange couplings and copulations, which produce many kinds of unknown hybrid beings. The true, and truly troubling, Frankensteins of today are the offspring of unknown flirtations and attachments between biochemical and climatic agents – the remains of plastics, fertilisers, pesticides, carbon dioxide, methane, and so forth, as they mingle, unite, and redistribute on the ground, in water, and in air. Capitalism and neoliberalism thrive on obsolescence, and no added tags of sustainable or socially responsible production will change the direction of human economies whose sole purpose is profit.

Faulkner, in his time, presents us with a (bigger) picture, allowing us to see that the relations between human enterprise and nonhuman forces are a matter of give and take, of action and reaction, rather than a unilateral conquest or control of nature. The Mississippi, whose 'natural' tendency it is to meander, to swell and shrink with the seasons, and to change its course frequently, is also not a self-determining actor, nor is it a natural force that can be channelled easily into obedience and servitude, as Twain has made clear. Faulkner highlights the introduction of the 'Mexican cotton seed' as a quintessential development that did not just change the region's economy but also severely affected the landscape, the 'Old Man', and the life of living beings in crucial ways:

> it [the cotton seed] was clearing the land fast now, ploughing under the buffalo grass of the eastern prairies and the brier and switch cane of the creek and river bottoms of the central hills and deswamping the whole vast, flat, alluvial, delta-shaped sweep of land along the Big River, the Old Man: building the levees to hold him off the land long enough to plant and harvest the crop: he taking another foot of slope in his new dimension for every foot man constricted him in the old, so that the steamboats carrying the baled cotton to Memphis or New Orleans seemed to crawl along the sky itself. (Faulkner 1954: 6)

Notable, once again, is that nonhuman agents are presented as the driving forces of change. Calling the Mississippi 'Old Man' pays the river the respect of an independent being, who cannot easily or permanently be 'held off' from his path and who will take back the space he needs, even if in another dimension.[17] Hence trying to bully the Mississippi into submissive behaviour is not bound to succeed, either in Twain's or in Faulkner's account. Both authors take the river seriously as a character, even if with a twinkling eye. The Mississippi is granted a personality of his own, and we cannot help but recognise that he shares some significant characteristics with Latour's Gaia: he may not be as ticklish and sensitive, but he certainly follows his own course, and he will counter all human efforts that try to harness the direction of his flow in a cool, yet resolute, manner:

> The Old Man: . . . paying none of the dykes any heed at all when it suited his mood and fancy, gathering water all the way from Montana to Pennsylvania . . . and rolling it down the artificial gut of his victims' puny and baseless hoping, piling the water up, not fast, just inexorably,

until finally, after days of trepidation, 'he would enter the house and float the piano out of it and the pictures off the walls, and even remove the house itself if it were not securely fastened down' (Faulkner 1954: 9). Making palpable not just the sensitivity but also the personality and fortitude of nonhuman beings, whether rivers or the sea, rocks or trees, cows or bees, is one way in which literary texts take on and bestow agency in a more-than-human world. Reflecting back our own hubris from the perspective of a river is a way of telling our common geohistory differently, of making us sense the repercussions of our own actions. Calling the Mississippi 'Old Man', then, is more than an anthropomorphising metaphor: it pays the river the respect it deserves, showing his animate nature, his independent determination as well as his responsiveness to human action. The Mississippi is part of Gaia, the sphere we share with so many other beings, all of which have a will and tendencies of their own. Literary agency, then, is not (merely) a matter of narrative grammar or a way of granting natural entities a subject position. Rather, it is the ability of literary texts to make us sense the soul of other beings, the personality of rivers, the charisma of rocks, the respectable age of a tree. We all share the same envelope, are in it together, so to speak, and we need to take seriously all earthbound beings as forces to be reckoned with – their capacity to thrive, find their own way, strike back, and, in some cases, to vanish and go extinct.

Hence literary agency expresses two dimensions of literary practice: first, the ability of texts – through diction, tone, irony, and storytelling – to show us the world in new ways, and, second, the aesthetic experience of reading, of letting poetry and prose resonate in our imagination, through our senses, and with our own bodies. Literary agency, then, defines a lived relation between readers and texts, and literature appeals to us by enlisting our imagination, our sense of humour and terror both. In the end, literary agency depends on our capacity to sense the world beyond ourselves and to let us be moved. The alternative is not pretty, and Latour has warned us: there is no Mother Earth to lure us away from a suicidal path, if we are inclined to take it, and neither is there a deity or a sovereign able to digest what we have put into the world but no longer care about. We are literally walking on thin ice, and if we mess this one up, be assured, there is no Planet B.

Notes

I am grateful to Bill Brown for taking the time to carefully read and comment on this chapter; our conversation over the years continues to inspire my thinking. Many thanks to my other friends at the University of Chicago for their valuable feedback, especially Deborah Nelson, Edgar Garcia, Eric Slauter, and Kenneth Warren.

1. In 'Fictional Attachments and Literary Weavings', Yves Citton suggests a 'literary form of attention' as a way of expanding the scope of theoretical thinking (Citton 2016: 321).
2. Christopher Morris's *The Big Muddy: An Environmental History of the Mississippi and Its Peoples* (Morris 2012) presents an excellent historical account of life on and with the Mississippi in the Delta region.
3. *A Tale of Two Rivers*, the first part of PBS's *Great Projects* documentary series (*Great Projects* 2002), provides impressive footage of the flood of 1927 and the toll it took especially on the African-American population; it also shows the hubris of one of the nation's boldest engineering projects in the twentieth century that tried to control and regulate the Mississippi, North America's largest river system. A thirteen-minute excerpt from the documentary is available online: <www.youtube.com/watch?v=UGy4DgeaZNo> (last accessed 4 December 2018).
4. See especially his chapter 9, 'Situating the Beings of Fiction' (Latour 2013: 233–58).
5. 'The new climatic regime' is the stated topic of Latour's *Facing Gaia* (2017b), as given in the subtitle.
6. See Bill Brown, 'The Obsolescence of the Human' (Brown 2015).
7. See, for instance, Latour, *Reassembling the Social: An Introduction to Actor-Network Theory* (Latour 2005), and his essays 'Where Are the Missing Masses? The Sociology of a Few Mundane Artifacts' (Latour 1992) and 'Why Has Critique Run out of Steam? From Matters of Fact to Matters of Concern' (Latour 2004).
8. Latour continues to specify: 'In the old "pre-Copernican" system, there was a difference in substance between the zone under the Moon (sublunary) and the zone above the Moon (supralunary): the higher one climbed above the "corruptible" Earth, to the planets and then to the fixed stars, the higher one went in perfection' (2017b: 60n.46).
9. In fact, the damage caused by human manipulation is hardly of a kind that is visible, especially not from 'nowhere'. However, if you stand in the middle of Delhi or Beijing or Jakarta, you may see that you do not see very far on certain days, that there is something in the air, but it is hard to say how airborne carbon dioxide, lead, and many other active ingredients of what we inhale will interact with the pneumonic 'apparatus'.
10. Latour understands Lovelock's concept of Gaia to be '*wholly secular*', citing the latter's characterisation of the sublunary world as '"implying no external cause and spiritual foundation", and "thus belonging wholly to this world"' (Latour 2017b: 87).
11. In his 2014 essay 'Climate and Capital: On Conjoined Histories', the historian Dipesh Chakrabarty has pointed out the difficulty of squaring, in terms of scale, our understanding of human history, especially that of 'industrial civilization', with 'the history

of the earth system', or 'the history of life including human evolution on the planet' (Chakrabarty 2014: 1). If 'put on the same chart', as Latour suggests, the widely diverging scales of these two histories do not render anthropogenic impact on planet earth insignificant, but, to the contrary, 'put the burden of unprecedented *geological power* abruptly on that same humanity's shoulders' (Latour 2017b: 44).

12. All terms mentioned here can be found in Algirdas Julien Greimas and Joseph Courtés's *Semiotics and Language: An Analytical Dictionary* (Greimas and Courtés 1982), originally published in French in 1979; while the first six are recognisable as narratological, the latter two may be less so; yet all are essential for Latour's conception of agency as following from action rather than individual agents.

13. In *Facing Gaia*, Latour references Greimas and Courtés's *Semiotics and Language* twice, even calling it 'the bible of semiotics' (Latour 2017b: 49, 51, 56).

14. See my Introduction in *The Literary Life of Things: Case Studies in American Fiction*, which shows the extent to which Latour's thinking is indebted to narratology (Tischleder 2014: 15–44, esp. 28–34).

15. This paragraph on the Mississippi reproduces parts of an argument made in my essay 'Thinking Objects, Building Worlds: Why the New Materialisms Deserve Literary Imagination' (Tischleder 2018).

16. Latour explains the term as follows:

    If it is the world that interests us – and no longer 'nature' – then we must learn to inhabit what could be called a *metamorphic zone*, borrowing a metaphor from geology, to capture in a single word all the 'morphisms' that we are going to have to register in order to follow these transactions. (Latour 2017b: 58)

17. Calling the Mississippi 'Old Man', Faulkner evokes the cliché and the historical baggage associated with this name, most memorable in a scene of the film *Show Boat* (1936), in which Paul Robeson sings about the Old Man 'rolling along' while the film shows images of black men toiling with huge cotton bales on their backs: 'What does he care if de world's got troubles? What does he care if de land ain't free?' This scene clearly voices the indifference of the nonhuman world, of a river ignorant of human hardship, especially of the racial injustice and exploitation at its banks (*Show Boat* 1936).

Bibliography

Brown, Bill (2015), 'The Obsolescence of the Human', in Babette B. Tischleder and Sarah L. Wasserman (eds), *Cultures of Obsolescence: History, Materiality, and the Digital Age*, New York: Palgrave Macmillan, pp. 19–38.

Chakrabarty, Dipesh (2014), 'Climate and Capital: On Conjoined Histories', *Critical Inquiry*, 41:1, pp. 1–23.

Citton, Yves (2016), 'Fictional Attachments and Literary Weavings in the Anthropocene', *New Literary History*, 47:2, pp. 309–29.

Clarke, Bruce (2017), 'Rethinking Gaia: Stengers, Latour, Margulis', *Theory, Culture and Society*, 34:4, pp. 3–26.

Faulkner, William (1954), 'Mississippi', *Encounter*, October, pp. 3–16.

Great Projects: The Building of America (2002), DVD, produced by Great Projects Film Company. USA: PBS.

Greimas, Algirdas Julien and Joseph Courtés (1982), *Semiotics and Language: An Analytical Dictionary*, Bloomington: Indiana University Press.
Herman, David (2000), 'Pragmatic Constraints on Narrative Processing: Actants and Anaphora Resolution in a Corpus of North Carolina Ghost Stories', *Journal of Pragmatics*, 32, pp. 959–1001.
Latour, Bruno (1992), 'Where Are the Missing Masses? The Sociology of a Few Mundane Artifacts', in Wiebe Bijker and John Law (eds), *Shaping Technology/Building Society: Studies in Sociotechnical Change*, Cambridge, MA: MIT Press, pp. 225–58.
Latour, Bruno (2004), 'Why Has Critique Run out of Steam? From Matters of Fact to Matters of Concern', *Critical Inquiry*, 30:2, pp. 225–48.
Latour, Bruno (2005), *Reassembling the Social: An Introduction to Actor-Network Theory*, New York: Oxford University Press.
Latour, Bruno (2013), *An Inquiry into Modes of Existence: An Anthropology of the Moderns*, Cambridge, MA: Harvard University Press.
Latour, Bruno (2016a), 'On Not Joining the Dots', Radcliffe Institute, Harvard University, 22 November, <www.youtube.com/watch?v=wTvbK10ABPI> (last accessed 8 November 2018).
Latour, Bruno (2016b), 'Life among Conceptual Characters', *New Literary History*, 47:2, pp. 463–76.
Latour, Bruno (2017a), 'Why Gaia Is Not a God of Totality', *Theory, Culture and Society*, 34:2–3, pp. 61–81.
Latour, Bruno (2017b), *Facing Gaia: Eight Lectures on the New Climatic Regime*, Cambridge: Polity.
Morris, Christopher (2012), *The Big Muddy: An Environmental History of the Mississippi and Its Peoples, from Hernando De Soto to Hurricane Katrina*, New York: Oxford University Press.
Show Boat (1936), film, directed by James Whale. USA: Universal.
Tischleder, Babette B. (2014), *The Literary Life of Things: Case Studies in American Fiction*, Frankfurt am Main: Campus.
Tischleder, Babette B. (2018), 'Thinking Objects, Building Worlds: Why the New Materialisms Deserve Literary Imagination', in Frank Kelleter and Alexander Starre (eds), *Projecting American Studies: Essays on Theory, Method, and Practice*, Heidelberg: Winter, pp. 225–39.
Twain, Mark (1944), *Life on the Mississippi*, New York: Heritage Press.

10

Three Problems of Formalism: An Object-Oriented View

Graham Harman

Formalism in Aesthetics

We are concerned in this chapter with what seems like a well-worn academic topic: aesthetic formalism.[1] Since we will approach this topic from the standpoint of object-oriented ontology (OOO), we should first say something about the persistent danger of an overly literal understanding of OOO's use of the term 'object'. That is to say, many readers expect an object-oriented interpretation of anything to exclude human beings and focus entirely on solid, material, inanimate things. No doubt a renewed focus on the inanimate is one of the tasks of OOO, given the excessively low status of nonhuman entities throughout the modern period in such disciplines as philosophy, literary studies, and political theory.[2] It is true that OOO reinterprets the human being as just another kind of object, even if an especially interesting one. Yet this has nothing to do with the supposed atrocity of 'reducing subjects to objects', as if OOO's procedure were to treat free and thinking subjects as if they were no better than useful commodities like corn or coal. For our purposes, 'object' simply refers to any unified reality that cannot be explained away in terms of its internal pieces ('undermining'), its external effects ('overmining'), or through the combination of both methods simultaneously ('duomining') (Harman 2013a). The point of referring to human beings as 'objects' is not to reduce them to manipulable solid materials, but rather to *protect* humans – and all other objects – from being reduced to something they are not.

We return now to 'formalism'. Though it seems to be one of those words, much like 'realism', that has different and even opposite meanings depending on the context in which it is employed, it is easy enough to define the term for our purposes. Let us use 'formalism' provisionally to refer to the doctrine that works of art are autonomous, self-contained entities largely independent of the biographical, historical, or sociopolitical contexts in which they were composed. This entails, for instance, that Shakespeare's plays or Picasso's paintings can be considered as encapsulated works able to travel across space and time, rather than as mere expressions of the situation from which they emerged: the life of a pleasant provincial outsider in Elizabethan London, or an energetic Spanish womaniser in the bohemia of Montmartre.

The root of such formalism can be found in the philosophy of Immanuel Kant, a towering figure in whose shadow everyone still dwells. Though formalism in our sense can be found in all three of his great *Critiques*, it is especially prominent in his ethical philosophy (Kant 2003, 2002, 1987). Above all, in order for an action to count as ethical for Kant, it cannot be motivated by any hope for favourable consequences. If I do something from the wish to go to heaven or fear of going to hell, if I want to have a good reputation in my community, or if I simply hope to sleep soundly at night with a good conscience, all such motivations treat ethics as a means to an end. For this reason, ethical actions cannot be an attempt to attain some beneficial result, nor can unethical actions – lying is the most famous example – be justified by their favourable outcomes in certain scenarios. Kant is even suspicious of purportedly ethical actions undertaken with too much warmth, joy, or good cheer, and seems to prefer instances of cold and flinty dutifulness. An action is ethical when it is undertaken for its own sake alone, however difficult it may be to find examples of pure ethical behaviour. Famously, this means that ethics must be governed by the 'categorical imperative', a duty binding universally and without exception: act in such a way that your action could be a universal law binding in all circumstances; act according to duty; act always so as to treat other human beings as ends in themselves rather than as means to an end. Kant's ethical outlook is nicely summarised in the following passage from his *Groundwork of the Metaphysics of Morals*, a sort of highly condensed version of the *Critique of Practical Reason*:

> There is one imperative that, without being based upon and having as its condition any other purpose to be attained by certain conduct, commands this conduct immediately. This imperative is **categorical**. It has to do not with the matter of the action and what is to result from it, but with the form and the principle from which the action itself follows; and the essentially good in the action consists in the disposition, let the result be what it may. This imperative may be called the imperative **of morality**. (Kant 1998: 27)

Although I am not aware of Kant ever using the term 'formalism' in an aesthetic context, he is rightly considered the grandfather of formalist aesthetics. Along the same lines as his ethical theory, Kant holds that the beauty of an artwork must be distinct from its personal agreeableness for me or anyone else. A literary work that presents vegetarian university professors in a favourable light might be expected to please me, given that I meet this description myself. As a native of Iowa, I might be naturally inclined to overrate the stature of Grant Wood, the most famous visual artist to have emerged from my home state. Such personal considerations may interfere with my ability to form a disinterested judgement of aesthetic beauty in these cases. Beyond this, Kant considers beauty to be 'in the eye of the beholder' in an eminently philosophical sense. Judgements of beauty pertain not to artworks themselves, but to the transcendental faculty of judgement belonging to all humans. Somewhat surprisingly, this holds not only for beauty, but also for those overpowering cases that fall under the heading of the sublime: experiences of measureless size or power. Kant considers the sublime to be an experience of infinity: not because any given thunderstorm, waterfall, or earthquake is truly infinite, but because the sublime surpasses my cosmic minuteness to such a degree that it *seems* absolutely large or powerful by comparison with myself. For Kant, the sublime is thus a matter of the 'human' side of the equation rather than the 'world' side to no less a degree than beauty.

We should note that aesthetic formalism since Kant has actually tended to invert this way of looking at things, treating the artwork itself rather than the human faculty of judgement as what is truly autonomous from its surroundings. Formalist criticism in literature and the visual arts – architecture is a more intricate case – starts by walling off the artwork from its surroundings, deliberately downplaying the sociopolitical or biographical factors that gave rise to the work or that speak to its past or present relevance. A good example of this inversion is the thought of the eminent art critic and historian Michael Fried, who is famously horrified by any 'theatrical' conception of art. Singling out minimalism for especial condemnation, Fried in the early phase of his career rejects art that works by provoking some sort of reaction in the spectator; indeed, he holds that theatre is nothing less than the death of art (Fried 1998). Though Fried reverses Kant's emphasis from the human subject to the closed-off nonhuman art object, this reversal still presupposes the privilege of disinterested contemplation and objective judgement, and entails a horror at any attempted fusion between human and nonhuman elements. In this way, the Kantian perspective is preserved in all its essentials: even if upside down, and even if Fried is sometimes misleadingly paired with Kant's successor and ontological rival G. W. F. Hegel, as in Robert Pippin's treatment of the theme (Pippin 2014). Elsewhere, I have shown in more detail why Fried cannot be linked any more closely with Hegel than can his one-time mentor, Clement Greenberg.[3]

It is true that OOO looks at first like a perfect match for aesthetic formalism, at least insofar as formalism pertains to the non-relational closure of any thing from its surroundings. After all, object-oriented thought is known for its insistence on the autonomy of objects from their relations, and this in turn seems to lead directly to the suppression of factors lying beyond the bounds of the artwork itself (Harman 2014b). Nonetheless, there are at least three problems with traditional formalism that OOO finds it necessary to modify:

The first was the principal topic of my 2016 book *Dante's Broken Hammer* (Harman 2016a). Namely, Kant insists not just on any old autonomy, but on an unjustified taxonomical one involving two specific classes of beings: (a) humans, and (b) everything else. Max Scheler already made a powerful criticism of Kantian ethics on this very point (Scheler 1973, 1992: 98–135). Although Scheler agrees with Kant's defence of the autonomy of ethical actions from any ulterior purpose or consequence, what he rejects is Kant's assumption that ethics requires the separation of humans from the world. What he gives us instead is an ethics of love or passion, much like Dante: one in which the basic ethical unit is not the dutiful human divorced from anything in the world, but a human–world dyad or compound in which the ethical person feels called by some personal, professional, or national ethical vocation. I do not just perform duties in a vacuum, but act in accordance with my rank-order of values. In just about any passage from Scheler's ethical writings, we find more emphasis on the role of objects than in Kant's own ethics. The following example is typical of Scheler:

> It follows that any sort of rightness or falseness or perversity in my life and activity are determined by whether there is an objectively correct order of these stirrings of my love and hate, my inclination and disinclination, my many-sided interest in the things of this world. (Scheler 1992: 98)

The ordering of values is different in one's own case from that of all other humans, though it is not for that reason beyond praise or blame: my individual rank-order may be despicable, degenerate, or at least imbalanced in some way deserving of criticism or punishment. But the truly important point is that the basic unit of ethics is not – as in Kant – a human subject considered apart from the rest of the cosmos, but the human as involved with this or that object of its passion.[4] In this way, Scheler hints at a broader possible criticism of the modern taxonomy of humans and world, one that was eventually undertaken in the 1990s by Bruno Latour (Latour 1993). It is not hard to imagine a Scheleresque critique of Kant extended to the aesthetic realm, and in some ways Fried attempts this in spite of himself, through his eventual admission that Édouard Manet was not really an anti-theatrical artist (Fried 1996). It follows that there is no reason to exclude the human element from the art object, as if this human presence on the scene were some sort of extraneous theatrical contamination. Instead, 'theatricality' must be embraced, since there is no artwork without a human beholder, and no love for art without individual or collective aesthetic vocations that prefer specific beauties to others. Here once more, the autonomous unit of aesthetics is neither the transcendental human faculty of judgement nor the artwork lying at a pristine distance, but the hybrid entity made up of me *and* the artwork. In short, Kant spoils his powerful notion of autonomy by assuming that this must mean either human autonomy from the object, or the object's autonomy from human beholders, instead of an autonomy of the compound they form from whatever lies outside it. That is the first problem with formalism as viewed from an object-oriented standpoint: its specific fondness for splitting the world into two taxonomical zones, one of them 'human' and the other 'world'. As if our frail newcomer species deserved to make up a full half of ontology, while everything else – black holes, dark energy, red giants, comets, minerals, pelicans, snakes, and atoms – were to be crammed into the other half!

The second problem concerns formalism's tendency to turn into holism. It is of course true that the formalist's first move is to exclude all sociopolitical, biographical, or economic context from our consideration of an artwork. There would be no formalism if the work were allowed to blend seamlessly into its surroundings, as the New Historicists among others wish: as if Shakespeare's plays were basically no different in kind from the census registries or prison documents of Elizabethan England (Greenblatt 2005). But once the artwork has been safely walled off from its social context, formalist critics have a strange tendency to turn the interior of the artwork into a holistic hall of mirrors. For the New Critics, for instance, every element of a poem gains its meaning only from the total context of all the other elements, as if 'beauty is truth, truth beauty' took its significance entirely from what preceded this slogan in the famous 'Ode on a Grecian Urn' of Keats (Keats 1977: 344–5). The same tendency can be found in the formalist art criticism of Clement Greenberg, who so disparages content in painting that the only function he allows it is to point knowingly to the flat, non-illusionistic canvas background lying beneath it (Greenberg 1986: 9; Harman 2014c). Hence, the second failing of formalism comes from its overstating the mutual interdependence of the various individual elements of any given work, though we know from both history and personal experience that literary works often exist in variant versions, or were modified in numerous ways up to the last minute, without necessarily leading to any important change in the work as a whole. I have considered this question in particular in a 2012 article entitled 'The Well-Wrought Broken Hammer' (Harman 2012).

The third and most obvious failing of formalism, one I have written about less often in the past, is its excessive exclusion of the world outside the artwork from our experience of that work. Picasso's *Guernica* certainly has aesthetic merit apart from its powerful cry against the brutality of Luftwaffe intervention in the Spanish Civil War, though it is equally certain that the painting would not be what it is if it were merely a fantasy of a *possible* act of violence in some *possible* war. Just as Fried's ban on theatricality needlessly excludes much artwork from the 1960s and beyond (happenings, performance art, conceptual art, landscape art) from the sphere of valid modern art, aesthetic formalism – especially in the visual arts, though not always in literature – leaves us empty-handed in considering possible interactions between artworks and the sociopolitical or biographical sphere. We should of course retain formalism's anti-holistic resistance to viewing, say, Shakespeare's plays as just another product of their time and place. Among other things, those plays have proved able to travel in a way that is not true of census registries or prison documents or menus from the inns of that era. It cannot be the case that *all* aspects of the environment of an artwork are reflected there as if in a gleaming, multifaceted mirror. Like any other object, an artwork is open to certain environmental influences while closing its doors to others. Yet it is obvious that artworks interact with *some* range of environmental features, just as the autonomy of individual humans from the world does not contradict our intimate dependence on oxygen, food, and water. Essentially, our goal is to expand Scheler's insight beyond his critique of Kantian ethics. How do we go about 'Schelerising' the arts? While formalism legitimately entails the autonomy of the artwork and the exclusion of one kind of holism – the kind that allows artworks to bleed too easily into their sociopolitical contexts – it cannot mean the exclusion of humans from the world or of artworks from human concerns. It must be a formalism whose formal units are compounds that glue together the artwork with some – but not all – of the environmental factors lying beyond the physical bounds of the artwork itself.

For discussing this third failing of formalism, I propose a brief object-oriented treatment of *Uncle Tom's Cabin*, though we will limit ourselves here to the remarks of two important critics of that work. It is hard to think of any novel, or indeed any art of any genre, whose sociopolitical effects have been more pronounced. Harriet Beecher Stowe's wildly successful novel – it sold more copies in the nineteenth century than any book but the Bible – was a crucial factor in galvanising opposition to American slavery, and in giving rise to the civil war that ended that abhorred institution (Stowe 2010). No self-respecting intellectual could view the liberation of the slaves in 1865 as anything but a positive result. Insofar as *Uncle Tom's Cabin* helped lead to this result, few intellectuals would wish to condemn the existence of the book. Nonetheless, it would be shocking today if we were to meet a serious literary person who would call it the greatest novel ever written, or even one of the twenty greatest, though it probably tops all others in terms of benevolent social effects. When we encounter *Uncle Tom's Cabin* on lists with titles such as 'the one hundred greatest novels ever written', we tend to assume that it makes the list for reasons of sociopolitical rather than literary merit. For even in a time like ours, when the humanities have come under crushing atmospheric pressure to behave as servants of progressive politics, many progressives would still describe Stowe's novel as hopelessly sentimental, improbable, or awash in its own brand of condescending racism.

Needless to say, the sociopolitical relevance of *Uncle Tom's Cabin* is not merely a thing of the past. The end of legalised American slavery in 1865 obviously did not heal the racial wounds of the country once and for all; as of 2019, the situation is becoming noticeably worse. The title character of Stowe's novel gave rise to what is still one of our nation's most brutal insults: to call an African-American male an 'Uncle Tom' remains a devastating way to write him off as passive and servile, as unwilling to stand up for his own rights, as complicit with the ruling power – even if there are fairer ways to interpret the Uncle Tom character of the book. The continuing relevance of the novel to its specific context can be further illuminated by a thought experiment like the earlier one with Picasso's *Guernica*. If we imagine that *Uncle Tom's Cabin* were simply an outlandish horror novel published in a slavery-free 1852 America, followed by further decades and centuries of placid racial harmony, its status today might be something like 'freakish product of pessimistic popular culture' rather than 'enduring pillar of the American literary canon'. Furthermore, although *Uncle Tom's Cabin* is certainly good enough to have travelled abroad, it does not travel quite as well as many classics. The experience of a European reading the book will not be commensurate with that of an American who reads it, and the experience of a white American reading it will no doubt be awkwardly different from that of Americans of African ancestry. All things considered, *Uncle Tom's Cabin* is perhaps the showcase example of a novel that seems to have everything to do with its context, and hence the one that a purely formalist approach is least equipped to handle.

Rather than give a detailed analysis of the novel itself, for which a chapter of this brevity is not the right place, we limit ourselves here to a pair of incisive essays that take completely opposite tacks. The editor of the Norton Critical Edition of *Uncle Tom's Cabin*, Elizabeth Ammons, wonderfully arranges for some illuminating friction with the first pair of scholarly essays at the close of the volume. First, we find a scathing indictment of Stowe's novel as sentimental closet racism devoid of literary merit, penned by no less a figure than James Baldwin. This is followed immediately by a ringing endorsement of the book, authored by the eminent feminist critic Jane P. Tompkins. Baldwin seems to reject the notion of 'protest novels' altogether, while Tompkins reads *Uncle Tom's Cabin* favourably as a gateway to feminist revolution. Speaking in the terms established earlier, Baldwin occupies something like a formalist position, and Tompkins an anti-formalist one. It will be more convenient to start with Baldwin's essay.

Contra: James Baldwin

We begin with what Baldwin rejects. He tells us bluntly that *Uncle Tom's Cabin* is 'a very bad novel' characterised by 'self-righteous, virtuous sentimentality' (Baldwin 2010: 533). 'Sentimentality' is no throwaway insult by Baldwin, but functions as a technical term for something he openly loathes: 'the ostentatious parading of excessive and spurious emotion'. This puts him in roughly the same place as Fried's opposition to theatricality in painting, *mutatis mutandis*. Yet Baldwin pursues the theme with a greater degree of vehemence than Fried: 'the wet eyes of the sentimentalist betray his aversion to experience, his fear of life, his arid heart; and it is always, therefore, the signal of secret and violent inhumanity, the mask of cruelty'. Stowe is accused of 'virtuous rage' and a worldview in which 'black equates with evil and white with grace' (Baldwin 2010: 535). Deserving or not, this is beautifully written invective against an author he considers not just bad, but dangerous. Yet Baldwin's target is broader than Stowe and her famous novel. It is not just that she happens to be a cruel sentimentalist who wrote a bad book. The real problem is the genre of the protest novel itself, which Baldwin formalistically holds to be directly opposed to the search for truth. By truth, he tells us that he means 'a devotion to the human being, his freedom and fulfilment; freedom which cannot be legislated, fulfilment which cannot be charted' (2010: 533). The opposite of this, he holds, is 'a devotion to Humanity which is too easily equated with a devotion to a Cause; and Causes, as we know, are notoriously bloodthirsty'. Baldwin follows this with a statement against politically conscious art that might even get him into trouble in today's intellectual climate, mocking the supposed 'Responsibility' of the novelist, 'which seems to mean that he must make formal declaration that he is involved in, and affected by, the lives of other people and to say something improving about this somewhat self-evident fact' 2010: 534). And finally: 'The "protest" novel, so far from being disturbing, is an accepted and comforting aspect of the American scene ... [Its] report from the pit reassures us of its reality and its darkness and of our own salvation' (2010: 536).

So much for what Baldwin rejects. What does he support? Aside from what he calls 'truth' and 'freedom', another key word in his arsenal is 'paradox'. The following is a fine summary of Baldwin's aesthetic credo:

> only within [the] web of ambiguity, paradox, this hunger, danger, darkness, can we find at once ourselves and the power that will free us from ourselves. It is this power of revelation which is the business of the novelist, this journey toward a more vast reality which must take precedence over all other claims. (Baldwin 2010: 534)

The term recurs later when, not implausibly, he condemns America as a 'country devoted to the death of the paradox' (2010: 538). Before moving on to Tompkins's rather different view of *Uncle Tom's Cabin*, I want to insist that there is much of value in what Baldwin says here about literature. Above all, in his defence of paradox and rejection of political virtue-signalling as the prime source of aesthetic quality, Baldwin shows himself to be a staunch opponent of literalism in the arts, and thus he is a comrade of OOO in its rejection of all literalism in the arts.[5]

We call something paradoxical or ambiguous when it seems to possess contradictory qualities. It is worth noting that this was one of the definitions that Aristotle gave of substance: it can have opposite qualities, as when Socrates is happy at one moment and sad at the next, or perhaps happy and sad in different ways in one and the same moment (Aristotle 1999). Aristotle's definition implies that every real substance is paradoxical or ambiguous, and this entails further that nothing can be equated with the sum total of qualities it possesses, since we have already seen that a substance is partly indifferent to its qualities. At the beginning of this chapter, there was a brief discussion of the OOO concepts of undermining, overmining, and duomining. What I did not mention above is that every form of knowledge is necessarily either a form of undermining (reducing a thing downward to its components), overmining (reducing it upward to its effects), or duomining (reducing it in both directions simultaneously). Baldwin's insistence on paradox in literature implies that literature is not a form of knowledge, but something else; after all, paradox is the signal of a reality that does not convert easily into any list of definite qualities. In OOO terms, the sociopolitical protest novel is primarily a form of overmining; to this extent it reduces the work of literature to a literal message, whether or not Baldwin is right that the message of *Uncle Tom's Cabin* is a narrowly theological one that flatters readers as to their salvation. By the same token, Aristotle's insistence on the paradoxical nature of substance, much like Socrates' claim that he knows nothing and has never been anyone's teacher, means that philosophy itself – like literature – is also not a form of knowledge. Along with the irreducibility of a serious literary work to any particular literal meaning, literature makes extensive use of metaphors and other figures of speech, none of which can be translated neatly into any definite literal statement.[6]

If OOO has any gripe at all with Baldwin's views on literature as expressed in his piece on *Uncle Tom's Cabin*, it would be with his prominent use of the words 'truth' and 'freedom'. What is wrong with these two words, which generally have such a positive ring to them? As for 'truth', unlike paradox, it generally suggests that one can gain direct access to what is true by following the proper intellectual or other revelatory procedures. To do this would mean that in principle we could witness the things of the world in their naked truth, which means in turn that we could correctly apprehend their properties. Yet this would eliminate the very ambiguity that Baldwin otherwise champions, and champions rightly in my view. For this reason, I would prefer that we keep paradox and ambiguity in our toolbox while downplaying the more familiar notion of 'truth', which seems inevitably paired with the literalism that Baldwin otherwise so skilfully assaults. The same holds for 'freedom', the word with the most incomparably good press throughout the modern period. For who could oppose human freedom? Who would argue instead for human bondage, especially in connection with a novel protesting the existence of slavery? The problem with freedom in its philosophical – rather than political – sense is its suggestion that human attachment to the world is somehow inherently oppressive, that the road to happiness and excellence involves ripping ourselves loose from attachments: as if human thought (just as in Kantian formalism) were essentially something other than the world, something that ought to be purified or separated from it.

We have seen that Baldwin critiques *Uncle Tom's Cabin* from a position that might be called formalist, insofar as he judges the novel as an autonomous work apart from its undeniable political effects and judges it a failure in that respect. Hence, Baldwin seems to prefigure the same path of evaluating the novel that one would expect from a OOO-influenced critic today. Given that object-oriented literary theory joins formalism in opposing any sort of holism that would drown the work in its historical context (while also attacking formalism for a different sort of holism that takes an overly relational approach to the elements *inside* a given artwork), there would appear to be no way, in Baldwin's wake, to argue for the literary merit of *Uncle Tom's Cabin*. Yet we might also wish to counter this possible OOO prejudice, looking for ways in which the context and influence of a work *can* be of relevance to it. And here we must put aside Baldwin and turn to a critic who does try to save Stowe's novel by examining its context. I speak of Jane P. Tompkins, whose treatment of *Uncle Tom's Cabin* first appeared as a journal article in 1978.

We recall that Baldwin attacks Stowe's novel for two different sorts of reasons. The first is that by positioning itself as a 'protest novel', it becomes too involved with a righteous-sounding cause external to the literary work itself, and thus fails to live up to the mission of literature. The second is that, even if we forget the political position taken by the book and focus only on its internal literary workings, these are every bit as bad. According to Baldwin, the chief internal flaw of the work is sentimentality, which he defines as 'the ostentatious parading of excessive and spurious emotion'. But we need to be careful here, for I suspect that Baldwin is engaged in a common sleight of hand that one often encounters among critics working in any genre. Yes, it may seem that Baldwin is merely complaining about the 'ostentatious parading' of emotion that is 'excessive' and 'spurious'. It is tempting for the reader to bite on this hook, since we all like to think of ourselves as aesthetically repulsed by cases of ham acting, melodramatic films, maudlin novels, and the like. Consider Michael Fried's complaints about 'theatricality' in painting, a case where we readily agree with Fried that there are numerous examples of overly staged tableaux. But alongside these persuasive critiques of *bad* emotion in writing and *bad* theatricality in painting, what Baldwin and Fried are really trying to suggest is that *all* emotion and *all* theatricality are bad. In Fried's case this is obvious, since he goes out of his way to emphasise Diderot's anti-theatrical tradition in French painting, despite his concession that the Diderotian tradition eventually collapses around the time of Manet (Fried 1988, 1996). In Baldwin's case the matter is less obvious, though I think just as decisive. Evidence of this comes late in his essay on *Uncle Tom's Cabin* when he praises Richard Wright's character Bigger Thomas, the disturbingly detached murderer/rapist anti-hero of *Native Son* (Baldwin 2010: 538). While Baldwin is no doubt correct that Bigger's life in Chicago is 'controlled, defined by his hatred and fear', this hatred and fear have evidently been so compressed into Bigger's interior that my primary impression of him is one of emotional deadness. Baldwin nearly concedes this point when he calls Bigger 'so exactly opposite a portrait' of Uncle Tom himself. And then there are Wright's own anti-sentimentalist leanings, made clear in his explanatory essay 'How "Bigger" Was Born', in which he recalls with horror how an earlier piece of his writing made a young white woman cry (Wright 2005a). He tells us that this led him to conceive of *Native Son* as a work that would generate no tears at all: and for most readers it probably does not, despite the horrific tale it relates. Now, although Baldwin and Wright are clearly motivated in their anti-sentimentalist attitudes by the specific features of American race relations, and the ways in which white authors and readers try to squirm off the hook by taking ostentatiously virtuous liberal positions on it, they are also part of the Western intellectual tradition – however excluded from it they may feel in other ways. When we take this into account, we can see that their anti-sentimentalist attitude is derived no less than Fried's from the Kantian modernism that wants to interpret the human subject as something basically cool and detached.

Pro: Jane P. Tompkins

Let us turn now to Jane Tompkins. As an ardent feminist, Tompkins has an obvious political motive for being less harsh on sentimentality than Baldwin, Wright, and Fried: it is well known that women are habitually and unfairly accused of overly emotional reactions and schmaltzy identification with less-than-serious film and literary characters. Tompkins summarises this negative attitude as follows: 'twentieth-century critics have taught generations of students to equate popularity with debasement, emotionality with ineffectiveness, religiosity with fakery, domesticity with triviality, and all of these, implicitly, with womanly inferiority' (Tompkins 2010: 540). She also cites Nathaniel Hawthorne's unfortunate 1855 complaint about the 'damned mob of scribbling women' (Tompkins 2010: 542). She laments further the way that New Historicists have ignored so many of the successful American woman novelists of the nineteenth century, not to mention the fact that even feminists have joined in the ridicule of such literary figures as 'Susan Warner, Sarah J. Hale, Augusta Evans, Elizabeth Stuart Phelps, her daughter Mary . . . and Frances Hodgson Burnett' (2010: 540). If we are too quick to join the critical tradition in dismissing such authors, we will be guilty among other things of forgetting 'literature's most avid readers – women' (2010: 541). Unfortunately,

> these women are generally thought to have traded in false stereotypes, dishing out weak-minded pap to nourish the prejudices of an ill-educated and unemployed female readership. Self-deluded and unable to face the harsh facts of a competitive society, they are portrayed as manipulators of a gullible public who kept their readers imprisoned in a dream world of self-justifying clichés. (2010: 541)

In fact, Tompkins argues, these authors practised an important literary genre that enjoyed great public interest in its time: 'the sentimental novel, whose chief characteristic is that it is written by, for, and about women' (2010: 541).

Before discussing why Tompkins finds this tradition has such political importance (which she does not distinguish sharply from purely literary importance) we should explain why OOO is largely in agreement with her defence of sentimentality, despite our otherwise extensive formalist sympathies. It is true that we must preserve our capacity for the critical rejection of artworks that play too lazily or manipulatively with our feelings. Films such as *Charlotte's Web* and *Old Yeller* bring copious tears to the eyes of children, and even to the eyes of adults who enjoy reliving their childhood attachment to talking cartoon creatures and fictional animals. During adulthood we gain a more nuanced view of attachment, along with a more stoical resolve in confronting inevitable loss, and hence *Charlotte's Web* and *Old Yeller* soon fade from any respectable list of one's favourite films. Certain paintings and photographs present emotions so preposterously fabricated or staged that we cannot take them seriously. Refined aesthetic taste may be strongly inclined to expel 'the ostentatious parading of excessive and spurious emotion'. Yet it may also be necessary that we turn down the volume and frequency of our ridicule to prevent 'false positives', and for a compelling philosophical reason. For it is only natural that in a modern world where human thought is treated as something utterly different in kind from everything else in the cosmos, thought comes to be treated as something basically alienated from the world. In other words, thought is treated as if it were basically duped by things unless it adopts a position of admirably distant and cynical reserve. It is not just sentimental nineteenth-century middle-class women who depart from this paradigm. The same already held true for Dante, who was passionate about so many things – and who was by modern standards laughably sentimental about Beatrice, a woman he barely met in the flesh before her early death, even if we call this a case of 'courtly love' and try to diminish its sincerity in this way. But from a OOO standpoint, the main purpose of aesthetics is not critique, but involvement: writing is good primarily if it earns the reader's absorption. Now, the best way to engage the reader's attention is not to capture their intellectual interest, which is always somewhat faint and feeble compared with our various animal energies. Nor is the point to flatter the reader's nihilistic alienation from puppies and rainbows. Instead, if we hope to earn the reader's conviction, we must earn their emotional investment. Histrionics must of course be avoided, but not all theatre is histrionic; excessive and spurious emotion should be expunged from one's writing, as Baldwin suggests, but few would argue that *all* emotion is excessive and spurious. As for *Uncle Tom's Cabin*, it cannot be rejected on the basis of sentiment alone, but only through a consideration of whether the sentiments it displays are really too false or extreme. We should also stand ready to condemn, aesthetically, work in which emotion is cold and lacking – as when the characters are too detached, posing as thinking subjects removed from a world that seems in danger of alienating them the moment they stoop to taking it seriously. I think here of Jean-Paul Sartre's *Nausea* (which is not ageing well in my own life as a reader) and even of Wright's aforementioned *Native Son*, whose bleakness seems to make it work better as a political statement, as a 'protest novel', than as literature in the sense that Baldwin means.

To summarise, the necessary autonomy of a literary work from its context does not entail that the characters and reader ought also to be autonomous from the entities with which they are involved. Ultimately, the topic of literature is not the observing transcendent subject alienated from a world that is something utterly different in kind, but the loves and other passionate bonds between characters and objects and readers and objects. What is at issue is fascination with the world: not the cool detachment of the pseudo-hip Brooklyn barista who would only answer my questions not with words, but with infinitesimal movements of the head never exceeding a centimetre. May he freeze forever near the base of Dante's hell, where he would be a good fit according to the Florentine poet's cosmology, which does not reward detachment.

But a different question is also important here, a question concerning what is external to the literary work. If formalism is about excluding effects on the outside world from a consideration of literature itself, what are we to make of a novel like *Uncle Tom's Cabin*, which was 'spectacularly persuasive' (Tompkins 2010: 557) and enjoys much of its acclaim for that very reason? In fact, Tompkins does not spend much time discussing the role of Stowe's novel in ending slavery, perhaps because that story is already well known. But another reason may come from Tompkins's sense, or at least her sense of Stowe's sense, that the mere legal erasure of slavery is not enough:

> The political and economic measures that constitute effective action for us, [Stowe] regards as superficial, mere extensions of the worldly policies that produced the slave system in the first place . . . [S]he recommends, not specific alterations in the current economic and political arrangements, but rather a change of heart. (2010: 549)

Note that this itself is also a formalist move insofar as it champions the spirit over the letter, or the background over the foreground: as in Heidegger's focus on Being over visible individual beings, Greenberg's insistence on the flat canvas background over the pictorial content that he dismisses as mere 'literary anecdote', or Marshall McLuhan's dictum that the content of any medium is no more important than graffiti on the atomic bomb (Harman 2013a).

Yet the 'change of heart' recommended by Stowe is not unconnected with the external world; indeed. according to Tompkins it is meant to pave the way for a sweeping women's revolution intended to transform human civilisation as a whole. What Stowe aims at, Tompkins says, is not just the liberation of the slaves, but a remaking of the human world in the image of Christian love as exemplified in the boundless care of motherhood (Tompkins 2010: 557). Tompkins calls our attention to Stowe's work with her sister Catherine Beecher, as displayed in an ambitious 1869 work entitled *The American Woman's Home*. In this book, 'a wealth of scientific information and practical advice is pointed toward a millenarian goal' (Tompkins 2010: 558). Far from a frivolous avoidance of serious political issues, Tompkins argues, the Stowe sisters' obsession with domestic concerns in this book 'is the prerequisite of world conquest, defined as the reformation of the human race through proper care and nurturing of its young'. This nurturing extends to such points of detail as the assertion that 'the bed frame is to be fourteen inches wide, and three inches in thickness' (2010: 558–9). In short, 'the home, rather than representing a retreat or a refuge from a crass industrial-commercial world, offers an economic *alternative* to that world, one which calls into question the whole structure of American society' (2010: 560).

Thus we have seen that Tompkins offers a positive reading of the very features of *Uncle Tom's Cabin* that lead Baldwin to dismiss it as subliterary rubbish. She also defends the sentimentalism that Baldwin abhors, and though she does so primarily on feminist political grounds, they are perfectly compatible with OOO's non-political argument that sentimental attachment belongs at the heart of the literary enterprise. Ignoring Baldwin's denunciation of the protest novel as a properly literary genre, Tompkins praises *Uncle Tom's Cabin* both as an anti-slavery novel ('probably the most influential book ever written by an American') and as an important contribution to a theory of politically subversive matriarchy (2010: 558). On this point we would still join Baldwin in wondering whether this is really the role of literature per se. But the time has come to draw some more general conclusions.

Conclusions

The main intellectual virtue of the concept of 'autonomy' is that it prevents premature mixing of everything with everything else. If Kant had not placed autonomy at the foundation of his ethics, it would have been difficult to sift truly ethical actions from those undertaken for mainly selfish reasons. If he had not distinguished what is beautiful in art from what is merely agreeable, art criticism might degenerate into mere expressions of personal reaction. Like any other philosophy, this modern formalism of Kant has its vices, and before discussing Baldwin and Tompkins, we identified three of them.

The first was the Kantian formalist taxonomy, which splits up the world into two and only two kinds of things: humans and nonhumans. This standpoint makes it urgent for Kant that, whether in ethics or aesthetics, there must be no cross-contamination between humans and any of the trillions of other things known as nonhumans. To appeal to results in ethics, or to objects in art, is to spoil what ought to be a self-contained process unfolding on the human side of the divide. I responded to this first vice of formalism by speaking in favour of sentimentality. Though I too hate cloying and manipulative emotion, the aloof human subject is such a philosophically unjustified model that I would almost rather read a children's book about kittens and unicorns than take another tour of Sartre's *Nausea*, much though I loved it in high school. The unit of literature, like the unit of ethics, is the human's sincere absorption in something that they are not: as in Dante, contra Sartre and his tiresome alienation.

The second vice of formalism was its tendency to lapse into holism. With the outside world safely walled off from access, the literary work was to become a perfect machine in which all elements responded hypersensitively to all others. My response to this vice was outlined in 'The Well-Wrought Broken Hammer' (Harman 2012), and primarily involved treating the literary work as made up of countless internal components that might be rearranged in different ways without violating the sacrosanct vision of the author. A historical parallel for this might be the impersonal stocks of national myth in which various characters perform slightly different actions in different retellings of the same stories, or with contemporary superheroes who are recreated constantly in ever-different adaptations without thereby losing their identity.

The third vice concerns formalism's tendency to over-exclude the outside world. Tompkins's essay on *Uncle Tom's Cabin* reminded us how obtuse the results of this can be. For in the case of Stowe's novel, the American Civil War has retroactively become part of the novel itself, and Tompkins even makes a plausible case for a sweeping feminist project at the base of the novel. On one level, we must resist the effort to historicise literary works, since – in the spirit of Baldwin – to reduce literature to a political cause (or a cultural consequence) is to let it blur into the world as a whole, and thus loses sight of the distinct challenges posed by literature in contrast with those of politics and society. Yet with every literary work, there is the possibility of forging a link between a work and some aspect of its context, and with some literary works there is no way to avoid this: *Uncle Tom's Cabin* is one such example, and so is the New Testament, if we are permitted to consider the latter document as literature. In cases of this sort, we have gone beyond literature strictly speaking, and entered the realm of hybrids or compounds. A better word would be the evolutionary biologist Lynn Margulis's 'symbiosis', in which two life forms join up to become a new third one (Margulis 1999).[7] If literary works sometimes (not always) hook up or symbiose with their surroundings, this is because they cease being literature in the strict sense and enter a different life cycle more comparable to that of the Bible. So it is with *Uncle Tom's Cabin*.

Notes

1. It was only while revising the final draft of this chapter that I first read Caroline Levine's wonderful book *Forms: Whole, Rhythm, Hierarchy, Network* (Levine 2015), so refreshing for its polite way of replacing numerous clichés and pieties with fresh ideas. The similarities between Levine's approach and my own are significant enough for me to prefer to deal with them separately elsewhere. But it can be said that our major point of agreement is our shared wish to extend the topic of 'form' into numerous spheres from which it is currently excluded. Meanwhile, our major disagreement is that Levine's heavy commitment to the 'affordances' (potential relations) of forms separates her from the object-oriented insistence that forms are mutually cut off from one another in a rather severe way that makes relations the exception rather than the rule. Yet the points of agreement are both numerous and encouraging. Among them is a shared view that half of the so-called 'New Formalism' movement – the half that Marjorie Levinson terms 'activist formalism' in her helpful overview 'What is New Formalism?' (Levinson 2007: 559) – grants excessive priority to narrowly political forms.
2. On the political role of inanimate things see Graham Harman, *Bruno Latour: Reassembling the Political* (Harman 2014a), as well as a fine article by Peer Schouten, 'The Materiality of State Failure' (Schouten 2013).
3. See my *Art and Objects* (Harman 2019). For a different sort of argument as to why Fried and Hegel are not a good match, see Knox Peden, 'Grace and Equality, Fried and Rancière (and Kant)' (Peden 2018).
4. Another book that makes a strong case for the role of inanimate objects in human ethics is Alphonso Lingis, *The Imperative* (Lingis 1998).
5. See my discussion of Marcel Duchamp in chapter 6 of *Art and Objects* (Harman 2019).
6. See Harman, *Object-Oriented Ontology*, chapter 2 (Harman 2018).
7. I applied Margulis's concept of symbiosis to the question of social theory in my book *Immaterialism* (Harman 2016b).

Bibliography

Aristotle (1999), *Metaphysics*, J. Sachs (trans.), Santa Fe: Green Lion Press.
Baldwin, James (2010), 'Everybody's Protest Novel', in Harriet Beecher Stowe, *Uncle Tom's Cabin*, 2nd edn, Elizabeth Ammons (ed.), New York: W. W. Norton, pp. 532–9.
Fried, Michael (1988), *Absorption and Theatricality: Painting and Beholder in the Age of Diderot*, Chicago: University of Chicago Press.
Fried, Michael (1996), *Manet's Modernism: or, The Face of Painting in the 1860s*, Chicago: University of Chicago Press.
Fried, Michael (1998), 'Art and Objecthood', in Michael Fried, *Art and Objecthood: Essays and Reviews*, Chicago: University of Chicago Press, pp. 148–72.

Greenberg, Clement (1986), *The Collected Essays and Criticism, Vol. 1: Perceptions and Judgments*, Chicago: University of Chicago Press.
Greenblatt, Stephen (2005), *Will in the World: How Shakespeare Became Shakespeare*, New York: W. W. Norton.
Harman, Graham (2012), 'The Well-Wrought Broken Hammer: Object-Oriented Literary Criticism', *New Literary History*, 43:2, pp. 183–203.
Harman, Graham (2013a), 'Undermining, Overmining, and Duomining: A Critique', in Jenna Sutela (ed.), *ADD Metaphysics*, Aalto: Aalto University Research Design Laboratory, pp. 40–51.
Harman, Graham (2013b), 'The Revenge of the Surface: Heidegger, McLuhan, Greenberg', *Paletten*, 291/292, pp. 66–73.
Harman, Graham (2014a), *Bruno Latour: Reassembling the Political*, London: Pluto.
Harman, Graham (2014b), 'Art without Relations', *ArtReview*, 66:66, pp. 144–7.
Harman, Graham (2014c), 'Greenberg, Duchamp, and the Next Avant-Garde', *Speculations*, 5, pp. 251–74.
Harman, Graham (2016a), *Dante's Broken Hammer: The Ethics, Aesthetics, and Metaphysics of Love*, London: Repeater.
Harman, Graham (2016b), *Immaterialism: Objects and Social Theory*, Cambridge: Polity.
Harman, Graham (2018), *Object-Oriented Ontology: A New Theory of Everything*, London: Pelican.
Harman, Graham (2019), *Art and Objects*, Cambridge: Polity.
Kant, Immanuel (1987), *Critique of Judgment*, Werner S. Pluhar. (trans.), Indianapolis: Hackett.
Kant, Immanuel (1998), *Groundwork of the Metaphysics of Morals*, M. Gregor (trans.), Cambridge: Cambridge University Press.
Kant, Immanuel (2002), *Critique of Practical Reason*, Werner S. Pluhar (trans.), Indianapolis: Hackett.
Kant, Immanuel (2003), *Critique of Pure Reason*, Norman Kemp Smith (trans.), London: Palgrave Macmillan.
Keats, John (1977), *The Complete Poems*, London: Penguin.
Latour, Bruno (1993), *We Have Never Been Modern*, Catherine Porter (trans.), Cambridge, MA: Harvard University Press.
Levine, Caroline (2015), *Forms: Whole, Rhythm, Hierarchy, Network*, Princeton: Princeton University Press.
Levinson, Marjorie (2007), 'What is New Formalism?', *PMLA*, 122:2, pp. 558–69.
Lingis, Alphonso (1998), *The Imperative*, Bloomington: Indiana University Press.
Margulis, Lynn (1999), *Symbiotic Planet: A New Look at Evolution*, New York: Basic Books.
Peden, Knox (2018), 'Grace and Equality, Fried and Rancière (and Kant)', in Mathew Abbott (ed.), *Michael Fried and Philosophy*, Kindle edn, pp. 189–205.
Pippin, Robert (2014), *After the Beautiful: Hegel and the Philosophy of Pictorial Modernism*, Chicago: University of Chicago Press.
Sartre, Jean-Paul (1975), *Nausea*, Lloyd Alexander (trans.), New York: New Directions.
Scheler, Max (1973), *Formalism in Ethics and Non-Formal Ethics of Values: A New Attempt toward the Foundation of an Ethical Personalism*, Manfred Frings and Robert Funk (trans.), Evanston: Northwestern University Press.
Scheler, Max (1992), 'Ordo Amoris', in Max Scheler, *Selected Philosophical Essays*, David Lachterman (trans.), Evanston: Northwestern University Press, pp. 98–135.

Schouten, Peer (2013), 'The Materiality of State Failure: Social Contract Theory, Infrastructure and Governmental Power in Congo', *Millennium: Journal of International Studies*, 41:3, pp. 553–74.
Stowe, Harriet Beecher (2010), *Uncle Tom's Cabin*, 2nd edn, Elizabeth Ammons (ed.), New York: W. W. Norton.
Tompkins, Jane P. (2010), 'Sentimental Power: *Uncle Tom's Cabin* and the Politics of Literary History', in Harriet Beecher Stowe, *Uncle Tom's Cabin*, 2nd edn, Elizabeth Ammons (ed.), New York: W. W. Norton, pp. 539–61.
Wright, Richard (2005a), 'How "Bigger" Was Born', in Richard Wright, *Native Son*, New York: Harper, pp. 431–62.
Wright, Richard (2005b), *Native Son*, New York: Harper.

11

A Field of Heteronyms and Homonyms: New Materialism, Speculative Fabulation, and Wor(l)ding

Helen Palmer

But what about making the world, this world, the old one?

(Le Guin 1989: 46)

The imagination is a tool of resistance ... Welcome to the future.

(Womack 2013: 24)

The satellites are spinning
A new day is dawning
The galaxies are waiting
For planet Earth's awakening

(Ra 2005: 331)

Black existence and science fiction are one and the same.

(*Mothership Connection* 1995)

We wield 'science fiction' voice and word to manifest world-paradigms necessary for our survival. Empire does not welcome this. *Ride with us against empire*.

(Metropolarity n.d.)

Prologue: THE FIELD

In a Taiwanese restaurant in downtown Sydney, a group of IT managers were quizzing her about the field she worked in. Haltingly, she surmised that the field was probably many interconnecting fields, and that her own background was both literary and philosophical, and that language was material, and the scope for innovation in language could be political and could be used to make material changes in the world, particularly in terms of new materialism and intersectional feminism. She said that new materialism was a field concerned with the matter that made up the world.

One of the IT managers had a glint in his eye. He wanted, he said, to know a bit more about this field. Where was the field? How big was the field? Who created the field? Who else was in the field? Was camping allowed in the field?

In a similarly ludic vein she addressed his queries earnestly, seriously, one by one, and between them sprouted a Field of unknowable dimensions. The meandering directions of the furrows ploughed in The Field were expressed via the medium of rapid-flowing arm movements; the colour of her interlocutor's tent in his agreed patch of The Field was decided upon; they discussed the implications of holding raves in The Field; the merits of camouflage versus fluorescent clothing in The Field; the presence of cows in The Field; what the cows ate in The Field. He began to ask her whether he would actually be permitted in The Field, but then stopped himself. If The Field operated according to a flat ontology, owned by both everyone and no one, he reasoned, then why would he need to ask her permission?

She said: all are welcome in The Field.

She did not say: Fredric Jameson might call The Field a formalist's prison-house.

She did not say: Lewis Carroll's generic 'it', usually described as 'a frog or a worm', might well be found in The Field.

She did not say: Noam Chomsky might call The Field a furiously sleeping colourless green idea (Jameson 1972; Carroll 2001: 53; Chomsky 1957: 15).

Fields, then, she thought later on as she switched off the light, are clearly unstable concepts with differing material realities. All well and good, but beyond a quasi-Wittgensteinian highlighting of the limits of our articulation of the boundaries of abstraction and concretion, what was it about this reductio *of the concept of the academic field that might be useful? Maybe it could be useful because it demonstrated the unique position of new materialism and speculative fabulation to enact worlds; to verb nouns; to story stories; to make matters matter; or to world wor(l)ds . . .*

Fictocriticism at the Lip of the World

We shape something when we utter it. Symbolism posits this shaping as a deferral, but it does not need to be seen this way. 'I say: a flower! and outside the oblivion to which my voice relegates my shape, insofar as it is something other than the calyx, there arises musically, as the very idea and delicate, the one absent from every bouquet' (Mallarmé 2001: 25). The step beyond this is the materialist disavowal of symbolic substitution in favour of realisation: the actual presence of the absent flower. Pioneer of Australian fictocriticism Stephen Muecke refers to Mallarmé's flower in his essay 'The Fall':

> We fall for the one who resembles a flower; this is the operation of a romantic percept as old and as complicated as the bouquet. But to know the structure of the plant (or the text) as a concept, is to be able, incredibly, to climb out again, wet, dripping, exhausted, on the lip of the world again. (Muecke 2002: 112)

This essay examines the 'lip of the world', as Muecke puts it, as the movable boundary between fiction and reality, and the concept of wor(l)ding as the problematisation of the distinction between 'lip' and 'world'. The absent/real flower is like the field that emerged from the conversations outlined above. It could be posited in terms of a projected ideality: a utopia, uchronia, or perhaps a combination of the two. As both *ou-* and (incorrectly) *eu-topos*, utopia is both not-place and good-place. Similarly, uchronia operates as the temporal version of this. One of the meanings of 'to speculate' (etymologically, to observe; later, to pursue truth through thinking; later still, to pursue profit through market value buying/selling), therefore, may be to operate as though the posited *ou* of utopia/uchronia has been granted ontological stability beyond its original projection.

The material realisation of a linguistically or symbolically deferred object inhabits the transversal, interpenetrating worlds of speculative fiction, speculative fabulation, science fiction, and a number of other related areas. The blending of these worlds is an ongoing process. There is now nothing unusual about a text that blends elements of fiction, poetry, scientific discourse, and philosophical reasoning. Muecke summarises the state of things with respect to the interpenetration of these worlds: 'The whole artifice of literary criticism was built up in order to do one thing really; to unmask the secrets of art. And the fiction was always there re-enchanting the world by putting on the beautiful masks again and again' (Muecke 2002: 108). The following discussion positions diverse expressions of speculative writing as wor(l)ding; it considers these processes and their contemporary political valency. And for this endeavour we begin predictably, albeit briefly, with Martin Heidegger, whose grammatical iterations and idiosyncrasies form an important part of his ontology, if only to depart from him.

Worlding from Heidegger to Haraway

Heidegger's work sometimes includes sentences comprising a noun which is then refracted into multiple grammatical forms. '*Das Ding dingt*' ('The thing things'), the translators quote him in an explanatory footnote in *What Is a Thing?* (Heidegger 1967: 8n.3), drawing our attention to the link between the noun *Das Ding* ('the Thing') and the verb *bedingen*, 'to cause or condition'. Heidegger performs a similar etymological linkage with 'worlding' and 'world' in 'The Origin of the Work of Art':

> The world is not the mere collection of the countable or uncountable, familiar and unfamiliar things that are just there. But neither is it a merely imagined framework added by our representation to the sum of such given things. The *world worlds*, and is more fully in being than the tangible and perceptible realm in which we believe ourselves to be at home. (Heidegger 1971: 44–5)

The work of art, for Heidegger, sets up a world. The performativity of the noun that repeats itself as a verb or gerund; the world's worlding is the setting up of the world. What, then, is the relationship between wording and worlding; in what ways could we say that the linguistic signifier 'worlds'? Jean-François Lyotard argues for the 'thickness' of the signifier in *Discourse, Figure*, which lends a certain sense of materiality to the signifier relevant to the present discussion. For Lyotard, language possesses a 'world-function', which worlds as it words:

> [O]ut of what it designates, every utterance makes a world, a thick object waiting to be synthesized, a symbol to be deciphered, but these objects and symbols offer themselves in an expanse where showing is possible. This expanse bordering discourse is not itself the linguistic space where the work of signification is carried out, but a worldly type of space, plastic and atmospheric, in which one has to move, circle around things, make their silhouettes vary, in order to utter such and such signification heretofore concealed. (Lyotard 2011: 83)

It is clear that what Lyotard is gesturing towards is a materiality of language. This is the worlding which occurs within all wording; write wor(l)ding. With a few exceptions (see particularly Avanessian and Hennig 2015, 2018), the phenomenon of language's materiality is still not much written about within new materialist circles due to the positing of new materialism as superseding the linguistic turn (see Barad 2003; Ahmed 2008; van der Tuin 2011). Rather than disavow language, however, we may continue to think language *as* matter in dynamic and complex ways. In order to determine what constitutes a process of wor(l)ding, the environment from which it emerges in its contemporary guise, and most importantly, its political valency in terms of reimagined futures and pasts, I will now look at a number of manifestations of wor(l)ding, all related to science fiction in different ways: from Donna Haraway's material-semiotic and later employment of the heteronym Terrapolis to ontologically unstable signs on the street to Afrofuturism's alternative realities, futures, and pasts.

'We are not immediately present to ourselves. Self-knowledge requires a semiotic-material technology to link meanings and bodies', Haraway writes (Haraway 1988: 585). We know from Haraway's earlier work that her conjoining of the material and the semiotic is important in understanding her work. In 'The Promises of Monsters' she uses the term '"material-semiotic actor" to highlight the object of knowledge as an active part of the apparatus of bodily production' (Haraway 2004: 67). Pointing towards the poem as an object with language as an actor, she describes bodies as objects of knowledge and 'material-semiotic generative nodes' (2004: 68). This move is about the insertion of the discursive and the artificial into nature and biology. In this context, it should not be forgotten that it is literature to which Haraway turns as her model for what she calls the apparatus of bodily production, using specifically Katie King's description of the 'apparatus of literary production' (Haraway 2004: 68). This model is extended to encompass the production and reproduction of bodies and other objects of value in scientific knowledge projects. This is the inspiration for Haraway's concept of the material-semiotic actor. In 'The Promises of Monsters' she charts the relationship between science fiction and a series of concepts that we would now claim are distinctly new materialist: 'Science fiction is generically concerned with the interpenetration of boundaries between problematic selves and unexpected others and with the exploration of possible worlds in a context structured by transnational technoscience' 2004: 70). Science fiction also informs Haraway's reading of Trinh T. Minh-ha's concept of 'inappropriate/d others':

> If Western patriarchal narratives have told that the physical body issued from first birth, while man was the product of the second birth, perhaps a differential, diffracted feminist allegory might have 'inappropriate/d others' emerge from a third birth into an SF world called elsewhere – a place composed from interference patterns. (Haraway 2004: 70)

It is clear when Haraway is sketching out her version of worlding that she is keen to separate her use of the term from Heidegger's: 'Finished once and for all with Kantian globalizing cosmopolitics and grumpy human-exceptionalist Heideggerian worlding, *Terrapolis* is a mongrel word composted with a mycorrhiza of Greek and Latin rootlets and their symbionts' (Haraway 2016: 11). Wor(l)ding for Haraway manifests itself in the SF sense: 'a risky game of worlding and storying; it is staying with the trouble' (2016: 13).

Some of her earlier thinking around the conception of worlding can be seen in her *Companion Species Manifesto* (2003) as in her subsequent reference to Alfred North Whitehead's process philosophy, specifically concerning his theory of prehensions. 'Reality is an active verb, and the nouns all seem to be gerunds with more appendages than an octopus' (Haraway 2003: 6), she writes, and of course tentacularity rears its tendrils later for her not merely as a figure but as an active mode of thought. Here we are explicitly made aware of the noun-as-gerund, active world*ing*, which in Haraway's most recent work is put into effect in the creation of Terrapolis: 'a story, a speculative fabulation, and a strong figure for multispecies worlding' (Haraway 2016: 10). As speculative fabulation and as heteronym (both terms discussed below), Terrapolis is Haraway's own particular 'matter-realising' (Braidotti 2013: 95) of The Field.

Agential Realism and the Material-Discursive

The shifting of noun to infinitive to gerund in the various theorisations of worlding ('world'–'to world'–'worlding') is also an important constituent part of Karen Barad's agential realism. Akin to Haraway's use of the gerund in the term world*ing*, Barad speaks of matter*ing*: 'In an agential realist account, matter does not refer to a fixed substance; rather, *matter is substance in its intra-active becoming – not a thing but a doing, a congealing of agency*' (Barad 2007: 151). Barad's account of agential realism works by means of entangling the material with the discursive. For Barad, matter 'is not a linguistic construction but a discursive production in the posthumanist sense' (2007: 151). Matter itself for Barad is always simultaneously a noun and a verb, because matter means mattering – or, as she writes it, matter(ing). The wor(l)dings discussed here are matter(ings).

The shift from materiality understood as thing to materiality understood as a doing is most clearly outlined in Barad's agential realism, which emerges from her unique reading of Niels Bohr's work. Bohr's development and critique of classical physics culminates, in Barad's words, in the following result: '*the nature of the observed phenomenon changes with corresponding changes in the apparatus*' (Barad 2007: 106). For Barad, Bohr thus demonstrates the inseparability, or entanglement, of the phenomenon and the apparatus, of matter and meaning. Epistemologically: '*No inherent/Cartesian subject–object distinction exists*' (Barad 2007: 114). Barad's reading of Bohr's epistemological framework results in the following statement: 'referentiality must be reconceptualised. The referent is not an observation-independent object but a phenomenon' (Barad 2007: 120). Bohr, according to Barad, situates practice within theory, and as a result, the processes of 'method, measurement, description, interpretation, epistemology, and ontology are not separable considerations' (Barad 2007: 120–1). Barad's reading of Bohr demonstrates that instead of taking words and things as separate and even opposing kinds of existents, we can take hold of both these existents simultaneously. Agential realism for Barad is a posthumanist theory of performativity that understands the primary ontological unit as the phenomenon. Phenomena for Barad are 'dynamic topological reconfigurings/entanglements/relationalities/(re)articulations of the world' (2007: 141). It is precisely this inseparability of matter and discourse that can allow wor(l)ding to take place.

Speculative Topoi: Afrofuturism as Uchronia

> *Ustopia* is a word I made up by combining utopia and dystopia – the imagined perfect society and its opposite – because, in my view, each contains a latent version of the other. (Atwood 2011: 66)

We could say that the 'fields' referred to so far are speculative topoi, of which a speculative spectrum already exists: from utopia to dystopia. As Margaret Atwood states above, it is possible for these to be conflated. The concept of dystopia is just as prevalent in discussions of contemporary world politics as it is in literary academia. In May 2017, for example, a conference called Dystopia Now was held at Birkbeck University in London. It is no longer surprising, nor is it an exaggeration, to say that dystopia *is* now. We see signatures of dystopia now everywhere. The Dystopia Now conference was held by the Centre for Contemporary Literature, but the topic bleeds outwards into all aspects of life. Dystopia really is now. The blurring of fiction and 'real life' is hardly a new phenomenon, but there are signs of a more intense perception of dystopia, heretofore understood exclusively in terms of a future-looking literary genre, as already happening in our reality, right now. Consider the statement below.

> Post Apocalyptic Fiction has been moved to our Current Affairs section.

This statement was written on a blackboard outside a New York bookstore in 2016 and was shared widely on social media. The literalisation of the radical genre-shift from fiction to 'real-life' demonstrates the incredulity with which humans are currently facing the world, and the increasing applicability of categories of fiction to lived experience. One effect of this phenomenon is the potential for categories of fiction to have material effects on lived experience. As a genre, science fiction has the potential to foretell scientific developments in the 'real' world, and the nature of speculation makes it harder to see where the fiction ends and the real begins. What is interesting about this kind of writing is that it relates real life to fiction in a very direct way. It demonstrates that the blurring of these realms is no longer confined to academic spheres. Perhaps dystopia is no longer a speculative topos; perhaps it has already been taken up in processes of wor(l)ding.

Wor(l)ding is, then, a particular blending of the material and the semiotic that can be perceived in what we call science fiction, speculative fiction, SF. Among other things, this transdisciplinary blend is apt to blur the boundaries between subject and environment, just as in Barad's agential realist account discussed above. Science fiction is particularly useful in demonstrating the multifarious inseparability of subject and object. As Atwood outlines in the introduction to her book on the topic, SF in its multiple contested forms and subgenres deals with 'those imagined other worlds located somewhere apart from our everyday one: in another time, in another dimension, through a doorway into the spirit world, or on the other side of the threshold that divides the known from the unknown' (Atwood 2011: 8). Science fiction is constituted by the wor(l)ding of an alternative topos; the 'SF world called "elsewhere"' mentioned by Haraway and quoted above. It comes as no surprise to those for whom 'other' has been an identifiable political category that the reimagining of these 'elsewheres' carries particular political-subjective applicability. This is why Afrofuturism is so important to this discussion. The wor(l)dings discussed below afford and create alternative spaces for those denied their place in the spaces already existing.

The alternative reimagining of pasts is sometimes called uchronia, although spatial or geographical descriptors are still widely used.[1] In June 2015, photographer Maciek Pozoga and musicologist Christopher Kirkley collaborated on an exploration of sound and image called 'Uchronia: The Unequivocal Interpretation of Reality' (Pozoga and Kirkley 2015). Exhibited in Bamako, Mali, the premise of the exhibition was speculative and political: what would have happened if a Malian emperor rather than Christopher Columbus had discovered America? This story was a development or continuation of a story that Pozoga had read about online, namely that in 1311 the Malian emperor Abubakari II left West Africa to explore the Atlantic Ocean. Pozoga's aim with this project is described by Helen Jennings as wanting 'to capture a sense of surface disorientation through the lens of folklore and science fiction thereby creating a space where it's the Azawad rebels and imperialist hangover that are unreal' (Jennings 2015). Whilst the 'Uchronia' exhibition speculates on historical narratives in order to produce a uchronia, other examples of Afrofuturist art and literature speak of a more mythological temporality. The cycle of birth, death, and renewal is given an Afrofuturist treatment in Tonya Liburd's poem 'Contemplation' (2016) by means of a mythic intertwining of trees, earth, and ancestral spirituality. The speaker of the poem digs herself an early grave, fatigued with the feeling that the entire earth amounts to an 'elsewhere' for her. In a few lines the entirety of human civilisation's trajectory of racial injustice is charted: 'as human civilization went on and on ... black-skinned men / pounded spikes, hammered tracks ... everything controlled by pale-skinned men, who miser'd / knowledge / and had guns'. The poem's speaker becomes entwined with the roots of trees and the earth itself: 'rich loam attached to my eyelashes'. At the end of the poem the speaker rises newly empowered, 'a creature of the Earth like any other', and is deferred to by the men she comes across, 'elder to eldest'. The poem draws to a close as the speaker is endowed with a 'new purpose' (Liburd 2016: 3). The temporal manipulation and the creation of alternative mythologies are common aspects of futurism in its initial manifestation at the beginning of the twentieth century. Both Italian and Russian futurists played around with the concept of time and created grand mythologies whilst differing wildly in their political agendas, yet neither used their futurism for specifically emancipatory purposes, or to redress the balance of racial injustice.[2] This is Afrofuturist writing as wor(l)ding, the creation of an alternative poetic world which has implications beyond the text.

Afrofuturism is a highly pertinent example of wor(l)ding because the world as it stands is already experienced as an elsewhere by people of colour. 'I'm black. I'm solitary. I've always been an outsider', states Octavia Butler in the *LA Times* in 1998 (Warrick 1998). This spawns the need for new alternative topoi. This is the argument of Sun Ra, Afrofuturist pioneer, in the classic film *Space Is the Place*:

> I'm not real. I'm just like you. You don't exist in this society. If you did, your people wouldn't be seeking equal rights. You're not real. If you were, you'd have some status among the nations of the world. So we're both myths. I do not come to you as a reality; I come to you as the myth, because that's what black people are. Myths. (Ra 1974)

Ra is persuading the black youths of Oakland to join him, arguing that they may as well create their own reality because they do not currently have the status of 'reality',

> since this planet for thousands of years has been up under that law of death and destruction, it's moving into something else which I choose to call MYTH, a MYTH-SCIENCE, because it's something that people don't know anything about. That's why I'm using the name MYTH-SCIENCE ARKESTRA, because I'm interested in happiness for people, which is just a myth, because they're not happy. I would say that the synonym for myth is happiness. Because that's why they go to the show, to the movies, they be sitting up there under these myths trying to get themselves some happiness. (Ra quoted in Sinclair 2010: 28)

It is important to point out that the multidirectional temporal aspect of Ra's Afrofuturism is evident in his constant use of ancient Egyptian mythology as already on display in his name, which is taken from the Egyptian sun god Ra. For Ra the Afrofuturist, whilst ancient Egypt remained 'his single lodestar where African mythology was concerned' (Lock 1999: 74), this turn to ancient Egypt was in essence future-oriented.

Sofia Samatar's epic piece 'Notes Toward a Theory of Quantum Blackness' contains statements such as 'All models of quantum blackness attempt to develop a new geometry' (Samatar 2016). As the author states in a brief prefatory comment, the poem is about 'blackness as gravity'. The scientific hypotheses are used speculatively, as pointers towards alternative types of thinking, but the message is clear: the existing structural systems are racially unequal and therefore new systems must be invented. 'Blackness cannot be integrated with quantum mechanics at very high energies. At lower energies, it is ignored; to address energies at or higher than the Planck scale, a new theory of quantum blackness is required.' The language of scientific observation and measurement is woven amongst the objects and signs of racial injustice and slavery, rendered in phrases such as 'the curvature of space-time is caused by the unequal distribution of mass / energy', and 'Plot the distance between bullet and flesh ... Between throat and hair. Between hunger and time of day' (2016). These interweavings both critique and affirm scientific methodologies, ultimately advocating a more nuanced branch of 'woke' futurist thinking which is at the heart of Afrofuturism.

Samatar's poem is acknowledged as part of a larger conversation involving the Black Quantum Futurism Collective. An artistic and literary collaboration between Camae Dennis and Rasheedah Phillips, the collective outlines Black Quantum Futurism as a practice (BQF) in three modes: Future Visioning, Future Altering, and Future Manifestation. According to Phillips, a BQF creative (she uses the noun to describe someone operating from a BQF perspective) 'exploits the fact that the future can alter the present and the present can alter the past' (Phillips 2015: 19). The use of 'quantum' here is careful: in the *Black Quantum Futurism: Theory and Practice, Vol. I* Phillips produces a 'BQF Correspondence Chart' in which various quantum phenomena are presented alongside African spiritual and religious phenomena, as well as physical descriptions and real-world correspondences. For example, wave-particle dualism described in physical terms is mapped onto the ancient Egyptian concept of the Tuat, Ka, and Qeb (Ankh Amen) and then described in certain 'real-world' manifestations (2015: 76–7). These impressive transhistorical wor(l)dings are uchronic in the sense that the unit of quanta is speculatively sourced in ancient times, thereby achieving precisely the 'elsewhere' of a future-present-past 'retrocausality' that Philips outlines.

Steampunk is another uchronic subgenre of science fiction that has been given an Afrofuturist makeover in recent times. Nisi Shawl's *Everfair* (2016) rewrites parts of history in order to create alternative futures. The novel explores the horrific Belgian colonisation of the Congo through imagining how things could have been if the native populations had learned about steam technology earlier. The utopian/uchronic Everfair is a haven not only for the native populations of the

Congo, but also for slaves escaping from other colonised places. As Shawl notes at the beginning:

> The steampunk genre often works as a form of alternative history ... I like to think that with a nudge or two events might have played out *much* more happily for the inhabitants of Equatorial Africa ... Of course steampunk is a form of fiction, a fantasy, and the events within these pages never happened. But they *could* have. (Shawl 2016: 7)

The modality of the '*could* have' in Shawl's excerpt above is important; it speaks of a vital contingency which is discussed further below. To what degree, then, are Afrofuturist steampunk fiction and quantum blackness material-semiotic actors or causes? We need only look as far as the proliferation of Afrofuturism itself to discern material effects: films, comics, poetry, fiction, theory, visual art, and music, to name just some examples of this flourishing. If we take 'material' in its financial understanding, the commercial success of the film *Black Panther* and the artist Janelle Monáe demonstrates this very clearly. *Black Panther* contains another uchronic wor(l)ding wherein the fictional nation Wakanda, in possession of the invaluable element of vibranium (somewhat resonant with Flann O'Brien's omnium, discussed below), flourishes and yet masquerades as a third world country to the outside world. Monáe's vast inventiveness in terms of her own personae includes the heteronym of messianic ArchAndroid Cindi Mayweather. As Monáe states in a feature in *Blues and Soul*:

> [T]o me the android will represent a new Other – just like any of us who've ever been considered 'the minority' at some time can feel like 'The Other!' And so I'm basically asking people to think about whether we'd DISCRIMINATE against this new 'Other' ... And what makes the ArchAndroid herself very special is that she represents the MEDIATOR between the haves and the have nots, the minority and the majority. (Lewis 2018)

The alignment of the android with the Other shows why the function of the heteronym is of particular use within Afrofuturism: it allows the 'have nots' to reimagine and reinvent. In Harawayesque, material-semiotic terms, articulations such as these are themselves signifiers with material effects in the world.

Wor(l)dings: Speculative Fabulation, Hyperstition, Fictioning, Myth-Science

Where else can we find comparable processes of wor(l)ding, and what are the factors that differentiate them? Warwick's CCRU (Cybernetic Culture Research Unit) defined what they called hyperstition as the process in which fiction is not opposed to the real. Rather, reality is understood to be composed of fictions – consistent semiotic terrains that condition perceptual, affective and behavioural responses ... Rather than acting as transcendental screens, blocking out contact between itself and the world, the fiction acts as a Chinese box – a container for sorcerous interventions in the world. (CCRU 2004: 278)

Hyperstition has been discussed and perceived at various significant points as the creation of fictophilosophical concepts: for example, Luciana Parisi describes Laboria Cuboniks' Xenofeminist Manifesto as 'an exercise in hyperstition: a thought experiment or an enabler of the future' and Haraway's cyborg figuration as 'a radical hyperstitional attempt at exposing the alien or denaturalised fabrication of gender' (Parisi 2017: 215, 217). Similarly, Simon O'Sullivan has used Lyotard's claim that art can multiply the fantasies of realism in order to develop his related concept of 'fictioning', and then, specifically, 'science-fictioning', departing from and incorporating the Afrofuturist concept of myth-science (O'Sullivan 2017). Citing Haraway, O'Sullivan draws our particular attention to the transition from 'world' to 'worlding' that we see in her work and compares this with his own examination of the transition from 'fiction' to 'fictioning' (Gunkel, Hameed, and O'Sullivan 2017: 13). The temporal paradox of science-fictioning, according to O'Sullivan, is

> how to be in the world but not wholly of that world; the important part being that there is no attempt to solve this paradox, rather it is made manifest. This is fictioning as mythopoiesis: the imaginative transformation of the world through fiction. (O'Sullivan 2016: 6)

As O'Sullivan and others are aware, we can trace this hyperstitional fictioning-as-mythopoiesis back to Henri Bergson's notion of *fabulation*, sometimes translated as 'myth-making', such as in *The Two Sources of Morality and Religion*. This myth-making faculty for Bergson is not merely the imagination; it is 'a very clearly defined faculty of the mind, that of creating personalities whose stories we relate to ourselves' (Bergson 1977: 195). *Fabulation*, or its English translation 'myth-making', for Bergson, is no less than a 'fundamental demand of life' and 'to be deduced from the conditions of existence of the human species' (Bergson 1977: 196). Myth-making links up ancient tales with contemporary novels, and, according to Bergson, the entire development of the human race. 'If the human species does exist, it is because the very act which posited man with his tool-contriving intelligence, with the necessary continuation of his intellectual effort, and the danger arising from such a continuation, begot the myth-making function' (1977: 197). Whilst Bergson's function here has a religious purpose, Ridvan Askin analyses the Bergsonian concept of fabulation as taken up by Gilles Deleuze and Félix Guattari in his theory of differential narratology and demonstrates that in Deleuze and Guattari the concept is secularised. Askin goes further than Deleuze and Guattari in his presentation and use of the fabulation function, widening its scope from merely fabulation as fiction to a more general Deleuzian speculative narratology in which fabulation's true function is 'the production of stories in the general sense of narrative rather than in the restricted sense of fiction' (Askin 2016: 69). For Askin, narration is by definition creative and speculative: 'It all boils down to this: in order to narrate, one has to make use of fabulation. In order to speculate, one has to tell a story' (2016: 70).

For a literary example of such hyperstitional, fabulatory imaginative transformation, let me briefly turn to a work which we might call speculative in the above sense and which definitely stretches the boundaries of the absurd, with the full knowledge of definitions being a slippery illusion of solidity in a watery landscape, and with the knowledge that the work would not have been called speculative at the time of publication: Flann O'Brien's *The Third Policeman*. The fictional and almost-but-not-quite-nonsensical philosopher de Selby's identification of a speculative element is relevant to this discussion and deserves a place in the speculative Field: omnium.

> 'You are omnium and I am omnium and so is the mangle and my boots here and so is the wind in the chimney.'
> 'That is enlightening', I said.
> 'It comes in waves', he explained ...
> 'Some people', he said, 'call it energy but the right name is omnium because there is far more than energy in the inside of it, whatever it is. Omnium is the essential inherent interior essence which is hidden inside the root of the kernel of everything and it is always the same ...
> Some people call it God.' (O'Brien 1996: 109–11)

What we have here is a playful, speculative, typological, conceptual persona for the driving force that illuminates, energises, and infuses everything. Omnium: one name for all. While the book was not published before the 1960s, it was written in the 1940s. De Selby almost proposes a kind of speculative vitalism which makes very direct reference to Bergson's philosophy in terms of his notion of the *durée* in order to reanimate a tantalisingly partial Bergsonian world: human existence is a succession of infinitely brief static experiences, and therefore a journey is a series of infinitesimal pauses. Its pleasing neological inventiveness, the engagement with (then) contemporary philosophical theories, and the knowing use of the fabulation function is at least historically interesting. More recently, these earlier examples of wor(l)ding have been refigured, refabulated, and reformed. For example, Elizabeth de Freitas' Laboratory of Speculative Sociology, in her contribution to the 2017 special issue on new materialism of *The Minnesota Review*, is to be understood in a number of different ways simultaneously. It is 'not only or essentially a thermodynamic system but also a quantum event, by which all individuation of object or person is the effect of wave diffraction and temporal permutations', she maintains (de Freitas 2017: 117). When de Freitas writes, in the past tense, that '[g]radually, researchers turned to a more haptic conception of diffraction, one more truly based in the feeling of intensity when two waves meet' (2017: 117), there is a sense that this knowingly fictional fragment might actually foretell the future trajectory of new materialist research into diffraction. This would then be the very action of speculative fabulation: the fiction materialises the real. To elucidate further how speculative fabulation engenders its own materiality, which can then have real spatio-temporal consequences, I will now turn to the use of heteronyms and homonyms.

Wor(l)dings: Heteronymy, Homonymy, and Contingency

What place might '-nym' word-creatures occupy in the Field? Surely this suffix (meaning 'name', from the Greek *onoma*) leads to a relatively limited nomenclature-type thinking. Homonyms – words which have the same pronunciation and spelling but are different in meaning – and heteronyms – words which have the same spelling but different pronunciation and meanings – both have potential to create a speculative proliferation of material-semiotic realities, as the examples below demonstrate. Both homonymy and heteronymy reduplicate worlds through words.

'*Don Quixote* is an accidental book, *Don Quixote* is unnecessary. I can premeditate writing, I can write it, without incurring a tautology' (Borges 1962: 50), we read in Jorge Luis Borges's short story 'Pierre Menard, Author of the *Quixote*'. Indeed, the story makes use of a homonym-like process in which identical articulatory marks or sounds made by the character Pierre Menard produce a replica of Cervantes's *Don Quixote* which is somehow different from the original. It is not a tautology. The difference between the identically written texts, according to the fictional reviewer, is their temporal position. The events taking place since the original publication of Cervantes's work contribute palimpsestically to the richness of the allusions to be found in the rewrite, and the result is an argument for the significance of context. Things matter differently according to their position, which is why the relation between the *Quixote* of 1605 and the *Quixote* of 1939 is analogous to that between homonyms: a rewriting, identical, but not a copy. Homonymy in this sense demonstrates a spatio-temporal, material-semiotic heterogeneity.

The Borgesian process of productive repetition with(out) difference has provoked further twenty-first-century iterations. In 2016 artist Ami Clarke replicated a chapter of former options trader Elie Ayache's book *The Blank Swan: The End of Probability* (which is itself inspired by the Borges story), and argued that this did not constitute a copy. Economic speculation requires the prediction of future events, which is yet another type of wor(l)ding, another type of field. Ayache's *The Blank Swan* (2010) is a critical response to Nassim Nicholas Taleb's *The Black Swan: The Impact of the Highly Improbable* (2007). Taleb's imagined polar worlds of Extremistan and Mediocristan are speculative topoi, they are toponyms. Perhaps they are heterotopias. The supreme law of Mediocristan is as follows: '*When your sample is large, no single instance will significantly change the aggregate or the total.*' In Mediocristan, called a 'utopian' province by Taleb (with speculative tongue firmly in speculative cheek), single events do not really affect the scale of the topos as a whole. The supreme law of Extremistan, by contrast, is as follows: '*In Extremistan, inequalities are such that one single observation can disproportionately impact the aggregate, or the total.*' Variation within distributions is far less constrained, making it harder to make reliable predictions from data. According to Taleb, wealth and almost all social matters are from Extremistan (Taleb 2007: 32–3). The title of Taleb's work, *The Black Swan*, pertains to an unpredictable improbable event which is then explained and made to seem less random. Taleb suggests both Google and 9/11 as examples of black swans.

Ayache's response book *The Blank Swan* counters these ideas very directly. Instead of discussing probability, he discusses contingency. Quantum mechanics, for Ayache, is the 'Black Swan of all Black Swans' (Ayache 2010: 15). The following description he provides echoes Barad in its foregrounding of the inseparability of phenomena and context:

> The quantum phenomenon has the peculiarity of not being separable from its context of manifestation. Depending on the experimental set-up (or context of experiment) the quantum object may disclose itself either as a particle or as a wave, and there is no way we could counterfactually argue, in one context, what the object may have been in the other. (Ayache 2010: 15)

For Ayache, it is contingency which must be compared with writing: for him 'the writing process and the pricing process are two special kinds of processes that do not take place in possibility or in probability, like the traditional stochastic processes' (Ayache 2010: xv). Ayache argues that neither possibility nor probability is a sufficient strategy for the paradoxical dimension wherein one can do something different from predicting history, which is impossible, or replicating it, which is empty. It is contingency, as advocated in Quentin Meillassoux's *After Finitude*, which Ayache believes is the necessary mode of thinking. More radical than chance, more self-defining than probability or possibility, contingency is the modality of modality. Meillassoux points out that contingency means that anything may happen, even that the invariants of the world remain invariants: 'Contingency is such that anything might happen, even nothing at all, so that what is, remains as it is' (Meillassoux 2009: 63). Contingency is similarly defined by Robin Mackay as 'the attempt to think events that take place but *need not take place*: events that could be, or could have been, otherwise' (Mackay 2011: 1). It is clear that contingency and narrative are vitally linked, but how might this be useful for the thinking of material-semiotic realities? According to Mackay, we must 'refuse simply being trapped in a (postmodern) state of mourning for lost certainties' (Mackay 2011: 4). In terms of contingency and narrative, it is interesting that Michael Jay Lewis defines contingency in this context as either 'accident' or 'apposition', both of which are significant for the wor(l)ding function. Whether one or both of these understandings of contingency are employed, its role in narrative as wor(l)ding is clear, and expressed by Lewis in terms of schemas: 'The translatability of the significance of one schema (a fictional one) into the logic of the next (a non-fictional one) is indicated, in part, by the ability of factors such as contingency' (Lewis 2012: 101). For Lewis, contingency is 'the universe's constituent unit' (2012: 114).

Contingency is also an important factor when thinking through the literary function of the heteronym, as we see in Alain Badiou's reading of Pessoa. The literary heteronym is a concrete but fictional alter ego, in contrast to a pseudonym, which is but a 'false name', that is, a different name for one and the same person. 'And so I created a non-existent coterie, placing it all in a framework of reality', writes Pessoa in his letter of 1935 to Adolfo Casais Monteiro (Pessoa 2001: 257). Pessoa's use differs significantly from the linguistic understanding of the heteronym, in which words have the same spelling but different pronunciations and different meanings. Famously, Pessoa developed scores of alternative personae who were cast as distinct characters and authors with their own distinct biographies, works, styles, and theories. Some were poets, some were critics. Ricardo Reis, Alberto Caeiro, and Álvaro de Campos all are and are not Fernando Pessoa. Pessoa's heteronyms, for Badiou, are

> opposed to the anonymous inasmuch as they do not stake a claim upon the One or the All, but instead originarily establish the contingency of the multiple ... For the real universe is at once multiple, contingent, and untotalizable. (Badiou 2005: 44)

It is interesting in Badiou's description that 'contingency' is highlighted here too. Again, it is literary writing that is presented as the medium of contingency. Badiou describes Pessoa's works as 'thought-poems' and reserves the highest praise for his oeuvre, placing Pessoa before any philosopher of modernity, attributing to him simultaneously Platonic and anti-Platonic trajectories and describing his poems in philosophical terms: 'a veritable philosophy of the multiple, of the void, of the infinite. A philosophy that will affirmatively do justice to this world that the gods have forever abandoned' (Badiou 2005: 45). Every heteronym is therefore a wor(l)ding, and this is where a creative and generative philosophy can begin to be thought.

Another example of a discussion of the function of the heteronym can be found in Kodwo Eshun's *More Brilliant than the Sun: Adventures in Sonic Fiction* (1998). This text is full of rhetorical flourishes similar to those we see in Haraway, including a literary heteronym for the world. Haraway's heteronym for the world in *Staying with the Trouble* is Terrapolis (Haraway 2016), whereas Eshun's in *More Brilliant than the Sun* is the Futurhythmachinic Discontinuum (Eshun 1998: 10). A wor(l)ding; a peopled world; both homonym and heteronym functioning synecdochally not just as signature but as what we might call entireosphere. Eshun takes his inspiration from Sun Ra's myth-science in populating a future-past of the world of electronic music that both is and is not our recognisable world.

Eshun builds on the avant-garde and jazz foundations laid down by Ra in the 1970s, moving the musical genres forward into the realms of disco, breakbeat, house, and techno. It is on the subject of early acid house music where Eshun's language really shifts into a gear of phonetic matter*ing* (to use Barad's term) that demonstrates the power of wor(l)ding. He calls upon the strategies of both homonym and heteronym whilst enacting their powers of wor(l)ding in the creation of his replica world of the Futurythmachinic Discontinuum. In this context, he writes about the pioneering acid house DJ Phuture:

> OJ Pierre's heteronym Phuture substitutes the 'f' in future for the 'pH' of the chemical formula and the ph of phono. Ph makes the phuture sound synthetic and phono-chemical. Ph is to sound as silver is to vision. Ph is the silver prefix, the word concentrate. The future becomes a phuturistic Pharmatopia. With Phuture, the sound of the future separates from the look of the phuture. Vision and sound, heteronym and homonym, split off, run away from each other. (Eshun 1998: 94)

Eshun's language does not just evoke; it renders material. Sound and shape effects wor(l)ding through a synthesis of elements: the polysemous, polysensory 'Ph' mentioned above is a prime example. The signature of the name splinters into its material fragments. Not only is the sign thick; the sign is also sharp. Fragments shored against our ruins, or perhaps, fragments assembled to make and remake the world. As Ursula Le Guin so beautifully states,

> To make a new world you start with an old one, certainly. To find a world, maybe you have to have lost one. Maybe you have to be lost. The dance of renewal, the dance that made the world, was always danced here at the edge of things, on the brink, on the foggy coast. (Le Guin 1989: 48)

Epilogue: THE FIELD

The sultry February night was thick with shimmering halfsmearings, halfsmatterings, as she surfed between sleep and waking at the lip of the world. Propped up on the nightstand was a postcard emblazoned with the words WORD THE WORLD BETTER (Foley 2017).

It struck her that personae and topoi . . . or, in the neologononsensical night, persoi and toponae . . . of Haraway and Eshun were not so different. To wor(l)d was to populate the Field with heteronyms and homonyms. Haraway's strings and critters crawled, knotted, entwined themselves around The Field of Terrapolis, as did Eshun's silver prefixes, punctuating, perforating, aerating The Field of the Futurrhythmachinic Discontinuum. To wor(l)d was to fabricate and fabulate, without knowing the outcome, because it was the only thing left to do.

Notes

1. Coined by Charles Renouvier in *Uchronie, l'utopie dans l'histoire: esquisse historique apocryphe du développement de la civilisation européenne tel qu'il n'a pas été, tel qu'il aurait pu être* (Renouvier 2010).
2. For a comparative discussion of Russian and Italian futurism, see Palmer 2014.

Bibliography

Ahmed, Sara (2008), 'Imaginary Prohibitions: Some Preliminary Remarks on the Founding Gestures of the "New Materialism"', *European Journal of Women's Studies*, 15:1, pp. 23–39.
Askin, Ridvan (2016), *Narrative and Becoming*, Edinburgh: Edinburgh University Press.
Atwood, Margaret (2011), *In Other Worlds: SF and the Human Imagination*, London: Virago.
Avanessian, Armen and Anke Hennig (2015), *Present Tense: A Poetics*, London: Bloomsbury.
Avanessian, Armen and Anke Hennig (2018), *Metanoia: A Speculative Ontology of Language, Thinking, and the Brain*, London: Bloomsbury.
Ayache, Elie (2010), *The Blank Swan: The End of Probability*, Chichester: Wiley.
Badiou, Alain (2005), *Handbook of Inaesthetics*, Alberto Toscano (trans.), Stanford: Stanford University Press.
Barad, Karen (2001), 'Re(con)figuring Space, Time, and Matter', in Marianne DeKoven (ed.), *Feminist Locations: Global and Local, Theory and Practice*, New Brunswick: Rutgers University Press, pp. 75–109.
Barad, Karen (2003), 'Posthumanist Performativity: Toward an Understanding of How Matter Comes to Matter', *Signs: Journal of Women in Culture and Society*, 28:3, pp. 801–31.
Barad, Karen (2007), *Meeting the Universe Halfway: Quantum Physics and the Entanglement of Matter and Meaning*, Durham, NC: Duke University Press.
Bergson, Henri (1977), *The Two Sources of Morality and Religion*, R. Ashley Audra and Cloudesley Brereton (trans.), Notre Dame: University of Notre Dame Press.
Borges, Jorge Luis (1962), 'Pierre Menard, Author of the *Quixote*', Anthony Bonner (trans.), in Jorge Luis Borges, *Ficciones*, New York: Grove Press, pp. 45–63.
Braidotti, Rosi (2013), *The Posthuman*, Cambridge: Polity.
Carroll, Lewis (2001), *Alice's Adventures in Wonderland* and *Through the Looking-Glass*, Ware: Wordsworth.
CCRU (Cybernetic Culture Research Unit) (2004), 'Lemurian Time War', in Davis Schneiderman and Philip Walsh (eds), *Retaking the Universe: William S. Burroughs in the Age of Globalization*, London: Pluto, pp. 274–91.
Chomsky, Noam (1957), *Syntactic Structures*, The Hague: Mouton.
Clarke, Ami (2016), *Author of the BLANK Swan*, London: Banner Repeater.
De Freitas, Elizabeth (2017), 'The Laboratory of Speculative Sociology', *The Minnesota Review*, 88, pp. 116–26.
Eshun, Kodwo (1998), *More Brilliant than the Sun: Adventures in Sonic Fiction*, London: Quartet Books.
Eshun, Kodwo (2003), 'Further Considerations on Afrofuturism', *CR: The New Centennial Review*, 3:2, pp. 287–302.
Foley, Jessica (2017), 'Word the World Better', Postcard, part of *Engineering Fictions* box set of scores, CONNECT Centre, Dublin, <www.engineeringfictions.wordpress.com> (last accessed 18 October 2018).
Gunkel, Henriette, Ayesha Hameed, and Simon O'Sullivan (2017), 'Futures and Fictions: A Conversation between Henriette Gunkel, Ayesha Hameed and Simon O'Sullivan', in Henriette Gunkel, Ayesha Hameed, and Simon O'Sullivan (eds), *Futures and Fictions*, London: Repeater, pp. 1–20.
Haraway, Donna (1988), 'Situated Knowledges: The Science Question in Feminism and the Privilege of Partial Perspective', *Feminist Studies*, 14:3, pp. 575–99.

Haraway, Donna (2003), *The Companion Species Manifesto: Dogs, People, and Significant Otherness*, Chicago: Prickly Paradigm Press.

Haraway, Donna (2004), 'The Promises of Monsters: A Regenerative Politics for Inappropriate/d Others', in Donna Haraway, *The Haraway Reader*, London: Routledge, pp. 63–124.

Haraway, Donna (2016), *Staying with the Trouble: Making Kin in the Cthulucene*, Durham, NC: Duke University Press.

Heidegger, Martin (1967), *What Is a Thing?*, W. B. Barton, Jr. and Vera Deutsch (trans.), Chicago: Gateway.

Heidegger, Martin (1971), 'The Origin of the Work of Art', in Martin Heidegger, *Poetry, Language, Thought*, Albert Hofstader (trans.), New York: Harper and Row, pp. 15–87.

Jameson, Fredric (1972), *The Prison-House of Language: A Critical Account of Structuralism and Russian Formalism*, Princeton: Princeton University Press.

Jennings, Helen (2015), 'Maciek Pozoga and Christopher Kirkley Create a Bamako Dreamscape through Photography, Music and their Afrofuturist Imaginings', *Nataal*, <http://nataal.com/uchronia/?rq=Uchronia> (last accessed 18 October 2018).

Le Guin, Ursula K. (1989), 'World-Making', in Ursula K. Le Guin, *Dancing at the Edge of the World: Thoughts on Words, Women, Places*, New York: Grove Press, pp. 46–8.

Lewis, Michael Jay (2012), 'Contingency, Narrative, Fiction: Vogler, Brenkman, Poe', *SubStance*, 41:2 (128), pp. 99–118.

Lewis, Pete (2018), 'Janelle Monae: Funky Sensation', *Blues and Soul*, 1088, <http://www.bluesandsoul.com/feature/554/janelle_monae_funky_sensation/> (last accessed 10 October 2018).

Liburd, Tonya (2016), 'Contemplation', *The Cascadia Subduction Zone: A Literary Quarterly*, 6:3, p. 3, <http://www.thecsz.com/past-issues/csz-v6-n3-2016.pdf> (last accessed 18 October 2018).

Lock, Graham (1999), *Blutopia: Visions of the Future and Revisions of the Past in the Work of Sun Ra, Duke Ellington, and Anthony Braxton*, Durham, NC: Duke University Press.

Lyotard, Jean-François (2011), *Discourse, Figure*, Antony Hudek and Mary Lydon (trans.), Minneapolis: University of Minnesota Press.

Mackay, Robin (2011), 'Introduction: Three Figures of Contingency', in Robin Mackay (ed.), *The Medium of Contingency*, Falmouth: Urbanomic, pp. 1–8.

Mallarmé, Stéphane (2001), 'Crisis in Poetry', in Mary Ann Caws (ed.), Manifesto: A Century of Isms, Lincoln: University of Nebraska Press, pp. 24–6.

Meillassoux, Quentin (2009), *After Finitude: An Essay on the Necessity of Contingency*, Ray Brassier (trans.), London: Continuum.

Metropolarity (n.d.), *Metropolarity*, <http://metropolarity.net/> (last accessed 1 May 2018).

Mothership Connection (1995), film, directed by John Akomfrah. London: BFI.

Muecke, Stephen (2002), 'The Fall: Fictocritical Writing', *Parallax*, 8:4, pp. 108–12.

O'Brien, Flann (1996), *The Third Policeman*, Normal: Dalkey Archive.

O'Sullivan, Simon (2016), 'Myth-Science and the Fictioning of Reality', *Paragrana*, 25:2, pp. 80–93.

O'Sullivan, Simon (2017), 'From Science Fiction to Science Fictioning: SF's Traction on the Real', *Foundation: The International Review of Science Fiction*, 128, pp. 74–84.

Palmer, Helen (2014), *Deleuze and Futurism: A Manifesto for Nonsense*, London: Bloomsbury.

Parisi, Luciana (2017), 'Automate Sex: Xenofeminism, Hyperstition and Alienation', in Henriette Gunkel, Ayesha Hameed, and Simon O'Sullivan (eds), *Futures and Fictions*, London: Repeater, pp. 213–30.

Pessoa, Fernando (2001), *The Selected Prose of Fernando Pessoa*, Richard Zenith (ed. and trans.), New York: Grove Press.
Phillips, Rasheedah (2015), 'Black Quantum Futurism: Theory and Practice – Part One', in Rasheedah Phillips (ed.), *Black Quantum Futurism: Theory and Practice, Vol. I*, Philadelphia: Afrofuturist Affair/House of Future Sciences Books, pp. 11–30.
Pozoga, Maciek and Christopher Kirkley (2015), 'Uchronia: Imagining an Alternate History Where a Malian Emperor Discovered America', *Vice*, 17 September, <https://www.vice.com/en_uk/article/zng5be/uchronia-0000744-v22n9> (last accessed 28 May 2018).
Ra, Sun (2005), *The Immeasurable Equation: The Collected Poetry and Prose*, James L. Wolf and Hartmut Geerken (eds), Stuttgart: Waitawhile.
Renouvier, Charles (2010), *Uchronie, l'utopie dans l'histoire: esquisse historique apocryphe du développement de la civilisation européenne tel qu'il n'a pas été, tel qu'il aurait pu être*, Whitefish: Kessinger.
Samatar, Sofia (2016), 'Notes Toward a Theory of Quantum Blackness', *Strange Horizons*, 29 February, <http://strangehorizons.com/poetry/notes-toward-a-theory-of-quantum-blackness/> (last accessed 28 May 2018).
Shawl, Nisi (2016), *Everfair*, New York: Tor.
Sinclair, John (2010), 'It Knocks on Everybody's Door', in John Sinclair (ed.), *Sun Ra: Interviews and Essays*, London: Headpress, pp. 19–30.
Space Is the Place (1974), film, directed by John Coney. Berkeley: North American Star System.
Taleb, Nassim Nicholas (2007), *The Black Swan: The Impact of the Highly Improbable*, New York: Random House.
van der Tuin, Iris (2011), 'New Feminist Materialisms', *Women's Studies International Forum*, 34:4, pp. 271–7.
Warrick, Pamela (1998), 'An Alternative Universe', *LA Times*, 18 October, <http://articles.latimes.com/1998/oct/18/magazine/tm-33581> (last accessed 28 May 2018).
Womack, Ytasha L. (2013), *Afrofuturism: The World of Black Sci-Fi and Fantasy Culture*, Chicago: Chicago Review Press.

12

Emerson's Speculative Pragmatism

Ridvan Askin

In the introduction to a special issue of *Speculations* on *Aesthetics in the 21st Century* that I co-wrote with my colleagues Andreas Hägler and Philipp Schweighauser, we argued that the recent speculative turn in continental philosophy is but 'German Idealism redux' (Askin, Hägler, and Schweighauser 2014: 38). Graham Harman rejected this idea in an interview, at least with respect to his own project, and suggested that the speculative turn owed much to romanticism instead (Cogburn 2015). If one follows Frederick Beiser's account of romanticism as a particular variant of German idealism (Beiser 2003), however, one can easily reconcile these different views: in this vein, the recent speculative turn could indeed be seen as a revamping and recasting of German idealist concerns, divided, roughly, into a Kantian-scientist wing (Brassier), a Hegelian-absolutist wing (Meillassoux), and a romantic wing (Harman, Grant, Shaviro, Morton).[1] Like Evan Gottlieb in this volume (chapter 6) and a previous book, in which he traced how the romantic project 'continues to resonate with our most pressing philosophical and ethico-political challenges today' (Gottlieb 2016: 224), I wish to explore some of the romantic roots pertinent to the contemporary debate, complementing Gottlieb's focus on British romanticism with a discussion of its American counterpart, notably Emersonian transcendentalism.[2] Given that some proponents of the new materialisms – I am particularly thinking of Jane Bennett and her vital materialism here – likewise draw on the romantics, such an endeavour promises to be particularly timely and fruitful. Apart from providing new insights into both Ralph Waldo Emerson's thought and Emerson scholarship, the present chapter should thus also help to put into relief one of the most crucial sources of the recent speculative turn. While the thrust and focus of the chapter will thus be on Emerson, I will at strategic points emphasise the debt that much of contemporary continental thought owes the romantics and transcendentalists. Not only do I hold that speculative realism, at least in what I have called its romantic guise, is but a continuation of speculative idealism, but also that, similarly, the new materialisms could well have been labelled the new idealisms. Both the idealism of the late eighteenth- and early nineteenth-century romantics and the realism and materialism of the late twentieth and early twenty-first century ultimately strive to fuse the ideal with the real and material, a programme that

Jean-Jacques Anstett in his introduction to Friedrich Schlegel's *Philosophische Vorlesungen* referred to as 'realidealism', the 'realization of the ideal and the idealization of the real' (Anstett 1964: xv; my translation), and Elizabeth Grosz recently expressed in her idea of a 'material-ideal' world (Grosz 2017: 14).[3]

As to Emerson, with his poetic and highly paratactic style and his reliance on the essay form, he espouses what I believe is best described as a speculative pragmatism, with the emphasis on 'speculative'. I will attempt to give this expression some consistency.[4] In a nutshell: like all pragmatists, Emerson adheres to an empiricist account of rational human inquiry. Unlike the pragmatists, he nevertheless maintains that this empiricism ultimately rests on a foundational matrix of ideas. This foundational, transcendental layer is indeed not accessible by means of rational inquiry. Only art is able to yield it. Thus, art becomes the most important human practice.

The trajectory I have chosen to flesh out this programme is as follows: I will begin with a brief outline of Emerson's romanticism, follow this up with considerations concerning the fundamental relation between metaphysics and aesthetics for Emerson, move on to the more specific relation between aesthetics and the work of art with literature as its prime example, and end with some thoughts on the relation between art and ethics. What emerges at the end of this trajectory is an understanding of art as the primary means of metaphysical inquiry apt to disclose the fundamental nature of being. In Emerson's idealist framework, such ontological disclosure concurrently amounts to the unearthing of the ethical injunction to attune oneself to the idea. Emerson's speculative pragmatism accordingly preaches 'the practice of ideas, or the introduction of ideas into life' (Emerson 1971a: 35). The primary site of such practice, that is, the paradigmatic speculative pragmatist enterprise, is precisely art; hence the form that Emerson's writings take.

Emerson's Romantic Programme in Outline

The philosophical reception of Emerson during roughly the past hundred years is marked by two major tendencies. The first of these pits him as the romantic precursor of American pragmatism and even as a pragmatist *avant la lettre*. Russel B. Goodman's *American Philosophy before Pragmatism* (2015) constitutes one of the most recent manifestations of this tradition. The second tendency goes back to Stanley Cavell and reads Emerson as a sceptic rather than a pragmatist.[5] Arguably, in literary studies the first of these tendencies is more widespread, mostly due to the pioneering work of Richard Poirier (Poirier 1966, 1987, 1992).[6] In any case, what the pragmatist and the scepticist reading have in common is that they underemphasise the speculative and outright metaphysical aspects of Emerson's thought. Simply put, these readings do not do justice to Emerson's transcendentalism. This assessment should not be misunderstood as a reiteration of Cavell's own similar-sounding misgivings about the pragmatist vein of Emerson scholarship (Cavell 2003b: 215–23). On the contrary, as I see it, Cavell's own take on Emerson, based on ordinary language philosophy as it is, is itself not speculative and metaphysical enough. But Emerson's transcendentalism is metaphysical all the way down.[7] The metaphysics Emerson espouses is that of idealism. For Emerson, transcendental ideas ground and determine empirical states of affairs. More precisely still, Emerson's idealism is an objective or speculative idealism as it posits 'a realism concerning ideas' (Dunham, Grant, and Watson 2011: 4): transcendental ideas constitute the real, fundamental matrix of any empirical entity whatsoever. Such a conception also has far-reaching ethical repercussions, as henceforth only those who manage to access the realm of ideas can be said to be living their life to the fullest, to be thoroughly self-aware, in short, to be one with their idea. Emerson's notion of self-reliance names precisely this ethical imperative: attune thyself to the world of ideas!

This metaphysical architectonic becomes decidedly romantic to the extent that it acknowledges the Kantian ban on the thing-in-itself, or, in more romantic parlance, the absolute, when it comes to its inaccessibility by means of conceptual thought while at the same time upholding its accessibility in principle.[8] Emerson is thus indeed a sceptic with respect to rational thought. Acknowledging the conceptual inaccessibility of the absolute while still insisting on its accessibility in principle, as Emerson and the romantics do, leaves but one road to travel: that of *aisthesis* or intuition. This is why the romantics in general and Emerson in particular insist so much on intuitive thought or *aesthetic* vision, why they cling 'all the more firmly to the powers of an *intuitive* reason ... a doctrine of intellectual intuition, which they identified with aesthetic feeling or perception' (Beiser 2002: 355): it provides the one and only access to the realm of ideas we have. This is also why works of art and, due to their linguistic make-up, particularly literary works assume such a pivotal role in romanticism and its American variant, transcendentalism: art and literature, in affording acute aesthetic experience, provide the royal road to the realm of ideas while at the same time manifesting it objectively in the given work. Literary works and works of art are objectivised *aisthesis*. In the words of Jane Kneller, the early romantics' revolutionary insight consisted in 'the *self-conscious*, *methodological* recognition of both the limitations of human knowledge (our inability to know either nature or ourselves in their entirety), and at the same time of the ineliminable, natural human drive to surpass those limitations' (Kneller 2007: 28).[9] For the romantics, such surpassing is the business of art: 'Where philosophy must stop ... poetry may begin', Kneller accordingly remarks (Kneller 2007: 130).[10]

It is Beiser, however, who argues this point most emphatically, leaving no doubt as to how the romantics thought we could overcome those limitations:

> One of the most remarkable traits of the early German romantics was their belief in the metaphysical stature of art. Almost all the young romantics ... made aesthetic experience into the criterion, instrument, and medium for awareness of ultimate reality or the absolute. Through aesthetic experience, they believed, we perceive the infinite in the finite, the supersensible in the sensible, the absolute in its appearances. Since art alone has the power to fathom the absolute, it is superior to philosophy, which now becomes the mere handmaiden of art. (Beiser 2003: 73)

This romantic conundrum of the relations between our cognitive limitations, metaphysics, aesthetics, and art as described by Kneller and Beiser arguably finds its most succinct expression in the following passage from Schelling's *System of Transcendental Idealism*:

> The whole of philosophy starts, and must start, from a principle which, *qua* absolutely identical, is utterly nonobjective. But now how is this absolutely nonobjective to be called up to consciousness and understood – a thing needful, if it is the condition for understanding the whole of philosophy? That it can no more be apprehended through concepts than it is capable of being set forth by means of them, stands in no need of proof [as this is what Kant had already proved]. Nothing remains, therefore, but for it to be set forth in an immediate intuition, though this is itself in turn inconceivable, and, since its object is to be something utterly nonobjective, seems, indeed, to be self-contradictory. But now were such an intuition in fact to exist, having as its object the absolutely identical, in itself neither subjective nor objective, and were we, in respect of this intuition, which can only be an intellectual one, to appeal to immediate experience, then how, in that case, could even this intuition be in turn posited objectively? How, that is, can it be established beyond doubt, that such an intuition does not rest upon a purely subjective deception, if it possesses no objectivity that is universal and acknowledged by all men? This universally acknowledged and altogether incontestable objectivity of intellectual intuition is art itself. For the aesthetic intuition simply is the intellectual intuition become objective. (Schelling 1978: 229)[11]

Emerson's programme falls squarely into this romantic paradigm, which, accordingly, is also expressed in the very form of his own textual production: adequate philosophy, that is, thought, has to proceed poetically. In this vein, Emerson's poetic and highly paratactic style and his reliance on the essay form are part and parcel of his overall literary-philosophical programme.

Speculative Metaphysics and Aesthetics

Let us now turn to Emerson's texts, beginning with a passage from one of his most famous essays, 'Nature':

> The greatest delight which the fields and woods minister, is the suggestion of an occult relation between man and the vegetable. I am not alone and unacknowledged. They nod to me and I to them.... Yet it is certain that the power to produce this delight, does not reside in nature, but in man, or in a harmony of both. It is necessary to use these pleasures with great temperance.... Nature always wears the colors of the spirit. (Emerson 1971a: 10)

Emerson here postulates an occult relation between the human and the vegetable, and the spiritual nature of nature, its being enveloped in spirit. This suggests that the occult relation between vegetable and human goes precisely through spirit, that spirit is that occult relation. But note that this relation is occult only for us humans. For the vegetable, there is nothing occult here, no secret to be disclosed. Vegetables simply inhabit the relation. They stand forth in it, they stand forth in spirit. It is this standing forth which in turn serves as a reminder to us that this relation, that spirit, is indeed the case. But what exactly makes us notice this? What entices us to see vegetables as more than just food, as more than mere matter in its utility? Whence this 'greatest delight' that the 'fields and woods minister' as Emerson says? It is here that aesthetics enters the stage, as the answer is of course: the beauty of nature. In one of his earliest lectures, Emerson already takes up precisely this conundrum:

> The beauty of the world is a perpetual invitation to the study of the world. Sunrise and sunset; fire; flowers; shells; the sea – in all its shades, from indigo to green and gray, by the light of day, and phosphorescent under the ship's keel at night; the airy inaccessible mountain; the sparry cavern; the glaring colours of the soil of the volcano; *the forms of vegetables*; and all the elegant and majestic figures of the creatures that fly, climb, or creep upon the earth – all, by their beauty, work upon our curiosity and court our attention. *The earth is a museum.* (Emerson 1939: 6, my emphases)

Not only is the world beautiful, and it is this beauty which entices us to inquire into its constitution, but '[t]he earth is a museum'. Given the context of its occurrence, this little phrase amounts to a distillation of much of Emerson's philosophy, as it evokes the museum in three senses: first, as the temple of the muses; second, as library or place of study (these two determinations derive directly from the Greek *mouseion*); and third, as the place for the exhibition of beautiful works. Seen this way, the earth, or more generally matter – it is telling that Emerson speaks of earth rather than world here – becomes the site of divine inspiration, of the proper use of thought, and the contemplation of beauty. The phrase thus encapsulates the Emersonian interrelation of metaphysics and aesthetics, that is to say, the relation of matter, spirit, beauty and the perception of beauty, and thought. Let us zoom in on Emerson's understanding of the relation between matter and spirit first.

In the first couple of programmatic pages from his lecture on 'The Transcendentalist', Emerson sketches not only this relation but also that between the materialist and idealist. The latter relation he characterises in the following manner: 'Every materialist will be an idealist; but an idealist can never go backward to be a materialist' (Emerson 1971b: 202). Why will every materialist be an idealist, and why is the reverse trajectory – an idealist becoming a materialist – impossible? In order to answer this question, we need to have a closer look at what materialism and idealism entail for Emerson. In his characterisation of these two philosophical doctrines in the first couple of pages of 'The Transcendentalist', Emerson classifies experience, the senses, facts, history, and nature as pertaining to matter and as ontologically subordinate to Thought, consciousness, and higher Nature. In other words, Emerson maintains that ideas ground and subsume matter, which is to say that idealism grounds and subsumes materialism. This is why materialists are bound to become idealists and why the latter will never become materialists: materialists have not reached the ground yet, they need to dig deeper in order to uncover it, in order to unearth the unconditioned condition, that is, the absolute. This is precisely the trajectory the idealist has already undertaken: idealists, far from disavowing matter, have, enticed by its beauty, taken to inquire into it. This inquiry has led them to the ground of matter, and it turns out that this ground – the unconditioned condition or the absolute – is the idea. Materialists are, fundamentally, still on their way to the ground – this is why they will become idealists eventually and why idealists can never become materialists; they have already discovered the prodigious realm of ideas underlying the realm of matter. They are adherents of a kind of enhanced materialism, of what Julian Young, in a discussion of Schelling's philosophy, calls 'ecstatic materialism' (Young 2013: 92). Much current materialist thought essentially amounts to a contemporary version of such late eighteenth- and early nineteenth-century romantic ecstatic materialism, from Bennett's recently proposed vital materialism, positing a 'vitality intrinsic to materiality' (Bennett 2010: 3), to Manuel DeLanda's neo-materialism, with its emphasis on 'matter's inherent creativity' (DeLanda 1997: 16), which Bennett quotes, on the 'form-generating resources which are immanent to the material world' (DeLanda 2002: 10), and on matter's 'spontaneous capacity to generate pattern without external intervention' (DeLanda 2002: 28).[12] For Emerson's idealist, '[e]very natural fact is a symbol of some spiritual fact' (Emerson 1971a: 18). The idealist 'manner of looking at things', Emerson adds, 'transfers every object in nature from an independent and anomalous position without there, into the consciousness' (Emerson 1971b: 202).

We have now determined both the nature of matter as natural fact or object of nature, and the relation between these objects and ideas such that ideas ground and subsume objects. While I do not think that a more specific determination of this relation – whether it is one of mimesis, or emanation, or expression – is necessary for the aims of this chapter (but see for example Stievermann 2007), the nature of ideas indeed needs to be further qualified. Is the transference of things 'into the consciousness' tantamount to a mentalism and thus a rejection of metaphysics proper? In other words, is Emerson a Kantian? Worse yet, is the sage of Concord but an unsystematic and flowery epigone of the sage of Königsberg? Emerson's pervasive theological rhetoric and onto-theological language incessantly evoking the One, the First Cause, Being, God, and so on make this rather implausible. Add to that his thoroughly un-Kantian conception of reason (indebted to Coleridge) as a visionary faculty, a veritable *sensus divinitatis*, and I believe we can firmly rule out the mentalism option.[13] It is in this anti-mentalist vein that he alleges: 'Mind is the only reality, of which men and all other natures are better or worse reflectors. Nature, literature, history, are only subjective phenomena. . . . [Human] thought, – that is the Universe' (Emerson 1971b: 203). While a cursory glance at these brief passages might actually suggest that, in their reduction of everything objective to the subjective and their positing of the coextensiveness of the human mind with the universe, they are endorsements of mentalism, such a reading would overlook that Emerson accords humans the same rank and level as 'all other natures', namely that of reflection: humans by no means constitute – in all senses of the word – reality but merely mirror it, the 'only reality' being Mind (with a capital M). There is no difference in kind between humans and nonhumans, merely a difference in degree – they are 'better or worse reflectors', as Emerson says. Without doubt, humans are the best reflectors for Emerson. This is not just because humans can think and thus, by dint of this simple fact, already constitute the best mirror of Mind, but particularly because their thought has the capacity to reveal this very fact. Human thought is reflective in two senses: first, by means of its sheer existence, it best reflects Mind; second, in its execution, in thinking, it is able to reflect on its very own nature – it is self-reflective. The result of such self-reflection is of course the disclosure of the first sense of reflection, namely that it is reflective of Mind. It is thus, by proxy, that Mind in-itself is revealed. Human thought's capacity of self-reflection ultimately provides the ground for both the Emersonian ethics of self-reliance and the primacy of aesthetics in his thought, a primacy that becomes manifest in the very form of his writings.

With Theodor W. Adorno, one could even invoke another kind of self-reliance here that nevertheless resonates profoundly with Emerson's own notion. For in their penchant for imagery and their highly paratactic style, Emerson's essays constitute paradigmatic examples for Adorno's understanding of the essay form and what he calls its 'aesthetic autonomy' (Adorno 1991: 5) – importantly, Adorno, rather than availing himself of the Greek form 'Autonomie', uses the German word 'Selbständigkeit' here, which easily translates as self-reliance (and Emerson's self-reliance is often translated as 'Selbständigkeit' in turn). The essay's 'aesthetic autonomy', Adorno writes, 'is easily accused of being simply derived from art, although it is distinguished from art by its medium, concepts, and by its claim to a truth devoid of aesthetic semblance' (1991: 5). For Adorno, the essay form manages to synthesise art and philosophy, intuitive and conceptual thought, without subsuming one under the other. Rhetorical 'association, verbal ambiguity, and … relaxation of logical synthesis … are fused in the essay with the truth-content' (1991: 21), Adorno accordingly states. It is precisely such fusion, such synthesis without sublation, that Emerson and the romantics aspire to. In its synthesis of the literary and the philosophical, the essay lends itself at the same time to aesthetic vision and conceptual reflection and self-reflection – it enables both *aisthesis* and the simultaneous conceptual reflection on *aisthesis*.

Let us tackle Emerson's aesthetics next, then. Further determining the role of aesthetics for his programme will also pave the way for the discussion of his ethics. As already pointed out, aesthetics furnishes the royal road of access to Mind in-itself, *aisthesis* being the primary discloser and revealer. Emerson says as much when he maintains: 'whatever belongs to the class of *intuitive* thought, is popularly called at the present day *Transcendental*' (Emerson 1971b: 206, my emphasis). That is, intuitive, not conceptual, thought gives us the conditions of experience. Returning to these initial passages of 'The Transcendentalist', we can see that for Emerson experience is a question of matter and materialism. This means that empiricism and materialism are synonymous for Emerson or at least that they are intimately related. Since we have already established Mind or Spirit as the condition of matter, a truly metaphysical condition, it becomes clear that intuitive thought's revelatory power lies in the fact that it amounts to a veritable becoming-Mind, a becoming-Spirit. It is very much in this vein that Bennett, for example, speaks of the 'human participation in a shared, vital materiality', insisting that humans very much '*are* vital materiality' (Bennett 2010: 14, emphasis in the original). For Emerson, the paradigmatic site of such participation and becoming is the work of art.

Aisthesis and the Work of Art

This is the case because the work of art is intuition materialised. In making intuition an object of encounter in the work of art, art is the prime facilitator of human thought's self-reflexivity. Art is self-reflexivity at work. In other words, the work of art materialises the relation between the empirical and the transcendental, between matter and ideas. The work of art is the very material manifestation of the relation between the material and the immaterial – it affords an aesthetic experience both of this relation and, by proxy, of the otherwise inexperienceable domain of ideas. The work of art is a veritable speculative experiment in metaphysics. And, since it affords experiences of the inexperienceable in so far as it affords an experience of the transcendental, its method is that of a transcendental empiricism. More precisely, the work of art is the method of transcendental empiricism. It thus becomes the Schellingian 'only true and eternal organ and document of philosophy' (Schelling 1978: 231).

I should note here that I borrow the term 'transcendental empiricism' from Deleuze, where it names what Deleuze calls the transcendental use of the senses, that is, a speculative employment of *aisthesis*: 'Empiricism truly becomes transcendental', Deleuze says, 'and aesthetics an apodictic discipline, only when we apprehend directly in the sensible that which can only be sensed, the very being *of* the sensible' (Deleuze 2004: 68). This being of the sensible is precisely not 'the given but that by which the given is given' (2004: 176). As such it is

> in a certain sense the imperceptible [*insensible*]. It is imperceptible precisely ... from the point of view of an empirical exercise of the senses in which sensibility grasps only that which also could be grasped by other faculties, and is related within the context of a common sense to an object which also must be apprehended by other faculties. Sensibility, in the presence of that which can only be sensed (and is at the same time imperceptible) finds itself before its own limit, the sign, and raises itself to the level of a transcendental exercise: to the 'nth' power. (2004: 176)

As I see it, Deleuze's programme, with its emphasis on the primacy of aesthetic knowledge and the powers of intuition, is essentially an extension of the romantic project. And in its general framework, Deleuze's transcendental empiricism is indeed a romantic method. That is why it is such an apt term for capturing Emerson's own theorisations.[14]

It is in this sense that, when speaking of literature in order to provide examples for his metaphysics, Emerson maintains: "'Tis not Proclus, but a piece of nature and fate that I explore. It is a greater joy to see the author's author, than himself" (Emerson 1983a: 137). The author's author is precisely the idea, Mind, or God, which the author makes tangible in their work. This making tangible of the otherwise intangible and ephemeral by the work of art amounts to what Emerson calls the 'deification of art' (1983a: 137). Expressed in other, more secular, words: it is the saturation of art with metaphysics.

This entire conundrum is made explicit in Emerson's essay 'The Poet'. The poet – the quintessential romantic artist – is, Emerson declares, 'a beholder of ideas, and an utterer of the necessary and causal' (Emerson 1983b: 6). The poet beholds the empirical and material, sees through it all the way down to its ideal ground, and – and this is crucial – instantiates this ground in the work of art (in this case the poem). This is possible precisely because the empirical and material world is amenable to such intuitive or aesthetic disclosure:

> Things admit of being used as symbols, because nature is a symbol, in the whole, and in every part. Every line we can draw in the sand, has expression; and there is no body without its spirit or genius. All form is an effect of character; all condition, of the quality of the life; all harmony, of health; (and, for this reason, a perception of beauty should be sympathetic, or proper only to the good.) The beautiful rests on the foundations of the necessary. The soul makes the body.... Here we find ourselves, suddenly, not in a critical speculation, but in a holy place, and should go very warily and reverently. We stand before the secret of the world, there where Being passes into Appearance, and Unity into Variety. The Universe is the externization of the soul. (1983b: 8–9)

In a nutshell: the effect of art is to give us the real. Of course, with Emerson the really real is the ideal. As already stated, Emerson champions a realism of ideas. Emersonian transcendental ideas pre-exist and coexist with empirical matter. Only art is able to disclose this pre- and coexistence.

Such disclosure is not just a matter of epistemology and ontology, however. In the passage I have just cited, note the curious talk of 'character', 'life', and 'health' and the parenthetical remark that the 'perception of beauty' *should* be 'proper ... to the good'. For Emerson, aesthetics – understood here in the sense of the perception of beauty – directly relates to ethics: it is, or should be, proper to the good (presumably, this relation can fail – indeed, such failure constitutes one of the main points of criticism that Emerson voices about the America of his time, for example in the famous first passages of 'Nature'). This is because Emerson conceives of being in good Platonist–Christian fashion as the unity of the True, the Good, and the Beautiful. And art, as the primary discloser of being, is thus directly related to both Truth and the Good. That it is related to Truth is implicit in its disclosure function, in its being the method of accessing and exhibiting the real. But how exactly is it related to the Good? This is what we will be looking at next.

Art and Ethics

Before we can determine art's relation to the Good, we have to determine Emerson's ethics at large. I have already mentioned in passing that his ethics is one of self-reliance, as most famously proposed in his eponymous essay (Emerson 1979a). Why self-reliance, and what exactly does it amount to? We have already established that all of nature, including the human, is nothing but a symbol, a representation, or a cipher of Spirit, Mind, God, the One, and so on. Here is Emerson again, expressing this relation as it pertains to the human:

> a man is only a relative and representative nature. Each is a hint of the truth, but far enough from being that truth, which yet he quite newly and inevitably suggests to us. If I seek it in him, I shall not find it. (Emerson 1983a: 133)

This short passage not only makes explicit that humans, like all of nature, like all existing things, are but representations of their conditioning ground, but also stresses that precisely because of this we will never attain that ground by turning to the other – 'If I seek it in him, I shall not find it.' The other is but a representation and I can only apprehend them as such. I will note their representational nature, but I will not be able to discern that which they represent. I simply cannot penetrate the other's soul. In order to do so I would literally have to become them. There is only one soul I can possibly access and that is my soul. Since Spirit, God, the One, and so on is in all things, it is also in me. This is what Emerson's ethical ideal of self-reliance essentially means: that one conscientiously and firmly stands in and on the grounds of being, that one undergoes what in Deleuzo-Guattarian parlance we might call a becoming-molecular or a becoming-zero. 'We are not in the world,' Deleuze and Guattari maintain, 'we become with the world; we become by contemplating it. Everything is vision, becoming. We become universes. Becoming animal, plant, molecular, becoming zero' (Deleuze and Guattari 1994: 168). If one compares these lines to the famous 'transparent eye-ball' passage in Emerson's 'Nature' essay, the affinity between Deleuze and Emerson becomes even more apparent: 'I become a transparent eye-ball. I am nothing. I see all. The currents of the Universal Being circulate through me; I am part or particle of God' (Emerson 1971a: 10). For both thinkers, the subject becomes self-reliant and autonomous only by availing itself of the powers of *aisthesis* in order to immerse and ultimately dissolve itself in the currents of a universal and cosmic becoming. The good life is the life in unison with the cosmos, the One, the idea or God, what Bennett calls 'the strange and incomplete commonality with the out-side' (Bennett 2010: 17). The following central passage from 'Self-Reliance' makes this explicit:

> What is the aboriginal Self on which a universal reliance may be grounded? What is the nature and power of that science-baffling star, without parallax, without calculable elements, which shoots a ray of beauty even into trivial and impure actions, if the least mark of independence appear? The inquiry leads

us to that source, at once the essence of genius, of virtue, and of life, which we call Spontaneity or Instinct. We denote this primary wisdom as Intuition, whilst all later teachings are tuitions. In that deep force, the last fact behind which analysis cannot go, all things find their common origin. For the sense of being which in calm hours rises, we know not how, in the soul, is not diverse from things, from space, from light, from time, from man, but one with them, and proceeds obviously from the same source, whence their life and being also proceed. We first share the life by which things exist, and afterwards see them as appearances in nature, and forget that we have shared their cause. Here is the fountain of action and of thought. Here are the lungs of that inspiration which giveth man wisdom, and which cannot be denied without impiety and atheism. We lie in the lap of immense intelligence, which makes us receivers of its truth and organs of its activity. When we discern justice, when we discern truth, we do nothing of ourselves, but allow a passage to its beams. (Emerson 1979a: 37)

Far from denoting any kind of individualism, Emersonian self-reliance names the becoming-other or what one could call the metaphysical alienation of the subject, as its innermost self or soul comes to coincide with Bennett's 'out-side' (Bennett 2010: 3, 17), what Meillassoux famously referred to as 'the *great outdoors*' (Meillassoux 2009: 7), and the romantics call the absolute (Being, the One, Idea, God, etc.). Emersonian self-reliance thus amounts to the subject's relinquishing of itself, its veritable *kenosis*. The more I turn inwards, the more I become aware of my Self, the more distant I become to myself as I follow a line of flight into absolute Being, the One, and so on. The Good is only to be found in an interiority that at the same time is but absolute exteriority.

How exactly is the *kenosis* of Emersonian self-reliance related to aesthetics and, ultimately, art? In the passage quoted above this relation remains rather implicit. But Emerson voices it quite explicitly on a number of occasions. Thus, in 'Nature' we read that 'Beauty is the mark God sets upon virtue' (Emerson 1971a: 15). Emerson here clearly establishes an intrinsic relation between aesthetics and ethics: everything beautiful is also virtuous and, conversely, everything virtuous is beautiful. Note that with virtue, we are now no longer just dealing with questions of thought and theory but also with those of action and praxis. 'Ever does natural beauty steal in like air, and envelope great *actions*' (Emerson 1971a: 15, my emphasis), Emerson accordingly writes. Thought and action are thus closely entwined both with one another and with the things of nature and nature at large. This is how Emerson characterises the triangulation of thought, thing, and action:

The intellect searches out the absolute order of things as they stand in the mind of God .... The intellectual and the active powers seem to succeed each other in man ... each prepares and certainly will be followed by the other. Therefore does beauty, which in relation to actions ... comes unsought, and comes because it is unsought, remain for the apprehension and pursuit of the intellect; and then again, in its turn, of the active power. Nothing divine dies. All good is eternally reproductive. The beauty of nature reforms itself in the mind, and not for barren contemplation, but for new creation. (Emerson 1971a: 16)

To sum up: beauty makes us think and act. Both things and actions are beautiful and thus create more thought and more actions, which also create things, such as artworks, and so on ad infinitum. This is why Emerson can maintain that '[t]he axioms of physics translate the laws of ethics' (1971a: 21) and that '[a]ll things are moral' (1971a: 25). They all reference – point to – Spirit, they 'hint and thunder to man the laws of right and wrong. . . . The moral law lies at the centre of nature and radiates to the circumference' (1971a: 26). Emersonian morality is thus not a question of judgement (as in Kant, for example) but of a veritable onto-ethics. Thought alone, being finite, cannot quite render the infinite Spirit or God grounding and producing it. Thought needs action to complement it. Actions are 'the perfection and publication of thought' (1971a: 28), as Emerson has it. But these actions precisely cannot or should not be actions blind to the workings of spirit. Otherwise, they would miss the ground and go astray – they would become unethical. The following passage from 'The Over-Soul' captures these relations – between thought and action, and that which grounds them – poignantly:

> If we consider what happens in conversation, in reveries, in remorse, in times of passion, in surprises, in the instructions of dreams, wherein often we see ourselves in masquerade – the droll disguises only magnifying and enhancing a real element, and forcing it on our distinct notice, – we shall catch many hints that will broaden and lighten into knowledge of the secret of nature. All goes to show that the soul in man is not an organ, but animates and exercises all the organs; is not a function, like the power of memory, of calculation, of comparison, but uses these as hands and feet; is not a faculty, but a light; is not the intellect or the will, but the master of the intellect and the will; is the background of our being, in which they lie, – an immensity not possessed and that cannot be possessed. From within or from behind, a light shines through us upon things, and makes us aware that we are nothing, but the light is all. A man is the facade of a temple wherein all wisdom and all good abide. What we commonly call man, the eating, drinking, planting, counting man, does not, as we know him, represent himself, but misrepresents himself. Him we do not respect, but the soul, whose organ he is, would he let it appear through his action, would make our knees bend. When it breathes through his intellect, it is genius; when it breathes through his will, it is virtue; when it flows through his affection, it is love. (Emerson 1979b: 161)

'Soul' is yet another name for the animating principle underlying and grounding all human thought and all human action that is itself just the human aspect of the cosmic power Emerson calls over-soul in his eponymous essay. Importantly, this power becomes manifest only in and through action, whether it be artistic, moral, or affectionate. But as we have seen, it is only artistic action, that is, the creation of artworks, that is apt to materialise and objectivise this power.

Conclusion

Overall, one can thus say that Emerson's philosophy can only be called pragmatist to the extent that it is also speculative. In other words, Emerson's philosophy is a speculative pragmatism, and artistic creation qua transcendental empiricism is its method. The method of transcendental empiricism discloses the ontological make-up of things, that is, the domain of ideas. At the same time, this ontological disclosure amounts to opening up to the ethical imperative: attune thyself to the idea! This injunction to attune oneself to the idea is the speculative pragmatist imperative par excellence, as only action that is not forgetful as to its generation in the idea, that is in attunement with the idea, will be true to the Good, the Beautiful, and the True, the unified trinity at the heart of being. Emerson's speculative pragmatism thus amounts to 'the practice of ideas, or the introduction of ideas into life' (Emerson 1971a: 35). The work of art is the site in which all these relations are brought together, congealed, and exhibited; art, then, is the ultimate speculative pragmatist practice, 'the practice of ideas'. Hence the form that Emerson's writings take. And hence Emerson's self-characterisation that he is 'in all [his] theory, ethics & politics a poet' (Emerson 1939: 18).

Notes

The present chapter is a translation, reframing, reworking, and elaboration of parts of my 'Emersons politisches Denken und die Dichtung' ('Emerson's Political Thought and Literature') (Askin 2018). I would like to thank Philipp Schweighauser, Marc Nicolas Sommer, and my co-editors for their incisive comments on various draft versions.

1. Of course, this is not to suggest that these thinkers are mere epigones or even just adherents of Kant, Hegel, and the romantics, respectively. In fact, for Ray Brassier and Quentin Meillassoux, the relationship with their philosophical forebears is more like how Gilles Deleuze once famously described his relation to Kant, namely as that to an 'enemy' (Deleuze 1995: 6), but an enemy worth having – I think Kant and Hegel are the enemies closest to Brassier's and Meillassoux's hearts. In the case of what I call the romantic wing, the relation seems to be more positive and straightforward as these thinkers quite openly and affirmatively draw on the romantic legacy: apart from Harman, this is also true of Iain Hamilton Grant, whose philosophical project is precisely that of a renewal of Schellingian thought, Steven Shaviro, who espouses Deleuze and particularly Whitehead in their romantic leanings (Shaviro 2014: 56–60), and Timothy Morton, who started out as a scholar of romanticism and keeps coming back to romantic authors and texts in his more recent ecotheoretical and speculative oeuvre (Morton 1994, 2012; see also Gottlieb 2016: 38, 46, 87–8).
2. The way I propose to limn the current landscape of continental speculative thought diverges from Gottlieb's to the extent that he includes Brassier and Meillassoux among

the heirs to the romantic legacy. But even in Gottlieb's book, Brassier arguably functions more as a kind of critical foil, and Meillassoux mostly serves to introduce the problems of correlationism and contingency (Gottlieb 2016: 143–87). This is because, I would argue on roughly Beiserian grounds, both thinkers hark back to German idealism, but not its romantic version. Gottlieb continues to press his romantic reading of Meillassoux in his contribution to this volume (Chapter 6).

3. Let me emphasise that the real and material must not be conflated: while materialisms are by default realisms, the inverse is not the case. Harman, for example, emphatically insists that his realism is not a materialism (Harman 2010). The reconciliation of the ideal with the real and that of the ideal with the material are two closely related projects, which may, but do not necessarily, overlap.

4. I will derive this characterisation directly from Emerson's writings. As such, it has affinities but is not synonymous with Brian Massumi's employment of the term: 'Ultimately, the thinking of speculative pragmatism that is activist philosophy belongs to nature. Its aesthetico-politics compose a nature philosophy. The occurrent arts in which it exhibits itself are politics of nature' (Massumi 2011: 28). One should note already here that I use 'pragmatism' in its most general sense, as a rich account of experience coupled with the 'insistence on attending to the practical' (Bacon 2012: 14).

5. To be clear, Cavell merely places Emerson among the thinkers displaying '*obsessions with the ordinary that [are] the equivalent of something* (not everything) philosophy knows as skepticism' (Cavell 2003a: 144, my emphasis) and ultimately differentiates what he famously termed Emerson's 'perfectionism' from such scepticism. The way I read it, however, Cavell's account of perfectionism, in its insistence on the ordinary, language, and writing, and its 'accept[ance] [of] the separation of the world' (2003a: 148), is just another symptom of scepticism.

6. For a crisp and very informative overview of the reception history of Emerson in American and literary studies, see the two entries by Glen Johnson and Randall Fuller in *Ralph Waldo Emerson in Context* (Johnson 2014; Fuller 2014).

7. This is not to deny that there are explicitly metaphysical readings of Emerson; it is just to say that they do not constitute a dominant critical paradigm (yet). For examples of decidedly metaphysical readings see Schulz 2012: esp. 82–98; Stievermann 2007; and Urbas 2016.

8. This is not to suggest that the romantic absolute is reducible to the Kantian thing-in-itself, particularly since the post-Kantian discourse on the absolute in large parts derives from Kant's discussion of the term in the first *Critique*'s passages on transcendental ideas (Kant 1998: A321–40/B378–98, esp. A324–8/B381–4). The point is rather that for the romantics, there is a world beyond representation that can nevertheless be accessed, albeit not by means of conceptual thought. Andreas Arndt, for example, emphasises precisely this point in his chapter on Schlegel in a recent monograph on the post-Kantians he co-authored with Walter Jaeschke (Jaeschke and Arndt 2012: 230–3). In Dalia Nassar's crisp formulation, '[f]or the romantics . . . the absolute was both an epistemological and a metaphysical idea: a cognitive ideal and an existential reality', the very 'ground of being and knowing' (Nassar 2013: 2, 259).

9. Of course, this diagnosis, given that it applies equally well to him, would make Kant himself a romantic or at least a proto-romantic. This is indeed the case for Kneller, but only to the extent that the early romantics end up being close to Kant (rather than the other way around), even assuming 'the anti-speculative position of Kantianism' (Kneller 2007: 7). While there is no doubt that the romantics derived their most pressing

problems from Kant, particularly from his third *Critique*, I very much follow Beiser in insisting that their attempted solutions consisted in reintroducing speculation in the guise of speculative intuition or *aisthesis*. The philosophical scholarship on the romantics is deeply divided precisely on this issue, with the divide being personified by Beiser and Manfred Frank, respectively. For a primer on this debate, see the two essays by Beiser and Frank in *The Relevance of Romanticism* edited by Nassar (Beiser 2014; Frank 2014), Nassar's own monograph (Nassar 2013), and the ensuing discussion staged by the online forum *Critique* involving two extended, critical review essays by Richard Fincham and Reed Winegar and Nassar's reply (Fincham 2015; Winegar 2015; Nassar 2015).

10. Kneller makes this claim in the context of her discussion of Novalis and, in accordance with her position outlined above, immediately proceeds by toning it down, asserting the unlikelihood that Novalis actually 'believed that poetry could ... unveil the absolute' (2007: 130).

11. This passage is replaced in the author's copy with a crisper and slightly less technical formulation, which, however, drops the explicit reference to art, the reason I opted for the original wording. Here is Schelling's revised version:

    The whole of philosophy starts, and must start, from a principle which, as the absolute principle, is also at the same time the absolutely identical. An absolutely simple and identical cannot be grasped or communicated through description, nor through concepts at all. It can only be intuited. Such an intuition is the organ of all philosophy. – But this intuition, which is an intellectual rather than a sensory one, and has as its object neither the objective nor the subjective, but the absolutely identical, in itself neither subjective nor objective, is itself merely an internal one, which cannot in turn become objective for itself: it can become objective only through a second intuition. This second intuition is the aesthetic. (1978: 229n.1)

12. One should note that while Bennett is upfront about her reliance on romanticism – she references Emerson's fellow transcendentalist Henry David Thoreau in this context (Bennett 2010: 2) and emphasises the crucial role of looking, seeing, and perceiving, that is, of aesthetics and *aisthesis* (2010: 4–5) – DeLanda would probably want to disown my characterisation of him as a neo-romantic. But see also Gottlieb's discussion of DeLanda in the context of romantic poetry, particularly Coleridge (Gottlieb 2016: 77–86). As an aside, given the current ubiquity and dominance of neo-materialist thought and given that Timotheus Vermeulen and Robin van den Akker align their much-discussed diagnosis of what they call our contemporary metamodernity with 'an emergent neo-romantic sensibility' (Vermeulen and van den Akker 2010), we might indeed be living in neo-romantic times.

13. Admittedly, Emerson is not always very clear on this point. In 'Nature' he even asserts:

    A noble doubt perpetually suggests itself ... whether nature outwardly exists.... In my utter impotence to test the authenticity of the report of my senses, to know whether the impressions they make on me correspond with outlying objects, what difference does it make, whether Orion is up there in heaven, or some god paints the image in the firmament of the soul? ... Whether nature enjoy a substantial existence without, or is only in the apocalypse of the mind, it is alike useful and alike venerable to me. (Emerson 1971a: 29)

For Coleridge's understanding of reason, which in turn is indebted to Schelling, see for example Coleridge 2004: 555–60. Coleridge is without doubt Emerson's and the transcendentalists' main source when it comes to classical German philosophy and the early German romantics. On Emerson's transatlantic relations, see David Greenham's and Samantha C. Harvey's recent monographs and Stanley Cavell's classic essay 'Emerson, Coleridge, Kant (Terms as Conditions)' (Greenham 2012; Harvey 2013; Cavell 1988).

14. In this context, it is worth noting that both Bennett and DeLanda are Deleuzians of sorts. In fact, quite a few new materialists and many of the thinkers associated with what I have called speculative realism's romantic wing heavily lean on and borrow from Deleuze's philosophy and metaphysics. This is true of, for example, Grant, Shaviro, Levi Bryant, Rosi Braidotti, Claire Colebrook, and Elizabeth Grosz, to name but a few. Given that throughout his career, Deleuze was very much invested in reconciling the ideal with the real and material, culminating in an understanding of the brain as precisely the synthesis of idea and matter expressed in phrases like 'Thought-brain' and '[t]he brain is the *mind* itself' (Deleuze and Guattari 1994: 210, 211), this should not come as a surprise.

Bibliography

Adorno, Theodor W. (1991), 'The Essay as Form', in Theodor W. Adorno, *Notes to Literature, Vol. I*, Rolf Tiedemann (ed.) and Shierry Weber Nicholsen (trans.), New York: Columbia University Press, pp. 3–23.

Anstett, Jean-Jacques (1964), 'Einleitung', in Friedrich Schlegel, *Philosophische Vorlesungen 1800–1807: Erster Teil*, Jean-Jacques Anstett (ed.), Munich: Ferdinand Schöningh, pp. xiii–xxxv.

Askin, Ridvan (2018), 'Emersons politisches Denken und die Dichtung', in Michael Festl and Philipp Schweighauser (eds), *Literatur und Politische Philosophie: Subjektivität, Fremdheit, Demokratie*, Paderborn: Wilhelm Fink, pp. 101–22.

Askin, Ridvan, Andreas Hägler, and Philipp Schweighauser (2014), 'Introduction: Aesthetics after the Speculative Turn', *Speculations*, 5, pp. 6–38.

Bacon, Michael (2012), *Pragmatism: An Introduction*, Cambridge: Polity.

Beiser, Frederick C. (2002), *German Idealism: The Struggle against Subjectivism, 1781–1801*, Cambridge, MA: Harvard University Press.

Beiser, Frederick C. (2003), *The Romantic Imperative: The Concept of Early German Romanticism*, Cambridge, MA: Harvard University Press.

Beiser, Frederick C. (2014), 'Romanticism and Idealism', in Dalia Nassar (ed.), *The Relevance of Romanticism: Essays on German Romantic Philosophy*, Oxford: Oxford University Press, pp. 30–43.

Bennett, Jane (2010), *Vibrant Matter: A Political Ecology of Things*, Durham, NC: Duke University Press.

Cavell, Stanley (1988), 'Emerson, Coleridge, Kant (Terms as Conditions)', in Stanley Cavell, *In Quest of the Ordinary: Lines of Skepticism and Romanticism*, Chicago: University of Chicago Press, pp. 27–49.

Cavell, Stanley (2003a), 'Aversive Thinking: Emersonian Representations in Heidegger and Nietzsche', in Stanley Cavell, *Emerson's Transcendental Etudes*, David Justin Hodge (ed.), Stanford: Stanford University Press, pp. 141–70.

Cavell, Stanley (2003b), 'What's the Use of Calling Emerson a Pragmatist?', in Stanley Cavell, *Emerson's Transcendental Etudes*, David Justin Hodge (ed.), Stanford: Stanford University Press, pp. 215–23.

Cogburn, Jon (2015), 'An Interview with Graham Harman', Edinburgh University Press Blog, 10 September, <https://euppublishingblog.com/2015/09/10/an-interview-with-graham-harman/> (last accessed 17 October 2018).

Coleridge, Samuel Taylor (2004), *Coleridge's Poetry and Prose: Authoritative Texts, Criticism*, Nicholas Halmi, Paul Magnuson, and Raimonda Modiano (eds), New York: W. W. Norton.

DeLanda, Manuel (1997), *A Thousand Years of Nonlinear History*, Cambridge, MA: MIT Press.

DeLanda, Manuel (2002), *Intensive Science and Virtual Philosophy*, London: Continuum.

Deleuze, Gilles (1995), 'Letter to a Harsh Critic', in Gilles Deleuze, *Negotiations, 1972–1990*, Martin Joughin (trans.), New York: Columbia University Press, pp. 3–12.

Deleuze, Gilles (2004), *Difference and Repetition*, Paul Patton (trans.), London: Continuum.

Deleuze, Gilles and Félix Guattari (1994), *What Is Philosophy?*, Hugh Tomlinson and Graham Burchell (trans.), London: Verso.

Dunham, Jeremy, Ian Hamilton Grant, and Sean Watson (2011), *Idealism: The History of a Philosophy*, Durham: Acumen.

Emerson, Ralph Waldo (1939), *The Letters of Ralph Waldo Emerson, Vol. 3*, Ralph L. Rusk (ed.), New York: Columbia University Press.

Emerson, Ralph Waldo (1966), 'The Uses of Natural History', in Ralph Waldo Emerson, *The Early Lectures of Ralph Waldo Emerson, Vol. I: 1833–1836*, Stephen E. Whicher and Robert E. Spiller (eds), Cambridge, MA: Harvard University Press, pp. 5–26.

Emerson, Ralph Waldo (1971a), 'Nature', in Ralph Waldo Emerson, *The Collected Works of Ralph Waldo Emerson, Vol. 1: Nature, Addresses, and Lectures*, Robert E. Spiller and Alfred R. Ferguson (eds), Cambridge, MA: Harvard University Press, pp. 1–45.

Emerson, Ralph Waldo (1971b), 'The Transcendentalist', in Ralph Waldo Emerson, *The Collected Works of Ralph Waldo Emerson, Vol. 1: Nature, Addresses, and Lectures*, Robert E. Spiller and Alfred R. Ferguson (eds), Cambridge, MA: Harvard University Press, pp. 201–16.

Emerson, Ralph Waldo (1979a), 'Self-Reliance', in Ralph Waldo Emerson, *The Collected Works of Ralph Waldo Emerson, Vol. 2: Essays: First Series*, Joseph Slater, Alfred R. Ferguson, and Jean Ferguson Carr (eds), Cambridge, MA: Harvard University Press, pp. 25–51.

Emerson, Ralph Waldo (1979b), 'The Over-Soul', in Ralph Waldo Emerson, *The Collected Works of Ralph Waldo Emerson, Vol. 2: Essays: First Series*, Joseph Slater, Alfred R. Ferguson, and Jean Ferguson Carr (eds), Cambridge, MA: Harvard University Press, pp. 157–75.

Emerson, Ralph Waldo (1983a), 'Nominalist and Realist', in Ralph Waldo Emerson, *The Collected Works of Ralph Waldo Emerson, Vol. 3: Essays: Second Series*, Joseph Slater, Alfred R. Ferguson, and Jean Ferguson Carr (eds), Cambridge, MA: Harvard University Press, pp. 131–45.

Emerson, Ralph Waldo (1983b), 'The Poet', in Ralph Waldo Emerson, *The Collected Works of Ralph Waldo Emerson, Vol. 3: Essays: Second Series*, Joseph Slater, Alfred R. Ferguson, and Jean Ferguson Carr (eds), Cambridge, MA: Harvard University Press, pp. 3–24.

Fincham, Richard (2015), 'Richard Fincham on Dalia Nassar's "The Romantic Absolute"', *Critique: Discussing New Books on Kant, German Idealism and Beyond*, 5 October, <https://virtualcritique.wordpress.com/2015/10/05/richard-fincham-on-dalia-nassars-the-romantic-absolute/> (last accessed 25 November 2016).

Frank, Manfred (2014), 'What Is Early German Romantic Philosophy?', in Dalia Nassar (ed.), *The Relevance of Romanticism: Essays on German Romantic Philosophy*, Oxford: Oxford University Press, pp. 15–29.
Fuller, Randall (2014), 'Critics: 1948–2013', in Wesley T. Mott (ed.), *Ralph Waldo Emerson in Context*, Cambridge: Cambridge University Press, pp. 274–82.
Goodman, Russell B. (2015), *American Philosophy before Pragmatism*, Oxford: Oxford University Press.
Gottlieb, Evan (2016), *Romantic Realities: Speculative Realism and British Romanticism*, Edinburgh: Edinburgh University Press.
Greenham, David (2012), *Emerson's Transatlantic Romanticism*, Basingstoke: Palgrave.
Grosz, Elizabeth (2017), *The Incorporeal: Ontology, Ethics, and the Limits of Materialism*, New York: Columbia University Press.
Harman, Graham (2010), 'I Am Also of the Opinion that Materialism Must Be Destroyed', *Environment and Planning D: Society and Space*, 28, pp. 772–90.
Harvey, Samantha C. (2013), *Transatlantic Transcendentalism: Coleridge, Emerson, and Nature*, Edinburgh: Edinburgh University Press.
Jaeschke, Walter and Andreas Arndt (2012), *Die Klassische Deutsche Philosophie nach Kant: Systeme der reinen Vernunft und ihre Kritik 1785–1845*, Munich: C. H. Beck.
Johnson, Glen (2014), 'Critics: 1836–1948', in Wesley T. Mott (ed.), *Ralph Waldo Emerson in Context*, Cambridge: Cambridge University Press, pp. 265–73.
Kant, Immanuel (1998), *Critique of Pure Reason*, Paul Guyer and Allen W. Wood (eds and trans.), Cambridge: Cambridge University Press.
Kneller, Jane (2007), *Kant and the Power of Imagination*, Cambridge: Cambridge University Press.
Massumi, Brian (2011), *Semblance and Event: Activist Philosophy and the Occurrent Arts*, Cambridge, MA: MIT Press.
Meillassoux, Quentin (2009), *After Finitude: An Essay on the Necessity of Contingency*, Ray Brassier (trans.), London: Continuum.
Morton, Timothy (1994), *Shelley and the Revolution in Taste: The Body and the Natural World*, Cambridge: Cambridge University Press.
Morton, Timothy (2012), 'An Object-Oriented Defense of Poetry', *New Literary History*, 43, pp. 205–24.
Nassar, Dalia (2013), *The Romantic Absolute: Being and Knowing in Early German Romantic Philosophy, 1795–1804*, Chicago: University of Chicago Press.
Nassar, Dalia (2015), 'Reply to Richard Fincham and Reed Winegar', *Critique: Discussing New Books on Kant, German Idealism and Beyond*, 6 October, <https://virtualcritique.wordpress.com/2015/10/06/reply-to-richard-fincham-and-reed-winegar/> (last accessed 25 November 2016).
Poirier, Richard T. (1966), *A World Elsewhere: The Place of Style in American Literature*, Madison: University of Wisconsin Press.
Poirier, Richard T. (1987), *The Renewal of Literature: Emersonian Reflections*, New York: Random House.
Poirier, Richard T. (1992), *Poetry and Pragmatism*, Cambridge, MA: Harvard University Press.
Schelling, F. W. J. (1978), *System of Transcendental Idealism*, Peter Heath (trans.), Charlottesville: University of Virginia Press.
Schulz, Dieter (2012), '"A Man Is a Method": Emerson as Educator-Philosopher', in Dieter Schulz, *Emerson and Thoreau, or Steps Beyond Ourselves: Studies in Transcendentalism*, Heidelberg: Mattes, pp. 74–97.

Shaviro, Steven (2014), *The Universe of Things: On Speculative Realism*, Minneapolis: University of Minnesota Press.

Stievermann, Jan (2007), *Der Sündenfall der Nachahmung: Zum Problem der Mittelbarkeit im Werk Ralph Waldo Emersons*, Paderborn: Schöningh.

Urbas, Joseph (2016), *Emerson's Metaphysics: A Song of Laws and Causes*, Lanham: Lexington Books.

Vermeulen, Timotheus and Robin van den Akker (2010), 'Notes on Metamodernism', *Journal of Aesthetics and Culture*, 2:1, <http://www.tandfonline.com/doi/full/10.3402/jac.v2i0.5677> (last accessed 17 October 2018).

Winegar, Reed (2015), 'Reed Winegar on Dalia Nassar's "The Romantic Absolute"', *Critique: Discussing New Books on Kant, German Idealism and Beyond*, 4 October, <https://virtualcritique.wordpress.com/2015/10/04/reed-winegar-on-dalia-nassars-the-romantic-absolute/> (last accessed on 25 November 2016).

Young, Julian (2013), *The Philosophy of Tragedy: From Plato to Žižek*, Cambridge: Cambridge University Press.

PART IV

Ordinary Language Criticism: Reading Literature through Anglo-American Philosophy

Editor's Introduction

David Rudrum

The philosophical origins of the chapters in this section of the volume are noticeably older than those in the other sections; however, their uptake in literary studies is as recent and as contemporary as any of the debates found herein. Although the tradition of 'ordinary language philosophy' is traceable to two seminal texts from the mid-twentieth century – the pivotally important *Philosophical Investigations* by Ludwig Wittgenstein (1953) and *How to Do Things with Words* by J. L. Austin (1962) – the rich potential of its linguistic and philosophical insights for literary criticism remained largely untapped for decades. It is only in the early twenty-first century that, thanks to the pioneering efforts of philosophers like Stanley Cavell and literary critics like Marjorie Perloff, the thought of Wittgenstein and Austin has taken on a newfound importance for the study of literature, and an identifiable body of 'ordinary language criticism' has come into being, quickly developing into one of the more original and exciting new areas of interface between philosophy and literature.

There is probably a simple explanation for this delay. Throughout the twentieth century, most of the interdisciplinary dialogues that took place between philosophical and literary studies emerged from advances in continental philosophy. From the existentialism of Martin Heidegger, Jean-Paul Sartre, and Albert Camus to the poststructuralist formulations of Jacques Derrida, Emmanuel Levinas, and Gilles Deleuze, the key moments of confluence seemed largely to sidestep Anglo-American thought. However, drawing on the work of philosophers such as Stanley Cavell, Richard Rorty, and Donald Davidson, a literary criticism more indebted to the legacies of analytic philosophy than to those of phenomenology has gathered momentum.

For more than a century, Anglo-American thought has been dominated by the analytic tradition, and the precepts of logical positivism held a powerful sway over much of it until the later work of Wittgenstein and Austin. In this climate, there was comparatively little appetite for serious aesthetic discussion of any kind in Anglo-American philosophical circles, and almost none for the study of literature, since literary and fictional texts were precisely the kind of linguistic phenomena that logical positivists viewed as metaphysical, illogical, and therefore a hindrance to the philosophical pursuit of truth. Both Austin and the later Wittgenstein were openly hostile to this pattern of thinking, and their followers and successors became even more so.

Cavell and Rorty both sought repeatedly to question and to blur any possibility of distinction between literary and philosophical texts, and both drew on older currents in American philosophy to demonstrate that such distinctions were comparatively recent, highly artificial constructs. Rorty appealed to the pragmatist tradition, developing a somewhat postmodern view of the situatedness of human knowledge, and a radically anti-foundational critique of the Western philosophical tradition. Cavell turned instead to the transcendentalist tradition of Henry David Thoreau and Ralph Waldo Emerson, whose work he found pre-empted the investigations of the everyday as practised by Wittgenstein and Austin, in a way of thinking and of writing that is simultaneously literary and philosophical. Though there is much to differentiate these two approaches, there are nevertheless important convergences, too. Both take a startlingly deflationary stance towards the claims of traditional philosophy, and both insist on the profoundly textual (and hence literary) character of philosophical writing.

Ordinary language criticism is emphatically not a literary theory. It has no received canon of texts or thinkers. (Indeed, Rorty himself repudiates the label of ordinary language philosopher, on grounds that the 'ordinary' constitutes a philosophical foundation for an anti-foundational philosophy – something Cavell denies.) It lacks its own set of key terms to function as methodological shibboleths, and involves no repertoire of conceptual or critical moves. It is instead a style of thinking, or a way of working with language and with texts.

The first chapter in this section, by Ingeborg Löfgren, begins with a brief outline of ordinary language criticism, and the difficulties of defining it. Eschewing theoretical or methodological abstraction, it is a way of reading and of arguing best encountered in practice. Thus, she adduces an interpretative debate about George Orwell's classic novel *Nineteen Eighty-Four* – involving Rorty's reading of the novel, a set of criticisms made of his reading by Cavellian philosopher James Conant, and Rorty's replies to those criticisms – as a good example of ordinary language criticism at work. Through a detailed reading of these critical exchanges, and of the text itself, she goes on to elaborate the nature of the interpretative claims made by ordinary language critics, and how they relate to methodological issues such as paraphrase and authorial intention.

R. M. Berry's chapter also adopts a procedure of comparison and contrast, placing Cavell's philosophy alongside the work of some Marxist thinkers more familiar to literary scholars, like Theodor Adorno, Georg Lukács, and Fredric Jameson. This juxtaposition is mutually illuminating, because it sheds light on one of the most fundamental aesthetic questions: that of the nature of artistic autonomy. All these thinkers are agreed that the issue of the work of art's autonomy is the foremost issue at stake in the literature we call modernism. However, they diverge quite widely as to what this issue entails, what the term is taken to mean, and why it is important. For the Marxist critics, the problem of autonomy is, for obvious reasons, an essentially political question, whereas a superficial reading of Cavell's position might lead one to conclude that for him it is a formal question. However, through careful readings of Cavell's writings on Samuel Beckett and Wallace Stevens, Berry shows how Cavell is actually investigating the very conditions of possibility for autonomy – political and aesthetic.

Lastly, Bryan Vescio's contribution takes us in a new direction, by turning to the philosophy of pragmatist thinker Robert Brandom. Brandom is one of the more radical inheritors of Wittgenstein, for whom the issue of representation is at best a metaphysical distraction from the role of philosophy in elucidating the social practices that frame everyday linguistic behaviour. Arguing that, implicitly from Plato's cave to Descartes' dualism, and explicitly from Kant's critiques onwards, Western thought has been dominated by the concept of representation, Vescio demonstrates instead that a more fruitful, non-representational way of thinking about literary texts can be found in the concept of metaphor. Drawing on Davidson's writings on this topic, as well as on Rorty's pragmatism, he shows how the role that metaphors play in language is in many ways analogous to, and can indeed supplement and augment, the idea of an 'inferential semantics', as articulated in Brandom's thought. The potential of Brandom and Davidson's philosophies for the study of literature is then exemplified in a careful reading of Thoreau's masterpiece, *Walden* – a text which is shown to articulate its concerns about nature and everyday life using the vehicle of metaphor rather than that of representation.

All in all, then, the chapters in this section both introduce and instantiate ordinary language criticism, showing it at work in some of its most distinguished practitioners as well as in new readings and interpretations, and ending with a thought-provoking opening, suggesting a new approach that ordinary language critics would do well to consider.

13

Two Examples of Ordinary Language Criticism: Reading Conant Reading Rorty Reading Orwell – Interpretation at the Intersection of Philosophy and Literature

Ingeborg Löfgren

Introduction

What is ordinary language criticism (OLC)? This chapter offers a partial answer by presenting two examples of OLC that both emanate from the same interpretative debate. The focal point of this text is the interpretative conflict between philosophers James Conant and Richard Rorty regarding how to understand the relevance of objective truth in George Orwell's novel *Nineteen Eighty-Four*.[1] First, I will be taking Conant's contribution to that exchange as a working example of OLC. Next, I will offer my own, meta-critical analysis of the interpretative conflict between Conant and Rorty as a second example of OLC at work. Approaching this interpretative conflict on two different levels, raising slightly different yet related questions and concerns, will hopefully create both a clear overview of that conflict itself and a richer understanding of OLC and its varieties.

In the first part of the chapter, I will recount the interpretative conflict between Rorty and Conant and show how Conant's critique of Rorty, and embedded in it, his alternative reading of *Nineteen Eighty-Four*, constitutes an example of OLC – even if Conant himself does not label it such. Through Conant's critique, I will also show that Rorty, though being greatly influenced by Wittgenstein, cannot be considered as doing OLC. In this first part of the chapter, I will be focusing on elucidating Conant's critique of Rorty.

In the second part I will make my own OLC analysis of the interpretative claims on both sides of the debate. This conflict can easily be viewed in terms of two recurring problems in interpretative theory: that of over-interpretation or reading-in, and that of authorial intention and interpretations of literary works. I will clarify the logic of the conflict by making some grammatical remarks, in Wittgenstein's sense, in response to how these problems surface in the debate.[2] I intend by this to illuminate those theoretical issues beyond this particular exchange from an OLC point of view.

Ordinary Language Criticism

Before I turn to the two examples, let me just briefly elaborate on what I take them to be examples of. In the introduction to *Ordinary Language Criticism: Literary*

Thinking after Cavell after Wittgenstein, Kenneth Dauber and Walter Jost write the following about OLC:

> Since the ambition of ordinary language criticism is to return criticism to its grounds in the 'ordinary' or natural language we all speak, it is hardly even a rubric and offers little hope for systematic organization. We might go so far as to say that all criticism is really ordinary language criticism, that is, when criticism *is* criticism as opposed to something else (quasi-scientific theory, or ideology, or even nonsense). (Dauber and Jost 2003: xi)

There are two things I think we should note in this quote. The first concerns what the 'ordinary' in OLC means. OLC inherits its understanding of the ordinary from ordinary language philosophy (OLP). In particular, it is the American philosopher Stanley Cavell's continuation and understanding of that tradition, and the specific way Cavell has picked up and developed the theme of the ordinary in J. L. Austin's and Ludwig Wittgenstein's works, that has influenced OLC. 'Ordinary', in OLP and OLC, is not to be taken in contrast to 'unusual' or 'specialised', or as meaning 'the most common' ways of using language. So, what does it contrast with? As Toril Moi writes in *Revolution of the Ordinary: Literary Studies after Wittgenstein, Austin, and Cavell*: 'it seems justified to ask whether everything is ordinary language. What is *not* ordinary?' She goes on to answer as follows:

> Fundamentally, there is just ordinary language, language that *works*, and thus helps us to draw distinctions, to see the world more clearly ... [T]he opposite to this is not a different, non-ordinary language, but language that *idles*. In philosophy, this leads to metaphysics. (Moi 2017: 75)[3]

The opposite of ordinary language is language that has become empty, that has merely the illusion of meaning. This happens, not because of some inherent malfunction in language, but when we, as speakers, are unknowingly failing to give sense to our words. If we transpose this to criticism we get the following: if language is ordinary in the OLC sense when it works, then criticism fails to be 'ordinary' when it somehow fails to work as criticism; when it unwittingly abandons its own criteria and fails to adequately live up to its own claims. One way in which criticism can fail to be 'ordinary', and thereby fail as criticism in the relevant sense for OLC, is by being too deeply intertwined with philosophical commitments that are themselves examples of language idling.

Second, OLC can, therefore, not be a systematic methodology that dictates a certain way of reading. OLC is rather negatively defined; it claims that our ordinary ways of reading and talking about literary works are important; it suggests that we may need to reconnect ourselves to those practices when criticism has gone awry. But OLC does not claim that established readerly practices provide standards of correctness, or that our everyday critical practices never lead us astray. In *Must We Mean What We Say?*, Cavell writes: 'Ordinary language philosophy is about whatever ordinary language is about' (Cavell 2002: 95). Similarly, OLC favours no themes or topics, it is about whatever the art, music, film, or – in this case – literature it investigates is about. OLC has no preference for any genre or mode of literature, say, realist fiction, prose, or even written texts. OLC is equally compatible with modernist poetry, absurdist drama, Shakespearean tragedy, romantic opera, 1930s movies, pop songs, or what have you. All of these different styles and genres are understood as taking place within 'the ordinary', but this does not mean that OLC conflates them or claims they are at bottom the same. Clearly, they are not.

What, then, one might ask, individuates OLC from just any other criticism that works? According to Dauber and Jost, two things. OLC has to, in some manner, 'take as its point of departure the so-called ordinary language philosophy deriving especially from Ludwig Wittgenstein in the early twentieth century' (Dauber and Jost 2003: xi). This means, I take it, that any writing inspired by the OLP tradition, and concerned with aesthetic matters, might qualify as OLC. Furthermore, OLC offers an alternative to what Dauber and Jost label 'the dead end of contemporary critical theory' (2003: xi). This means that OLC has a critical edge; it problematises ways theory or philosophy (I take the terms to be interchangeable in this context) can sometimes distort, rather than clarify, the arts:

> [T]he attempt by some contemporary theorists to use theory as a means of mitigating or undoing reading altogether is what OLC critics would specifically oppose. Accordingly, where theorists today use theory to distance and even separate themselves from texts that they seem to feel too narrowly constrict them, OLC would employ theory to enable a fuller inhabitation of texts in a variety of ways ... OLC reverses direction from removal to reinvestment, to seeing from the inside. (2003: xi–xii)[4]

OLC is not against theory, or against interpretations that have a theoretical or philosophical outlook. It is, however, against the kind of theoretically aloof interpretation that almost, as it were, attempts to overcome, or replace, the work it purports to analyse. OLC opposes theories that try to lay down rules in advance for what you can and cannot do in reading, thereby curtailing the very adventure of reading.[5] While holding that suspicious reading offers one important, sometimes necessary, mode of interpretation, OLC rejects the notion that the hermeneutics of suspicious is always pertinent in criticism. Instead of thinking of theory/philosophy as something that penetrates the deceptive literary surface, enabling the reader to reach its hidden truths, OLC conceives of the interaction between philosophy/theory and literature in less violent and hierarchical terms: as a conversation between equals. In such a conversation both parties may reveal and find out more about themselves and their interlocutor than they could have done if philosophy/theory were from the start taken to be the trustworthy detective, forcing its suspect, literature, to confess (see Moi 2017: 175–95). It is through such anti-hierarchal, conversational ways of reading philosophy and literature together that theory's claim to dominance can be overcome, according to OLC. In the words of Cavell:

> I should like to stress that the way to overcome theory correctly, philosophically, is to let the object or the work of your interest teach you how to consider it. I would not object to calling this a piece of theoretical advice, as long as it is also called a piece of practical advice. Philosophers will naturally assume that it is one thing, and quite clear how, to let a philosophical work teach you how to consider it, and another thing, and quite obscure how or why, to let a film teach you this. I believe these are not such different things. (Cavell 1981: 10–11)

In response to this description of OLC, one question that may arise is: how does it differ from good old-fashioned close reading? Might the stress on the text itself, on it teaching us how to read it, evoke the suspicion that OLC promotes a kind of critical conservatism, perhaps even an ideologically suspect unwillingness to scrutinise texts from any other perspective than their own preferred self-understanding?

There are indeed certain similarities between close reading and OLC, if one stresses the aspects of attention to details, the focus on the reciprocity between form and content, the importance bestowed upon the reader's judgement and humility before the text. But what separates OLC from close reading and the New Critical idiom is that it has no predetermined focus – say on ambiguity, irony, paradox – nor does its conception of the literary work necessarily exclude the author and their intentions, historical and social context, power relations and politics, etc. In fact, OLC aspires to no general theoretical conception of 'the literary' or 'the meaning' of literature as such. On the contrary, OLC is fearful of what Wittgenstein labels our 'craving for generality' (Wittgenstein 1964: 17). This craving tempts us to define our concepts prior to specific investigations and readings – thus deciding beforehand what can be seen by them – rather than looking at different uses during our investigations and readings. Instead, OLC thinks that philosophising on concepts such as 'the author', 'the novel', 'subjectivity', 'character', 'context', etc., should be done in response to some concrete difficulty; when the critic encounters a text that actually creates some conceptual conundrum. A specific work, or an interpretation of a work, may show us that a concept is indeed in need of theorising. A case in point is the interpretative conflict between Rorty and Conant I am about to address, where the concept of truth in *Nineteen Eighty-Four* becomes something that requires theorising in order for us to grasp what is actually at stake in the novel.

Before I turn to that conflict, I think this characterisation of OLC also licenses us to call someone an ordinary language critic who has not labelled him- or herself thus. This is important for my claim that Conant is doing OLC, even if he has not himself described his work thus. In the next part of this chapter I will show how Conant's text is characterised by the features listed by Dauber and Jost, in ways relevant to both his critique of Rorty and his own reading of *Nineteen Eighty-Four*. Thereby we will also see that Rorty, though an admirer of Wittgenstein and someone who philosophises through readings of literature, can hardly be considered as doing OLC.

Freedom, Cruelty, and Truth: Rorty on *Nineteen Eighty-Four* and Conant on Why Rorty is Unable to Read Orwell

Rorty Reading Orwell

The interpretative conflict between Rorty and Conant can be said to boil down to what significance the concept of objective truth has for Orwell's dystopic novel *Nineteen Eighty-Four*. In his 'The Last Intellectual in Europe: Orwell on Cruelty', Rorty makes the quite astonishing claim, for anyone who has read Orwell's novel, that 'the question about "the possibility of truth" is a red herring' (Rorty 1989: 182). Instead, Rorty claims, the novel is centrally concerned with cruelty: 'I think the fantasy of endless torture – the suggestion that the future is "a boot stamping on a human face – forever" is essential to *1984*' (Rorty 1989: 182). At the time of its publication, the real importance of the novel was not that it warned against totalitarian societies' assault on the very idea of truth. Rather, Rorty writes, its accomplishment was that it 'sensitiz[ed] an audience to cases of cruelty and humiliation which they had not noticed' (1989: 173).[6] Regarding present-day readers, Rorty suggests, the work can teach us that cruelty is the worst thing you can do to someone – a view he equates with what it means to be a liberal – and that if we merely take care of freedom, then truth can take care of itself (1989: 173, 176).

Those who read the novel as significantly concerned with the defence of truth are committed, Rorty thinks, to a misguided philosophical position, namely, epistemological realism. Rorty takes this realist reading to be quite common among Orwell's critics. He finds, for instance, Lionel Trilling and Samuel Hynes guilty of it (Rorty 1989: 171–4).[7] His own reading is thus offered in contrast, and as an alternative, to such realist readings.

But what about all those numerous passages in *Nineteen Eighty-Four* that appear to speak against Rorty's interpretation – where the defence of truth seem absolutely central to the novel as a whole? Rorty is of course not unaware of them. One, which he cites himself, is the following:

> The Party told you to reject the evidence of your eyes and ears. It was their final, most essential command. [Winston's] heart sank as he thought of the enormous power arrayed against him, the ease with which any party intellectual would overthrow him in debate . . . . And yet he was in the right! . . . The obvious, the silly, and the true had got to be defended. Truisms are true, hold on to that! The solid world exists, its laws do not change. Stones are hard, water is wet, objects unsupported fall towards the earth's centre. With the feeling that he was speaking to O'Brien, and also that he was setting forth an important axiom, [Winston] wrote: *Freedom is the freedom to say that two plus two make four. If that is granted, all else follows.* (Orwell 1990: 84)[8]

This passage is not, however, to be taken as textual evidence of the importance of truth in the novel, according to Rorty. The point is not that two plus two equals four, but that you should be allowed to believe it and say it without getting hurt (Rorty 1989: 176). Commentators who have focused on the defence of truth instead, Rorty argues, typically conclude that:

> Orwell teaches us to set our faces against all those sneaky intellectuals who try to tell us that truth is not 'out there' ... Orwell has, in short, been read as a realist philosopher, a defender of common sense against its cultured, ironist despisers. On this reading, the crucial opposition in Orwell's thought is the standard metaphysical one between contrived appearance and naked reality. (Rorty 1989: 172–3)

In this quote Rorty signals awareness of how his own philosophical position regarding the concept of truth – that it is part of an outdated metaphysical vocabulary that we should rid ourselves of – can put him in unflattering proximity to O'Brien and the advocacy of Newspeak. But in Rorty's view, what is frightening about O'Brien is not his disregard for objective truth, but his taste for suffering. O'Brien is construed as a warning; this is what intellectuals become in a totalitarian society with no free outlet for intellectual talents – connoisseurs of pain (Rorty 1989: 176).

> Torture is not for the sake of getting people to obey, nor for the sake of getting them to believe falsehoods. As O'Brien says, 'The object of torture is torture'. For a gifted and sensitive intellectual living in a posttotalitarian culture, this sentence is the analogue of 'Art for art's sake' or 'Truth for its own sake', for torture is now the only art form and the only intellectual discipline available to such a person. (Rorty 1989: 180)

Consequently, when it comes to such pivotal passages of the book as when O'Brien, through torture, makes Winston say – and believe – that two plus two equals five, O'Brien is not doing that because truth, and the destruction of Winston's grasp of truth, are in any way important: 'The *only* point in making Winston believe that two and two equals five is to break him', Rorty writes (1989: 178).

In the end O'Brien rearranges those pieces into a creature who now 'loves' Big Brother. Producing such a Frankenstein's monster of a soul, however, 'is just an extra fillip', according to Rorty. The real object of the torture is the exquisite sound a mind makes as it is being ripped into shreds (Rorty 1989: 179).

Conant Reading Rorty and Orwell

In 'Freedom, Cruelty, and Truth: Rorty versus Orwell', Conant claims that 'there is a fairly literal sense in which Rorty is *unable to read* Orwell and that this inability is tied to an inability to free himself from certain philosophical preoccupations' (Conant 2000: 269–70). This is, I think, quite clearly something that qualifies as a kind of OLC critique: according to Conant, Rorty – in Dauber and Jost's words – uses philosophy as a means of mitigating or undoing reading altogether.

How then, is this undoing of reading through philosophical preoccupations executed? It is created through what Conant calls Rorty's 'obsession' with realism, an obsession he labels 'epistemologism' (Conant 2000: 270). Due to this obsession, Rorty can only envision two alternative readings of *Nineteen Eighty-Four*, Conant claims: either a realist reading that views the novel as centrally defending a metaphysical thesis about truth as correspondence with what is 'out there'; or an anti-realist reading, Rorty's own neo-pragmatist reading, in which the question of truth simply drops out as irrelevant. An irony of Rorty's epistemologism, Conant notes, is that he nevertheless remains in the clutches of the very form of metaphysical question he tries to dissolve:

> In his criticism of Realism, Rorty invariably formulates his rejection of a thesis of Realism in terms of a counterposed thesis. He thus invariably ends up affirming a thesis that has the same logical form as a thesis which the Realist affirms, but with one difference: a negation operator has been introduced into the content-clause of the thesis. Rorty ... ends up affirming an alternative answer to the Realist's question. He ends up claiming that there is something we cannot do or have which the Realist claimed we can do or have. (Conant 2000: 274)[9]

What Rorty fails to see, Conant claims, is that there is a variety of non-metaphysical ways of talking about the importance of objective truth, ways that are neither realist nor anti-realist, but simply ordinary. This is how Orwell speaks about truth, in *Nineteen Eighty-Four* and in other texts, and this is how Trilling's and Hynes's commentaries on the novel should be understood, Conant argues.

This brings out the second OLC characteristic in Conant's text: that he significantly draws on an OLP understanding of 'the ordinary' in his readings of Rorty and Orwell.

> In Wittgenstein's sense of 'ordinary'[,] ... *ordinary* contrasts (not with *literary* or *metaphorical* or *scientific* or *technical*, but) with *metaphysical*. In this sense of 'ordinary', the uses to which poetry and science puts language are as much part of ordinary language as calling your cat or asking someone to pass the butter ... Rorty's anti-metaphysical response bears the characteristic earmark of an *anti-metaphysical metaphysics* (be it Berkeley's, Hume's, Carnap's, or Derrida's): a recoil from the ordinary. (Conant 2000: 323nn.51–2)

Conant's claim is not that all these ordinary uses of language – literary, scientific, technical, etc. – are all the same and no more difficult than asking someone to pass the butter. The point is that there are language uses, most of our everyday language uses, that are not secretly fused with and founded upon metaphysics; that it is perfectly possible to use the word 'truth', and to find truth to be utterly important, without being committed to any metaphysics at all. In his response to Conant, Rorty makes it clear that he neither understands what Conant means by 'ordinary' uses of language, nor thinks they have any philosophical significance: 'Commonsensical remarks or platitudes can be used as objections to proposals for conceptual revision, but they should not be. Appeals to ordinary language are of no philosophical interest' (Rorty 2000: 345). And: '[I]f there were something like what Cavell calls "the Ordinary" – I doubt that I should have any interest in dwelling within it' (Rorty 2000: 349). This is enough to show, I think, that Rorty cannot be viewed as doing OLC.

What stands in the way of Rorty seeing these ordinary uses, Conant argues, is his preferred method of dissolving philosophical problems by dropping the vocabularies in which they are formulated (Conant 2000: 278). Words that Rorty identifies as essential to certain philosophical positions that he opposes work as philosophical triggers for him (Conant 2000: 281). In numerous texts, Conant reminds us, Orwell expressed thoughts he found important in precisely the kind of vocabulary Rorty deems suspicious, such as: 'The feeling that the very concept of objective truth is fading out of the world is – and should be – frightening' and 'There are objective historical truths. Historical facts are independent of what we say or believe happened in the past' (Conant 2000: 279).

Since Rorty can only hear such formulations as expressive of metaphysical statements, he must either excuse them as mere rhetoric or avoid them in order to lend credibility to his own reading of *Nineteen Eighty-Four*. It is thus Rorty, Conant thinks, who perversely reads 'every line of Orwell (and every line of Orwell commentary) through philosophical spectacles', and it is 'Rorty – not Trilling or Hynes – who attempts to enlist Orwell on one side of an argument between a Realist and an opponent of Realism' (Conant 2000: 284).[10] In this context Conant underlines how he and Rorty differ as readers of Wittgenstein:

> [Rorty is unable] to exercise the sort of discernment that Wittgenstein's later work is centrally concerned to impart: an ability to discern between ordinary and metaphysical *uses* of language ... In attacking (not the *use* that a philosopher makes of his words, but) *the words*, urging us to throw the words themselves away, Rorty would have us destroy (not only metaphysical houses of cards, but) precious everyday discursive resources and along with them the concepts (and hence the availability of the thoughts) which they enable us to express. (Conant 2000: 323 n.52)

The above point is vital for Conant's critique of Rorty's claim that the single purpose of getting Winston to believe that two plus two equals five is to cause Winston as much pain as possible. It is equally essential for Conant's alternative interpretation of that torture scene, and its relevance for our understanding of the importance of objective truth in the novel. This brings us to Conant's own reading and its third OLC characteristic: that of countering a theoretically aloof reading, in which Orwell looks like a neo-pragmatist, with a reading that theorises from inside the text.

Presenting his own interpretation of *Nineteen Eighty-Four*, Conant points out that Rorty has served us with a false conflict: why should we view O'Brien – or the novel as a whole – as concerned *either* with cruelty *or* with truth? Why can they not be concerned with both? Returning us to the text, Conant reminds us that there are several passages in the novel that become quite mysterious on Rorty's reading. The following quote, where O'Brien tells Winston why he is being tortured, is one example:

> We are not content with negative obedience, nor even with the most abject submission. When finally you surrender to us, it must be of your own free will. We do not destroy the heretic because he resists us: so long as he resists us we never destroy him. We convert him, we capture his inner mind, we reshape him. We burn all evil and illusion out of him; we bring him over to our side, not in appearance, but genuinely, heart and soul. (Orwell 1990: 267)[11]

Here O'Brien at least appears to declare a very strong interest, not just in tearing minds apart, but in putting them together again so as to make them completely obedient to the Party. If O'Brien was only interested in Winston's delicious pain, why devote so much time to arguing with Winston about historical facts and arithmetical truths? Why torture Winston in this specific way, Conant asks:

> The question is whether O'Brien's concern is merely with 'breaking' people (in which case truth and falsity can drop out as irrelevant), or whether it is with breaking them in a very particular way, namely in such a way that their minds can be subsequently enslaved. If the aim is to break Winston in such a way that he is able to believe only what the Party wants him to believe, then breaking his hold on the distinction between truth and falsity might not be irrelevant. What does it take to enslave a mind? (One might have thought the novel as a whole was concerned to explore this question.) (Conant 2000: 290)

There is another way than Rorty's of interpreting O'Brien as an emblem of intellectual life in a totalitarian society. Conant reaches that interpretation by appealing to Orwell's explicit aim with the novel: 'Orwell summed up what he "really meant to do" in *Nineteen Eighty-Four* by saying that his aim was to display "the *intellectual* implications of *totalitarianism*"' (Conant 2002: 291, quoting Orwell 1968b: 460). It is in the light of this aim that Conant thinks we should view the pivotal scene where Winston is tortured into believing two plus two is five. By crushing his hold on the concept of truth, the Party deprives Winston of the ability to form beliefs and draw conclusions on his own. That is the goal: 'It is this capacity of individuals to assess the truth of claims on their own that threatens the absolute hegemony of the Party over their minds' (Conant 2000: 299).

For Winston this prospect is horrifying: 'If the Party could thrust its hand into the past and say of this or that event, *it never happened* – that, surely, was more terrifying than mere torture and death' (Orwell 1990: 37).[12] Conant juxtaposes this quote with the following words from Orwell: 'The really frightening thing about totalitarianism is not that it commits "atrocities" but that it attacks the concept of objective truth' (Orwell 1968b: 88).[13] The reason why this is so horrifying in *Nineteen Eighty-Four* is not merely that Winston himself loses this capacity, but that the Party sets out to make this lack the normal condition of everyone – and may succeed in doing so.

Doublethink, reality control, and other Party strategies are only planned to be transitory in *Nineteen Eighty-Four*. Once the population has learned to do all this naturally, these strategies will no longer be required since there will be no alternatives to them in which to think. The same goes for Newspeak: the dictionary of Newspeak is important as long as people in Oceania still speak English (or Oldspeak, as it is called in Newspeak). But since the aim of Newspeak is to destroy all words that can invite heresies, words are destroyed in order to destroy thoughts: once that job is done, no one will be able to understand those dictionaries, because English, as we know it, will be gone. Here Conant underlines the similarity between O'Brien and Rorty: both want to do away with thoughts they find unfruitful by doing away with the *words* that express them. Both, for different reasons, find no need for the word 'truth' (Conant 2000: 308–15).[14]

This is the intellectual consequence of totalitarianism which Orwell warns against in *Nineteen Eighty-Four*, according to Conant: the very 'undermining of the possibility of your leading a life in which you are free to think your own thoughts – to have your own take on whether, for instance, something is an atrocity or not' (Conant 2000: 295). A person who can no longer make use of the concept of truth cannot be free. She no longer has the capacity to even crave such freedom. Nothing beyond 'goodthink' will be within her conceptual grasp.[15]

This means, Conant argues, that '[t]he central topic of Orwell's novel – the abolition of the conditions of the possibility of having an intellectual life – fails to come to view on Rorty's reading' (Conant 2000: 292).[16] It also means that Rorty's advice, that we should let go of truth and concentrate on preserving freedom, fails to make much sense within the world of the novel:

> According to Rorty's Orwell, if we take care of freedom, truth can take care of itself ... [T]his is roughly the opposite of Orwell's view. When 'the very concept of objective truth begins to fade out of the world', the conditions, not only for truth, but for freedom, are undermined ... The preservation of freedom and the preservation of truth represent a single indivisible task for Orwell – a task common to literature and politics. (Conant 2000: 310)

This brings us to a further way in which Conant's criticism can be said to be a critique from the inside. Conant takes seriously Rorty's aim to protect freedom. If freedom is not protected, but rather made impossible, by our letting go of the vocabulary of objective truth, this does not only mean that Rorty's reading of *Nineteen Eighty-Four* is faced with serious problems. It also means that Rorty's philosophy is faced with serious problems.

The Grammar of Interpretation: Authorial Intentions and Philosophical Heresies of Paraphrase

At this point, I hope to have established how Conant's text qualifies as OLC. However, so far, I have said nothing about to what extent Conant's critique of Rorty is fair, or whether his interpretation of *Nineteen Eighty-Four* is superior to Rorty's. Turning to these questions now, we see some familiar problems within literary hermeneutics being actualised by this conflict: if one of these readings is a misinterpretation and the other valid, what makes them so? If Conant's is valid, must Rorty's be invalid (and vice versa)? What does it mean for an interpretation to trump another? What is the relevance of both being philosophical readings of literature? What is the logic of this conflict?

To address these questions, let us look at Conant's most general critique of Rorty.[17] It can be broken down into two parts:

- Rorty fails to understand what Orwell writes (and how Orwell means what he writes) when it comes to the issue of objective truth in *Nineteen Eighty-Four*,

because

- Rorty is so philosophically obsessed with the conflict between realism and anti-realism that he *reads-in* that philosophical conflict into texts that contain his trigger-words.

I will assess this critique from an OLC point of view by asking two questions: to what extent does it matter that *Nineteen Eighty-Four* is fiction, a novel, when it comes to

1. the relevance that appeals to authorial intentions have?
2. the difference between a reading that is informed by a philosophical outlook/concern in a benign way, and a reading that makes philosophical paraphrases/over- or mis-interpretations in order to facilitate a philosophical argument?

Question (1) is important here because, while Conant offers a very strong case against any claim that Rorty's reading captures what Orwell wanted to say with *Nineteen Eighty-Four*, it is unclear whether Rorty's reading makes that type of claim, or that it needs to in order not to misread the work (or fail to read it altogether).

Question (2) is important because it could be argued that Conant is also informed by philosophy in his reading of *Nineteen Eighty-Four*, namely by the OLP tradition, which certainly guides his understanding that Orwell uses words like 'truth' ordinarily. One could therefore ask what makes Conant's OLC reading any less of a distortive philosophical paraphrase than Rorty's neo-pragmatic reading of *Nineteen Eighty-Four*.

In other words, this conflict gives me occasion to address, from an OLC perspective, the seemingly perennial questions within literary theory about authorial intention and the limits of, and criteria of validity in, literary interpretation. Here, these questions will be addressed more specifically with regard to philosophical readings of literature. This meta-critical, theoretical, analysis will constitute the second example of OLC that this chapter offers.

Literary Works and Authorial Intentions

If we begin with the first issue, that about authorial intentions, it seems clear that Rorty did not attempt to make an interpretation of *Nineteen Eighty-Four* that in any way depends on what *Orwell* wanted to say. Rorty explicitly declares that his reading 'is not a matter of wanting to have [Orwell] on my side of a philosophical argument' (Rorty 1989: 173), and in his response to Conant's critique he writes:

> My reading of [Orwell] was not intended to claim him as a fellow pragmatist, but to explain why one could be a non-Realist and still have one's moral horizon expanded by *1984*, why one could agree with O'Brien's coherentism and still be intrigued, fascinated and appalled by O'Brien's way of coming to terms with the absence of freedom ... The idea was to say how the book looks when seen through non-Realist eyes ... Had Orwell taken an interest in such arguments, I imagine, he would have sided with the Realists. (Rorty 2000: 344)[18]

Rorty admits that there are passages where he sounds as if he wants Orwell on his side (2000: 349n.3).[19] Conant, therefore, has reason to read Rorty this way. But if we accept Rorty's comments on this matter, which I think we should, those passages should be viewed as unfortunate and unsubstantial with regard to the main gist of the interpretation. So, what happens to Conant's claim that Rorty misinterprets the work because he fails to see what Orwell meant? Must Rorty focus on what Orwell wanted to communicate in order to make a valid interpretation?

No. Readers of imaginative literature are not obliged to read for authorial intentions. Usually when we read a philosophical text we are, and should be, interested in what the author meant. We can certainly read literature in this way too, and in Orwell's case it can seem particularly pertinent to do so. But we do not have to, which is why I conclude that the first part of Conant's critique – that Rorty's reading fails because he cannot read (what) Orwell (meant) – does not hit home.

Conant, on the other hand, is indeed reading *Nineteen Eighty-Four* with the purpose of understanding how Orwell intended us to read it. This is a reading one could describe as intentionalist – if that term were merely shorthand for any reading interested in what the author wanted to convey with a text. But as that term, to my ears at least, is too deeply rooted in the notion of intentionalism, it does not fit Conant's position. Intentionalism in literary hermeneutics claims that the correct or best reading of a work is that which captures (as closely as possible) what the author intended to say.[20] It can be contrasted with the opposite theoretical position, anti-intentionalism, which claims that what the author meant with his or her work is irrelevant to what the literary work means as an aesthetic artefact.[21] The latter might be a fair description of Rorty's position, if we look at other texts he has written on the subject (see Rorty 1992). Conant, as far as I know, has no such general stance on authors' intentions and literary works. In this particular reading of *Nineteen Eighty-Four*, he finds Orwell's intentions important. But he does not espouse the theoretical claim that valid literary interpretations require that readers aim for authors' intentions. And that is, in my view, to his credit.

I do not think this conflict should be viewed in terms of the debate between intentionalism and anti-intentionalism. In fact, I think that debate itself is a red herring. It exemplifies quite well the attempt to mitigate or undo reading through theory that Dauber and Jost declared as inimical to OLC; it is an attempt to lay down rules, from the outside of theory, about what we must – or must not – do as readers in order to adequately capture 'the meaning' of a work.

From my OLC perspective, the questions of whether authorial intentions are relevant in literary interpretation or not, whether they should be seen as belonging to the 'inside' or the 'outside' of texts, are not questions that can be assessed, as it were, in general. In fact, as general questions I think they are only seemingly meaningful. The relevance of authorial intention has to be assessed piecemeal, in response to specific works and specific questions and claims about those works – not through theoretical definitions of interpretative validity, or of 'literary meaning', made in advance, and before the unruly act of reading begins.

The point is not that we never need to theorise on these matters – say, on the concept of authorial intention in literature – but that we should do so precisely when we need that theorisation: when we encounter some specific problem in our critical practice that requires philosophical clarification. We should not assume, gripped by our craving for generality, that unless we make clear our general view on 'the relevance of authorial intention for literary interpretation' (as if all the various ways we might give that expression meaning could be reduced to one thing), we are unfit to do our interpretative job.

Conant and Rorty have quite different interpretative aims: one is interested in the author's intentions in *Nineteen Eighty-Four*, the other is not. In this regard, both exemplify ordinary ways we interpret literature, and both have their place in everyday readerly practice. If we are to pass judgement on which reading is the better in this particular case, we have to look at something other than who is interested in what the author meant and who is not.

Literary Works and Philosophical Paraphrases

What then, about the claim that Rorty's reading is flawed because he makes a distorting philosophical paraphrase of *Nineteen Eighty-Four*? That is, can he be charged with missing the relevance of truth in *Nineteen Eighty-Four* because he *reads-in* his own obsession with realism into the novel?

Here my answer is: yes. Regardless of Orwell's intentions, Rorty, in fact, ignores important sections in *Nineteen Eighty-Four* foregrounding truth. He also ignores

O'Brien's explicit explanation about why Winston is being tortured. Here is one such scene:

> 'No!' exclaimed O'Brien. His voice had changed extraordinarily, and his face had suddenly become both stern and animated. 'No! Not merely to extract your confession, nor to punish you. Shall I tell you why we have brought you here? To cure you! To make you sane! Will you understand, Winston, that no one whom we bring to this place ever leaves our hands uncured? We are not interested in those stupid crimes that you have committed. The Party is not interested in the overt act: the thought is all we care about. We do not destroy our enemies, we change them. (Orwell 1990: 265)

One may, of course, think that O'Brien is lying to Winston here. But I see little textual evidence fuelling that suspicion. Winston, for one, thinks that O'Brien means what he says:

> 'By the time we had finished with [Jones, Aaronson and Rutherford] they were only shells of men. There was nothing left in them except sorrow for what they had done, and love of Big Brother. It was touching to see how they loved him. They begged to be shot quickly, so that they could die while their minds were still clean.' His voice had grown almost dreamy. The exaltation, the lunatic enthusiasm, was still in his face. He is not pretending, thought Winston; he is not a hypocrite; he believes every word he says. (Orwell 1990: 268)

These passages are hard to square with Rorty's reading of O'Brien as only concerned with causing Winston pain, and not with enslaving his (and everyone else's) mind. So even if we dismiss any reference to the aims of the author, Conant's and Rorty's interpretative claims are still opposed with regard to the relevance of the concept of objective truth in the novel.

In that conflict, I would say that Conant's reading trumps Rorty's. This is not because if we have two opposing interpretations, and one is valid, then the other must be invalid. I am not defending monism in interpretation. As Cavell reminds us in *Pursuits of Happiness*, it is part of the grammar of interpretation that there has to be room for more than one – though not all need to be of equal standing.[22] The reason Conant's reading trumps Rorty's is quite simple and ordinary: it is because he can make better sense of central passages of the novel and of the novel as a whole.

This is also why Rorty, but not Conant, can indeed be charged with making a distortive philosophical paraphrase, with reading-in his philosophical obsessions in the novel. Philosophical readings are not distortive per se. Both Conant and Rorty are readers guided by philosophical concerns and conceptions. Rorty, however, avoids reading certain passages of the novel in order to preserve his philosophical interpretation, he ignores central parts of the work in order to make a philosophical point.

What is wrong with doing that? Can you not do that? Well, you can do it, but then that is what you have done; you have – to speak with Dauber and Jost – used philosophy as a means of mitigating or undoing reading; you have distanced yourself from the work as if it too narrowly constricts you. Doing that comes at a price, and the price might be that you have pushed yourself outside of criticism, that what you do is no longer criticism.[23] Whether that is a price worth paying of course depends on what you take yourself to have gained by it. Perhaps you rather think of it as broadening the criteria of literary interpretation, changing the game from inside? Games do change in these ways. But how do you know if you have succeeded? This brings us to questions about the limits of interpretation, the sharedness of our criteria of critical validity, and what kind of authority we appeal to when we make interpretative claims.

Acknowledging the Vulnerability of Interpretative Claims

All interpretations, of course, suffer from omissions and blind spots. That is part of their grammar: you emphasise some parts of a work and not others. Only the work itself can say exactly and all of what it says.[24] This means that it is the job of the interpreter to make discerning choices, to judge what is central and not. In this evaluative task we can, and do, disagree.

So how do we judge whether an interpretation is valid or an over-interpretation? If our normal condition allows for plenty of disagreement on this matter, it can seem a hopelessly subjective task, drenched in uncertainty. Or as Cavell writes about interpretative claims: 'How can serious people habitually make such *vulnerable* claims? (Meaning, perhaps, claims so *obviously* false?)' (Cavell 2003: 83). Cavell hardly thinks interpretative claims are false by default – that there is no such thing as interpretative validity; he does not espouse interpretative scepticism. Interpretations are, however, vulnerable in ways that claims that are either true or false (in a more straightforward manner) are generally not. They are vulnerable because as much as they are claims – to community and shared intelligibility – they are invitations to others to try to see what I see.

As a literary interpreter, I can, and should, present evidence of different sorts in favour of my reading: quotes from the work, comments by the author, facts about literary conventions or historical facts at the time the work was written, etc. – in short: material we critics consider relevant for the kind of reading I make and the kind of interest I take in a text. Readers of my interpretation will, however, have to make up their own minds whether they see these connections the way I do, or even see them at all. I have no way of proving that my reading holds. The 'proof' is in the eating of the pudding: in what I make others see in the work.[25] If I have displayed all the textual evidence I can think of, and pointed out the pattern I find, there is nothing more for me to do: 'I have reached bedrock, and my spade is turned' (Wittgenstein 2008: §217). What my interpretations crave – and are vulnerable to – is not proof or disproof but acknowledgement or rejection by fellow readers. The risk that I may go too far, that I may read-in, cannot be cleared out in advance. On that subject, Cavell writes:

> '[R]eading in', as a term of criticism, suggests something quite particular, like going too far even if on a real track. Then the question would be, as the question often is about philosophy, how to bring reading to an end. And this should be seen as a problem internal to criticism, not a criticism of it from outside ... [T]he moral I urge is that this assessment be made the subject of arguments about particular texts. (Cavell 1981: 35)[26]

What is the difference between seeing the risk of reading-in as something internal to criticism and seeing it as something we need to tackle from the outside? One outside strategy would be to create a theory of interpretative validity – say, that we must read, or must avoid reading, for the author's intention in order to get literary meaning – and then regulate our criticism accordingly. But that would be precisely to yield to interpretative scepticism by trying to refute it head-on; it would be to yield to the misconception that we need such a theory to ground our critical practice, or anything goes. But as David Rudrum points out: 'Claims made in literary criticism and in any discussion of aesthetics are ... in an important sense groundless; in fact, they seek to secure their own grounding' (Rudrum 2013: 17). This means that the proper way to deal with interpretative scepticism – say, the fear that there are no common criteria of validity, or no real difference between valid and invalid readings – is to acknowledge the truth in it (not that *it* is true!): namely, that occasionally we do not share criteria, our claim to community remains unanswered, and we do not recognise what the other is doing as criticism at all.

The fact that we disagree, however, takes place against a backdrop of a shared practice of reading. OLC's way of treating the risk of reading-in as 'internal to criticism' is to view the assessment of validity as something done from the inside of reading, every time, case by case.[27] What separates philosophical interpretations of literature that are clarifying from distortive paraphrases can thus not be settled on a general, theoretical level. It can only be assessed through the act of reading itself, by our reading particular interpretations and their particular claims. This is what I take myself to have done in assessing Rorty's and Conant's interpretations. What I appealed to then were, I take it, our common criteria of validity in literary interpretation, not to a theory of interpretative validity.

But what about my appeals to Cavell and the OLP tradition? Is that not appealing to theory? Perhaps in a minimal sense, but not in the sense of laying down theoretical rules for what counts as interpretative validity or literary meaning. The authority of Cavell's grammatical reminders does not reside in his being an 'authority' within OLP, but in that we, as critics, who are equally authoritative in using our common, ordinary, critical terms, acknowledge those reminders as being expressive of what we mean by our words. Likewise, my authority in claiming that Rorty reads-in, and that Conant's reading trumps Rorty's, is no greater and no less than any other critic's and has the same source: our sharing the practice and criteria of criticism. Our criteria cannot protect us from experiencing interpretative conflicts, mistakes, and disagreement as to whether a specific interpretation has played itself outside the game of criticism or changed its rules, etc. That is what can make criteria so disappointing, make them seem in need of theoretical underpinning. Criteria do not guarantee success – they 'only' make conflict, mistake, and disagreement possible at all, just as they make attunement, success, and agreement possible at all.

If our ordinary criteria of criticism can be disappointing in this way, OLC can seem equally disappointing, for anyone on the lookout for the next intellectual fashion. OLC offers no hip theory, no trendy methods, and no exclusive jargon by which I can claim authority and importance. OLC puts its trust in literature and its readers, convinced they are enough for criticism to flourish. OLC wants to return us critics to the ordinary language where we – not some theory – speak. This also means daring to hear and claim my own voice, shouldering responsibility for my language. In criticism I have to acknowledge myself as a reader, acknowledge that my reading exposes me – my prejudices, my blind spots, my hobby horses – beyond my knowledge and control; that I am – or at least may be – read and known in return. This condition of literary interpretation is as blissful as it is terrifying. Which in turn, I think, hints at why we might be tempted to escape reading, by means of theory, in the first place.

Notes

I am grateful for the generous financial support I have received from Birgit och Gad Rausing Stiftelse för humanistisk forskning and Riksbankens jubileumsfond: The Swedish Foundation for Humanities and Social Sciences, while working on this chapter.

1. See Rorty 1989, 2000; Conant 2000.
2. Wittgenstein's 'grammar' denotes something like the logic, the discursive and conceptual possibilities, that you learn as you learn your mother tongue. Grammatical remarks and reminders are produced in order to dissolve some specific philosophical confusion. They are not intended to describe logical relations in language in general, or to reveal any new knowledge. They are supposed to merely make us aware of something we already know but fail to appreciate while philosophising, thus leading us to philosophical bewilderment:

   > Something that one knows when nobody asks one, but no longer knows when one is asked to explain it, is something that has to be called to mind. (And it is obviously something which, for some reason, it is difficult to call to mind.) (Wittgenstein 2008: §89)

3. We will see later in this chapter that Conant offers a similar understanding of 'the ordinary'. See also Wittgenstein 2008: §§116–19.
4. What this 'seeing from the inside' means will hopefully become clear through examples of how this notion is used in OLC, in the subsequent two parts of this chapter.
5. Moi 2011 discusses this succinctly.

6. That is, it made leftist intellectuals see what was going on in the Soviet Union differently. This should not be understood 'as a matter of [it] stripping away appearance and revealing reality' but as 'a redescription of what may happen or has been happening – to be compared, not with reality, but with alternative descriptions of the same events' (Rorty 1989: 173).
7. Rorty is referring to Trilling 1971 and Hynes 1971.
8. Also quoted by Rorty 1989: 172.
9. Conant's critique of Rorty here is isomorphic with Cavell's critique of the anti-sceptic who tries to refute the sceptic head-on by claiming that we *do* know whatever it is that the sceptic denies that we know. That, according to Cavell, is not to cut ties with scepticism (see Cavell 1999: 37–48).
10. Conant does not deny that there may very well be Realist readings of Orwell; he thinks that Peter Van Inwagen is an example of such a Realist reader. But as Rorty is still captured in the same form of reading as Van Inwagen – a reading that centres on a dispute between Realism and anti-Realism, 'neither [of them] allows for a reading of the novel which takes the author to identify with the sentiments of his protagonist but doesn't take such identification to commit the author to Realism' (Conant 2000: 283).
11. Also quoted by Conant 2000: 340n.197.
12. Also quoted by Conant 2000: 297.
13. Also quoted by Conant 2000: 295; this can be compared to what Winston reads in *The Theory and Practice of Oligarchical Collectivism*, by Emmanuel Goldstein: 'The two aims of the Party are to conquer the whole surface of the earth and to extinguish once and for all the possibility of independent thought' (Orwell 1990: 201).
14. See also Orwell's 'Appendix: The Principles of Newspeak' (Orwell 1990: 312–25).
15. 'Goodthink' means, roughly, orthodoxy: to think in alignment with the Party (Orwell 1990: 317).
16. This of course means that Conant and Rorty have quite different views on what an intellectual – and a liberal – is (see Conant 2000: 291–5, 310–11).
17. '[T]here is a fairly literal sense in which Rorty is *unable to read* Orwell and ... this inability is tied to an inability to free himself from certain philosophical preoccupations' (Conant 2000: 269–70).
18. This quote does seem to affirm Conant's claim that Rorty construes his own reading on the assumption that we must embrace either a Realist reading or an anti-Realist reading, and that the Realist is the most common one.
19. One such unfortunate passage is the following: 'As evidence that this way of reading the last part of *1984* is not entirely factitious, I can cite a column which Orwell wrote in 1944' (Rorty 1989: 176). If what Orwell meant to say is irrelevant, then this column should also be irrelevant. Other such lapses are when Rorty writes about what Orwell does and claims, such as: 'Orwell did not invent O'Brien to serve as a dialectical foil ... He invented him to warn us against him' (Rorty 1989: 176); 'I take Orwell's claim that there is no such thing as *inner* freedom, no such thing as "autonomous individual," to be ... that there is nothing deep inside each of us, no common human nature ... to use as moral reference point' (Rorty 1989: 177).
20. See, for instance, Hirsch 1967; Juhl 1980; Carroll 2002; for a recent defence of 'extreme intentionalism', see Stock 2017.
21. In this camp we find such, in other respects antagonistic, texts as Wimsatt and Beardsley 1982 and Fish 1980.

22. '[F]or something to be correctly regarded as an interpretation ... there must be conceived to be competing interpretations possible, where "must" is a term not of etiquette but of (what Wittgenstein calls) grammar, something like logic' (Cavell 1981: 36).
23. Could such failed criticism work as something else, say, as philosophy? I will have to leave this question open. In fact, I think it should remain open, as a question left for case-by-case assessment. However, since I agree with Cavell's view that we should look at philosophy as a form of – or something analogous to, say, literary – criticism, it is not obvious what the contrast between criticism and (good) philosophy would be within an OLC understanding (see Cavell 1984). One could argue that while Rorty's reading of *Nineteen Eighty-Four* may fail as literary criticism, as an interpretation of the work, Rorty's main concern is not to be faithful to the text, but to make a philosophical point. I cannot go into a detailed discussion about how we should respond to such a complaint here. I can say, though, that I read Rorty as indeed making some substantial interpretative claims about *Nineteen Eighty-Four*, claims that have to be answerable to the text if we are to take seriously the notion that his reading of *Nineteen Eighty-Four* is supposed to achieve something philosophically. Otherwise, the reference to *Nineteen Eighty-Four* appears to do no philosophical work and could be dropped. Conant argues that it is precisely Rorty's philosophical shortcomings that are revealed in his shortcoming as a reader of Orwell: that these two things, in this particular case at least, go hand in hand.
24. But with regard to *that* sense of 'exactly' and 'all', interpretation can neither fail nor succeed in capturing 'it' either. To capture 'it' is not a logically possible goal for an interpretation. It would not make sense to even try. I discuss this as being part of Cleanth Brooks's confusion in 'The Heresy of Paraphrase', where he tries to argue that there is a substantial something that a paraphrase cannot say which the poem says (see Löfgren 2015: ch. 6).
25. On the impossibility of proof on these matters, see Cavell's excellent discussion in 'Aesthetic Problems of Modern Philosophy', especially his discussion on what validates the wine tasters' judgements (Cavell 2002: 73–96).
26. Colin Davis has a rather different reading of this passage from mine. He sees it as indicative of Cavell espousing what Davis calls 'overreading'. My view is rather that Cavell is here acknowledging that the risk of overreading is one we cannot avoid, and that our fear of that risk should not deter us from brave and experimental readings. Nevertheless, Cavell concedes that reading-in is a real risk and that there is such a thing as going too far (see Davis 2010: 139–40).
27. In 'Music Discomposed', Cavell writes: 'you cannot tell from outside; and the expense in getting inside is a matter for each man to go over' (Cavell 2002: 209). In this quote Cavell is discussing how we expose fraudulence in modernist art, but the point holds equally well for how to expose over-interpretation in literary interpretation.

Bibliography

Carroll, Noël (2002), 'Andy Kaufman and the Philosophy of Interpretation', in Michael Krausz (ed.), *Is There a Single Right Interpretation?*, University Park: Pennsylvania State University Press, pp. 319–44.
Cavell, Stanley (1981), 'Introduction: Words for a Conversation', in Stanley Cavell, *Pursuits of Happiness: The Hollywood Comedy of Remarriage*, Cambridge, MA: Harvard University Press, pp. 1–42.

Cavell, Stanley (1984), 'The Politics of Interpretation', in Stanley Cavell, *Themes Out of School: Effects and Causes*, San Francisco: North Point Press, pp. 27–60.

Cavell, Stanley (1999), *The Claim of Reason: Wittgenstein, Skepticism, Morality, and Tragedy*, Oxford: Oxford University Press.

Cavell, Stanley (2002), *Must We Mean What We Say? A Book of Essays*, updated edn, Cambridge: Cambridge University Press.

Cavell, Stanley (2003), 'The Avoidance of Love: A Reading of King Lear', in Stanley Cavell, *Disowning Knowledge: In Seven Plays of Shakespeare*, updated edn, Cambridge: Cambridge University Press, pp. 39–123.

Conant, James (2000), 'Freedom, Cruelty, and Truth: Rorty versus Orwell', in Robert B. Brandom (ed.), *Rorty and His Critics*, Malden: Blackwell, pp. 268–343.

Dauber, Kenneth and Walter Jost (2003), 'Introduction: The Varieties of Ordinary Language Criticism', in Kenneth Dauber and Walter Jost (eds), *Ordinary Language Criticism: Literary Thinking after Cavell after Wittgenstein*, Evanston: Northwestern University Press, pp. xi–xxii.

Davis, Colin (2010), *Critical Excess: Overreading in Derrida, Deleuze, Levinas, Žižek, and Cavell*, Stanford: Stanford University Press.

Fish, Stanley (1980), *Is There a Text in This Class? The Authority of Interpretive Communities*, Cambridge, MA: Harvard University Press.

Hirsch, E. D. (1967), *Validity in Interpretation*, New Haven: Yale University Press.

Hynes, Samuel (1971), 'Introduction', in Samuel Hynes (ed.), *Twentieth Century Interpretations of 1984*, Englewood Cliffs: Prentice Hall, pp. 1–19.

Juhl, P. D. (1980), *Interpretation: An Essay in the Philosophy of Literary Criticism*, Princeton: Princeton University Press.

Löfgren, Ingeborg (2015), 'Interpretive Skepticism: Stanley Cavell, New Criticism, and Literary Interpretation', PhD thesis, Litteraturvetenskapliga inst. Uppsala Universitet.

Moi, Toril (2011), 'The Adventure of Reading: Literature and Philosophy, Cavell and Beauvoir', in Richard Eldridge and Bernard Rhie (eds), *Stanley Cavell and Literary Studies: Consequences of Skepticism*, New York: Continuum, pp. 17–29.

Moi, Toril (2017), *Revolution of the Ordinary: Literary Studies after Wittgenstein, Austin, and Cavell*, Chicago: University of Chicago Press.

Orwell, George [Eric Blair] (1968a), *The Collected Essays, Journalism, and Letters of George Orwell, Vol. III: As I Please, 1943–1955*, Sonia Orwell and Ian Angus (eds), London: Secker and Warburg.

Orwell, George [Eric Blair] (1968b), *The Collected Essays, Journalism, and Letters of George Orwell, Vol. IV: In Front of Your Nose, 1945–1950*, Sonia Orwell and Ian Angus (eds), London: Secker and Warburg.

Orwell, George [Eric Blair] (1990), *Nineteen Eighty-Four*, London: Penguin.

Rorty, Richard (1989), 'The Last Intellectual in Europe: Orwell on Cruelty', in Richard Rorty, *Contingency, Irony, and Solidarity*, Cambridge: Cambridge University Press, pp. 169–88.

Rorty, Richard (1992), 'The Pragmatist's Progress', in Umberto Eco, Richard Rorty, Jonathan Culler, Christine Brooke-Rose, and Stefan Collini (eds), *Interpretation and Overinterpretation*, Cambridge: Cambridge University Press, pp. 89–108.

Rorty, Richard (2000), 'Response to Conant', in Robert B. Brandom (ed.), *Rorty and His Critics*, Malden: Blackwell, pp. 342–50.

Rudrum, David (2013), *Stanley Cavell and the Claim of Literature*, Baltimore: Johns Hopkins University Press.

Stock, Kathleen (2017), *Only Imagine: Fiction, Interpretation and Imagination*, Oxford: Oxford University Press.

Trilling, Lionel (1971), 'Orwell on the Future', in Samuel Hynes (ed.), *Twentieth Century Interpretations of 1984*, Englewood Cliffs: Prentice Hall, pp. 24–8.

Wimsatt, W. K. and Monroe C. Beardsley (1982), 'The Intentional Fallacy', in W. K. Wimsatt, *The Verbal Icon: Studies in the Meaning of Poetry*, Lexington: University Press of Kentucky, pp. 3–18.

Wittgenstein, Ludwig (1964), *Preliminary Studies for the 'Philosophical Investigations' Generally Known as The Blue and Brown Books*, New York: Harper and Row.

Wittgenstein, Ludwig (2008), *Philosophical Investigations: The German Text, with a Revised English Translation*, G. E. M. Anscombe (trans.), 50th anniversary edn, Malden: Blackwell.

14

Stanley Cavell and the Politics of Modernism

R. M. Berry

I do not know whether to argue, or merely to treat as unavoidably obvious, that the problem for any philosophical account of literature is the present. My hesitancy is that, were I to argue it, those practising the version of philosophy or literature I would be arguing against would not disagree with me or, if they did, would not recognise themselves in the terms of my argument. When in *Philosophical Investigations* §128 Wittgenstein remarks, 'If someone were to advance *theses* in philosophy, it would never be possible to debate them, because everyone would agree to them' (Wittgenstein 2009: 56), I take him to be describing a refinement of this problem. It is the problem of recognising what one is presently doing, or perhaps the problem of recognising its social and political significance, when the context appears perfectly ordinary. If we characterise this problem as a lack of either critical or historical consciousness, then that should not mislead us into thinking it can be addressed by more – or by a more critical – consciousness. Recognising the context necessary to any action is itself an action and remains as subject to that context as any other. If one fails to recognise the significance of one's present context, or if one finds it too ordinary to dwell on, then what prevents one's own consciousness from becoming its product, if not the unconscious instrument of its social domination? It is hard to see how any philosophical account of literature could be called political in any but a pejorative sense without answering this question. And that is at least one way the present becomes a problem.

My aim in what follows will be to show how what has been characterised as the autonomy of modernist literature, or perhaps only as its ambition to attain an unattainable autonomy, far from a metaphysical displacement of politics, is itself modernism's politically significant work. I begin with contrasting two ways of looking at modernism's relation to its contemporary context, the first of which I take to be exemplified by Fredric Jameson's dialectical criticism and the second of which I understand to characterise Stanley Cavell's philosophical aesthetics. What I find helpful about Jameson's account is that, like the criticism of Lukács or Adorno, it spells out with unsurpassed coherence what is often operative but unelaborated in the work of other critics, especially those who share Jameson's conviction that modernist literature and its social, economic, technological, and political context are inseparable. Although my enthusiasm is for Cavell's modernism, I am only secondarily interested in exposing any shortcomings of Jameson's. On the contrary, one gain of the comparison is to bring out Cavell's and Jameson's compatibilities. However, my justification for contrasting them is to better highlight what Cavell calls presentness, the distinctive achievement of modernist literature and art, and this will mean explaining how writing with little or no explicitly political content does concretely political work. My literary exemplars, Samuel Beckett and Wallace Stevens, are both taken from the period Jameson has called 'late modernism', the time when, in *A Singular Modernity*, he claims the ostensibly non-political aesthetic ideology of modernism develops (Jameson 2002: 164–72). If my account is convincing, it will show that what Jameson and other commentators have interpreted as a solipsistic inflection of historical modernity is better understood, both in modernist philosophy and in modernist literature, as a problem, not of knowledge, but of time.

The Problem of Autonomy

At the start of his long essay on Samuel Beckett's *Endgame* (Cavell 2002: 115–62), Cavell contrasts his reading of the play with those of Martin Esslin and Lukács, both of whom, despite their opposite assessments, take Beckett's work to be continuous with its contemporary world. Cavell quickly dismisses Esslin, whose nihilistic enthusiasms sound as though he has forgotten what art is, but Cavell lingers on Lukács, repudiating his critique while carefully differentiating it from the socialism Lukács claims to represent. What complicates Cavell's response is that what he calls Lukács's 'classical demand' – 'that the artist achieve perspective which grants independence from the world within which [the artist] is centered' (Cavell 2002: 116) – is Cavell's, too. For Lukács, of course, this demand is met through Marx's theory of production, which provides a perspective on society distinct from society's own. Because modernists like Joyce, Kafka, and Beckett abandon this perspective, foregrounding the seemingly autonomous activity of consciousness and imagination, their work becomes for Lukács a social symptom, embodying the alienated subject's inverted image of itself. Although Cavell finds such an account blind, he agrees that, following the modernists' disenchantment with realism, the relation of what happens in a work to what happens in the world its audience inhabits becomes an issue. He describes the situation this way:

> [I]n modernist arts the achievement of the autonomy of the object is a *problem* – the artistic problem. Autonomy is no longer provided by the conventions of an art, for the modernist artist has continuously to question the conventions upon which his art has depended, nor is it furthered by any position the artist can adopt, towards anything but his art. (Cavell 2002: 116)

Exactly why no political position can provide the critical perspective that a position towards art can, or just how, if questioning social conventions will not secure an artist's independence, questioning aesthetic conventions is supposed to – these are things Cavell does not explain, or not unless his whole philosophy is an explanation. However, one point seems clear: if Cavell considers Lukács blind, that is not because he thinks Lukács's description of the critical function of realism is inaccurate or because he simply disagrees with Marx's account of alienation. When he accuses Lukács of taking *Endgame* 'much as any corrupted audience takes it', Cavell is not saying Lukács is mistaken. He is saying that Lukács's description of the problem of autonomy is not a description. It is the problem itself.

The most sophisticated recent practitioner of Lukács's mode of criticism is Fredric Jameson, whose abstract, intricately mediated version of Marxism offers a more capacious assessment of modernist art and literature than his forerunner's. Like Cavell, Jameson takes the word 'autonomy' to name the problem modernism confronts – in aesthetics, philosophy, psychology, and economic relations (Jameson 2002: 161, 120–4, 154–5, 91) – but for Jameson the problem is that things have become autonomous, or appear so, while for Cavell the problem is more nearly that things have been deprived of autonomy, or appear so. However, for both, the critic's task is to determine how modernist art and literature, in confronting this or any problem, relate to their world. In a departure from classic reflection theory, Jameson develops a dialectical model of base and superstructure in which Lukács's social totality is reconceived as a dynamic reciprocal interaction (Jameson 1991: 302). Despite the dependence of all interpretation on historical framing, the relation of modernist works to the history of modernity is for Jameson never direct. Although this deferral of totalisation mitigates the worst of Lukács's dogmatism, it exacerbates the problem of autonomy, since modernism represents in Jameson's history the period when the interactivity of work and world grows increasingly attenuated. Whereas in a 'high or classic' modernist like Joyce the autonomy of consciousness and imagination still presupposes an absolute or utopian dimension (Jameson 2002: 168), thus projecting a realisable future, in a 'late modernist' like Beckett or Stevens aesthetic autonomy becomes total, 'involv[ing] a constant and self-conscious return to art about art' (Jameson 2002: 198). Although Jameson differentiates this late modernist 'ideology' of aesthetic autonomy from the historical experience of 'autonomisation' – that is, of our increasing independence from our creation – his narrative recounts how during modernism the reciprocal interaction of representation and reality, self and other, word and meaning, devolves into countless independent entities (Jameson 2016: 141–2). And the conclusion of Jameson's story is much as Lukács imagined: art's critical perspective vanishes. As Jameson says of *Waiting for Godot*,

> We will have understood something fundamental about late modernism by grasping everything that came to seem unacceptable to Beckett himself in the allegorical schema that staged the British Empire (Pozzo) in its relationship to its colonies in general and Ireland in particular (Lucky). (Jameson 2002: 201)

When Cavell says that, for modernism, autonomy is 'the artistic problem', he does not mean that the modernists' disenchantment with realism is the problem. Although Cavell shares Jameson's and Lukács's sense that with historical modernity a kind of alienation occurs – a process in which subjects disengage from their social and material surroundings – he does not think that the absence of explicitly political content in works by Beckett, Stevens, Anthony Caro, Jackson Pollock, or Arnold Schoenberg is any failure to respond to it. On the contrary, the achievement of autonomy is, in Cavell's account, the concrete form of modernism's response. A particularly clear example occurs late in Cavell's *Endgame* essay where, having described the dramatic predicament as a curse on all creation, he announces that the predicament can be resolved, the curse ended, by removing the audience from the theatre (Cavell 2002: 156–7). What transforms this social alienation into social perspective is *Endgame*'s recognition that creation will not end, or not in the way resolution requires, merely by removing the human beings present. Instead, it is the *concept* of an audience that must be removed, which Beckett accomplishes, according to Cavell, by 'our feeling that no one in the place, on the stage or in the house, knows better than anyone else what is happening, no one has a better right to speak than anyone else' (Cavell 2002: 158). Cavell's idea is that the invisible wall which in traditional theatre separates observers from participants can, like every other human construction, be dismantled, and when its undoing is more than just a representation, that is, when it is embodied in the actors' movements and continuous with the sound of Beckett's words and manifested in the material surroundings of the theatre itself, then the relation of what happens in the work to what happens in the world undergoes a change. Although describing it is as difficult as changing, a result is that *Endgame*'s vestiges of political reference – the action's setting in an apparent bomb shelter amid what sounds from Clov's descriptions like the aftermath of a nuclear holocaust – figure only secondarily. With the audience's removal, differences in historical perspective, in what some may know about the Cold War that others do not, cease to count. Instead, the change, if what happens on stage occurs to anyone, happens before you know it.

What makes Lukács's account of modernism look to Cavell like the problem it means to describe is its dependence on a stark difference in historical perspective, on what the critic knows that the modernist – as far as her historical consciousness is represented by her work – does not. In Jameson's account, the starkness of this difference is mitigated by the reciprocal interaction of the modernist's quest for autonomy and the progress of autonomisation, but in neither Lukács's nor Jameson's history is modernism's so-called 'inward turn', its 'introspective probing of the deeper impulses of consciousness' (Jameson 1991: 312), what modernist writers and artists intend it to be – that is, a realistic response to their situation. On the contrary, it seems unclear whether there would be any history for Lukács or Jameson to narrate if aesthetic autonomy, at least as they describe it, were realisable. In Cavell's account, by contrast, aesthetic autonomy is a *practical* problem, where that means that, in the absence of any framing narrative, the work's relation to its world must be discovered in its working. In truth, the autonomy of modernist literature and art just is this discovery. One source for Cavell's account is Wittgenstein's *Philosophical Investigations*, where our relation to the world is continually threatened, not by our failure to know it, but by our determination to know it better than we do. In a passage recalling issues raised by modernist painting, Wittgenstein wonders how we are able to see a given picture as a man walking up a steep path leaning on a stick: 'Might it not have looked just the same if he had been sliding downhill in that position?', he asks, adding, 'Perhaps a Martian would describe the picture so' (Wittgenstein 2009: 60). One point of this passage seems obvious: namely, that even the most automatic response occurs within a behavioural context or, in Wittgenstein's idiom, a '*Lebensform*' or 'form of life'. When Jameson says of modernism's 'inward turn' that 'those feelings, expressed in connection with the self, could only come into being in correlation with a similar feeling about society and the object world' (Jameson 1991: 312), he is making a related point. Change the context, and our experience of the world changes, too. But a second point seems more controversial. Is Wittgenstein saying that we just *do* see the picture as a man walking uphill, that, in our context, we could not also experience it as a man sliding downhill? Does not our ability to make sense of Wittgenstein's question presuppose our seeing it from more than one perspective? And if that is true, then is he implying that we relate to our world like aliens?

Alienation, autonomy, separateness, all comprise a practical aesthetic problem because of what in *The Claim of Reason* Cavell calls 'the truth of skepticism' (Cavell 1999: 45): not that we can never know our contemporary social and material world, or even that we can know it only from our own perspective, but rather that our relation to the world is not based on knowing. What it is based on, according to Wittgenstein according to Cavell, is '*Übereinstimmung*', which Anscombe translates as 'agreement' but Cavell, preserving the musical overtones of Wittgenstein's German, translates as 'attunement'. The idea is that if we are to inhabit a social and material world, then it is not necessary for our opinions about that world to agree, but it is necessary for us to be attuned to, to agree in, the way they are expressed. Moreover, if we are to represent that world in art, then it is necessary that our different ways of inhabiting it be sufficiently in tune that artists and audiences can recognise that represented world as ours. Finally, if we are to account critically for our world's representation, then it is necessary, not that our accounts harmonise, but that what counts as criticising, giving accounts, and representing be in fundamental accord. When in *Philosophical Investigations* §241 (Wittgenstein 2009: 94) Wittgenstein describes fundamental agreement as agreement in form of life, he means that what is necessary is '*Übereinstimmung*', not so much in what we say and do as in how we say and do it. However, what is *not* necessary, according to Wittgenstein according to Cavell, is attunement itself. In truth, nothing occurs more automatically in *Philosophical Investigations* than our disengaging from, relating like aliens to, or treating as independent of us any representation of our world. To experience this alienation for ourselves, we need only see what Wittgenstein's example of the Martian makes obvious: that between a picture of a man walking uphill and a picture of his sliding downhill in the same position, no material difference exists. If, despite the two pictures' indistinguishability, all of our contemporaries see only one, then how are we to represent what we see? Certainly not by trying to paint the second picture. It is as though art's meaning and its materiality had divided, making the significance formerly immanent in colour and figure seem artificially imposed. When Cavell calls autonomy 'the artistic problem', he may mean what Jameson means, that the autonomisation characteristic of modern production has so overtaken our world that even artistic creation now seems alienating, or he may mean that, to achieve perspective on our world, art must create a new form of life. But either way, our attunement has become an issue.

There is an oppressiveness to the modern world, at least as we know it, a curse or fate or historical necessity from which, in Cavell's account, modernist literature and art struggle for their independence, and even if not reducible to a particular form of social or economic organisation, it remains inseparable from any politics worthy of the name. What makes our world's annihilation in *Endgame* exactly as oppressive as the world itself is not that all human beings have been eliminated. It is that this annihilation was not literal annihilation. A preposterous few have been spared, making the plot's only action – that of Hamm's telling his story – humankind's last justification for being there. Cavell's idea is that for Hamm to ignore this task, to refuse to account for inequitable suffering and death, would be to deny his humanity, but that does not mean Hamm or any human is equal to it (Cavell 2002: 143–5). This dividedness, this human alienation from the experience of humankind, is the curse, and every perspective on it just curses creation all over. When Jameson claims that an 'empirical examination' of any modernist work will reveal a 'realist core', a 'starting point' in 'some commonsense experience of a recognisably real world', and so concludes that 'the work of art and the realm of art itself can never become truly autonomous' (Jameson 2002: 120), we can experience this same dividedness in ourselves. We will hardly disagree that, when we 'empirically examine' one of Hamm's sentences – e.g., 'Moments for nothing, now as always, time was never and time is over, reckoning closed and story ended' (Beckett 1958: 83) – a number of candidates for its 'realist core' come to mind: e.g., disillusionment, missed opportunities, fruitless labour, boredom. But such a 'core' makes Beckett's words peripheral, since it can be known without them, so we may also feel reluctant to agree. If we ask from what oppressiveness, if only they could 'become truly autonomous', Beckett's words would struggle for independence, it would not be from 'some commonsense experience of a recognisably real world', without which they would not be words. A more obvious candidate would be Jameson's story of autonomisation, in which their meaning and materiality divide. If the political work of *Endgame* must occur before all stories, before what happens on stage and what happens in our world can need relating, how is such fundamental attunement found?

Democracy and Narrative

As Andrew Norris has remarked, Stanley Cavell is not usually considered a political philosopher, if only because 'he expresses almost no interest in political institutions such as the state or in the violence to which it claims a monopoly' (Norris 2006: 15). However, as Norris and other commentators have observed, to experience the political dimension of Cavell's writing, one need only notice its most controversial feature, its use of the first-person plural pronouns 'we' and 'us'. When Cavell says of *Endgame*, 'Words, we feel as we hear them, *can* mean in these combinations, and we want them to, they speak something in us' (Cavell 2002: 130), we do not just feel addressed, respectfully included, or acknowledged; we feel implicated, and unless we stop reading, we will want to know in what, for what, how far. What can make Cavell's writing feel oppressive is not just that – like his literary models, Wittgenstein and J. L. Austin – he often speaks in an ostensibly universal voice, or even that this form of assumed agreement can seem presumptuous, but that Cavell's saying what we say, mean, feel, and want raises the stakes on *dis*agreement. If I disagree with Jameson's statement that 'consciousness and subjectivity are unrepresentable' (Jameson 2002: 57), then I disagree about his words' relation to a world we both inhabit, and experience, documents, quotations, and examples can support our respective positions, but if I disagree with Cavell's statement, then it no longer goes without saying how far we both inhabit a world, and what disagrees is not just his statement with mine, but what counts for us as making statements, that is, what counts as a combination of words about whose relation to the world we can meaningfully disagree. Experiences, documents, quotations, and examples can still support our positions, but only so far as they clarify or make concretely imaginable points of disagreement that, to be more than just alienation, must find their support in how Cavell and I live. In other words, what I disagree with Cavell about is not only to whom the pronoun 'we' refers, but how that collectivity is represented, where its representation is less an issue of accurate description than one of embodiment (Gibson 2007: 76–7), that is, of which of my or Cavell's words, intentions, feelings, desires, thoughts, and actions are instances of it. No statement I can make about my group's behaviour will, of itself, make Cavell's and my differences real. To achieve my independence, I must do as Cavell does to achieve his: I must find out in practice, experimentally, how far the social and material world I inhabit depends on my attunement with people like Hamm, Beckett, Cavell.

If it is correct to say that 'the modern world' refers to the historical period in which our world's creation becomes autonomised, happening – either in appearance or in fact – increasingly without our participation, then in Cavell's reading of *King Lear*, what is at issue in the abdication scene is the modern world (Cavell 2002: 285–94). The scene's traditional aporia – how Lear could fail to know what is obvious to everyone in the audience, that his daughter Cordelia loves him, that her sisters Regan and Goneril are merely playacting – is not the modern issue. On the contrary, as Cavell demonstrates, that aporia has a solution: Lear knows everything everybody else knows. He banishes Cordelia, while rewarding her sisters, because he wants a theatrical performance, wants a public representation of love, not the thing itself, and is willing, or thinks he is, to pay for it. The modern issue, which will occupy Cavell for the remainder of his career, is how audiences from the Renaissance to the present could have imagined they knew what Lear did not, since, if Cavell is right, Lear's intentions were as obvious as his daughters'. Although not resolving this second issue, the 'truth of skepticism' makes it practical, reinterpreting modern epistemology, not as a problem of knowledge conditions, but as a problem of time. The crucial passage (Cavell 2002: 320–2) occurs when, in comparing Shakespearean drama with tonal music, Cavell describes our following what happens in *King Lear* as our experiencing its plot's direction in what happens only *now*. The relevant contrast is with ordinary experience – that is, with our experience of ordinariness – in which, for example, 'a remark which begins a certain way can normally have only one of a definite set of endings' (Cavell 2002: 321). Cavell's idea is that, in *Lear*, this automatic character of everyday speech and action, its definite range of implication, is at issue, so that the direction taken by each character's life – not just why anything said or done ends as it does, but where and how it even begins – is being decided in *this* scene. It is as though the world we inhabit were, if not created and annihilated, then shaped and tested, in every word. Knowing in such a context means discovering, not narrating. Everything necessary to knowing Lear's intentions – that is, to knowing how a performance in exchange for wealth and power becomes preferable to feelings impossible to predict or control – is embodied on stage. All that makes knowing a problem is living as though we already know.

When Cavell says that 'nothing is deeper than the fact, or the extent, of agreement itself' (Cavell 1999: 32), he is saying that the democratic basis of our participation in modern society is comprised, not of laws or rules or norms or beliefs, but of forms of agreement of which every participant is an equally authorised representative (Laugier 2006: 30–5). That such fundamental attunement is manifest in the lives of all does not mean that, regardless of context, I will know how to act like one of us. On the contrary, how far I am able to speak and act in tune with others must be determined experimentally, in practice, by trying out the behaviour that seems to me to accord with my group and then seeing what happens. No one's attunement will be perfect, and no society, not even the most oppressive, will or could discount every variation, but it is precisely the discord between my sense of our attunement and others' sense of it that enables me to discover both who my group is and who I am, where that is an issue of how far I can locate my meaning in others and theirs in me. And, of course, there will be times when I want to disagree, want to make an issue of my independence, embodying in opposition to my society the forms of life apart from which I consider 'us' meaningless. But the point is that, assuming 'us' refers to those with whom I share a world, disagreements over how deeply we are attuned are not just ordinary political disagreements. When in *Philosophical Investigations* §246 Wittgenstein declares it nonsense to say only *I* can know whether I am in pain, he is not making a technical point about language (Wittgenstein 2009: 95–6). He is addressing a confusion that, in the modern world, occurs almost automatically. The confusion involves our feeling autonomous, free to think and act as we choose, precisely where our lives are most deeply bound together, and feeling limited, constrained in what we can desire and express, precisely where each of us is choosing to live as we do. Wittgenstein's clarification – that others cannot be differentiated from me by their not knowing my pain, since I do not *know* my pain either; I *have* it – means to be jarring. It is as though we had forgotten how differently it feels to know what is happening and to undergo it. To acknowledge this difference, to feel jarred by it, is to discover my alienation from my kind.

As long as we live as though the difference in what is happening to others and what is happening to us is a difference in what each of us knows, in our historical perspective, we cannot hope to discover history's direction in what is happening now. No one knows better than anyone else how deeply human beings are attuned. No perspective is superior. If I still feel, even after reading Wittgenstein, that sufferers know what is happening as no one else possibly could or, conversely, that no one in the throes of pain could possibly know what is happening to him or her as well as a journalist, historian, social scientist, or physician, then my discord with Wittgenstein is over what is happening, not just over my relation to it. Perhaps Wittgenstein convinces me that I have become confused, that, in reality, my knowing hunger, despair, or torture depends neither on its happening to me nor on my having more information about its historical context and social or material causes than any sufferer. Still, if I am to know what is happening, I must do more than just be convinced. I must also respond, live, act like someone who knows what hunger, despair, or torture is, and that means acknowledging what, in the modern world, is most confusing: that even when what happens to others is not happening to me, it happens for everybody in the same time. Knowing becomes a problem in *Lear*, not just because we must recognise Lear's preference for commodity relations over personal relations, but because so much of what happens in a theatre accords with it. Finding it obvious that, even after a lifetime at court, Lear does not know flattery as well as we do means locating the cause of Lear's tragedy in his apparent misrecognition at the beginning. However, nothing in the abdication scene – not Lear's banishing of Cordelia, dividing up of his kingdom, or divesting himself of wealth and power – makes the play's ending inevitable (Cavell 2002: 322). For Lear to get all he paid for, his daughters need only to continue behaving as in the past, accommodating their father's vanity and weakness, and so avoiding the social awkwardness of having to acknowledge either, and if this domestic hypocrisy turns monstrous, nothing in the play suggests that it is because Regan and Goneril are predisposed to cruelty. On the contrary, it is merely that Lear persists in their family's old deceit, scene after scene, even when his daughters have stopped. From his abdication to his death, all Lear wants is to know life without having to discover it for himself – experimentally – and if we cannot tell what is happening, that is not because we are less adept at reading his mind than his daughters. It is because our whole reason for attending theatre is that we want to know life without risk, too.

Interpreters of Cavell's philosophy generally agree about what represents its most unsettling conclusion: that if I ask why I should behave towards what others count as hunger, despair, or torture as though I *know* it is hunger, despair, or torture, then no answer of the form my question anticipates will satisfy me. However, there is less agreement on how Cavell answers the question that seems to follow: why, then, is its counting as hunger, despair, or torture neither a matter of my personal choice nor a result of my society's dictation? When Cavell takes the theme and moral of *Philosophical Investigations* to be the subject's correct relation to society (Cavell 1999: 329), he is recognising a problem about my relation to the world that, although manifest in how I represent the world, is not solved by representing it differently. In Wittgenstein's philosophy, the subject's relation to society is not the relation of a part to a whole, an event to a structure, or an elaboration to a system. It is the relation of a present to a past, and that means that my questioning what hunger, despair, and torture really are yields no satisfying answer, not because the answer would be nonsense, but because my question is not a question. It is an experiment, a test. That is, I am trying to discover, to find out in practice, how deeply I am implicated in what has amounted to suffering for my society so far. In *Philosophical Investigations* §185 (Wittgenstein 2009: 80–1), Wittgenstein narrates the puzzling case of a pupil who, having learned to write down series of numbers in the form 0, n, $2n$, $3n$, etc., responds exactly as we would do when told n equals 2, writing down 0, 2, 4, 6, 8, etc. However, on reaching 1,000, he writes 1,004, 1,008, 1,012, etc. The significance of the case appears when Wittgenstein imagines our trying to explain the pupil's mistake to him. When we say that he should have continued adding 2 as before, the pupil replies, 'But I did go on in the same way!' Apparently, our disagreement with this pupil is not just over how he applies the formula, $n = 2$, after 1,000. If his reply is truthful, he has *always* been applying it differently, has *from the beginning* seen or thought he saw implications in how we count that we do not see. And the possibility of his and our becoming attuned, that is, of our ever learning to count in the same way, depends on one or both of us discovering something previously missed, something basic to our systems of numbers unacknowledged till now.

The political aim of Cavell's signature practice, of his saying what we say, mean, feel, want, think, and do, is to address a problem of the kind Marx addresses when declaring, 'Life is not determined by consciousness, but consciousness by life' (Marx 2010: 656). It is a problem that arises when how problems are addressed comes to operate independently of the form of life in which those problems arise. Although Cavell's elaboration of this problem resembles Adorno's critique of dehumanised rationality more than Marx's economic history, the function of Cavell's 'we' is to make its solution practical. In his philosophy, society changes for the same reason that what I say, mean, feel, want, think, and do changes: because if a real question arises about what it now means to be us, accounting for what it meant in the past will constitute no satisfying answer. Counting what is presently happening as hunger, despair, or torture is not choosing how to count it, because discovering my implication in suffering is not selecting among options. It is acknowledging that, in the present of what my society calls 'enhanced interrogation', virtually everything I say, mean, feel, want, think, and do embodies the knowledge that it is torture. And it is meaningless to say that this embodied knowledge has been dictated to me by my society, since, given the depth of discord that 'enhanced interrogation' manifests, it is no longer clear what, if anything, the phrase 'my society' means. Either words and actions like mine really are representative of who we are, in which case my society is not who it thinks it is, has become deeply confused, and needs a jarring reminder, or my society has never been who I thought it was, in which case I have always been participating in a form of social practice, of life, I am just now discovering. But either way, our disagreement is not over how to represent suffering correctly – or not if by 'represent' we mean describe, measure, depict, etc. There is no verifiable information, no fact about water-boarding that, if only included in our accounts, would enable us all to count in the same way. In the present of such a practice, what divides us is basic, fundamental, deep. Trying to narrate it, to recount how suffering is misrecognised, would be as pointless as trying to tell Lear that Cordelia is the one who really loves him. How far we still share a world no longer goes without saying.

When taking up in 1965 the question of whether compositions by Schoenberg or Webern are really atonal, and, if so, whether they still count as music, Cavell describes watching an accomplished musician discuss and perform these works, recording his impression that, despite similarities to Beethoven's music, they constitute 'a new world'. He concludes:

> Moreover, but still perhaps even more rarely, we may find ourselves *within* the experience of such compositions, following them; and then the question whether this is music and the problem of its tonal sense, will be – not answered or solved, but rather they will disappear, seem irrelevant. (Cavell 2002: 84).

Two points want stressing. First, the question Cavell initially takes up, the question whether atonal compositions count as music, had something unsatisfying about it. Apparently, what Cavell wants to know, what he believes anyone listening to atonal music is trying to discover, is something that, once known, makes that question seem merely academic. Cavell never answers it. And, second, how he discovers what he wants to know is by participating. That is, he concentrates on the musician's behaviour, tries out for himself her ways of speaking and acting, experiments, until he can follow what happens in the composition. Cavell never implies that what one discovers in this way is less amenable to articulate expression than our widely institutionalised knowledge of tonal music. In fact, on the final page of *Must We Mean What We Say?* he makes explicit what one discovers: namely, 'what it is about sounds in succession that *at any time* has allowed them to be heard as presentness' (2002: 353). The idea is that atonal compositions disclose a new world, but not new in the way that, for earthlings, Mars would be new; rather, new in the way that, for someone after a victorious struggle with despair or disease or injustice, earth is new. In other words, atonal compositions acknowledge something real, there to be heard any time music is heard, and that, had Beethoven not already been attuned to it, he could not have composed tonally. Nothing makes this knowledge harder to acquire than knowledge of music at any time, or nothing except what makes self-knowledge hard to acquire. I would describe the difficulty this way: were the man I am to meet the man I was, nothing I know now could make me see what was happening then, what, whenever I look back on it, seemed to mean nothing at the time – unless both versions of me, past and present, were to change. And that can only happen in the present.

Presentness

When Cavell says that the autonomy of the modernist work 'is no longer ... furthered by any position the artist can adopt, towards anything but his art' (2002: 116), he is not espousing the concept of autonomy Jameson criticises, that is, a concept in which art's relation to itself displaces its relation to the world. Cavell's point is that the aesthetic practices in which Western artists and their audiences have traditionally agreed, those conventions we call representational, no longer provide what our fundamental agreement, our '*Übereinstimmung*', provides: namely, freedom from any need for mediation. Jameson describes the situation perfectly:

> For better or for worse, art does not seem in our society to offer any direct access to reality, any possibility of unmediated representation or of what used to be called realism. For us today, it is generally the case that what looks like realism turns out at best to offer unmediated access only to what we think about reality, to our images and ideological stereotypes about it. (Jameson 1991: 150).

Like Lukács, Jameson takes this situation to mean that, from late modernism to the present, art becomes politically significant primarily as a social symptom (Jameson 1991: 151), while Cavell takes it to mean that continuing to treat modernist works as Lukács does, as representations, is likely itself to become a social symptom. But for Cavell, modernist art becomes politically significant, not by representing forms of mediation, but by happening for everybody, if at all, only in the same time. In *Endgame* something is happening. As Cavell notes, Hamm first asks about it in the present continuous tense, 'What's happening, what's happening?' (Beckett 1958: 13), then, near the end, switches to the past, 'What's happened? . . . What has happened?' (1958: 75). That the time difference is material, that, despite the return of the play's opening tableau (1958: 84), something really has changed, is evidenced by the appearance of the 'small boy' (1958: 78), but our difficulty answering Hamm's questions, our difficulty knowing what this change means or even telling much difference, is not just that the boy's identity is being withheld. It is that nothing follows inevitably from anything else, nothing happens by the end that, if known from the beginning, would alter the script. If an invisible wall still divides us, no difference of perspective maintains it. Cavell describes the divide this way: 'That what is now happening to them is not now happening to us is our only difference from them – the deepest, the only unbreachable difference there is between two people: that they are two' (Cavell 2002: 159). Or in a phrase, our differences are history.

In Cavell's modernism, the work of art and literature consists of discovering fundamental agreement. When Cavell speaks of aesthetic autonomy, this discovery is what he has in mind. It connects the work to our world. The specific form it takes in *Endgame* is what Cavell calls 'hidden literality' (2002: 119). Some examples are Clov's remark, while handling an alarm clock near the end, that he is 'winding up' (Beckett 1958: 72) or Hamm's line, 'Forgive me', which sounds like an apology but literalises into an imperative, 'I said, forgive me!' (1958: 7). Cavell describes our experience of such lines: '[Beckett's] words strew obscurities across our path and seem wilfully to thwart comprehension; and then time after time we discover that their meaning has been missed only because it was so utterly bare – totally, therefore unnoticeably, in view' (Cavell 2002: 119). Although peculiarly significant in Beckett's mature writing, hidden literality effects a change in our relation to the aesthetic medium that is characteristic of modernist achievement generally. When Hamm asks, 'Do you believe in the life to come?', Clov's reply – 'Mine was always that' (Beckett 1958: 49) – discloses in Hamm's words something to be heard at any time but that went unacknowledged when voiced. It is as though our agreement in language, our attunement in how we express ourselves, were alienated in Hamm's question about how reality should be represented and discovered only afterwards, when Clov's literalisation jars us. But Cavell's conclusion (2002: 119) that 'it is *we* who had been willfully uncomprehending, misleading ourselves in demanding further, or other, meaning, where the meaning was nearest' attributes this alienation, not to modernity and the progress of autonomisation – or not immediately – but to our determination to overcome it. We miss what happens when Hamm speaks because we demand more from Beckett's words than meaningless materiality. That we thus contribute to their meaninglessness does not mean autonomisation has become inescapable. We are creating this confusion, after all. But it does mean that the world we share, if dependent for its reality on how we represent it, is annihilated already. Discovering fundamental agreement is not agreeing on what Beckett's words mean. It is acknowledging what, when known, is known too late.

That what happens in modernist literature and art happens before we know it is the preoccupation of Cavell's essay on Wallace Stevens, the late modernist about whom he and Jameson have both written at length. In their accounts, the problem of Stevens's poetry is its autonomy, its freedom from the authority or dictation of anything external, and in both, its claim to make the world happen, as though the meaning of history and poetry were simultaneous, is its political stake. However, in Jameson's version, the autonomy of Stevens's poetry displaces the world, becoming, not merely a symptom of autonomisation, but its aesthetic ideology (Jameson 2016: 220). In Stevens's early volume, *Harmonium* (1923), the object of experience is repeatedly represented alongside the process of experiencing it, making their relation poetry's work. Jameson calls this situation 'the quintessential Kantian moment in which, as contemporary middle-class subjectivity is forced back inside its own head, the idea of the thing peels off the "thing itself," now forever out of reach' (Jameson 2016: 218). Within such a philosophical context, 'Thirteen Ways of Looking at a Blackbird' (Stevens 1982: 92–5) becomes an allegory of the object's retreat:

> When the blackbird flew out of sight,
> It marked the edge
> Of one of many circles.

Here the modern subject appears as a circle, or perhaps as its absent centre, within the circumference of which the object, dark in itself, remains visible as far as the edge. However, beyond this perimeter, what Jameson calls 'the dynamics of autonomisation' continue (Jameson 2016: 218). As he explains, 'the autonomisation of image from thing, idea from image, name from idea' (2016: 220) is a historical experience, not a linguistic theory, but once language is experienced as itself an object, it submits to this same autonomising, dissolving into separate styles, connotations, idioms, tropes, grammars, accents. Stevens provides no perspective on this historical process, according to Jameson, because its separation is what he wants. Poetry can redeem meaningless materiality, can 'take the place / Of empty heaven and its hymns' (Stevens 1982: 167), only because words have separated from the world, functioning independently. The result is, in Jameson's description, 'an astonishing linguistic richness on the one hand and an impoverishment or hollowness of content on the other' (Jameson 2016: 208). Despite its verbal ingenuity, Stevens's poetry can in the end 'designate nothing but itself' Jameson 2016: 221).

For Cavell, by contrast, the problem of autonomy in Stevens's writing has less to do with its independence from reality than with its independence from philosophy, particularly from the philosophical distinction between form or medium and content; but his principal difference with Jameson is that, for Cavell, the problem of autonomy already exists in the description of the problem, making still more fundamental the problem of how to write about it. To bring this writing problem out, Cavell quotes from Stevens's posthumously published essay, 'A Collect of Philosophy':

> According to the traditional views of sensory perception we do not see the world immediately but only as the result of a process of seeing and after the completion of that process, that is to say, we never see the world except the moment after. (Cavell 2006: 70).

Cavell acknowledges that, to American philosophers contemporary with Stevens, this description would have sounded very confused, contrasting either seeing with itself or after with nothing before. But, Cavell asks, what if, instead of failing to write in a form professional philosophers considered meaningful, Stevens were addressing a problem professional philosophy failed to consider, one for which writing in the form of poetry would be advantageous? In 'Thirteen Ways of Looking at a Blackbird', Cavell locates such a problem in the fifth stanza:

> I do not know which to prefer,
> The beauty of inflections
> Or the beauty of innuendoes,
> The blackbird whistling
> Or just after.

Here, the issue of experiential immediacy does not involve an intervening subjectivity but, as in Stevens's prose version, an intervening delay. A sound, the bird's whistling, is contrasted with what, if anything, is made of it later, and if the poem shows no decided preference for either, or no more than Kant shows for the noumenon, it at least recognises a sense in which sounds and their significance, inflections and their innuendoes – or just matter and meaning – can be experientially distinct. Day in, day out, we hear sounds of which we make nothing. Any bird call we recall seems the rarest exception. Instead of the philosopher's problem, the problem of confusing reality with what Jameson calls our 'ideological stereotypes' (Jameson 1991: 150), Stevens's problem is that the world can call to or on us perpetually, finding us away.

This problem of our failure to be present when the world calls is what modernist literature, in struggling for its autonomy, struggles to overcome. In 'Thirteen Ways of Looking at a Blackbird', the struggle is to be on time for a social event, a marriage, one uniting creatures in immediate relation.

> A man and a woman
> Are one.
> A man and a woman and a blackbird
> Are one.

Nothing seems more obvious than that this stanza (stanza IV) describes nothing, that it is not, or not in any normal sense, the representation of a state of affairs, either imaginary or real. On the contrary, its writer knows himself divided, of three minds in stanza II – or confesses himself so in the recent past – each mind as capable of flying off in its own direction, of surpassing the limits of what he can see, as any blackbird. If there is a sense in which, either speaking or writing stanza IV, he is now in his right mind, no longer beside himself, it can only be that he means, not to be describing a union, but to be performing one. In other words, the blackbird, man, and woman are, prior to the poet's words, living estranged, their affections in some sense alienated, and if not utterly divorced from what is happening, then separated. The work of the poem would then be to make their marriage more than a mere 'linguistic richness' impoverished of content, to find words that would join them, would authorise the work. Cavell describes it as 'finding how to appear to reality early', arriving before objects 'are given to us or dictated to us; or before, we might say, the division hardens between objects and subjects' (Cavell 2006: 71). Such a time is 'earlier than philosophers now imagine to be possible' (Cavell 2006: 71), which is to say, in Jameson's narrative, before 'the quintessential Kantian moment' (Jameson 2016: 218). The idea is that, once our language has divided into a 'realist core' (Jameson 2002: 120) and a periphery of styles, tropes, connotations, idioms, accents, grammar, etc., whatever we say about the union of man, woman, and blackbird, rather than joining us fundamentally, will sound like an 'ideological stereotype' (Jameson 1991: 150).

The undivided language the poet seeks must be one in which human beings are in fundamental agreement, are already attuned, but not such that, whenever that attunement is represented, questions of what 'we' means – especially in reference to a man, a woman, and a bird – never occur to anyone. Quite the opposite: such questions will seem to follow inescapably from an attunement so fundamental, as though our modernity automatically made an issue of it. In stanza VIII, the poet attempts to write both in and about this pre-philosophical language:

> I know noble accents
> And lucid, inescapable rhythms;
> But I know, too,
> That the blackbird is involved
> In what I know.

It is hard to avoid hearing this stanza as a rejoinder, that is, as an emphatic no, no, no, no to some sceptical denigration of the poet's work. It is as if one of his three minds had said poetry involved the externals of knowledge only, were separate from its 'realist core'. The implication is that what feels 'inescapable' in a poem is not its meaning but merely its cadence, a matter of inflections, rhythms, accent patterns, etc. The poet's 'must' in stanza XII would then be fanciful:

> The river is moving.
> The blackbird must be flying.

Unless carried away with these words, we know that between the flight of a blackbird and what a man or woman finds moving, whether a river or an eye, there can be no implication. In reality, the world is known an object at a time, as separable from how we feel about it as any meaning from its corresponding sound. The poet's rejoinder to this philosophical turn of mind consists of no evidence, or not unless confessing to prior involvement with the blackbird counts as evidence. On the contrary, if a man and a woman and a blackbird are one, then the conjunction between them must be there already, in the words announcing it, so to speak, waiting to be discovered, acknowledged. That the three explicit self-references in the poem, stanzas II, V, and VIII, all involve a separation between what the poet knows and what happens, either in the poem or in writing it, suggests that this discovery, although identical with the poem itself, still awaits.

If Stevens's poem succeeds in marrying us to the world, then that is not because, after reading it, we know more than before about what it means for a man, a woman, and a blackbird to be one. It is because this marriage happens for everybody, if at all, only in the same time. Here is stanza XIII:

> It was evening all afternoon.
> It was snowing
> And it was going to snow.
> The blackbird sat
> In the cedar-limbs.

The final sentence sounds disarmingly prosaic, a verb and two unmodified nouns – assuming 'black' and 'cedar' do not count as modifiers – just the kind of assertion that, except in literature, might be verifiable. Nothing about its context or form suggests that it is meant other than literally. On the contrary, the earlier contrast (stanza VII) between imaginary and seen birds, where, unlike in stanza IV, a decided preference is shown for the latter, suggests that this thirteenth blackbird fulfils its poetic function by having none, by being neither less nor more than what we see in reading. I will not try to explicate such seeing here, except to insist, against a philosophical turn of mind, that it cannot be limited to anything less meaningful than words, say, to mere marks on a page or noises. Instead, what we must see, if we are to read stanza XIII at all, is a contrast in temporality. Identifying the time of the stanza's first two sentences is not easy, but suffice it to say that there is no period in which the afternoon and snowfall they describe could *have* happened. In both, the future permeates the present, eliminating the now in which anyone – even you or I – might have been there. I do not mean to imply that such a tense is impossible. In truth, I think it is the time in which we mostly live. I only want to claim that what the stanza's third and poem's final sentence describes never occurred in it. That I have seen photographs of blackbirds just means I can see what I was not present to see, and that I have seen paintings of blackbirds just means I can see what and how another has seen. But if, like the thin men of Haddam, I do not 'see how the blackbird / Walks around the feet / Of the women about you' (Stevens 1982: 93), then I *never* saw. I do not know which to prefer, the blackbird flying, whistling, walking, sitting, or just after. However, if the blackbird ever sat in the cedar-limbs, then it happened for everybody only now.

Acknowledgements

A version of this chapter appeared as 'Stanley Cavell und die politische Dimension der literarischen Moderne', in *Literatur und politische Philosophie: Subjektivität, Fremdheit, Demokratie*, Michael G. Festl and Philipp Schweighauser (eds), Paderborn: Wilhelm Fink, 2018, pp. 145–67.

Bibliography

Beckett, Samuel (1958), *Endgame*, New York: Grove Press.
Cavell, Stanley (1999), *The Claim of Reason: Wittgenstein, Skepticism, Morality, and Tragedy*, New York: Oxford University Press.
Cavell, Stanley (2002), *Must We Mean What We Say? A Book of Essays*, updated edn, Cambridge: Cambridge University Press.
Cavell, Stanley (2006), 'Reflections on Wallace Stevens at Mount Holyoke', in Christopher Benfy and Karen Remmler (eds), *Artists, Intellectuals, and World War II: The Pontigny Encounters at Mount Holyoke College, 1942–1944*, Amherst: University of Massachusetts Press, pp. 61–79.
Gibson, John (2007), *Fiction and the Weave of Life*, Oxford: Oxford University Press.
Jameson, Fredric (1991), *Postmodernism, or, The Cultural Logic of Late Capitalism*, Durham, NC: Duke University Press.
Jameson, Fredric (2002), *A Singular Modernity*, London: Verso.

Jameson, Fredric (2016), *The Modernist Papers*, London: Verso.

Laugier, Sandra (2006), 'Wittgenstein and Cavell: Anthropology, Skepticism, and Politics', in Andrew Norris (ed.), *The Claim to Community: Essays on Stanley Cavell and Political Philosophy*, Stanford: Stanford University Press, pp. 19–37.

Marx, Karl and Friedrich Engels (2010), 'From *The German Ideology*', in Vincent B. Leitch (gen. ed.), *The Norton Anthology of Theory and Criticism*, 2nd edn, New York: W. W. Norton, pp. 655–6.

Norris, Andrew (2006), 'Introduction: Stanley Cavell and the Claim to Community', in Andrew Norris (ed.), *The Claim to Community: Essays on Stanley Cavell and Political Philosophy*, Stanford: Stanford University Press, pp. 1–18.

Stevens, Wallace (1982), *The Collected Poems*, New York: Vintage.

Wittgenstein, Ludwig (2009), *Philosophische Untersuchungen / Philosophical Investigations*, 4th rev. edn, G. E. M. Anscombe, P. M. S. Hacker, and Joachim Schulte (trans.), Malden: Blackwell.

15

Inferentialist Semantics, Intimationist Aesthetics, and *Walden*

Bryan Vescio

Metaphor is the dreamwork of language.

(Davidson 1984: 245)

Sentences which suggest far more than they say, which have an atmosphere about them, which do not merely report an old, but make a new, impression; sentences which suggest as many things and which are as durable as a Roman aqueduct; to frame these, that is the *art* of writing. Sentences which are expensive, towards which so many volumes, so much life, went; which lie like boulders on the page, up and down or across; which contain the seed of other sentences, not mere repetition, but creation.

(Thoreau 1906a: 418–19)

As Richard Rorty demonstrated some forty years ago in his first book, *Philosophy and the Mirror of Nature* (Rorty 1979), the mainstream of philosophy has been dominated by the metaphor of representation. From the birth of metaphysics in the ancient Greek desire to distinguish reality from its dim imitations on the wall of Plato's cave to the birth of modern epistemology in René Descartes' worries about whether the mind can accurately represent even the surfaces of things, Rorty's book traces the persistence of this metaphor in the Western philosophical imagination. But he also both heralds and promotes a powerful counter-current that emerged in the twentieth century in thinkers like John Dewey, Ludwig Wittgenstein, and Martin Heidegger, who attempted to weed out this metaphor and free philosophy from its tiresome oscillation between certainty and scepticism. The important innovation these philosophers made was to identify language as the source of human awareness and meaning by conceiving of linguistic meaning in terms of social practices rather than representations.

This effort continues today in the work of philosophers like Robert Brandom, whose inferentialist semantics fills in the details of the social practice picture of language recommended by the later Wittgenstein. While the anti-representationalist views of Rorty, Brandom, and others have made considerable inroads in many areas of philosophy, however, they have had almost no discernible effect on the philosophy of art, where aesthetics is still dominated by the metaphor of representation. One reason their linguistic approach has seemed incompatible with philosophical aesthetics is the lingering influence of Immanuel Kant, whose representationalist aesthetics downplays the role of language in producing aesthetic value. The metaphor of representation has modelled epistemology on perception, and aesthetic experience and value seem to be even more closely dependent on perception than knowledge does. Consequently, aesthetics has seemed in the first instance to be about inner episodes or experiences that are independent of and prior to the mediations of language, rendering the literary arts special and derivative cases, even in works like Kant's that rank them among the highest of arts. But even as they promise greater clarity and certainty, metaphors of representation in aesthetics engender the same problems of scepticism that they do in epistemology, and these problems are felt most keenly by those responsible for teaching literature and the arts. In this chapter, I will argue for an alternative, anti-representational aesthetic that dissolves these problems, an aesthetic of intimation that parallels Brandom's semantics of inference, by supplementing his account with Donald Davidson's theory of metaphor. I will demonstrate the value of this aesthetic by intervening in the ongoing debate about Henry David Thoreau's aesthetic practice in his classic *Walden, or Life in the Woods* (Thoreau 1906b). Because Thoreau's appreciation of the beauty of nature is so often seen as hostile to linguistic characterisation, my redescription of it will suggest how an intimationist aesthetic can account for all the aesthetic phenomena philosophers have tried to explain, from highly conceptualised works of poetry to artworks in non-linguistic media to the simplest phenomena of nature itself.

Kant's Representationalist Aesthetics

One of the main threads of Rorty's story about the demise of the metaphor of the mirror of nature is the later Wittgenstein's repudiation of the earlier representationalist theory of language he had advanced in his *Tractatus Logico-Philosophicus* (Wittgenstein 2003). Wittgenstein begins his posthumously published *Philosophical Investigations* (Wittgenstein 1958) by rejecting the idea that language is primarily a medium for representing the world, in favour of the idea that it is a collection of social practices he refers to as 'language games' or 'forms of life'. This idea gained enormous influence in both philosophy of language and philosophy of mind in the second half of the twentieth century. Instead of conceiving of language as mediating between mind and world, or subject and object, it encourages the view that language is a practical tool for coping with the world, and in the philosophy of language it sparked such ideas as Davidson's claim in 'A Nice Derangement of Epitaphs' that there is no difference between 'knowing a language and knowing our way around in the world generally' (Davidson 1986: 446). Similar anti-representational considerations led Wilfrid Sellars to propose in 'Empiricism and the Philosophy of Mind' his doctrine of 'psychological nominalism', which holds that '*all* awareness . . . is a linguistic affair' (Sellars 1963: 160). More recently, Brandom, a younger colleague of Sellars, has identified language use with the ability to play 'the game of giving and asking for reasons' in his monumental book *Making It Explicit*, which he characterises as 'filling in' the details of Davidson's theory (Brandom 1994: 152–3).[1] All these views have loomed large in Rorty's ambitious anti-foundationalist efforts to dissuade philosophers from continuing to pursue metaphysical and epistemological questions at all. The more an anti-representational conception of language is advanced, the larger the role language seems to play in the life of the human mind.

Language has not, however, come to play nearly as significant a role in the philosophy of art, where philosophers have been notably reluctant to see aesthetic awareness as a linguistic affair, and not coincidentally, have tended to persist in adopting representational metaphors for their understanding of aesthetic experience and value.[2] One reason must surely be the long shadow Kant's *Critique of Judgment* (Kant 1914) still casts over the philosophy of art. Here Kant continues his first two critiques' novel response to the gap between subject and object Descartes posited, not by anchoring certainty to an outer realm of things represented but by determining the universal laws governing the inner realm of representations. The role of language in Kant's three critiques has been a matter of some dispute, but Michael N. Forster's recent discussion provides a balanced and compelling account.[3] He notes that while Kant assigns to language only 'an inessential and subordinate role' (Forster 2014: 83) in the three critiques, other writings, both early and late, suggest that Kant was influenced by the idea that thought is in fact dependent on language, a view enthusiastically embraced by his contemporaries Johann Georg Hamann and Johann Gottfried Herder. Forster concludes that Kant 'only acknowledges some sort of causal dependence of human beings' thought and concepts on language, but still believes that thoughts and concepts are in their essential nature separable from and sovereign over language' (2014: 94). And in his three critiques, Forster suggests, Kant deliberately suppresses any sense of the dependence of thought on language in order to distance himself from the much stronger claims of Hamann and Herder.

The critical phase in Kant's career, in which he de-emphasised the role of language in thought, coincides with the period in which he developed his most influential ideas about aesthetics.[4] In his book *Kant and the Empiricists: Understanding Understanding*, Wayne Waxman argues for the continuity between the Kant of the three critiques and the British empiricists, with whom he is usually contrasted, on the basis of their shared doctrine of 'sensibilism', which Waxman defines as 'the thesis that all our ideas – perceptions, in Hume's terminology, representations in Kant's – originate in (are coeval with) being perceived and have no existence prior to or independently of their immediate presence to consciousness in perception' (Waxman 2005: 3). Language, on this model, is nothing more than a vehicle for conveying these prelinguistic or extralinguistic ideas to other minds – as Waxman puts it, sensibilists 'regarded ideational thought as master and linguistic discourse as slave' (2005: 109). The effect of sensibilism is 'to strip away from thought everything related to public discourse' and to render human cognition and experience a private transaction between the individual mind and the world. 'In Kant's case', Waxman writes, 'human intelligence was conceived very much in terms of the individual, isolated, conscious intelligence' (2005: 102).

The aesthetic Kant propounds in *The Critique of Judgment* is clearly derived from this representationalist view of the human mind that denies a significant role for the conventions of public discourse. One aspect of aesthetic judgements that Kant emphasises is their immediacy. He says that a term of aesthetic value like 'beautiful' 'always signifies something which pleases immediately' (Kant 1914: 51). Since language, for Kant, is a medium of expression, it can play no part in immediate aesthetic judgements. In fact, for Kant, aesthetic judgements bypass concepts entirely, since such judgements 'must refer the object immediately to my feeling of pleasure and pain, and that not by means of concepts' (1914: 61). One reason that Kant takes the 'free beauty' of natural phenomena, as opposed to the 'merely dependent beauty' of works of art, as the paradigm case of aesthetic value is that the former is perceived more directly, without the mediation of concepts or purposes:

> But if we regard a thing as a work of art, that is enough to make us admit that its shape has reference to some design and definite purpose. And hence there is no immediate satisfaction in the contemplation of it. On the other hand a flower, e.g., a tulip, is regarded as beautiful; because in perceiving it we find a certain purposiveness which, in our judgment, is referred to no purpose at all. (1914: 90)

And for Kant, because no concept is 'capable of being adequate to' the 'aesthetic ideas' that all works of art express, such ideas 'cannot be completely compassed and made intelligible by language' (1914: 197). In *The Critique of Judgment*, Kant develops an aesthetic that, like his theories of cognition and action in the other two critiques, is based on private, inner representations rather than public discourse.

But this approach to the aesthetic creates problems that will be familiar to many of those who teach literature and other works of art. On the one hand, Kant insists that all aesthetic judgements make claims to universality. He needs this sense of universality to distinguish the beautiful from the merely pleasant, asserting that

> this claim to universal validity so essentially belongs to a judgment by which we describe anything as *beautiful*, that if this were not thought in it, it would never come into our thoughts to use the expression at all, but everything which pleases without a concept would be counted as pleasant. (1914: 59)

On the other hand, though, because judgements of beauty bypass concepts, they cannot be justified by publicly available reasons or criteria:

> If we judge Objects merely according to concepts, then all representation of beauty is lost. Thus there can be no rule according to which anyone is forced to recognise anything as beautiful. We cannot press [upon others] by the aid of any reasons or fundamental propositions our judgment that a coat, a house, or a flower is beautiful. (1914: 62)[5]

So as teachers of literature or other arts, Kant's aesthetic asks us to force upon students' attention monuments of beauty that we take to be worthy of study – not just for us, but for everyone – and yet when students dispute our judgements, we can provide them with no reasons or criteria to justify our selections. Because Kant's theory of aesthetic value, along with its many descendants, cuts off aesthetic judgement from public norms of justification, it appears to make any sort of education that seeks to cultivate students' appreciation for works of art either impossible or a mere exercise in bullying. This pedagogical shortcoming alone should inspire us to seek an alternative to Kant's legacy of representationalist aesthetics.

From Inferentialist Semantics to Intimationist Aesthetics

Abandoning this model and reclaiming art as a conceptual, even linguistic phenomenon might solve these problems, but a primary motivation for continued resistance to that move is that language is typically viewed as a medium for representing 'direct' and 'unmediated' sensations or perceptions. So denying that language is a medium and the explanatory role of representation in philosophy more generally, as philosophers in the wake of Wittgenstein have increasingly done, should alleviate this concern. The most important recent philosopher to have done so is Brandom, who has helpfully condensed the complex, technical arguments in his 1994 magnum opus *Making It Explicit* into a shorter, less technical introduction titled *Articulating Reasons: An Introduction to Inferentialism* (Brandom 2000a). He explicitly sets himself against 'a representational paradigm' that he says

> reigns not only in the whole spectrum of analytically pursued semantics ... but also in structuralism ... and even in those later continental thinkers whose poststructuralism is still so far mired in the representational paradigm that it can see no other alternative to understanding meaning in terms of signifiers standing for signifieds than to understand it in terms of signifiers standing for other signifiers. (Brandom 2000a: 9–10)[6]

By contrast, he portrays his project as a form of 'conceptual pragmatism' that 'offers an account of knowing (or believing, or saying) *that* such and such is the case in terms of knowing *how* (being able) to *do* something' (Brandom 2000a: 4). What people do that determines the meaning of their content or beliefs, Brandom claims, is to participate in the social practice he calls 'the game of giving and asking for reasons', in which the meaning of any assertion is what other moves in the game – what other assertions – it commits or entitles one to, hence the name Brandom gives to his programme: 'inferentialist' semantics. The meanings of sentences are therefore not to be found in what they or the terms they comprise represent but rather in the patterns of linguistic behaviour they evince. Thinking of language as action leaves no room for the distinction between form and content, which is just the distinction between representations and what they represent. And thinking of language and meaning in terms of social cooperation rather than inner representations leaves no explanatory role for mental faculties operating on inner representations. Brandom writes, 'I do not see that we need – either in epistemology or, more important, in semantics – to appeal to any intermediaries between perceptible facts and reports of them that are noninferentially elicited by the exercise of reliable differential responsive dispositions' (2000a: 205–6).[7]

Brandom makes an acute observation about the sources of representationalism that suggests that the revolution he proposes against it in semantics should inspire a parallel revolution in aesthetics:

> Classical empiricist philosophy of mind takes immediate perceptual experiences as the paradigm of awareness or consciousness. Classical empiricist epistemology takes as its paradigm of empirical knowledge those same experiences, to which it traces the warrant for and authority of all the rest. As the tradition has developed, it has become clearer that both rest on a more or less explicit semantic picture, according to which the content of experience, awareness, and knowledge is to be understood in the first instance in *representational* terms: as a matter of what is (or purports to be) represent*ed* by some represent*ing* states or episodes. (Brandom 2000a: 24–5)

As we have seen, the aesthetics of even the anti-empiricist Kant also takes this kind of representation as its paradigm. But some critics of Brandom have charged that his views on language, which make everything depend on giving and asking for reasons, leaves no room for the apparently irrational, or at least a-rational, activity of art. Charles Taylor puts the charge this way:

> A serious attempt in prose to set out true judgments about the beauty of things (aesthetics), the virtues of life (ethics), or the nature of God (theology) has to draw on uses of language, in Cassirer's broad sense, which are disclosive. I mean the uses which either without asserting at all, or going beyond their assertive force, make something manifest through articulating it. (Taylor 2010: 35)

Brandom's reply is to say 'that every autonomous language game must *include* practices of giving and asking for reasons', though it need not be confined to such practices (Brandom 2010: 303). Here at least, Kant's aesthetic seems to have the edge on Brandom, since Kant does include such a mysterious, disclosive function of language in his argument that reasons for aesthetic value cannot be given and are beside the point, while Brandom's inferentialism never explains how the apparently unreasonable demands of art can be satisfied within the game of giving and asking for reasons.[8]

Fortunately, though, while Brandom describes himself as filling in the details of Davidson's philosophy of language, in this case an aspect of Davidson's philosophy can help furnish the aesthetic component of Brandom's inferentialist semantics. In his essay 'What Metaphors Mean', Davidson offers a radical new theory of metaphor that makes a startling claim: 'We must give up the idea that a metaphor carries a message, that it has a content or meaning (except, of course, its literal meaning)' (Davidson 1984: 261). The crux of Davidson's argument is that when metaphors acquire definite meanings in addition to their literal ones, they are said to 'die'. As long as it is 'alive', a metaphor does not produce any 'special meaning, a specific cognitive content' (1984: 262), but rather 'prompts or inspires' us to notice an indefinite number of things (1984: 263) – which is to say that its literal meaning gives it a clear enough inferential role, but that its strangeness and even obvious falsity prod us towards assigning it a new role that is as yet diffuse and indefinite. As Rorty remarks in his essay 'Unfamiliar Noises: Hesse and Davidson on Metaphor', while Davidson's metaphors may not possess special meanings themselves, their power and value are ultimately measured not in the idle or disinterested pleasure Kant associates with the aesthetic but in their effects on the social practices that Brandom calls the game of giving and asking for reasons: 'People's linguistic repertoires are thus enlarged, and their lives and actions changed in ways they cannot easily articulate' (Rorty 1991a: 170). Moreover, Davidson suggests that these effects of metaphor can be produced not only by a single phrase or sentence, but by an entire text, when he discusses the effect of T. S. Eliot's poem 'The Hippopotamus'. He concludes this discussion by saying, 'The poem does, of course, intimate much that goes beyond the literal meaning of the words. But intimation is not meaning' (Davidson 1984: 256). What Davidson has done in his theory of metaphor, then, is to identify an aesthetic effect of at least literary texts – intimation – that performs exactly the disclosive function Taylor associates with art while remaining firmly planted in a pragmatic, inferential, and decidedly non-representational account of language compatible with Brandom's.

Near the end of his essay, Davidson suggests that this function need not be restricted to literary texts, but could also be applied to visual arts and natural phenomena, and there seems to be no reason it could not characterise the aesthetic effects of music or other arts as well:

When we try to say what a metaphor 'means', we soon realize that there is no end to what we want to mention. If someone draws his finger along a coastline on a map, or mentions the beauty and deftness of a line in a Picasso etching, how many things are drawn to your attention? You might list a great many, but you could not finish since the idea of finishing would have no clear application. How many facts or propositions are conveyed by a photograph? None, an infinity, or one great unstatable fact? Bad question. A picture is not worth a thousand words, or any other number. Words are the wrong currency to exchange for a picture. (Davidson 1984: 263)

Indeed, as Rorty points out, the continuity between metaphors and non-linguistic phenomena is that much stronger on Davidson's account because it abandons representationalism:

> For, by putting metaphor outside the pale of semantics, insisting that a metaphorical sentence has no meaning other than its literal one, Davidson lets us see metaphors on the model of unfamiliar events in the natural world – *causes* of changing beliefs and desires – rather than on the model of *representations* of unfamiliar worlds, worlds which are 'symbolic' rather than 'natural'. (Rorty 1991a: 163)

Like Kant's aesthetic, the one Davidson outlines is not amenable to criteria because there are no ready-made inferential roles or conventions under which to subsume it: 'There are no instructions for devising metaphors; there is no manual for determining what metaphor "means" or "says"; there is no test for metaphor that does not call for taste' (Davidson 1984: 245). It drops the claim to universal validity in Kant's judgements of beauty, but by identifying the value of metaphor with its effects on the game of giving and asking for reasons, it allows critics and teachers to discuss and debate those effects with their students by making them explicit:

> The critic is, so to speak, in benign competition with the metaphor maker. The critic tries to make his own art easier or more transparent in some respects than the original, but at the same time he tries to reproduce in others some of the effects the original had on him. In doing this the critic also, and perhaps by the best method at his command, calls attention to the beauty or aptness, the hidden power, of the metaphor itself. (Davidson 1984: 264)

Davidson begins his essay by suggesting that '[m]etaphor is the dreamwork of language' (1984: 245), and the central accomplishment of his essay, when placed in the context of Brandom's inferentialist paradigm, is to make room for dreaming beyond the metaphor of representation.

But why identify the aesthetic effect Davidson describes with aesthetic value in general? The answer lies in its social function, which Brandom alludes to in a later essay titled 'Vocabularies of Pragmatism: Synthesizing Naturalism and Historicism'.[9] Brandom describes two different perspectives from which to evaluate differing 'vocabularies', or relatively stable sets of linguistic practices: 'the perspective of the *naturalist*' and 'the perspective of the *historicist*' (Brandom 2011b: 136). The former perspective thinks of vocabularies as 'evolutionary coping strategies' for improving our chances of survival and getting what we want, 'whether rooted in our biology, in the determinate historical circumstances under which we reproduce our social life, or in idiosyncrasies of our individual trajectories through the world' (2011b: 136–7). The latter thinks of them primarily as tools that 'make it possible to frame and formulate new ends' (2011b: 137). Pragmatism, according to Brandom, is the view that synthesises these two perspectives, allowing us to see our linguistic practices both as satisfying the naturalistic purposes we already have and as satisfying our historicist purpose of growth through the continual invention of new purposes. On Davidson's and Rorty's account, it is metaphor that accomplishes this latter purpose by allowing sudden, vertical leaps out of horizontal, inferential patterns, enabling 'people's linguistic repertoires [to be] enlarged, and their lives and actions changed in ways they cannot easily articulate' (Rorty 1991a: 170). That is why at the end of his essay Rorty praises metaphors as 'indispensable instruments of moral and intellectual progress' (1991a: 172). Inferences, after all, can only be made within vocabularies, not between them – the whole point of what Brandom calls 'the vocabulary vocabulary' is to call attention to different sets of linguistic practices that lack inferential connections with one another. An intimationist aesthetic, then, is not just an optional extra that may be grafted onto Brandom's inferentialist semantics, but a necessary addition that explains as inference cannot the large-scale shifts from one vocabulary to another. Brandom also assimilates this distinction between naturalism and historicism to Rorty's distinction between the public and the private, suggesting that the former results mainly in the pursuit of public ends while the burden of the latter mostly falls to individuals in private.[10] Synthesising the two perspectives, Brandom suggests, means making room in our public projects for these private ones:

> There is no reason that the vocabulary in which we conduct our public political debates and determine the purposes toward which our public political institutions are turned should not incorporate the aspiration to nurture and promote its citizens' vocabulary-transforming private exercises of their vocabularies. (Brandom 2011b: 153)

On this view, the effects Davidson attributes to metaphor are not just isolated aesthetic effects but rather perform a social function commensurate with the role the arts and aesthetic value play in the lives of individuals and the culture as a whole.[11]

Metaphor and Intimation in *Walden*

Given that representational metaphors continue to dominate contemporary philosophy of language and art, it should not be surprising that they also tend to inform literary critics' appraisals of the aesthetic practices of important writers. This is especially true in discussions of Thoreau and his masterpiece, *Walden, or Life in the Woods*, in part because his book is itself about the aesthetic appreciation of nature and both it and his other writings are rife with incompatible statements about what that appreciation entails. The dominant understanding of Thoreau's aesthetic is that he valued direct sense impressions above all else, shunning the mediations of language and conceptualisation. In *American Renaissance*, F. O. Matthiessen says that Thoreau was most 'intent to study the exact evidence of his senses' (Matthiessen 2009: 98), and in her 2009 study *Passions for Nature: Nineteenth-Century America's Aesthetics of Alienation*, Rochelle L. Johnson sums up Thoreau's aesthetic by saying it 'assumes that there is deep value in the sensory experience of natural phenomena' (Johnson 2009: 207). Yet many passages in Thoreau's writings, such as the one from his journal that I quoted in my epigraph, locate the sources of aesthetic value rather in human language and its effects. Again and again Thoreau denies the possibility of passively receiving or recording sensory experience, most famously even suggesting in his journal that humanity must be the measure of all things when he writes, 'That is, man is all in all, Nature nothing, but as she draws him out and reflects him' (quoted in Hansen 1990: 137). Although she also cites a passage in *Walden* in which Thoreau appears to repudiate metaphor, Johnson accurately notes that the book itself is so saturated with metaphor that it 'calls more attention to him and his metaphor making than it does to the material world' (Johnson 2009: 200–1). In spite of all the confusion surrounding Thoreau's aesthetic, the most notable consensus that has emerged among critics in recent years is that it attempts to bridge the gap between subject and object, and thus between humanity and the rest of the natural world. Johnson quotes Laura Dassow Walls's claim that Thoreau sets out 'to close the gap between self and nature' (Johnson 2009: 207). David Faflik writes that Thoreau, in his aesthetics of 'surface', 'discovered a middle ground between subject and object' (Faflik 2013: 81). Rick Anthony Furtak cites a journal entry in which Thoreau questions the distinction between 'things as they appear' and things 'as they are' (Furtak 2012: 113). And Olaf Hansen finds that the allegorical mode in which Thoreau writes resists the choice 'between absolute subjectivity on the one hand and absolute objectivity on the other' (Hansen 1990: x). Perhaps an intimationist aesthetic, which valorises metaphor and overcomes the distinction between subject and object by abjuring the metaphor of representation altogether, might bring some clarity to Thoreau's aesthetic practices in *Walden*, whatever it is he thought he was doing.

The first thing to notice about Thoreau's aesthetic in *Walden* is that even though its subject matter is the beauty of natural phenomena, it is clearly opposed to the representationalist aesthetic Kant models on perception and sensation. In his important 1973 book *Literary Transcendentalism: Style and Vision in the American Renaissance*, Lawrence Buell says that Thoreau's writing 'is not content to stay on the descriptive level alone' but rather is constantly 'playing with the significance of things' (Buell 1973: 73) and creating an 'atmosphere in which one is induced to look for meanings' (1973: 74). Hansen also notes that Thoreau 'hardly ever leaves the observation stand alone' (Hansen 1990: 134), and Furtak cites the way Thoreau consistently links 'beauty' with 'significance' in his journal (Furtak 2012: 113, 120).[12] Moreover, as Buell points out, Thoreau's writing emphasises 'message and tone at the expense of aesthetic symmetry and logical precision' (Buell 1973: 74). These characterisations of Thoreau's writing fly in the face of Kant's idea of the aesthetic, which downplays the role of meaning in aesthetic value in favour of formal unity. Even more significantly, *Walden* realises Thoreau's aesthetic in its abundant use of metaphor. It is the metaphors of *Walden* that are most memorable and that survive in common language, metaphors like 'sucking the marrow out of life', 'off the beaten path', 'marching to a different drummer', and 'castles in the air'. The sentences in which he coins these metaphors are just the kinds of sentences he says epitomise the art of writing in the journal entry I took as my epigraph, sentences that 'suggest much more than they say' and that 'do not merely report old, but make a new, impression', sowing 'the seed of other sentences, not mere repetition but creation' (quoted in Hansen 1990: 137–8). This passage is also an apt description of Davidson's conception of metaphor, and Thoreau's references here to 'suggestions' and 'impressions' rather than meaning suggest a process of sowing 'seeds of other sentences' that is more akin to Davidson's notion of intimation than to Brandom's notion of inference. What is missing entirely from this description, as from so many of Thoreau's other passages on writing, is any hint of the metaphor of representation. In *Walden*, furthermore, he celebrates poetry, the art of writing, not as a medium distancing us from life but as 'the work of art nearest to life itself', contrasting it in this regard with more representational forms of art: 'It may be translated into every language, and not only be read but actually breathed from all human lips; – not be represented on canvas or in marble only, but be carved out of the breath of life itself' (Thoreau 1906b: 114). His aesthetic practice, and at least these versions of his aesthetic theory, add up to something that looks a lot like an intimationist aesthetic, redeeming the role of language in creating and establishing aesthetic value.

Many contemporary critics, however, now read Thoreau as practising an aesthetic that is directly opposed to one based on intimation. While the intimationist aesthetic takes the effects of metaphor as the model for aesthetic value in general, Johnson argues that Thoreau, particularly in his journal and his later works, makes 'a general shift away from metaphor and toward conveying the literalness of natural phenomena through description' (Johnson 2009: 191), a shift that captures what Johnson calls 'nature's truth' by letting the world speak for itself.[13] For Johnson, the shift away from metaphor is a shift away from an 'aesthetic of alienation', since metaphor distorts and anthropomorphises nature, creating distance between it and humanity. But this idea depends on the assumption that language in general is a representational medium between self and world, and that literal language represents the world more accurately and directly. That is exactly the view of language Johnson espouses and attributes to Thoreau when she says that 'words serve as linguistic signifiers of other things' (Johnson 2009: 193). This assumption that literal language is a clear medium of representation while metaphor is a distorting one leads Johnson to devalue *Walden*, which she concedes is 'immersed in expression through metaphor' (Johnson 2009: 192), in favour of Thoreau's later, supposedly more literal works. She does, however, find the roots of Thoreau's later aesthetic in one passage in *Walden* near the beginning of the chapter on 'Sounds', in which he warns of the 'danger of forgetting the language which all things and events speak without metaphor, which alone is copious and standard' (Thoreau 1906b: 123). But this passage is ambiguous: instead of renouncing metaphor, it might simply be stressing the continuity between the aesthetic effects of metaphor and those of natural phenomena that Davidson and Rorty stress – the fact that natural phenomena produce the same effects on our linguistic behavior as metaphor. What prevents Johnson from seeing that possibility is her own attachment to the metaphor of representation, which makes representational transparency the only kind of continuity with nature she sees as worthwhile. But when the representationalist view of language is abandoned, there is no need to worry about the kind of 'alienation'

Johnson describes: the only sense in which humanity can become alienated from the natural world is by adopting metaphors for our relation to it that portray it as something apart from us. That is just what the metaphor of representation does, and the irony of Johnson's reading of Thoreau is that it depends entirely on just this metaphor – an anthropomorphising one at that, since it attributes to nature its own 'truth' and 'significance' apart from humanity's.[14]

Faflik offers a similar reading of Thoreau's aesthetic, which he describes as 'shallow', not in the sense that it is trivial or superficial, but rather in the sense that, unlike that of other transcendentalists, it prefers surfaces to depths. Faflik notes the way Thoreau oscillates between recommending diving to great depths and remaining on the surface, particularly in *Walden*. From an intimationist point of view, this idea is promising, since it might be used to make the anti-representationalist point that there is nothing behind or within language or a text that constitutes its meaning. Unfortunately, Faflik proves to have something more like Johnson's 'literal' aesthetic in mind when he explains that by an aesthetic of surface he means 'a "mood" of hypersensitive receptiveness to "things" as "things"' (Faflik 2013: 79). In the same way that Johnson talks about metaphor as distorting and alienating, Faflik describes language in general, by way of a quotation from W. J. T. Mitchell, as an 'opaque, distorting, arbitrary mechanism of representation', adding, 'In surface, however, we forgo the "distorting" forces of depth, and so perhaps come closer to achieving unmediated meaning in our reading than is otherwise possible within any image-dependent sign system' (Faflik 2013: 79). Again, he identifies Thoreau's enemy as image or symbol, much as Johnson identifies it as metaphor. While Faflik is perhaps more careful to qualify his reading than Johnson, calling only for something 'closer to unmediated meaning' and ultimately arguing that Thoreau's surface aesthetic occupies a middle ground that is '[n]either too direct nor too distant, neither fully mediated nor unmediated' (Faflik 2013: 81), only the idea of language as a representational medium makes this language of 'distance' and 'mediation' intelligible in the first place. But again, Thoreau's text provides scant reason to assimilate the metaphor of 'depth' to the metaphor of 'representation'. A key moment in Faflik's reading is his discussion of Thoreau's efforts to plumb the depths of the pond itself, defying the local myth that it is bottomless with the exact measurements he produces. Faflik reads this episode as a triumph of surface aesthetics, presumably because it finds a secure bottom in what was thought to be bottomless. But Thoreau's point, yet another resolutely metaphorical or symbolic one, is surely to demonstrate that he has probed depths that his neighbours in and around Concord have not – after all, the episode clearly echoes the most famous passage in the book, in which he describes his reasons for abandoning the town and striking out for the woods: 'I wanted to live deep and suck out all the marrow of life, to live so sturdily and Spartan-like as to put to rout all that was not life' (Thoreau 1906b: 101). Here, 'depth' indicates not representational content but passionate intensity and even practical necessity. Depth is indeed a crucial metaphor in *Walden*, but it is rarely if ever used to indicate meaning in a representational sense. Like Johnson, Faflik projects his own representational assumptions about language and the aesthetic onto Thoreau's work.

In the conclusion of her book, Johnson admits that '[m]etaphors themselves ... are not the problem' (Johnson 2009: 221), pointing out that environmentalists use the device Rorty called an 'indispensable tool for moral and intellectual progress' in 'creating new, more environmentally sustainable metaphors for nature' (2009: 234). Particularly in the light of an intimationist aesthetic, it is certainly possible to read Thoreau as using individual metaphors and the grand metaphorical structure that is *Walden* as a whole to suggest a new vocabulary for talking about the relationship between self and world, humanity and nature. Critics like Johnson and Faflik miss this opportunity because they only see Thoreau through the lens of the old vocabulary of representation.[15] Johnson advocates a sense of continuity with and humility towards nature, but she only understands those terms in the context of the particular kind of breach between humanity and the rest of the natural world that is posited by the metaphor of representation, a breach she describes when she suggests that 'the best we can do in terms of understanding nature is to recognise the space that is the gap between our consciousness (the "inside") and the world (the "outside")' (2009: 222). Critics seem to agree in reading Thoreau as trying to heal this breach, but they neglect the possibility of doing so by repudiating the metaphor that opens it in the first place. Perhaps we should read Thoreau as intimating a new vocabulary that redefines our continuity with and humility before nature in non-representational terms, as positing a naturalism without mirrors[16] in which a sense of causal rather than epistemological dependence is sufficient for both continuity and humility.[17] An intimationist aesthetic that finds value in *Walden*'s abundance of metaphors and attempts to reproduce some of their effects makes such a reading possible.

Representationalist aesthetics begin with the model of sensation and perception and attempt to apply that model, sometimes with great difficulty, to linguistic phenomena like literary texts. An intimationist aesthetic, which takes all awareness to be a linguistic affair, reverses that process, identifying a particular aesthetic effect of literary texts that can also be achieved by non-linguistic phenomena. Because of its copious use of metaphor to find beauty and significance in the phenomena of nature, Thoreau's *Walden* is among the best demonstrations of how the idea of intimation can account for aesthetic experience and value in general, in spite of critics' efforts to read representational metaphors into it. Thoreau has frequently been called a proto-pragmatist, and the ways in which he anticipates an intimationist aesthetic, itself a consequence of pragmatism, provide further reason to apply that label to him. In *Walden* he describes what he takes to be the role of philosophy: 'It is to solve some of the problems of life, not only theoretically, but practically' (Thoreau 1906b: 10). Matthiessen suggests how this view affected Thoreau's aesthetic practice when he wrote: 'What he responded to as beauty was the application of trained skill to the exigencies of existence' (Matthiessen 2009: 188). Furtak, who also associates Thoreau with pragmatism, echoes this sentiment in his description of Thoreau's approach to writing: 'Furthermore, the literary process of articulating a vision of the world cannot be detached from the practical task of inhabiting it' (Furtak 2012: 116). Even in his lonely errand of private self-transformation in the wilderness Thoreau maintained firm practical contact with 'the problems of life', and his work is also a prime example of the ways in which what Brandom describes as the naturalist and historicist perspectives can be synthesised. The problem both Thoreau and an intimationist aesthetic in general help solve by replacing a representational aesthetics with one rooted in the social practices of language is to restore the meaning and value of art to the realm of the practical, not only refusing to sacrifice the work of dreaming but making it the primary business of life.

Notes

1. Brandom does, however, qualify the idea shared by most pragmatists that language should be seen as a tool. The reason, he says, is because tools are used to serve existing purposes, and the function of language is to make it possible to have purposes to begin with: 'The essence of specifically discursive practice – the practice of deploying *concepts* – is precisely its engendering of this capacity to entertain an indefinite number of novel beliefs, and to frame an indefinite number of novel ends' (Brandom 2011a: 81). This is one reason he argues for the primacy of 'historicist' purposes, as we will see below.
2. This is even true of some versions of pragmatist philosophy of art, including that of Dewey in *Art as Experience* (Dewey 1989). Richard Shusterman has more recently championed Dewey in his criticisms of 'textualist pragmatism', the form of pragmatism rooted in the philosophy of language that I am recommending, in books like *Practicing Philosophy: Pragmatism and the Philosophical Life* and *Pragmatist Aesthetics: Living Beauty, Rethinking Art* (Shusterman 1997, 2000). I have demonstrated the ways in which both Dewey and Shusterman remain indebted to representationalist metaphors in chapter 3 of my book *Reconstruction in Literary Studies: An Informalist Approach* (Vescio 2014: 75–105).
3. Forster's essay is included in a recent collection called *The Linguistic Dimension of Kant's Thought: Historical and Critical Essays* (Schalow and Velkley 2014), whose essays mostly aim at recuperating an important role for language in Kant's thought.
4. My criticisms of Kant only apply to his idea of the beautiful, and I will not discuss the other source of aesthetic value he discusses, the sublime.
5. In his essay 'The Place of Language: From Kant to Hegel' in Schalow and Velkley's collection, Robert Wood argues not only that language is not bypassed in Kant's aesthetic but that it is essential to all three of the central topics discussed in the critiques: 'In all three orders, what is involved is inter-human communication which, though grounded in feeling in the aesthetic order, nonetheless requires linguistic communication as essential mediation' (Wood 2014: 37). While it is true that Kant repeatedly notes that aesthetic judgements must be universally communicable, this idea still makes language, regarded as medium, the slave of its foundational master, non-linguistic or prelinguistic ideas. And because Kant explicitly denies language access to these foundational aesthetic ideas, he denies the possibility of justifying the judgements they ground.
6. The 2010 collection *Reading Brandom: On Making It Explicit* (Weiss and Wanderer 2010), which contains essays on Brandom and his responses to them, is instructive in illustrating the clash between representationalist and anti-representationalist intuitions. Time and time again Brandom's critics insist that what is missing from his work is a sense of truth or meaning that admits of the idea of representation, and Brandom's responses mostly amount to different ways of saying that his critics are begging the question in favour of representation.

7. While Rorty and Brandom agree that 'experience' cannot justify beliefs, the main point on which they differ is whether facts can do so. Rorty thinks Brandom's commitment to the idea of facts making beliefs true or false is a residual commitment to representationalism. For the issues at stake, see Rorty's essay 'Robert Brandom on Social Practices and Representations' (Rorty 1998), as well as their exchange in *Rorty and His Critics* (Brandom 2000b), where Brandom first published his essay 'Vocabularies of Pragmatism' (Brandom 2011b).
8. Practically the only other effort to bring Brandom's ideas to bear on aesthetics and literary theory is Phillip Stambovsky's *Philosophical Conceptualization and Literary Art: Inference, Ereignis, and Conceptual Attunement to the Work of Poetic Genius* (2004). Stambovsky, too, attempts to find a place within Brandom's inferentialist framework for something like the disclosive effects I attribute to metaphor, which Stambovsky describes as the way 'literary art can amplify and transformatively enlarge the inferential form' (2004: 11) of philosophical concepts. Unfortunately, instead of turning to Davidson to define this function, Stambovsky relies on ideas from Heidegger, Rudolf Otto, and William Desmond that reintroduce representational metaphysics.
9. One consequence of deriving an aesthetic theory from pragmatist philosophy of language rather than representationalist epistemology is that the aesthetic must be regarded as a set of social practices rather than as a particular class of inner representations.
10. Rorty's public/private distinction is obviously very different from the one Kant has in mind in distinguishing the mental representations involved in aesthetic judgements from public discourse. While the latter is the distinction between the inner realm of the mind and social practices outside it, the former is the distinction between social practices that require consensus and those that do not.
11. Curiously, Kant anticipates much of Davidson's conception of what metaphors accomplish in his discussion of the aesthetic idea, a notion his commentators often overlook or dismiss. Such ideas even seem, for Kant, to be associated with metaphor:

> Thus Jupiter's eagle with the lightning in its claws is an attribute of the mighty king of heaven, as the peacock is of his magnificent queen. They do not, like *logical attributes*, represent what lies in our concepts of the sublimity and majesty of creation, but something different, which gives occasion to the Imagination to spread itself over a number of kindred representations, that arouse more thought than can be expressed in a concept determined by words. (Kant 1914: 109–10)

Kirk Pillow makes this connection in his essay 'Jupiter's Eagle and the Despot's Hand Mill: Two Views of Metaphor in Kant' (Pillow 2014), but he associates Kant's view of metaphor with the 'interactionist' view of Max Black instead. Black's views are the primary critical target of Davidson's essay on metaphor because they attribute special meanings to metaphors beyond their literal ones. Kant's obscure and incommunicable 'aesthetic ideas' indeed play an analogous role to that of Black's special 'metaphorical meanings', and both result from thinking of language as a medium for conveying the non-linguistic. The advantage of Davidson's view on metaphor, which follows from his wider view of language as a set of social practices rather than a medium, over both Black's and Kant's is that it accounts for metaphors' mysterious effects by positing nothing beyond the resources of ordinary language. Davidson naturalises metaphors without depriving them of any of their power.

12. E. D. Hirsch makes a distinction between 'meaning' and 'significance', in his *Validity in Interpretation* (Hirsch 1967), that provides one way of understanding the effects of metaphors, given Davidson's claim that they have no special meanings of their own, though Hirsch distinguishes between 'meaning' and 'significance' by suggesting that the former requires authorial intent while the latter does not. Davidson, on the other hand, is more inclined to see the 'intimations' of metaphors as intended by their authors. For a discussion of Hirsch that appears to assimilate his idea of 'significance' to Davidson's 'intimation', see Rorty's essay 'Texts and Lumps' (Rorty 1991b).
13. The aesthetic Johnson attributes to Thoreau is not Kant's aesthetic, but merely the other side of the coin that is put in play when aesthetic experience and value are conceived in terms of representation. It is, one might say, the 'empiricist' counterpart to Kant's 'rationalist' or 'idealist' aesthetic, finding aesthetic value in the unconceptualised 'content' of a representation rather than in its unconceptualised 'form'.
14. Another problem, of course, with the aesthetic Johnson finds in the later Thoreau is that it raises all the same problems of scepticism that representationalism always raises. How can we ever tell if a writer has adequately captured 'nature's truth' or significance rather than merely projecting the human versions onto nature? The reply that we can tell by looking for literal rather than metaphorical language doesn't help because literalness may only be the language we currently agree upon – literal language can be false.
15. According to Johnson, 'metaphors are just as likely to partake of culturally constructed systems of value as they are to convey fresh modes of perception' (Johnson 2009: 199). That is probably because her understanding of metaphor is informed mostly by the theory of George Lakoff and Mark Johnson, whose claims about metaphors really only apply to metaphors after they have 'died' or become a part of a culture's conventions. That is one reason she thinks metaphor is unable to capture the kind of natural meaning that 'resists representation in conventional uses of language' (Johnson 2009: 181). But as Davidson shows, metaphors like those that Thoreau creates in *Walden* are decidedly unconventional uses of language, and they are potential sources of 'fresh modes of perception' as long as they remain alive.
16. This is, in fact, the title of a book by another contemporary pragmatist philosopher, Huw Price, and it might well have served as a subtitle for *Walden* (Price 2011).
17. Johnson is quite right to say that in *Walden* nature functions 'largely as a means to self-cultivation and as a symbol of the possibility of human enlightenment' (Johnson 2009: 191), but this can only be the lack of humility with which she charges Thoreau if he is neglecting an additional duty to represent nature accurately.

Bibliography

Brandom, Robert B. (1994), *Making It Explicit: Reasoning, Representing, and Discursive Commitment*, Cambridge, MA: Harvard University Press.
Brandom, Robert B. (2000a), *Articulating Reasons: An Introduction to Inferentialism*, Cambridge, MA: Harvard University Press.
Brandom, Robert B. (ed.) (2000b), *Rorty and His Critics*, Oxford: Blackwell.
Brandom, Robert B. (2010), 'Reply to Charles Taylor's "Language Not Mysterious?"', in Bernhard Weiss and Jeremy Wanderer (eds), *Reading Brandom: On* Making It Explicit, New York: Routledge, pp. 301–4.

Brandom, Robert B. (2011a), 'Analyzing Pragmatism: Pragmatics and Pragmatisms', in Robert B. Brandom, *Perspectives on Pragmatism: Classical, Recent, and Contemporary*, Cambridge, MA: Harvard University Press, pp. 56–82.

Brandom, Robert B. (2011b), 'Vocabularies of Pragmatism: Synthesizing Naturalism and Historicism', in Robert B. Brandom, *Perspectives on Pragmatism: Classical, Recent, and Contemporary*, Cambridge, MA: Harvard University Press, pp. 116–57.

Buell, Lawrence (1973), *Literary Transcendentalism: Style and Vision in the American Renaissance*, Ithaca: Cornell University Press.

Davidson, Donald (1984), 'What Metaphors Mean', in Donald Davidson, *Inquiries into Truth and Interpretation*, Oxford: Clarendon Press, pp. 245–64.

Davidson, Donald (1986), 'A Nice Derangement of Epitaphs', in Ernest LePore (ed.), *Truth and Interpretation: Perspectives on the Philosophy of Donald Davidson*, Oxford: Blackwell, pp. 433–46.

Dewey, John (1989), *The Later Works of John Dewey, 1925–1953, Vol. 10: 1934, Art as Experience*, Jo Ann Boydston (ed.), Carbondale: Southern Illinois University Press.

Faflik, David (2013), 'Deep Thought, Shallow Aesthetic: Reading Surface Meaning in Thoreau', *American Literature*, 85:1, pp. 61–91.

Forster, Michael N. (2014), 'Kant's Philosophy of Language?', in Frank Schalow and Richard L. Velkley (eds), *The Linguistic Dimension of Kant's Thought: Historical and Critical Essays*, Evanston: Northwestern University Press, pp. 81–104.

Furtak, Rick Anthony (2012), 'The Value of Being: Thoreau on Appreciating the Beauty of the World', in Rick Anthony Furtak, Jonathan Ellsworth, and James D. Reid (eds), *Thoreau's Importance for Philosophy*, New York: Fordham University Press, pp. 112–26.

Hansen, Olaf (1990), *American Individualism and Practical Intellect: American Allegory in Emerson, Thoreau, Adams, and James*, Princeton: Princeton University Press.

Hirsch, E. D. (1967), *Validity in Interpretation*, New Haven: Yale University Press.

Johnson, Rochelle L. (2009), *Passions for Nature: Nineteenth-Century America's Aesthetics of Alienation*, Athens: University of Georgia Press.

Kant, Immanuel (1914), *The Critique of Judgment*, J. H. Bernard (trans.), 2nd edn, London: Macmillan.

Matthiessen, F. O. (2009), *American Renaissance: Art and Expression in the Age of Emerson and Whitman*, New York: Barnes and Noble.

Pillow, Kirk (2014), 'Jupiter's Eagle and the Despot's Hand Mill: Two Views of Metaphor in Kant', in Frank Schalow and Richard L. Velkley (eds), *The Linguistic Dimension of Kant's Thought: Historical and Critical Essays*. Evanston: Northwestern University Press, pp. 107–33.

Price, Huw (2011), *Naturalism without Mirrors*, Oxford: Oxford University Press.

Rorty, Richard (1979), *Philosophy and the Mirror of Nature*, Princeton: Princeton University Press.

Rorty, Richard (1991a), 'Unfamiliar Noises: Hesse and Davidson on Metaphor', in Richard Rorty, *Philosophical Papers, Vol. 2: Objectivity, Relativism, and Truth*, Cambridge: Cambridge University Press, pp. 162–72.

Rorty, Richard (1991b), 'Texts and Lumps', in Richard Rorty, *Philosophical Papers, Vol. 2: Objectivity, Relativism, and Truth*, Cambridge: Cambridge University Press, pp. 78–92.

Rorty, Richard (1998), 'Robert Brandom on Social Practices and Representations', in Richard Rorty, *Philosophical Papers, Vol. 3: Truth and Progress*, Cambridge: Cambridge University Press, pp. 122–37.

Schalow, Frank and Richard L. Velkley (eds) (2014), *The Linguistic Dimension of Kant's Thought: Historical and Critical Essays*, Evanston: Northwestern University Press.

Sellars, Wilfrid (1963), 'Empiricism and the Philosophy of Mind', in Wilfrid Sellars, *Science, Perception, and Reality*, New York: Humanities Press, pp. 127–96.

Shusterman, Richard (1997), *Practicing Philosophy: Pragmatism and the Philosophical Life*, New York: Routledge.

Shusterman, Richard (2000), *Pragmatist Aesthetics: Living Beauty, Rethinking Art*, 2nd edn, Lanham: Rowman and Littlefield.

Stambovsky, Phillip (2004), *Philosophical Conceptualization and Literary Art: Inference, Ereignis, and Conceptual Attunement to the Work of Poetic Genius*, Madison: Fairleigh Dickinson University Press.

Taylor, Charles (2010), 'Language Not Mysterious?', in Bernhard Weiss and Jeremy Wanderer (eds), *Reading Brandom: On Making It Explicit*, New York: Routledge, pp. 32–46.

Thoreau, Henry David (1906a), *The Writings of Henry David Thoreau, Journal II: 1850–September 15, 1851*, Bradford Torrey (ed.), Boston: Houghton Mifflin.

Thoreau, Henry David (1906b), *The Writings of Henry David Thoreau, Vol. 2: Walden*, Boston: Houghton Mifflin.

Vescio, Bryan (2014), *Reconstruction in Literary Studies: An Informalist Approach*, New York: Palgrave.

Waxman, Wayne (2005), *Kant and the Empiricists: Understanding Understanding*, New York: Oxford University Press.

Weiss, Bernhard and Jeremy Wanderer (eds) (2010), *Reading Brandom: On Making It Explicit*, New York: Routledge.

Wittgenstein, Ludwig (1958), *Philosophical Investigations*, 3rd edn, G. E. M. Anscombe (trans.), New York: Macmillan.

Wittgenstein, Ludwig (2003), *Tractatus Logico-Philosophicus*, C. K. Ogden (trans.), New York: Barnes and Noble.

Wood, Robert (2014), 'The Place of Language: From Kant to Hegel', in Frank Schalow and Richard L. Velkley (eds), *The Linguistic Dimension of Kant's Thought: Historical and Critical Essays*, Evanston: Northwestern University Press, pp. 29–52.

PART V

Embodiment as Ethics: Literature and Life in the Anthropocene

Editor's Introduction

Frida Beckman

Concern about the environment, about ecology, and about the destructive if not devastating effect of the human species on what until recently was simply referred to as 'nature' is hardly new to either philosophy or literature. Even if we were to limit ourselves to the more recent history of the public acknowledgement of the fact of climate change – most explicitly accounted for with the concept of the Anthropocene – the field is, like most fields, too rich to account for over the course of a few pages or chapters. The concept's prehistory includes the agricultural development of some twelve thousand years ago, the inventions and advancements of the industrial revolution beginning some two hundred and fifty years ago, scientific discoveries such as the first pointers towards the impact of burning coal on global temperature some one hundred and thirty years ago, the mathematical calculations indicating increasing temperatures some seventy years ago, and Rachel Carson's *Silent Spring* some fifty-five years ago, which was, in turn, important to the increasing public and political awareness and activist engagement with environmental concerns some fifty years ago. Some thirty years ago, French philosopher Michel Serres outlined the 'objective violence' done to the earth superseding the 'subjective violence' of interhuman wars in his book *The Natural Contract*. And some twenty years ago, Paul Crutzen brought the concept of the Anthropocene to public consciousness, essentially suggesting that human life has had such a fundamental impact on earth and the climate that we need to recognise the history of this impact as a new geological epoch.

In the millennial years that have followed Crutzen's remark, this terminology, alongside the increasing urgency and tangibility of climate change, has assisted in formulating and bringing together the fields of philosophy and literature in novel and vital ways. With its profound implications for thinking about the prerequisites as well as the effects and limits of human life as we have known it in Western modernity, this 'game changer', as Claire Colebrook puts it, puts pressure on the humanist tradition as a whole. Human narratives appear, she notes, increasingly parochial in the face of the geological temporality and logic with which we have tampered without being able to grasp the implications. This parochialism can be said to include concepts and conceptions central to philosophical and literary investigations alike, concepts such as subjectivity, identity, temporality, and history.

This parochialism and its implications are also fundamentally ethical and representational. The ethical and representational challenges are, of course, many, but I would like to point specifically to what has emerged as a key dilemma. To begin with, the increasing pressures of climate change and its implications for the present as well as the future have generated a more acute awareness of the precariousness and ethics of embodiment. Questions such as where life will be possible, for how long life will be possible, what kind of life will be possible, and under what conditions life will be possible challenge abstract humanist ideals and bring long-existing problems of inequality, geopolitics, and anthropocentrism into sharper relief. It seems we have already decided, however – built in, as it were, in the logic of capitalism and liberalism themselves – that some lives can and must be sacrificed. These include numerous nonhuman species, numerous human lives in exposed areas and situations, and many if not all lives of future generations of human and nonhuman species alike.

In this light, and in the face of these long-term implications and geological dimensions, the narratives that we have used to try to account for embodied and situated life stories seem profoundly inadequate to do so. The vastness of geological temporality is nothing new to science but it has not previously been of much concern for literature. Western modern literature and the novel in particular are built on an interest in the fate of individual destinies to the extent that efforts to move beyond temporalities pertaining to them put pressure on the novel form itself. Efforts to accommodate this pressure are, indeed, increasingly common, as for example in the works of David Mitchell and Jeanette Winterson, works that try to situate the brevity of human life in relation to larger temporalities and implications. As Adam Trexler shows in what is one of the first book-length studies on the topic, what he calls 'Anthropocene fiction' novels composed in the context of this awareness challenge key literary components including time, setting, character, and representation.

This section of our collection offers four contributions all of which explore these ethical and representational challenges to philosophy and literature in different ways. Thus, we can see how Astrid Bracke, in 'Living to Tell the Story: Characterisation, Narrative Perspective, and Ethics in Climate Crisis Flood Novels', brings together philosophical investigations of climate change ethics with what has emerged as a research field called econarratology. With the help of a set of 'flood novels' – *The Flood* (2004) by Maggie Gee, *The Ship* (2015) by Antonia Honeywell, and Clare Morrall's *When the Floods Came* (2015) – Bracke explores the ethical dimensions of climate change – who gets to survive and whose perspective gets to be formulated – against the narratological conditions that enable or disable such storytelling. Addressing the ethics of privilege as well as intergenerational responsibility, she explores how central narrative components such as characterisation and narrative perspective are challenged in literature that strives to explore the ethical dimensions and implications of climate change.

In the next contribution, 'Contemporary Anthropocene Novels: Ian McEwan's *Solar*, Jeanette Winterson's *The Stone Gods*, Margaret Atwood's *Oryx and Crake* and *The Year of the Flood*', Robert P. Marzec explores how each of these novels interrogates the challenges of climate change. More specifically, he explores the portrayal in these novels of what he calls 'the scopic human', a species particular to well-to-do parts of the world and characterised by its insistence on overconsumption in combination with persistent externalisation of ecological responsibility. This is a sort of human that affects environments 'on a planetary scale' while simultaneously denying 'being a part of those environments'. The novels Marzec explores all portray and problematise this scopic creature and illuminate the ethical implications of the rationality that underpins it. They thereby point to the way in which the scopic human is the 'individualised embodiment of the accident' called the Anthropocene, the notion of the accident understood in Paul Virilio's sense as a component not incidental but integral to the substance of modern existence itself. This modern existence is governed by neoliberal political practices, which, under the auspices of sustainability, nonetheless require the continued externalisation of the problem of climate change. Literature is essential here, Marzec argues, as it enables a potentiality, an imagining of forms of human individuality and space-time beyond the otherwise seemingly inevitable prospect of extinction.

Approaching these challenges to philosophical and literary discourse posed by climate change quite literally, the third contribution to this section adopts a formally experimental mode. In 'The Day of the Dark Precursor: Philosophy, Fiction, and Fabulation at the End of the World', Charlie Blake suggests that where literary fiction and philosophy as separated and as conceived in their more traditional formats struggle to find the tools to investigate our Anthropocene present, what is sometimes called 'theory-fiction', or 'philosophiction', or 'fictocriticism' might be more attuned to investigating such challenges. Indeed, his own contribution is itself an example of such a hybrid mode of expression, a mode he traces through philosophers and authors such as Georges Bataille, Gilles Deleuze and Félix Guattari, Luce Irigaray, William S. Burroughs, Jorge Luis Borges, and Kathy Acker. Drawing on Deleuze's concept of 'fabulation', that is, an opening towards the 'people yet to come', Blake engages philosophy and literature to set up a 'fabulating machine', as a 'map and compass' to navigate through the 'post-Anthropocene age'. Such a machine enables a 'transversal ethics' as it opens for an engagement with climate change beyond the disciplines.

The fourth and last contribution to this section, finally, expresses an Anthropocene ethics in the form of literature. Indeed, Adrian Parr's poem 'So to Speak' rubs our faces in the injustice of environmental crisis by refusing to allow us to distance or shield ourselves from it with the help of scientific or academic discourse. Letting beautiful and ugly words and worlds meet, the poetic form allows Parr to show us a world in which the earth is cracking from heat and hunger on the one side while those inhabiting the other are getting high on artificial success, all while the migratory birds hover somewhere in between. Parr's poem reminds us that we not only need to interrogate the parochiality of human narratives but also to continue exploring and embracing ways in which literature can enable us to re-engage with the world.

While obviously not exhaustive of the field, the four chapters of this section do introduce and elaborate on many of the literary and philosophical key thinkers, writers, and concerns of the Anthropocene.

16

Living to Tell the Story: Characterisation, Narrative Perspective, and Ethics in Climate Crisis Flood Novels

Astrid Bracke

Global warming is linked to increased flooding in most European countries, as well as in other areas around the world (Alfieri et al. 2018: 1–9). In Britain, changing environmental and climatological circumstances will make floods twenty times more likely by 2080, affecting at least twice as many people as are currently at risk from flooding. Floods are literal and figurative symbols of climate change. The image of the flood captures feeling overwhelmed as a result of climate crisis and the fear of sudden rather than gradual environmental collapse when the moment of no return has been passed. It is hardly surprising, then, that so many twenty-first-century British fictions imagine a very wet future for Britain. In this chapter I discuss a number of postmillennial British flood fictions that explore the ethical dilemmas of climate change. By bringing literary studies – especially ecocriticism and narratology – into conversation with climate ethics, I show how characterisation and narrative perspective foreground problematic issues of privilege and inequality. The novels explored moreover test the limits of narrating climate crisis by challenging the significance of knowledge and the nature of narrative itself in the Anthropocene.

Increased cultural awareness of environmental crisis shows in the rise of what critics and reviewers have called 'climate fictions': genre and literary fictions about changing political, socio-economic, cultural, and environmental changes due to climate change.[1] The novels that I focus on in this chapter can be said to constitute a subgenre, that of the climate crisis flood novel.[2] These works are part of a tradition of flood narratives going back to origin stories such as the Bible, the epic of Gilgamesh, and Greek and Roman mythologies, as well as a British tradition of novels including Richard Jefferies's *After London* and *The Drowned World* by J. G. Ballard (Jefferies 1885; Ballard 2012). As I show in what follows, in Maggie Gee's *The Flood*, Antonia Honeywell's *The Ship*, and Clare Morrall's *When the Floods Came* (Gee 2004; Honeywell 2015; Morrall 2015) floods provide a lens through which to explore the large-scale socio-economic and political crises caused and exacerbated by environmental change.

The issues that climate crisis presents are ethical as much as socio-economic, political, and cultural problems: '[p]reserving the conditions for the continuation of human life on our planet', Robin Attfield suggests, 'has become an ethical issue, as have responsibilities with regard to the rest of the biosphere' (Attfield 2010: 183). Stories such as those I examine in this chapter are optimally suited to exploring these ethical issues. They ask questions about who gets to survive, who is most affected, and whose story gets told. They explore issues of privilege, of survival, and of blame. In a time of global climate crisis, novels function as experimental spaces in which actual and imagined circumstances are played out, in which ethical and moral dilemmas are considered, and in which the changing world can be explored. The novel produces 'new perspectival forms with which to picture the world' (Boxall 2013: 7), and its imaginative capacities 'have made it a vital site for the articulation of the Anthropocene' (Trexler 2015: 23). In this chapter, I bring flood fiction together with recent philosophical work on especially the ethics of climate change. I will demonstrate how novels may be approached as moral test tubes in which the dilemmas of the Anthropocene are played out, including the ethical challenges raised by environmental change. In doing so, the novels engage directly with climate ethics, and particularly intergenerational ethics.

My reading of twenty-first-century flood fictions is informed by ecocriticism and narratology, and the field that is developing at the intersections of these fields, econarratology.[3] Since its inception in the 1990s, ecocriticism has been concerned with studying representations of nature, emphasising how textual landscapes are founded in real, physical landscapes.[4] Surprisingly, it has been relatively slow to engage with climate crisis. For many ecocritics, 'climate change [was seen] as a human incursion into ecosystems or Nature writ large, rather than a process that inextricably binds together human and nonhuman systems' (Trexler 2015: 17). Since the late 2000s, ecocriticism has become increasingly concerned with environmental crisis, and particularly with the challenges that it poses to the imagination. Scholarship on the topic can be said to roughly fall into one of two categories: the normative, prescriptive approach to climate crisis novels, or the objective, descriptive approach, as Adeline Johns-Putra delineates it (Johns-Putra 2016). In the first, critics read novels and other texts in order to distil lessons from them. Seen from this perspective, novels should answer questions about how we should live in a time of climate change, or even how to prevent a worsening of climate change. This stance fits in well with ecocriticism's activist roots, and with those who see literary criticism as a form of real-world action. Those critics approaching literature from the second perspective focus on the representation of climate crisis in literature, paying especial attention to the tension between an event generally perceived as almost un-narratable, and the narrative constraints posed by the novel as a form. This chapter is an example of the second kind of ecocritical scholarship, especially in its focus on the narratological dimensions of climate crisis flood novels, and the narrative challenges posed by climate change. It discusses, as Pieter Vermeulen puts it, 'the resources of the literary narrative *not* to shape ethical and political action, but rather to come to terms with the finitude of human life', and in this case, the fate of human narratives (Vermeulen 2017: 870).

In the following pages, I will bring these perspectives into dialogue with moral philosophy and climate ethics. Much like ecocriticism, philosophy has also been slow to engage with climate change: Martin Schönfeld noted in 2010 that 'there is as yet no systematic, concerted, or rational inquiry into the phenomenon of climate and its ontological and meta-ethical aspects' (Schönfeld 2010: 21). As the criticism I engage with shows, a growing body of philosophical work is developing that explores particularly the moral and ethical challenges presented by climate crisis. I use these perspectives in combination with econarratology to focus on ethical issues central to *The Flood*, *The Ship*, and *When the Floods Came* through the narratological concepts of characterisation and narrative perspective. In the chapter's coda, I turn to the narrative challenges that climate change poses.

Characterisation and Privilege

Flood fictions constitute a particularly productive subgenre of climate fiction because they explicitly tackle the spatial and temporal challenges that the Anthropocene poses to the human imagination. The flooded landscape localises climate crisis by providing a confined space in which the societal, political, and environmental dimensions of the Anthropocene are played out. Moreover, flood fictions build on older narratives while simultaneously extending into the future through climate predictions, thereby establishing a timeline of past and future climate change. Flood fictions as I define them have two main characteristics: first, they use flooding as a literal and figurative image of climate crisis, and second, they internalise the effect of climate change on cultures and societies through narrative fragmentation and language erosion. I will explore this second aspect in the coda to this chapter, in which I briefly discuss how the breaking apart of narrative and language reflects the novels' concern with narratives and knowledge in the (flooded) Anthropocene.

In all three novels that this chapter focuses on, floods have devastated Britain. *The Ship* and *When the Floods Came* are set roughly fifty to eighty years after their publication dates – towards the late twenty-first century. In *The Flood*, the temporal setting is vaguer – indeed, its textual world as a whole is more unfamiliar than that of the other two novels. Throughout, as Sarah Dillon remarks, *The Flood* creates 'alternative worlds that are uncomfortably close to, yet different from, our own' (Dillon 2007: 386). For example, the characters refer frequently to Hesperica, a country on which the country in the novel – Britain, supposedly – has become practically dependent. On a closer look, Hesperica is modelled on the United States, and the novel's initial readers in the 2010s will have easily picked up a reference to Tony Blair from the two main political figures in the novel: Mr Bliss and Mr Bare. Gee's novel also differs from Honeywell's and Morrall's in its narrative perspective by switching between first and third person. Moreover, unlike the other two novels, it focuses on a handful of characters who are not related. *The Ship* and *When the Floods Came*, on the other hand, centre on two families. In *The Ship*, the main character is Lalage, a teenager whose father has filled a ship with five hundred people from all over the globe in an attempt to save them from an increasingly violent and unstable world. *When the Floods Came* is about Roza, a young woman in her early twenties who lives with her parents and siblings in an abandoned flat outside Birmingham. Both works draw explicitly on familiar climate crisis discourse. In *The Ship*, floods have devastated low-lying deltas such as Bangladesh and the Netherlands, and the latter country has also been lost to floods in *When the Floods Came*. Roza mentions that water temperatures in Iceland are still rising, 'after fifty years of warming' (Morrall 2015: 81), and that environmental measures implemented by the government in the past did not stop the floods (Morrall 2015: 7). While neither Lalage nor Roza explicitly uses the phrase 'climate crisis', the events that they mention have become so much a part of climate change discourse that readers will make this connection themselves. In *The Flood*, on the other hand, the actual cause of the near-constant flooding in the novel remains much more implicit. While the incessant rain at the beginning of the novel may very well be a consequence of environmental change, the massive flood that kills the characters at the end of the work is supposedly caused by an asteroid that triggers a tsunami.

Amidst all the political, social, and economic upheaval in the novels, however, the narrators and main characters are fine. Their position shows just how privileged the perspective is that the novels depict. In the middle of national, if not global, crises, Roza, Lalage, and the characters in *The Flood* survive, even thrive. They, as Lalage slowly realises, are better off than most other people around the world. Aboard the ship she hears the stories of people who lost everything: they tell her how their homes were lost in floods, their parents died in pandemics, and their children were killed for food. She, on the other hand, grew up 'in a proper flat, with food and clothes and locks on the door, and because we had these things, it seemed to me that they were available, and anyone who lived without them was making a choice' (Honeywell 2015: 6). The reader is consequently provided with the perspective of the survivors, the lucky few who, due to the narrative perspective, seem the norm. Such exceptionalism is a recurring trope in flood stories. In the epic of Atrahasis a flood is the gods' way of dealing with overpopulation, much as in Ovid's *Metamorphoses* it is Jove's punishment for a humankind corrupted by crime. Similarly, in Genesis, humankind's wickedness leads God to flood the earth, saving only one man and his family: Noah. While the names of those saved differ, all of these ancient flood stories have in common that only the very special survive: the immortal, the divine, and the devout.

The survival of one character or a group of characters in flood stories is often a narrative inevitability: without a survivor, there is no one to tell the story, and arguably, no story to tell, unless an omniscient perspective is chosen of the kind more common in Victorian literature than in twenty-first-century fiction.[5] More importantly, stories require a character or characters that the audience can sympathise with. In the case of these climate crisis flood novels, exceptionalism becomes more than a narratological necessity: it becomes an ethical problem. Not only is the reader likely to empathise with a privileged perspective, they are also likely to underestimate the consequences of climate crisis. How people respond to climate crisis in everyday life remains relatively unexplored: much is to be learned about 'what individuals and groups actually *do* and *believe* when it comes to considering others (including non-human species) as potential targets for ethical consideration in the context of climate change' (Markowitz, Grasso, and Jamieson 2015: 469). At the same time 'people's beliefs about who (or what) should be considered as morally significant are likely to play an important role in shaping our individual and collective responses to climate change' (Markowitz, Grasso, and Jamieson 2015: 469). Narratives provide particularly apt spaces in which to explore such actions and beliefs, emotions, and thoughts. The question of who counts is played out in several ways in the novels. In *The Flood* the separation between the haves and the have-nots is foregrounded through its characterisation, yet broken down by events in the novels. Lottie and Harold, two of the novel's main characters, are amongst those who are wealthy and have remained relatively sheltered from the effects of the floods – much like those who attend one of the main events in the novel, the 'End of the World gala'. The line between the haves and have-nots becomes increasingly thinner as the floods become worse: 'nothing was separate any more. The walls had become thin as paper. Thieves moved through doors and windows like smoke. The rage round the Towers spread out in slow ripples' (Gee 2004: loc. 1257). As Lalage realises in *The Ship*, the survival of the few often happens at the expense of the many. In order to fill the ship with sufficient supplies, her father, Michael, hoards goods that could have saved others in the present, and not just his own people in the future. Lalage feels that 'they had altered the world's balance – that the ship was not so much an escape from hunger as the cause of it' (Honeywell 2015: 111). Unlike her father, she is aware of the role of mediated responsibilities in a time of crisis: responsibilities in which 'there is one or another kind of distance or gap between action and foreseeable impacts' (Attfield 2010: 184). An everyday example of mediated responsibility is how the decision of consumers in one area of the world to buy a certain product creates the incentive for producers to pollute in another part of the world. In his exploration of mediated responsibilities, Attfield notes that it is frequently uncertain what the impact of a certain action is – or if it will even have an impact. The decision of one consumer may arguably make them feel as if they are not personally responsible for the working or living conditions of people they will never meet, living thousands of kilometres away. Similarly, Michael's hoarding of supplies has no immediate effect on others as far as he can, or wants to, see. While environmental change is forcing us to rethink our ethical responsibilities (Attfield 2010: 193), Michael ignores these. Instead, the sociopolitical and economic collapse is an opportunity for him to live his dream: once the ship leaves the harbour, he becomes a leader, a saviour admired by hundreds.

In *When the Floods Came*, Roza and her family are also saved – without really having to do anything themselves. At the beginning of the novel, Roza lives an extremely sheltered life, with little to no contact with what remains of the British population. That she and her family survived at all is because of their immunity to Hoffman's disease, a contagious illness that has killed much of the British population. Towards the end of the novel, it is suggested that Roza and her family are even more exceptional when they are literally saved from the flood. After a stranger attempts to kill her and her family – and succeeds in murdering her fiancé – Roza and her family are airlifted out of the floods by a Chinese helicopter. Apparently, Roza and her brother Boris were so much appreciated by the Chinese company they worked for that the Chinese sent a rescue mission halfway across the world when they believed them to be in trouble. A new life awaits the family in Brighton, the government seat. This event reinforces a belief that Lalage expresses in *The Ship*: she and the others aboard are 'the good people who had escaped from the bad people' (Honeywell 2015: 125). In this sense, the novel explicitly engages with the question that Claire Colebrook argues is central to post-apocalyptic literature and film: 'What is it about humanity that one would want to accept?' (Colebrook 2014: 190). In other words, which elements of humanity and humankind are worth saving, or, to put it differently, make the survival of the human species worthwhile?[6] In post-apocalyptic flood novels such as *The Ship* the answer to this question is either those smart enough to work the system, like Lalage's father, are worth it, or those who are lucky enough to be saved by others, like Roza and her family and the people aboard Michael's ship in *The Ship*. Survival, then, is often presented as primarily a consequence of having the right genes, or knowing powerful people, and worth is often not what makes people survive: it is their mere survival that somehow suggests that they are worthy.

First-Person Narration and Privilege

A sense of exceptionalism and privilege is expressed in these novels not just through characterisation, but also through narrative perspective. By means of their first-person perspectives, *The Flood*, *The Ship*, and *When the Floods Came* reinforce an emphasis on survival as available only for the lucky few. All three novels are narrated by a first-person narrator, participating in and reporting on events. As such, the narrators are the sole centres of focalisation: the reader only gets to see the textual world through the eyes of Lalage, Roza, and, to some extent, an unnamed narrator in *The Flood*. In *The Flood* the narrative perspective is complicated by the work's structure: the first and last sections of the novel – titled 'Before' and 'After' respectively – are told by an unnamed first-person narrator. The rest of the novel is embedded in this frame-tale, and is told from a third-person narrative perspective.[7] In any novel, narrative perspective and focalisation colour the reader's interpretation of events. As David Herman puts it,

> to say that an event or object or participant is focalised in a certain manner is to say that it is perspectivally indexed, structured so that it has to be interpreted as refracted through a specific viewpoint and anchored in a particular set of contextual coordinates. (Herman 2002: 302–3)

The phrase 'refracted through a specific viewpoint' is important here: the narrators' experiences of climate change in the novels preclude any kind of view outside of their own. For the reader, then, an alternative perspective on (the consequences of) environmental crisis is not available within the novel.

Yet a first-person narrative perspective may not only have problematic effects. Extending my analysis of narrative perspective in flood fictions through Tim Mulgan's work on future-oriented second-personalism shows that the first person may provide a conversation with future people that might influence the choices we make today.[8] The 'second person' in Mulgan's sense is the other who is affected by our current choices, but whom we will never meet, and therefore struggle to take into account when we make choices that have consequences for the future. In flood fictions it is the first-person narrative perspective that achieves the kind of second-personal perspective Mulgan advocates. The characters in these novels live in what Mulgan calls a 'broken world'. In such a broken world, 'resources are insufficient to meet everyone's basic needs, a chaotic climate makes life precarious, each generation is worse-off than the last, and our affluent way of life is no longer an option' (Mulgan 2018: 536). The difficulty that people have in imagining this future makes literature a particularly apt and productive thought experiment.[9] A key element of second-personalism as Mulgan defines it is that people recognise their own obligations towards other people. This happens when the people in the broken world 'acknowledge the importance of favourable conditions' (Mulgan 2018: 539), and particularly how they lost these conditions because of the actions of their forebears. Through fictional future people – as in novels, for instance – those in the present become more aware of their obligations. In other words, for early twenty-first-century people to take responsibility for the future and future people, fictional future people should – literally – speak to them, as happens in flood fictions. Both Roza and Lalage are acutely aware that the circumstances they are living in are the result of what people in the past did or did not do. In conversation with her mother, for instance, Roza learns that the anti-pollution laws that were passed when her mother was younger caused economic collapse because tourists stopped coming to Britain. Moreover, the laws, she thinks, 'were pointless, far too late to be of any use' (Morrall 2015: 7). In *The Ship*, Lalage is even more explicit: 'I was angry at the stupidity of the generations before mine that had brought us to this place' (Honeywell 2015: 36). The future's explicit reference to the past also has a narratological effect: it establishes a sense of futurity, enabling the reader to place the stories in time. Readers tend to compare the fictional world to their own, actual world. Through a series of spatial and temporal cues provided by the narrative, the reader tries to place the narrative in respect to their own time. For instance, if a novel describes the discovery of the steam engine, the reader will place the story in a past relative to their own time – if the novel is populated by artificial intelligence, they will place it in the future. Marie-Laure Ryan terms this process of interpretation the principle of minimal departure, suggesting that

> we construe the central world of a textual universe ... as conforming as far as possible to our representation of AW [the actual or real world]. We will project upon these worlds everything we know about reality, and we will make only the adjustments dictated by the text. (Ryan 1992: 51)

Interestingly, dystopian fiction often depicts the future as a return to the past: Lalage describes, for instance, how 'pleasure islands that had been raised from the oceans melted back into them as though they had never existed' (Honeywell 2015: 1–2).

Nonetheless, dystopian post-apocalyptic novels such as flood fictions primarily contain cues that create a sense of futurity. Roza's and Lalage's reflections on their past – our present – are temporal cues that enable a reader's transportation from their own time into the future; a movement made arguably easier if a reader is able to sympathise with a first-person narrator.

The first-person perspective of these flood fictions, then, achieves several things: it foregrounds a problematic sense of privilege that the reader might apply to their own chances of survival, and downplays the severity of climate crisis. At the same time, the perspective plays a role in achieving the kind of second-personal justification that Mulgan proposes is central to thinking through the consequences of our current actions on future people. The principle of minimal departure achieved through temporal cues is furthermore strengthened by the use of first-person narrators, possibly allowing readers a smoother transition into the future. Before turning to the novels' concern with narratives and knowledge in the Anthropocene, I want to explore one final consequence of the first-person perspective, namely the role it plays in thinking through intergenerational ethics in the novels.

Climate change is an inherently intergenerational issue. Even if all emissions were to end tomorrow, the climate would continue to change for the worst for centuries to come. In especially *The Ship* and *When the Floods Came*, the intergenerational dimension of environmental crisis is played out through the children, teenagers, and young adults that populate the novels. Lalage is sixteen years old, a teenager about to have a child of her own. Her father's ambitious plan to equip a ship for five hundred people to spend the rest of their lives on is explicitly an intergenerational project, an attempt to give his child a better future, despite the fact that he and his forebears contributed to what Mulgan calls a 'broken world'. Lalage's father tells her: 'I wanted you to have a chance to live with higher thoughts than where to find food' (Honeywell 2015: 77). Here he repeats a well-known feature of environmentalist discourse: that the current generation has to save the planet for future generations, for our children and grandchildren. Lalage, interpreting this not as an act of care, but as a burden, promises her unborn child that she will never say this – although her decision to leave the ship to seek an alternative at the end of the novel may come down to the same thing. This kind of future-thinking, or what Lee Edelman (2004) has called 'reproductive futurism',[10] has been critiqued especially by queer scholars, who have explored the extent to which, as Catriona Sandilands puts it, 'the future Child serve[s] as a naturalizing alibi for a narrowly, even destructively, hetero-reproductive present' (Sandilands 2014: 309). In much environmentalist discourse, the child functions as a symbol for the future, as a reason for current sacrifice and struggle – much as Michael tries to gloss over the ethical issues surrounding his ship by telling Lalage he wanted to secure a better future for her. In *When the Floods Came* the association between children and the future is so strong that children are frequently kidnapped because they are so rare. Those that have survived 'belong to an exclusive club' (Morrall 2015: 83). They are, Roza's father tells her, 'like heirlooms', not echoing the past, but representing the future (Morrall 2015: 77). The privileged position of Roza and her family shows once more in the fact that her parents have four children, and lost none of them to disease or violence. Yet as the novel progresses, a disturbing fact emerges about Roza's youngest sister, Lucia. She is not, in fact, the family's 'first' Lucia. The first Lucia was lost in a flood. A little while later, another girl – the 'second' Lucia – was found wandering near the flats. The family adopted her without ever really making explicit to Lucia or each other that this is an odd situation, made even more disturbing when Aashay, the mysterious stranger, explains to Roza that there are markets for children. Roza and her family, he explains, are '[Lucia's] third owners, not the second ... Where she came from originally isn't the point. She's a child, and she's currency' (Morrall 2015: 318). The importance that is placed on children in *The Ship* and *When the Floods Came* raises questions central to intergenerational ethics:

> Can future people be understood to have rights? In particular, can they be understood to have rights vis-à-vis currently living people? Can currently living people through their actions affect how and whether those rights are fulfilled or violated? What obligations, if any, do currently living people stand under owing to the rights that future people will have, and to the (possible) impact of their actions on future people? (Sanklecha 2017: 3)

The Ship and *When the Floods Came* in particular provide relatively straightforward answers to these questions: previous generations did have a duty towards the future people depicted in these works, and they failed.

Yet the discussion of intergenerational ethics and the future of humankind can, and should, be taken a step further. From an environmentalist perspective the issue should not be working for a better future for our children and grandchildren, but rather having fewer, or no, children at all. As Garrard suggests, '[p]erhaps we need not to be taught to love nature more, but to love children less' (Garrard 2012b: 56), a point reinforced by Lawrence Buell's argument that environmental sustainability goals 'should assign a higher priority to curtailing world population increase' (Buell 2016: 24). In his discussion of climate ethics and population policy, Philip Cafaro argues along similar lines as Garrard and Buell: '[e]nding human population growth is almost certainly a necessary (but not sufficient) condition for preventing catastrophic global climate change' (Cafaro 2012: 48). Population control is rarely mentioned by policymakers, politicians, and environmentalists (Cafaro 2012: 48), even though reducing population growth is both cheaper and more effective than many of the other measures put forth to alleviate climate crisis. As Cafaro puts it, 'less people is the environmental gift that keeps on giving' (Cafaro 2012: 7). The issue is not merely the effect that current populations have on future people, but also the hardships inflicted on people today because of overpopulation: 'the real point of population control', Garrett Hardin proposes, 'is not to reduce population *per se*, but to reduce misery among the living' (Hardin 1993: 262). Overpopulation no doubt plays a role in the global collapse that has taken place in *The Ship*. In that novel the new government instates a form of population control by executing en masse those that cannot identify themselves. In *When the Floods Came* people are subject to rigorous testing for disease prior to marriage and before being allowed to have children. In the latter novel, Hoffman's disease has considerably reduced the population, especially in Britain, thereby suggesting a kind of restored balance, although it does not lead to a world that can be seen as anything but broken. In *The Flood* the tsunami at the end does away with much of the population of the city in which the novel is set (even though most, if not all, of the characters survive in a kind of afterlife).

Nonetheless, some critics might argue that climate fictions such as the flood novels I focus on in this chapter evade the biggest issue facing us today, namely the possibility of the complete extinction of the human species. Rather than being confronted with the devastating and deadly consequences of climate crisis, the reader is provided by these novels with a way out. Such an escape from crisis is routinely offered by many contemporary (post-)apocalyptic stories. Much as the narrators survive in *The Flood*, *The Ship*, and *When the Floods Came*, so does the hero of the 2014 film *Interstellar* – by aiding the discovery of a new planet – and the misunderstood genius in the 2017 film *Geostorm*, who essentially fixes the climate.[11] In focusing on survival and adaptation and, in the case of the films, expressing a sense of techno-optimism, these narratives keep us from asking whether the human species should survive at all. Colebrook critiques post-apocalyptic film and literature for precisely this reason. She suggests that

> [a]n entire genre of what has come to be known as post-apocalyptic film and literature currently and repeatedly, with ever increasing verve, plays out a fantasy of human near-disappearance and redemption, and does so precisely when our energies ought to be focused on what humans have done to the planet and how they might desist from so doing. (Colebrook 2014: 197)

Instead, she advocates thinking of narrative beyond the human, and going beyond current forms and modes of narrative: 'one might say that climate change should not require us to return to modes of reading, comprehension and narrative communication but should awake us from our human-all-too-human narrative slumbers' (Colebrook 2014: 25). Colebrook, like other critics, points out that contemporary apocalypticism is not so much about the world about to end as it is about survival.[12] According to Renner, twenty-first-century apocalyptic stories, such as the television series *The Walking Dead*,

> do far more than simply affirm our suspicions that our current world is corrupt and encourage us to delight in its destruction. Today's apocalyptic tales appeal to a yearning for experiences that will reveal the undiscovered heroic potential in the most average of us all and establish a new community in which the truly worthy are rewarded. (Renner 2012: 206–7)

In especially *The Ship* and *When the Floods Came*, the protagonists are saved because they are worthy – unlike in *The Flood*, where everyone, regardless, lives on in the afterlife. Imagining the future and even establishing a kind of dialogue with fictional future peoples, then, may not only have the potential benefit of creating awareness and leading to better choices in the present; it might indeed lessen the perceived need for action, as long as the ultimate extinction of the human species (as explored by Colebrook) is not addressed.

Coda: The Trouble with Narratives

A growing body of ecocritical scholarship is concerned with the narrative challenges posed by environmental change. The most frequently mentioned issue is that of the sheer scale of climate crisis, both temporally and spatially.[13] As Garrard suggests, '[n]one of the traditional forms in literature, film, or television documentary is unproblematically suited to capturing the geographical and temporal scale, complexity, and uncertainty of climate change in particular' (Garrard 2009: 709). Climate crisis requires 'creative ways of drawing public attention to catastrophic acts that are low in instant spectacle but high in long-term effects' (Nixon 2011: 10). Some of these creative ways are suggested by Richard Kerridge, when he provides an overview of genres suited to depicting environmental crisis (Kerridge 2014). In a similar vein Heise has argued for the database as a more suitable narrative genre than more traditional formats, and, much as Timothy Morton has, for experimental collage in the modernist tradition (Heise 2010, 2016; Morton 2010). As literary and cultural scholars, ecocritics have been keen to emphasise the role that narratives might play in a time of climate crisis: (new) narratives, they hold, might be required to move 'environmentally oriented thought into the future', rather than 'shackle environmentalism to outdated templates' (Heise and Carruth 2010: 3). While the immediate effect of narratives on environmental awareness is contested,[14] the new narratives argument avoids an issue that resurfaces in much contemporary literature: the fragmentation of narratives themselves. Climate crisis affects narratives, knowledge, and literature to such an extent that in addition to the future loss of material objects it entails the loss of the very novels' structural coherence; the novels themselves fall apart structurally. Vermeulen suggests that environmental change and the possibility of human extinction have begun to alter the function of narrative:

> [U]nderstood as a mode of knowledge, and as a technology through which cultural knowledge is archived in the present, narrative no longer only serves as a way of (cognitively) organising and emplotting human experience, but also as a way of (affectively) apprehending the end of possible human life. (Vermeulen 2017: 867)

Likewise, flood fictions are not only about the finitude of humankind; they also – quite literally – depict the finiteness of narratives. They suggest that not only humankind, but also the fate of literature, relies on survival: without it, there is neither a story to tell, nor someone to tell it (or read it, for that matter).[15] Yet while the flood narrative as it surfaces in the novels discussed above is invested in a story of survival, it cannot prevent that story of survival from cracking, as floods also entail the destruction of literature, of knowledge, and even of storytelling itself.

In all three flood novels, narratives, especially in book form, play an important role: one of the characters in *The Flood* works for a publishing company about to lose its entire archive to the floods, and both Lalage in *The Ship* and Roza in *When the Floods Came* are enchanted when they come across (digital) libraries. In their worlds, books have become scarce. Books and stories, the novels suggest, are important: they provide a connection to the past that Lalage's father is keen to sever in *The Ship*, and consolation to Roza, who insists on taking her copy of *Birds of the British Isles* with her when she travels – as a way of 'touching the past' (Morrall 2015: 117). Narratives, then, are consoling and comforting, providing connections of some sort, especially in a time of crisis. As Derek Attridge proposes, literary works may offer 'profound consolation' to their readers: 'this happens when the experience of the work enables the reader to reconceive his or her situation' (Attridge 2004: 77). Or, as cognitive narratologists hold, narratives help us make sense of the world. It is hardly surprising, then, that the loss of narratives, knowledge, and books coincides in the novels with extensive socio-economic, political, and cultural collapse, caused or exacerbated by climate crisis. This emphasis on narratives and knowledge is the second main characteristic of flood fictions as I define them. In these works, the loss of written narratives and knowledge to the water and chaos of climate change becomes a symbol, even a synecdoche, for the loss of Western civilisation on the one hand, and a reference to the epistemological uncertainty inherent in the Anthropocene on the other.

Some climate crisis novels go even a step further than the novels I have discussed so far: they do not only depict the loss of narratives, they embody it. In novels such as Margaret Atwood's *Oryx and Crake* (Atwood 2003) and Cormac McCarthy's *The Road* (McCarthy 2006), in which a kind of language entropy takes place, 'the exhaustion of narrative is the corollary to the death of the planet', according to Peter Boxall (Boxall 2013: 217).[16] Megan Hunter's *The End We Start From* (Hunter 2017) depicts another flooded London. The novel's fragmented nature, combination of narrative levels, and use of language illustrate what climate crisis, and floods in particular, do to knowledge, to storytelling, and to the way in which we try to make sense of the world. Hunter's novel is highly experimental, consisting of brief passages of text in which an unnamed narrator describes a massive flood that makes London uninhabitable and which subsequently leads to armed conflict in England. Floods have seeped into the narrative of *The End We Start From*, filling it with gaps and uncertainties about the novel's world and the characters that populate it. The narrator's language is moreover saturated with watery similes and her attempts to find the exactly right description to capture the unimaginable effects of the flood. The fragmented nature of the novel symbolises the epistemological uncertainty that characterises climate crisis: despite the models and predictions offered by organisations such as the Intergovernmental Panel on Climate Change, despite the resolutions and conventions, the form and consequences of climate crisis are essentially unknown. Floods are especially hard to predict: while scientists agree that the severity and frequency will increase, floods are in essence very local events, influenced by not only rainfall, but also the particular environment and landscape (Whitfield 2012; Alfieri et al. 2018). The fragmented story told in *The End We Start From*, then, is not only a consequence of the devastating flood, but also embodies the destruction of the familiar world in the most powerful way any text can: by falling apart.

Flood novels present particularly apt spaces in which to imagine and think through climate crisis. Not only do the floods depicted in them correspond to realities and future predictions for many parts of the world, they are also instantly recognisable and relatively easy to picture. Moreover, since they take place in a necessarily constricted environment, flood fictions provide a useful environment for thinking through changing human relationships and the ethical dilemmas that result from climate crisis. How these relationships are played out in novels, and the picture this presents of environmental change, are significantly shaped by narrative elements such as characterisation and narrative perspective. The flood fictions I have explored present an experiment in intergenerational ethics, and hint at the potential benefits of imagining future people and coming face to face with the second person as defined by Mulgan. Yet the loss of narratives in flood fictions and the breaking apart of the very narratives that make up these novels also reflect the deep uncertainty at the heart of the Anthropocene, and the challenges this poses to narratives. A conversation between literary studies and climate ethics foregrounds the ethical issues that we need to face in the present, no matter whether the future holds future people, or human extinction.

Notes

1. The term 'climate fiction' was first coined by Dan Bloom. Adam Trexler's *Anthropocene Fictions: The Novel in a Time of Climate Change* provides the first book-length exploration of the genre, although he prefers to use the term 'Anthropocene fictions' (Trexler 2015).
2. Other British works that can be said to be part of this subgenre include Sarah Hall's *The Carhullan Army* (Hall 2007), Sam Taylor's *The Island at the End of the World* (Taylor 2009), and Megan Hunter's *The End We Start From* (Hunter 2017). Floods are a feature of many climate crisis novels outside of Britain as well, for example Barbara Kingsolver's *Flight Behaviour* (Kingsolver 2012), Nathaniel Rich's *Odds Against Tomorrow* (Rich 2013), and Jeff Vandermeer's *Borne* (Vandermeer 2017). Waterless floods are prominent too, for example in *The Year of the Flood* (Atwood 2009) and *The Trees* (Shaw 2016).
3. As defined by Erin James: '[econarratology] maintains an interest in studying the relationship between literature and the physical environment, but does so with sensitivity to the literary structures and devices that we use to communicate representations of the physical environment to each other via narratives' (James 2015: 23). See also Bernaerts et al. 2014, Lehtimäki 2013, and Herman 2011 for narratologists exploring the intersections of ecocriticism and narratology.

4. While a number of proto-ecocritical works have been identified over the years – for example Leo Marx's *The Machine in the Garden* (Marx 1964), Raymond Williams's *The Country and the City* (Williams 1973), and Joseph Meeker's *The Comedy of Survival* (Meeker 1974) – the field is generally held to have originated from the first anthology of ecocritical works, *The Ecocriticism Reader* (Glotfelty and Fromm 1996). The most comprehensive introductions to date remain Greg Garrard's *Ecocriticism* (Garrard 2012a), *The Oxford Handbook of Ecocriticism* (Garrard 2014), and the *Cambridge Companion to Literature and Environment* (Westling 2014).
5. Indeed, even a third-person perspective often entails the survival of one or several humans. See also Vermeulen's exploration of 'found narratives', studied by a future historian or archaeologist (Vermeulen 2017).
6. For an exploration of extinction and human worth, see also Sanklecha 2017.
7. Interestingly, both the 'Before' and 'After' section are told after the catastrophe has taken place in the novel, from the point of view of what might be thought of as the afterlife.
8. Mulgan bases his second-personal intergenerational ethics on Stephen Darwall's work on the ethical significance of the second-person standpoint (see Darwall 2009).
9. Mulgan himself composes a kind of post-apocalyptic short story in his article, including passages written from the perspective of a future philosopher, reporting on the broken world in which she lives and confronting the business-as-usual approach taken by most people.
10. Sandilands summarises Edelman's argument in *No Future* as follows: 'contemporary politics are dominated by the figure of the Child in a logic in which the kernel of futurity is seen to reside in the innocent child's wellbeing' (Sandilands 2014: 308).
11. For a useful overview of films dealing with climate crisis, and some of the research on their reception, see Svoboda 2016.
12. See also Tate 2017. Karen Renner suggests that Biblical apocalypse, of course, never meant 'the end of the world', but rather the end of the earthly existence and, hopefully, the beginning of existence in heaven (Renner 2012: 204). See also Buell 2016 and my own discussion of apocalypse as a problematic narrative in *Climate Crisis and the 21st-Century British Novel* (Bracke 2018).
13. See, for instance, Timothy Clark's discussion of scale (Clark 2015) and Weik von Mossner 2014. Ursula Heise's *Sense of Place and Sense of Planet* (Heise 2008) is the first extensive ecocritical discussion of scale. A critique of discourses on climate crisis and scale is provided by Derek Woods (Woods 2014).
14. For research on *The Day After Tomorrow* see Hulme 2009: 213–14; Svoboda 2016.
15. See also Garrard's discussion of imagining a world without humans, or 'disanthropy' (Garrard 2012b).
16. Boxall neglects the fact that while in both novels written narratives and written knowledge are lost, oral narratives survive. Relating the loss of narratives to the loss of civilisation, as Boxall and many novels do, presents a very Western perspective that is admittedly problematic.

Bibliography

Alfieri, Lorenzo, Franceso Dottori, Richard Betts, Peter Salamon, and Luc Feyen (2018), 'Multi-Model Projections of River Flood Risk in Europe under Global Warming', *Climate*, 6:16, pp. 1–19.

Attfield, Robin (2010), 'Mediated Responsibilities, Global Warming and the Scope of Ethics', in Ruth Irwin (ed.), *Climate Change and Philosophy: Transformational Possibilities*, London: Continuum, pp. 183–96.
Attridge, Derek (2004), *The Singularity of Literature*, London: Routledge.
Atwood, Margaret (2003), *Oryx and Crake*, New York: Anchor.
Atwood, Margaret (2009), *The Year of the Flood*, London: Bloomsbury.
Ballard, J. G. (2012), *The Drowned World*, New York: W. W. Norton.
Bernaerts, Luc, Marco Caracciolo, Luc Herman, and Bart Vervaeck (2014), 'The Storied Lives of Non-Human Narrators', *Narrative*, 21:1, pp. 68–93.
Boxall, Peter (2013), *Twenty-First-Century Fiction*, Cambridge: Cambridge University Press.
Bracke, Astrid (2018), *Climate Crisis and the 21st-Century British Novel*, London: Bloomsbury.
Buell, Lawrence (2016), 'Anthropocene Panic: Contemporary Ecocriticism and the Issue of Human Numbers', *Frame*, 29:2, pp. 11–27, <http://www.tijdschriftframe.nl/29-2-perspectives-on-the-anthropocene/1449/> (last accessed 8 January 2019).
Cafaro, Philip (2012), 'Climate Ethics and Population Policy', *WIREs Clim Change*, 3, pp. 45–61.
Clark, Timothy (2015), *Ecocriticism on the Edge: The Anthropocene as a Threshold Concept*, London: Bloomsbury.
Colebrook, Claire (2014), *Death of the PostHuman*, Ann Arbor: Open Humanities Press.
Darwall, Stephen (2009), *The Second-Person Standpoint*, Cambridge, MA: Harvard University Press.
Dean Moore, Kathleen and Michael Nelson (eds) (2010), *Moral Ground: Ethical Action for a Planet in Peril*, San Antonio: Trinity University Press.
Dillon, Sarah (2007), 'Imagining Apocalypse: Maggie Gee's *The Flood*', *Contemporary Literature*, 48:3, pp. 374–97.
Edelman, Lee (2004), *No Future: Queer Theory and the Death Drive*, London: Duke University Press.
Gardiner, Stephen (2011), *A Perfect Moral Storm: The Ethical Tragedy of Climate Change*, New York: Oxford University Press.
Garrard, Greg (2009), 'Ian McEwan's Next Novel and the Future of Ecocriticism', *Contemporary Literature*, 50:4, pp. 695–720.
Garrard, Greg (2012a), *Ecocriticism*, 2nd edn, London: Routledge.
Garrard, Greg (2012b), 'Worlds Without Us: Some Types of Disanthropy', *SubStance*, 41:1, pp. 40–60.
Garrard, Greg (ed.) (2014), *The Oxford Handbook of Ecocriticism*, Oxford: Oxford University Press.
Gee, Maggie (2004), *The Flood*, Kindle edn, London: Saqi Books.
Glotfelty, Cheryll and Harold Fromm (eds) (1996), *The Ecocriticism Reader*, Athens: University of Georgia Press.
Hall, Sarah (2007), *The Carhullan Army*, London: Faber and Faber.
Hardin, Garrett (1993), *Living Within Limits: Ecology, Economics, and Population Taboos*, Cambridge: Cambridge University Press.
Heise, Ursula (2008), *Sense of Place and Sense of Planet*, Oxford: Oxford University Press.
Heise, Ursula (2010), 'Lost Dogs, Last Birds, and Listed Species: Cultures of Extinction', *Configurations*, 18:1/2, pp. 49–72.
Heise, Ursula (2016), *Imagining Extinction: The Cultural Meanings of Endangered Species*, Chicago: University of Chicago Press.

Heise, Ursula K. and Allison Carruth (2010), 'Introduction to Focus: Environmental Humanities', *American Book Review*, 32:2, p. 3.
Herman, David (2002), *Story Logic: Problems and Possibilities of Narrative*, Lincoln: University of Nebraska Press.
Herman, David (2011), 'Storyworld/Umwelt: Nonhuman Experiences in Graphic Narratives', *SubStance*, 40:1, pp. 56–181.
Honeywell, Antonia (2015), *The Ship*, London: Weidenfeld and Nicolson.
Hulme, Mike (2009), *Why We Disagree About Climate Change*, Cambridge: Cambridge University Press.
Hunter, Megan (2017), *The End We Start From*, London: Picador.
James, Erin (2015), *The Storyworld Accord: Econarratology and Postcolonial Narratives*, Lincoln: University of Nebraska Press.
Jefferies, Richard (1885), *After London*, e-book, Project Gutenberg, <http://www.gutenberg.org/ebooks/13944> (last accessed 8 January 2019).
Johns-Putra, Adeline (2016), 'Climate Change in Literature and Literary Studies: From Cli-Fi, Climate Change Theater and Ecopoetry to Ecocriticism and Climate Change Criticism', *WIREs Clim Change*, 7, pp. 266–82.
Kerridge, Richard (2014), 'Ecocritical Approaches to Literary Form and Genre: Urgency, Depth, Provisionality, Temporality', in Greg Garrard (ed.), *The Oxford Handbook of Ecocriticism*, Oxford: Oxford University Press, pp. 361–76.
Kingsolver, Barbara (2012), *Flight Behaviour*, London: Faber and Faber.
Lehtimäki, Markku (2013), 'Natural Environments in Narrative Contexts', *Storyworlds*, 5, pp. 119–41.
Markowitz, Ezra M., Marco Grasso, and Dale Jamieson (2015), 'Climate Ethics at a Multidisciplinary Crossroads: Four Directions for Future Scholarship', *Climatic Change*, 130, pp. 465–74.
Marx, Leo (1964), *The Machine in the Garden*, Oxford: Oxford University Press.
McCarthy, Cormac (2006), *The Road*, New York: Knopf.
Meeker, Joseph (1974), *The Comedy of Survival: Literary Ecology and a Play Ethic*, Tucson: University of Arizona Press.
Morrall, Clare (2015), *When the Floods Came*, London: Sceptre.
Morton, Timothy (2010), *The Ecological Thought*, Cambridge, MA: Harvard University Press.
Mulgan, Tim (2018), 'Answering to Future People: Responsibility for Climate Change in a Breaking World', *Journal of Applied Philosophy*, 35:3, pp. 532–48.
Nixon, Rob (2011), *Slow Violence and the Environmentalism of the Poor*, Cambridge, MA: Harvard University Press.
Renner, Karen (2012), 'The Appeal of the Apocalypse', *Lit: Literature Interpretation Theory*, 23:3, pp. 203–11.
Rich, Nathaniel (2013), *Odds Against Tomorrow*, New York: Farrar, Straus and Giroux.
Ryan, Marie-Laure (1992), *Possible Worlds, Artificial Intelligence and Narrative Theory*, Bloomington: Indiana University Press.
Sandilands, Catriona (2014), 'Queer Life? Ecocriticism After the Fire', in Greg Garrard (ed.), *The Oxford Handbook of Ecocriticism*, Oxford: Oxford University Press, pp. 305–19.
Sanklecha, Pranay (2017), 'Should There Be Future People? A Fundamental Question for Climate Change and Intergenerational Justice', *WIREs Clim Change*, 8, pp. 1–11.
Schönfeld, Martin (2010), 'Field, Being, Climate: Climate Philosophy and Cognitive Evolution', in Ruth Irwin (ed.), *Climate Change and Philosophy: Transformational Possibilities*, London: Continuum, pp. 21–31.

Shaw, Ali (2016), *The Trees*, London: Bloomsbury.

Svoboda, Michael (2016), 'Cli-Fi on the Screen(s): Patterns in the Representations of Climate Change in Fictional Films', *WIREs Clim Change*, 7, pp. 43–64.

Tate, Andrew (2017), *Apocalyptic Fiction*, London: Bloomsbury.

Taylor, Sam (2009), *The Island at the End of the World*, London: Faber and Faber.

Trexler, Adam (2015), *Anthropocene Fictions: The Novel in a Time of Climate Change*, Charlottesville: University of Virginia Press.

Vandermeer, Jeff (2017), *Borne*, New York: Farrar, Straus and Giroux.

Vermeulen, Pieter (2017), 'Future Readers: Narrating the Human in the Anthropocene', *Textual Practice*, 31:5, pp. 867–85.

Weik von Mossner, Alexa (2014), 'Science Fiction and the Risks of the Anthropocene: Anticipated Transformations in Dale Pendell's *The Great Bay*', *Environmental Humanities*, 5, pp. 203–16.

Westling, Louise (ed.) (2014), *The Cambridge Companion to Literature and the Environment*, Cambridge: Cambridge University Press.

Whitfield, P. H. (2012), 'Floods in Future Climates: A Review', *Journal of Flood Risk Management*, 5, pp. 336–65.

Williams, Raymond (1973), *The Country and the City*, London: Chatto and Windus.

Woods, Derek (2014), 'Scale Critique for the Anthropocene', *Minnesota Review*, 83, pp. 133–42.

17

Contemporary Anthropocene Novels: Ian McEwan's *Solar*, Jeanette Winterson's *The Stone Gods*, Margaret Atwood's *Oryx and Crake* and *The Year of the Flood*

Robert P. Marzec

Jeanette Winterson's *The Stone Gods*, Margaret Atwood's *Oryx and Crake* and *The Year of the Flood*, and Ian McEwan's *Solar* are all novels dealing with environmental issues, and may be classified by some as climate change fiction, or 'cli-fi'. But they have something else in common. Each confronts from a different angle the transiting of humans from the Holocene into the Anthropocene, a transition that forces our species to come to grips with the enormous consequences of anthropogenic, planet-wide climate change. A good percentage of these global environmental changes that humans of the twentieth and twenty-first centuries have produced is irreversible. It will be 'highly unlikely', for instance, for us to keep below a 2 °F increase, according to the latest report from the Intergovernmental Panel on Climate Change (IPCC 2014), and more likely that the increase will be at least 3 °F. Even if we were by some miracle able to go carbon-neutral tomorrow, sea levels would still rise at least a metre, imperilling an unimaginable number of people living in cities and along shorelines around the planet. At the same time these immensely destructive forces are abominably denied or downplayed, and in some cases maliciously ignored by entities and individuals in both the corporate and the public world. By taking up this unprecedented challenge of the Anthropocene, Atwood, McEwan, and Winterson interrogate some of the reasons why humans repudiate or ignore the very large-scale forces they have come to be. In the process, each author articulates forms of human potential and human embodiment that constitute ethical and feasible alternatives to the anthropogenic norm.

In *Solar*, I will argue, McEwan presents us with a normalised form of Anthropocene human subjectivity manifest in the character of Dr Michael Beard, a Nobel-Prize-winning physicist – intelligent and aware of technological forms of sustainability, yet comically self-destructive and blithely unaware of his own extreme threat to ecosystems. The novel's focus on the specific kind of single-minded science espoused by Beard is instructive for understanding the seductive character of neoliberal discourses of sustainability. There are of course multiple approaches to sustainability, many of which are valuable to the future of human–ecological relations. But Beard's commitment to the logic of his scientific discipline gives us an exemplary case of the kind of siloed logic that fails to consider the complexity of ecological relations continually violated by neoliberalism with its structural commitment to breeding self-centred individuals, and its ruthless prioritising of economic development. Atwood's *Oryx and Crake* delivers a similar kind of anti-hero in Crake, an engineer capable of creating a perfectly sustainable species. Yet Crake is callously blind to the collateral damage wrought by massive genetic engineering efforts, and will go so far as to help engineer the almost total annihilation of the human species. Atwood continues this storyline in *The Year of the Flood*, focalising the efforts of a politically active environmental group called God's Gardeners, a radical assemblage that attempts to maintain a biocentric disposition within a culture dominated by a militarised governmentality. In her novel *The Stone Gods* Winterson interrogates the kind of Anthropocene subjectivity generated by neoliberalism's unholy marriage to today's security society polity, as articulated by theorists and scholars like Gilles Deleuze, Michel Foucault, and Ken Booth.[1] The future world of *The Stone Gods* is made up of temporally short-sighted humans, evacuated of political sensibilities and devoted to immediate material desires. In this contracted form of Enlightenment autonomous individualism, humans are incapable of preparing for the future, and, as such, are sentenced to an endless repetition of environmental destruction. In *The Stone Gods*, political governments have vanished and the state is thoroughly merged with the free-market machine, run by a global corporate entity called MORE-*Futures*. MORE-*Futures* advances economic and military solutions for all sociality, overseeing daily existence with an expanding array of security technologies. The discourse of security ensures that forms of scientific progress are caught within increasingly restrictive and unsustainable technologies. The novels therefore all confront the key environmental impediments of our time, factors, as I will articulate more fully below, that have led to the rise of the Anthropocene.

Against these considerable Anthropocene forces, Atwood, McEwan, and Winterson also present us with radically different forms of human subjectivity, ones directed more to an ecologically and sociologically embedded existence that offers more holistic capacities for existing. In Winterson's *The Stone Gods*, the characters of Spike and Billie illustrate the need for non-military, anti-neoliberal practices. Billie's intellectual meditations on the ontological origins of anti-ecological meaning-making, coupled with Spike's assertions of quantum theory, tender alternative potentials for a more sustainable existence. *Solar's* ecologically minded Tom Aldous and McEwan's satiric narration – with its periodic intervention of poststructuralist theories of linguistic construction – reveal forms of embedded existence that serve as a productive counterpoint to Beard's single-minded instrumental thinking. Lastly, Atwood's *The Year of the Flood* considers the successes and failures of a social movement that would seek to fully deconstruct these impediments. In following the efforts of the God's Gardeners, the novel offers up an ecologically embedded political movement that provides various methods for breaking the Anthropocene's self-destructive cycle.

The Geological, Scopic Human

On an almost daily basis scientists acquire more evidence of how the Anthropocene is unlike any other period in human and modern planetary environmental history.

By now the oft-repeated litany of widespread ecological decline is well known to scholars working in the environmental humanities: massive extinction (more than two-thirds of the planet's species likely to be functionally extinct by 2100); substantial sea-level rise (at least a metre but most likely more by 2100); loss of island nations, some as soon as mid-century; temperature increase of (as of this writing) more than 2 °F, but more likely 3 °F (and possibly close to 6 °F according to some modelling scenarios); massive migration of 'climate change refugees' (18 million in Bangladesh alone); increased water- and food-security issues[2] in political hotspots like Sub-Saharan Africa; normalised hotter temperatures (with Phoenix, Arizona, for instance, seeing up to sixty days above 115 °F each year by 2100, as opposed to one day above 115 °F in the last twenty years); expansion of ocean dead zones; and more. Not typically connected to this list are the co-constituent liminal transgressions that are equally symptomatic of human activity in the Anthropocene: the genetic engineering of entire agricultural systems; the technological imperative to develop artificial intelligence and robotic systems capable of infiltrating all levels of social existence and eliminating the need for what we used to think of as the workforce; the ramping up of defence budgets and initiatives related to climate change and the increased insecurity it promises to bring; the war against the humanities – which includes multiple fields of study that were, prior to the Anthropocene, considered to be indicators of the highest achievements of the human species; the degrading of science as fantasy (happening inside and outside academia); and the general decline of ontological inquiry and any form of thought that fails to fit easily into the market-driven imperatives of neoliberalism.

Atwood, McEwan, and Winterson all in different ways underscore the importance of situating the Anthropocene, which is generally understood exclusively in terms of ecological matters, within the broader military, economic, and technological framework I briefly outline above. Expanding this framework is important because the Anthropocene as a workable concept is still in its infancy, despite the widespread use of the word in multiple disciplines. Though new efforts are under way to identify earlier stages of the Anthropocene back through previous centuries and in relation to more complex historical, cultural, and political forces, these remain part of sporadic scholarship emerging only within the last few years.[3] In emphasising the theoretical challenges in our critical interrogation of 'geological scale' human subjectivity, Dipesh Chakrabarty's essays 'Postcolonial Studies and the Challenge of Climate Change' (2012) and 'The Climate of History: Four Theses' (2009) effectively brought the name 'Anthropocene' to the attention of scholars working in various disciplines in the humanities.

Although the concept of the Anthropocene can be dated to Paul Crutzen's pronouncement in 2000, similar proclamations had been made by a number of philosophers impacting several humanities disciplines. Michel Serres, for instance, wrote in 1995 that humans had begun to act as 'tectonic plates' (Serres 1995: 16). Prior to that Paul Virilio had spoken repeatedly about a widespread transformation in humanity's relation to technology, in which humans had become subject to a dangerously limited relationship to technological production: one in which the 'substance' of technology (including the workings and understanding of the technological artefacts we produce) had come to be replaced by a paltry cognisance of technological failure (Virilio 2007: 11). We have become so accustomed, Virilio argued, to widespread Anthropocene-scale technology (he, of course, did not use the word Anthropocene) as a matter of fact that we do not think of its essential nature, let alone its impact on steering human and nonhuman existence in a particularly self-destructive direction. Rather our attention has been reoriented towards the fear of potential technological breakdowns. As a consequence, we submit ourselves to increasingly asphyxiating forms of security to ensure the continuing functioning of the system. Moreover, the breakdown itself, argues Virilio, is part of the very essence of technological production in the modern age: the car is the invention of the car crash; the nuclear power plant is the invention of the meltdown (or the bomb); and we can add without hyperbole, given the overwhelming amount of scientific evidence, the contemporary human is the invention of a new geological age (Virilio 2003: 6).

Solar, *The Stone Gods*, and *Oryx and Crake*, each in its different manner, explore with great precision the apparently boundless scope of today's human subjectivity – what I will refer to throughout the rest of this chapter as the *scopic human*; that is, a form of human subjectivity materialised in a spatio-temporal continuum of exceeding scope. From the start it should be recognised that the scopic human is not a universal entity. This species of human can be found mainly in its acts of overconsumption and negatively externalised environmental impacts. Primarily, the scopic human seeks to expand its reach by activating the kind of global assemblages that comprise today's human technological architecture. The scopic human has its antecedents in capitalism's growth into an immense global plateau, constantly deploying flows in every direction, putting a colonised form of desire to work by organising 'lack' (gaps in development) across the landscape in order to aggrandise evermore territory; or to use Deleuze and Guattari's apt phrasing in their critique of capital, lack is 'created, planned and organized through social production' (Deleuze and Guattari 1983: 28). The capitalist assemblage generates the free-floating subject, which, in its coupling with the deterritorialising assemblage of capitalism, becomes the geological human, affecting environments on a planetary scale, while denying, at the same time, being a part of those environments. It is the kind of environmentally disembodied individual found in the (post-)industrialised world, but it can also be found in the urban elite camps of the so-called third world. McEwan's Michael Beard, Atwood's Crake, and Winterson's President of MORE-*Futures* exemplify this subjectivity.

Ian McEwan's *Solar*

Beard is a Nobel Prize winner, a shrewd thinker, and a highly knowledgeable physicist sought the world over. He holds 'honorary' university positions, sits on 'a royal commission on science funding', speaks on radio shows 'in layman's terms about Einstein ... [and] quantum mechanics', serves as a consulting editor for scholarly journals, attends conventions, and lives 'weary of himself' as a world 'celebrity' in his field (McEwan 2010: 16).

Despite his extensive knowledge and accomplishments, Beard nonetheless remains blind to his own extremely astigmatic, transcendentally dangerous understanding of complex ecological relations. He is 'vaguely aware' of global warming, yet he has no patience for those who attempt to live a more sustainable existence, such as his graduate assistant Thomas Aldous. Aldous, excited about tackling environmental problems from multiple angles, takes a multidisciplinary approach to the environmental problems of the Anthropocene. Aldous, whose specialism is particle physics, encourages Beard to consider solar energy, battery-storage development, artistic representations of alternative ecological relations articulated in novels, and documentaries detailing the effects of climate change. Aldous essentially asks Beard to adopt radically different intellectual processes in order to fundamentally rethink his disconnected world view and unsustainable set of behaviours (2010: 28–32). He is the character that first presents Beard with the idea of photovoltaics, which Beard rejects as 'the essence of a crank' (2010: 31). Beard's disdain for people like Aldous, and any genuine environmentalism, is rampant. He even goes so far as to plan in advance an intellectual blitzkrieg against a group of ecologists concerned about the negative effects of engineering the oceans:

> There was ... a scheme that fascinated him ... The idea was to dump many hundreds of tons of iron filings in the ocean, enriching the waters and encouraging the plankton to bloom. As it grew, it absorbed more carbon dioxide from the air. The precise amount could be calculated in order to claim carbon credits, which could be sold through the scheme to heavy industry. If a coal-burning company bought enough, it could rightfully claim that its operations were carbon-neutral. The idea was to get ahead of the competition before the European markets were fully established ... Some marine biologists, no doubt with secret plans of their own, had heard rumors of his scheme and had been arguing in the press that interfering with the base of the food chain was dangerous. They needed to be blasted out of the water with some sound science. Beard already had two pieces ready for publication, but it was important to hold back until the right moment. (2010: 217–18)

The idea of an iron-seeding experiment stems from the economically influenced, geoengineering school of climate change solutions. Such solutions are beloved by neoliberals attempting to 'solve' the problem of global warming through market mechanisms (a case in point is carbon trading, a scheme that has been shown time and again to fail in its promise to reduce greenhouse gases) (see Hoag 2011). McEwan is referring to an experiment here that has been tried more than once by geoengineers working in the Arctic. Iron seeding essentially turns the ocean into even more of a carbon sink than it is, which threatens ocean ecosystems. Such schemes are worth less than the time it takes to set them up. A best-case scenario would see a reduction of less than one eighth of the over eight billion metric tonnes of carbon dioxide we are currently putting into the atmosphere annually. The carbon dioxide would be eaten by microscopic 'diatoms', which die and sink to the ocean floor after the food source of iron depletes (Biello 2012). But the conditions for maintaining such a dodgy scenario are dubious. Even if everything works as planned the carbon dioxide only stays on the ocean floor a maximum of 200 years. In addition, iron-seeding schemes can easily backfire, potentially producing an overabundance of plankton that eat up oxygen, thereby creating ocean dead zones where essentially nothing can live (like the one in the Gulf of Mexico at the mouth of the Mississippi River).

The point to draw from this is not that Beard lacks intelligence. His accomplishments in the field of quantum physics are clear, and the iron-filing scheme is comprehensible and convincing according to its own internal logic. If we are to discover the disposition of Beard's subjectivity as an individual of the Anthropocene, we need to critically assess this logic from a different angle. We need to question the viability of the logic based on its essential character. Beard's mode of reasoning is teleological and sequential in nature, which means that in its very assiduous efficiency it fails to think the *con*sequential aspects of its actions. This very type of sequential thinking, which has been an influential form of intelligence since the age of the Enlightenment, is militaristic in its aggressivity. Even the open-minded Aldous is swayed by teleological sequentiality in his attempt to solve the problems of greenhouse gas production via photovoltaics. He is not the only one who believes in this magic sustainability bullet: solar energy is one of the most compelling solutions to climate change. Many solutions to climate change, such as the idea of 'carbon-neutrality' and certain conceptions of 'sustainability', equally lend themselves to a sequential set of thought processes that by definition fail to see their consequentiality.

Beard in fact, oddly recognises the consequences of Aldous's single-minded obsession with photovoltaics in his very dismissal of Aldous as foolish: 'The essence of a crank was, first, to believe that all the world's problems could be reduced to one and solved. And second, to go on about it nonstop' (McEwan 2010: 31). Aldous's articulation of solar energy as the ultimate clean solution and the stepping stone to a new industrial revolution is logically sound in its own unique framework. There is no doubt that the replacement of petroleum sources of energy with solar energy would put an end to the worst emissions of anthropogenic greenhouse gases. Anyone serious about climate change, and serious about putting an end to the corporate empire of petroleum and its history of environmental injustice, cannot see the move in that direction happen fast enough. Yet in presenting solar as a magic bullet we overlook the very consequential human obsessions with production and overconsumption, which will undoubtedly continue with the move to solar energy and other renewable resources. At such a moment the idea of solar energy is transformed into the *telos* of a sequential solution that, in fact, turns out to be a continuation of the anthropogenic forcing of planetary environments.

We can effectively identify the limitation of this linear train of thought in almost all of Beard's attempts to rationalise. After Aldous's death Beard pilfers Aldous's work on photovoltaics, claiming it as his own. This unethical act in itself is not a sign of Anthropocene subjectivity. The problem, rather, lies in the precise form of his thinking in the wake of this event. His reasoning is linear, all-subsuming, and presumptively caught within the liberal humanist myth of world-system transcendence. His hyper-monomaniacal devotion to marketing photovoltaics is one symptom of this. McEwan merges this with Beard's intense addiction to alcohol and food, which increases in intensity the more he becomes addicted to photovoltaics. But we should not dismiss this as some form of character flaw. Assigning this to the level of immoral behaviour on the part of an individual misses the point. Beard's addictive behaviour is obviously emblematic of the kind of overconsumption that prevails among privileged subjects living in the Global North and West. And his inability to see that behaviour as one of the key forms of anthropogenic forcing causing climate change is also his inability to see beyond his own intellectual framework. Towards the end of the novel, when Beard changes his mind and adopts solar energy as the ultimate answer, the paradox of his absurd behaviour and his absurdly rigid logic becomes clear.

We see this logical contradiction in a conversation that Beard has with his American corporate partner Toby Hammer. Hammer is funding Beard's photovoltaics project, but he has also heard that climate change may be a hoax, and that the planet may be cooling, not warming. In addressing Hammer's concerns, Beard blithely describes the extreme impact climate change is having on the world:

> Here's the good news. The UN estimates that already a third of a million people a year are dying from climate change. Even as we speak, Bangladesh is going down because the oceans are warming and expanding and rising. There's drought in the Amazon rain forest. Methane is pouring out of the Siberian permafrost. There's a meltdown under the Greenland ice sheet that no one really wants to talk about ... Two years ago we lost forty percent of the Arctic summer ice. Now the eastern-Antarctic is going ... Toby, listen. It's a catastrophe. Relax! (McEwan 2010: 251)

In an example of risk management turned on its head, Beard transforms catastrophe into a marketing incentive. According to this logic, without the existing and growing threats generated by global warming the technology of photovoltaics would be worthless. This is more than a symptom of capitalism; it is a sign that Virilio has determinately identified as the *accident* – purposefully built into a generalised system of production and reproduction.

Here it is worth pausing a bit to consider Virilio's conceptualisation of this idea: what he calls the 'accidental thesis' (Virilio 2007: 6). Virilio's work has long considered the ontology of human environmental relations and their impacts. The concept of the accidental thesis discloses the essential character of production in the Anthropocene. Conventional reason grasps accidents as the unintentional consequences of modern phenomena, whether it be the car accident, or the toxins from commercial farming, or the meltdown of a nuclear power plant. Against this view Virilio takes a proper ecological stance: accidents should not be explained away as unwanted side effects; rather they are an ontological indicator of the primary substance and form of thought of our modern era. Rather than coding the accident as an error in human design, or even as a limitation in the reliability of materials, which can, it is proposed, be solved through greater 'security measures' and more robust technological know-how, Virilio reads the accident as a symptomatic event. In today's world, the accident is not an incidental side effect, but rather an intended incident. In becoming 'a clearly identifiable historical phenomenon', the accident reveals the essence of modernity's technoscientific mode of production: 'The invention of the substance is also the invention of the "accident"' (Virilio 2007: 6). The accident is 'built in', so to speak, from the beginning: 'The shipwreck is indeed the "futuristic" invention of the ship, the air crash the invention of the supersonic plane, and the Chernobyl meltdown, the invention of the nuclear power station' (2007: 6). Accidents, therefore, are not an unexpected breakdown in the substance and production of existence; accidents are the primary substance of existence itself – the confirmation of and justification for more technological advancement, 'states of exception' (to invoke Giorgio Agamben's theorisation of political existence; see Agamben 2005), and security.

This brings us full circle back to the evolution of the scopic human: the human as a geological force which we can now understand to be the ultimate practice of individualisation in the Anthropocene. The Anthropocene names that age in which ecological breakdown reveals the full achievement of technology's accidental essence. It is in this way that Virilio comes to define ecological disasters as the 'clinical symptom' of the enfolding of the accident into the substance of existence (Virilio 2003: 7). To this we can now add the scopic human as the individualised embodiment of the accident – the entity which, through technological development, has expanded its reach and dominion on a global scale. Furthermore, this ontological relationship between the scopic human and the accident opens the way to rethinking the discourse of technical rationality, as embodied in the figure of Beard and the unidirectional character of his reasoning. As Virilio argues, the accidental, in addition to being a term for describing the substance of technological production, equally names a state of mind. In technology's constant push for development, the precise knowledge of technology outpaces human understanding. Even the 'specialist' involved in the production of new technological advances does not completely know the mechanism of a technological apparatus, necessarily working only on a particular component of the apparatus made up of heterogeneous and discipline-specific generated parts. Consequently, the curious activity of accepting products without understanding how they work becomes a naturalised state for the human user. Instrumentality begins to disappear from human consciousness. Great sophistication and greater impact bring great incomprehension, and consciousness changes its field of recognisability away from the understanding of operations towards an obsession with the accident: 'consciousness now exists only for accidents' (Virilio 2007: 6). In turn, intelligibility begins to emerge out of the demand for greater security. As we will see, this re-focalisation of intelligence manifests itself sharply in Atwood's *Oryx and Crake* and Winterson's *The Stone Gods*. To return to McEwan's *Solar*, Beard's evangelical 'good news' that climate change is killing a third of a million people a year, sending half of Bangladesh into oblivion, and melting the polar ice caps is a symptom of the essential connection between his rationality and the accident: the 'catastrophe' so necessary to his logical enterprise. In this sense, photovoltaics are not a solution for the transformation of humanity's unsustainable existence; they are the integral element in a logical economy that depends on the accident for its justificatory and productive power. Put differently, solar energy will not change the scopic human's desire for ever greater reach; it will only enable the geologic desire for mass consumption to continue its ever-increasing pace.

But to talk about overconsumption is to articulate only a percentage of what it means to be a subject in the Anthropocene. Acts of overconsumption in and of themselves are not peculiar to the Anthropocene era. What does make them a sign of the Anthropocene is articulated obliquely by Beard in the story he tells corporate interests in his attempt to peddle Aldous's photovoltaic formula. In the story itself we see the framework that makes the Anthropocene possible:

> What's at issue is the creation of another industrial revolution ... Coal and then oil have made our civilization, they have been superb resources, lifting hundreds of millions of us out of the mental prison of rural subsistence. Liberation from the daily grind coupled with our innate curiosity has produced in a mere two hundred years an exponential growth of our knowledge base. The process began in Europe and the United States, has spread in our lifetime to parts of Asia, and now to India, China, and South America, with Africa yet to come. (McEwan 2010: 171)

In this passage, I want to argue, we see the central motor of the Anthropocene dramatised. The (his)story narrated here matches the sequential movement we have seen before in Beard's processes of reasoning. But nowhere is the consequential scope of the sequestered, near-sighted train of thought more revealing. Modern human 'civilisation', with its accumulated 'knowledge' and 'liberation' of human potential, is by definition anthropogenically (I am tempted to say 'anthropogenetically') self-destructive. In other words, the human establishment of civilisation is from its very beginnings oriented towards large-scale violence. No matter that this understanding of civilisation is Eurocentric, colonialist, and racist to the core (in Beard's story of modern humanity, knowledge, advancement, and civilisation spread from the West to the South and the East — that is, to peripheral spaces and constituencies that presumably had no progress or sophistication of their own). It is just as alarmingly modern-centric in its conception of 'civilisation', 'knowledge', and 'culture'. According to Beard, only within the last 200 years has humanity begun to genuinely think and develop. The last 10,000 years (or more, if we want to go back further than the agricultural revolution) of human thought and accomplishment are absolutely erased in this drama. In this radically foreshortened sequence of events, with the beginning of intelligence and progress located at the start of the industrial revolution, Anthropocene rationality cordons off all alternative possibilities to its singular, closed-loop narrative.

Here the closed nature of the Anthropocene narrative reveals its most toxic feature. Having defined and sealed off the pathways of thought, the rationality made visible can subsequently present itself as organic and disinterested, and therefore not actively (humanly) manufactured. The purity of this logic is not disinterested in the typical sense of being ahistorical and apolitical, as so often mentioned throughout the modern and contemporary period of philosophical theory. Beard knows that he is being political by working directly with political and politically non-neutral organisations. And he applies his arguments with recourse to specific historical frameworks, as manifest in the passage's historical timeline. Rather, the nature of his intellectual disinterestedness lies in his tying of rationality to the 'liberation' of humanity from the earth: the Anthropocene narrative identifies the beginning of true reason with a new and empowering Genesis myth. The birth of the human originates with the erasure of earthly relations. This erasure of earthly limitations will eventually evolve into the desire for the restriction of all limitations as the human epoch picks up speed and technological 'advancements' increase in scale. Thus, the original impulse to transcend earthly limitations (which in turn establishes the earth as a limitation) constitutes the first 'scaling up' in the birth of the Anthropocene human. From its beginning the civilised human enters existence as a scopic creature, attempting to create a boundless human 'ecosystem'. From these heights, Beard can gleefully find value in planetary destruction being a 'catastrophe'.

Margaret Atwood's *Oryx and Crake*

We find a similar sequential teleology and scopic boundlessness in the character of Crake from Atwood's *Oryx and Crake* – though, as we will see, with a twist. In *Oryx and Crake* the political and scientific elite live in securitised compounds, while the remainder of humanity live in deteriorated and crumbling cities called 'pleeblands' (Atwood 2005: 27). Crake works in the most exclusive of compounds 'OrganInc', which is run by the security defence and corporate administration called 'CorpSeCorps' (2005: 27). CorpSeCorps, similar to Winterson's MORE-*Futures*, is essentially the reigning form of government in both *Oryx and Crake* and *The Year of the Flood*. It has evolved to take the place of any form of federal or state governing bodies. Its power is only kept in check by other defence and corporate compounds located in different regions throughout the Western world. The sociopolitical architecture is basically a form of walled and militarised regionalism, with corporations serving up a heavily security-focused governmentality. Knowledge produced within one corporate compound is closely guarded, and the employees of each compound have to 'be on constant alert' (2005: 27). Scientists, entrepreneurs, and engineers working in the compounds produce 'hardware, ... software, ... hostile bioforms, ... weapons of every kind' (2005: 28).

The character of Jimmy serves as a poor inheritor of the immense and rich arts and humanities tradition. He is a weak counterpart to the character of Crake – the engineer genius who can outwit any intellectual opponent, and who is coveted by the most powerful of corporations. Though Jimmy's father compares the compounds to feudal walled castles and cities, the militarised basis of political reality described in the novel more tellingly resembles one of the future geopolitical scenarios found in the Millennium Ecosystem Assessment (MA) Scenarios, a set of four speculative future narratives developed at the United Nations and the World Bank in 2005 in response to the planet-wide degradation of ecosystems (Millennium Ecosystem Assessment 2005). The social system of *Oryx and Crake* most closely matches the 'Order from Strength' MA scenario, which is based on the idea of what the MA refers to as 'barbarization'. 'Order from Strength' is a scenario characterised by a 'regionalized and fragmented world concerned with security and protection', with enclosed markets within civil and political society 'paying little attention to common goods' (Millennium Ecosystem Assessment 2005: 225). People take an 'individualistic attitude toward ecosystem management' (Millennium Ecosystem Assessment 2005: 225). Ecosystems are the last things on people's minds, and if they are addressed at all, it is out of a reactive need to confront negative ecological feedbacks.

The inventive Crake thrives in this world. In honing his intellect, he adopts a form of rationality that functions according to a teleological impulse assumed to be consistent and wholly convincing. Unlike Beard, Crake does not approach the problems of humanity's unsustainable relationship to the environment from the standpoint of allowing the species to continue its self-destructive, overly consumptive behaviour patterns. In the many arguments with his best friend Jimmy, a non-scientist who studies art and literature, Crake's lucid logic always wins the day. This is made possible because, in the same manner as Beard, he presumes that thinking is an organic process, grounded in unchallengeable certainties. His 'logic' epitomises the self-fulfilling logic of the engineer, a modern subject whose technological prowess is made possible by the same horizon of history provided in Beard's narrative. As with Beard, the sequential character of that logic diminishes any serious consideration of its collateral consequences.

When giving Jimmy a tour through the CorpSeCorps lab, Crake introduces him to the kind of engineering marvels invented for scopic human consumption: algae wallpaper crafted to change colour depending on a person's mood, algae bathroom towels designed to soak up more water, and a headless, brainless chicken grown solely for its breast meat. The possibility that the algae might someday end up as waste leaking into a river system, potentially causing an outbreak resulting in the depletion of oxygen in the water ecosystem, never enters the engineers' heads. In the same vein Crake introduces Jimmy to a new form of natural security system. Called 'wolvogs', they are a bioengineered amalgam of wolves and dogs designed to work 'better than an alarm system' (Atwood 2005: 205). 'They're bred to deceive', Crake tells Jimmy. 'Reach out to pet them, they'll take your hand off' (2005: 205). In their construction of the animal, the engineers assume that a widely dispersed myth about a certain breed of dog is in fact an organic truth: Crake tells Jimmy that they have added 'a large pit-bull component' to the genetic mix (2005: 205). Like most who lack discipline-specific knowledge about domesticated animals, Crake assumes that aggressiveness is in the pit bull's genes, whereas the specialist associated with domesticated animals understands that any such aggressiveness in not at all natural but contextual and arises in and through specific acts of training. Of course, one could conclude this to be Atwood's own lack of knowledge about bull terriers, but considering Atwood's otherwise rich ecological reflections, it would be difficult to argue that she believes species attributes to be so completely genetically hardwired. More importantly, the point is that this assumption on the part of Crake reflects a larger pattern. The 'truth' of aggressiveness is wholly logical to Crake, yet its basis in a mythology that surrounds the species and not in sound science stems from his intellectual assumption that species are inherently wired to be of a specific disposition. Like Beard, he considers his logic to be buttressed by an ontological guarantee.

Beyond this initial level Crake and Beard part ways. The more we see Crake's arguments with Jimmy staged in the novel, the more we begin to discern that his reasoning is ultimately governed by a securitising imperative. His is a militarised mentality, swiftly manoeuvring to outwit any thought heterogeneous to his own by conceptualising that thought as an opponent to be overthrown. In a paradox of hubris, he reveals the logical conclusion of his own tenacious and unrelenting but equally suffocating rationality. In the following passage Jimmy recounts an argument during which he presented Crake with human language and the potential for multiple forms of human creativity:

> It's comforting to remember that *Homo sapiens sapiens* was once so ingenious with language, and not only with language. Ingenious in every direction at once.
> Monkey brains, had been Crake's opinion. Monkey paws, monkey curiosity, the desire to take apart, turn inside out, smell, fondle, measure, improve, trash, discard – all hooked up to monkey brains but monkey brains all the same. Crake had no very high opinion of human ingenuity, despite the large amount of it he himself possessed. (2005: 99)

In this passage we see Jimmy's nostalgia for humanity's past historical capacity for language wisdom (which he, himself, disappointingly lacks), and Crake's aggressive response. Crake, in essence, deploys an unsophisticated, pedestrian definition of what biologists that study primates refer to as a 'nested hierarchy' that includes simians (the scientific term for monkeys) and other ape-like creatures (Pumain 2006: 82). The prosaic 'monkey' names an inaccuracy symptomatic not only of Crake's lack of knowledge about the field (or perhaps his disdain), but his indifference towards forms of inquiry that do not match the truculent engineering logic he considers to be a pure form of rationality. The core of that purity lies in its style of defensive strategy. 'Monkey', in this example, is a misrepresentation that collapses the complex nested hierarchy of numerous species of primates. As a designator it no doubt signifies Crake's misanthropy, but it is also invoked to belittle any alternative point of view. Deployed as a defensive manoeuvre it is indicative of Crake's general dismissal of any field of study (and the fields he dismisses are multiple) not reflective of mechanistic, security-driven intelligence.

The teleological endowment of species with an innate end has obvious consequences (the example of CorpSeCorps's chicken engineering is not far from the treatment of chickens in factories that exist today). Yet Crake's involvement in the ultimate engineering masterpiece serves as an alarming example of what can go wrong when forms of teleologically sequential intelligence ground themselves in organic truths – which, as I have been arguing, is the defining structure of thought in the Anthropocene. In seeking a solution to the anthropogenic enervation of ecosystems Crake takes the position that human identity is inherently unsustainable, therefore leading him to the logical conclusion that the species must be eliminated. The early stages of this determination are orchestrated around the introduction of the 'BlyssPlus Pill', a form of prophylactic based on the concept that humans are 'monkeys' (in Crake's definition of the word). As Crake tells Jimmy, BlyssPlus was designed 'to take a set of givens, namely the nature of human nature, and steer these givens in a more beneficial direction than the ones hitherto taken' (Atwood 2005: 293). That 'nature', as identified by Crake, is based on the pseudo-Freudian, pop-psychology axiom that humans are essentially sexual creatures governed by 'sexual energy'. In this interpretative framework, complex historical events such as war are nothing more than 'misplaced sexual energy' (2005: 293). Crake and his lab mates at CorpSeCorps consider that unsatisfied sexual energy 'to be a larger factor than the economic, racial, and religious causes often cited' (2005: 293). From this assumption they identify an inherent flaw in humans: humans are 'partially monogamous with polygamous and polyandrous tendencies' (2005: 293). This inherent conflict, they argue, leads 'to jealousy', 'violence', and 'feelings of low worth' (2005: 294). They find an ideal solution to the dilemma in a study of an extinct species, the bonobo chimpanzee, which was 'indiscriminately promiscuous', 'not pair-bounded', and spent most of its life 'when it wasn't eating, engaged in copulation' (2005: 294). The BlyssPlus pill thus protects users against sexual diseases, provides them with 'an unlimited supply of libido and sexual prowess, coupled with a generalized sense of energy and well-being' (2005: 294). To boot, it slows down the ageing process.

As Crake leads Jimmy to the paradisaical climax of his argument, he articulates the benefits of BlyssPlus in a manner that sounds strikingly similar to Beard's reverence for solar energy:

> Such a pill, he said, would confer large-scale benefits, not only on individual users – although it had to appeal to these or it would be a failure in the marketplace – but on society as a whole; and not only on society, but on the planet. The investors were very keen on it, it was going to be global. It was all upside. There was no downside at all. He, Crake, was very excited about it. (2005: 294)

Here we can plainly see Crake's sequential teleology leading directly to the scopic nature of human thought in the Anthropocene: the pill is 'large-scale'; it will benefit all of society and the planet; marketing will make it 'global'; and there is 'no downside at all'. To add to it, the pill also acts as 'a sure-fire one-time-does-it-all birth-control pill' (2005: 294) that will sterilise both sexes. In harnessing the inferred essence of what it is to be human – sexual energy – the pill solves the problem of planetary population at the same time.

If the aggressive disposition of this solution is not enough to reveal the combative, bellicose character of Crake's logic, his clarification to Jimmy of the need for such a pill does. When Jimmy ironically asks Crake if he is being altruistic in his concern for humanity's future, he responds:

> 'It's not altruism exactly', said Crake. 'More like sink or swim. I've seen the latest confidential Corps demographic reports. As a species we're in deep trouble, worse than anyone's saying. They're afraid to release the stats because people might just give up, but take it from me, we're running out of space-time. Demand for resources has exceeded supply for decades in marginal geopolitical areas, hence the famines and droughts; but very soon, demand is going to exceed supply *for everyone*. With the BlyssPluss Pill the human race will have a better chance of swimming.' (2005: 294–5)

Crake's apocalyptic justification for mass sterilisation and chemical manipulation brings forward a second aspect of the Anthropocene's configuration: the circumstance of living in the end-time. The scope of human actions produces a situation demanding an equally immense scopic course of action. At least this is what Crake assumes, on the basis of an inherent anthropological identity. Thus, we see the endpoint of the closed-loop Anthropocene narrative, an ending predetermined from the narrative's very beginning. Like photovoltaics, the pill becomes a magic-bullet solution, one which Crake will push to its logical conclusion by transforming BlyssPluss into a deadly virus, which eventually kills off most of the human population on the planet. The potential for humans to move their behaviour towards a more sustainable mode of existence never appears as a possibility for Crake any more than for Beard. The narrative categorically forbids any consideration of such a possibility.

At such a point Crake's way of thinking – *the* mode of thought generated by the Anthropocene's narrative – reveals its hidden commitment to destruction. The presumption that engineering is an ontologically organic and neutral form of thought generates an increasingly unstable, accident-driven system, responding to each new crisis with another crisis, and ultimately responding to the potential elimination of the human race by eliminating the human race. This refusal to see the limitations of his intellectual horizon divulges the inherent contradiction of his own science of reasoning. By revealing these contradictions, we can begin to see how *Oryx and Crake* stands as a novel that deconstructs the limitations of not only engineered solutions to Anthropocene dilemmas, but the very idea of thought that engenders these solutions.

Jeanette Winterson's *The Stone Gods*

Winterson's *The Stone Gods* pushes the consequences of scopic subjectivity and teleological sequentiality to even greater depths. The novel is divided into four distinct time periods, traversing two different worlds and some 65 million years. It opens on

'Orbus', an earth-like planet that can only support human life for another fifty years due to anthropogenic climate change. It is an example of what the earth will be like if the spew of greenhouse gases continues under a business-as-usual plan. The CO_2 has risen to 550 parts per million (ours breached 410 ppm in April of 2017). It also provides a persuasive and unsettling example of what the geopolitics of neoliberalism will become in 50–100 years.

In *The Stone Gods*, government as we know it no longer hides its corporate connections behind lobbying mechanisms. The new politics combines scientific leaders in the fields of engineering and artificial intelligence, corporate entrepreneurs and leaders, and military and security specialists. This new amalgam is called MORE-*Futures*. MORE-*Futures* takes the approach of scientists like Steven Hawking and engineers like Elon Musk, who argue that we need to colonise Mars to ensure the future survival of humanity. In the novel the saviour planet is called Planet Blue. Sixty-five billion years behind Orbus in terms of ecological development (dinosaurs are at the top of the food chain), Planet Blue needs to be extensively developed if it is to support Orbus's advanced culture. MORE-*Futures* decides that the top of the food chain needs to be wiped out. To do so, MORE-*Futures* scientists drop a nuclear device on a nearby asteroid, changing its course to crash on Planet Blue. The impact, it is thought, will destroy most of the dinosaurs, secure the ecosystem, and thereby create a new geological age more properly suited to the needs of the human species. Unfortunately, MORE-*Futures*' scientists' calculations are off. The impact wreaks havoc, and the carefully calculated plan ends up making life on Planet Blue impossible for humans for at least another 65 million years. The last two sections of the novel take place precisely that many years later, when we discover that Planet Blue is our earth, and humans are once again on the verge of ecological collapse. Earth is in the midst of recovering from a third world war, which has left a large portion of the population living lives of heavy radiation sickness.

The novel dramatises unlike any other the consequences of closed-loop teleological thought, and its connection to immense scopic proportions. At the same time, the novel confronts what we might characterise as the ultimate irony of Anthropocene humanism. In the fanatical desire to expand human impact to a geological scale, the human desire to conquer the mystery and complexity of intelligence results in a socially generated deep dissatisfaction with human limitations. The world's leading scientists turn away from the human species to concentrate their efforts on artificial intelligence. From out of this misanthropy MORE-*Futures* creates 'Spike', a female android capable of accessing the entire sum of human knowledge. The goal of Spike is articulated by the President of MORE-*Futures*:

> The Robo *sapiens* is a corrective. No major decisions that impact on the lives of others will be taken without running all the data through her ... She will be linked to a vast Mainframe computer – something no human can be. It will be like having all of the Nobel Prize winners working together for the good of mankind. And because she isn't motivated by greed or power, because she isn't political or ideological, she can arrive at the best solutions. (Winterson 2007: 133)

Despite scientists' efforts to escape the limitations of human intelligence, they nonetheless conceptualise Spike as the quintessence of Anthropocene logic, specifically in the form of neoliberalism's ultimate fantasy of freedom from political accountability. She is conceived as an entity that will finally offer humans an indisputably pure form of intelligence, thinking outside and beyond any contextual fetters. She stands as the ultimate destroyer of all ecological limits – in all senses of the term, biological and metaphorical. She is designed to be the disembodied Market, freed from any bureaucratic interests and speaking truths unchained by all interests.

Except Spike turns out to be very much the opposite of this fantasy. For Spike, intelligibility is not defined by the teleologically neutral form of sequential thought endorsed by her makers. She slips through the surveillance system of MORE-*Futures* to live on the fringes of London, living with the 'incurables ... and freaks' that make their home beyond the militant security and the culture of hyperconsumption of the corporate city (2007: 179–80). Rather than accept the objectivity and post-politics-based logic of 'accountability' valorised by MORE-*Futures*, Spike rejects these and other predetermined assumptions about the nature of meaning-making. She embraces what one might call the irreducible groundlessness of knowledge, which opens a passage to a less scopic and more embedded subjectivity. Her specific pathway to this radical contingency is in and through the language of quantum physics.

At a pivotal moment in the novel, Spike confronts her friend Billie. Billie brings up the axiomatic materiality of the last and recent war that swept through the city, chiding Spike for her quantum theories, which collapse the artificial barriers between reality and illusion. In response, Spike recasts the reality of the war as a radically contingent materiality, in spite of its unquestionable facticity:

'I don't want to be told that reality is an illusion'.
    'But it is ...' said Spike ...
    '[W]as it an illusion when the fireball blew our temperate lives into melt-down? Were the bombs an illusion? The gutted streets? Did I imagine I was crying?'
    'It was too late by then', said Spike. 'What happened did happen. But not before it was so powerful an idea that it took shape and form and ripped through the thin skin that separates potential from event'.
    'I hate when you talk like this'.
    'I merely observe that this is a quantum Universe and, as such, what happens is neither random nor determined. There are potentialities and any third factor – humans are such a factor – will affect the outcome'.
    'And free will?'
    'Is your capacity to affect the outcome.' (2007: 180–1)

Spike names the seemingly hardwired and empirical reality for what it is: an ideologically constituted and galvanised existence that can only be changed if that ideology is confronted as the illusion it is. 'Illusion' here should be understood in its most radical sense: not as an indication of something 'false', but as a metaphor denoting an ontological disposition that breaks open the presumably logical rational/irrational binary (articulated in this passage in terms of the 'random' and the 'determined'). The bulwark of rationality, seemingly standing in opposition to irrationality, is exposed as being one of the two sides of the same coin, and not a true opposite. The opposite of rationality is a different mode of rationality, one that 'rip[s] through the thin skin that separates potential from event' (2007: 181).

Spike uses quantum physics to intimately embrace the Nothingness that lies at the heart of existence: '"This is a quantum universe", said Spike, "neither random nor determined. It is potential at every second. All you can do is intervene"' (2007: 62). Billie herself considers this radical potentiality in terms of her own identity and its relation to her specific historical context:

> I am a lost manuscript, surfacing in fragments, like a message in a bottle, a page here, a page there, out towards an unknown shore. It has been the same all my life because my mother set the numbers that way, coded me, programmed me, and although it is possible to play with the numbers, I can't break the shape. Determinism versus Freewill is a false study – unhelpful, a time-waster. Life has never been All or Nothing – it's All and Nothing. Forget the binaries. (2007: 127)

In this passage Billie articulates three levels of fundamental, constitutional embedding. She combines quantum physics' collapse of the barrier between Determinism and Freewill, All and Nothing, with the materiality of her own identity – her genetic 'coding' and her bodily 'shape' – and extends that to the register of language, seeing herself as a 'lost manuscript', embedded in the quantum nature of reality at the level of corporeal reality, the level of individual corporeal reality, and the level of language. It is within the metaphor of the circulation of her identity as a manuscript 'surfacing' into existence in 'fragments' with no predetermined teleological end, moving outwards 'towards an unknown shore', that Winterson achieves the most precise and compelling articulation of the embedded nature of the subject and its existence. This embeddedness offers a new form of circulation untethered from any transcendent regulating principle, from any self-enclosed sequentiality that would lead, in its unchained growth, to the rise of the scopic subject.

Margaret Atwood's *The Year of the Flood*

Atwood takes this form of an embedded circulation within the play of immanent relations into a more specifically ecological register. In opposition to the sequential logic of Crake and the conservative oligarchy of CorpSeCorps operative in *Oryx and Crake*, in her sequel *The Year of the Flood* she attempts to think an embedded ecological politics through the radical collective of the God's Gardeners. Through the God's Gardeners Atwood crafts a successful and growing environmental movement. The organisation is composed primarily of scientists, engineers, and artists, but also of people from the pleeblands who join the Gardeners along the way. In crafting the God's Gardeners collective Atwood confronts two of the largest twenty-first-century coordinating cultural regimes:

religion and science. As we learn a bit more than halfway through the novel, the collective was conceived as a solution to the split between science and religion: 'their goal [was] the reconciling of the findings of Science with the sacramental view of Life' (Atwood 2009: 240).

We see the same kind of ontological critique appearing in this novel as in *The Stone Gods*. Again, the target is the human species, but here the critique manifests itself in the framework of religion and social movements, rather than the more rarefied form of quantum physics. Atwood's framework is specifically biological in its focus, and through an expansive, immanent conception of the planet's heterogeneous biological community she develops the image of an ecological 'matrix' (2009: 161) meant to dethrone the human as an autonomous, sovereign subject. She achieves this most openly through the character of Adam One – the leader of the God's Gardeners:

> We are inclined to overlook the very small that dwell among us; yet, without them, we ourselves could not exist; for every one of us is a Garden of sub-visual life forms. Where would we be without the Flora that populate the intestinal tract, or the Bacteria that defend against hostile invaders? We teem with multitudes, my Friends – with the myriad forms of Life that creep about beneath our feet, and – I may add – under our toenails.
>
> True, we are sometimes infested with nanobioforms we would prefer to be without, such as the Eyebrow Mite, the Hookworm, the Pubic Louse, the Pinworm, and the Tick, not to mention the hostile bacteria and viruses. But think of them as God's tiniest Angels, doing His unfathomable work in their own way, for these Creatures, too, reside in the Eternal Mind, and shine in the Eternal Light, and form a part of the polyphonic symphony of Creation. (2009: 160)

Adam One articulates here a biocentric ethics, envisioned through a conception of subjectivity in a circulation other than that of the kind that obtains in neoliberal humanism and its attendant rule of unequally distributed democracy. Here the circulation of the human species is not to be found in any economic register (capitalist or otherwise), or in any anthropocentric social formation (democratic or otherwise), but through the immanent flow of the ecosystem. More importantly, the immanent flow visualised here is in no way oriented towards anthropocentric concerns. It is not the pets or livestock of humans imagined here (what we typically consider when we think about the 'nonhuman' in our attempt to supposedly get beyond the human with discourses such as animal rights). Rather it is the kind of biodiversity typically off the charts when it comes to the human capacity to envision the nonhuman: the flora and bacteria of the intestinal tract, and nanobioforms found on the body. Atwood opens the door to rethinking the Human and its identity from the standpoint of biology. For instance, there are over 100 trillion cells in the human body, and only one in ten of these cells are human. What happens to our notions of 'human sovereignty', 'autonomy', and 'individuality' when faced with these kinds of immanent, indwelling circulatory flows?

Adam develops even further this expansion of the body, moving increasingly outwards to build a radical form of exteriority:

> Consider also His works in the Earth! The Earthworms and Nemotodes and Ants, and their endless tilling of the soil, without which it would harden into a cement-like mass, extinguishing all Life. Think of the antibiotic properties of Maggots and of the various Moulds, and of the honey that our Bees make, and also of the Spider's web, so useful in the stopping of bloodflow from a wound. For every ill, God has provided a remedy in His great Medicine Cabinet of Nature! ...
>
> When next you hold a handful of moist compost, say a silent prayer of thanks to all of the Earth's previous Creatures. Picture your fingers giving each and every one of them a loving squeeze. For they are surely here with us, ever present in that nourishing matrix. (2009: 160–1)

The image of the 'nourishing matrix' provides life for humans (the 'great Medicine Cabinet of Nature'), but also extends beyond the human to include the 'soil' from which all life is possible. Definitions of life expand in rich diversity as they are uncoupled from the anthropocentric imaginary, enabling a different kind of self-realisation of species from their own distinct and embodied ecological circulations. This enables a vision of the world not from the human standpoint but from the expanding diversity and value of species-specific vitality. In this heterogeneous, species-specific imaginary the 'soil' is released from the customary human-centred imaginary, with its agricultural demand for monocropping, high yields, insecticides, herbicides, genetically engineered crops, and so on (all of which result in a massive erosion of the soil), which is replaced with an awareness of the 'soil' as a signifier of all the lives that came before, the 'teaming multitude' of 'Earth's previous Creatures' that made the soil/life possible.

Is this expansion still not scopic in nature? Certainly there is an enlarged scope of consciousness being encouraged in Adam's reimagination of God's Creatures as 'Earth's Creatures'. Yet the growth here contains none of the aggressive transcendence and unquestionable sequential logic indicative of Beard and Crake. Nor can it be said to be a conception enabling the Human to become a geological force, as we have seen to be the main feature of Anthropocene subjectivity. The key lies in the expansion of anthropocentric specificity to species-specificity. Adam One makes this trans-species move in his first encounters with the general public in the pleeblands. When spreading his 'ecological word' in his initial attempts to build the flock of the God's Gardeners, he speaks of a different 'measure'. Addressing a crowd of reluctant sewage workers, he foregrounds this ontological critique:

> My dear Friends. My name is Adam One. I, too, was once a materialistic, atheistic meat-eater. Like you, I thought Man was the measure of all things ... In fact, dear Friends, I thought measurement was the measure of all things! Yes – I was a scientist. I studied epidemics. I counted diseased and dying animals, and people too, as if they were so many pebbles. I thought that only numbers could give a true description of Reality. (2009: 40)

In decentring the human – 'Man' – as the locus of all knowledge production, Adam One opens the door to diverse grounds for measurement, and to the very concept of measurement. As Amitav Ghosh argues in his powerful work *The Great Derangement: Climate Change and the Unthinkable*, the problems of the Anthropocene – global warming, species extinction, mass starvation – are problems 'not [of] a measure to be left to the individual conscience' (Ghosh 2016: 133). In other words, what Adam offers in these revisions of human and biological reality is the ecological concept of the *Umwelt* – the constitutionally different conception of the environment first developed by the bio-semiologist Jakob von Uexküll (Uexküll 2010: 212). *Umwelt* is one of two common German words for 'environment', but the term refers to something considerably different from what 'environment' is typically taken to mean in English. *Umwelt* is species-specific, and delineates the defining spatio-temporal relations peculiar to a given living entity. It considers the different grounds of measuring and coordinating that obtain in different creatures. Agamben, in his analysis of Uexküll's concept, articulates it as follows:

> Too often ... we imagine that the relations a certain animal subject has to the things in its environment take place in the same space and in the same time as those which bind us to the objects in our human world. This illusion rests on the belief in a single world in which all living beings are situated. (Agamben 2004: 40)

Put differently, flows of space, time, and energy do not exist in the same way for humans as they do for other species, such as honey bees, horses, polar bears, or beavers. The environments – *Umwelten* – of each are fundamentally different and hold different significances and potentialities. Human-centred systems, even human conceptions of immanence (be it political or ontological), focalise the significances specific to humans, and the architecture of these significances more often than not tear through and jeopardise the heterogeneous *Umwelten* of other species. Uexküll's word for this human-centred ecosystem is *Umgebung* – the other German word for environment. We can take Uexküll's concept, which is essentially biological in its focus and framework, and extend it to the register of politics. Adam One builds an ecological politics, I want to claim, not only immanent in the people of the God's Gardeners, but also immanent in the lifeworlds of nonhuman entities. As such he offers the most radical conception of embeddedness, more so than any of the other characters from the novels we have been analysing here.

Conclusion

By now it is becoming a truism to say that the Anthropocene names an era in which humans become a geological force. We characterise this 'forcing' in terms of the individual's scopic reach, as aided by anthropocentric technology, and name that different 'ecosystem' more accurately with Uexküll's term for the human environment: *Umgebung*. Dealing with the immensity of that force, which lies beyond the capacity of any single human – despite the human's scopic pretensions – constitutes a different kind of problem. But left unchecked, the widespread loss of habits, the erosion of the polar ice caps, the destitution of millions of climate change refugees, the death of countless species ... the list goes on: the repercussions of Anthropocene subjectivity and its predominant logical economies will lead to problems that lack any solution. For those species that have already become functionally extinct, there will never be a solution to the effects of anthropogenic forcing on their habitats. For those communities of people already on the move from the loss of their land due to sea-level rise, there is no solution that will bring back their land. To those who have died from drought, the drought never ended. For those attempting to stall the spread of such loss, the challenges are formidable. For the humanities, that challenge can take many forms, and one of those forms is the envisioning of alternative forms of thought and political creativity. As I hope I have begun to show, the novels analysed here offer key insights into the limitation of what counts as intelligence and empirical, rational thought in the Anthropocene, and what promises come from thinking new attempts to unmake our defensive sovereignty. In such a way we might generate more embedded modes of existence.

If Virilio reveals the self-destructive nature of a closed, accidental system seeking to extend its reach into infinity, then Jacques Rancière offers us a way to reconsider how to imagine and restage our political commitments, so that we might reach a different, more sustainable form of life. Politics, as Rancière defines it, involves an act of speech that 'gauges the gap between speech and the account of it' (Rancière 1999: 26). The 'account' named here describes the platform of human potential orchestrated by the powers that be. As such, politics 'is primarily the conflict over the existence of a common stage and over the existence and status of those present on it' (1999: 26–7). It is an activity that makes appear the power, agendas, prejudices, violence, and injustice inherent in the 'distribution of places and roles' 1999: 28). It comprises a battle over the rules governing the appearance of existing (and potentially existing) places and roles: 'Political activity is whatever shifts a body from the place assigned to it ... It makes heard a discourse where once there was only noise; it makes understood as discourse what was once only heard as noise' (1999: 30). In this sense, politics is not about known objects and places but exclusively about form, the appearance of formations in and through the confrontation of power politics and an egalitarian struggle not previously given formation in the field of the visible – a struggle that makes the field of a new visible appear as such. It is a process of 'subjectification against identification', that is, of the creation of different forms of subjective being against the norm (1999: 37). To return to Ghosh's *The Great Derangement*, the point is to 'find a way out of the individualizing imaginary in which we are trapped' (Ghosh 2016:135).

As Ghosh argues, fiction's ontological ammunition of the subjunctive 'as if' enables novelists to conceive 'of the world other than it is':

> the great irreplaceable potentiality of fiction is that it makes possible the imagining of possibilities. And to imagine other forms of human existence is exactly the challenge that is posed by the climate crisis: for if there is any one thing that global warming has made perfectly clear it is that to think about the world only as it is amounts to a formula for collective suicide. (2016: 128)

Atwood's, McEwan's, and Winterson's novels imagine these new forms of human individuality, which in turn engender new spaces, and new forms of imagination and thought. They introduce new bodies, new potentials for human subjectivity – embedded in new formations that connect All and Nothing, that realise species-specific ecologies, and that unlock politics from its addiction to the kind of planetary manipulation that has brought us to the Anthropocene and the brink of extinction.

Notes

1. Here I speak of the paradigmatic shift identified by Foucault – from 'disciplinary societies' to the globalisation of the 'security society' (see Foucault 2008: 19). Deleuze, who picks up on Foucault's 'disciplinary societies', which he defines as sets of enclosures or 'moulds', later argues that, post-World War II, society has been orchestrated according to the different ontological force of 'control', one that operates not as a mould but as a 'modulation' (see Deleuze 1992). This generalised transition to security eventually sees the rise of 'critical security studies', by Booth and others (see Booth 2005).
2. 'Food security' – a concern that now saturates agricultural disciplines in addition to political and social science disciplines, and orchestrated by global governance bodies like the United Nations – is another symptom of the security society polity (see Ingram, Erickson, and Liverman 2010).
3. See, for instance, Roy Scranton's wartime experiences reformulated to think the Anthropocene's 'end of civilisation', James R. McNeill and Peter Engelke's connection of fossil fuels to 'acceleration', and Jason W. Moore's critique of the term and preference for 'capitalocene' (Scranton 2015; McNeill and Engelke 2014; Moore 2016).

Bibliography

Agamben, Giorgio (2004), *The Open: Between Man and Animal*, Stanford: Stanford University Press.
Agamben, Giorgio (2005), *State of Exception*, Chicago: University of Chicago Press.
Atwood, Margaret (2005), *Oryx and Crake*, New York: Random House.
Atwood, Margaret (2009), *The Year of the Flood*, New York: Random House.
Biello, David (2012), 'Controversial Spewed Iron Experiment Succeeds as Carbon Sink', *Scientific American*, 18 July, < https://www.scientificamerican.com/article/fertilizing-ocean-with-iron-sequesters-co2/> (last accessed 8 January 2019).
Booth, Ken (2005), *Critical Security Studies and World Politics*, Boulder: Lynne Rienner.
Chakrabarty, Dipesh (2009), 'The Climate of History: Four Theses', *Critical Inquiry*, 35:2, pp. 197–222.
Chakrabarty, Dipesh (2012), 'Postcolonial Studies and the Challenge of Climate Change', *New Literary History*, 43:1, pp. 1–18.
Deleuze, Gilles (1992), 'Postscript on the Societies of Control', *October*, 59, pp. 3–7.
Deleuze, Gilles and Félix Guattari (1983), *Anti-Oedipus: Capitalism and Schizophrenia*, Minneapolis: University of Minnesota Press.
Foucault, Michel (2008), *The Birth of Biopolitics: Lectures at the Collège de France, 1978–1979*, New York: Palgrave Macmillan.
Ghosh, Amitav (2016), *The Great Derangement: Climate Change and the Unthinkable*, Chicago: University of Chicago Press.

Hoag, Hannah (2011), 'The Problems with Emissions Trading', *Nature*, 25 November, <https://www.nature.com/news/the-problems-with-emissions-trading-1.9491> (last accessed 1 November 2017).

Ingram, John, Polly Erickson, and Diana Liverman (2010), *Food Security and Global Environmental Change*, New York: Routledge.

IPCC (Intergovernmental Panel on Climate Change) (2014), *Climate Change 2014: Synthesis Report*, Geneva: IPCC.

McEwan, Ian (2010), *Solar*, New York: Random House.

McNeill, James R. and Peter Engelke (2014), *The Great Acceleration: An Environmental History of the Anthropocene Since 1945*, Cambridge, MA: Harvard University Press.

Millennium Ecosystem Assessment (2005), *Ecosystems and Human Well-Being: Scenarios, Vo. 2*, Washington, DC: Island Press.

Moore, Jason W. (2016), *Anthropocene or Capitalocene? Nature, History, and the Crisis of Capitalism*, Oakland: PM Press.

Pumain, Denise (2006), *Hierarchy in Natural and Social Sciences*, New York: Springer.

Rancière, Jacques (1999), *Disagreement: Politics and Philosophy*, Minneapolis: University of Minnesota Press.

Scranton, Roy (2015), *Learning to Die in the Anthropocene*, San Francisco: City Lights.

Serres, Michel (1995), *The Natural Contract*, Ann Arbor: University of Michigan Press.

Virilio, Paul (2003), *Unknown Quantity*, London: Thames and Hudson.

Virilio, Paul (2007), *The Original Accident*, Cambridge: Polity.

von Uexküll, Jakob (2010), *A Foray into the Worlds of Animals and Humans: With a Theory of Meaning*, Minneapolis: University of Minnesota Press.

Winterson, Jeanette (2007), *The Stone Gods*, London: Mariner Books.

18

The Day of the Dark Precursor: Philosophy, Fiction, and Fabulation at the End of the World – A Fictocritical Guide

Charlie Blake

Kleptomancy – divination by theft, whether from oneself or another. Self-quotation to the point of infinite regress, either through pure spatial or linear repetition or a temporal transection of that repetition. A divinatory fugue said to be induced by standing between two parallel mirrors illuminated from above by an all too pellucid moon. A symptom of certain forms of chronic neologophilia in cases of transmodal anxiety syndrome. Sometimes a synonym for a déjà vu within a déjà vu.[1]

Time here ... will be defined ideally by a reversal where the image is unlinked and the cut begins to have an importance in itself. The cut, or interstice, between two series of images no longer forms part of either of the two series: it is the equivalent of the irrational cut, which determines the non-commensurable relations between images.

(Deleuze 1989: 213)

The end of the world is a seemingly interminable topic – at least, of course, until it happens.

(Danowski and De Castro 2017: 24)

Preface

The following text belongs to a long and venerable tradition of found objects and manuscripts whose sense is subsequently unravelled to suit the exigencies of readers or viewers or listeners from a time and place far removed from its initial genesis and production. It can, nonetheless, be fairly accurately dated as having been written down at various points in or between 2018 and 2052 in the common era system, although subject to a certain temporal dislocation between those dates, as was becoming increasingly commonplace in that period. From this approximate dating, however, it is safe to say that it may be read as both a guide to and an extrapolation from certain tendencies in then recent fictocritical discourse as those tendencies had emerged as both an exercise in experimental, speculative fiction and an internal commentary on that process and its context and possible implications under the aegis of the accelerating crisis of the Anthropocene. The structure is fairly straightforward: there are four sections of mythopoeically oriented narration, commentary on or elaboration of various aspects of the crisis and its consequences for human and nonhuman elements as the crisis unfolds, and this is conveyed through the traditional narrative techniques of character, voice, mode, location and context:

> Prologue
> Barnacle Love (a Scherzo for J. G. Ballard)
> The Spindle and the Lyre (a Lecture)
> Singularity and Dispersion (a Delayed Introduction and Commentary)
> Epilogue

If the sections entitled 'Prologue', 'Barnacle Love', 'The Spindle and the Lyre' and the 'Epilogue' are essentially fictional or at least quasi-fictional in their elaboration, the intervention of the fourth section entitled 'Singularity and Dispersion' disrupts this pattern and is of a more overtly critical, philosophical, reflective, diffractive, and theoretical nature, albeit one as reminiscent at times of the digressive style and unreliable narration of, say, the heirs of Miguel de Cervantes or Laurence Sterne or even Vladimir Nabokov as of the more formal, scholarly, or critical introduction. Indeed, its position just prior to the very brief 'Epilogue' is, perhaps, telling in this context. Finally, as the inclusion of a prologue and epilogue would seem to indicate, while the sections may be read in any order the reader so chooses in pursuit of the 'irrational cut' of thought or sense or meaning in the flow of images, it is probably advisable on first reading at least, and while the content is being initially absorbed and processed, to follow the advice of the King of Hearts in Lewis Carroll's exemplary fable to 'begin at the beginning ... and go on till you come to the end: then stop', as it is also, as the editors have recently discovered (although this is of course in no way mandatory), to read it aloud to oneself in the pre-modern and incantatory fashion, rather than silently as was the general convention of the times in which it was presumably written.

Prologue

Later that same day, as the dying sun hung low and heavy in the sky, he gazed for a moment at the ragged script unfurling beneath him as his pen scurried back and forth across the page, back and forth, forth and back, adding, deleting and adding some more. 'Are we inside the mirror or outside the mirror?' he asked himself. 'If one, then the other too, of course ...', a voice replied from behind or beyond the page. 'For we are verbs as much as we are pronouns and pronouns as much as we are nouns and nouns as much as we are the various tricks of narrational focus or modality or diegesis or topical/tropical glitching and gliding', the voice added. He looked up and saw himself looking back at himself. Ran his left index finger slowly along his left eyebrow. A little like Kafka. A little like Burroughs pretending to be Kafka. Looked down. The voice continued. 'And so to be outside the mirror is, of course, to be inside the mirror and vice versa ...

... Everybody knows that.'

Silence followed. A slow, sweet silence. A long, slow, sweet, wet drip of silence, now slithering and sliding down and across the walls of the cavern, down and down again to where the prisoners were chained together, so very far from the sunlight. So very far from the crystalline stars and the bloated sun and the all too pellucid moon. So very far from either source or lichtung. Here instead, a single lightbulb swinging in the gloom. In the intricate darkness. Carving through the darkness. In the invisible breeze. An insolent metronome of flickering light. From some vagrant future. Yours and mine. In the intricate darkness. Yours and mine. In the recalcitrant darkness still curling around and above a broken tesseract of now barely flickering screens. Still curling around and above a savage entropy, itself swirling and sweeping backwards through time in whorls and waves, crashing and lapping and gyring recursively on the shoreline of now. Images of the ghosts of the missing people to come in the quantum spray.

In and out. Flickering. The missing people to come. Fabulating ontographies. Out and in.

Then gone.

And yet.

And yet, high above, far nearer the dying, rotting sun so high above, it finally became clear to him that something had indeed been scribbled down on the page before him, something pliant and yet preserved, dark and yet luminous, at least as it appeared in his mind's eye on the page as it unfurled beneath him and before him. As it scrolled down the screen of his mind's eye, sliding into the between and the beyond of his noetic vision before falling falling falling into newly wrought vector spaces, spaces like cosmic bubbles in which intermedial clusters of rapidly spinning hieroglyphics and strange new intensities were in the process of being born. Unfolding next and sequentially and at unbearable velocities into planes and metaplanes and xenoplanexes, into spinning hyper-geometries and scalar transmodalities, into arrays and extrapolations of myriad transverse symmetries – all of them orthogonal, perhaps, to our own more desultory toposophical conventions, but still graspable, somehow, through the immanence and imminence of the human or posthuman sensorium and its enfolding imaginarium. Still identifiable, that is, from the net of its raw, unprocessed cognition, as captured and then processed, he noted, by minor adjustments to his post-simian wetware apparatus. Actively captured, that is, by exploratory tendrils and tentacles, then reintegralised via the slow process of inscription, along with, in this instance, the detritus of a swiftly vanishing sea, a sea whose glimmering wash and weft still swept the vestiges of the ruined university around him and above him.

New Cross Gate, London, 2052

Barnacle Love (a Scherzo for J. G. Ballard)

Monsters on the shore – As with every intertidal zone, lower climes are filled with monsters. Sea stars and whelk snails live by devouring helpless, immobile barnacles – but at the same time, they are damaged by the Sun's desiccation if they venture too high.

(Palumbi and Palumbi 2014: 79)

> [I]f you see such a semiotic barnacle, scrape it off.
>
> (Haraway 2016: 169)

Later that same day, Theodora and I took a long walk along the seashore and marvelled at the jewel-encrusted buildings that had somehow survived the metastases of the dreamcancer,[2] vibrant, lapidary cathedrals of supplicant arches and vine-strangled towers rising above the shimmering waves like something from a canvas by an imaginary union of Max Ernst and M. C. Escher. Then, a little further down the coast, we marvelled once more at the iridescent spiralling bioformations still accreting in, around and just above those dangerous waters, as they swirled and lapped and licked with soft azure tongues the old worn steps that would once have led down to the circular harbour. 'For these are waters', – as my companion noted and as we observed as we walked and talked beneath the dying mats of moss and lichen on the harbour wall – 'for these are waters', she continued, 'waters and waves within and beneath which, amidst the tangled web of confluvial life and above the strands of ebb and tideflow, a softly pulsing throb of reflected and refracted solar flaring from the rotting sun will very soon raise these waters' temporal ambience to a near Venusian intensity of heat and time in the shimmering black sunfire and from thence like gunfire vaporise those same waters to nothing . . .'

. . . and yet, to our delight, as we ambled along the shoreline in the early morning mists ~ and then to our further delight as we walked on and as the fieriest tendrils of the savage noonday eschaton burned and spat and flared and sizzled backwards through time and then spread out across and through time as a fan of incandescent and rapidly accelerating cilia on and through the vermilion sands and the pearlish brown rocks that jutted above them and the bubbling, silver-veined mud beneath those rocks and then vitrified the footsteps we had left behind us on the palimpsest beach as we walked and talked . . .

'. . . oh will you? won't you?' she asked, 'will you? won't you? will you join the dance? . . .', she asked . . .

. . . and yet, and yet as we walked beneath those exquisite coral arches and adamantine bridges and obsidian terraces and talked of cabbages and kings and other such things, and yet, and yet even in all this ~ those ancient and venerable Crustacea, the acorn barnacles we had come to see still clung to those same glistening, fractured hieratic rocks. Static, sliding and serpentine, slithering and still, caught, it seemed at times, as though in the zigzag eye of the photographer's flash. Caught as the object of a moment in an infernal dance between the fractured gaze of the burning eye of the rotting corpse of the ancient sun so very high above and the lapping cauldron of emergent death and life so very deep below. Barnacles. Scuttling in slow-motion updownstillwards as an etching of motion, of Brownian ecstasy, like a Viola-frame unravelling in quasi-time, in different velocities, paddling first like dancing spinning vacuoles in incrementally abbreviated spirals, voids and curlings, rising next from a place where monsters of the briny deep, newly enhanced, neuro-circuited and bio-temporised by the vagrant outliers of quasi-legal scientific research, were still predating on the living delicacies clinging to those same rocks in the intervals between night and day ~

Though here I must digress before I have even truly begun (he continued). And so I will now continue to continue by confessing to a small, avolutionary, spatio-temporal conceit, or even deceit, conducted, I suppose, for the sake of a certain 'literary symmetry', as my mentor once described it . . .

. . . and so, and so it goes, and so to rewind a little, thus and this, thus it was that while harvesting some newly discovered varieties of barnacle in an archipelago of the South China Sea I received an urgent message via sinowave™ from Theodora. We had last met at a colloquium on the machinic resurrection of late twentieth-century philosophers in the ruins of Goldsmiths College, University of London, in the previous year (see Blake 2018: *passim*), and had promised one another to meet up again this summer at a symposium being held on the coast of Madagascar at the Institute of Nissological Studies, a centre for teaching and research which had quite recently been established there by the eminent nissologist and doyen of vanishing archipelagos Professor Diane Morgan of Vincennes, Paris, under the aegis of the many-breasted goddess of love and law, along with the goddess's consort, our sweet and barbarous friend and ally, the shattered muse of ecstasy and annihilation, Dionysia. I had up until that point, I must confess, been somewhat lost in my beloved schizo-cartographical musings and meanderings, sketching out moments and instants of past and future intertidal extinction, then branching out these moments and instants as heuristically freighted extensions in blips, bars, lines, planes, vectors, metaplanes, and xenoplanexes: as hypostitional models, in effect, in all directions and none. 'Weaving meo-ontosophical tapestries for bored apocalypticians' (as Theodora had once half-joked to me on the fast train to Uppsala), 'even after the event of cosmicide itself!' And yes I indeed was, as she had so astutely observed, still effectively weaving meo-ontosophical tapestries for bored apocalypticians such as myself (doodling in the waiting room of my cosmic pessimism, as another meo-ontosophical ally had once put it). And yet, as Theodora also knew so well (and had for many centuries, it often seemed, but how could that be?), beneath all that theatrical nihilism I had always nurtured a deep and melismatic yearning for undiscovered ends, for the sweet harmonies of light and voice and mycelial connection as much as for the darker, earthier, dissonances of time, loss, and absence. And thus it was, Janus-like and contrary as ever, I carried with me in heavily annotated paperback my copies of Charles Darwin's four volumes on barnacles, within which he had started to establish patterns in species diversity through a meticulous taxonomy of these remarkable Crustacea some ten years before the publication of *The Origin of Species*.

Oh yes. Darwin. The fifth great Misteress of Suspicion (after Marx, Nietzsche, Lovelace, and Freud). Precursor of both temporal warping and proxy-line immortality. The naturalist, the geologist, the loomist, the vampire, and the time traveller in some hyperstitional (or hypostitional) loop/anomaly – dreaming into being from a nineteenth-century study in southern England the Möbius strip of transcontinental psychic epidemiology in the early to mid-twenty-first century. Double agents from another dimension too, of course. And so. To facilitate this manoeuvre I was looking specifically at those overlapping few weeks when old Shanghai sunk beneath the plasticene waves and the superplutocrats began to move en masse in venal swarms to the fast-expanding resorts of the Arctic and sub-Arctic Riviera. When ancient African gods were resurrected in accelerating waves of furious retribution against the drone-drenched demonocracies of the Old West – fomenting techno-wars (as if we could forget) with organic avatars and the time-extracted metrics of delivery and termination. But when she called me that afternoon I was resting rather than working or even contemplating (my vitrified shellspawn, arrayed in blue-green vitrine) – swinging gently, that is, in my soft hammock beneath the cool blue stratum of the boat (as it creaked gently in the waters) and reading a late twentieth-century visionary fiction called *Pussy, King of the Pirates*. It was one of Theodora's favourite texts, and she had given it to me in London after acquiring it herself on the upper level of the notorious Urverk bar in downtown Uppsala some years before.

'Oh Zeno dearest', she had said, 'dearest Zeno, *please* do come and hear my presentation next week if you can! And be my respondent too, perhaps? It would be so lovely to see you again! We could go walking on the beach and observe ghost barnacles on that beautifully poisonous shore!' And so it was, some three days later, here I was. Miraculate and, unusually for me, nearly solvent. And then, newly arrived, there she was too, standing on the tarmacate waiting for me. I watched her for a moment. As I always did. As I always will.

Oh Theodora, (once saint and martyr of old Alexandria, now remade, remodelled, reanimated, repurposed, reborn, like Dionysus or the Nazarene she thought to herself, but different too, lipstick, scent and circuitry, silk and chrome, and flexible carbon boots on the cracked, black tarmacate), paused, shook her head a little, just a touch to dissipate the haze of travel and exhaustion, bit her lip, brushed a lock of stray, golden, blue, and purple hair from her eyes, eyes now of obsidian now of gold now of vermilion, now of ultra-violet or infra-red, and now she closed those tired, opalescent eyes tight tight tight shut, long dark lashes interlocking, eyebrows furrowed, and now took a long, slow, deep, endless breath, allowed her mind to still for a moment, like a rough pebble in a mountain stream. And then, after looking into herself and having established from this inward glance how much time she still had available before the darkness fell, looked down deeply into herself, into the simian wetware apparatus she was wearing, deep into the heat and heart of the flesh and circuitry, and searched then with human digits to check her physical and topographical coordinates, her actual as well as her virtual location. Having calculated the distance between where she now stood and her target, she looked up again at the mazy empyrean, at the vast abrupt.

Gazing. Thoughtful. Dreaming. Wistful.

> *Oh, my sweet muse. Oh, my distaff muse. Oh, my shattered muse. My sweet and holy protectoress. My dark and holy precursor. Time-shattered crystals falling like snow. Falling and calling from innumerable futures entagliated. Trapped though in a singular past. Frozen now in Baltic amber. Africa. Sweet Africa. Woven in French tapestries. Stained in English*

> *glass. Etched on quantum particles and the aureoles of distant and dying suns. Etched in the Egyptian sand, sea and sky. Africa. Written on swirling waters. Written on the hot, desert wind. Alexandria. Lost city. Sunken city. So long ago. Satan's last and listless gambit. Heat and surcease. Don't get distracted now. Wait! Look! Open your eyes!*
>
> (Blake 2018: 229)

Then she turned to look at me. And so, next, a brief embrace, the briefest of embraces, then a kiss, then a longer kiss, a pause, and then, in due course, one more kiss, longer, slower, slowest, and then, in due course, we slipped sideways ~ turning ~ a spectral switch of horiscene ~ and then chronoscene ~ then chthulucene ~ to transverscene.

Turned away, that is, from the old ruined landing site by that half-dismantled pier of jutting rusting bones and salt-worn pornwood. Now here then rather than there then ~ that is ~ then. OK? Here. Now here in this softly muted and yet elegantly fashioned cocktail bar. (Virilio's Bar, that is, adjoining the ultra-luxurious Café Nemo next to the Hilbert hotel where we were staying.)

Gaze steady now. Deep so deep into my eyes. Rays of heavenly polychromatic light spectrally suffused. Like mediaeval optics or specularities times twice. Polychromatically profane. Obscene. Double Fast Naked Fast Naked. Double Silhouette. Dark Vine Sex. Divine dissipation. As intense as the tropical night to come. A shift of one foot. Rustle of fabric. Lemurs across the rooftops. A look. Upwards. Ghosts in transit.
Forest waves. Night waves.
Dying sun.

Now here in this softly muted and yet elegantly fashioned cocktail bar, arrayed in retro-black and silver and chrome and set in quasi-symmetry against the tracings of faux Chinoiserie falling from the ceiling, with spiral vino-stands and concentrically arranged Japanese beer slots in dull grey on either side (if you can visualise it), arrayed, that is, also, with shot silk curtains veined with neurographics of the Great Accident, shading the chronoscene – here on this reckless and piratical sliver of the Malagasy coast where she now clicks and now whirrs and hums and is now about to start, a small and yet super-attentive halo of an audience super-splayed around her feet, her mirror boots, plugging and un-plugging and re-plugging themselves into the vinculum.

She paused for a moment. Closed her eyes. Tongue darted between lips, in and out. Fast. Twice. Three times. Forked and lascivious. Control. Opened her eyes. Dilated from black slits. Obsidian slits. Magenta now. Wide. Looked around. Up. Down. Now.

Then, pointedly, she looks towards me and projects now a quotation from Plato and another from Maurice Blanchot and another from Georges Bataille and another from Donna Haraway in the air just above us and between us, giving us all a moment to peruse it, collectively. Arches a single eyebrow, the left one, as if to make sure we are paying her *full* attention now.

Pauses for silence. Purses her lips. Incipit.

The Spindle and the Lyre (a Lecture)

> When feminine divinities even imperceptibly govern discourse, becoming still exists.
>
> (Irigaray 2013: 23)

> [W]e may catch ourselves looking forward to what will in no time be staring you larrikins on the postface in that multimirror megaron of returningties, whirled without end to end.
>
> (Joyce 2012: 554)

Minutes to go.[3]

One of the more curious moments in Plato's oeuvre comes in the concluding book of *The Republic*, where after Socrates has made his most complete statement yet on the separation of philosophy and myth or literature – speculative writing, in effect – the reader is taken to a tale of katabasis and anabasis with a moral that both extends the theme of justice that runs throughout the ten books and at the same time seemingly contradicts the injunction against the poet or artist as a citizen of the ideal polity. The argument in books three and ten of *The Republic* is well known, but in brief, Plato's position as expressed via Socrates is that poetry (and more problematically, myth) detracts from truth and justice, the pursuit of which is understood as the basis of the ideal state, and does so by virtue of its use of mimesis, which is an imitation of things in the world that are themselves imitations of the forms and thus doubly distanced from the source of light. From the sun. The phantoms of fiction in this sense are like the shadows on the cave wall far from the solar truth in his famous simile, shadows whose enjoyment is at best a distraction from the pursuit of the true way and at worst a degeneracy of the intellect in favour of pure sensation. Famously, Aristotle sought to rescue the poets and artists and audiences and readers from his teacher's derision by the creation of a poetics and the development of an aesthetics. Poetics in this case can be understood as Aristotle's recuperation of the poetic for philosophy, as part of the *organon*, in that it conceptualises the poetic and thus returns it to the pursuit of truth, justice, order, and so forth, the pursuit that Plato excluded it from. This is, of course, in keeping with Aristotle's more general project to provide what we might now call a scientific account of everything that is or has been or could be or indeed could never be, from voids to vacuums to tetrachords to time machines to ballistics to barnacles and so on. What this initial quarrel established by Plato sets up is a tension between the poetic (or the literary/artistic) and the philosophical that resonates through history from that moment to the present, and which generates an enigmatic and often paradoxical tension that is also the source and indeed the engine behind much if not all of the productivity in both fields of reflection and endeavour. Perhaps no one has described this tension quite so well as Blanchot, who notes in *The Writing of Disaster* that:

A philosopher who would write as a poet would be aiming for his own destruction. And even so, he could not reach it. Poetry is a question for philosophy which claims to provide it with an answer, and thus to comprehend it (know it). Philosophy, which puts everything into question, is tripped up by poetry, which is the question that eludes it. (Blanchot 1995: 50)

Aside from the generically male poet in this passage, who now seems so oddly and anachronistically 'merely male', this statement, with its characteristically abstruse and Blanchotian gesturing towards some kind of aesthetic or cognitive revelation that never actually arrives, perfectly captures the evasive moment of resolution which never resolves itself between the philosophical and the literary modes of apprehension and movement, whether textually, dialectically, or otherwise. But it is in the next section of Plato's *Republic* in book ten that we find this moment of impossibility and conceptual incongruity most eloquently and vividly realised. In this section we move, somewhat surprisingly considering the injunction we have just left, to a mythical tale of an ordinary Pamphylian soldier called Er who dies and is reborn so as to tell of what he has witnessed in the underworld, in the land of the dead. Here he sees many things over a specified period of time, notably the noble dead choosing the form of their rebirth as human or nonhuman. Here Orpheus, upon whose abject failure to rescue Eurydice from Hades in the myth Blanchot pins the essence of the gift of creativity itself, decides to be reborn as a swan, thus abandoning his lyre for a lifetime of monogamous quietude and, one assumes, radical uncreativity. But more striking than any of this is the spindle of necessity whose stem and hook are made of adamant, while its whorl consists of various substances ... one is bound to picture it as if there were first a large, hollow whorl, with its insides completely scooped out, and with a second, smaller one lying snugly inside it. If this image is not bizarre enough, we discover further whorls within whorls within whorls making up this extraordinary mechanism of fate, and then the central function of its motion and meaning personified through a combination of Pythagorean number and mythical entities:

> And the spindle turned on the knees of Necessity, and up on each of the rims of the circles a Siren stood, borne around in its revolution and uttering one sound, one note, and from all the eight there was a concord of a single harmony. And there were three others who sat round at equal intervals, each one on her throne, the Fates, daughters of Necessity, clad in white vestments with filleted heads, Lachesis, and Clotho, and Atropos, who sang in unison with the music of the Sirens, Lachesis singing the things that were, Clotho the things that are, and Atropos the things that are to be. (Plato quoted in Lao 2007: 43)

Of course, there are many readings of the significance of this machine, from the Pythagorean to the parodic, but what is this machine for us now, for philosophy and poetry and art under a dying sun and a weeping moon, what is this spindle of necessity in the world to come, after the end of the world, that is, for the missing people to come, that is, other than a miraculating machine as Gilles Deleuze and Félix Guattari once borrowed this extraordinary image from the records of Daniel Paul Schreber via the case study of Freud? A miraculating machine as a fabulating machine, that is, like the writing machine of Franz Kafka in his famous story of the penal colony, but in this case a machine built not to punish or inscribe the law of punishment and cruelty as judgement so much as to invent new dreams between the poles of chance and necessity, like something from the Casino of Lost Objects or an image drawn from an as yet unwritten story by the soon to be resurrected Argentinian poet of crossed destinies, or even a real casino mechanism, a radical contingency generator, pulled out of an imaginary Las Vegas into another story completely, and creating that story as a reflection on its philosophical origins in conflict and loss. Like Saint Jerome's visions of the women of Rome and the temptations of the heart and the flesh and the soul and the intellect that came to him via Satan's radio as he moved from station to station in the barren heat of the desert of Chalcis, but translated for another age and another mechanism of desire and dereliction. Or like a broken-down Elvis or Sinatra or Kanye or a glitching Marilyn Marilyn Marilyn or Rihannana or Gagagaga dadadadada flickering holosophographically in the pixilated ruins of a man's-man's-man's world, or so it seems (but it don't mean nothing … nothing … nothing), and many other such visions and revisions and elisions. Indeed, it may be, as we sit here watching the sky crack open and the oceans flair and acidify and our identities merge, it may be that this fabulating machine is the only machine we have left to dream with, the only map and compass we have left for the post-Anthropocene age we are so hastily creating for ourselves and our children of selves and for the dreams we have left to dream in the short time we still have available to us on this blue and fragile world.

After the lecture had concluded and questions had been asked and responded to, Theodora and I sat in the café thinking together about this fabulating machine that is also a spindle of necessity that is also an engine of contingency and invention, thinking together about the talk she had just given on this dream of Plato and the lyre of Orpheus and the missing people to come at the end of the world, gazing together next at a bedraggled coffee-table book on the famous unicorn tapestries that had until so recently hung in museums in Paris and New York, and then at a monochrome picture of a figure scribbling in a darkened room in a ruined and flooded city and then at a picture of another figure about to walk from the wings onto a stage in front of an invisible audience and then at an image of a leaf floating and circling high above another city or perhaps many cities and then finally at a picture of you, dear reader, opening a book or screen or holosphere and finding yourself gazing back at yourself in the mirror of the print and discovering that this very moment of conceptual copulation, of selective narcissistic bibliosexuality, of involuntary iteration, now, here, in the heart of the flesh of the universal book, in the rustle of its virtual pages, in which you gather the random sweepings of print and page and pixel before you into a singular moment of logos and see yourself gazing back at yourself and see yourself retrospectively casting sense and un-sense back to now and forward to now again so closing the loop of understanding and discovering again that yes, today is the day of the dark precursor and always was and always will be.

Yes.

'Perhaps it's time to leave now', I said to Theodora, as she raised her eyes from the book and looked deep into mine. 'Yes', she said, 'you're right. I think it's time to go.'

Singularity and Dispersion (a Delayed Introduction and Commentary)

> True it never *was*. Yet because they loved, it was
> A pure creature. They left it room enough.
> And in that space, clear and un-peopled,
> It raised its head lightly and scarcely needed
> Being.
>
> (Rilke 2001: 175)

> Everything happens and nothing is recorded
> In these rooms of the looking glass,
> Where, magicked into rabbis, we
> Now read the books from right to left.
>
> (Borges 1964: 60)

Of late, in certain critical or speculative circles and networks, and particularly in those circles and networks concerned with the notion of the Anthropocene or its cognates – or a fortiori with the post-Anthropocene and its various supposedly retroactive causalities[4] – it has become almost de rigueur to note that in the face of an ever-expanding array of doom-laden scenarios confronting our world and our increasingly fragile species, one of the more illuminating tools for the forensic and therapeutic investigation of these dark projections and of our potential responses to them is not so much the formal essay or lecture or public debate, or even the documentary, so much as an often freely associative hybrid of, say, philosophy, fiction, mathematics, and scientific report, sometimes termed theory-fiction, or philosophiction or fictocriticism, or some variant on that hybridisation.[5] That such should be, or at least might well be, the case should not perhaps really surprise us that much in this derelict age in which we find ourselves, any more than it might have in any former age, for in an extended sense (and allowing the scientific report as such and newly specialised areas of mathematics such as set theory, category theory, and mereotopology, not to mention computational aesthetics, diagrammatics, data geometry, schizo-cartography, and geotraumatics, to be rather later guests at the literary-philosophical banquet), the apparently recent move to theory-fiction or fictocriticism on the edges of academic discourse could be viewed as being merely the latest (and possibly the last, as in final, or terminal) manifestation of a more consistent human tendency. This is a tendency in the critical reflection on life and creativity that may well have emerged with the birth of writing or even before (we can only speculate), and might be said to dip in and out of sight and fashion as different schools and expert-systems rise and fall, but in essence can certainly be argued to extend back, so far as our fragmentary records allow, to pre-Socratic intellectuals such as Heraclitus and Parmenides in the Western tradition, as well as their contemporaneous equivalents in China, Africa, Western and Central Asia, and the Indian subcontinent in the so-called axial age.[6] For what is at stake here is not merely the recording of affect, percept, concept, calculation, and event transcribed as marks scratched on wood or stone or papyrus or skin or even mist, fire, and running water (*pace* Heraclitus or Siddhartha or Lao Tzu or the mythical Hermes Trismegestus), but the opening and closing of human time itself through the coactively bio-isomorphic status of writing itself, of inscription itself, of the logos itself, as thinking not just in time, but on time, around time, and through time.

This is writing that may be understood in a certain mode and in a broadly Derridean sense as an *arche*-writing, certainly, but more specifically, more usefully, and perhaps more cybernetically in this context, it can also be grasped as the switch or governor of that opening and closing of time, of that systole and diastole of contingency and chronoplasticity, as also of the multidimensional looms involved in weaving and distributing patterns of data, affect, information, and light that render themselves to our transient consciousness in exponentially intricate tapestries of number, sense, and soma. This is writing apprehended as an attenuated event operating at the deepest and swiftest levels of meaning, mattering, and textuality,[7] an event whose process and mechanism of attenuation is, and by virtue of that process and mechanism, unavailable to our direct consciousness except as a fleeting and entirely contingent diagram of cybernesis or topology, or more indirectly – and in many cases this may well be the same thing – as a piece of music or a poem or an image or an equation or an inscription, a fragment of speech or narrative or code, or even a smear of light in the sky or a fleeting daydream. What is at stake, then, as a consequence and at an operational level, at a level more directly available to ordinary human consciousness in the quotidian production of meaning or significance, that is, as also to its primary, secondary, and tertiary memory systems,[8] is writing as a machine, as a report or account or balancing up or summing up of its constituent elements, or as a statement of law as retribution, distribution, command, and control within a local rather than a universal context, as it was in the earliest known iterations of writing as law such as the code of Hammurabi, sixth king of the first Babylonian dynasty, in the eighteenth century BCE. More pertinently, what is also at stake for this account, as it adumbrates selectively its underlying concern with the ontology of fiction and fictional entities and events more generally, is writing as the generator of pseudo-ontologies and conceptual or affective topologies of being, of 'beings of fiction' as Bruno Latour has described them (Latour 2013: 233–59), and thus, by extension, of the traditional categories of myth and fiction, drama and poetry, film and fantasy, of the fleeting daydream as much as the epic, and of the poetics and aesthetics and critical or analytical commentaries attendant upon these forms of expression, diegesis, and mimesis. This is in contrast, of course, to the supposed purity and rigour and logical auto-surveillance – even to the transcendental or foundational qualities – of writing as philosophical analysis or conversation or dialectic in the Socratic tradition (a contrast which has, of course, haunted the Western literary and philosophical imagination, as we have seen above, since Plato's expulsion of the poets and artists from his ideal society some two and a half millennia ago). Moreover, and bearing in mind this distinction between art or poetry, on the one hand, and philosophy, on the other, and by way of a sociocultural context for the melange of genres and the intricate metalinguistic levels that this distinction can so easily generate, this understanding of the marks and morphemes of writing as either literary (or fictional) and philosophical (or critical-analytical) is not to be considered here or in the quasi-fictional fragments that precede this commentary as a merely spatial arrangement of fundamentally temporal forms and utterances, especially as metaphysically enhanced by its potentially ironic relation to by now archaic and long-abandoned intellectual vogues such as poststructuralism or postmodernism or deconstruction or speculative realism, and ornamentally displayed – curated even – for the gallery, the archive, the museum, or the library of human imagination through the ages, but one defined by its own tendency to strategic conflation or disappearance. Indeed, it is not unfair to claim that we are living through an era of multiplicitous accelerations in which a theory and its immediate progeny may flash in and out of web presence or prescience with an extraordinary alacrity, retaining influence even as it self-dismantles.

Perhaps a cogent example of this phenomenon might be given through one of the more significant examples of this tendency from the first decade of the twenty-first century, Reza Negarestani's vertiginously projective fictocritical-theory-novel *Cyclonopedia: Complicity with Anonymous Materials*. This was a literary-philosophical-mythological-mereotopological event whose publication in 2008 spawned near-instant critical acclaim and anatomisation[9] at the same time as its author began gradually but decisively to distance himself from its more delirial post-Deleuzo-Guattarian/Bataillian libidinal materialism, its emergent 'tiamaterialism', to embrace an ostensibly more rigorous, bracing, and decidedly neo-rationalist philosophical-computational aesthetic, an aesthetic tracing out retro-projections of artifical general intelligence (AGI) synthesis via Wilfrid Sellars and others, for example, before moving forward to a resurrection (via Robert Brandom and others) of Hegel for the computational age.[10] Negarestani's case is interesting for a number of reasons, not least its intellectual density and ambitious scope, but it is especially notable for the present context in that it exemplifies a dilemma that inevitably arises when talking or writing about something as potentially ephemeral as theory-fiction, in that it raises the question of whether – in this instance – *Cyclonopedia* was somehow exemplary of a new fictocritical genre in the process of emerging from a roiling sea of theory, reflecting as it did so on disciplinary transitions moving deep beneath the lapping waves of everyday discourse, like accelerated tectonic plates in the creation of a new conceptual continent, or merely a brief and unique divergence from patterns of theoretical-fictional hybridisation. That Negarestani had and has since been working in the art world more often than in mainstream academia is significant too for reasons that are also more generally convergent with the present discussion or chapter (or 'work') in terms of both its method and its methodology, if not its momentum. They are convergent with this discussion in that it may be said to operate with a set of styles and techniques drawn from the art world as much as from academia as such, a set of styles and techniques in which *ekphrasis* may be taken as a fundamental operating principle for a start. In addition, this is an operative principle accompanied by a certain pathos towards the work-as-process-and-event. A pathos whose inspiration and momentum might be further characterised as involving an unlikely marriage between, on the one hand, the gravity and evasiveness of Blanchot's pursuit of the source and origin of art in the tragic error of Orpheus in his essay on that theme as elsewhere in his work, and on the other, the tightly controlled conceptual anarchism and tactical irony of the post-Internet artist Seth Price, who opens his art-novel *Fuck Seth Price* with the following:

> He drifted through a thick and obscure world, observant but incapable of action. It took him a while to understand that he wasn't dreaming, but moving through the real world and actual life, only it was no longer his life, because his body and all its doings were no longer under his control. (Price 2015: 8)

To make this pathos function effectively as a working critical axiomatic or at least *stimmung* from which to generate statements about its aim and object that are also part of that aim and object, or are at least mirrored by them (vertically as well as horizontally), certain assertions need to be absorbed by the reader at this point, not so much as eternal verities but as transitional and transactional coordinates or sub-axioms or operative functions. These are functions that may be said to operate, for example, through the consumption and internalisation of an image of the following list or snapshot of the genealogy of the ephemeral category of literary-philosophical commentary called theory-fiction or fictocriticism, as that category itself applies reflexively to this textual installation called 'The Day of the Dark Precursor'. This image once internalised may then be considered as a working but ultimately contingent and thus entirely disposable map of what follows and precedes this statement. Accordingly, if then the contemporary genealogy of theory-fiction may be said in general, and provisionally, to locate its origins in a blend of the cosmic horror of H. P. Lovecraft, the erotothanatropics of Bataille, and the generally unclassifiable project of Deleuze and Guattari, and also traces out various strands of lineage through Sterne, Herman Melville, Carroll, Arthur Conan Doyle, Burroughs, Clarice Lispector, Walter Benjamin, Jorge Luis Borges, Kathy Acker, J. G. Ballard, Hélène Cixous, Blanchot, Luce Irigaray, Pierre Klossowski, Cindy Sherman, Vilém Flusser – and more recently Nick Land, Negarestani, Renee Gladman, China Miéville, Tacita Dean, Donald Glover, Janelle Monáe, and Thomas Ligotti – it also embraces any moment and quite promiscuously any text or image or concept or code or meta-code that furthers its ravenous hybridity, so long as that text, image, concept, or code, etc., has or can be assigned a value that might then be described as philosophical or theoretical as well as fictional.

To forestall at this stage any possible disappointment (and please leave the auditorium quietly if you wish to exit before the interval), it should be made clear that there will be no attempt here as in the sections that preceded this commentary to reference or analyse any further the history, genealogy, or thematics of this general tendency or of this emergent fictocritical mentality and its attendant mode of production/consumption/subversion, as I have no doubt there are others far better qualified than the present commentator to take on this undoubtedly invaluable academic exercise. Rather, and considering this ravenous hybridity of critical bricolage as an aspect of what has been elsewhere described as *phenomenophagism*,[11] this brief delayed introduction merely comments on the blending of fiction, philosophy, fabulation, and marine biology (a combination certain elements of which have, of course, a notable precedent in Aristotle, or at least in the exploded version of Aristotle bequeathed to us via Arabic, medieval, and Renaissance scholars, a precedent that extends experimentally, and perhaps arguably in the case of philosophy, through Melville and Lovecraft, Flusser, Ballard, Irigaray, and Miéville) that seeks to at least begin to interrogate the era we are living through and the one we are about to enter with the textual and conceptual tools available to us in this emergent critical form and related media. It should be considered, therefore, not so much as a critical survey or argument per se, but more – and by specifically deploying the 'lecture', 'colloquium', and 'academic report' formats as *mise en abymes* – as an interrogation of the limits and possibilities of a certain manifestation of theory-fiction in the face of the coming ecoclasm. This is a process itself framed within a more spectral theory-fiction that is in turn framed by and within a broader project of affective and conceptual engineering that embraces installation, performance, post-Internet, and sound art (by way of an archiving of the vanishing present) as well as the more conventional travails of academic publication. But these are, of course, merely retrospective promises and hints that might or might not have been fulfilled by the text above, thereby raising the question of the promise as a philosophical or theoretical problem when it comes to the pseudo-ontologies and statements of fiction. So what of fabulation and the 'people to come', then, as hinted towards in the Deleuzian mode of the subtitle?[12] What of the Dark Precursor of the title itself?[13] Is this entity from Deleuze's arguably most important philosophical book the key to this text – or merely what Alfred Hitchcock used to describe in relation to his film-plots as a MacGuffin? Well, as keys (or MacGuffins) go, incongruity and paradox may well be considered the master here, far more so perhaps than Deleuze's fabulation per se, or at least far more so in any direct or obviously denotational sense. The radical incongruity of the post-Internet artist Price, whom we have mentioned before, which combines music, sound, and the moving image with achronic commentary and fragmented speculation in ways that deliberately exacerbate the differences between these vehicles and which thereby refuse to allow ordinary sense to link them into any consistent or congruous pattern, can then, in this case, be treated as the master key that opens the lock to reveal further keys and further locks as well as a number of keys that appear to have no locks and vice versa. In this sense the practice of systematic incongruity and inconsistency which we identify here – of the unreliable narrator of traditional narrative fiction abducted and transferred to the creative nonfiction of theory, criticism, and cultural or philosophical commentary – can be said to parallel the more general art-theoretical conversation Price adumbrates and for which it is both an effect and a precursor. For as he notes in his art-critical guide *Dispersion*, of the art he produces as part of the detritus of Conceptualism and a conversation about that detritus and its rearrangement, this is a form of post-Conceptualism that remains, perhaps necessarily, 'radically incomplete', and quoting Martha Rosler, is an

> 'as if' approach, where the Conceptual work cloaks itself in other disciplines (philosophy being the most notorious example), provoking an oscillation between skilled and de-skilled, authority and pretence, style and strategy, art and not-art. (Price 2002)

Nor is this mood or pathos the province of the plastic arts and their written or critical legacy alone, but it may be said to permeate the 2010s in a number of ways. A parallel stylistic ennui in the ostensibly literary arena may be found in the work, for instance, of the novelist Jarett Kobek, who in *I Hate the Internet* and *The Future Won't Be Long* has made it abundantly clear that he is writing deliberately bad novels with no redeeming novelistic features whatsoever, as this reflects – and reflects upon – the experience of the reading and writing subject in a web-addicted world in ways that a good novel never could. Thus we have, as one critic put it: 'in the place of realistic characters and a coherent plot … Twitterish one-liners, bloggy opinions and chatter about celebrities' (Newman 2017), and no attempt made to redeem this relentless Kardashian superfluity, or even give it the satirical bite that might feasibly be claimed of Price. And yet, for some readers Kobek defines the age and its literary supplement as accurately as if not more so than more traditional novelists such as Zadie Smith, Don DeLillo, Margaret Atwood, or Dave Eggers. In essence, however, the presiding spirit of this perception of the times we now live in long precedes it, having lived on the coast of modern-day Turkey in the sixth century BCE. Here, Heraclitus, the 'weeping philosopher', generated a series of gnomic statements some of which have come down to us as fragments, such as this one: 'The fairest order in the world is a heap of random sweepings' (Heraclitus 1979: 85). Thus, if the world or universe is chaos, the capacity of psyche to conceive it holistically is order. It is this apparent disjunctive synthesis of chaos and the logos, characterised by the human ability to make sense of chaos as a partner of and precursor to the order of sense (and not, perhaps, the sense of order) rather than as a polarity, that characterises for this writer the critical spirit of the age in its writing and reading, which, as well as being inherently chaosophical in the manner described in relation to the schizo-analytic cartographies of Guattari, is haunted transversally by a spirit of paradox as old as philosophy itself. But the spirit of paradox must combine with the more delinquent and vagrant spirit of the times in every dice throw, for such is the engine of the chronoplasticity to come. And what we find now in this combinatorial conceptualism is not so much the 'waning of affect' once predicted by Fredric Jameson (1991: 10) as the defining ethos of postmodernism, but rather a conscious heightening of its artificial tones and timbres as a kind of affective engineering which is also as a mode of cognitive navigation and negotiation appropriate to the era of the Anthropocene/post-Anthropocene malaise. What this also indicates in terms of contemporary critical method is a certain aleatory shift, combining the illusion of forward momentum associated with classical dialectics and the essay form generally with the aesthetic of drift and digression associated with the various trans-generic forms and expressions of experimental literature and art, from Sterne and the Baroque through the golden age of experimental modernism to the diaspora of post-Internet creativity represented, at least in the Anglosphere, by figures such as Price and Kobek, but also by elements of collage, pastiche, and montage in, say, experimental electronic music, olfactory art, trans-urban performance, Afrofuturism, and parallel currents of creative and critical activity. What these art-critical products also suggest are new ways of reading the spectral landscape of the Anthropocene and its inhabitants, human or otherwise, organic or nonorganic, and even of reading the traces of the missing-people-to-come who haunt retroactively its derelict forests and poisoned wastelands and ruined cities and acidified oceans. But significantly, these are ways still rooted in the most ancient philosophical examples, such as those that have survived from the weeping philosopher himself.

So in this discussion we have moved backwards and forwards and via a series of knight's moves, taking in some of the ancient battles identified by Plato and Aristotle in the Western tradition, dipping into the warm jacuzzi of continental philosophy's sensual flirtation with the literary, and the metafictional fascination with the mirror. We have also hinted, albeit very indirectly via pararga, at the bracing conceptual showers and ontological vicissitudes of analytic philosophy's infatuation with the unicorn. We will, however, delay discussion of this latter arresting anomaly for a moment until its relation, along with that of the existence or otherwise of unicorns, to the broader issue of contemporary philosophy and contemporary fiction (or ancient fiction read with contemporary eyes) and imminent ecocatastrophe has been more clearly delineated – or not, as the case may be. Indeed, because of the often vagrant nature of its subject matter (and as should by now be evident to the reader if she has got this far), this process of delineation, definition, and triangulation requires a plethora of techniques and misdirections from both the literary and the philosophical traditions, from vagrant epigraphs – increasingly inadmissible in much academic writing – to broken-off lectures, random stage directions, and sometimes incongruous dramatic or speculative digressions that appear to lead nowhere. The movement between these elements will sometimes be as smooth as the radio segue of a seasoned disc jockey and at other times as abrupt as the jump cut in the early films of Jean-Luc Godard or its equivalent in the temporal (or possibly static) philosophy of Deleuze. At this stage, however, and for reasons more cartographic than conceptual or dialectical, we must conclude by adumbrating at the very least the lines of connection between those elements as they manifest in the contemporary capitalist imaginary and through the scholarly and critical shoots and tendrils being sent out from that imaginary into the thin and foetid air of the world beyond and without the human.

In terms of both momentum and drift, then, what has been central both to the reflexive and recursive conceits deployed in this presentation, and to the argument or arguments (for why be singular when you can be plural?) these conceits will help to begin to trace out and bring into profile, is the possible emergence of new forms of corporeality and embodiment aligned with the rehearsal of a transversal ethics appropriate to an age in which the 'human' is quite possibly on the edge of a moment of either radical transformation or radical termination. Thus and by a process of commodious vicus of recirculation, we must return to the initial conditions through which we first entered this text – via, that is, the opening and master epigraph concerning kleptomancy or divination through theft, that is, deployed as method to the point of autopoetic implosion, and rather more achronically to the following: an improvisation on the theme of marine biology and philosophical trouble drawn from a biosophical instruction from Haraway and the mythopoetics of early Ballard, a singular moment in a more general poetics of creation from some lines scavenged, dismantled, and detourned variously from Plato, Lucretius, Darwin, Carroll, Rainer Maria Rilke, Borges, Acker, Blanchot, Bataille, Lispector, and Saint Jerome, and what might be called – and will be called in this instance – a noetics of ontological adjacency in myth and imagination, the latter to be transmitted imminently and once again, in this instance, from the near future via an antiquated public address system in a dilapidated theatre in the West End of London just after the death of coral via human agency and just prior to the Great Flood . . .

Epilogue

He stopped writing, raised his head and grasped the edge of the desk to acknowledge the acceleration of his pulse and heart rate and the dopamine rush lifting his attention upwards and outwards. Writing this now, as history and record, multivalent and transmedial, not knowing who will read it on battered and rain-soaked fragments in some future scenario as the planet earth flames and flares and arches its back in readiness for astral penetration. There would be much stopping and starting now, he knew that much. Much breathing in and breathing out, deep and heavy, systole and diastole, zeroes and ones and up and down and left and right and here and there. Here and there. There. Here. Now. He looked down. He could hear the ripple of the audience moving and motioning through the adjacent auditorium, adjacent in a different time (chronically but not spatially proximous, that is), to find their seats for the show. He closed his eyes and allowed that ripple to sieve and grow and pull him back through the space that had opened up momentarily in the crack between worlds. Between their world and his world and our world. Now he was there, here, now, like an oculus rifting and hovering above the concept, like Vertov's camera eye upgraded by Alphanet, expanding into audition and haptics and maybe even olfactics. In the theatre beside the stage. In the book behind the page. On the beach of a ravaged world. Behind the screen like a two-way mirror.
Watching.
Reading.
Listening.
Aware of you.

Notes

1. On the promise and perils of kleptomancy as a practice of creative nonfiction, a form of divination by textual or intellectual theft, whether from oneself or others, and a fictocritical style and methodology employing autopoiesis to the point of self-implosion, see Blake 2018.
2. On the Great Accident or 'Great Collapse' and the attendant cognitive metastases of the so-called 'Dreamcancer', see Blake 2015: 369–90.
3. Title of a cut-up textual experiment generally attributed to William S. Burroughs and/or Brion Gysin initiated at a party in Paris, possibly at the infamous Beat Hotel (see Burroughs, Gyson, Beiles, and Corso 1960).
4. 'Post-Anthropocene' as suggested by a wide spectrum of critical and fictional texts, from Colebrook 2014 and Weisman 2008 to a range of material from the mid-1990s to a spectrum of speculative and science fiction from the 1960s to the present and beyond.
5. An attempt to systematise fictocritical strategies may be found in Haas 2017. Also of some interest, albeit from the non-standard or non-philosophical perspective that characterises his oeuvre generally, is Laruelle 2015.
6. The notion of an axial age between roughly 800 BCE and 300 BCE in which a great intellectual and cultural transformation took place in various parts of the globe, a transformation with enormous intellectual and cultural implications for the development of the species, has a number of precedents, but was first systematised by the German philosopher Karl Jaspers in the 1940s and has since been elaborated by Karen Armstrong amongst others (see Jaspers 2011; Armstrong 2006).
7. In this sense following Karen Barad's observation that meaning and matter (or mattering) are not separate elements but 'inextricably fused together' (Barad 2007: 3).
8. The idea of distinguishing between primary, secondary, and tertiary memory, in which tertiary memory is recorded memory as this has come to characterise a new and panhuman form of retention and potential intellection via artefacts, is developed from Edmund Husserl by Bernard Stiegler in Stiegler 1998.
9. Notably in the collection *Leper Creativity*, based on a symposium held at the New School in New York City in 2011 (Keller, Masciandaro, and Thacker 2012).
10. It can be safely assumed that many of these strands will have come together in Negarestani's monograph *Intelligence and Spirit*, which was still unpublished at the time of writing.
11. On phenomenophagism and the related theme of cosmicide, see Blake 2014: 91–109.
12. A useful critical elaboration of the related notions of fabulation and the people to come in Deleuze may be found in Bogue 2010.
13. The dark precursor famously makes an appearance in *Difference and Repetition*, dramatically preceding thunderbolts exploding between different intensities (Deleuze 1994: 119).

Bibliography

Acker, Kathy (1996), *Pussy, King of the Pirates*, New York: Grove Press.
Armstrong, Karen (2006), *The Great Transformation: The World in the Time of Buddha, Socrates, Confucius and Jeremiah*, London: Atlantic Books.
Barad, Karen (2007), *Meeting the Universe Halfway: Quantum Physics and the Entanglement of Matter and Meaning*, Durham, NC: Duke University Press.
Blake, Charlie (2014), 'The Animal that Therefore I Am Not: Inhuman Meditations on the Ultimate Degeneration of Bios and Zoe via the Inevitable Process of Phenomenophagism', in

Patricia MacCormack (ed.), *The Animal Catalyst: Towards Ahuman Theory*, London: Bloomsbury, pp. 91–110.

Blake, Charlie (2015), 'A Thousand Chateaus: On Time, Topology and the Seriality of Serial Murder', in Edia Connole and Gary S. Shipley (eds), *Serial Killing: A Philosophical Anthology*, London: Schism Books, pp. 369–90.

Blake, Charlie (2017), 'The Elves of (Dis)integration: Velosophy, Hyperstition and the Ontography of the Arcane', in Graham Freestone and Charles Johns (eds), *Parasol 1: Journal of the Centre for Experimental Ontology*, Lincoln: Parasol Press, pp. 62–79.

Blake, Charlie (2018), 'The Shattered Muse: Mêtis, Melismatics and the Catastrophical Imagination', in Patricia MacCormack and Colin Gardener (eds), *Ecosophical Aesthetics: Art, Ethics and Ecology with Guattari*, London: Bloomsbury, pp. 217–44.

Blanchot, Maurice (1981), *The Gaze of Orpheus*, Lydia Davis (trans.), New York: Station Hill Press.

Blanchot, Maurice (1995), *The Writing of Disaster*, Ann Smock (trans.), Lincoln: University of Nebraska Press.

Bogost, Ian (2012), *Alien Phenomenology, or What it's Like to be a Thing*, Minneapolis: University of Minnesota Press.

Bogue, Ronald (2010), *Deleuzian Fabulation and the Scars of History*, Edinburgh: Edinburgh University Press.

Borges, Jorge Luis (1964), *Dreamtigers*, Mildred Boyar and Harold Morland (trans.), Austin: University of Texas Press

Burroughs, William S., Brion Gysin, Sinclair Beiles, and Gregory Corso (1960), *Minutes to Go*, Paris: Two Cities.

Colebrook, Claire (2014), *Death of the Posthuman: Essays in Extinction, Vol. 1*, Ann Arbor: Open Humanities Press.

Danowski, Déborah and Eduardo Viveiros de Castro (2017), *The Ends of the World*, Rodrigo Nunes (trans.), Cambridge: Polity.

Deleuze, Gilles (1994), *Difference and Repetition*, Paul Patton (trans.), London: Athlone Press.

Deleuze, Gilles and Félix Guattari (1980), *A Thousand Plateaus: Capitalism and Schizophrenia*, Brian Massumi (trans.), Minneapolis: University of Minnesota Press.

Guattari, Félix (2009), *Chaosophy: Texts and Interviews 1972–1977*, Sylvère Lotringer (ed.), David L. Sweet, Jared Becker, and Taylor Adkins (trans.), Los Angeles: Semiotexte.

Haas, Gerrit (2017), *Ficto/Critical Strategies: Subverting Textual Practices of Meaning, Other, and Self Formation*, New York: Columbia University Press.

Haraway, Donna J. (2016), *Staying with the Trouble: Making Kin in the Chthulucene*, Durham, NC: Duke University Press.

Heraclitus (1979), *The Art and Thought of Heraclitus: An Edition of the Fragments with Translation and Commentary*, Charles Kahn (trans.), Cambridge: Cambridge University Press.

Irigaray, Luce (2013), *In the Beginning*, London: Bloomsbury Press.

Jameson, Fredric (1991), *Postmodernism, or, The Cultural Logic of Late Capitalism*, Durham, NC: Duke University Press.

Jaspers, Karl (2011), *The Origin and Goal of History*, London: Routledge.

Joyce, James (2012), *The Restored Finnegans Wake*, Danis Rose and John O' Hanlon (eds), London: Penguin.

Keller, Ed, Nicola Masciandaro, and Eugene Thacker (eds) (2012), *Leper Creativity: Cyclonopedia Symposium*, New York: Punctum Books.

Kobek, Jarett (2016), *I Hate the Internet*, New York: Serpent's Tail.

Kobek, Jarett (2017), *The Future Won't Be Long*, London: Serpent's Tail.
Lao, Meri (2007), *Seduction and the Secret Power of Women: The Lure of Sirens and Mermaids*, Rochester, VT: Park Street Press.
Laruelle, François (2015), *Photo-Fiction, a Non-Standard Aesthetics*, Drew S. Burk (trans.), Minneapolis: Univocal.
Latour, Bruno (2013), *An Inquiry into Modes of Existence: An Anthropology of the Moderns*, Catherine Porter (trans.), Cambridge, MA: Harvard University Press.
Lispector, Clarice (2014), *Água Viva*, Stefan Tobler (trans.), London: Penguin.
Negarestani, Reza (2008), *Cyclonopedia: Complicity with Anonymous Materials*, Melbourne: Re.press.
Negarestani, Reza (2018), *Intelligence and Spirit*, Falmouth: Urbanomic.
Newman, Sandra (2017), 'The Future Won't Be Long by Jarett Kobek Review – Follow-up to I Hate the Internet', *The Guardian*, 21 December, <https://www.theguardian.com/books/2017/dec/21/future-wont-be-long-jarett-kobek-review> (last accessed 12 June 2018).
Palumbi, Stephen R. and Anthony R. Palumbi (2014), *The Extreme Life of the Sea*, Princeton: Princeton University Press.
Price, Seth (2002), *Dispersion*, <http://www.distributedhistory.com/Disperzone.html> (last accessed 12 June 2018).
Price, Seth (2015), *Fuck Seth Price*, New York: Leopard.
Rilke, Rainer Maria (2001), *The Poetry of Rainer Maria Rilke*, A. S. Kline (trans.), Kindle edn.
Stiegler, Bernard (1998), *Technics and Time 1: The Fault of Epimetheus*, Richard Beardsworth and George Collins (trans.), Stanford: Stanford University Press.
Weisman, Alan (2008), *The World Without Us*, London: Virgin Books.

19

So to Speak

Adrian Parr

The mud bakes tough and slow
the sun casts a dusty glow.
Drought slowly sinks
down hard and low.
Here it comes, ready or not:
An unforgiving thirst cracks open the land.
As hunger makes a stand.

Here come the people
spinning out an escape
kidnapped by birthplace,
and the apple of no one's eyes.

The planet bears witness
when flowers drop at an officer's feet
Gentle dissent
Now charged with causing offence

Eco-warriors took to the sky last night.
Civil disobedience now a threat to the state
For trying to make the world a better place.
A kiss planted on a riot cop's helmet
lands her in cuffs for sexual violence.

Into the streets that have no name,
the well-oiled machine
where everyone and everything is fair game.
It's a hell of a gamble.

Tight corrugated iron boxes
slipping over, under, and

through sloppy muck
just barely standing up.

On the fringes there is never more,
barely enough
it's always tough.
Not even a back-breaking eighty hours a week
will get you by.
The ends just never meet.
That is unless you get high.

'Because we're so lazy, right?'

Even down here
at the bottom of the ladder
new ladders form.
From the bully to the priest.
Faith beats on and on
and tyranny takes a punch.

Gang boys strut and deliver their stuff.
And still,
dignity persists,
insists,
on just a little respect.
Can you believe this!
How fuckin' hard can it get?

Take a deep breath.

'Cause kids are still playing
kicking ball
and throwing paper planes.
A game of tag
through open sewers and over rusty roofs they leap.
All smiles.
One falls in the trash pile.
Laughter lets loose.

The rush of a moment's pride has slipped by.
Babes now strut the sidewalk.
'I'll be anything you want me to be', she says defiantly.
'A thangettie thang thang
And a rompety
pump, hump, thump.'

Bootie goes on sale
alongside a mother selling carrots and kale.
Both cost ten shillings.
Both hoping today falls quietly away.
Quite the choice,
wouldn't you say?

Give one good reason why!
Well, as the saying goes:
Shit happens huh!

Life is left black and blue.
bratat,
crack,
crack.
An old man steps aside,
looks the other way.

On the other side,
up high,
electrified and sound,
gated and endlessly gay.
More room than anyone knows what to do with.
Where everything costs an arm and a leg
and the air . . . whoo hoo it's squeaky clean.
Nobody's ever quite satisfied.
A life of maybe, just maybes,
and the sky's the limit.
Ahhhh just losin' track of time
when opportunity blooms at the end of line.

Google-eyed with speculative smiles
everything is greener on the other side.
Who wants to be a millionaire, overnight?
Hell yeah!

Whose side?
My side?
Your side?
Their side?
Whose side are you on, anyway?
G-d, oil, and guns!

Thumbs up,
singing and quivering
to a squeaky-clean
pop queen
who's jiggling and wiggling out a love song.
'Is that the way you want it?'
Her soft porn voice throbbin'
you'd never know she'd just turned thirteen.

Fast forward …
pearly whites are shining, thriving,
sky-diving boundless prospects.
Shouting, 'I'm sooooo happy and u know it.
Cause I'm gonna show it.'

The saccharin taste of success,
prowess,
doing the very best.
Ahhh it's the best of the best.
Stuck in a pissing contest.
The latest,
and don't forget –
greatest dance in the joint.

Cut the crap – it's the luck of the draw.

Buyer's market!
Seller's market!
Winners and losers
of all stripes and colours
from the streets that have no name
to the secured enclaves of fame,
fortune,
foolishness,
and don't forget those good Samaritans.
Smiles so smug
they barely crease a cheek.

Loose change takes a shot at
'Too ugly to prostitute'
'Too stoopid to steal'
Ladies first.
Just kiddin'.

Across the street:
'Seeking kindness',
gets a cruel slap on the wrist,
a professional nod and brisk clap on the back:
'Good morning and have a nice day!
Now let me be on my way.'
No need for a guilt trip,
Just movin' on up
'Hey, ain't nothing wrong with that.'

Up at ya!

How quickly the crow flies
from sipping bubbly
to sniffing meth,
once four walls and a roof
now a bus shelter and a wooden stoop.
See, it gotcha too.

The birds no longer migrate
all condemned to refugee-state.
Even drinking and clean breathing come at a price.
Our forests are disappearing
polar bears are drownin'
and the seasons are no more.
With a few monkeys left in the banana patch
and all the rest, trying to get in
on the winnings.

And the future looks on and sighs …

Even the straightest of arrows can curl
in a world divided against itself.
The formula is earthshattering:
'It's entirely up to you.
Just give it a whirl.'

Says who?
Don't lie!
You freak!
There is no grand design.
No external threat.
No one will save ya.

Nulla, nada, niente.
Some say Gucci, others Prada.
Throw in a couple of fakes
Hey ... whatever it takes!
Another political jacko holdin a finger up – hey yo!
waitin' to see which way the wind blows
and a hell of a lot of making something outa nothin'
that's how it goes.

A few major players
placing bets.
Most are outta sight. Outta mind.
Oh and yeah: the thief, got away.
Environmentalists, now terrorists.
This is as good as it gets.

All in another day's work for empire-business.

Along the horizon a new power risin'.
The climate waivers
Storms are surging
Clouds are shakin'
above a new generation
Standin' up for the earth
'There is no planet B'
'The debate is over'

An elite cut of activists
partners with the corporatists.
Conservation International and Wal-Mart get tight
Greenpeace and McDonalds make it right.
Hey, its sink or swim.
Everybody wants the win-win
Except the losers!

So to speak ...

PART VI

Politics after Discipline: Literature, Life, Control

Editor's Introduction

Frida Beckman

Relations between political development, philosophical inquiry, and literary modes of expression and reading are always at least implicit in the literary modes themselves. Even when not thematically foregrounded, literary characters and events mirror conceptions of individuals and their actions as they emerge from specific societal conditions and ontological and epistemological presuppositions. But while everything is political in minor literature, to borrow Gilles Deleuze and Félix Guattari's formulation, major literature tends to put the spotlight on the fate of the individual and consign politics to the basement. Analogously, reading and interpretation, even if not explicitly politically motivated, are, as the history of literary scholarship and its various schools show, themselves activities that cannot be separated from historical and philosophical and sometimes explicitly political conditions and concerns. In addition to more or less overt thematic depictions of the political in literature and to the more or less overtly political readings of literature, literature is also often – some would argue always – related to the political by means of form. These relations are multiple and include, for example, religious-philosophical motivations, as in the epic with is allegorical heroes; philosophical-political ones, as in the experimental cut-up techniques used by William S. Burroughs; and political-economic ones, as in what Virginia Woolf sees as the twisted texts produced by female writers without a room of their own.

One of the particular configurations of the conditions of and challenges to literature in the present can be traced to changing political logics and to the demise of humanist ideals that traditionally have shaped it. These changing logics have been described by Michel Foucault and post-Foucauldian theory as the shift from the disciplinary society of subjects and institutions to a biopolitics on the scale of populations and further on to neoliberalism and control societies. Moving away from the identities, subjects, and institutions of disciplinary society, Western contemporaneity is seen to be increasingly shaped by a more fluid politics of control that functions by acting directly on life itself. Such politics is less about constructing individuals and more about continuously manipulating 'dividuals', affects, and desires. Politics thus becomes more intimate while also less visible. And just as the classical distinction between public and private becomes increasingly hard to identify, so are the limits of the political in literature. What is political literature today, and what are the thematic and formal preoccupations and challenges of and to literature after discipline?

The four contributors to this section tackle these questions in various ways. In the first chapter, 'Literary Study's Biopolitics', Rey Chow situates the decline of the academic study of literature in the context of biopolitics. While biopolitics is most often associated with life in its physical forms, Chow insists that intellectual life too – and this includes language as well as literature – can and should be understood as governed by such principles. Chow's approach is different from what she identifies as the more common strategy in contemporary engagements with the relation between literature and biopolitics, which involves tracing predominantly thematic concerns with various forms of biopolitics as they are formulated and expressed in literary texts. What she wants to interrogate instead is literature itself as caught up in this biopolitical conditioning of the present. Tracing the wrestling with language and meaning from Foucault's *The Order of Things* (*Les mots et les choses*, 1966) to Franco Moretti's *Distant Reading* (consolidated and published as a book in 2005), Chow shows how this wrestling, in its most recent turn to graphs and algorithms, is, to some extent, coextensive with the study of biological systems and economic models. Predicting the increasing expansion of methods using numbers, formulas, and big data in literary studies, she notes how this rhymes well with ever-increasing demands on utility and problem-solving within the humanities and the corporatisation of the university at large.

In the second chapter, 'We Have Been Paranoid Too Long to Stop Now', Frida Beckman and Charlie Blake look at how the thematic, formal, and hermeneutic conditions of literature and philosophy may be affected by changing political structures. Two main dimensions of this problem are addressed. The first one concerns the form of the modern novel and its historical and formal reliance on disciplinary models. Tracing a historical line that begins with the theories and representations of the subject in Descartes and *Don Quixote*, the investigation dwells on a discussion of the paradoxical insistence on the individual in the modern novel as it emerges along the disciplinary modes of power in the eighteenth and nineteenth centuries and ends, finally, with how the novel, traditionally so reliant on discipline, is affected by the different modulations of control. The second concern addressed is shaped by the many new modes of reading that have been proposed due to a discontent with, or suspicion towards, the hermeneutic practices that dominated the second half of the twentieth century. With the aim of historicising and contextualising such practices and their crises, the authors find the need to evaluate the revaluation of paranoid reading initiated by Eve Kosofsky Sedgwick in the late 1990s and the various kinds of alternative readings that have been proposed in the decades since then.

Where the first chapter of this section is concerned with the general conditions of literature in an age of biopolitics and the second chapter offers a philosophical-historical contextualisation of the more specific problems of literary form and reading in control society, the third chapter zooms in on an even more intimate interrogation of the thematic and formal challenges to literature in the present. In 'Securing Neoliberalism: The Contingencies of Contemporary US Fiction', David

Watson takes a close look at theories of neoliberalism and how they relate to those of risk, contingency, securitisation, control, and biopolitics. He then compares these theories to both more traditional and emergent structures of literary narrative. That contingency is both 'a problem and resource for narrative and for plot structures' is nothing new, he notes, but contemporary literature engages with and is to some extent shaped by the more politically dominant role of contingency and risk associated with the present. While presenting a wide array of theories and literary texts, he offers a closer look at Colson Whitehead's *The Intuitionist* (1999) and Jennifer Egan's *A Visit from the Goon Squad* (2010) in order to exemplify and illustrate the preoccupation with contingency and temporality in contemporary fiction.

The final chapter in this section, 'Automatic Art, Automated Trading: Finance, Fiction, and Philosophy', explores yet another dimension of contemporary literature as it wrestles with political realities. Arne De Boever shows how finance novels – and examples here include Bret Easton Ellis's *American Psycho* (1991), Teddy Wayne's *Kapitoil* (2010), and Michel Houellebecq's *The Map and the Territory* (2012) – constitute an ideal site for understanding the nature of the politics of algorithmic control. More specifically, De Boever scrutinises the role of art, and particularly abstract art such as Jackson Pollock's, in such novels. Tracing contemporary finance economy and its challenges to literature, film, and art and, conversely, how literature and film have engaged with contemporary finance economy, De Boever suggests that outlining these challenges helps us towards accounting for ways in which individual and collective lives are governed after discipline.

20

Literary Study's Biopolitics

Rey Chow

The decline of literature as a subject of academic study is indisputable in today's world, but seldom is this decline approached as a form of biopolitics. In contemporary literary and cultural studies, the term 'biopolitics' (coined by the Swedish political scientist Johan Rudolf Kjellén) is usually associated with Michel Foucault's efforts to politicise the institutional management of human life as it enters history in modern times. As invoked by Foucault in works such as the first volume of *The History of Sexuality*, *'Society Must be Defended'*, and *The Birth of Biopolitics* (Foucault 1978, 2003, 2008), biopolitics has to do with historically evolving systems of sovereignty, discipline and control (including surveillance, pathologisation, and penalisation), and knowledge production. Above all, the discussions in these works reiterate Foucault's stated interest in the governance of human populations through the abstract permutations of a quantity-driven scientific field such as statistics.

My use of the term 'biopolitics', though also closely tied to Foucault, follows a somewhat different trajectory. First, in an old-fashioned humanistic manner, I associate 'life' as much with intellectual work involving semiotic systems as with the physical dimensions of human existence as defined within the frames of biodiversity and ecology. Because language plays a crucial role in the creation of imaginary worlds that are indispensable to human life, language and literature should, to my mind, be acknowledged as part of biopolitics (even though such acknowledgement is not currently fashionable). Second, and perhaps more importantly, the emergence of literature as an object of interest in modernity has a history that is coextensive with the politics of discourse formation. This history is part institutional, part practical, part national-geographical, and always language-oriented. In the Foucauldian sense of discourse, such a history is animated and mediated not only through literature's internal dynamics but also through its coevolution and competition with other histories of discursive ruptures. From this perspective, it is Foucault's *The Order of Things* (Focuault 1970), with its analyses of modern discourses' emergences both from their historical predecessors and in their contemporaneous relations with one another, which foreshadows his subsequent discussions of the politics of life.

For are not the academic and social pathways of biology, political economy, and literature – the three emergent, mutually affecting disciplines of knowledge production as featured in *The Order of Things*, corresponding to the contents of life, labour, and language – inherent in the organisation of modern life, in ways that are replete with struggles for legitimacy, dominance, and survival? This biopolitics – the contentious strife for the governance of life through discourse rationalisation (and its attendant modes of objectification) – is what I would like to foreground as literary study's special contribution.

More typically, of course, when biopolitics is invoked in relation to literature, the tendency is rather to treat biopolitics as an empirical reality, one that is then reflected or expressed in the medium of literary writing. To the extent that biopolitics is regarded as some kind of extratextual happening, it is interchangeable with an entire series of themes in literary study, from the proletarian struggle against capitalism in the days of Karl Marx and Friedrich Engels, to the rise of the nation-state, working-class lives, domestic and non-domestic forms of desires, anticolonial and antislavery insurgence, globalisation, and environmental issues in the age of the Anthropocene, among others. For reasons just mentioned, my aim in this chapter is to pursue an alternative line of inquiry. Instead of treating literature as a type of expressive or reflective activity (however complex), and instead of attributing to this activity a mysterious capacity for resisting or contesting the reality around it (in a type of academic speech act that has become predictable and banal), I would like to pose the following biopolitical questions. How does literary study live and die in the vast historical shifts from a world that, once upon a time, seemed organised, indeed dominated, by language, to one in which language no longer enjoys the privilege of being the exclusive or indispensable key to knowledge? What are some of the modern and contemporary efforts to save literary study? What kind of picture emerges when literary study is situated within the institutional struggles for power and survival in the ongoing realignments of discursive networks in the global corporate university?

Evicting Language

> This evictive state naturally corresponds to a plenitude of virtualities: it is an absence of meaning full of all the meanings.
>
> (Barthes 1977: 42)

The contemporary world, we are often told, is characterised by postmodern motifs such as an incredulity towards metanarratives; incommensurability among different forms of knowledge; the commodity- and nostalgia-driven cultural logic of late capitalism; play with artistic forms from collage and pastiche to repetition and citation; and general cultural relativism. For those working in the literary humanities, these motifs also necessitate a reflection on the status of language. How to describe postmodernity's inheritance, if it may be so called, of modernity's fraught relation to language? What is the nature of that fraught relation?

In the Anglo-American context, T. S. Eliot's well-known experiments with language in his early poetic work, experiments that are as morally pessimistic as they are stylistically innovative, are characteristic of high modernism's twin (one might say schizophrenic) approach. In the poem 'The Love Song of J. Alfred Prufrock', for instance, the relationship of the poet to language is implicitly homologised to a balding middle-aged man's haunting by his own sexual impotence. While this anxiety about an age-old medium that seems increasingly unreliable and untrustworthy shapes literary modernism's classic sense of its own predicament ('It is impossible to say just what I mean!' (Eliot 1970: 16)), the lack of fit, the widening gap, between words and things (what Samuel Beckett's tragicomic plays dramatise as a prevailing condition of unhappiness) also proves to be a source of immense artistic productivity, as modernist writings in different genres, by canonical authors such as James Joyce, Virginia Woolf, Gertrude Stein, and innumerable others, have shown. From modernity's perspective, then, the incontrovertible epistemic issue seems to be the sense of a definitive transformation of language's status in relation to representation.

Importantly, this transformation is commonly conceived of and narrativised or lyricised as a loss, perhaps even a fall: language, once in possession of a sovereign overview of the world like a polished windowpane, is now said to have become opaque, impenetrable, and unwilling or unable to communicate. (In today's biomedical terms, we could say that this is a story of language's becoming *autistic*, that is, experiencing insurmountable difficulty communicating with the outside world.) This nostalgic imagining of language's bygone potency (or state of eloquence) can perhaps be included among the metanarratives whose increasing untenability has, according to Jean-François Lyotard, come to define the postmodern condition. Whether language was ever really the master of representation, the collective mournful belief – one that has powerfully influenced philosophical and artistic thinking about the modern world – is that it has, somehow, slipped and fallen from this magical, originary status.

In response to language's putative demise, scholars of the literary humanities of earlier generations have typically attempted to defend language's relevance by portraying an antagonism and incompatibility between humanistic learning, on the one hand, and science and technology, on the other. Martin Heidegger, for instance, is an outstanding example of a philosopher who tries to reanimate language – to bring it back to life – in this manner. For Heidegger, speaking about poetry, language is not only the dwelling of Being; it is also equipped with the mystical power to interpellate, to invite and bid things to come forth by being named. Poetic language is a calling-out in which presence is sheltered in absence, and what is brought near remains still at a distance (Heidegger 1971: 189–210). Similarly turning to poetic language as a way to reclaim humanistic learning's universal significance, the Anglo-American New Critics – Allen Tate, I. A. Richards, William Empson,

Cleanth Brooks, W. K. Wimsatt, J. C. Ransom, Monroe Beardsley – exemplify the poem appreciated in isolation as an organic whole, whose reality is deemed independent of history and authorial intention. 'A poem should not mean / But be': in this well-known proclamation from Archibald MacLeish's 'Ars Poetica' (MacLeish 1926: 126–7), one detects a purist desire for the artistic or literary work to be (understood as) ontologically self-sufficient, as though any swerve into meaning would amount to a detraction or contamination. Once ontological self-sufficiency has been elevated to the place of a supreme moral virtue, it becomes an ideal to which everyone aspires. The postmodern trends in multiplying narratives, in particular narratives about the self, may in this light be seen as a continuation of the ongoing revitalisation and reinvention of (the relevance of) poetic language. The label 'postmodern' (rather than modern) simply means that anyone now should be entitled to such poetic rebirth and renewal: however trivial or eccentric, every human being's life story ought to be given a chance to be told and actualised afresh as an organically complete poem, with a value in and of itself. To this end, the celebration of multicultural diversity and of multi-ethnic literatures in North American academic institutions is, historically speaking, both a symptom and an extension of the unfinished, New Critical literary project.

In *The Order of Things* (1970), Foucault, too, offers a memorable analysis of this story of language's dislocation. Foucault's point of departure is, however, notably different in that he does not approach language by way of an essential function (such as naming) or by way of a putatively organic entity (such as a poem). Using Jorge Luis Borges's fantastic Chinese encyclopedia to show how language divides, multiplies, and arranges the universe differently in another civilisation, he prepares the stage for historicising the story of language's transformation, making us realise that the lingual properties to which Western civilisation has long been accustomed may be just local flora and fauna. Because of this self-consciously comparative method based on historical shifts and relative values, and also because Foucault refrains from demonising science and technology in the manner characteristic of many of his literary contemporaries, his discussion of the mutations of language in modernity remains highly instructive. As the book's original title indicates, *Les mots et les choses* is about the emergence of a certain epistemic void – that is to say, an increasing rift, since early modern times, in the relationship, the assumed linkage, between words and things. Although Foucault admittedly partakes of the modernist tendency to project a linguistic plenitude retrospectively onto former time periods, his treatment of the plenitude's disappearance is remarkably divergent.

According to Foucault, language's decline from the happy, intimate condition of being continuous with the world – in what he calls language's demotion to the mere status of an object – has led to three types of compensation, in three main areas of knowledge production. In what we call the humanities and the interpretative social sciences (*les sciences humaines*), Foucault writes, techniques of exegesis specialising in the discovery and disturbance of buried, muted, or unconscious meanings become key to scholarly undertakings. The works of Marx, Friedrich Nietzsche, Bertrand Russell, and Sigmund Freud are exemplary of this specialisation. In the realm of literature, on the other hand, a type of avant-garde creative writing looms on the horizon, deriving its power paradoxically from language's awareness of its own newly historical uselessness. Rather than being in communication/communion with the world in a seamless fashion, this type of writing radically withdraws into itself, taking on an unintelligibility that becomes, in turn, the hallmark of an artful, self-referential quality, a quality that henceforth distinguishes literary language as such. Although Foucault's examples are French, his discussion of literature in these terms is a little reminiscent of the Anglo-American New Critics' notion that a poem should not mean but be. To this extent, he corroborates a largely Western European and North American diagnosis of literary writing's becoming an autistically closed-off world – in what, biopolitically speaking, might be called discourse mutation and differentiation – in the course of modernity.

When reconsidered in light of the two other sets of power realignments portrayed in the book (political economy and biology), Foucault's depiction of the emergence of modern literature (in France) suggests that the story of literary writing is also one about speciation and specialisation as well as processes of (dis)empowerment understood in close relation to these biologically inflected terms. The estranged state in which, according to Foucault, literature finds itself in the modern West – the state of impotent power – is where we continue to find the proliferation of experimental and avant-garde arts today.

In the area of knowledge production that may be broadly labelled scientific, Foucault argues, the newly emergent, deepening abyss between words and things has led instead to the construction of a neutralised language, one that would be so thoroughly stripped of accidents and alien elements that 'it could become the exact reflection, the perfect double, the unmisted mirror of *a non-verbal knowledge*' (Foucault 1970: 296, my emphasis). If language in the other knowledge domains has become conjectural and speculative, requiring ever-more nuanced interpretation to the point of rendering all claims to certitude relative, in the scientific domain language remains bound to the optimism of 'a search for a logic independent of grammars, vocabularies, synthetic forms, and words' (1970: 297). This search materialises in symbolic logic, a discipline intent on 'representing the forms and connections of thought *outside all language*' 1970: 297, my emphasis).[1]

Rather than dismissing science on the basis of the ills of instrumentalism and mercantilism, then, Foucault makes the refreshing move of showing science itself as participating in language's historical mutation process, albeit taking up a different kind of niche. As a type of discourse, science continues to dream of, indeed to strive towards, being a language that corresponds to reality – a language, in other words, that is somehow able to keep itself free of the chaos, derangement, and ambiguity in which other forms of knowledge production increasingly find themselves. While also confronted with modernity's language crisis, scientific discourse takes the form, according to Foucault's description, of a mode of enunciation or signification whose most fundamental attribute lies in its aspiration to speak and write without words, without the metaphoric clutter, noise, and messiness of linguistic mediation. Scientific discourse rigorously adopts the ideal and practice of objectivity that, as Lorraine Daston and Peter Galison argue, arose in the mid-nineteenth century as a radical epistemological therapy against the fear of subjective errors, against the threat of subjectivity as errancy. 'Objectivity is to epistemology what extreme asceticism is to morality' (Daston and Galison 2007: 374), they write.

Dreaming Denotation

In an interesting parallel to – or perhaps as a result of? – this scientific vision of a zero degree of representation and, by implication, the ideal of transcribing thought directly without language, attempts to make use of scientific-looking graphs and diagrams can be found repeatedly in the theoretical writings of well-known thinkers in the literary humanities and interpretative social sciences. For a preliminary list, recall the figures used by Ferdinand de Saussure to discuss the relation between the linguistic signifier and signified; Heidegger's crossing-out of Being, which subsequently transmutes into Jacques Derrida's line-across that puts words and concepts (and the metaphysics of presence they conjure) 'under erasure'. Worth noting also is the interesting prominence of the mathematical and the geometrical in some of Heidegger's unique observations, as for instance, the jug that holds in the form of a void (see the chapter 'The Thing', Heidegger 1971: 165–86). Heidegger's fondness for etymologies, accordingly, may be understood as a fondness for organising words that visibly and vocally correspond to one another as though they belong in a series. (What are etymologies if not graphic and sonic sets?) The work on language can thus be analogised to archaeology, with the aim of establishing connections among buried, broken fragments of meaning. (Although he did not continue to pursue it, this connection between language and archaeology was clearly behind Foucault's musings in *The Archaeology of Knowledge* (Foucault 1972).) There are also Claude Lévi-Strauss's structures of myth and mathematical charting of kinship relations; Barthes's staggered rectangles for explaining the semiotic workings of ideology or myth; Jacques Lacan's bars, diagrams, and knots for signalling the absences that constitute the subject; A. J. Greimas's and Fredric Jameson's semiotic squares for describing the behaviour and circulation of linguistic, cultural, and ideological data; Foucault's references to lists, tables, and calligrams; Gilles Deleuze's folds, vectors, and rhizomes ... The list goes on. How can we begin to understand these remarkable but rarely discussed pictorial occurrences in the theoretical writings so intimately linked to literary study?

One possible explanation is that such graphs and diagrams lend the study of human language and culture respectability through the fashionable aura of systematicity (resulting from optical consistency). Be that as it may, what remains intriguing, from the stance of a postmodern world inundated with virtual images, seems something of a different order (if only because 'respectability' tilts the issue a little too hastily in the direction of an acquiescence to institutional power, of what might be called STEM envy). Indeed, can we not venture a speculation along the historical lines I am describing – namely, that even for theoretical thinkers whose bread and butter is language (the language of myth, philosophy, fiction, and history), graphs and diagrams offer the allure of instantaneous transmission and illumination, of a type of perceptual immediacy that seems impossible with cumbersome words?

To see this allure, let us consider the contemporary enthusiasm for a technology such as PowerPoint. What this technology provides, of course, is the convenience of a standardised format for public presentation by way of projectable visual arrangements of contents. While doing so, meanwhile, it announces something else – namely, the suggestion that what is written in language *can* become accessible in visibly grab-able modules of information (summary points). This accessibility is often presented in the form of a cutting-up of narrative's forward movement, but this cutting-up, a rendering into parts, materialises not through reduction but rather through addition. Visually, supplementary items such as bullet points, paragraph spaces, enlarged fonts, colours, and so on are *added* to the contents through computer software, even though the point, ostensibly, is to minimise language's elaborateness, to help extract what is imagined as the gist, core, or essence of an argument (as if this were indeed possible through such visual manipulations). The gist, core, or essence, so to speak, is thus literally grafted onto writing itself as a prosthesis, an extra collection of settings which, henceforth, competes for attention as the (putatively) more precise and more intelligible version of what is being presented.

As this rather crude example indicates, even in the simplest of cases the appearance of diagrammatic icons and alignments serves a function other than that of direct communication. For if such icons and alignments distinguish themselves visibly from the procession of the printed words, such a distinction also carries with it the implication of what Barthes, in his analysis of the rhetoric of the image, refers to as denotation. Defining denotation in contrast to connotation, as 'a message by eviction, constituted by what is left in the image when the signs of connotation are mentally deleted', Barthes calls this evictive (or evicted) state of intelligibility the 'utopian character of denotation' (Barthes 1977: 42). Going along the structural linguistic grain of his argument, we can say that denotation amounts to the supposition of an assured arrival at the destination of meaning, as opposed to the errancy, the drifting and digressing, that linguistic connotation is all about. (For T. S. Eliot, such drifting and digressing finds its fitting personification in 'the women [who] come and go / Talking of Michelangelo' (Eliot 1970).) Denotation is about putting a stop to these errant movements once and for all.

In the context of theoretical discourse, the use of graphs and diagrams gives to denotation, an abstract ideal, a palpably objectified, material shape. Often referred to as illustrations, such graphs and diagrams are visual aids, devices intended to help us understand what is happening in (spite of) the verbal text. But practical experience tells a different story: more often than not, the illustrations are a source of puzzlement and confusion. The question that is rarely asked is the one posed succinctly by Barthes: 'What is the signifying structure of "illustration"? Does the image duplicate certain of the informations [*sic*] in the text by a phenomenon of redundancy or does the text add a fresh information to the image?' (Barthes 1977: 38). In a similar vein, when discussing Lacan's interest in topology – 'with its progressively more and more mind-boggling objects, from the Moebius strip, the Klein's bottle and the torus to cross-cap, the Borromean knot and the whole theory of knots, all of which take off from Lacan's early and ample use of schemata and graphs' – Mladen Dolar points to the heart of the matter:

> It would seem that the topological objects were meant to serve the purpose of giving an 'illustration' or a spatial demonstration of his theoretical propositions. This purpose immediately entailed a reversal, I suppose not unintended, for *what was designed to facilitate understanding (or was it ever?) was far more difficult to grasp than the thing it was supposed to render intelligible and, rather, served as an impediment, itself in need of explanation.* Gradually the topological objects and paradoxes, and particularly the knots, lost their status of illustrating something and became the thing itself, the focus of interest and elaboration in itself, the very way that theory should proceed, embodying something that cannot be rendered in any other way. (Dolar 2011: 123, my emphasis)

As it assumes the form of nonverbal knowing, of a thinking outside of language, what begins as a seemingly scientific, because denotative, act, in spite – or perhaps because – of its ambition to discern and record (thought) objectively, ends up rejoining the literary and artistic forces of modernity to become an exercise in esoterism, in which objectivity seems indistinguishable from solipsism, from the arcaneness of intransitive (because self-referential) speech. Offering the semblance of positivity and universality, the graphs and diagrams are simultaneously cryptic and enigmatic, their readily visible forms impenetrable even to sophisticated readers, who are typically at a loss as to what they mean without detailed explanations, without a careful reconsideration of the words.[2]

The coexistence of such polarities of meaning-making suggests that diagrammatic denotation – or more precisely, the diagram-as-denotation – needs to be rethought as an epistemic conundrum, one in which the ongoing modernist sense of a crisis of language continues to play itself out in the form of a collective fantasy. This is the fantasy that language is somehow disposable, that if we could simply find a way to get to the bottom of things – geometrically, algebraically, statistically, or whatever – we *ought* to be able to arrive at that utopian, evicted state of not needing language altogether. Beyond the dots, the lines, the curves, the circles, the squares, the numbers, and other figures on the page, there persists a wish and a demand, bestowing on diagrammatic denotation the import of something excessive, something obscene.

To put it differently, when they are used in theoretical writings in the literary humanities and interpretative social sciences, the graphs and diagrams serve in effect as a little theatre where the unresolved relationship between words and things stages itself as a spectacle, calling attention to what, to borrow a phrase from Franco Moretti, seems a 'total *heterogeneity of problem and solution*' (Moretti 2005: 24). Side by side with the words, the diagrams appear as something like a language, albeit one that dreams of being without language; something like writing, albeit one that dreams of doing without writing. In their proximity to words, the graphs and diagrams yearn, as though with a kind of mimetic desire, to take language's place, to usurp writing's hold on abstraction by becoming the preferred native informants of thought.

Is not our contemporary nanotechnology with its infinite imaging capabilities, set into motion with simple manipulations such as keystrokes, clicks, taps, and finger swipes, as well as text-messaging operations limited to 140 characters and discharged with abbreviated spellings and emoticons, part of the same dream, the same ecstasy? Perhaps this entangled relationship between the verbal and the graphic in the aftermath of the historical emergence of objectivity needs to be made part of our re-evaluation of the coexistence, however fraught, of the humanities and the sciences? If the postmodern condition is indeed about the end of (the possibility of) metanarratives, it is high time we abandoned the metanarrative of the antagonism and incompatibility between these two areas of knowledge production, to make way for an alternative view of their uneven coevolution in the age of informatics. In particular, what does and could this coevolution mean for the study of literature?

Rescuing Literary Study

> From the abode of noise and impropriety, where nobody was in their right place, to the asshole gringos handing him bullshit about sovereignty, democracy, and human rights. This is what comparative literature could be, if it took itself seriously as *world literature*, on the one hand, and as *comparative morphology*, on the other.
>
> (Moretti 2005: 90)

Within the Anglo-American university, the turn of the twenty-first century has seen serious attempts to reanimate the study of literature. Under the rubrics of postcolonial, Anglophone, Francophone, world, planetary, neuro, environmental, and other similarly timely connections, scholars seek to restore to literature its due relevance in a relentlessly chimerical world. In particular, geopolitical considerations have emerged as a compelling form of reasoning, wherein movements of peoples, languages, and cultures have led to creatively new ways of reading texts (for instance, by way of issues of migration, de-territorialisation, and translation). As literary critics and historians hunker down in their increasingly specialised pursuits, however, relatively little has been said about how literature continues to be produced, with or without changes, as an object of study in an age when numbers, formulas, and algorithms dominate. *Exactly how to think about the literary object in the era of mass quantification? What is this object? By what processes is it constituted and objectified? By what processes might it be reconceptualised and remade?* This cluster of questions seems to bypass scholars even as they scrutinise writings produced under different historical circumstances. Yet if we follow Foucault's lead in *The Order of Things* and take seriously the coevolution of languages or disciplinary discourses – so that certain practices of language study, for instance, can be shown to be epistemically coextensive with certain theorisations of biological systems or economic models – we might have some means of grappling with these eminently interdisciplinary and, I contend, biopolitical questions. Franco Moretti's work offers some provocative suggestions in this regard.[3]

With a critique of close reading as his strategic point of departure, Moretti takes aim at the method that has constituted the literary object for decades in the Anglo-American context. A practice of concentration based on the contemplation of words; a skill-cum-spiritual exercise supposed to deliver the truth of a text regardless of the author's intentions, biographical details, and other extraneous circumstances surrounding the text's production: once the point is underscored that what constitutes literary study and its objects is simply the repeated intensive examination of a few canonical texts by a select group of people,[4] close reading, like the Church, is de-sacralised. This challenge of the doxa sets the euphoric tone of the debates to come, precisely because it carries the equivalent of a blasphemous charge and reformist aspiration. However radical close reading was in its heyday as a necessary intervention in the study of literature, the realisation that such focus on the text is possible only when the volume and variety of texts involved are restricted, indeed suppressed, means that close reading needs to be historicised and, as it were, put in its place. Although close reading a play by William Shakespeare, a poem by William Wordsworth, or a novel by Jane Austen used to be an activity taken for granted in a university setting where the English department is usually the largest unit of the literary humanities, in the aftermath of Civil Rights and multiculturalism, repeated close readings of these authors have come to seem, in the eyes of some, parochial. Even in the context of English itself as an evolving field, there needs to be room nowadays for more 'exotic' contemporary authors such as J. M. Coetzee, V. S. Naipaul, Kazuo Ishiguro, Jamaica Kincaid, Timothy Mo, and Zadie Smith. And things are much more complicated once other languages and canons enter the picture. Alongside the multiplicity of a single text, a single phrase, or a single word, which close reading is so adept at revealing, other forms of multiplicity – such as demographics, together with the existential and political demands they bring – loom with persuasive claims to legitimacy.

Against the time-honoured method of close reading, Moretti introduces what he calls abstract models for literary history; specifically, he shows how a use of graphs, maps, and trees enables him to foreground interconnections among textual elements (that is, generic, geographical or locational, and stylistic variations) that are otherwise inaccessible. In contrast to the intensive pondering of a small number of individual texts, Moretti's visual models allow for a wide range of literatures to be scanned in a comparative manner, frequently in association with historical developments in different parts of the world. Among other merits, the use of graphics avoids the pitfalls of a trendy, moral instrumentalisation of so-called world literature that, not unlike traditional close reading, is often based on selective, indeed eclectic, analyses of very few sample texts.

At this juncture, a difficulty arises that typically results from an endeavour to overturn accepted custom: the questioning of such custom is indubitably needed and justified, but the alternatives are far from satisfactory. Distant reading, Moretti's ambitious antidote to close reading, is a fascinating case in point not least because of Moretti's admirable intellectual vision.[5] In the book *Graphs, Maps, Trees*, he proposes the titular trio of artificial constructs as examples of distant reading, in which 'the reality of the text undergoes a process of deliberate reduction and abstraction' and, accordingly, distance is 'not an obstacle, but a *specific form of knowledge*' (Moretti 2005: 1). The aim of this new method, he suggests, is 'a more rational literary history' (2005: 4).

When viewed in light of the aforementioned paradoxes of diagrammatic denotation, however, Moretti's project appears to partake – albeit on a much larger and more replicable scale – of the fantasy shared among some of our foremost literary and cultural theorists: the fantasy of being unencumbered by language. As a well-intentioned attempt to update and rescue literary study by broadening its geopolitical reach, distant reading seems the latest rejoinder to those graphs and diagrams whose 'utopian' character, as Barthes points out, consists in the wish for an eviction – that is, for a language that has been vacated and, preferably, can be left on the side. The irony of this wishful thinking does not escape Moretti himself. An expert and experienced reader of literature, Moretti is the first to call attention to the fundamental problem with such an eviction – the fact that the abstract visual figures he proposes cannot stand alone without the help of words: 'to make sense of quantitative data, I had to abandon the quantitative universe, and turn to morphology: evoke form, in order to explain figures' (2005:24). Rather than *reducing* the text, then, as Moretti believes,[6] the abstract visual figures have actually *added* another dimension, a numerical frame, to the literary texts in question. What this means is that henceforth, when studying novels, readers will need to contend not only with their verbal significations but also with the graphs, maps, and trees Moretti has introduced.

In this construction of a new object for literary study, what is the status of the visual material itself? If, as a speculative program, distant reading is meant to explore 'the true nature of the historical process' (Moretti 2005: 29), by charting the links among textual elements that are otherwise not apprehended, what is the relation between the graphs, maps, and trees, on the one hand, and Moretti's own verbal explanatory accounts, on the other? Where the visualised data is explained, it seems, it is always in terms of a *new* knowledge, however tentative, to be acquired.

Visualisation, in other words, is a method of structuration that sharpens correlations by making them readily perceptible and *graspable*. In a manner not unlike the enigmatic visual figures adopted by theorists from Lacan to Deleuze, Greimas, and Jameson, there seems, in Moretti's discussions, an implicit equation of visualisation (in its positivistic mode) with recognition, access, and knowability – an equation that belongs, as I have been suggesting, in the collective fantasy of diagram-as-denotation. Although there is nothing transparent about the graphs, maps, trees, and other similar optical figures, all of which are coded data – no such representation can signify, can 'mean', without verbal explanation – they are nonetheless treated and presented as though they were code-free. In actuality, then, one type of mediation, language, has simply been superseded by another type of mediation, computation.

The disjuncture between close reading, which specialises in metaphorical depth, the inner dynamics of language, and most of all a select repertoire of texts, on the one hand, and, on the other, distant reading, which favours geographical expanse, comparative interactions among diverse literary productions and lineages, and the prospects of an extensive, indeed limitless global archive: this disjuncture is symptomatic of the problems confronting most practitioners of literary study today. And once it is realised that such study cannot with any good reason be confined to a particular language as used strictly by one group of readers, writers, and speakers, comparativism ineluctably follows, only henceforth to be dogged by meta-comparative questions, not least of which would be those regarding the often incommensurate assumptions about comparison as a practice across genres, forms, languages, time periods, and cultural traditions. Different languages' renderings of a similar-seeming word, for instance, may render apparently straightforward quantitative findings dubious and unreliable. As Moretti puts it in a more recent conversation: 'the problem is when you start to zoom in' (Heise 2017: 273). Moreover, though open-ended by design, the quantitative approach has ironically led to a 'reprovincialisation' of literary study (2017: 276), because computational research on different literatures tends to be conducted routinely, if not exclusively, in the national languages in which the literatures are written. By the same token, the overwhelming bulk of the work done in the so-called digital humanities has been on English and American corpora (2017: 276).

The problems are clear but the solutions, whenever proposed, seem only to generate other problems – hence Moretti's astute observation that there is a total heterogeneity of problem and solution. The numerous calls in recent years to reconceptualise literary study – in terms of republicanism, circulation, untranslatability, postcoloniality, and non-Anglophonic cultural pluralism – as well as the erudite debates pro and contra world literature (Casanova 2007; Damrosch 2003; Apter 2013; Cheah 2016; Mufti 2016), are part and parcel of what I propose to call the biopolitics of literary study. In this biopolitics, played out in academic institutions across the globe, it is a savvy navigation of vast distances in both time and space, as opposed to a contemplative groping in the dark labyrinths of language, that, I suspect, will gain increasing currency. Distant reading (and an affiliate like surface reading), in which the utopian promise of language's eviction goes hand in hand with the fundraising potential of data mining and archiving as well as with denotative diagramming: this materially generative research pathway is likely to be the niche in which literary study will be able to have some kind of future life in the corporatised university setting.

These institutional efforts to rescue literary study – of which database compilation is simply one prominent example – can also, and unavoidably, seem subjective and random, precisely because they are democratising exercises. Once opened up and diversified, literary study's raw materials and epistemic boundaries tend to become infinitely (re)negotiable: such materials and boundaries may be as easily disparaged and dismantled as they are assembled, in manners that resemble some receptions of installation art exhibits. For instance, if the comings and goings in a village in a nineteenth-century French or English novel can be graphically calculated to reveal economic or sociological patterns, what about happenings in a town setting in some twentieth-century African novels? Or, if Biblical allusions can be systematically charted in the linguistic styles of some European fiction, why not chart Zen Buddhist allusions in the linguistic styles of some East Asian fiction? And so on. Where would such a list of possible computational projects begin and end? Who should decide how far artificial intelligence and Big Data should go in helping to refashion the literary object, and for whom?

Meanwhile, as higher education morphs into a transnational business enterprise, replete with name-brand monitors, investment portfolio managers, designated goods producers (the instructors), and worldwide customers (students and their parents), initiatives to streamline and market literary study as a tangible product are well under way. Witness the hefty and pricey literary histories, companion volumes, and handbooks, commissioned by publishers such as Harvard, Oxford, Cambridge, Wiley-Blackwell, Routledge, Palgrave, and their competitors, and aimed virtually exclusively at libraries as buyers. Assorting literary writings by way of national languages, geographical regions, genders, ethnicities, sexual orientations, and popular thematics, these so-called 'books' are usually manufactured through entrepreneurial teamwork, in a relay from editors (the foremen and content managers) to authors (the assembly-line labourers, recruited to churn out the goods in accordance with pre-set formats),[7] to an invisible entourage of copyediting, production, and marketing personnel.

The biopolitics of literary study is the politics of finding – or, just as easily, losing – one's way in these large, impersonal realities of our time. On the one side lies a dazzling abundance of fictional talent: novels, short stories, plays, and poems written in different languages and formats; serialised television dramas; and film scripts, in addition to the canonical classics composed in different languages and made available in different translations. As in ages past, there is no shortage of excellent creative writing, whose richness and ubiquity defy even the most diligent efforts of perusal and cataloguing. On the other side, meanwhile, proliferate the utilitarian strategies of institutional control and monetary capture, in and with which the twenty-first-century university has become a proactive partner and collaborator. As academics, we face the bureaucratisation (that is, regimentation) of every aspect of teaching and learning, even as we are bombarded by incessant appeals to 'free' and 'enhance' our basic habits, including the tools we use to read, write, and communicate, through commodified technologisation. These mutually reinforcing dynamics suggest that the biopolitics of literary study cannot be effectively challenged by social activism and its sponsorship of particular populations – such as workers, women, gay people, subalterns, and disabled people – each with its variant of literary output, as such identity-based productions of resistance are by now normativised constituents of the politicisation of global culture. Instead, this biopolitics stands to remind us that literary study, too, needs to be rethought as a mutating life form, whose existence hitherto does not have to mean that its existence is guaranteed or inevitable. In the corporatised university, in particular, literary study's seasoned capacity for engaging with deeply humanistic issues – pain, suffering, deceit, error, illusion, dissent, hatred, conflict, and failure – seems today as much a potential for the discipline's continued institutional diminution as it is a potential (as some colleagues will no doubt want to argue) for its continued survival. This is simply because engagements with such humanistic issues have been steadily shifting to the academic sectors with 'problem-solving' missions. Alongside such academic sectors as global health, public policy, environmental ethics, international relations, and social justice – and their specialised quantifications and professionalised rationalisations – how can the non-problem-solving work of language and literature be (again) of import? Can it? The challenge facing literary study's practitioners seems nothing less than making way for their object's evolvement into a new niche: to change, indeed to reinvent, the literary itself qua object.

Notes

Some of the arguments in this chapter are drawn, in revised form, from my earlier article 'On the Graphic in Postmodern Theoretical Writing' (Chow 2011).

1. Although Foucault did not name them, his discussion calls to mind the venerable pedigree of philosophers in the analytic tradition – Friedrich Ludwig Gottlob Frege, Russell, Ludwig Wittgenstein, Rudolf Carnap, and A. J. Ayer, among others – who were preoccupied with or haunted by the idea of a perfectly neutral language.
2. This is why, as Barthes points out in his analysis of ideology (mythology), the language of modern mathematics, which is supposed to resist interpretation, tends under some circumstances to become an easy prey to ideology. Against such resistance, for instance, ideology can simply turn a formula such as $E = mc^2$ into a mythical signifier for 'mathematicity' itself (see Barthes 1973: 132–3).
3. See Moretti's discussion of how a change of the object can be brought about by quantification, while in comparative literary study of the novel the status of the object has remained unchanged.
4. See the chapter 'Conjectures on World Literature' in Moretti 2013: 43–62.
5. '[P]roblems without a solution are exactly what we need in a field like ours, where we are used to asking only those questions for which we already have an answer' (Moretti 2005: 26).

6. Elaborating on what literary maps do, Moretti writes:

    > you *reduce* the text to a few elements, and *abstract* them from the narrative flow, and construct a new, *artificial* object like the maps that I have been discussing ... Not that the map is itself an explanation, of course: but at least, it offers a model of the narrative universe which rearranges its components in a non-trivial way, and may bring some hidden patterns to the surface. (Moretti 2005: 53)

7. In one such anthology to which I am a contributor, *A New Literary History of Modern China* (Wang 2017), authors were required to begin their essays uniformly with a specified date and an important incident, so as to be consistent with the format of the publisher's volumes on other national literary histories.

Bibliography

Apter, Emily (2013), *Against World Literature: On the Politics of Untranslatability*, New York: Verso.
Barthes, Roland (1973), *Mythologies*, Annette Lavers (trans.), London: Paladin.
Barthes, Roland (1977), 'Rhetoric of the Image', in Roland Barthes, *Image-Music-Text*, Stephen Heath (ed. and trans.), New York: Hill and Wang, pp. 32–51.
Casanova, Pascale (2007), *The World Republic of Letters*, M. B. Debevoise (trans.), Cambridge, MA: Harvard University Press.
Cheah, Pheng (2016), *What Is a World? On Postcolonial Literature as World Literature*, Durham, NC: Duke University Press.
Chow, Rey (2011), 'On the Graphic in Postmodern Theoretical Writing', *Twentieth-Century Literature*, 57:3/4, pp. 372–9.
Damrosch, David (2003), *What Is World Literature?*, Princeton: Princeton University Press.
Daston, Lorraine and Peter Galison (2007), *Objectivity*, New York: Zone.
Dolar, Mladen (2011), 'The Burrow of Sound', *differences*, 22:2/3, pp. 112–39.
Eliot, T. S. (1970), 'The Love Song of J. Alfred Prufrock', in T. S. Eliot, *Collected Poems, 1909–1962*, London: Faber and Faber, pp. 13–17.
Foucault, Michel (1970), *The Order of Things: An Archaeology of the Human Sciences*, Alan Sheridan (trans.), London: Tavistock.
Foucault, Michel (1972), *The Archaeology of Knowledge*, A. M. Sheridan Smith (trans.), New York: Pantheon.
Foucault, Michel (1978), *The History of Sexuality, Vol. 1*, Alan Sheridan (trans.), New York: Pantheon.
Foucault, Michel (2003), *'Society Must Be Defended': Lectures at the Collège de France 1975–1976*, Mauro Bertani and Alessandro Fontana (eds), David Macey (trans.), New York: Picador.
Foucault, Michel (2008), *The Birth of Biopolitics: Lectures at the Collège de France 1978–1979*, Graham Burchell (trans.), New York: Palgrave Macmillan.
Heidegger, Martin (1971), *Poetry, Language, Thought*, Albert Hofstadter (trans.), New York: Harper Colophon.
Heise, Ursula (2017), 'Comparative Literature and Computational Criticism: A Conversation with Franco Moretti', in Ursula Heise (ed.), *Futures of Comparative Literature*, London: Routledge, pp. 273–84.

Lyotard, Jean-François (1984), *The Postmodern Condition: A Report on Knowledge*, Geoffrey Bennington and Brian Massumi (trans.), Minneapolis: University of Minnesota Press.
MacLeish, Archibald (1926), 'Ars Poetica', *Poetry*, 28:3, pp. 126–7.
Moretti, Franco (2005), *Graphs, Maps, Trees: Abstract Models for Literary History*, New York: Verso.
Moretti, Franco (2013), *Distant Reading*, New York: Verso.
Mufti, Aamir (2016), *Forget English! Orientalisms and World Literatures*, Cambridge, MA: Harvard University Press.
Wang, David Der-wei (ed.) (2017), *A New Literary History of Modern China*, Cambridge, MA: Harvard University Press.

21

We Have Been Paranoid Too Long to Stop Now

Frida Beckman and Charlie Blake

For those eager to look behind the scenery of everyday life and see how everything is actually connected, for those not just paranoid but trained in the art of reading about paranoia, or perhaps for those trained in reading about paranoid reading and schooled in old-fashioned notions like intertextuality, it will, quite possibly, be relatively easy to see how our chapter title points back to a well-known revaluation of paranoid reading from the 1990s: Eve Kosofsky Sedgwick's essay 'Paranoid Reading and Reparative Reading; or, You're So Paranoid, You Probably Think this Introduction Is about You' (Sedgwick 2002), first published in 1997. Sedgwick here looks back to the paranoid reading practices she herself and many with her conducted in the 1980s as well as to what she sees as an overdetermined relationship between what Paul Ricœur famously described as the hermeneutics of suspicion and critical theory, a relationship that, Sedgwick argues, has yielded a 'privileging of the concept of paranoia' (2002: 125). Sedgwick's purpose here is not to reject paranoid reading but to suggest that its overwhelming influence on critical theory may have suppressed and misplaced other, 'weaker', and perhaps 'reparative' practices of reading. Quite apart from sharing with Sedgwick a penchant for old tunes and their titles, we should make it clear from the outset that we also share with her an interest in critically revisiting earlier modes of reading in order to test their usefulness in the face of contemporary concerns and preoccupations. This interest is one that has been adopted by many working in the field of literary and critical theory over the past two or maybe three decades – a period which, it hardly needs to be stressed, coincides with the rapid ascendancy of the World Wide Web and the concomitant explosion of online culture. Indeed, and in the way of a kind of excess of clambering up meta-levels of reading practice, it has been pointed out that '[o]ne way to describe "the way we read now" is to say that we don't read at all' (Price 2009: 120). But whether or not this tendency is directly or only indirectly related to such developments, there does seem to have emerged during this period a very particular set of preoccupations with how we read – and more specifically, how we read how we read.

Rita Felski traces this renewed interest in the topic back to Sedgwick's essay and then – via a pragmatic genealogy of form and intervention – through contributions to the field including Bruno Latour's examination of why critique has 'Run Out of Steam' in 2004, Elisabeth Strowick's 'Comparative Epistemology of Suspicion' from 2005, Stephen Best and Sharon Marcus's proposition about surface reading from 2009, Heather Love's discussion of a 'descriptive turn' in 2010, and Felski's own essay on what may come after suspicion (Felski 2011: 218). To this list we may add, for example, Antonio Negri's revisiting of the role of critical theory in the age of Empire (Negri 2007), Marcus's 'just reading' from the same year (Marcus 2007), Timothy Bewes's discussion of 'generous reading' or reading 'with the grain' (Bewes 2010), Franco Moretti's *Distant Reading* consolidated in book form in 2013 (Moretti 2013), and, indeed, Felski's continued work in this area, including, notably, her book *The Limits of Critique* (Felski 2015). In different ways, each of these critics revisit the function of critique today and the modes of reading that have dominated literary criticism since the 1970s. Although their arguments and proposals are different and although they do not always agree with each other, a central starting point is the urge to break free from what Sedgwick describes as the 'mandatory injunction' to approach texts, more or less explicitly, by means of a hermeneutics of suspicion and the concomitant privileging, as she sees it, of paranoia in contemporary critical practices (Sedgwick 2002: 125).

While certainly sharing the conviction that critique and reading should not be shaped by established, closed, or conclusive models, we wish to suggest here that in order to understand such contemporary preoccupations with the ways and hows of reading, we need an expanded understanding of an integral relation between modern conceptions of the individual and of the experience of paranoia together with the particular history that paranoia shares with both the history of the novel and modern epistemology and ontology. Furthermore, we need to situate this contemporary preoccupation with ways of reading in relation to the equally contemporary challenges to politically engaged readings. This chapter will, accordingly, begin the process of illuminating incrementally the dark, paranoid, philosophical dimensions from which the novel at least partially emerged alongside modern epistemology and ontology and trace the consequences of that relative simultaneity of emergence for some recent and contemporary styles of reading. It will do so, moreover, against a background in which the philosophical investigations of reality, subjectivity, knowledge, fear, power, the communication of ideas and affects, and the arrangements of society, instigated in and by the work of René Descartes, Thomas Hobbes, and John Locke in particular, will be used to orient the themes of the individual, the world, and the status of paranoia and paranoid reading in the emergent novel and its historical legacy. Tracing relations between the novel's paranoid and individual-centred origins and contemporary shifts in biopolitics that seem to move it away from the individual as a central target and mode of power, we will try to better understand some of the recent challenges to the novel form and to novel reading.

To begin with, then, it is our contention that the rise of paranoia as an aspect of the human condition is, as we will illustrate via examples from Descartes to Philip K. Dick and beyond, contemporaneous with the rise of the modern generally and especially with a number of central elements in modern European philosophy, such as in the early modern era's most significant form of portable media and focus of representation, expression, and moral questioning: the novel. The articulation of the condition of paranoia as 'paranoia' in the clinical, psycho-social, political, fictional, or popular sense is a slightly later development, of course, though one which can, we believe, be deployed retroactively without danger of anachronism because of this (initially unnamed) simultaneity with the rise of the novel and the birth of early modern European philosophy. All are in a sense a response to a seismic shift in human understanding of the world from an essentially theocentric to an anthropocentric model, with all the attendant anxieties this shift brought in its wake. In terms of paranoia's naming as 'paranoia' in and of itself and its clinical definition and evolution within the field of psychoanalysis, the founder of this essentially twentieth-century discipline, Sigmund Freud, sets the scene with his discussion of the extraordinary case of Daniel Paul Schreber, whose *Memoirs of My Nervous Illness* from 1903 remains one of the central texts referred to within the psychoanalytic case study genre, and especially so after Freud's comments on this case were published in 1911. The essence of Freud's understanding of paranoia here and elsewhere (an essence still evident after numerous elaborations by and subsequent to Freud, it should be noted) may be found in some notes from a correspondence with Wilhelm Fliess from 1895, where, in a brief report called 'Draft H', he writes that 'the purpose of paranoia is ... to fend off an idea that is incompatible with the ego, by projecting its substance into the external world' (Freud 1966: 209).

After Freud, this image of projection is developed most significantly by Melanie Klein and those who draw on the Kleinian corpus, for whom paranoia is not merely the product of repression leading to projection (and introjection) but the basis of a universal 'position' which the human subject occupies as an inevitable result of its relationship with its primary object – in essence, the maternal figure and the body parts and economies of giving, taking, protection, and abandonment, and exchange thereof. Thus the 'paranoid schizoid position' (Klein 1984: 2) splits the universe of the child into an absolute and seemingly Manichaean vision of the good mother/bad mother or good breast/bad breast, and fear and aggression are consequently both projected outwards to external subjects and objects and introjected inwards, where they lodge as shards of affect and agency. Central here is Klein's notion of 'projective identification' (1984: 8) in which elements of the self are projected to the within of another and enfolded by the object of that projection, whether human or otherwise, thereby enabling, if only symbolically, partial or complete control of him or her or it (as a pre-emptively defensive tactic against threat or attack). But this unconscious projection inevitably carries with it the terror of its inverse, of being controlled from within oneself by someone or something from outside. This is, of course, a central feature of clinical persecutory delusion, as well as of many novels and films dealing with the anxieties of modernity and modern technology, from mysterious implants that command one's behaviour from within, to rays from outer space or government agencies that infiltrate the brain, to general 'voices in the head', to possession by demonic or alien forces or the setting up of an immersive artificial reality by those same forces to persecute or control the individual by controlling their epistemological coordination of thought or experience, or even their very ontological foundations as subjects that exist in space and time.

For Jacques Lacan, paranoia was the catalyst for his revisioning of Freud and reinvention of psychoanalysis in the 1930s. This revisioning and reinvention were negotiated via his encounter with the surrealist movement and the 'paranoid-critical' method of Salvador Dalí in particular, as well as the influential reading of Hegel's *Phenomenology of Spirit* and most notably the master–slave dialectic from that work by Alexandre Kojève (1969). In essence, building on both Freud and Klein and with the additional inputs described above, paranoia at this early stage for Lacan is about the 'imago' or projected image, which in the case of the pre-conceptual child is characterised by a constant fear of 'aggressive disintegration' (Lacan 1980: 4) involving fragments of self, disjointed limbs, mutilation, evisceration, bursting, nihilation, the body in pieces – all of which combine to form a fundamentally paranoid and existentially untenable conception of self and world. These terrifying images are necessarily disavowed if the self is to hold together at all and as such, projections of a future self-mastery – images of completion and individuation – emerge to enable the human subject to function. From 1936, Lacan's focus on paranoia per se shifts to his adaptation of Henry Wallon's mirror-stage or mirror-phase and thereby initiates the Lacanian revolution in psychoanalysis. The enormous complexity and frequent obscurity of Lacan are clearly beyond the scope of this brief survey of paranoid positions, but what is important to retain here is that for Lacan paranoia is effectively the condition of knowledge itself and thus fundamental to human subjectivity and individuation.

This stress on paranoia and individuation continues in the work of Lacan's one-time pupil Félix Guattari, who, along with Gilles Deleuze, is possibly Lacan's most influential critic in the field of desire and subjectivity. What the earlier Guattari retains and develops, however, and in ways that will feed into his and Deleuze's political vision of paranoia and schizophrenia in the two volumes of *Capitalism and Schizophrenia* (*Anti-Oedipus* (1972) and *A Thousand Plateaus* (1980)) is what Guattari, in *Molecular Revolution*, calls 'the coefficient of collective paranoia' (Guattari 1984: 86).[1] This is in effect a modelling or reorientation of lines of transversality – notions of exchange and communication that escape the subject/object polarity – and the ways in which they subvert and reconfigure the paranoid consciousness that underpins various social, bureaucratic, and institutional groupings, including states and the discipline of psychoanalysis itself. These lines of transversal connection and disconnection, which for Guattari can be creatively manipulated to establish new kinds of subjectivity and revolutionary micro-political action, are inherently bound up with the process of individuation. Thus, he claims that 'the tendency of the individuation of desire is always towards paranoia and individualism' (1984: 87). In his subsequent work with Deleuze, this claim is elaborated and developed, and what is crucial here for the discussion that follows is the necessary link between paranoia and the individual human subject as in some way mutually co-determinate.

When viewed in the dark mirror of paranoia, the centrality of the individual in the novel and to the activity of novel reading itself indicates significant parallels to and reflections of these paranoid dimensions of knowledge, thought, and experience. Through negotiating multiple fragments and elements within the domains of philosophy and literature, as well the various political forces that configure and reconfigure the individual as a nexus of discipline and control in industrial and post-industrial societies, the novel works to forge new machineries of subjectivity in the face of constant ethical and epistemological challenges and existential doubts. With its central focus on the individual subject, the novel thus constitutes a stage on which the dramas of defending the self – and indeed, the very notion of the self – against its various real or imagined enemies are played out. The modern epoch of the European novel emerged, as Guido Mazzoni notes, as it was ready to secure 'an unprecedented linguistic space' for 'the existence of private, common individuals' (Mazzoni 2017: 19).[2] Mazzoni ascribes this opening space to the liberation from two previous traditions: the imperative of normative morality of art in the Platonic Christian tradition and a classicist poetics of style insisting on separation (2017: 18). While tracing the emergence of the novel back to the sixteenth century (and thus pointing to a longer history than that which Watt outlines in his influential if often challenged study *The Rise of the Novel* (2000)), Mazzoni shows how a key factor moulding the individual as the novel takes its modern shape during the late eighteenth and early nineteenth century is the way it is necessarily circumscribed by laws and institutions. Unlike the epic and mythological heroes capable of changing and shifting destinies on a cosmic scale, the common people that are given space in the modern novel are determined by their role in what Daniel Defoe calls the 'middle station of life', where the actions of individuals are subordinated to the social order (Defoe 1994: 8–13). This means that the increasing attention to the individual in the novel is to a particular sort of individual – one that is elevated to importance despite but also because of their unspectacular and necessarily restricted particularity.

The innovations appearing with the modern novel, Watt notes, are closely linked to the individualist focus of the empiricists during the seventeenth century (Watt 2000: 144–5). Understood in its general sense, the modern novel form shares with modern epistemology an ambivalent preoccupation with the nature and conditions of the individual in its restrictions and capacities as a 'knowing subject'. Philosophical analyses of the novel's individualist focus refer back to the Cartesian cogito and its internal reflection on self-certainty, and to the individualism outlined by Hobbes and Locke and later influentially formalised by C. B. Macpherson. Thus, for example, when Defoe defied the theoretical and literary tradition of his day by subordinating the plot to the centrality of the development of the individual character, Watt notes how he also provided 'as defiant an assertion of the primacy of individual experience in the novel as Descartes' *cogito ergo sum* was in philosophy'

(Watt 2000: 34). At the same time, these philosophical and literary histories share a recurring sense of doubt regarding the nature and conditions of this individual in relation to the external world and external reality. If it is on the individual, rather than fate or God or some other higher force, that we must rely to get to the truth and the real, then unhampered access to an objective and correct interpretation of reality becomes critical. Thus it is in the shift from a theocentric to an anthropocentric universe that characterises the gradual transitions of modernity from faith to reason that the individual and paranoia – individuation as paranoia – paranoia as individuation – emerge. The relatively fixed reality produced by God is incrementally replaced by the dangerously mutable realities produced by the sovereign individual.

At this point it is, perhaps, crucial to differentiate between and make explicit two idealities of self; two idealities drawn from the lineage of modern philosophical argument and engagement, that is, that have become centrally operative in the construction of the prismatic self of the novel from the time of its inception through its development to the present. To begin with, we have the internal and rationally – almost mathematically – configured *cogito ergo sum* of Descartes. The post-Cartesian 'subject' is a figure born of a method of radical doubt and a potential existential terror over its own existence, let alone that of the world around it. To push his own preconceptions about knowledge as far as he can, that is, to be absolutely sure that he is not basing his knowledge on false grounds, Descartes decides to suppose that in the place of a good and truthful God, there is 'some malicious demon of the utmost power and cunning' employing 'all his energies in order to deceive me'. This way, all external things – the sky, the air, etc. – are 'merely the delusions of dreams which he has devised to ensnare my judgment'. In order to make sure that such a demon, should it exist, has no power to impose on him, Descartes also relinquishes his certainty about his own bodily experiences and perceptions: 'I shall consider myself as not having hands or eyes, or flesh, or blood or senses, but as falsely believing that I have all these things.' Ultimately, and famously, the only certainty he allows himself to arrive at is being confident that he is capable of thinking. Importantly, this certainty, which takes the shape of the famous *cogito ergo sum*, is possible only by being acutely aware of the possibility of deception: 'he will never bring it about that I am nothing so long as I think that I am something' (Descartes quoted in Nadler 1997: 45). In pre-empting the paranoiac socialities of, say, Thomas Pynchon's *The Crying of Lot 49* (1965), this is also the subject who wonders – in a manner that presages the ontological unmooring of the replicants by the ever-visionary Dick in *Do Androids Dream of Electric Sheep?* (1968). And although within his own terms Descartes succeeds in quelling the malign genius of cosmic deception, as numerous commentators have noted subsequently, this victory is only achieved by an essentially scholastic evasion of cosmic doubt via what many consider an equally cosmic and rationally unfounded leap of faith, disguised as a philosophical argument for the existence, omnipotence, and goodness of a supreme deity who would, by definition, absolutely forbid so universal an epistemological perversion as this deception to permeate creation.

Interestingly, such evasions seem less manageable in the novel. Steven Nadler notes how 'precisely the same philosophical problem is raised both in the first major work of modern philosophy and in the first modern novel', and this, he points out, is a problem with a paranoid foundation: 'in the face of the possibility of ongoing deception by some powerful and malicious being, how can we possibly trust our sensory and rational faculties to provide us with true and reliable knowledge?' (Nadler 1997: 42). Referring, of course, to Miguel de Cervantes's *Don Quixote*, and pointing to the distinct similarities between Cervantes's and Descartes' work, Nadler even suggests that Descartes may have read Cervantes's novel before articulating his famous dictum. And even if he did not, Nadler argues, it seems relevant to compare the predicaments of Descartes' mediator and those of Don Quixote (1997: 43). Both Descartes and Cervantes, Nadler notes further, would both have encountered the scholastic notion of the 'enchanter' or 'deceiver' in their intellectual development 1997: 42). John Farrell further underlines the importance of such comparisons from a synchronic perspective as he notes that the culture and era from which Descartes' demon arises is the same that constructs 'Don Quixote and his malicious enchanters' (Farrell 2006: 114). In this light, the particularities of Don Quixote's madness may also be seen as an expression of Cartesian doubt *avant la lettre*. But the end results differ. Importantly, Farrell notes, Descartes' demon is conquered and the doubts dismissed, while Don Quixote's 'bedevilment' reaches no such resolution (2006: 115). In addition, and as Nadler points out, the similarities between the two are different in implication because, whereas Descartes' method of doubt is intended to be universalisable, Don Quixote's madness is fascinating exactly because of his particularity, a particularity that must also, as Nadler underlines, 'represent something recognizably general in order to live up to the expectations of a literary character' (Nadler 1997: 55).

A second ideality with a foundational impact on modern conceptions of the individual can be traced back to the work of Locke,– and arguably to Hobbes before him. Here, we can discern the outlines of the liberal individual/individualist who will dominate so much Western political discourse in the centuries that follow, leading in due course to the reign of 'possessive individualism' specified by Macpherson. The seventeenth-century political theories of the self, developed centrally by Hobbes and Locke, Macpherson suggests, conceive of the individual 'as essentially the proprietor of his own person or capacities, owing nothing to society for them'. In addition, the individual is part of neither a moral nor a social whole but is determined rather by his ownership – if of nothing else, then at least of his own person (Macpherson 1962: 3). Outlining the assumptions of this possessive individualism as it emerged from seventeenth-century political theory, Macpherson notes how they take freedom to be fundamentally related to an independence from the will of others, except when doing otherwise suits the interests of the individual concerned (1962: 263–4).[3] The post-Lockean 'individual' is the product of a perpetual negotiation between power and property and the radial extensions of the self and the socius. Therefore, and as with the Cartesian cogito, possessive individualism comes with its own kind of paranoia. Where Descartes' demon made him retreat to that core of thought that he saw as inviolable, Hobbes's and Locke's empiricist approach necessarily directs their concerns for the potential manipulations of the self outwards. Because denying the senses *tout court* is not an option within their theoretical premise, it is the information that these yield that needs to be approached with suspicion.

This ambivalence – the centrality of experience to knowledge that necessarily means an interrogation of the nature of experience itself – is reflected in an ambivalent approach to the individual and its relation to the external world. Distrust and suspicion become inevitable. Thus, for example, Farrell points out, the political philosophy of Hobbes diverges from that of Aristotle centrally in that while the latter based his assumptions on the idea of the political animal as finding gratification in an ordered society, the former bases his on the assumption that men are naturally hostile to such cooperation unless it is imposed upon them by a sovereign force of some kind. This distrust constitutes a central reason for Hobbes's emphasis on individual self-possession – no one else can be fully trusted – but also for his understanding of the irrationality, self-deceptiveness, and violence at the heart of the self (Farrell 2006: 122–6). Hobbes's view of social life, Farrell suggests, is that of a 'shadowy forum where solipsisms do not meet but cross' (2006: 126). Locke's epistemology is typically associated with a more confident approach to the individual but it too, Farrell goes on to show, relies on suspicion. The Lockean subject can ultimately know of nothing other than its own ideas and their interrelation. It can have no real knowledge of the external world and should therefore try to limit its influences. But as it has to live in relation to the external work, it must base its knowledge, even as it is imperfect, on the senses. This makes Locke's model paradoxical, Farrell underlines. As he puts it, 'If skepticism can lead to peace and withdrawal from concern with the world, combined with suspicion it can create the sense that the struggle to define one's reality against the persuasions of others has no proper basis on which to proceed' (2006: 237).

Thus, the modern self in its novelistic and novelised variants is potentially haunted by two species of paranoiac fear which, however covert their operation, substantially determine how that prismatic self organises the fictional world – the scenery – around it, and by extension, how we do something similar with the world into which we find ourselves – to borrow from Martin Heidegger – 'thrown'. On the one hand, then, in its Cartesian form, the self may doubt its own existence, or that of the world around it – as does Horselover Fat in Dick's *Valis* (1981) – or that of others in that world – as does Mark Schluter in Richard Powers's *The Echo Maker* (2006) – or view the world as nothing other than plasterboard and paint – as does Ragle Gum in Dick's *Time Out of Joint* (1959) – or perhaps, in the more contemporary data-saturated milieu that most of us now spend our lives negotiating, as an algorithm put together by an errant, mischievous, and quite possibly malign game player – as in Harlan Ellison's 'I Have No Mouth and I Must Scream' (1967) – or as a giant corporation keeping us from true reality by means of social media – as in Dave Eggers' *The Circle* (2013). This way, a small glitch in the elaborate system you took for natural reality might at any time expose it as but 'delusions of dreams', which, as Descartes puts it, a demon 'has devised to ensnare my judgment', as it has Ed Fletcher when he arrives too early at work and finds that reality has not yet been properly adjusted, in Dick's short story 'Adjustment Team' from 1954. On the other hand, the senses and the body constitute crucial tools for the ostensibly upright citizen or hero or bourgeois subject, as it is forever haunted by the possibility of a radical 'otherness' unsettling individual self-possession. This might be an 'otherness' ranging from the sheer, darkly sinister, carnivalesque strangeness of the scenes of the fair coming to town in Charles Dickens's ostensibly realist 1854 novel *Hard Times*, to the preoccupation with haunted houses or properties or possession in the supernatural sense, or the absolute re-barbarianisation of the world in zombie apocalypse or post-apocalypse in the American novel and movie of the second half of the twentieth century. Thus, power and property and how we can possibly know and trust what we see are as much a part of the incipient paranoia of the literary form as the more ontological terrors of a loss of self or the exposure of the world we know as a deception, as in Jack Finney's 1954 novel and Don Siegel's classic film adaptation, *Invasion of the Body Snatchers* from 1956. So it is that we find in these and in innumerable other examples in the novel and its increasingly diverse progeny that epistemological paranoia and ontological paranoia, the two main sources from which a myriad of paranoiac philosophical and literary or filmic tributaries descend, always finally meet under the aegis of a perpetual fear of deception.

Accordingly, emerging alongside the evolving individualism of modernity and its epistemological and ontological investments of and in paranoia, it seems unsurprising that literature from this period onwards evinces an interest in paranoid plots and thematics. Furthermore, it is important to note how the novel is certainly not a passive recipient or reflector of philosophical concerns, but plays a part in shaping modern conceptions of the individual through cultural parallelism and exchange. Where the epics and allegories of earlier periods conveyed communal values and systems, the novel's depiction of the particularities of characters supposedly like you and me makes claims on the emergent humanist belief in the individual. Depicting ordinary individuals in ordinary settings is also a way of laying claims to representation, that is, to defining the nature of the individual in the first place in terms of context and milieu. In fact, could not the novel as a form be a sort of Cartesian demon presenting us with 'delusions of dreams' that are 'devised to ensnare [our] judgment'? Or, if our own perception of reality is susceptible to the natural hostility and persuasions of other men, as Hobbes claims, is not the novel a potential tool for manipulating our beliefs within or even beyond the control of the sovereign? Such doubts lift paranoia from the level of plot – where paranoid protagonists look over their shoulders suspecting vicious demons, states, communists, or aliens – to the level of the reader, who might begin to ask to what extent their schooling and, as some would have it, normalisation and subject identification as liberal or disciplinary subjects are shaped by the themes, structures, plots, and modes of characterisation of the novel. In other words, readers of the novel might start interrogating the extent to which the novel tradition is related to their perception of themselves as subjects capable of rational thought and agents in charge of their own destinies. Such questions lead us to link the epistemological influences on the novel as a form to the social and political conditions shaping the time of its modern development.

The centrality of the role of industrialisation generally to the formation of the novel and the 'economic individualism' consolidated not least in early realist novels (Watt 2000: 144) has been well noted. Emerging alongside the industrialism of late eighteenth- and early nineteenth-century Europe, the novel in its modern form also emerged alongside the array of disciplinary controls theorised by Michel Foucault, a central element of which is the training and normalisation of subjects. In his theorisation of disciplinary power, Foucault sees how the sovereign power formations of pre-industrial society are increasingly replaced, from the seventeenth and eighteenth century onwards, with forms of power that rely less on right and sovereign rule and more on controlling and managing individual bodies by means of normalisation and discipline (Foucault 2003: 31). Foucault insists that we need to forsake theories of sovereignty, such as those Hobbes posits in the 1651 *Leviathan*, that see society as made up of distinct individualities united by the state, the latter constituting society's head, or heart, or soul. Instead, Foucault argues, power should be analysed by means of the power-effects that construct subject positions (2003: 29). It is a mistake, he suggests, 'to think of the individual as a sort of elementary nucleus' that can be subordinated or destroyed by power. Rather, and from the perspective of disciplinary power, it becomes clear that

> one of the first effects of power is that it allows bodies, gestures, discourses, and desires to be identified and constituted as something individual. The individual is not, in other words, power's opposite number: the individual is one of power's first effects. (2003: 29–30)

However, Foucault suggests, focusing in particular on the period from the nineteenth century to the present, a system of rights is superimposed on disciplinary power so as to conceal its true workings. In other words, the real locus of power – disciplinary control by means of training and normalisation – is hidden behind an articulation of sovereignty of the state as well as of the individual.

On top of the philosophical ambivalence regarding the individual subject, then, the novel also needs to negotiate a continually generative process of political ambivalence. New Historicists have noted how the formation of novelistic expression occurs in interrelation with the disciplinary mode of power Foucault theorises. More than that, they have suggested that the novel form becomes informed or even complicit in concomitant arrangements of structures and processes of power/knowledge. Jeremy Tambling, for example, observes that literary texts during the nineteenth century are not only informed by but also 'aware of' the power structures emerging alongside them (Tambling 1995: 23). Similarly, and with more emphasis, D. A. Miller suggests that the novel is not only shaped by but is also an actual part of such disciplinary power (Miller 1988: 20). This means, then, that at the same time that the idea of the liberal subject becomes key to literary form, as we have seen via Descartes, Locke, and Hobbes, this idea is undermined if we acknowledge the functions of disciplinary power, that is, the way it constructs this subject in the first place. Or as Miller puts it, more astutely:

> the point of the exercise, relentlessly and often literally brought home as much in the novel's characteristic forms and conditions of reception as in its themes, is to confirm the novel-reader in his [sic] identity as 'liberal subject,' a term with which I allude not just to the subject whose private life, mental or domestic, is felt to provide constant inarguable evidence of his constitutive 'freedom,' but also to, broadly speaking, the political regime that sets store by this subject. Such confirmation is thoroughly imaginary, to be sure, but so too, I will eventually be suggesting, is the identity of the liberal subject, who seems to recognize himself most fully only when he forgets or disavows his functional implication in a system of carceral restraints or disciplinary injunctions. (1988: x)

What Miller describes here is the ways in which the formal structures that the novel develops in order to accommodate the adventures of the unique individual serve to maintain a sense of interiority, which it is in the very nature and interest of disciplinary society to both promote and undermine. In order to conform to the demands placed on a good subject in disciplinary society, the individual needs to maintain the sense of selfhood that the novel helps in constructing. And as Foucault notes, the increasing focus on individual life in literature serves the micro-political function of providing subjects with the 'correct training' by means of objectification and normalisation (Foucault 1977: 192–3). From this perspective, then (and bearing in mind that this applies more directly to the tradition of realism in the novel than to the more fragmentary or experimental forms of radically interior or exterior or entropic or machinic forms of narrative identity associated with certain strands of Anglophone literary modernism in, say, James Joyce, Virginia Woolf, Samuel Beckett, Gertrude Stein, or Wyndham Lewis), the idea of the liberal subject – with its roots, as we have seen, in Descartes, Hobbes, and Locke – is promoted in a novel form that has to hide, or forget, or disavow, the disciplinary power that undermines those conceptions of subjectivity in the first place. Such a Foucauldian conception of the individual subject as shaped by societal structures and processes of power/knowledge, in other words, creates an ambivalent and contradictory impulse to the knowing subject and the attendant possessive individualism shaping the novel's epistemological heritage.

But if we are to pursue such an angle on the political formations and function of the individual subject, we need to acknowledge that for all the uses of Foucault's disciplinary model in relation to the novel as to many other institutions arising in modernity, his more recently published lectures on biopolitics point towards a theory of power that is not primarily concerned with the individual. Where the disciplinary structures that he had formerly identified worked by training and shaping individual subjects, life under the biopolitical regime he outlines in his lectures at the Collège de France towards the end of the 1970s allows for subjects to think and move like populations – stochastically, as molecularities, as shifting constellations of auto-generative subjectivity – thereby shifting the overall machinery of power's focus from the individual subject per se to the broader sweep of biopower and governmentality. Life itself becomes the target here, on a scale from the most minute to the level of species and populations. In such a 'permanent matrix of political power', he suggests, there is no need for structures of power relying on subjection and sovereignty (Foucault 2008: 303) but rather, power works by means of control over all levels and shapes of life. This form of biopower does not replace discipline but coexists with it; what he calls 'the body-organism-discipline-institutions series' is complemented with a series of 'the population-biological processes-regulatory mechanisms State' (Foucault 2003: 250).[4] It seems apparent, however, that once we get to later views concerning the developments and the social and political effects of digital technologies, particularly Deleuze's (1995) elaboration of Foucault's theories in terms of control, the modulatory power of biopolitics is of increasing importance. Departing from Foucault's theories on discipline, Deleuze observes how the central relevance of institutions and their training of subjects under discipline is increasingly moderated under late capitalism by new technologies and new forms of power that in themselves no longer rely on institutions and individuals for control. Power under the regime of control is not dependent on such larger entities, but functions more by means of the direct modulation of affects and desires.

In other words, Foucault's work on biopolitics and Deleuze's elaboration of his theories suggest that, increasingly, control mechanisms work not primarily by means of disciplinary modes of training and normalisation intent on moulding individuals, but rather by exercising a constant and more intricate modulation and minute calibration of 'dividuals'. The individual is no longer the primary target of control. Rather, as David Savat notes, such control recognises patterns, flows, and movements, registers effects, and adjusts the environment in an undetectable manner (Savat 2013: 48–53). While the disciplinary subject is constructed in advance of events, and thus trained to behave in a correct manner for all eventualities, the subject under control is constructed simultaneously with events. This means that the subject is not a subject at all but itself an event: the individual turns into the 'dividual', an ostensibly human subject transformed or elaborated from its historically iterated liberal identity into variant sets of malleable configurations of data, configurations which can then be quantified and reshaped by emergent technologies of power and control in the so-called 'Societies of Control' that Deleuze extrapolates from and after Foucault. This newer mode of control comes with a shift of perception and awareness. The control exercised under discipline is, Savat points out, experienced by its subjects; it is even something that they 'ideally impose upon themselves, so as to make themselves into good individuals' (2013: 50). The subject checks itself against registers of normality and standards and, ideally, strives towards its expected form.

But control as modulation cannot be experienced in the same way: it is not interested in 'making specific forms' or even 'good' standardised individuals, but rather works by means of anticipating, identifying, and predicting patterns and flows (2013: 50). This way, it becomes virtually impossible for the subject under control to adjust to, or indeed resist, its environment simply because that environment continually anticipates its moves and desires (2013: 53–4). The control, as Savat puts it, is subtler but also more unmitigated: it 'has already occurred prior to a subject's arrival or eventuation' (2013: 54).

In this light, readings interested in how the novel constructs individuals will need to take into account not only how notions of the individual shaped by Cartesian and Hobbesian ideals may be affected by the individual's subjection to political correction and training in a disciplinary fashion, but also the potential further implications of the shifts in biopolitics on such construction of individuals, as well as on the novel's potential political function in 'training' such individuals in the first place. This is not to suggest that developments of discipline, biopolitics, and control are sequential, or to claim that literature is bound to sequentiality. Rather, what we may see exemplified by, but by no means restricted to, the English novel from its origins to its establishment as the dominant genre of the era, such as in *Robinson Crusoe* (1719), *Tristram Shandy* (1759–67), *Frankenstein; or, The Modern Prometheus* (1818), *Wuthering Heights* (1847), and *Vanity Fair* (1847–9), are layerings, with disciplinarity a bottom layer in which autonomy is emergent and yet always already determined by societal structures – which might or might not be ideological but could also be governmental. Of course, discipline does not exclude biopower, or vice versa, so in a way the shifts outlined here merely generate new and collective possibilities for paranoia that embrace not merely the individual or the group – as for example in novels and their audiovisual progeny such as *Rosemary's Baby* (1967, with a film version in 1968), *The Conversation* (1974), and *The X-Files* (1993–2002) – or the 'total society' – as in *We* (1924, with adaptations in 1982 and 2016), *Nineteen Eighty-Four* (1949, with various subsequent adaptations), and *The Matrix* (1999) – but also species, as in Howard Hawks's *The Thing from Another World* (1951, remade by John Carpenter as *The Thing* in 1982) and George Romero's seminal zombie trilogy, *Night of the Living Dead* (1968), *Dawn of the Dead* (1978), and *Day of the Dead* (1985), and its many imitations.

But although paranoid fiction thus develops more overt mechanisms for dealing with the more generic paranoia of the novel tradition as we have outlined it here, this still does not explain how the novel would incorporate the flow of 'dividualisation', which speaks to a different temporality of anticipation that does not quite fit with the negotiation between individual and environment as we have come to recognise it. Nancy Armstrong points to the novel's formal reliance on establishing a sense of the individual and its relation to community, and notes that changing societal, cultural, and political structures may challenge the novel format (Armstrong 2011: 8). She points to novels by writers such as Ian McEwan, David Mitchell, and Nicola Barker as illustrative of such challenges, as they create 'nonindividuals' existing within 'microworlds' and thereby call for new ways of understanding both humanist categories and the novel form (2011: 9–10). But there is a long way ahead for a literary form that has always relied so intimately on the individual, however fraught its history. Under the regime of control, Savat notes, there is a simultaneous production of essence and event, of solid form and flow, and what emerges is a competition between the two – essence and event – in what becomes a 'twin antagonistic process' between the production of individuals and the flow of 'dividuality' (Savat 2013: 57). How, if at all, can and need the already troubled negotiations between ideas of the liberal subject and disciplinary structures in the novel work to negotiate this additional dilemma that seems to undermine the individual as the most central component of liberal society? Novels that address questions of control and technology directly, such as Eggers's *The Circle* (2013) and Patrick Flanery's *I Am No One* (2016), evince thematic preoccupations with control and its threats to humanist conceptions of the subject, but they do not come with formal challenges to match. While such novels turn towards digitalised contemporaneity and do address the threats to the idea of the individual subject that contemporary control poses, such threats ultimately play the same role as earlier ones – they are windmills. One reason for such formal hesitation may be found in the novel's historical and foundational reliance on the individual, as outlined here. Because the novel has always been concerned with the negotiation between the individual and the threats towards it, and because disciplinary modes of power have haunted the liberal subject of the novel from its youth, these are also the structures most readily available. Indeed, and as Timothy Melley suggests, the prevalence of paranoia in a post-war context suggests 'a broad cultural refusal to modify a concept of self that is no longer wholly accurate or useful' (Melley 2000: 14–15).

And here, finally, it is time to return to Sedgwick and her concern over a tradition of paranoid reading as outlined at the beginning of this chapter. We are fully aware that our own reading has itself been of the paranoid inclination, but we are also convinced that such a reading is important for our understanding of the interlinked relation between individualism, paranoia, and the novel historically, and for our recognition of the challenges to the novel posed by developing formations of power. In this sense, we have also embraced paranoia in that it, as Sedgwick puts it, 'insists on being both "a way of knowing" and "a thing known"' (Sedgwick 2002: 131). But we are also eager to recognise, with Sedgwick, that paranoia, in being both anticipatory and retroactive, tends to construct rigid temporal relations that obscure our view of other possibilities and contingencies (2002: 146). The rigid temporality of paranoia, she notes, pre-empts the painful but also potentially relieving and, most importantly, ethically and politically enabling realisation that things both past and present may have been and may be different from what we know (2002: 146). Thus, for example, the 'drop-dead-elegant' diagrams of the 'Foucauldian paranoid' may award us with, 'narratability, a body, cognition' but also delimit the potential for struggle (2002: 131–2). Here, we would like to propose that the shift from the individual to the dividual, even as it opens up new venues for paranoia, also opens towards the potential of 'thinking otherwise' that 'the paranoid imperative' that we have identified throughout modern philosophy as well as literature has prohibited (Sedgwick 2002: 133). Even as control mechanisms point to hitherto unmatched levels of manipulation and surveillance, theories of control also potentially interfere with the relation between the conception of the individual and paranoia in these fields as they have been outlined here in several key ways. Conceptions of control and the dividual do not have to disavow external influences on the self because they recognise that there is no such inviolable thinking or self-possession to begin with. In addition, the differing temporality of the dividual disables the sort of narratability, body, and cognition that the Foucauldian model constructs.

Deleuze (1995) historicises his argument about the dividual by pointing to changing mechanisms in a post-war context and the 'control society' consolidating during this period, but it is important to note that this is a historicisation of power mechanisms rather than of the 'dividual' itself. Although technological and geopolitical developments have adapted to, and perhaps contributed to, the more minute modes of control that do not rely on institutions and individuals, as stated earlier, the recognition of subjectivities beyond the delimitations of the individual is not necessarily disabling. Instead, such theories can help by recognising and making space for conceptions about the self beyond the individual. As we saw via Guattari earlier, institutional and disciplinary groupings are supported by a paranoid consciousness that tends towards individualism. For Guattari, such individualism is born of an individuation of desire that is concomitant with paranoia. As with his conception of 'the coefficient of collective paranoia' (Guattari 1984: 86), this creation of subjectivity is intimately intertwined with the individuation of desire that leads to paranoid individualism. For Guattari, importantly, this is related to transversal connections that can also yield a more productive and politically resistant micro-politics, but because of the paranoid tendency towards individuation, desire is repeatedly tied up in formations such as institutions and individuals. But central to such conception is not only the link between individualism and paranoia but also the way it carries another possibility. Because the individual is not the starting point but a result of a paranoid capture of an otherwise open transversal process of connection and disconnection, the process could also generate other modes of agency. This way, paranoid individuation may be loosened with the help of what Sedgwick, via Klein, calls a 'reparative impulse'. This is an impulse towards addition and accretion, a position that 'undertakes a different range of affects, ambitions, and risks' (Sedgwick 2002: 149–50), because to get out of the paranoid position requires courage – it requires an 'often risky positional shift' away from the patterns we know, or think we know (2002: 137).

And as we have shown in this chapter, these are patterns of paranoia, patterns that seem so intimately bound up with notions of the individual that the one cannot seem to do without the other. The question is the extent to which the shifts and transitions regarding the political function of the individual create a double consciousness around the experiential dimension of liberty or freedom for the individual and the socius, and the extent to which this generates new forms of paranoia that are themselves mapped out and explored through the strategic narrative designs of the novel. Paranoid responses to these transitions from disciplinarity to biopolitics could arguably be echoed in the implicit structures of reading generated by the novel at different stages and in different settings: where disciplinarity per se works alongside (or beneath) the focus on individual consciousness in modernism, for example; or even in surrealist experimentation, to effect a transition in the paranoid mode from pure disciplinarity via the ascendancy of notions of personal liberty (of affect or action or interpretation) to control. Because what, ultimately, is the multiplication of reading practices that we pointed to at the beginning of this chapter – surface, distant, generous, reparative reading – but a response to the uncertainty of how and what texts mean and how we might know them? Without in any way suggesting that the methods these practices propose are similar, what they do have in common is the sense that the ways of reading – primarily those practices of symptomatic reading that have shaped literary studies since the 1970s – are not yielding sufficient, or even correct, answers. Repeatedly, this sense of insufficiency is framed in terms of a shifting politics, one that is based not on secrecy but, quite on the contrary, on visibility and even on the spectacular. Sedgwick wonders what 'a hermeneutics of suspicion and exposure has to say to social formations in which visibility itself constitutes much of the violence' (2002: 140) and Best and Marcus even suggest that the once almost paranoid assumption that domination is always veiled 'now has a nostalgic, even utopian ring to it' (Best and Marcus 2009: 2). What is suggested – if by nothing else, then by the very decision to look for some kind of 'variation on, supplement to, or critique of' symptomatic reading (2009: 6), as do the contributors to the special issue of *Representations* called 'The Way We Read Now' to which Best and Marcus's essay serves as introduction – is that the search for hidden meanings and deceptive structures might lead us down the wrong path. Indeed, as Beckman has suggested elsewhere in that same vein, strategies of looking for hidden structures might even conceal from us the workings of a politics taking place in broad daylight (Beckman 2016). Surely, and even when this is not addressed explicitly in these proposals for new ways of reading, changing political structures have implications for our perceptions and conception of the individual subject and its modes or capacities for recognising such structures and their interrelation to cultural expression. Whatever certainties we might have felt in the past – even if they were only by means of a methodology based on suspicion – have been replaced by doubt and uncertainty about our ability to read in the first place. In other words, is not the crisis in critique and the proposing of various forms of alternative ways of reading very much itself a sign of paranoia?

Positing these various engagements with how we read today in terms of paranoia is not in any way to disparage them, but rather to align them with a philosophical and literary history of individualism and paranoia, as well as to try to situate them as an expression – or perhaps even as a symptom – of a historical point in time that comes with new challenges to these notions. Even though few of the new ways of reading proposed have been situated in relation to shifts in biopolitics and to control mechanisms explicitly (apart from Beckman's), many of them emerge from a sense that we are facing new social and political challenges that require new kinds of responses. The paranoid dimensions of modern philosophy and literature as outlined here – from Descartes through Hobbes and Foucault and from Cervantes to Dickens to Dick – are, as we have shown, shaped by an insistence on the individual and the concomitant pitfalls of deception. Perhaps the new configurations of power consolidating over the last few decades are leaving an imprint, if not on the literature itself so much – indeed, as we suggested a moment ago, and although novels do address the challenges of the control society thematically, we have struggled to locate clear examples of novels taking such challenges onboard formally – then on modes of reading or concerns regarding such modes. If symptomatic reading and its more outspoken relative, paranoid reading, are felt to be insufficient today, this may be in part because we sense that as reading subjects, we will not learn enough from such practices. We have got paranoid, if you will, about our own paranoia. This might mean revisiting or even abandoning paranoid reading as we thought we meant it, but we are not sure that this means that we can slough off paranoid defences of the self. Ultimately, then, we agree with Sedgwick that we need a 'more ecological view of paranoia' (2002: 146–7). As we have tried to show in this chapter, we propose that such ecology does not preclude the historical and structural role of paranoia in the constitution of individualism and the novel alike. We need to keep paranoia in mind, not only to better understand the history of modern epistemology and literature, but also in responding to the responses and reading the reading of reading that are taking place today. Indeed, we have been paranoid a little too long to stop now.

Notes

1. This retention arguably also feeds into Deleuze's later adaptation of Michel Foucault's disciplinarity to his own notion of control and his further development of the notion of the 'dividual' as a product of post-disciplinarity.
2. This discussion of the novel in the context of Mazzoni, Ian Watt, and C. B. Macpherson is quite similar to Frida Beckman's discussion of the topic in her essay 'Control and a Minor Literature' in her edited collection *Control Culture* (Beckman 2018).
3. It has been suggested by Etienne Balibar that Macpherson, in his eagerness to identify a coherent system of possessive individualism, misreads Hobbes and creates unity where there is not one (Balibar 2002: 300–1). But of most importance to the present argument is that both thinkers have had a strong influence on notions of individuality in relation to ownership of the self and that these theories, in turn, have had a formative influence on the novel.
4. It has been argued recently, however, that Foucault's elaboration on biopower led him to move away from the disciplinary model to one of biopower and biopolitics and that this in turn generated a dialogue, in his work, with an emergent neoliberalism. This means, as the collection *Foucault and Neoliberalism* edited by Daniel Zamora and Michael C. Behrent indicates (Zamora and Behrent 2015), that Foucault's elaboration of the economy of disciplinary subjects and subjectivities in the mid-1970s is not quite so clear cut as an earlier generation of Anglophone critics and Foucauldians have tended to make out.

Bibliography

Armstrong, Nancy (2011), 'The Future in and of the Novel', *Novel: A Forum on Fiction*, 44:1, pp. 8–10.
Balibar, Etienne (2002), '"Possessive Individualism" Reversed: From Locke to Derrida', *Constellations*, 9:3, pp. 299–317.
Beckman, Frida (2016), *Culture Control Critique: Allegories of Reading the Present*, London: Rowman and Littlefield.
Beckman, Frida (2018), 'Control and a Minor Literature', in Frida Beckman (ed.), *Control Culture: Foucault and Deleuze after Discipline*, Edinburgh: Edinburgh University Press, pp. 180–92.
Best, Stephen and Sharon Marcus (2009), 'Surface Reading: An Introduction', *Representations*, 108:1, pp. 1–21.
Bewes, Timothy (2010), 'Reading with the Grain: A New World in Literary Criticism', *differences*, 21:3, pp. 1–33.
Defoe, Daniel (1994), *Robinson Crusoe*, London: Penguin.
Deleuze, Gilles (1995), 'Postscript on Control Societies', in Gilles Deleuze, *Negotiations: 1972–1990*, Martin Joughin (trans.), New York: Columbia University Press, pp. 177–82.
Farrell, John (2006), *Paranoia and Modernity: Cervantes to Rousseau*, Ithaca: Cornell University Press.
Felski, Rita (2011), 'Suspicious Minds', *Poetics Today*, 32:2, pp. 215–34.
Felski, Rita (2015), *The Limits of Critique*, Chicago: University of Chicago Press.
Foucault, Michel (1977), *Discipline and Punish: The Birth of the Prison*, Alan Sheridan (trans.), London: Penguin.
Foucault, Michel (2003), *Society Must Be Defended: Lectures at the Collège de France, 1975–76*, Mauro Bertani and Alessandro Fontana (eds), David Macey (trans.), New York: Picador.
Foucault, Michel (2008), *The Birth of Biopolitics: Lectures at the Collège de France, 1978–1979*, Michel Senellart (ed.), Graham Burchell (trans.), Basingstoke: Palgrave Macmillan.
Freud, Sigmund (1966), *The Standard Edition of the Complete Psychological Works of Sigmund Freud, Vol. 1: Pre-Psycho-Analytic Publications and Unpublished Drafts 1886–1899*, James Strachey (gen. ed. and trans.), London: Hogarth Press.
Guattari, Félix (1984), *Molecular Revolution: Psychiatry and Politics*, Rosemary Sheed (trans.), London: Penguin.
Klein, Melanie (1984), *The Writings of Melanie Klein, Vol. 3: Envy and Gratitude and Other Works (1946–1963)*, Roger Money-Kyrle (gen. ed.), New York: Free Press.
Kojève, Alexandre (1969), *Introduction to the Reading of Hegel*, New York: Basic Books.
Lacan, Jacques (1980), *Écrits: A Selection*, Alan Sheridan (trans.), London: Tavistock.
Macpherson, C. B. (1962), *The Political Theory of Possessive Individualism: Hobbes to Locke*, Oxford: Oxford University Press.
Marcus, Sharon (2007), *Between Women: Friendship, Desire, and Marriage in Victorian England*, Princeton: Princeton University Press.
Mazzoni, Guido (2017), *Theory of the Novel*, Cambridge, MA: Harvard University Press.
Melley, Timothy (2000), *Empire of Conspiracy: The Culture of Paranoia in Postwar America*, Ithaca: Cornell University Press.
Miller, D. A. (1988), *The Novel and the Police*, Berkeley: University of California Press.
Moretti, Franco (2013), *Distant Reading*, New York: Verso.
Nadler, Steven (1997), 'Descartes's Demon and the Madness of Don Quixote', *Journal of the History of Ideas*, 58:1, pp. 41–55.

Negri, Antonio (2007), 'Art and Culture in the Age of Empire and the Time of the Multitude', *SubStance*, 36:1, pp. 48–55.

Price, Leah (2009), 'From *The History of a Book* to a "History of the Book"', *Representations*, 108:1, pp. 120–38.

Savat, David (2013), *Uncoding the Digital: Technology, Subjectivity and Action in the Control Society*, Basingstoke: Palgrave Macmillan.

Sedgwick, Eve Kosofsky (2002), 'Paranoid Reading and Reparative Reading, or, You're So Paranoid, You Probably Think this Essay Is about You', in Eve Kosofsky Sedgwick, *Touching Feeling: Affect, Pedagogy, Performativity*, Durham, NC: Duke University Press, pp. 123–51.

Tambling, Jeremy (1995), *Dickens, Violence and the Modern State: Dreams of the Scaffold*, Basingstoke: Macmillan.

Watt, Ian (2000), *The Rise of the Novel: Studies in Defoe, Richardson and Fielding*, London: Pimlico.

Zamora, Daniel and Michael C. Behrent (eds) (2015), *Foucault and Neoliberalism*, Cambridge: Polity.

22

Securing Neoliberalism: The Contingencies of Contemporary US Fiction

David Watson

One of the most conspicuous developments in the study of contemporary US fiction has been the turn towards neoliberalism as an explanatory and periodising framework, as can be seen in the increasing interest in exploring this fiction in connection with neoliberalism's economic, political, social, and cultural ascendancy from the early 1970s to the present. To periodise contemporary US fiction in this fashion entails making sense of how 'literary culture responds to the neoliberal moment and . . . how neoliberalism has fundamentally altered the trajectory of contemporary literature production', as Mitchum Huehls and Rachel Greenwald Smith explain in their introduction to the recent essay collection *Neoliberalism and Contemporary Literary Culture* (Huehls and Greenwald Smith 2017: 15). The appearance of neoliberalism as an analytical category organising the study of contemporary fiction may seem relatively belated in comparison with its manifestation in the social sciences, with this project really gaining traction only after the financial crisis of 2007–8, which provided it with some of its theoretical and political urgency. Even given this short time span, the critical and theoretical projects taking part in this intervention in our understanding of the contemporary are by no means uniform. While some scholars aim to show how literary culture grapples with financialised American neoliberalism, its waxing and waning, and its economies of credit and debt (see La Berge 2014; McClanahan 2018), others focus on how literary critical and theoretical categories such as affect (Smith 2015) and critique (Huehls 2016) are implicated in, and even shaped by, the logic of neoliberalism. Other critics, operating in a somewhat different key, focus on neoliberalism as a mode of subjectification, drawing attention to emergent neoliberal identity formations, whether violent political subjectivities (Elliot 2018) or entrepreneurial forms of the self (Johansen 2017), and to how neoliberalism reorganises older identity formations, including that of the citizen-subject (Cherniavsky 2017), and selectively incorporates within its market logic previously marginalised identities in the name of ideologies of diversity and selective tolerance (see Duggan 2012; Hong 2015). Finally, approaches that seek to depict neoliberalism as an ontological frame for contemporary literary cultures aim at identifying possibilities for aesthetic autonomy within its saturating atmosphere (N. Brown 2012), or at reading contemporary literary culture as testifying to the uneven global distribution of neoliberalism and identifying thereby literary possibilities outside of its purview (see essays in Brouillette, Nilges, and Sauri 2017).

If there is a shared historical account underwriting these divergent projects it is that of the liberalisation of the market since the 1970s, the rise of finance capital, and attendant processes of deregulation, privatisation, and free trade. It also includes narratives concerning the fragmentation of communal bonds, the rise of the *homo economicus* and the citizen-consumer, the waning of the welfare or social state, and the recoding of political and ethical values in market terms. If there is a shared logic linking these projects, it is that the political as well as economic transformations and state restructuring associated with neoliberalism go hand in hand with the market-mediated transformation of the population, the citizen-subject, and culture. Accordingly, neoliberalism is suspected of transmogrifying 'every human domain and endeavour ... according to a specific image of the economic' (W. Brown 2015: 10). This conceptualisation of neoliberalism, or rather neoliberalisation, is perhaps best captured by Michel Foucault's description of the rise of *ordo-* and neoliberalism, which he argues instantiates a shift to the 'use of the typical analysis of the market economy to decipher non-market relationships and phenomena which are not strictly and specifically economic but what we call social phenomena' (Foucault 2008: 240). From this perspective, it is not just that there is no outside to a neoliberal market logic; it self-reflexively provides an explanatory regime for its own workings and expansion. That is as much to say that according to this logic, neoliberalism provides the principles of intelligibility whereby we understand the extensions of a market rationality to non-economic domains of life, including literary culture and contemporary fiction.

The literary critical turn towards neoliberalism is underwritten, in part, by the increasing prominence in contemporary fiction of what Alison Shonkwiler has described as the 'financial imaginary', broadly speaking 'the formal project ... of imaginatively grasping the historical and cultural processes by which the seeming realities of the economy are reconceived as phenomena of virtuality and representation' (Shonkwiler 2017: ix). Novels such as Teddy Wayne's *Kapitoil* (Wayne 2010) and Peter Mountford's *A Young Man's Guide to Late Capitalism* (Mountford 2011) have mapped and given representational form to the global unfolding and asymmetries of the neoliberal economy, while Gary Shteyngart's *Super Sad True Love Story* (Shteyngart 2010) engages with the national debt of the United States and with the often racialised politics of credit evaluation. Meanwhile, operating at a more intimate scale, Viken Berberian's *Das Kapital: A Novel of Love and Money Markets* (Berberian 2010) and Jonathan Franzen's *Freedom* (Franzen 2010) have tested the capacity of narrative realism to explore the potential intersections between neoliberalism and affective, relational structures. In Franzen's novel, for instance, the neoliberal credo 'free markets foster competition' (Franzen 2010: 118) provides the novel with an interpretative and metaphoric network for mapping a set of familial and love relationships developing in tandem with the deregulation and growth of the neoliberal market during the 1970s and 1980s. Franzen overtly historicises his narrative by connecting it to the neoliberal economy, but neoliberalism functions equally well as a periodising framework for other contemporary works of fiction sharing in Shonkwiler's financial imaginary.

But at the same time as there has been an increase in fiction about the neoliberal economy, something has been developing in contemporary fiction that, following Shonkwiler, we may very well call a security imaginary. Novels such as Jess Walter's *The Zero* (Walter 2006) have given representational form to the contemporary permutations of the national security state, while Alex Shakar's *Luminarium* (Shakar 2011) and Dave Eggers's *The Circle* (Eggers 2013) have, respectively, mapped the intersections between the security state and the entertainment industry, and narrated the evolution of a surveillance society. What we may term the contemporary risk society, attuned to security risks and dangers, particularly environmental hazards caused by human action, has provided the context within which we need to read numerous works of fiction such as Nathaniel Rich's *Odds Against Tomorrow* (Rich 2013) and Ben Lerner's *10:04* (Lerner 2014). At the same time, the impact of the expanded contemporary security state, as well as a heightened security consciousness, on modes of racialisation, migration, humanitarian interventions, and the ways we imagine global connectivity has haunted novels such as Amy Waldman's *The Submission* (Waldman 2011), Bob Shacochis's *The Woman Who Lost Her Soul* (Shacochis 2013), and Atticus Lish's *Preparations for the Next Life* (Lish 2015), as well as a host of others. Taken together, these novels suggest that contemporary fiction imagines for the reader how the security state operates within and impacts on a globally interconnected world. Moreover, this fiction gives narrative form to an endless array of risks, contingencies, and unpredictable futures exacerbating present-day insecurities. A character in Don DeLillo's *Point Omega* (DeLillo 2010) suggests that if stories inoculated us against terror once upon a time, they now take part in an 'endless counting down' (2010: 45) to an unnamed and unimaginable catastrophe. If so, we may very well suggest that this catastrophism, or rather security imaginary, of contemporary fiction has developed concurrently with, and in the shadow of, the financial imaginary of contemporary literature concerning Shonkwiler and other critics reading this fiction in relation to the neoliberal present.

How do we periodise this fiction of risk, danger, and security in relation to neoliberalism? Is this periodising term sufficiently capacious to serve as an explanatory framework for this literature? In what follows, I argue that rather than our dispensing with the term at this juncture, neoliberalism needs to be rethought as not exclusively an economic formation but a particular mode of understanding and engaging with risk, uncertainty and contingency. In being so rethought, the term would allow us to periodise and think together the divergent strands of contemporary literary production and its imaginaries of finance and security. Later on, I will turn to a set of contemporary novels – Colson Whitehead's *The Intuitionist* (Whitehead 1999) and Jennifer Egan's *A Visit from the Goon Squad* (Egan 2011) in particular, but also Don DeLillo's *Falling Man* (DeLillo 2007) – that provides us with the means with which to think the complexities of the neoliberal present and the terms whereby we understand as well as periodise its culture. Before such an undertaking, however, it is worthwhile pondering how and why we need to rethink the category of neoliberalism within literary studies to include concepts such as risk, contingency, and security. In other words, why modify the terms whereby we periodise the contemporary? Such a project necessarily takes as its starting point the insistence in contemporary scholarship that there is no such thing as a single object called neoliberalism (Collier 2012: 186). It is a plurality – a set of economic policies concerned with market-oriented reform and deregulation, a political ideology resistant to collectivist, planned, and socialised modes of government, a sociocultural condition in which 'market competition, with its calculus of credit and debt, is ... made into a necessary precondition for all potential actions' (Shaviro 2010: 8), and so on. The different meanings attaching themselves to the term cannot necessarily be resolved by recasting them as sequential stages in the diachronic evolution of something to be called neoliberalism, either. There is good reason, as Aihwa Ong and Jamie Peck have respectively argued, to imagine neoliberalism as an assemblage, as a set of discrepant processes and practices assuming different shapes when deployed within divergent spaces, a hybrid mobile technology entering into alliances with disparate political, economic, and social formations wherever it is deployed (Ong 2007; Peck 2010). There is no pure, essential neoliberalism from this perspective.

This resistance to essentialising neoliberalism has enabled, usefully for my purposes, accounts that associate neoliberalism not, in the first instance, with an economic rationality, but with certain orientations towards such categories as risk, contingency, uncertainty, security, and insecurity. Pat O'Malley, for instance, suggests that neoliberalism should be thought of in terms of a double and contradictory relationship towards risk and uncertainty. He argues that neoliberalism entails the valorisation of embracing risk, and the identification of risk-taking with freedom or, that is to say, a new entrepreneurial ethos. But simultaneously, he argues that 'with respect to risk – that is risk minimisation or avoidance of harmful risk – responsibility is expanded and personalised' (O'Malley 2004: 76). Thus, within the logic of neoliberalism, risk and uncertainty both form part of an entrepreneurial, market rationality, and indicate the boundaries of this rationality, the problem space where it gives way to processes of risk privatisation and management – the expansion of a logic of security. Mitchell Dean similarly associates neoliberalism with a world in which contingencies of various kinds have become endemic: 'what is emergent', he argues, 'is a neoliberal regime founded on a narrative of evolution of ecological, economic and social systems in the direction of greater complexity and subject to unpredictable catastrophe' (Dean 2014: 159). Exposure to contingencies, from Dean's perspective, is foundational to the neoliberal narrative, and neoliberal governance takes such contingencies as the complex referent object of its rule. So, a basic question: how do these accounts of the contingencies of neoliberalism, or rather of the space occupied by the contingent within it, relate to others that stress the economic logic of the neoliberal period? Perhaps more to the point: what are their implications for a literary criticism intent on periodising contemporary fiction within a neoliberal framework?

We can situate and contextualise Dean's and O'Malley's interventions by noting that they form part of the literature on governmentality that, inspired by Foucault's work on biopolitics, seeks to connect contemporary modes of governance to concepts of risk and security. Briefly, within this framework, biopower seeks to identify certain risks and dangers to what Foucault called the species-body (the economy, population, or society), and deploys an apparatus of security to mitigate the threat (Dean 2010: 29). This deployment occurs at the level of the species-body but also at that of the individual body, that of the biopolitical subject incited to govern itself by managing its own security and insecurity. Part of this adjustment to risks, however, entails identifying an uncertain future with freedom and opportunities for the entrepreneurial self, with risk and uncertainty emerging as preconditions for neoliberal modes of freedom. Turning this account into a description of neoliberalism echoes in many ways Foucault's diagnosis of liberalism in *The Birth of Biopolitics* as a 'political culture of danger' (Foucault 2008: 66) in which the economic interests and freedom of the individual need to be balanced with collective interest and security. This brings Foucault to the statement that 'strategies of security' are both 'liberalism's other face and its very condition' (2008: 65). The literature on governmentality would have us believe that the contemporary interplay between risk-taking, understood in terms of neoliberal freedom and economic rationalities, and strategies for securing the self and society is at the same time the obviated face of neoliberalism and its condition of possibility.

Bringing questions of security and risk into discussions of neoliberalism has several consequences. Among others, it demands that we pay attention to the intertwining and co-construction of contemporary market rationalities and what Stephen Graham describes as the 'ever-broadening landscape of "security" blending commercial, military and security practices with increasingly fearful cultures of civilian mobility, citizenship and consumption' (Graham 2011: 73). In addition to attending to how an economistic logic extends into every sector of politics and culture, with these domains becoming largely intelligible in terms of economic value, we would consider as well how a logic of security links and reaches from 'the most private spaces of being to the vast flows and conflicts of geopolitics' (Burke 2002: 2), thereby constituting societies and subjects in terms of their security and insecurity. Our narrative of the contemporary would account both for the growth of the governmental and nongovernmental security sector, and for the expansion of constructs of security that 'have come to dominate everyday life in the US imperial state' (Grewal 2017: 2), as Inderpal Grewal puts it, as well as for the rapid growth of finance capital and the ongoing financialisaton of everyday life, with finance increasingly becoming identified as a 'way to develop the self' (Martin 2002: loc. 202). It would focus attention on how the partially privatised carceral wing of the security state has replaced the welfare state as a way of managing subjects and populations excluded from or threatening the economic freedoms and benefits of neoliberalism (see Camp 2016). Similarly, the historical archive of neoliberalism would include histories of the 'imperial ... and racial formations' (Stoler 2016: 22) forming part of the history of the security state, in addition to, for instance, the histories of the implementation of neoliberal policies in the 1970s in the so-called developing world before they were brought to bear on the UK and the US in the 1980s. These conjunctures, homologies, and intersecting histories might ask of us to rethink neoliberalism as an assemblage of economic and security logics or systems ceaselessly describing and redescribing the contemporary. They might too ask of us to reconsider accounts identifying neoliberalism with a straightforward waning of the state and the political, drawing attention instead to the politics of securitisation, and the role of the state in economic and security governance.

From one widely circulating perspective, this conjuncture between security and economic neoliberalism may indicate that neoliberalism should be identified with what Ulrich Beck and Anthony Giddens have described as a self-reflexive 'risk society', in which risk emerges as the principal mode of sociopolitical organisation (Beck 1992; Giddens 1999). This position is a widespread one that associates risk with the permanent potential for crisis, damage, and peril. Yet it is not clear at all that this account exhausts the role assigned to risk and uncertainty within the neoliberal framework. Within the neoliberal economy, risk is connected with 'ideals of opportunity, performance, gain and value' (Roitman 2014: 75) as much as it is with narratives of threat. That is as much as to say that risk plays a crucial role in the neoliberal logic of the entrepreneurial subject and organisation: risk-taking for gain is a discourse of opportunity and freedom for that part of the population able to undertake and live with risks. Moreover, increased exposure to contingencies translates into value creation in financial speculation. Risk is then not exclusively something that neoliberal formations seek to externalise and defend against; it is at the same time constitutive of the neoliberal economy and its identification of risk-taking with a particular kind of freedom.

One way into the contemporary conjuncture between the neoliberal economy and security is by focusing, then, on the variety of differentiated roles played by contingency – the aleatory, the uncertain, the incalculable or unknown, risk, chance – within these formations. In *After Finitude: An Essay on the Necessity of Contingency*, Quentin Meillassoux revives philosophical interest in the question of why there is something rather than nothing, that is to say whether being is necessary or contingent. Because this world is fundamentally contingent for him and exists for no reason, he argues that '[t]here is no reason for anything to be or to remain the way it is; everything must, without reason, be able not to be and/or be able to be other than it is' (Meillassoux 2009: 60). For Meillassoux the only necessity is the contingent nature of the world. But, alongside contemporary philosophy, contingency has a place as well within the long history of neoliberalism and within contemporary biopolitics, as it has within literary criticism, as we shall see soon. Within the history of economic neoliberalism, the concept returns us to the work of the Austrian economist Friedrich August Hayek and his rejection of rational constructivism. In his late *The Fatal Conceit: The Errors of Socialism*, Hayek summarises this major theme in his work by returning to the question of reason: 'By "reason properly used" I mean reason that recognises its own limitations and, itself taught by reason, faces the astonishing fact, revealed by economics and biology, that order generated without design can far outstrip plans men consciously contrive' (Hayek 1988: 8). We may suggest that the key problematic for Hayek is information. Lacking a vantage point outside of the self-generating, emergent order of the market – or of a different ecology for that matter – the state or an economic actor has imperfect information concerning this order, which is continually reshaped, in turn, by the operator's actions and observations, as well as those of others working within the same system. The complexity of this situation imbues it with uncertainty; its contingencies move it outside the purview of rational planning and intervention by the state. In this precise sense, we may very well say that '*human rationality has become increasingly irrelevant*' (Mirowski and Nik-Khah 2017: 18) to the neoliberal market. More recently, Michael Dillon and Luis Lobo-Guerrero have argued that within our contemporary biopolitical imaginary, contingency has been identified as the 'definitive property of life' (Dillon and Lobo-Guerrero 2009: 14). To be a living thing, in all of its emergent complexity, means first of all, from this perspective, to be a finite, contingent being. At the same time, the contingent is also intrinsic for them to the 'bioeconomy in which the properties of living things are employed to create value' (2009: 14). This argument secures a central role for contingency within contemporary imaginaries of life and the neoliberal economy by identifying the contingent as the referent object of contemporary biopolitics. From Hayek to Dillon and Lobo-Guerrero there is a persistent association of biological life and the economy with the contingent. Dillon and Lobo-Guerrero usefully add to this series of associations that if life is to be understood in terms of the contingent, then contingency emerges as the 'definitive epistemic object of rule' (2009: 14). Governance, the apparatus of security, takes as its object of rule life understood as a contingent formation.

It may be the case, then, that contingency defines the operational fields of the economy and security within neoliberalism. In fact, it appears that the contingent creates the conditions of possibility for the market and contemporary apparatus of security. Arguing in relation to the neoliberal economy, Elena Esposito suggests that 'without uncertainty, the economy could not function or exist' (E. Esposito 2013: 110). Contingency, for her, provides the foundation for innovation and creativity. Moreover, what is priced and traded on financial markets in the form of derivatives is commodified contingency: the risks associated with a future entity are measured, divided, transferred, priced, and traded in an attempt to leverage the future, or at least its contingencies. In many ways, Esposito's analysis of the neoliberal economy echoes Dillon's argument that within contemporary biopolitics, security takes the contingent as its problem and operational space: contingency, Dillon suggests, is 'the epistemic object for biopolitics of security in the 21st century inasmuch as it characterizes the understanding of human life as an emergent and creative entity to whose promotion and development biopolitics are now committed' (Dillon 2008: 314). It is not just that security addresses itself to uncertainty, protecting human life against external dangers. Life, what Foucault would call the species-body, is dangerous to itself because of its contingent nature, the same nature that is also responsible for its complexity and freedom. Security, from this vantage point, does not simply protect life against itself, but aids, calibrates, and manages its adaptive emergence as well. The contingent, within neoliberalism, appears to be situated at the intersection of the economy and security, capital, and governance. Security seeks to promote life through its management; the market seeks to profit from its commodification.

One way of making sense of this apparently paradoxical relation between neoliberalism and contingency may very well be to rethink neoliberalism according to the biopolitical immunitary paradigm offered by Roberto Esposito. In Esposito's work, immunity functions, among other things, as a way of navigating and resolving what he takes to be a paradox within biopolitical philosophy. For Esposito, Foucault's account of biopolitics, in which he makes life central to the operations of power and rule, pulls in two different directions: biopolitics appears to name both a thanatopolitics and a vitalist politics of care. Turning to the concept of immunity to resolve this tension, Esposito argues that immunity projects operate by protecting life through its negation. 'To survive', he writes, 'the community, every community, is forced to introject the negative modality of its opposite, even if the opposite remains precisely a lacking and contrasting mode of being of the community itself' (R. Esposito 2011: 52). In this formulation, the contrastive vectors towards life and death associated with biopolitics turn out in an ironic, aporetic fashion to be one and the same. More importantly, the logic of the immunitary paradigm provides a way of grasping the contrastive tendencies within neoliberal formations to exploit and valorise risk and uncertainty, even while seeking to manage and defend against contingencies.

The topology of the immunitary paradigm, which focuses attention on what is internal or external to a given formation, may obscure, however, the temporal dimensions of the handling of the contingent within neoliberalism. Accordingly, Martijn Konings insists that if neoliberalism is to be understood as 'an intervention in the logic of contingency' (Konings 2018: loc. 450), we also need to make sense of its particular temporality, its embrace of a speculative orientation. For Konings, this does not mean that neoliberalism is driven by prediction, which would associate it with the rational constructivism rejected by Hayek. Rather, if the logic of neoliberalism is characterised by its engagement with the uncertain and contingent, neoliberal reason should be understood as orienting itself towards an unknown and incalculable future – a propensity that according to Steven Shaviro gestures towards a 'close affinity ... between economic speculation and fictional speculation' (Shaviro 2011: 5) in science fiction. The point of the logic of neoliberalism then becomes to strategise around an unpredictable future, to speculate about its probabilities, to exploit it on the market, to attempt to shape it – to 'bend the production of the future around one's own position' (Konings 2018: loc. 280) – rather than to make it an object of knowledge. Konings is mainly concerned with the world of speculative finance, which he takes to be the emblematic sector of the neoliberal economy rather than its commodity culture, but he associates the temporality of the market strikingly with the security logic of pre-emption, arguing that a key aspect of neoliberal governance is to pre-emptively engage with potential rather than definite threats. Indeed, the speculative logic Konings is interested in has long been viewed as a hallmark of the contemporary neoliberal security apparatus. Accordingly, Melinda Cooper writes in her *Life as Surplus* (2008) about what she terms the 'neoliberal politics of security' that

> In this sense the new discourse of catastrophe risk establishes our affective relation to the future as the only available basis for decision making, even while it recognizes the inherently speculative nature of this enterprise. What it provokes is not so much fear (of an identifiable threat) as a state of alertness, without foreseeable end. It exhorts us to respond to what we suspect without being able to discern; to prepare for the emergent, long before we can predict how and when it will be actualized; to counter the unknowable, before it is even realized. In short, the very concept of the catastrophe event seems to suggest that our only possible response to the emergent crisis (of whatever kind – biomedical, environmental, economic) is one of speculative pre-emption. (Cooper 2008: 83)

Neoliberal security takes as its referent objects the dangers posed by an unknown future about which it can speculate and against which it can strategise without achieving certainty about the nature of the threat. 'It is not a matter of mobilising the security discourse *in spite of the fact* that we do not know what is to come', Peter Burgess argues, 'it is far more a matter of mobilising *because* we do not know' (Burgess 2011: 4). As with finance, the contingent nature of the unknowable future introduces a speculative element into neoliberal security. We may very well imagine the neoliberal economy and security to be speculative genres working on the contingent, profiting from it, seeking to tame it and the insecurities it produces.

The place of contingency within the logic of neoliberalism appears to be secured, but what does the contingent and its speculative logics have to do with literature and the situation of contemporary fiction? One way of approaching this question is to think of the contingent as a problem and resource for narrative and for plot structures. It is in this sense that Fredric Jameson, in his *The Antinomies of Realism*, reserves a place for the contingent in his account of realism and its narratives. In his discussion of Eric Auerbach and Gustave Flaubert's *Madame Bovary*, Jameson notes that the realist narrative works against classification and genre trappings, doing so to escape narratives of predestination and plot structures with predetermined endings. He writes,

> older conceptions of destiny or fate are challenged by newer appeals to that equally ideological yet historically quite distinct notion of this or that 'reality', in which social and historical material rises to the surface in the form of the singular or the contingent. (Jameson 2013: 143)

This new mode of temporality – that of the incalculable, open future – and of representing the real – as singular, contingent material resistant to classification – are joined by an 'interiorization of chance' (2013: 202) that for Jameson renders interiority an experience of contingency. Realism, as an aesthetic mode and ideology, turns to contingency to produce a formal rupture with other aesthetic modes, and installs the contingent as a constitutive given of the world and the human. Turning to contemporary fiction, though, Jameson scathingly observes that the undetermined future promised by the contingencies of the classical realist novel lingers on in recent fiction and surprisingly resonates with 'a late-capitalist and consumerist present eager to persuade us that nothing is irrevocable and that everything is possible' (2013: 184).

Whatever we make of Jameson's judgement, which appears to reiterate for contemporary fiction the alliance between neoliberalism and contingency pursued here, it is undoubtedly the case that contingency as a concept is important to contemporary US fiction. Whitehead's debut novel, *The Intuitionist*, makes, for instance, for a productive counterpoint to Jameson's comments on contemporary fiction and contingency. In the novel, Lila Mae Watson, the first African-American elevator inspector in the unnamed city of the novel, is drawn into an ongoing quarrel between different factions in the Elevator Inspectors Guild. She is an Intuitionist, who inspects elevators through a type of affective and tactile communion with the aura of the elevator, while the faction arrayed against the Intuitionists trusts in traditional Empiricism and inspects elevators through the scientific measurement of stress indicators. When an elevator Lila Mae has inspected has an unexpected free-fall, she suspects it has been sabotaged and goes on the run to clear her name. She uncovers in her quest the fact that James Fulton, the founder of Intuitionism, was African-American passing as white. Accessing Fulton's unpublished archive, Lila Mae discovers a manuscript draft describing what is called 'The Black Box', a mysterious device that will enable a 'second elevation' (Whitehead 1999: 61) freeing all from the city and its economy. The novel gestures in the direction of a utopian future of racial uplift and social mobility, which it contrasts with its repeated suggestions that unnamed and invisible African-American labour forms the backbone of its unnamed city, reminiscent in many ways of New York, and its economy. As Lila Mae discovers, though, Fulton's work, including this utopian promise of an elevation to a world that *'will look like Heaven but not the Heaven you know'* (1999: 241), may perhaps be an elaborate joke, a hoax. In his reading of the novel, Ramón Saldívar argues that by making Lila Mae the keeper and inheritor of Fulton's hoax, Whitehead is engaging in a '"postrace" aesthetic' (Saldívar 2013: 15) driven by 'persistent ironic impulses towards utopian desires that remain impervious to the real' (2013: 12). Rather than activating straightforwardly an open future of untrammelled possibilities, as Jameson expects of the fiction of the neoliberal present, *The Intuitionist* cites even while suspending the possibility of such a future, thereby rendering ironic neoliberal promises of uplift and mobility.

While the foreclosed utopian temporality of *The Intuitionist* resists recuperation in the terms provided by Jameson, its engagement with contingency testifies to the subsistence of this realist concern in contemporary fiction. One way into this dimension of the novel is provided by Lauren Berlant, who argues that the novel is organised around a catastrophic event, the elevator crash, which 'induces and reveals a shared history of crisis within the ordinary whose terms the powers that be want to control' (Berlant 2008: 852). For Berlant, the novel is about adapting and affectively relating to a 'history of crisis ordinariness' (2008: 852), which is to say the experience of the contingencies of the historical present. Such a reading of the novel directs us towards a passage Katherine Hayles identifies as the climax of the narrative (Hayles 2017: 185) in her discussion of the resonances between the novel and computational theory, in particular problems that fall into the category of the undecidable. The passage in question begins with Lila Mae's reflections on the Arbro corporation and its enforcer, 'Natchez', actually Raymond Coombs, who is searching for Fulton's plans for the black box, before opening into a discussion of catastrophic events, a falling elevator or the truth becoming known of Fulton's 'lie of whiteness' (Whitehead 1999: 239):

> Arbo and Natchez are merely unanswered questions. Their intrusion into her life is a matter of cause and effect, prospering along logical trajectories of greed, and only require adequate information to explain them. Time to sift the facts through her fingers and shake out the fine silt until what is left in her hand is what happened. But there is still the matter of Fulton and Intuitionism. She thinks, what passing for white does not account for: the person who knows your secret skin, the one you encounter at that unexpected time on that quite ordinary street. What Intuitionism does not account for: the catastrophic accident the elevator encounters at that unexpected moment on the quite ordinary ascent, the one who will reveal the device for what it truly is. The colored man passing for white and the innocent elevator must rely on luck, the convenience of empty streets and strangers who know nothing, dread the chance encounter with the one who knows who they are. The one who knows their weakness. (1999: 231)

In important ways this passage is about the question of what genre *The Intuitionist* belongs to, and how it understands its own narrative structure. It opens with the promises of the detective novel: there are 'unanswered questions' about a crime that can be answered by sifting through and weighing the evidence, and by arranging events in a causal, linear order. Yet the novel's narrative resists full identification with this genre. Its narratives concerning the dangers of racial passing and catastrophic events cannot be accounted for via the conventional optics of the detective genre. What resists this generic enclosure is the potential for a 'chance encounter' that will uncover the secret of passing, or for an unexpected accident, unpredicted and unpredictable, that will unveil the 'crisis ordinariness' of the historical present. What resists generic identification is being positioned within a racialised system wherein the subject is vulnerable to the knowing gaze of others, and relating insecurely to mechanical systems that could go haywire without a moment's notice. In short, the contingent, and the insecurity it heralds, short-circuits the novel's identification with the detective genre, as it does for future visions of neoliberal uplift. Or, as Saldívar argues, the contingencies of the narrative prevent it from belonging to any single genre, resulting in a 'hybrid narrative' combining 'alternative history, steampunk fantasy, detective noir fiction, and even old-style protest social realism'

(Saldívar 2013: 11). Rather than a formal adherence to contingency resulting in realism, as occurs in the history Jameson is interested in, here it produces an unstable amalgam of a realist mode and various often-fantastical genres.

By making the contingent foundational to his plot and its narratives of catastrophic accidents, anomalies beyond statistical prediction, and frustrated post-racial fantasies, Whitehead also seeks to install the contingent as the hidden truth of not only the historical present of the text but also the histories of progress and racial discrimination it is interested in. The dread and vulnerability associated with racial passing in this passage are generalised elsewhere as constitutive of race relations in the US. Accordingly, Lila Mae's father teaches her that 'white folks can turn on you at any moment ... They can turn rabid at any second: this is the true result of gathering integration: the replacement of sure violence with deferred sure violence' (Whitehead 1999: 23). Every encounter is imbued with the potential for unpredictable violence. Similarly, the elevator accident is not a singular, exceptional occurrence. Instead it speaks of a widespread potential for unforeseen accidents, 'instructing the dull and plodding citizens of modernity that there is a power beyond rationality' (1999: 230).

The narrative of *The Intuitionist* is obsessed with the outer edges of calculability, the incalculable, the unpredictable and contingent, what it calls the 'emissaries from the unknowable' (1999: 227). It is apt then that the novel makes it impossible to determine when its events are taking place. Daniel Grausam has persuasively argued that we should understand the novel's temporality as made up out of an accumulation of discrepant historical detail, with it thereby producing a 'multi-temporal now' (Grausam 2017: 121) resistant to periodisation in terms of this or that history of the present. Yet, for Grausam, the contemporaneity of Whitehead's work, including *The Intuitionist*, is assured because Whitehead puts 'economic issues at the heart of each book' (2017: 123), issues that resonate with those of the neoliberal present. While agreeing with Grausam, we may refine this point by suggesting that *The Intuitionist* asks to be read in relation to its neoliberal context not just because of its economic narrative, but because of its dalliance with the same 'emissaries from the unknowable' that appear to be preoccupying neoliberalism, whether considered as an economic form or a logic of security and governance.

Unlike *The Intuitionist*, Jennifer Egan's *A Visit from the Goon Squad* leaves little doubt as to its historical coordinates. Egan's novel consists of thirteen chapters addressing the perspectives of the same number of characters, with the chapters shifting backwards and forwards across past, present, and future. The novel's temporal setting includes the last decades of the twentieth century, the first decade of the twenty-first century, and the near future, with the narrative addressing concerns ranging from the rise of social media and the decline of the record industry to climate change, the aftermath of the 9/11 terrorist attacks, and the rise of commercial and governmental surveillance. Given this catalogue and the range of the novel's temporal setting, Egan's work may very well be read as offering a history of the present that includes narratives of its future.

Given its obvious contemporaneity, it is unsurprising that scholarship on Egan's novel has repeatedly situated it in relation to dominant tendencies within the logic of neoliberalism. In 'The Author as Executive Producer', Michael Szalay proposes, for instance, that Egan's novel should be understood in relation to prestige television and media conglomerates such as AOL–Time Warner, in particular its HBO division, whose 1999–2007 series *The Sopranos* inspired *A Visit from the Goon Squad*. For Szalay, Egan's novel mediates and self-reflexively inhabits this corporate media ecology. Noting that prestige television is increasingly valorised by literary authors, Szalay suggests that Egan struggles in the novel with the 'opportunities now afforded novelists by the rise of a newly prestigious and ostensibly literary television format' (Szalay 2017: 258). For example, entrepreneurs and creative workers fill the novel. The publicists, agents, journalists, musicians, actors, and record producers embody the creative portfolio of the 'transmedia novelist as she assumes different roles in the media industry' (2017: 257) on the basis of a novel incorporating and citing different forms of media ranging from music to, famously, a PowerPoint presentation. What Szalay is suggesting is that *A Visit from the Goon Squad* doubles and reflects, in the same way as Egan's authorial role, the corporate media ecology it inhabits. The point of this doubling is that Egan and the novel are self-positioned within the corporate media and gain access to the opportunities provided by it – the position of showrunner or executive producer for the author, and for the novel its transformation into a prestige television series such as *The Sopranos*. The author and the novel are imbued, then, with the potential of providing and acting as the 'template that coordinates otherwise far-flung media' (2017: 257).

Szalay's provocative argument accounts for a number of the features of Egan's novel and for claims she has made for it. Discussing, for instance, a proposed television adaptation of *A Visit from the Goon Squad*, Egan claims the novel has the potential for it: 'I did consciously ask the question of whether there would be a way to write a novel that would have the same kind of lateral feeling of a television series', she says to Dave Itzkoff in an interview, 'the same kind of sense of movement in all directions, but not necessarily forward. The movement from central to peripheral characters from season to season' (Itzkoff 2011). The novel is in a sense also about the migration of media content between different forms and platforms that Egan is hinting at in the interview. For example, the novel's final chapter introduces us to the Starfish, a 'kiddie handset' (Egan 2011: 347) with which young children can download music. Egan explains that this new demography resulted in the reinvention of artists' catalogues, with Biggie Smalls' 'Fuck You, Bitch' – a non-existent song – remixed to transform the offending bars into 'You're Big, Chief' (2011: 348). Her novel folds into itself narratives about adaptability of content, its distribution, and the developing media infrastructures supportive of this dissemination. It is not difficult, I would argue, to bring this interest into line with the economic logic of neoliberalism. Describing one aspect of this logic, Jeffrey T. Nealon argues that 'capitalism today seeks primarily to saturate and deepen – intensify – its hold over existing markets ... the intensities of finance (how do you squeeze more profits out of the stuff you already have?) become the linchpin practices of this risky new economy' (Nealon 2012: 26). Understanding Egan's novel as part of the contemporary corporate media ecology helps us to see how 'the intensities of finance' visible in, for example, the transformation of the house mortgage into securities and tradeable derivatives are also present, albeit in a different form, in what Szalay describes as, in effect, Egan's desire to leverage her novel within the corporate media environment of AOL–Time Warner. In this configuration, the author and the novel are intermediate figures. What is important is the shape the novel will assume in the future and the role the author plays in this transformation and mediation of her work. That we can read traces of this process within Egan's novel does little more than bear witness to the fact that it is self-reflexively interested in the neoliberal economic circuit it seeks to occupy.

This reading of Egan's novel in terms of media and neoliberal economies is, of course, quintessential of the tendency in critical engagements with contemporary fiction to read this fiction as operating in tandem with the larger logics and developments within the economic sphere. Without seeking to interrogate or dislodge such a reading, I would suggest it needs to be supplemented by readings informed by different interpretative protocols if we wish to attend to how Egan's novel resonates with and interrogates the variegated neoliberal present. What readings such as this one omit is the novel's preoccupation with contingency and the history of surveillance in the US. Egan's fidelity to the literary and imaginative potential of the contingent is testified to by its opening lines, taken from Marcel Proust's *In Search of Lost Time*, 'The unknown element of the lives of other people is like that of nature, which each fresh scientific discovery merely reduces but does not abolish' (Egan 2011: epigraph). From this perspective, we may very well think of the constellation of characters distributed across the thirteen discrete chapters of the novel as inhabiting a contingent field of appearance and disappearance. Characters appear and disappear, their connections to one another half glimpsed, their importance to the narrative uncertain. In the narrative, this uncertainty is temporalised: time is the 'goon' (2011: 145) of the title, forcing the characters in the narrative to encounter unexpected, often inimical, events. As Louise Amoore perceptively claims regarding the character system of the novel, 'Egan's novel deftly displays the persistence of the indeterminate elements, even in the face of a science and technology that would otherwise gather every fragment in the form of network analysis or semantic web' (Amoore 2013: 159). From a perspective such as Szalay's one might want to suggest that such an indeterminacy is helpful, in that it may provide the fragments and threads of unfinished, incomplete stories that may prove useful to develop for prestige television, especially given its tendency to shift back and forth between central and peripheral narratives. But Amoore is interested not in reading contemporary fiction in relation to the neoliberal present, but in identifying political possibilities within the neoliberal politics of security, a project for which she finds Egan's novel of heuristic value. She argues that the novel should be read within a framework attuned to contemporary security concerns with uncertain futures and investment in data and surveillance as rendering legible and actionable the risks endemic to neoliberalism. Noting that 'contemporary security seeks to write the life of the subject through data items' (Amoore 2013: 175), she identifies the indeterminacies of Egan's novel both with the contingencies security takes as its referent object and data profiling seeks to make transparent, and with a logic of potentiality resistant to security, a logic valorising 'the unanticipated effect, surprise event, and chance encounter' (2013: 161) – the categories Amoore posits as informing a politics beyond the logic of security.

Amoore's reading of Egan's novel in terms of its relation to neoliberal security explains for us why the novel constitutes a veritable catalogue of surveillance technologies, ranging from the military to the commercial. In fact, Egan's novel draws out the links between 'state surveillance and rampant consumer surveillance' (Johnston 2017: 161). Remarkably, if the novel is invested in narrating the future history of the neoliberal present, it associates this future with what we may term, rephrasing Berlant, a security ordinariness. In 'Pure Language', the final chapter of *A Visit from the Goon Squad*, a crowd moves through a future New York to gather for a concert in Lower Manhattan. As the crowd gathers in Lower Manhattan, military helicopters circle overhead, the 'too loud, too loud' sound of their rotor blades filling the crowd with unease, the 'price of safety' (Egan 2011: 368), as Alex, Egan's young music mixer observes. The crowd has lived through 'two generations of war and surveillance' (2011: 373), which have shaped the security architecture of the city:

> Before them, the new buildings spiralled gorgeously against the sky, so much nicer than the old ones (which Alex had only seen in pictures), more like sculptures than buildings, because they were empty. Approaching them, the crowd began to slow, backing up as those in front entered the space around the reflecting pools, the density of police and security agents (identifiable by their government handsets) suddenly palpable, along with visual scanning devices affixed to cornices, lampposts, and trees. The weight of what had happened here more than twenty years ago was still faintly present for Alex, as it always was when he came to the Footprint. He perceived it as a sound just out of earshot, the vibration of an old disturbance. Now it seemed more insistent than ever: a low, deep thrum that felt primally familiar, as if it had been whirring inside all the sounds that Alex had made and collected over the years: their hidden pulse. (2011: 368)

The scene is relatively brief, but it is among the most vivid in the novel's final chapter, and in its dramatic compression of details it effectively clarifies the nature of both Egan's imagined future world and its relation to the neoliberal present. Egan's future anterior identifies the September 11 attacks on the World Trade Centre, the unnamed fulcrum of this passage, as the point of emergence of a national security and surveillance state rendered visible here via a dense assemblage of spaces between buildings, the crowd, police, security agents, reflecting pools, handsets, scanning devices, lampposts, and trees. At once perfectly ordinary and a cause of unease, this securitisation of the public sphere sets up a background rhythm, a 'hidden pulse' of risk and security, against which the daily lives of the crowd are conducted. Yet the hidden pulse of risk and security synchronises the deployment of security technologies in Lower Manhattan with two generations of warfare abroad. Intimately linking war abroad and surveillance at home, this hidden pulse also animates the sound work of Alex, who produces and mixes songs for children, the primary audience for popular music in Egan's future. By inserting the whirring sound of the helicopter rotor blades into Alex's memories of the sounds he has digitalised and manipulated, Egan invites reflection on the relation between the digital manipulation of sound and the various visual and algorithmic profiling technologies characteristic of contemporary surveillance practices. Past, present, and future, daily life, affects of unease and safety, wars abroad, surveillance and the memories of a life immersed in music are connected in this periodising of the contemporary according to a security logic that forms part of the fabric of daily life.

It is hardly the case that this concern with surveillance and security is restricted in the novel to its future-set chapters. 'Safari' is chronologically the earliest of the chapters in the novel and depicts the Kenyan safari of a music executive, his girlfriend, children, and bandmates. The chapter is filled with proleptic sequences such as the following one:

> Thirty-five years from now, in 2008, this warrior will be caught in the tribal violence between the Kikuyu and the Luo and will die in a fire. He'll have had four wives and sixty-three grandchildren by then, one of whom, a boy named Joe, will inherit his *lalema*: the iron hunting dagger in a leather scabbard now hanging at his side. Joe will go to college at Columbia and study engineering, becoming an expert in visual robotic technology that detects the slightest hint of irregular movement (the legacy of a childhood spent scanning the grass for lions). He'll marry an American named Lulu and remain in New York, where he'll invent a scanning device that becomes standard issue for crowd security. He and Lulu will buy a loft in Tribeca, where his grandfather's hunting dagger will be displayed inside a cube of Plexiglas directly under a skylight. (2011: 71)

The safari gaze of the narrator in this chapter turns out to be a temporalising one, mapping for the reader the future trajectories of people and objects. The passage proleptically juxtaposes the pre-emptively terminated life of the grandfather, subsequently memorialised like a still life captured in Plexiglas, and Joe and Lulu's open-ended life in New York. In doing so it contrasts insecure and secure frames for life, acting like a security scanner, producing information about risks and potential for survival, even while drawing our attention to the development of various security technologies. These technologies, like the security scanner, are then also the technologies that will resurface in 'Pure Language' where the scanner is used at the concert, which Joe will attend and Lulu will help market, to identify threats via the data points of a crowd. The decades between the safari and the concert are then a history of the development of surveillance technologies and their application.

But something else may be occurring in this passage. Bruce Robbins has used it as the most salient example of Egan's narrative technique in the novel, which for him is saturated with proleptic narratives. As Robbins notes, prolepsis can be understood as indicating that the future is '*beyond human will and agency*' (Robbins 2012: 194), subject to the gods or to chance. As such Egan's proleptic narrative is an example of the writing of contingency, paradoxically making the unpredictable life courses of the 'warrior' and his family clear by anticipating and sketching out their future trajectories. Prolepsis is not prediction, not exactly, unless it is what we are left with after elements of chance or error have been subtracted from predictive narratives. Yet, by suspending narrative indeterminacy, Egan captures something of the indeterminacy and contingency implied by her equation of time with a violent goon. But from another perspective, this assaying of the life of the 'warrior', as Amoore notes, produces the transparent, knowable life trajectory that contemporary security discourse desires, but fails, to render legible (Amoore 2013: 166). Whatever the case may be, Egan's prolepses make clear that her narrative in the novel can be understood in terms of categories such as contingency and strategies of speculation. The indeterminacies and contingencies of her novel translate into future-oriented narratives, some fixed like that of the warrior, others open-ended. What occurs at the level of short textual segments such as the story of the 'warrior' is repeated at the level of the novel as a whole, when its final two chapters move into the future of the narrative's present. Some of those stories too are left open-ended, their outcome uncertain. Perhaps the most uncertain, because it speaks to the reader's contingency as well, is the depiction of climate change and environmental damage in the second-to-last chapter. The novel's narratives suggest and seek to teach an alertness towards such contingencies associated with the future. More narrowly, the position the novel assumes towards the unknown future intersects with, as much as it attempts to resist as Amoore argues, a neoliberal logic of security: it approaches the future with apprehension and with a concern for its calculability or incalculability.

Time is a problem for Egan's novel, and for a reading of it in the terms provided by neoliberalism. Time is opportunity, and to be identified with the possibility of the novel circulating and transforming within a contemporary corporate media ecology. It is also, as Egan puts it, a 'goon' – contingent, risky, dangerous – to be secured and approached with apprehension, if not predicted. What image of time we seek to foreground in our reading of the novel determines how we position it in relation to neoliberalism, also bifurcated by a temporal split between the time of finance and the economy, and the time of security and risk. The challenge posed by the novel, by neoliberalism, and by our periodising efforts may very well be how to think these times together, as part of the same field of contingency, opportunity, and danger.

It may be the case, then, that reading fiction in relation to the neoliberal present and its contingencies raises anew questions about the temporality of literary narratives, in particular about the speculative futures at play in how these narratives assay the many dangers and opportunities of the contemporary. If so, neoliberalism and contemporary fiction share a predisposition or attunement towards the future, both emerging as future-oriented modes of engaging with and taming the contingent and uncertain. Less speculatively, however, I want to turn here towards a scene from Don DeLillo's *Falling Man*. Towards the end of the novel, Keith Neudecker, a survivor of the September 11, 2001, attack on the World Trade Center, finds himself engaged in high-stakes gambling at a poker tournament. The narrator tells us that the 'money mattered but not so much ... There was the fact that they would all be dead one day ... The game mattered, the stacking of the chips, the eye count, the play and dance of the hand and eye' (DeLillo 2007: 228). DeLillo subtly alludes to the association of finance with gambling in this passage. The September 11, 2001, attack is present as well, overtly in the reference to the finite nature of life, less overtly in the atmosphere of unpredictability and uncertainty necessarily surrounding the gambling. But at the heart of the passage is its engagement with chance or rather contingency. In this game of chance, what matters more than the connotations of the scene is the gains and losses, speculative manoeuvres, strategising and calculating in the face of the unpredictable. To deploy a varied account of neoliberalism as a framework for periodising the contemporary is to pay attention to moments such as this in narratives, where contingencies come into play, and what remains to be decided is how to understand and approach the uncertain. To do so is not to negate or even to diminish the importance of the finance economy or security, but to pay careful attention to the productive and dangerous field of contingency that serves as their condition of possibility and yet, also, the problem space they seek to manage and leverage for profit.

We may wonder, in conclusion, whether understanding neoliberalism as both an economic and security formation may not provide a way of grasping the present moment in which, under the presidency of Donald J. Trump, neoliberalism appears to have entered into an alliance with an intensification of the workings of the national security sate. As Nikhil Pal Singh argues, 'Trump's ideology seems less a rejection of neoliberalism *tout court* than its acceleration ... a moment when the neoliberal market state merges with an increasingly politicized corporate realm alarmed about the terms of order and rule' (Singh 2017: 168). This alarm has resulted in a presidency whose first significant executive order was a travel ban targeting Muslims from seven countries. The Trump presidency can be understood thus far as resulting in the expansion of police powers and surveillance, and the increasing securitisation of migrant mobility. It can also be understood as being in many ways a continuation of neoliberal economic policies. While Trump appears to be in favour of protectionist economic policies and to disavow neoliberal globalisation, he otherwise seems to be intensifying the neoliberal agenda by announcing tax cuts for corporations and elites, further deregulating the market and financial services, and pushing back against the social state. In fact, Trump's economic vision appears to be driven by a commitment to deregulated markets and to unrestrained growth (Daly 2017: 86), the foundational principles of neoliberalism. Rather than witnessing a break with neoliberalism under the Trump presidency, we may be viewing one of its periodic transformations, as Trump's allegiance to unfettered markets and growth enters into alliance with his commitment to an authoritarian and increasingly brutal security state. Aihwa Ong has cautioned us to be attentive to 'the restless nature of the neoliberal logic and its promiscuous capacity to become entangled with diverse assemblages, thereby crystallizing political conditions and solutions that confound liberal expectations' (Ong 2007: 7). In our current neoliberal moment, that entails attending to mutations in the articulation of economic and security formations, their conjunctures, and the differences these transformations make in how we periodise and understand the contemporary and its culture.

Bibliography

Amoore, Louise (2013), *The Politics of Possibility: Risk and Security Beyond Probability*, Durham, NC: Duke University Press.

Beck, Ulrich (1992), *Risk Society: Towards a New Modernity*, London: Sage.

Berberian, Viken (2010), *Das Kapital: A Novel of Love and Money Markets*, New York: Simon and Schuster.

Berlant, Lauren (2008), 'Intuitionists: History and the Affective Event', *American Literary History*, 20:4, pp. 845–60.

Brouillette, Sarah, Mathia Nilges, and Emilio Sauri (eds) (2017), *Literature and the Global Contemporary*, New York: Palgrave Macmillan.

Brown, Nicholas (2012), 'The Work of Art in the Age of its Real Subsumption under Capital', *Nonsite.org*, 13, <https://nonsite.org/editorial/the-work-of-art-in-the-age-of-its-real-subsumption-under-capital> (last accessed 1 July 2018).

Brown, Wendy (2015), *Undoing the Demos: Neoliberalism's Stealth Revolution*, Cambridge, MA: MIT Press.

Burgess, J. Peter (2011), *The Ethical Subject of Security: Geopolitical Reason and the Threat Against Europe*, London: Routledge.

Burke, Anthony (2002), 'Aporias of Security', *Alternatives: Global, Local, Political*, 27:1, pp. 1–27.

Camp, Jordan T. (2016), *Incarcerating the Crisis: Freedom Struggles and the Rise of the Neoliberal State*, Oakland: University of California Press.

Cherniavsky, Eva (2017), *Neocitizenship: Political Culture after Democracy*, New York: New York University Press.

Collier, Stephen J. (2012), 'Neoliberalism as Big Leviathan, or . . . ? A Response to Wacquant and Hilgers', *Social Anthropology*, 20:2, pp. 186–95.

Cooper, Melinda (2008), *Life as Surplus: Biotechnology and Capitalism in the Neoliberal Era*, Seattle: University of Washington Press.

Daly, Herman (2017), 'Trump's Growthism: Its Roots in Neoclassical Economic Theory', *Real-World Economics Review*, 78, pp. 86–97.

Dean, Mitchell (2010), *Governmentality: Power and Rule in Modern Society*, Los Angeles: Sage.

Dean, Mitchell (2014), 'Rethinking Neoliberalism', *Journal of Sociology*, 50:2, pp. 150–63.

DeLillo, Don (2007), *Falling Man*, New York: Scribner.

DeLillo, Don (2010), *Point Omega*, New York: Scribner.

Dillon, Michael (2008), 'Underwriting Security', *Security Dialogue*, 39:2/3, pp. 309–32.

Dillon, Michael and Luis Lobo-Guerrero (2009), 'The Biopolitical Imaginary of Species-Being', *Theory, Culture and Society*, 26:1, pp. 1–23.

Duggan, Lisa (2012), *The Twilight of Equality? Neoliberalism, Cultural Politics, and the Attack on Democracy*, Boston: Beacon Press.

Egan, Jennifer (2011), *A Visit from the Goon Squad*, New York: Anchor.

Eggers, Dave (2013), *The Circle*, San Francisco: McSweeney's Books.

Elliott, Jane K. (2018), *The Microeconomic Mode: Political Subjectivity in Contemporary Popular Aesthetics*, New York: Columbia University Press.

Esposito, Elena (2013), 'The Structures of Uncertainty: Performativity and Unpredictability in Economic Operations', *Economy and Society*, 42:1, pp. 102–29.

Esposito, Roberto (2011), *Immunitas: The Protection and Negation of Life*, Cambridge: Polity.

Foucault, Michel (2008), *The Birth of Biopolitics: Lectures at the Collège de France, 1978–1979*, New York: Palgrave Macmillan.

Franzen, Jonathan (2010), *Freedom*, London: Fourth Estate.
Giddens, Anthony (1999), 'Risk and Responsibility', *Modern Law Review*, 62, pp. 1–10.
Graham, Stephen (2011), *Cities under Siege: The New Military Urbanism*, London: Verso.
Grausam, Daniel (2017), 'The Multitemporal Contemporary: Colson Whitehead's Presents', in Sarah Brouillette, Mathia Nilges, and Emilio Sauri (eds), *Literature and the Global Contemporary*, New York: Palgrave Macmillan, pp. 117–33.
Grewal, Inderpal (2017), *Saving the Security State: Exceptional Citizens in Twenty-First-Century America*, Durham, NC: Duke University Press.
Hayek, Friedrich August (1988), *The Collected Works of Friedrich August Hayek, Vol. 1: The Fatal Conceit: The Errors of Socialism*, William W. Bartley III (ed.), London: Routledge.
Hayles, N. Katherine (2017), *Unthought: The Power of the Cognitive Nonconscious*, Chicago: University of Chicago Press.
Hong, Grace Kyungwon (2015), *Death beyond Disavowal: The Impossible Politics of Difference*, Minneapolis: University of Minnesota Press.
Huehls, Mitchum (2016), *After Critique: Twenty-First-Century Fiction in a Neoliberal Age*, New York: Oxford University Press.
Huehls, Mitchum and Rachel Greenwald Smith (2017), 'Four Phases of Neoliberalism and Literature: An Introduction', in Mitchum Huehls and Rachel Greenwald Smith (eds), *Neoliberalism and Contemporary Literary Culture*, Baltimore: Johns Hopkins University Press, pp. 1–18.
Itzkoff, Dave (2011), 'Jennifer Egan Discusses TV Plans for *A Visit From the Goon Squad*', *ArtsBeat*, 21 April, <http://artsbeat.blogs.nytimes.com/2011/04/21/jennifer-egan-talks-tv-plans-fora- visit-from-the-goon-squad/?_r=1> (last accessed 21 June 2018).
Jameson, Fredric (2013), *The Antinomies of Realism*, London: Verso.
Johansen, Emily (2017), 'Neoliberalism and Contemporary Anglophone Fiction', *Oxford Research Encyclopaedia of Literature*, <http://literature.oxfordre.com/view/10.1093/acrefore/9780190201098.001.0001/acrefore-9780190201098-e-185> (last accessed 18 June 2018).
Johnston, Katherine D. (2017), 'Metadata, Metafiction, and the Stakes of Surveillance in Jennifer Egan's *A Visit from the Goon Squad*', *American Literature*, 89:1, pp. 155–84.
Konings, Martijn (2018), *Capital and Time: For a New Critique of Neoliberal Reason*, Kindle edn, Stanford: Stanford University Press.
La Berge, Leigh Claire (2014), *Scandals and Abstraction: Financial Fiction of the Long 1980s*, New York: Oxford University Press.
Lerner, Ben (2014), *10:04*, New York: Farrar, Straus and Giroux.
Lish, Atticus (2015), *Preparation for the Next Life*, London: Oneworld.
McClanahan, Annie (2018), *Dead Pledges: Debt, Crisis, and Twenty-First-Century Culture*, Stanford: Stanford University Press.
Martin, Randy (2002), *Financialization of Daily Life*, Kindle edn, Philadelphia: Temple University Press.
Meillassoux, Quentin (2009), *After Finitude: An Essay on the Necessity of Contingency*, Ray Brassier (trans.), London: Continuum.
Mirowski, Philip and Edward Nik-Khah (2017), *The Knowledge We Have Lost in Information: The History of Information in Modern Economics*, New York: Oxford University Press.
Mountford, Peter (2011), *A Young Man's Guide to Late Capitalism*, New York: Houghton Mifflin Harcourt.
Nealon, Jeffrey T. (2012), *Post-Postmodernism: Or, The Cultural Logic of Just-in-Time Capitalism*, Stanford: Stanford University Press.

O'Malley, Pat (2004), *Risk, Uncertainty and Government*, London: Routledge.
Ong, Aihwa (2007), 'Neoliberalism as Mobile Technology', *Transactions of the Institute of British Geographers*, 32:1, pp. 3–8.
Peck, Jamie (2010), *Constructions of Neoliberal Reason*, New York: Oxford University Press.
Rich, Nathaniel (2013), *Odds Against Tomorrow*, New York: Farrar, Straus and Giroux.
Robbins, Bruce (2012), 'Many Years Later: Prolepsis in Deep Time', *The Henry James Review*, 33:3, pp. 191–204.
Roitman, Janet (2014), *Anti-Crisis*, Durham, NC: Duke University Press.
Saldívar, Ramón (2013), 'The Second Elevation of the Novel: Race, Form, and the Postrace Aesthetic in Contemporary Narrative', *Narrative*, 21:1, pp. 1–18.
Shacochis, Bob (2013), *The Woman Who Lost Her Soul*, New York: Atlantic Monthly Press.
Shakar, Alex (2011), *Luminarium*, New York: Soho Press.
Shaviro, Steven (2010), 'The "Bitter Necessity" of Debt: Neoliberal Finance and the Society of Control', pp. 1–9, <http://www.shaviro.com/Othertexts/Debt.pdf> (last accessed 18 August 2018).
Shaviro, Steven (2011), 'Hyperbolic Futures: Speculative Finance and Speculative Fiction', *The Cascadia Subduction Zone*, 1:2, pp. 3–5, 12–15.
Shonkwiler, Alison (2017), *The Financial Imaginary: Economic Mystification and the Limits of Realist Fiction*, Minneapolis: University of Minnesota Press.
Shteyngart, Gary (2010), *Super Sad True Love Story*, New York: Random House.
Singh, Nikhil Pal (2017), *Race and America's Long War*, Oakland: University of California Press.
Smith, Rachel Greenwald (2015), *Affect and American Literature in the Age of Neoliberalism*, Cambridge: Cambridge University Press.
Stoler, Ann Laura (2016), *Duress: Imperial Durabilities in Our Times*, Durham, NC: Duke University Press.
Szalay, Michael (2017), 'The Author as Producer', in Mitchum Huehls and Rachel Greenwald Smith (eds), *Neoliberalism and Contemporary Literary Culture*, Baltimore: Johns Hopkins University Press, pp. 255–76.
Waldman, Amy (2011), *The Submission*, London: Windmill Books.
Walter, Jess (2006), *The Zero*, New York: Harper.
Wayne, Teddy (2010), *Kapitoil*, London: Duckworth.
Whitehead, Colson (1999), *The Intuitionist*, New York: Random House.

23

Automatic Art, Automated Trading: Finance, Fiction, and Philosophy

Arne De Boever

Introduction

In what follows, I want to show how contemporary finance novels – and more generally, cultural engagements with finance – can help us gain a better understanding of today's politics of control. By looking at the role of art in financial fiction and film, and considering the role of abstract expressionism and the paintings of Jackson Pollock in such works in particular, I propose to trace what art historian Pamela Lee in a very different but related context characterised as the 'digital legacy' of Pollock's much-discussed connection with Cold War politics, which is at the origin of today's politics of control. Lee considers Pollock in this context as part of a 'military-aesthetic complex' that, she suggests, has morphed into the algorithmic present. To develop this connection further, I argue, finance is a good place to look. Indeed, finance is one of the sites where today's post-disciplinary politics of algorithmic control is most obviously on display. With the help of art, literature, and film, I seek to develop a philosophical perspective, an episteme or mindset, that would help us gain insights into how today, after discipline, our individual and collective lives are governed.

In the first part of this chapter, I provide a brief overview of the contemporary finance economy. This is necessary both to understand the challenges that finance poses to art, literature, and film and to develop the philosophical perspective that would be able to capture the phenomenon of finance. I continue in the second part of the chapter by considering how literature and film have engaged the contemporary economy: the recurrent appearance of Pollock in some financial literature and film will guide my analysis here. In the third part of the chapter, I provide an art historical perspective on Pollock's role in the finance novel, which I tie to contemporary theories of politics. It is through this perspective that I gain insight into today's politics of algorithmic control, the origins of which can be found in Pollock's Cold War moment.

The Contemporary Economy: A Quick Sketch

With his general formula of capital, Karl Marx laid bare how capitalism turns money (M) into money that is worth more money (M′) through the intermediary of the commodity (C): M–C–M' is the formula that captures this movement (Marx 1990: 247–57). In order to keep this accumulation of money going, however, capitalism has in its recent history gone through various 'fixes'. David Harvey has written about capitalism's 'spatial fix' (Harvey quoted in McClanahan 2017: 12) in this context, namely the geographical expansion of its production and consumer markets. In Harvey's wake others, such as the scholar of debt Annie McClanahan, have considered what they call capitalism's 'temporal fix' (2017: 13). The latter refers to the ways in which neoliberal finance relies on the future to generate value in the present: its value-generation relies, for example, on the buying and selling of packages of mortgages that derive their value from a borrower's promise to pay the money that was lent to them back with interest. There is what Steven Shaviro has called a 'premediation' (Shaviro 2009: 32) of the future going on here that is different from capitalism's 'spatial' fix.

The temporal fix of financialisation arguably marks a shift in the general formula of capital, because the particular economy we find here no longer centrally revolves around the commodity that one learns about in Marx. Instead, commodities have been replaced by financial instruments like packages of mortgages, insurance policies, or student loans. I am thinking of the so-called collateralised debt obligations (CDOs), for example, that, in their toxic form, caused the crash of 2007–8; or of the student loan asset-backed securities (SLABs) that may become responsible for the next major market crash, since their sustainability depends on the unlikely fact of borrowers actually paying off their loans.

Added to that – to the 'what' of contemporary financial markets, the fact that they no longer revolve around commodities but around abstract and complex financial instruments – is the 'how' of contemporary markets. It is important to realise that the bustling trading floor that many still imagine when the stock market is evoked is, today, drastically outdated. It is an anachronistic representation of the market. The last human-occupied seat on the New York Stock Exchange was recently sold (Popper 2016; Detrixhe 2017); humans are still around on the trading floor, but they are largely there to supervise the trading that digital agents – algorithms – are doing. Such trading can happen very fast (hence the term high-frequency trading or HFT); in the case of an HFT-caused crash like the 2010 flash crash, for example, it happened so fast that neither humans nor computers were able to record the number of trades that took place during the market collapse. Abstract and complex, and fast as hell, this kind of capitalism – financial capitalism or finance – poses major challenges to representation: in theory, but also in the arts (the literary, visual, and performing arts). That challenge, which was already noted by the Marxist critic Fredric Jameson when he was writing about postmodernism as 'the cultural logic of late capitalism' (Jameson 1991), has only become more important since Jameson published his book. A Jameson-inspired project like Jeff Kinkle and Alberto Toscano's *Cartographies of the Absolute* (which deals with the mappings of finance) shows this well (Toscano and Kinkle 2015). The fact that Alison Shonkwiler has written in this context of a 'financial sublime' clearly marks this as an aesthetic challenge (Shonkwiler 2017).

How could art capture not only the baffling complexity of financial reality but also its stark, nonhuman character? How could it render the speed at which today's financial markets operate? These are important questions for artists who want to engage with the digital economy in their work. To put this in a different way: what kind of art would be attuned to the reality of the contemporary economy – fast, nonhuman, abstract, and complex? For those who thought that Jameson's book on postmodernism had settled the issue (and who had perhaps regretted that settling it through postmodernism risked leading too far away from actual finance, from a realism of actual finance), it has been interesting to see that in literature, for example, when it comes to novels about the 2007–8 financial crisis, realism is back; novelists are making a concerted effort to 'explain' finance to their readers in the aftermath of the crash.[1] But what kind of realism is needed here, given our financial situation? Certainly, it is not the aesthetic that the novelist Tom Wolfe, author of the financial novel *The Bonfire of the Vanities* (Wolfe 1987), advocated way back in 1989: a journalistic, social realism that would merely flex its epistemic muscle in the face of the increased abstraction and complexity of the financial world (Wolfe 1989). Novelists just ought to work harder, Wolfe admonishes, to 'bring the billion-footed beast of [financial] reality' (1989: 55) to terms: to stalk it, tame it, and render it accurately between the covers of a book. It seems, rather, that with the reality of markets today – with the reality of digitised trading environments in which nonhuman agents are acting at speeds that neither humans nor computers can fully record (or, as a consequence, regulate) – we are experiencing an ontological shift that in part gives the finger to old-school realism à la Wolfe. It would certainly need a little bit of Jameson's postmodernism mixed in. If Nassim Nicholas Taleb still considered today's markets within a probability model when he laid out his black swan theory of highly improbable market events (Taleb 2010), then derivatives trader and philosopher Elie Ayache clearly goes a step further with his theory of the market event as a blank swan, when he posits the market event as absolutely contingent (Ayache 2010). This is an 'anything could happen' position that characterises the human trader (and this figure is still central in Ayache's thought) as a kind of heroic agent who is perpetually responding to market events, and 'writing' (Ayache's term; Roffe 2014) the market's reality in response to those. Perhaps the appropriate aesthetic here would be more speculative than postmodern – perhaps we need a little sci-fi (science fiction) to render today's fi-fi (financial fiction) effective.[2]

I suggest this partly in view of the fact that the imagery that is often used to describe today's financial reality is, for lack of a better term, cosmic. It is the imagery of the universe, of the Big Bang and black holes. Perhaps Wolfe did get something right when he described the bondsmen of the 1980s as 'masters of the *universe*' (Wolfe 1987: 11, my emphasis). If his satire was said to target the testosterone- and cocaine-fuelled mastery evoked by that phrase, it also introduces the universe into the financial picture – and that particular emphasis was to prove prophetic. With its private, non-transparent, and largely unregulated HFT environments called 'dark pools' (Patterson 2012), contemporary finance has arguably entered the realm of the 'dark ideas' of physics (like 'dark matter' or 'black holes', for example). In the case of HFT, its association with black holes certainly seems justified even at a superficial level: while HFT is supposed to add liquidity to the market by increasing trading volume overall, it is clear that such an increase in volume merely creates a liquidity *effect*.[3] This means that when the chips are down, and the market appears to be in distress, HFT liquidity will disappear like snow under the sun, the clearest sign that HFT does not represent a real investment in the market. In other words, HFT has a kind of vacuum effect on the market that some have compared to the ways in which, within the horizon of a black hole, all the information gets sucked towards the extreme gravity of the centre; beyond the horizon, nothing gets out (as you may remember from Christopher Nolan's magisterial film *Interstellar*).

But there is more: it turns out that some of the actual science for HFT, some of its actual algorithms, were developed by physicists who were working on black holes. For example, Henry Laufer, the former head of the hedge fund Renaissance Technologies, did his PhD in astronomy at Princeton and wrote a book about black holes. There is a real confluence between astrophysics and finance that needs to be considered here. The sociologist Karen Knorr Cetina, who used to work on high-energy physics, has explored this conundrum in her work (Cetina 2014). I am also thinking of James Owen Weatherall's book *The Physics of Wall Street* (Weatherall 2013).

As Vincent Bontems and Roland Lehoucq point out in a book titled *Les idées noires de la physique* (*Dark Ideas in Physics*), the history of black holes begins in 1783 when the English physician and astronomer John Michell proposes that we think of a mass so large that even light does not travel at the speed required to escape its gravitation (Bontems and Lehoucq 2016: 85). The popular understanding of what later (in 1967) comes to be called a 'black hole' as some kind of 'cosmic vacuum cleaner' can be related to the limit of the black hole's sphere from which neither light nor matter can escape – the so-called horizon of the black hole (2016: 91). Contrary to the horizon on earth, which shifts with the position of its observer, the horizon of a black hole is absolute: 'It is a limit of space-time, independent from any observer, and it divides events into two categories' (2016: 88). Outside of this horizon, one basically finds the universe as we know it. Inside of it, light can no longer travel freely between two arbitrary points, because light is directed towards the centre of the black hole. Communication within the black hole is therefore severely limited. Light and matter cannot travel from the inside towards the outside, but only in the other direction.

Proof of the existence of black holes was delivered for the first time in 1971, when 'astrophysicists detect Cygnus X-1, a binary system whose characteristics suggest that it is a system formed by a black hole and a gigantic star' (Bontems and Lehoucq 2016: 89). Since 1971, as Bontems and Lehoucq point out, some twenty black holes have been discovered in our galaxy; the largest is located at the centre of the Milky Way. Coincidentally (or not?), the Nasdaq Stock Market, the world's first electronic stock market, was also opened in 1971; this is also when the Nixon administration, in response to the rising cost of the Vietnam War, unilaterally abolished the gold standard, thus bringing down the Bretton Woods system of international exchange (all currencies pegged to the dollar, and the dollar pegged to gold) that had been established after World War II. It was the beginning of the era of unbridled financial speculation. In short, we find here a historical – though perhaps more than historical, I am suggesting – coincidence of scientific and economic developments that lays the foundation for the cosmic reality of finance today.

Art in the Finance Novel

As a way into the challenges that such a reality poses to art, literature, and film, I propose to consider the art that is featured in the financial novel. I suppose it should not come as a surprise that financial novels are full of art. Bret Easton Ellis's *American Psycho* – which is a classic of the financial fiction genre and has been deemed by some 'the first neoliberal novel' (Williams 2013) – repeatedly invokes art, explicitly referring to works by Cindy Sherman, Eric Fischl, Julian Schnabel, Frank Stella, George Stubbs (the odd one out, for sure), and most memorably David Onica (Ellis 1991). With the exception of the Onica, which appears to be hung upside down in Patrick Bateman's apartment (as his soon-to-be-brutally-murdered ex-girlfriend points out), one really just comes across these artists and their works in passing: their paintings are mentioned in the novel in the same way that other commodities are. There is no depth to the engagement. They are merely there as markers of wealth.

Some (I am thinking of Dave Beech; Beech 2016) might argue that as such, these artworks are exceptional commodities whose value is in no way determined as it is with other commodities. Others (readers of Marina Vishmidt for example; Vishmidt 2012) may want to put some pressure on whether these artworks can even be called commodities. Perhaps it would be more accurate to characterise them (as per my discussion of capitalism and finance capitalism earlier on) as financial instruments through which speculative value is generated: as makers rather than merely markers of wealth. In his book *Conceptual Art*, Alexander Alberro has laid bare conceptual art's particular affinity with the financial era (Alberro 2003). It is worth noting that the first exhibition dedicated solely to conceptual art was in 1970, so right at the beginning of the financial, neoliberal era. Following this line of argument is in tension with the more common view of conceptual art as challenging the art market through its decommodification; in other words: by the fact that it takes the commodity out of the art market, conceptual art would share its dematerialisation with financial instruments – with the financialised art market. As such, the appearance of artworks in the financial novel may be not only a sign of wealth, but a kind of reminder from the realm of the aesthetic of how in the financial era wealth is generated. In other words, there might be something conceptual to the presence of non-conceptual artworks in the financial novel.

Even if art in the finance novel operates conceptually, then, it is still worth asking which art specifically can be found there. In *American Psycho* it is, with the exception of George Stubbs, contemporary art; and of course it would have to be contemporary art that appears in the financial novel as a value-generating instrument par excellence. Consider simply the collection of the Broad Museum in Los Angeles, which appears to hold together as an investment alone. It includes the usual suspects: Jeff Koons, for example – another icon of bad taste along with Bateman's Onica.

Another fitting example would be the Young British Artist Damien Hirst. Koons and Hirst both appear in Michel Houellebecq's financial novel *The Map and the Territory* (not Alan Greenspan's book about the 2007–8 financial crisis, which has the same title; Houellebecq's was published first; Greenspan 2013, Houellebecq 2012). *The Map and the Territory* opens with a description of the artist Jed Martin at work on a painting titled *Damien Hirst and Jeff Koons Dividing Up the Art Market* – a painting that in the same section of the novel he also destroys. When the novel's opening section ends with the artist 'seiz[ing] a palette knife [and] cut[ting] open Damien Hirst's eye' because he thinks he has been making 'a truly shitty painting' (Houellebecq 2012: 14) ('un tableau de merde', in the original French (Houellebecq 2013: 29), 'a shit painting'), the reader can appreciate the destruction of the painting in part because it brings down two icons of the art/monetary value conjunction, Hirst and Koons:

Catching the sticky canvas with one hand, he tore it in one blow, tipping the easel over onto the floor. Slightly calmed, he stopped, looked at his hands, sticky with paint, and finished the cognac before jumping feet first onto the painting, stamping on it and rubbing it against the floor until it became slippery. He lost his balance and fell, the back of his head hitting the frame of the easel violently. He belched and vomited, and suddenly felt better. (Houellebecq 2012: 14)

This scene comes at the beginning of a novel that is obsessively engaged with economics. It traces the career of a contemporary artist who starts out as a photographer, recording objects at the end of the era of industrial production (think Harvey/McClanahan again, or more precisely Giovanni Arrighi and the terminal crisis of capitalism (Arrighi 1994)), and experiences the first height of his career when he starts photographing Michelin maps – hence the novel's title. The Michelin maps also show up in Houellebecq's debut novel *Whatever* (*Extension du domaine de la lute*), which is a brilliant representation of life under post-Fordism (see Sweeney 2010). In both cases they are indicative of the problematic of realism that is central to Houellebecq's work. If in *Whatever*, the question was what kind of realism could do justice to life under post-Fordism, in *The Map and the Territory* that problematic is pushed in the direction of 'abstract' and 'complex' finance.[4] How to write a novel about the particular kind of value-generation that characterises our contemporary moment? Houellebecq does this, in my view very successfully (though James Wood predictably did not think so), through a realist novel about a contemporary artist.

So here, with the problematic of the map and the territory, we have another reason why art may be prominently present in financial fiction: as a reminder of the challenges that finance's abstraction and complexity pose to representation, which is something that I mentioned earlier on.

That reminder immediately raises what one could call the issue of scientific financial realism – the issue of whether the reality of finance, of today's financial markets, can be truthfully described and understood (and, ultimately, predicted). This conundrum comes to prominence in the second half of Houellebecq's novel, when, after a gruesome murder (whose victim is none other than the author Michel Houellebecq), *The Map and the Territory* abruptly shifts into detective novel mode. The detective, however, is married to Hélène, an economics professor whose 'interest in economics had waned considerably over the years', as the novel tells us:

> More and more, the theories that tried to explain economic phenomena, to predict their developments, appeared almost equally inconsistent and random. She was more and more tempted to liken them to pure and simple charlatanism; it was even surprising, she occasionally thought, that they gave a Nobel Prize for economics, as if this discipline could boast of the same methodological seriousness, the same intellectual rigor as chemistry, or physics. And her interest in teaching had also waned considerably. (Houellebecq 2012: 208)

While her husband does his utmost to trace a murder and understand a murderer in order to prevent him from striking again, the novel has Hélène doubting those same endeavours on the economic front. After their family dinner, the couple turn on the news, where a reporter discusses 'the crisis that had been shaking the financial markets for several days, and which threatened, according to some experts, to be even worse than that of 2008' (this scene is set in the near future, by the way; Houellebecq often engages in this kind of subtle science fiction). 'Did you hear what the expert said?', asks Hélène (2012: 210). 'Did you see his forecasts?'

> 'In a week's time we'll see that all his forecasts were wrong. They'll call another expert, even the same one, and he'll make new forecasts, with the same self-assurance ... ' She was shaking her head, upset, even indignant. 'How can a discipline that can't even manage to make verifiable forecasts be considered a science?' (2012: 210)

We are talking economics here, but these statements can also be applied to her husband's detective work. What Hélène is taking on is, in a sense, the expert's capacity to 'detect' the markets. And she is arguing that such detection, such a realism of the market, is impossible. Economics is not a science. One wonders, by analogy, whether police work is. Traditionally, the detective novel operates within the scientific paradigm. But here the spectre is raised (which we know if not from Paul Auster's *New York Trilogy* then from Friedrich Dürrenmatt's *The Pledge*

(*Das Versprechen*)) of a detective novel that would not.[5] Indeed, an entire countertradition of postmodern detective fiction has been built around this conceit, and is reactivated here in the speculative context of finance. The economics professor plants a seed of suspicion that the 'solution' that the detective novel, or detective work, provides is really illusory — that there can be no science of detecting reality, just as there can be no science of detecting the markets. *The Map and the Territory* deems this kind of realism impossible. Robin Mackay calls this position 'epistemology noir' (Mackay 2016).

Now, the context within which this impossibility plays out is, on the one hand, that of a financial crisis, and, on the other, that of a gruesome murder. But, and here is where I finally arrive at the core of my argument, it is also that of art. When the painter Jed Martin sees photographs of the site of the murder at the detective's office, he responds: 'It's funny ... it looks like a Pollock, but a Pollock who would have worked almost in monochrome' (Houellebecq 2012: 222). When he finds out what the images 'represent in reality' (2012: 222), he collapses. Later though, Martin will take his statement back, saying: 'You know, it's just a rather mediocre imitation of a Pollock. There are forms and drips, but the whole thing is arranged mechanically, there's no force, no vital *élan*' (2012: 224). It is perhaps this 'mechanical' removal from 'life' that anticipates the fact that in *The Map and the Territory*, Houellebecq's murderer *will* ultimately be found. Detection *is* possible. The murder is *no* Pollock, so it *is* possible to map it. Realism remains intact after all, but as 'mediocre imitation'. It is unclear in the novel whether this conclusion also applies to financial realism, to the mapping of the markets (the novel does not make this explicit, at least). For it might be, instead, that the markets are more like a Pollock than Houellebecq's murder scene — and therefore undetectable, as the detective's wife suggests. Pollock's presence in the financial novel is where this very issue gets played out.

Again, it is not surprising that there would be a Pollock in a finance novel. Together with Willem de Kooning and Mark Rothko, two other abstract expressionists, Pollock is one of the few contemporary artists on that dubious list of 'most expensive'.

But here too, there is more. In Teddy Wayne's finance novel *Kapitoil*, it is Pollock's paintings, or rather what Pollock has said about his paintings, that inspire the Qatar-born Karim Issar to develop an algorithm that can predict the fluctuations of oil prices. 'Then I enter an exhibit on the American Jackson Pollock', Issar (who is working hard on his English) writes in his journal.

> At first I do not enjoy his paintings. They are too chaotic and have no logic and organization like Mondrian's.... But then I see some quotations by Pollock about his paintings, such as: 'I don't use the accident — 'cause I deny the accident'... And I reevaluate that possibly Pollock's paintings have more value, because he has a philosophy similar to mine, which is that life is ultimately predictable. (Wayne 2010: 17)

Regardless of whether one can indeed draw this conclusion – predictability – from Pollock's action painting or automatic painting, here is where it ultimately leads Issar:

> I can use Pollock's ideas about denying the accident and about there being no center for a stock market program. Everyone else who writes programs to predict the stock market concentrates on the most central variables and incorporates a few minor ones. But what if I utilize variables that no one observes because they seem tangential, and I utilize *exclusively* these tangential variables? (2010: 17)

Thus, Issar's program is born, and it turns out to be wildly successful. It is Pollock, one of the most expensive contemporary artists, who is presented as having contributed to this financial boom. Pollock works here as a maker of wealth rather than as its mere marker.

Here too, as in Houellebecq, the tension between the natural and the artificial or the mechanic is in play. Recall that Pollock's work, in Houellebecq, is presented as having a 'vital *élan*' (this in opposition to the murder scene, which looks derivative). As is well known, Pollock drips, splatters, flings, and smears his paint. There is the famous whiplash stroke that the critics always talk about and that is impossible to miss in videos of Pollock painting. Issar seems to interpret Pollock's technique as mechanical. I think that may be a misreading. Certainly, in *Kapitoil*, Issar himself is presented as a mechanical man. Preparing for a Halloween party, his colleagues hand him a wrench and suggest he go as a mechanic (2010: 117). Later in the novel, he describes his own responses as robot-like. The novel's narrative is frequently interrupted by clunky breakdowns of reasoning, going from, say, point '1' to point '1.B.1.a.i' (2010: 147). Through all of his, *Kapitoil* presents Issar not merely as a bot – a descendant, I would argue, of 'automated teller' Patrick Bateman (to draw from Leigh Claire La Berge's perceptive reading of Ellis's novel (La Berge 2015: 136)) – but as a mechanical person whose calculated reasoning is in tension with his humanity (which ultimately prevails in the novel – as of course it would!). The question we are left with is to what extent that ultimate victory of humanity is already prefigured in Pollock's way of painting.

Compare and contrast Issar's rather limited association of Pollock with a certain kind of automation to how Pollock appears in Alex Garland's recent film *Ex Machina*, in which a character called Nathan Bateman[6] – inventor of 'Blue Book, named after Wittgenstein's notes, ... the world's most popular internet search engine', as the script puts it (Garland 2013: 37) – lets one of his employees in on the artificial intelligence (AI) called 'Ava' that he has created (Bateman's company sounds like a mashup of the Blue Brain project – the Lausanne-based project to create a synthetic brain modelled after the human brain – with Facebook and Google). Now, one of the scenes in which Bateman is trying to explain the reasoning that lies behind his AI's brain takes place in what the script refers to as 'the Pollock room' (2013: 28). The conversation happens in front of a Pollock painting; specifically, Pollock's painting *No. 5, 1948*, one of the most expensive paintings ever sold.

We do not learn this in the film, but Garland explains in an interview that the scene was supposed to be a lot longer (Britt 2015). In the longer version, it was suggested that Bateman made an AI recreate the original Pollock and then mixed up the paintings and destroyed one of them, 'and he had no idea which was the original and which was the fake', in a kind of literalisation of Pollock's 'automatic art' (2015).[7] But what sense of the automatic is in play here? Here is Bateman's understanding of it:

> Jackson Pollock. The drip painter. He let his mind go blank, and his hand go where it wanted. Not deliberate, not random. Someplace in between.... What if Pollock had reversed the challenge? Instead of trying to make art without thinking, he said: I can't paint unless I know exactly why I'm doing it. What would have happened? (Garland 2013: 59)

His employee replies: 'He never would have made a single mark' (2013: 59). Bateman concludes: 'The challenge is *not* to act automatically. It's to find an action that's *not automatic*' (2013: 59, my emphasis). This is what his AI project is all about. Again, though in a different way than in *Kapitoil*, it comes from Pollock — something that is suggested in the film not only through the conversation in the Pollock room but also by how the film visualises Bateman's office, which looks like a Pollock.

Once again, Pollock is not merely a marker of wealth, and specifically here of a certain kind of intelligence; he also helps make that intelligence. And this kind of intelligence is changing the financial industry today (I am thinking of algorithmic trading in particular). So even though *Ex Machina* is not about finance per se, there is a connection — and Pollock is like a portal here back into finance. Here too, the tension between the natural and the artificial is in play, as is evoked very much in the script's shuttling between natural settings (meadows, the mountains) and the glass, steel, and concrete architecture of Bateman's house — an opposition that Bateman's AI can be said to overcome. Both in *Ex Machina* and in *Kapitoil*, Pollock becomes the site where different understandings of AI are played out.

Why Pollock?

Regardless of how Pollock is mobilised in these various cultural representations, we should now finally also ask about this mobilisation as such — about whether it makes sense at all that Pollock would appear in these representations of finance and AI. At first sight, the ironies of the turn to Pollock in these contexts appear to be multiple: certainly, it is striking to see a painter whose work is generally associated with the Depression Era, and who from 1935 until 1943 was employed by the United States government (as part of the Works Project Association of Roosevelt's New Deal Federal Arts Project), aligned with high finance and extreme wealth in this way — even if his *No. 5, 1948* is now one of the most expensive paintings ever sold. As Frances Stonor Saunders notes in her seminal 'Yanqui Doodles' essay, Pollock, like other abstract expressionist artists, was 'producing subsidized art for the government and getting involved in left-wing politics' (Saunders 1999: 253). This was particularly true for Pollock, 'who in the 1930s had been involved in the Communist workshop of the Mexican muralist David Alfalo Siquieros' – and Saunders adds that 'several other Abstract Expressionists had all been Communist activists' (1999: 253). These artists were, then, not at all of the capitalist kind; rather, capital would be thrown at them in an attempt to depoliticise them.

In addition, one should note that even if Pollock himself insisted that his work was 'No chaos, damn it!' (Hammond 1998: 6), it was still about the freedom of human expression – and it seems odd to have it brought into alliance with AI here, which tends to be associated first and foremost with surveillance and what Frank Pasquale has recently called 'the black box society' (Pasquale 2015), in which freedom becomes a mere correlative of government, as Michel Foucault, lecturing in the mid-1970s, put it (Foucault 2008). One can think here of Gilles Deleuze's 'society of control' (Deleuze 1992) or the Belgian researcher Antoinette Rouvroy's notion of 'algorithmic governance' (Rouvroy and Stiegler 2016) as well. It should be noted, however, that whereas to some, 'Abstract Expressionism [was] evidence of a Communist conspiracy', to others it represented something entirely different: 'a specifically anti-Communist ideology, the ideology of freedom, of free enterprise' (Saunders 1999: 254), which of course would ultimately deliver precisely the very cynical notion of freedom that can be paired with the digital age.

If Foucault, at the end of the famous fifth section of the first volume of his *History of Sexuality*, in which he proposes the notion of biopolitics, imagines people in the future being amused by the obsession with sex as a site where our liberation could be found – if only we could get to the bottom of sex, then we would be free! – one could perhaps imagine a similar amusement with or even laughter at what is left of freedom in the digital age. If we can agree that the disciplinary power that Foucault associates with an anatomo-politics of the body may have waned, while the biopolitics of the population ('focused on the species body ... and effected through an entire series of interventions and regulatory controls' (Foucault 1990: 139)) has intensified into the psycho- and even neuro-politics of the mind and the brain, we can see that our notion of freedom has morphed along the way. It has transformed into something that is not so much disciplined or even the target of intervention or regulation (both of which Foucault associated with biopolitics (1990: 139)) but has rather become premediated, to hark back to Shaviro's term. Deleuze concisely anticipated all of this, after Foucault, in his 'Postscript' (Deleuze 1992). The data that we provide just by carrying our digital devices or through our activity online is gathered and used to establish a pattern that predicts what we might do tomorrow; today, our individual and collective free actions are used to bring tomorrow's freedom within the limits of control. Patterns – established through the most advanced computer science – are used, for example, to predict market behaviour and guarantee trading profit.

Pollock, one may be surprised to hear, is part of the history of such patterning. Art historian Pamela Lee has drawn out, not in a direct way but by carefully mapping out Pollock's historical moment, his place in the history of contemporary algorithmic culture – the 'digital legacy', as she calls it, of the historical moment of which Pollock was very much a part (Lee 2017). In her work on 'Think Tank Aesthetics', Lee puts Pollock's painting, which Pollock himself situated entirely within the representational and not the abstract (Pollock rejected the term abstract expressionism, as Lee points out), in dialogue with a Cold War intellectual and military culture. Thus, she lays bare Pollock's role in what in another chapter of the same book project she calls 'the military-aesthetic complex' (Lee 2011: 29). Here, Pollock's non-chaotic painting becomes part of a Cold War obsession with patterning, with the deciphering of abstract form into representation so that, for example, enemy behaviour could be predicted (and it is, of course, Saunders who has most convincingly laid out abstract expressionism's tie to the Cold War and the CIA in particular; Eva Cockcroft had done as much already in 1974 (Cockroft 1985)). Lee finds the discourse on patterns and patterning in anthropology, and notes the government's interest in it around 1947. Pollock's painting and the discourse around it, she suggests, need to be read within the same context, with a methodological overlap between all three disciplines – anthropology, the military, and art. At stake in a Pollock are the very same issues that fascinate those other fields at the time. And those issues continue, Lee argues, all the way into today's digital age.

In other words, while Pollock may seem to be out of place in cultural representations of finance and AI at first sight, a closer historical look – which I have provided here via Lee's work – forces one to reconsider. As I have shown, 'the military-aesthetic complex' in which Lee situates Pollock is a 'financial' complex as well, with 'financial' crucially replacing here the adjective 'industrial' that Lee's use of the phrase 'the military-aesthetic complex' elides. To see this means to look at Pollock and the politics of control with which his work is historically associated through the lens of the M-M' (financial) cycle rather than the M-C-M' (industrial) cycle that I discussed in the first section of this chapter.

Such a 'dematerialised' reading of Pollock goes against the mythology that is usually constructed around him. As Saunders points out in 'Yanqui Doodles', the myth of Pollock is very much a 'material' one: 'Everything about Pollock was right. Born on a sheep ranch in Cody, Wyoming, he entered the New York scene like a cowboy – hard-talking, heavy-drinking, shooting his way from the Wild West' (Saunders 1999: 254). Saunders adds, however: 'This was, of course, a mythical past. Pollock had never ridden a horse, and had left Wyoming as a young child. But the image was so apt, so *American*, and no one disbelieved it' (1999: 254). Although echoes of this kind of masculinity continue in the financial era, the materiality of the image (which can be tied to Pollock's already mentioned insistence on representation versus abstraction when it came to the characterisation of his work) also stands in tension with the abstraction of finance – arguably in the same way that the abstraction of a figure like Bateman in Ellis's *American Psycho* stands in tension with the extreme (and splattered, one might add) materiality of Bateman's brutal murders.

The time seems to have finally come, then, to start 'disbelieving': it seems clear that Pollock's work participated in the abstract, dematerialised culture that the myth (as well as Pollock himself through how he talked about his work) sought to keep at bay. This may then be just one further irony of his role in the finance novel, but one that nevertheless needs to be taken seriously, as I have shown. The institutionalisation of Pollock as a monument in post-World War II art is inseparable from the contemporaneous replacement of a politics of discipline with a politics of control. Pollock's recurrent appearance in contemporary financial literature and film, as the very inspiration for the design of the algorithms that govern today's financial markets and, more generally speaking, control our lives, is an important reminder of this.

Notes

I hinted at the possibility of this chapter in De Boever 2018: 234n.34. Versions of this chapter were presented at: International Cultural Studies Certificate Program, University of Hawaii, Manoa, Spring 2018; Leonardo Art, Science and Technology Lectures, Beijing (Central Academy of Fine Arts) and Shanghai (Chronus Art Center), Autumn 2017; The Association for the Study of the Arts of the Present, University of California, Berkeley, Autumn 2017. I am grateful for the feedback I received from the audience on those occasions.

1. I am thinking here of Cristina Alger's *The Darlings* (2012), for example, or Adam Haslett's *Atlantic Union* (2010), John Lanchester's *Capital* (2012), Jess Walter's *The Financial Lives of the Poets* (2009), Jonathan Dee's *The Privileges* (2010), and Meg Wolitzer's *The Interestings* (2013).
2. In their 'Fictions of Speculation' special issue of the *Journal of American Studies*, McClanahan and Hamilton Carroll highlight the shift of financial/neoliberal fiction to genre fiction. Why this shift? They argue, convincingly I think, 'that the complex origins and calamitous effects of contemporary financialization have required the more capacious epistemologies available to so-called "genre fiction"'; in other words, 'genre fiction limns a more complex ontology, suggesting the correlation between the spectrally virtual and the intractably material that also characterizes our contemporary moment of late late capitalism'. In their special issue, it is 'speculative fiction' that emerges as something like the 'genre' of the financial and neoliberal age (Carroll and McClanahan 2015: 657).
3. The algorithms are not interested in the value of actual stocks; they are merely interested in buying and selling at a very high speed in order to profit from minimal differences in price (so-called arbitrage) or from fees that various markets award for buying or selling (fees that can amount to substantial sums if you manage to buy or sell hundreds of thousands of times per day, for many days).
4. On the association of these terms with finance, see La Berge 2014.
5. Reza Negarestani's 'Requiem for the Detective Novel' has explored the limits of the 'deductive' detective novel in this context, considering what other modes of reasoning detective novels might pursue (Negarestani 2016). As will be clear, such a critique of the detective novel would exceed what Ben Parker, in a perceptive reading of the Sherlock Holmes stories, calls 'the method effect': if, as per Parker's argument, none of the clues provided in a Holmes story enables Holmes' deductive method – they merely create the method effect, whereas the method in fact always relies on some outside clue not available to the reader or to Holmes's assistant, Watson – the critique of the detective

novel I hint at here radicalises that 'outside'. Had the realism been more realist in a Holmes story — i.e., had it represented all the details that Holmes saw — then the stories would really have been illustrations of the deductive method. The situation I am interested in, rather, is one in which all the details would have been provided, but without success for the deductive method. Reality escapes deduction (see Parker 2016).

6. This name is a clear nod to the character Patrick Bateman in Bret Easton Ellis's novel *American Psycho* (1991). Patrick Bateman's last name was in turn a clear nod to the last name of Norman Bates, the psychotic character in Alfred Hitchcock's celebrated film *Psycho*, based on Robert Bloch's novel with the same title (see the second chapter in De Boever 2018: 51–77).

7. Philosopher Catherine Malabou also comments on this in her book *Morphing Intelligence: From IQ Measurement to Artificial Brains* (Malabou 2019), which was not yet published at the time of writing this chapter and which is based on her Wellek Lectures at the University of California, Irvine. I would like to thank Catherine Malabou for allowing me to read this book ahead of its publication.

Bibliography

Alberro, Alexander (2003), *Conceptual Art and the Politics of Publicity*, Cambridge, MA: MIT Press.
Arrighi, Giovanni (1994), *The Long Twentieth Century*, London: Verso.
Ayache, Elie (2010), *The Blank Swan: The End of Probability*, Chichester: Wiley.
Beech, Dave (2016), *Art and Value: Art's Economic Exceptionalism in Classical, Neoclassical, and Marxist Economics*, Chicago: Haymarket.
Bontems, Vincent and Roland Lehoucq (2016), *Les idées noires de la physique*, Paris: Les Belles Lettres.
Britt, Ryan (2015), 'Ex Machina Writer/Director Alex Garland Talks Robots, Consciousness, and Jackson Pollock', *Electric Lit*, 7 May, <https://electricliterature.com/ex-machina-writer-director-alex-garland-talks-robots-consciousness-and-jackson-pollock-c631736a5efe> (last accessed 9 January 2019)
Carroll, Hamilton and Annie McClanahan (2015), 'Fictions of Speculation: Introduction', *Journal of American Studies*, 49:4, pp. 655–61.
Cetina, Kartin Knorr (2014), 'What If the Screens Went Black?', in Beate Geissler, Oliver Sann, and Brian Holmes (eds), *Volatile Smile*, Nuremberg: Moderne Kunst Nürnberg, pp. 112–27.
Cockcroft, Eva (1985), 'Abstract Expressionism, Weapon of the Cold War', in Francis Frascina (ed.), *Pollock and After: The Critical Debate*, New York: Harper and Row, pp. 125–33.
De Boever, Arne (2018), *Finance Fictions: Realism and Psychosis in a Time of Economic Crisis*, New York: Fordham University Press.
Deleuze, Gilles (1992), 'Postscript on the Societies of Control', *October*, 59, pp. 3–7.
Detrixhe, John (2017), 'Why Robort Traders Haven't Replaced All the Humans at the New York Stock Exchange – Yet', *Quartz*, 26 September, <https://qz.com/1078602/why-the-new-york-stock-exchange-nyse-still-has-human-brokers-on-the-trading-floor/> (last accessed 9 January 2019).
Ellis, Bret Easton (1991), *American Psycho*, New York: Vintage.
Foucault, Michel (1990), *The History of Sexuality, Vol. 1*, Robert Hurley (trans.), New York: Vintage.

Foucault, Michel (2008), *The Birth of Biopolitics: Lectures at the Collège de France 1978–1979*, Michel Senellart (ed.), Graham Burchell (trans.), New York: Palgrave Macmillan.
Garland, Alex (2013), *Ex Machina*, <https://www.slguardian.org/wp-content/uploads/2016/06/Ex-Machina.pdf> (last accessed 9 January 2019).
Greenspan, Alan (2013), *The Map and the Territory: Risk, Human Nature, and the Future of Forecasting*, New York: Penguin.
Hammond, Anna (1998), '"No Chaos, Dammit": An Interview with James Coddington, Chief Conservator', *MoMA*, 1:7, pp. 6–11.
Houellebecq, Michel (2012), *The Map and the Territory*, Gavin Bowd (trans.), New York: Knopf.
Houellebecq, Michel (2013), *La carte et le territoire*, Paris: J'ai Lu.
Jameson, Fredric (1991), *Postmodernism, or, The Cultural Logic of Late Capitalism*, Durham, NC: Duke University Press.
La Berge, Leigh Claire (2014), 'The Rules of Abstraction: Methods and Discourses of Finance', *Radical History Review*, 118, pp. 93–112.
La Berge, Leigh Claire (2015), *Scandals and Abstraction: Financial Fiction of the Long 1980s*, Oxford: Oxford University Press.
Lee, Pamela (2011), 'Aesthetic Strategist: Albert Wohlstetter, the Cold War, and a Theory of Mid-Century Modernism', *October*, 138, pp. 15–36.
Lee, Pamela (2017), 'Pattern Recognition c. 1947', WHAP!: West Hollywood Aesthetics and Politics Lecture Series, West Hollywood Library, 26 November.
McClanahan, Annie (2017), *Dead Pledges: Debt, Crisis, and Twenty-First-Century Culture*, Stanford: Stanford University Press.
Mackay, Robin (2016), 'Epistemology Noir', WHAP!: West Hollywood Aesthetics and Politics Lecture Series, West Hollywood Library, 10 November.
Malabou, Catherine (2019), *Morphing Intelligence: From IQ Measurement to Artificial Brains*, Carolyn Shread (trans.), New York: Columbia University Press.
Marx, Karl (1990), *Capital: A Critique of Political Economy, Vol. 1*, Ben Fowkes (trans.), London: Penguin.
Negarestani, Reza (2016), 'Requiem for the Detective Novel', Talk at Bijou Theater, California Institute of the Arts, 14 November.
Parker, Ben (2016), 'The Method Effect', *Novel*, 49:3, pp. 449–66.
Pasquale, Frank (2015), *The Black Box Society: The Secret Algorithms that Control Money and Information*, Cambridge, MA: Harvard University Press.
Patterson, Scott (2012), *Dark Pools: The Rise of the Machine Traders and the Rigging of the US Stock Market*, New York: Crown Business.
Popper, Nathaniel (2016), 'Computerized Trading Firm to Take Over Barclay's N.Y.S.E. Seats', *The New York Times*, 26 January, <https://www.nytimes.com/2016/01/27/business/dealbook/computerized-trading-firm-to-take-over-barclayss-nyse-seats.html> (last accessed 9 January 2019).
Roffe, Jon (2014), 'The Writing of the Market: Interview with Elie Ayache', *Collapse*, 8, pp. 517–602.
Rouvroy, Antoinette and Bernard Stiegler (2016), 'The Digital Regime of Truth: From the Algorithmic Governmentality to a New Rule of Law', Anaïs Nony and Benoît Dillet (trans.), *La Deleuziana: Online Journal of Philosophy*, 3, pp. 6–27, <http://www.ladeleuziana.org/wp-content/uploads/2016/12/Rouvroy-Stiegler_eng.pdf> (last accessed 9 January 2019).

Saunders, Frances Stonor (1999), *The Cultural Cold War: The CIA and the World of Arts and Letters*, New York: New Press.
Shaviro, Steven (2009), *Post-Cinematic Affect*, Winchester: Zero Books.
Shonkwiler, Alison (2017), *The Financial Imaginary: Economic Mystification and the Limits of Realist Fiction*, Minneapolis: University of Minnesota Press.
Sweeney, Carole (2010), '"And Yet Some Free Time Remains . . .": Post-Fordism and Writing in Michel Houellebecq's *Whatever*', *Journal of Modern Literature*, 33:4, pp. 41–56.
Taleb, Nassim Nicholas (2010), *The Black Swan: The Impact of the Highly Improbable*, New York: Random House.
Toscano, Alberto and Jeff Kinkle (2015), *Cartographies of the Absolute*, Winchester: Zero Books.
Vishmidt, Marina (2012), 'Speculation as a Mode of Production in Art and Capital', PhD thesis, School of Business and Management, Queen Mary University of London, <https://qmro.qmul.ac.uk/xmlui/bitstream/handle/123456789/8707/Vishmidt_M_PhD_Final.pdf?sequence=1> (last accessed 9 January 2019).
Wayne, Teddy (2010), *Kapitoil*, New York: Harper Perennial.
Weatherall, James Owen (2013), *The Physics of Wall Street*, New York: Houghton Mifflin Harcourt.
Williams, Jeffrey J. (2013), 'The Plutocratic Imagination', *Dissent*, <https://www.dissentmagazine.org/article/the-plutocratic-imagination> (last accessed 9 January 2019).
Wolfe, Tom (1987), *The Bonfire of the Vanities*, New York: Picador.
Wolfe, Tom (1989), 'Stalking the Billion-Footed Beast: A Literary Manifesto for the New Social Novel', *Harper's Magazine*, November, pp. 45–56.

Notes on Contributors

Ridvan Askin is Postdoctoral Teaching and Research Fellow in North American and General Literature at the University of Basel. He is the author of *Narrative and Becoming* (2016) and the co-editor of *Literature, Ethics, Morality: American Studies Perspectives* (2015), *The Aesthetics, Poetics, and Rhetoric of Soccer* (2018), and *Aesthetics in the 21st Century*, a special issue of *Speculations* (2014). He is also the translator of *Die Pinocchio Theorie* (2018), a collection of several of Steven Shaviro's essays.

R. Scott Bakker is a critically acclaimed novelist and independent scholar.

Frida Beckman is Professor of Comparative Literature at the Department of Culture and Aesthetics, Stockholm University. She has published on literature, philosophy, sex, and politics and is the author of *Between Desire and Pleasure: A Deleuzian Theory of Sexuality* (2013), *Culture Control Critique: Allegories of Reading the Present* (2016), and *Gilles Deleuze* (2017), as well as the editor of *Deleuze and Sex* (2011) and *Control Culture: Discipline after Foucault and Deleuze* (2018).

R. M. Berry is Emeritus Professor and former Chair of English at Florida State University. His books include the novels *Frank* (2006), an 'unwriting' of Mary Shelley's *Frankenstein*, and *Leonardo's Horse*, a *New York Times* 'notable book' of 1998, as well as two collections of short fiction. He edited the fiction anthology *Forms at War* (2009) and the critical anthology *Fiction's Present: Situating Contemporary Narrative Innovation* (2007), co-edited with Jeffrey Di Leo. His criticism has appeared in *New Literary History*, *Philosophy and Literature*, *Symploke*, *Narrative*, and *Soundings*, as well as in a range of edited volumes, including *The Oxford Handbook of Philosophy and Literature*.

Charlie Blake is currently Visiting Senior Lecturer in Media Ethics and Digital Culture at the University of West London. A founding and executive editor of *Angelaki: Journal of the Theoretical Humanities*, he has co-edited a variety of theory collections and published variously on Blanchot and music, Deleuze and angelic materialism, Bataille and divine dissipation, death and xenosonics, posthuman paranoia and art in the age of parasite capitalism, the topology of serial killing, and the greater politics of barnacles, bees, and werewolves. His most recent work involves an improvisation inspired by Voltaire, Leibniz, and the philosophy of addiction.

Astrid Bracke writes on twenty-first-century British fiction and nonfiction, ecocriticism and narratology, climate crisis and floods. Her monograph *Climate Crisis and the Twenty-First-Century British Novel* was published in 2018. Her work has appeared in *English Studies*, *ISLE*, and *The Oxford Handbook of Ecocriticism*. She is Lecturer in British Literature at HAN University of Applied Sciences, Nijmegen.

Rey Chow teaches at Duke University, where she is Anne Firor Scott Professor of Literature. She is the author of numerous monographs on literature, film, critical theory, and cultural politics, including *Entanglements, or Transmedial Thinking about Capture* (2012) and *Not Like a Native Speaker: On Languaging as a Postcolonial Experience* (2014). With James A. Steintrager, she is the co-editor of *Sound Objects* (2018). An elected fellow of the American Academy of Arts and Sciences, Chow is currently also Distinguished Visiting Professor in the School of Modern Languages and Cultures, University of Hong Kong. Her writings have appeared in a dozen languages.

Claire Colebrook is Edwin Erle Sparks Professor of English, Philosophy, and Women's and Gender Studies at Penn State University. She has written books and articles on contemporary European philosophy, literary history, gender studies, queer theory, visual culture, and feminist philosophy. Her most recent book is *Twilight of the Anthropocene Idols* (2016, co-authored with Tom Cohen and J. Hillis Miller).

Arne De Boever teaches American Studies in the School of Critical Studies at the California Institute of the Arts, where he also directs the MA Aesthetics and Politics programme. He is the author of *States of Exception in the Contemporary Novel* (2012), *Narrative Care* (2013), *Plastic Sovereignties* (2016), and *Finance Fictions* (2018). His new book *Against Aesthetic Exceptionalism* will be published in 2019.

Nicky Gardiner is a PhD candidate and Associate Lecturer in Literary Theory at the University of Huddersfield, where he is researching representations of the corpse in contemporary fiction. He received his Master's degree from the University of Amsterdam and was awarded a research grant by the AHRC in 2015 to pursue a PhD exploring the intersections between the corpse and new materialisms in contemporary fiction. His research interests include theories of embodiment, poststructuralism, and posthumanism in contemporary literature and theory.

Alison Gibbons is Reader in Contemporary Stylistics at Sheffield Hallam University. She is the author of *Multimodality, Cognition, and Experimental Literature* (2012) and co-editor of *Mark Z. Danielewski* (2011), *The Routledge Companion to Experimental Literature* (2012), *Metamodernism: Historicity, Affect, and Depth after Postmodernism* (2017), and *Pronouns in Literature: Positions and Perspectives in Language* (2018). She has published widely in international peer-reviewed journals, including *Ariel*, *Contemporary Literature*, *Metaphor in the Social World*, *Narrative*, and *Textual Practice*.

Evan Gottlieb is Professor of English at Oregon State University, where he teaches classes on romanticism and literary theory. His most recent book is *Romantic Realities: Speculative Realism and British Romanticism* (2016).

Graham Harman is Distinguished Professor of Philosophy at the Southern California Institute of Architecture. His most recent books are *Object-Oriented Ontology: A New Theory of Everything* (2018) and *Speculative Realism: An Introduction* (2018).

Birgit Mara Kaiser is Associate Professor of Comparative Literature and Transcultural Aesthetics at Utrecht University. She studied sociology and literature in Bochum, Bielefeld, Madrid, and London and holds a PhD in Comparative Literature from New York University. Her research spans literatures in English, French, and German from the late eighteenth to the twenty-first century, with a special interest in aesthetics, affect, and subject formation. She also publishes in the fields of postcolonial literary studies and feminist new materialism. She is founding coordinator of *Terra Critica*.

Ingeborg Löfgren received her PhD in Literary Studies from Uppsala University in 2015. She has Master's degrees in both Philosophy and Literary Studies from the same university. Drawing on the works of Stanley Cavell, her research traces scepticism within theories of literary interpretation, in particular within New Criticism. Currently, she is working on a postdoctoral project on the literary philosophy of the Swedish novelist and activist Sara Lidman (1923–2004) from the perspective of Ordinary Language Criticism.

Robert P. Marzec is Professor of Environmental and Postcolonial Studies in the Department of English at Purdue University. He is the author of *Militarizing the Environment: Climate Change and the Security Society* (2015) and *An Ecological and Postcolonial Study of Literature* (2007). He is the associate editor of *Modern Fiction Studies* and has published articles in *boundary 2*, *Radical History Review*, *Public Culture*, *Postmodern Culture*, and *Elementa: Science of the Anthropocene*.

Helen Palmer is a Senior Lecturer in English Literature and Creative Writing in the Department of Humanities at Kingston University London. She is the author of *Deleuze and Futurism: A Manifesto for Nonsense* (2014). She has recently published work on new materialism and interdisciplinary practice, Deleuze and *Alice in Wonderland*, and some poetry in the *Minnesota Review*. She is currently writing a book on defamiliarisation, new materialism, and queer theory, and a novel set in Blackpool called *Pleasure Beach*.

Adrian Parr is the Dean of the College of Architecture, Planning and Public Affairs at the University of Texas at Arlington in the Dallas-Fort Worth metroplex. She is a UNESCO water chair and the producer and co-director of the award-winning documentary *The Intimate Realities of Water*. Her most recent publication is *Birth of a New Earth: The Radical Politics of Environmentalism* (2017).

Graham Priest is Distinguished Professor of Philosophy at the Graduate Center, City University of New York, and Boyce Gibson Professor Emeritus at the University of Melbourne. He is known for his work on non-classical logic, particularly in connection with dialetheism, on metaphysics, on the history of philosophy, and on Buddhist philosophy. His books include: *In Contradiction*, *Beyond the Limits of Thought*, *Towards Non-Being*, *One*, and *The Fifth Corner of Four*. For further details, see grahampriest.net

David Rudrum is Senior Lecturer in English Literature at the University of Huddersfield. He has published widely on the relationship between philosophy and literature, in books such as *Literature and Philosophy: A Guide to Contemporary Debates* (edited, 2006), *Stanley Cavell and the Claim of Literature* (2014), and *Supplanting the Postmodern* (co-edited with Nicholas Stavris, 2015). He has published in journals including *Philosophy and Literature*, *Narrative*, and *Textual Practice*, and is currently writing a literary history of trolling before the invention of the Internet.

Babette B. Tischleder is Professor of North American Studies and Media Studies at the University of Göttingen. Her books include *The Literary Life of Things: Case Studies in American Fiction* (2014) and the co-edited volumes *Cultures of Obsolescence: History, Materiality, and the Digital Age* (2015) and *An Eclectic Bestiary: Encounters in a More-than-Human World* (2019). Her current work is concerned with the ways in which critical and creative practices may tackle the ecological troubles and endangered futures in our multi-species world.

Josh Toth is Associate Professor of English at MacEwan University. He is the author of *The Passing of Postmodernism: A Spectroanalysis of the Contemporary* (2010) and *Stranger America: A Narrative Ethics of Exclusion* (2018), and co-editor of *The Mourning After: Attending the Wake of Postmodernism* (2007) and *Polyvocal Bob Dylan: Music, Performance, Literature* (2019). He is currently writing a book on contemporary metafiction.

Robin van den Akker is Senior Lecturer in Continental Philosophy and Cultural Studies as well as the Head of the Humanities Department at Erasmus University College Rotterdam. He has written extensively on the digitisation of social space and social time and contemporary arts, culture, aesthetics, and politics. His work has been translated into various languages, including Mandarin, Russian, German, and Spanish. He is co-editor of the collection *Metamodernism: Historicity, Affect, and Depth* (2017) and is currently working on a book about metamodernist tendencies in contemporary architecture.

Timotheus Vermeulen is a scholar and critic. He is Associate Professor in Media, Culture and Society at the University of Oslo. His research interests include cultural theory, aesthetics, and close textual analysis of film, television, and contemporary art. His latest book is *Metamodernism: Historicity, Affect, and Depth after Postmodernism* (2017), co-edited with Alison Gibbons and Robin van den Akker. He is currently completing a book on measures of depth in contemporary visual art, and preparing a project on the use of fiction as a method for truth-telling in twenty-first-century culture, with the working title 'The Second Society'.

Bryan Vescio is Professor and Chair of English at High Point University. His literary criticism focuses on American writers from the late nineteenth century to the present, particularly Cormac McCarthy. His theoretical work applies insights from pragmatist philosophy and contemporary analytic philosophy of language to literary and aesthetic theory, attempting to define the role of literary study in higher education today. He is the author of *Reconstruction in Literary Studies: An Informalist Approach* (2014), and is working on a new collection of essays titled *Dreaming as Doing: Literature and the Humanities in a Practical Age*.

David Watson is an Associate Professor in the Department of English at Uppsala University, where he specialises in American literature and culture. He has published on nineteenth-century and modernist American poets, nineteenth-century and contemporary novelists, and issues in transnational and translation studies. Currently, he is completing a monograph on *The Security Sublime: Contingency and Vulnerability in Twenty-First-Century American Fiction*. His most recent research is on neoliberalism, finance, and the contemporary American novel, as well as nineteenth-century vernacular writing.

Index

actor-network theory
  de-hierarchised relational ontology, 176
  human/nonhuman actants, 179, 183
  Latourian actors, 176
  overview of, 175–6
  in relation to literary theory, 175, 183
  role of networks, 176
  role of the human in, 182–3
Adorno, Theodor, 12, 240
aesthetic formalism, 199–200
aesthetics
  application of intimationist aesthetic to Thoreau, 306, 309–10
  Emerson's relation between aesthetics and ethics, 242, 244–5
  Emerson's relation between metaphysics and aesthetics, 237–8, 240–1
  inferentionalist semantics as antidote to, 302
  intimationist aesthetics, 303–5
  Kantian concept of, 300, 306
  representational aesthetics, 290, 297–8, 299, 300
  Thoreau's sources of aesthetic value, 305–6
  universality of aesthetic judgements, 300–1
affect
  affectivity in the nonhuman, 108
  affects and percepts of art, 4, 14
  in autofiction, 50
  and co-emergent subjects, 107
  corporeal existence and affectivity, 105
  detachment of in writing, 9
  end of in postmodernism, 44–5
  language as material-affective, 108–9
  in modernist and postmodernist art, 45–6
  and moral reasoning, 7
  in *The Scream* (Munch), 45
  the singularity of, 12–13
  structures of feeling in modernist literary contexts, 46–7
  thinking, speaking, affecting and being affected, the interrelation of, 108–9, 111–15

Afrofuturism
  Black Panther (Coogler), 224
  Black Quantum Futurism Collective, 223
  'Contemplation' (Liburd), 221–2
  as example of worlding, 222–4
  function of the heteronym, 224
  myth-science concept, 225
  'Notes Toward a Theory of Quantum Blackness' (Samatar), 223
  Space Is the Place (Coney), 222–3, 229–30
  as uchronia, 221–3
  'Uchronia: The Unequivocal Interpretation of Reality' (Pozoga and Kirkley), 221
Agamben, Giorgio, 357
agential realism, 219–20, 221
aisthesis, 236, 240, 241, 243
Akker, Robin van den, 25, 28–9, 59, 60
altermodernism, 26, 27
Ammons, Elizabeth, 204
Amoore, Louise, 442–3, 445
analytic philosophy, 1–2, 13, 255
Anglo-American New Critics, 396–7, 398
Anglo-American philosophy, 255
Anstett, Jean-Jacques, 235
Anthropocene
  the accident thesis, 344–5
  anthropocentric patterns of thought, 24
  closed nature of the narrative of, 346–7
  concept of, 340
  delimitation of human/nonhuman, 108
  as exemplified by the Mississippi delta, 182
  fictocriticism as a new way of reading in, 371–3, 375–7
  Gaia figure and the Anthropocene moment, 183–8
  humankind's use of technology in, 340–1, 344–5
  indicators of, 187
  living in the end-time, 351
  magic-bullet solutions, 343, 351
  mass solutions, 350

Anthropocene (*cont.*)
  prehistory of climate change and, 317
  sacrifice of human and nonhuman species in, 318
  situating of in wider social contexts, 340
  widespread ecological decline, 338, 339–40, 357–8
  see also climate change; climate crisis flood novels
Aristotle, 153, 154, 155, 205, 368, 375, 417
Armstrong, Nancy, 422
Arquilla, John, 43–4
art/artworks
  and access to the transcendental layer, 235, 241–2, 245–6
  affect in modernist and postmodernist art, 45–6
  in *American Psycho* (Ellis), 454, 455
  art and abstract expressionism in financial fiction, 450, 454–7
  autonomy as an artistic problem, 280–4, 289–90
  autonomy of artworks in formalism, 202, 209, 210
  conceptual art and the financial era, 454
  the creation of affects and percepts, 4, 14
  environmental factors and experiences of, 202–3, 209, 211
  formalist criticism, 200
  the human in relation to the art-object, 201
  Kantian concept of beauty in, 199–200
  modernist art as politically significant, 289–90
  nonhuman art objects, 200
  representational aesthetics, 290, 297–8, 299, 300
  and the Romantic aesthetic experience, 236–7, 240, 241
  social contexts of, 198, 202
  theatricality in, 201, 202, 204, 207
  as transcendental empiricism, 241
  use of intimationist aesthetics for, 303, 307
  worlding and, 217
Attfield, Robin, 321–2, 325
Attridge, Derek, 103, 332
Atwood, Margaret, 220, 221; *see also Oryx and Crake* (Atwood); *The Year of the Flood* (Atwood)
Austin, J. L., 255, 259
authorship
  anti-intentionalism, 269–70
  authorial intentions in ordinary language criticism, 268–70
  authors as narrators in autofiction, 49–51
  bloggers, 24
  death of the author (Barthes), 23, 24, 25, 46
  intentionalism, 269–70
  the modern author figure, 25
  self-publishing, 25
  women authors, 208
  writing as bodily practice (*écriture féminine*), 105, 107–8

autofiction
  10:04 (Lerner), 49–50, 51
  affect in, 50
  genre of, 48–9
  Kapow! (Thirlwell), 50–1
automodernism
  concept of, 76, 86
  posthuman subjectivities and, 87
  term, 22, 24, 27
autonomy
  alliance with automation, 24, 76, 86, 87
  of artworks in formalism, 202, 209, 210
  concept of, 210
  in Kantian ethics, 200–1, 210
  of modernist literature, 279
  within object-oriented ontology (OOO), 200
  the problem of within modernism, 280–4, 289–90
  within virtual humanism, 87–92
  in Wallace Stevens's poetry, 291–5
Ayache, Elie, 227, 228, 452

Badiou, Alain, 4, 229
Baldwin, James, 204–7, 211
Barad, Karen, 176, 219–20, 221
Barth, John
  'Autobiography', 46–7
  'Lost in the Funhouse', 46–7, 49
Barthes, Roland
  death of the author, 23, 24, 25, 46
  on denotation, 400
  on illustration, 400–1
  use of the pictorial, 399
Baudrillard, Jean, 23, 25–6, 45
Beckett, Samuel, 396
  Endgame, 280–1, 282, 284–5, 290–1
  Waiting for Godot, 281
Beiser, Frederick, 134, 236
Bennett, Jane, 175, 234, 239, 241, 243, 244
Bergson, Henri, 2, 225, 226
Berlant, Lauren, 438–9
Best, Stephen, 425
biopolitics
  biopower and the novel/individual relationship, 422
  contingency in relation to, 435
  discourse formation and, 394–5
  Foucault's theory of, 391, 394, 420–1, 433, 460
  Foucault's theory of power, 420–1
  immunitary paradigm, 436
  language and literature in, 394, 395
  of literary criticism, 405–7
  paranoid responses to the transition to, 424–6
  risks to the species-body, 433, 460
  term, 394
  the turn to, 391

Black Quantum Futurism Collective, 223
Blake, William, 10–11
Blanchot, Maurice, 368–9
blogging, 24
Bohr, Niels, 219–20
Bontems, Vincent, 453–4
Borges, Jorge Luis, 227
Bourriaud, Nicolas, 26–7
Brandom, Robert, 297, 298–9, 301–3, 304–5, 310
Buell, Lawrence, 306, 329
Bush, George W., 26
Butler, Octavia, 222

Cafaro, Philip, 329
Calle-Gruber, Mireille, 105
capitalism
    challenge of representation of finance capitalism, 451–2
    as the cultural logic of postmodernism, 26
    'how' of contemporary markets, 451
    Marx's formula of, 450–1
    temporal fix of financialisation, 451
    see also neoliberalism
Carson, Rachel, 317
categorical imperative, 199
Cavell, Stanley
    on atonal compositions, 289
    the attunement of human beings, 286–8
    autonomy as an artistic problem, 280–4, 289–90
    on autonomy in Wallace Stevens's poetry, 291–5
    contrasted with Fredric Jameson, 280
    on Emerson, Ralph, 235, 256
    experiences of ordinariness, 285–6
    interpretative claims, 272, 273
    language and representations of collectivity, 284–5
    and ordinary language criticism, 235, 255, 256, 259, 260–1
    as a political philosopher, 284–5
    political significance of modernist art, 289–90
    presentness, 280
    reading of *Endgame* (Beckett), 280–1, 282, 284–5, 290–1
    reading of *King Lear*, 285–6, 287
    representation of suffering, 287–9
    on the turn back to the everyday, 3
Cervantes, Miguel de, 416
Chakrabarty, Dipesh, 340
Chandler, James, 134
Childish, Billy, 25, 27, 28
chronoplasticity, 376–7
Citton, Yves, 192
Cixous, Hélène
    Algeria and the notion of human subjectivity, 110
    con-temporaneous affect, decision and subject in *So Close*, 109–10, 111–15
    corporeal existence and affectivity, 105
    the feminine mode of subjectivity, 105–7
    human sentience, 105
    the human subject in, 103–4
    in/exclusions of otherness in *So Close*, 110–11
    intertextuality with Kleist, 112
    language as material and corporeal, 108–9
    literature of, 102
    nonhuman others, 108
    philosophical work, 102
    and the relation of philosophy and literature in the works of, 103
    So Close, 104, 109–15
    writing as bodily practice (*écriture féminine*), 105, 107–8
Clarke, Bruce, 185
climate change
    within ecocriticism, 322
    ethical issues of, 318, 321–2, 324–5
    ethics of population control, 329–30
    floods as symbols of, 321
    future thinking in environmentalist discourse, 328, 329
    geoengineering solutions to, 342–3
    human narratives as parochialist, 317–18
    intergenerational ethics of, 328–30
    narrative challenges of climate change, 318, 331–2
    philosophy's engagement with, 322–3
    prehistory of, 317
    solar energy as a solution for, 343
    threat to humankind, 32–3
climate crisis flood novels
    consolative role of narratives, 332
    escape from crisis in, 330
    ethical issues of climate change in, 322
    exceptionalism of the narrators, 324, 330–1
    the finiteness of narratives in, 331–2
    floods as symbols of climate change, 321
    future-oriented second-personalism, 326–8
    genre of, 321, 323
    mediated responsibilities in, 325
    narrative loss embodied in, 332–3
    narratives and knowledge, 332
    narratological challenges of, 322
    see also The Flood (Gee); *The Ship* (Honeywell); *When the Floods Came* (Morrall)
cognitive science, 145–6, 152–3
Colebrook, Claire, 317, 326, 330
Conant, James, 256, 261, 262, 263–71, 273–4
Connor, Steven, 22–3
continental philosophy, 2, 255–6
contingency
    definition of, 228
    in *Falling Man* (DeLillo), 446
    in the financial markets, 452

contingency (*cont.*)
   in *The Intuitionist* (Whitehead), 438–40
   literary heteronyms, 229
   Meillassoux, Quentin on, 131–2, 228, 434
   and neoliberalism, 431–8, 446
   and realist narrative, 437–8, 439
   role in narrative worlding, 228
   and strong correlationism, 131–2
   in *A Visit from the Goon Squad* (Egan), 442, 444–5
Cooper, Melinda, 437
corporeality
   being human and, 105
   language as material-affective, 108–9
   writing as bodily practice (*écriture féminine*), 105, 107–8
   see also embodiment
correlationism
   contingency and strong correlationism, 131–2
   critiques of, 124, 133
   definition of, 123
   hyper-Chaos, 132, 133
   idealism as strong correlationism, 128
   legacy of, 134–5
   limitations of, 124
   Meillassoux's identification of, 122, 123–4
   object-oriented philosophy and, 124, 128
   strong correlationism and knowledge of the external world, 130–1
   strong correlationism in Shelley's poetry, 128–31
   vitalism as strong correlationism, 128
   weak and strong forms of, 125, 128
   weak correlationism in Wordsworth's poetry, 126–8
Critchley, Simon, 28
critical posthumanism
   concept of, 75
   How We Became Posthuman (Hayles), 75, 76, 79–82
   re-embodiment in, 80
Crutzen, Paul, 317, 340
Cuboniks, Laboria, 225
Curtis, Adam, 34, 35
cyberspace
   alterity in, 78–9
   as anarchic space, 78
   dissemination of knowledge in, 74
   dissolution of subjectivity in, 78
   material disembodiment in, 79–82, 86–7
   as postmodern environment, 76, 77–8, 86–7
   as (post-)postmodern environment, 77
   presence/absence binary, 80
   term, 77

Dauber, Kenneth, 257, 260, 263, 270, 272
Davidson, Donald, 303, 304, 307
de Man, Paul, 10
Dean, Mitchell, 432–3
deconstructionism, 8, 13, 58, 61, 103
Defoe, Daniel, 414
Deleuze, Gilles
   on art and the Cosmos, 2, 4, 11, 13
   becoming-molecular, 243
   coefficient of collective paranoia, 413, 424
   critique of capital, 341
   the dividual, 424
   fabulation, 225, 375
   forms of power, 421
   miraculating machines, 370
   on philosophical and literary modes of thought, 8–9
   society of control, 460
   transcendental empiricism, 241
   use of the pictorial, 399
DeLillo, Don
   Falling Man, 445–6
   Point Omega, 431
Dennett, Daniel, 145
denotation, 400–2
depth
   depthiness in metamodern fiction, 50
   end of in postmodernism, 44–5, 50
   lack of in Wahol's images, 45
Derrida, Jacques
   on deconstruction, 8, 13, 58
   on modernity, 23, 29
   philosophy of impossibility, 10
   and the relation of philosophy and literature, 9, 14, 103
   use of graphs, 399
Descartes, René, 74, 414, 415–16, 418
detective fiction, 456–7
Dickens, Charles, 36–7
digimodernism, 25–6, 27, 28
digital technologies
   aesthetic of the apparently real, 25
   automodernism, 24, 27, 28, 76, 86, 87
   birth of the modern internet, 78–9
   digimodernism, 25–6, 27, 28
   and the dissemination of knowledge, 74
   mashups, 24
   'You Are Not Your Browser History' (Thorp), 31–2
Dillon, Michael, 435
discourse
   biopolitics and discourse formation, 394–5
   future thinking in environmentalist discourse, 328, 329
   neoliberal sustainability discourses, 338–9
   scientific discourse, 398–9
Dolar, Mladen, 401
Don Quixote (Cervantes), 416
dystopia, 220

ecocriticism
  narrative challenges of climate change, 331–2
  normative approach, 322
  objective approach, 322
  see also climate crisis flood novels
Egan, Jennifer *see A Visit from the Goon Squad* (Egan)
Eggers, David, 48, 376, 431
  The Circle, 418, 423, 431
Eliot, T. S.
  experiments with language, 396
  'The Hippopotamus', 303
  'The Love Song of J. Alfred Prufrock', 396
  and the relation of philosophy and literature, 1, 13
  use of denotation, 400
Ellis, Bret Easton, 454, 455
embodiment
  of digital grotesques in *Super Sad True Love Story* (Shteyngart), 77, 84–5
  dis/embodiment in *Super Sad True Love Story* (Shteyngart), 82, 92–3
  ethical challenges of climate change, 318
  material disembodiment in cyberspace, 79–82, 86–7
  metaphoric embodiments in *Super Sad True Love Story* (Shteyngart), 85–6
  posthumanist dis/embodiment, 79
  re-embodiment in critical posthumanism, 80
  the scopic human as the individualised embodiment of the accident, 345
  transhumanist dis/embodiment, 75
  in *A Visit from the Goon Squad* (Egan), 65
Emerson, Ralph Waldo
  aesthetics/ethics relationship, 242, 244–5
  aesthetics/metaphysics relationship, 237–8, 240–1
  aisthetic vision, 236, 240, 243
  anti-mentalism of, 239–40
  the essay form, 240
  ethical ideal of self-reliance, 236, 243–4
  idealism of, 236
  materialism/idealism relationship, 238–9, 242
  'Nature', 237–8
  'The Over-Soul', 245
  'The Poet', 242
  romanticism of, 236
  'Self-Reliance', 243–4
  as speculative pragmatist, 235, 246
  transcendentalism of, 234, 235–6, 241–2, 245–6
  'The Transcendentalist', 238, 240
  in the works of Stanley Cavell, 235, 256
emotions
  emotional investment in artworks, 208–9
  as feminine, 207–8
  love and passion in ethical philosophy, 200–1
  sentimentality as a bad emotion, 204, 206–7
the Enlightenment, 6, 7, 23, 27, 35, 339, 343
Eshelman, Raoul, 59, 60

Eshun, Kodwo, 229–30
Esposito, Elena, 435
Esposito, Roberto, 436
Esslin, Martin, 280
ethical philosophy
  autonomy, concept of, 210
  categorical imperative, 199
  challenges of climate change, 318
  Emerson's aesthetics/ethics relationship, 244–5
  Emerson's ethical ideal of self-reliance, 236, 243–4
  ethical issues of climate change, 318, 321–2, 324–5
  ethics of love/passion, 200–1
  intergenerational ethics, 328–30
  Kantian concept of, 199, 200
  mediated responsibilities, 325
  separation of experience and desire, 7
existence
  Kantian concept of, 143
  properties of non-existent objects, 144–5
  the quantifier 'some', 142
  the verb 'exists', 142–3
extremism, 26

fabulation, 225–7, 370, 375
Faflik, David, 306, 308–9
Falling Man (DeLillo), 445–6
Fang, Lai Tze, 82
Farrell, John, 416, 417
Faulkner, William
  human/nonhuman actants, 193–4
  'Mississippi', 180–2
Felski, Rita, 183, 410–11
fictional objects
  causation and unity, 147–8
  Faulkner's 'Mississippi', 180–2
  fictional names that do not refer, 139–41
  fictional names that refer to existent objects, 141–2
  fictional names that refer to non-existent objects, 142–3
  the illusion of self, 148–9
  multiple drafts of the narrative self, 145–6
  names in fiction, 138–9
  principle of the difference of discernibles and, 139
  properties of, 144–5
  the self as a collection of perceptions, 146–7
  the self in Buddhist philosophy, 145
fictocriticism
  contemporary genealogy of, 374–5
  Cyclonopedia (Negarestani), 373–4
  and the notion of the Anthropocene, 371–3, 375–7
  overview of, 216–17

finance novels
  American Psycho (Ellis), 254, 455
  art in, 454–7
  challenge of representation in, 451–2
  conceptual art and the financial era, 454
  cosmic imagery for financial realities, 452–4
  financial imaginary of, 430
  The Map and the Territory (Houellebecq), 455–7
  neoliberalism and narrative realism, 430–1
  politics of algorithmic control, 450, 457–8, 460–1
  realism in, 451–2, 455–7
  role of art and abstract expressionism, 446
The Flood (Gee)
  first-person narrative perspective, 326–8
  privileged narrators of, 324
  role of book narratives, 332
  separation of the haves and the have-nots, 325
  temporal setting, 323
Fokkema, Aleid, 46
formalism
  aesthetic formalism, 199–200
  artwork's environmental factors and experiences of, 202–3, 209, 211
  definition of, 12, 198
  holism in, 201–2, 206, 211
  James Baldwin's critique of *Uncle Tom's Cabin* (Stowe), 204–7
  Kantian, 199
  separation of the human and the other, 200–1, 211
Forster, Michael N., 299
Foucault, Michel
  biopolitical theory, 391, 394, 420–1, 433, 460
  the disappearance of man, 23, 24
  historical mutation of language, 397–8
  on knowledge production, 398–9
  the rise of *ordo-* and neoliberalism, 430
  separation of truth from language, 4
  theory of disciplinary power, 419–20
Franzen, Jonathan, 430
Freitas, Elizabeth de, 226–7
Freud, Sigmund, 106, 412
Fried, Michael, 200, 201, 202, 204, 207
Fukuyama, Francis, 43
Funk, Robert, 66, 67
Furtak, Rick, 306, 309

Gaia project
  and the Anthropocene moment, 183–8
  as an autopoietic system, 185
  comprehension of through literary agency, 192–3
  conundrum of defining Earth, 185–6
  the Gaia figure, 183–4
  geo-agents, 189–90
  geological impact of humans, 187–8
  Latour's political ecology, 182
  narratological terms for, 188–9, 191
  overview of, 179–80
  science/humanities division and, 187
  the sublunary world contrasted with the Galilean view, 179, 183, 184–5, 187
Garland, Alex, *Ex Machina*, 458–9
Garrard, Greg, 329, 331
Gee, Maggie *see The Flood* (Gee)
Ghosh, Amitav, 357, 358
Gibson, William, 77
globalisation, 192–3
Goodman, Russel B., 235
Gottlieb, Evan, 234
Graham, Stephen, 433
Grausam, Daniel, 440
Greenberg, Clement, 200, 202
Greimas, Algirdas Julien, 188, 189, 190
Grewal, Inderpal, 433
Guattari, Félix
  on art and the Cosmos, 2, 4, 11, 13
  becoming-molecular, 243
  coefficient of collective paranoia, 413, 424
  critique of capital, 341
  fabulation, 225
  miraculating machine, 370
  on philosophical and literary modes of thought, 9

Habermas, Jürgen, 4, 7, 28, 57
Hall, Stuart, 43
Hansen, Olaf, 306
Haraway, Donna
  Terrapolis, 218, 219, 229
  worlding concept, 218–19, 225
Hardin, Garrett, 329
Harman, Graham, 124, 128, 133, 175, 176, 234
Hartmann, Franz, 152
Harvey, David, 451
Hassan, Ihab, 19, 74
Hawthorne, Nathaniel, 208
Hayek, Friedrich August, 434–5
Hayles, N. Katherine, 75, 76, 79–82, 88, 91, 439
Hegel, Georg Wilhelm Friedrich
  the classical, 64
  the Hegelian romantic, 69
  return to in post-postmodernism, 60–2
  the symbolic, 62–5
Heidegger, Martin
  grammatical iterations, 217
  on poetic language, 396
  relation of philosophy and literature, 4
  use of graphs, 399
Heise, Ursula, 331
Heraclitus, 376
Herman, David, 326

heteronymy
    in Afrofuturism, 224
    literary heteronyms, 229
    Terrapolis, 218, 219, 229
    in worlding, 227–8, 229–30
heuristics
    automaticity of application, 158
    dynamic vulnerability of, 165–6
    heuristic theory of meaning, 159–62
    selective consumption of, 158
    systematic nature of putative misapplications, 158
    visual cognition, 157–8, 162
Hirst, Damien, 455
historicity
    abstract models for literary history, 403–4
    end of in postmodernism, 44–5
    historical mutation of language, 397–8
    historicisation of close reading, 403
    in metamodern fiction, 51
history
    a bend of History, 43–4
    The End of History, 43
    re-start of, 43–4
Hobbes, Thomas, 416–17, 419
holism, 201–2, 206, 211
Honeywell, Antonia *see The Ship* (Honeywell)
Houellebecq, Michel, 455–7
human subjectivity
    Cartesian 'I', 74, 108–9
    Cixous's experiences of colonial violence in Algeria, 110
    co-emergent subjects, 107
    control and the humanist subject, 423–4
    corporeal existence and affectivity, 105
    dissolution of in cyberspace, 78
    the dividual, 421–2, 423–4
    the feminine mode of, 105–7
    fragmentation of in postmodernist fiction, 46–7
    in Hélène Cixous's work, 103–4
    holistic forms of human subjectivity, 339, 341
    intentional mediocrity and human's fundamental nature, 154–5
    Lacanian paranoia as fundamental for, 413
    within metaphysics, 99–100
    normalised form of Anthropocene human subjectivity in *Solar* (McEwan), 338
    paranoid schizoid position, 412–13
    post-Cartesian subject, 415–16, 418
    posthuman subjectivities, 87, 103–4
    within poststructuralism, 99
    theory of disciplinary control, 419–20
    thinking, speaking, affecting and being affected, the interrelation of, 108–9, 111–15
    transcendental, 3
    see also the self

humanism
    the Cartesian subject, 74, 108–9
    parochialism of in relation to climate change, 317–18
    reconciliation of technological advancement within, 88
    the Subject, 104, 107, 108
    see also critical posthumanism; posthumanism; virtual humanism
Hume, David, 146
Hume's problem, 122
Hunter, Megan, 332–3
Husserl, Edmund, 1–2, 3, 13
Hutcheon, Linda, 19, 47, 48, 58
hyperindividualism, 24, 28, 58
hypermodernism, 27, 28, 42, 57
hyperstition, 224–5

idealism
    of Emerson, Ralph, 236
    fusion with the real in romanticism, 234–5
    materialism/idealism relationship, 238–9, 242
    strong correlationism as, 128
identity *see* the self
inferentionalist semantics, 301–3
intergenerational ethics, 328–30
intimationist aesthetics, 303–5, 307
The Intuitionist (Whitehead)
    computational theory in, 439
    engagement with contingency, 438–40
    genre of, 439
    narrative of, 438
    temporal setting of, 440
Irigaray, Luce, 12

James, David, 48, 62
Jameson, Fredric
    autonomy in modernism, 281–2
    on autonomy in Wallace Stevens' poetry, 291–5
    cognitive maps, 45
    the contingent and realism, 437–8, 439
    contrasted with Stanley Cavell, 280
    on the cultural logic of capitalism, 451
    depthlessness, 50
    dialectical criticism, 279–80
    late capitalism and postmodernism, 26
    mediated version of Marxism, 281
    modernism's inward turn, 282–3
    the '1960s' transitional period, 43
    non-political aesthetic ideology of modernism, 280
    on postmodernism, 28, 44–5, 452
    representation in modern art, 290
    singular modernity, term, 22
    use of the pictorial, 399

Johnson, Rochelle L., 306, 307–8, 309
Jost, Walter, 257, 260, 263, 270, 272
Joyce, James, 9–10, 63, 281, 396

Kafka, Franz, 370
Kant, Immanuel
  aesthetics of, 298, 300, 306
  on the beautiful and the sublime, 199–200
  ethical outlook, 199, 200
  on existence, 143
  formalism and, 199
  influence on British romantics, 122, 125
  the problem of theory, 6–7, 10, 11, 13–14
  project of critique, 100
  role of language in human thought, 299
  strong correlationism's rejection of, 125
  transcendental schema, 122, 123
  universality of aesthetic judgements, 300–1
Kapitoil (Wayne), 430, 457–8
Kerridge, Richard, 331
Kirby, Vicki, 25, 27, 28, 107
Kirkley, Christopher, 221
Klein, Melanie, 412
Kleist, Heinrich von, 112
Kneller, Jane, 236
knowledge
  digital technologies and the dissemination of knowledge, 74
  Kantian theoretical knowledge, 6–7, 10, 11, 13–14
  knowledge production, 398–9
  literature as not a form of (paradox), 205
  narratives and knowledge in climate crisis novels, 332
Kobek, Jarett, 376
Konings, Martijn, 436–7
Koons, Jeff, 455
Kristeva, Julia, 5, 63, 105

Lacan, Jacques
  Cixous's critique of, 106
  interest in topology, 401
  on paranoia, 413
  use of the pictorial, 399
language
  anti-representational conceptions of, 298–9
  as data in *Super Sad True Love Story* (Shteyngart), 82, 85, 91–2
  denotation, 400–2
  digital mediation of language, 84–5
  dislocation of in postmodernism, 395–7
  distant reading via diagrammatic denotation, 403–6
  effect of sensibilism on, 299
  everyday language practices, 3
  Foucault on the historical mutation of, 397–8
  genotexts, 63
  Heidegger's grammatical iterations, 217
  historicist perspective, 304–5, 310
  for immediate aesthetic judgements, 300
  inferentionalist semantics, 301–3
  an intimationist aesthetic and, 309–10
  for knowledge production, 398–9
  linguist practices from the pragmatist view, 304–5
  linguistic meaning as social practice, 297
  as material-affective, 108–9, 218
  naturalist perspective, 304–5, 310
  phenotexts, 63
  poetic language, 396–7, 398
  replacement of by the pictorial, 399–402
  representationalist theory of language, 298
  role of in thought (Kant), 299
  T-ing communication (*A Visit from the Goon Squad*), 62–4
  truth's separation from, 5
  world-function of, 217–18
  see also ordinary language philosophy
Latour, Bruno
  actor-network theory, 175
  concept of nonhuman agency, 189
  focus on narrative, 182, 186, 188–9, 191
  on postmodernism, 33–4
  science/humanities division, 186–7
  on the separation of reason, 7
  significance of the Mississippi delta, 182, 189–92
  use of literary examples, 186
  see also the Gaia project
Le Guin, Ursula, 230
Lee, Pamela, 450, 460–1
Lehoucq, Roland, 453–4
Lerner, Ben, *10:04*, 49–50, 51, 431
Levinas, Emmanuel, 55, 58–9, 70
Lévi-Strauss, Claude, 399
Lewis, Michael Jay, 228
Liburd, Tonya, 221–2
Lipovetsky, Gilles, 24, 27–8, 57
literary agency
  definition of, 180, 194–5
  and the Gaia project, 192–3
  in the interstices of texts, 182
  of the Mississippi for Latour, 191–2
  and the nature of nonhuman actants, 194
literary criticism
  abstract models for literary history, 403–4
  the biopolitics of, 405–7
  criteria of timelessness, 1–3
  critique of close reading, 403, 405
  database compilation, 406
  distant reading via diagrammatic denotation, 403–6
  interpretative claims, 272–4

modes of reading, re-evaluation of, 410–11, 425
neoliberalism as an analytical category for contemporary US fiction, 429–30, 445
ordinary language philosophy within, 255–6
the political in, 391–2
in the 21st century, 402–3, 405
use of representational metaphor, 305
see also ordinary language criticism (OLC); paranoid reading
literature
as aesthetic experience in romanticism, 236–7, 241
becoming through, 9
centrality of the individual in the novel, 414–15, 417–18, 420, 422–3
climate crisis's challenge to, 331–2
control and the humanist subject, 423–4
disciplinary control in the novel, 422, 423, 424
disciplinary power and the novel, 419–20
emergence of, 8
the essay form, 240
formalist criticism, 200
geological temporality in, 318
global publishing markets, 406
industrialisation and the novel, 419–20
literary texts as agents of worlding, 180–2
literature and language in the biopolitical, 394, 395
metamodernism in, 47–50
modernist, 9–10, 279
the political in, 391
and the predicament of theory, 10
the question of literature, 153
relationship with philosophy, 1, 3–4, 5–6, 8–9, 13–14, 103, 418
security imaginary, 431
separation of philosophy and literature, 4–5, 7–8, 12–13
shift from fiction to 'real-life', 220–1
as symbiosis, 211–12
use of intimationist aesthetics for, 303, 307
in a web-addicted world, 376
Lobo-Guerrero, Luis, 435
Locke, John, 416–17
logical purity, 1
Lovelock, James, 183, 184, 185, 186, 188
Lukács, Georg, 280, 281, 290
Lyotard, Jean-François
on grand narratives, 23, 26
micronarratives, 28, 34
the postmodern condition, 31, 57, 75, 396
the world-function of language, 217–18

McCarthy, Tom, *Satin Island*, 30–1
McEwan, Ian *see Solar* (McEwan)
McGowan, John, 23

MacIntyre, Alasdair, 7
Mackay, Robin, 228
McLaughlin, Robert L., 47
Macpherson, C. B., 414, 416–17
Madsen, Michael, *Into Eternity*, 33
Malabou, Catherine, 61
Marcus, Sharon, 425
Margulis, Lynn, 211–12
Marx, Karl, 280, 288, 450–1
mashups, 24
materialism
ecstatic materialism, 239
materialism/idealism relationship, 238–9, 242
see also new materialisms
materiality
disembodiment of corporeal materiality, 79–82, 86–7
as a doing, 219–20
of language, 108–9, 218
the material-semiotic, 218, 221, 224, 227, 228
Matthiessen, F. O., 305, 309
Mazzoni, Guido, 414
meaning
deep information questions, 163–4
heuristic theory of meaning, 159–62
within human social cognition, 159
inexplicable properties of intentional phenomena, 154–5
meaning-talk as ecological, 162–3
practical meaning, 165–6
shallow information questions, 163, 165
systematic self-deception and, 160–2
theoretical meaning, death of, 164–5
theory of, 166–7
truth and meaning in *A Visit from the Goon Squad* (Egan), 56–7
mediocrity
exceptionalist critique of, 159–60
intentional mediocrity and human nature, 154–5
as reductive, 156–7
as scientistic, 156
as self-contradictory, 156
Meillassoux, Quentin
After Finitude, 122, 123, 124–5, 128, 131, 132–3
the arche-fossil example, 124
on contingency, 131–2, 228, 434
facticity, 131
and the great outdoors, 122, 123, 244
hyper-Chaos, 132, 133
identification of correlationism, 122, 123–4
L'Inexistence Divine, 122, 133
strong correlationism and the external world, 130–1
a 'World of justice', 133
see also correlationism

mentalism, 239–40
metafiction
  historioplastic metafiction, 61–2
  as neo-romantic, 65, 68
  postmodernist strategies of, 58
metamodernism
  concept of, 41–3
  cultural logic of, 41, 42, 43
  donkey-and-carrot double-bind metaphor, 29
  in literature, 47–50
  neo-romantic values and, 25, 27, 28, 62
  Notes on Metamodernism platform, 42
  oscillations in, 48, 59, 60
  shift from postmodern to, 43
  structure of feeling, 44
  temporal orientations, 51, 52
  see also autofiction
metaphor
  donkey-and-carrot double-bind metaphor, 29
  effects of in Davidson's theory of, 303–4
  intimationist aesthetics through, 303, 305, 307
  removal of metaphor from the model of representation, 297, 303–4, 307–8
  in Thoreau's *Walden*, 306–7, 308
metaphysics
  human subjectivity and, 99–100
  Wittgenstein's ordinary in contrast to, 264
Millennium Ecosystem Assessment (MA) Scenarios, 348
Miller, D. A., 420
Milton, John, 8
'Mississippi' (Faulkner), 180–2
modernism
  absence in, 64
  demise of and advent of postmodernism, 22–7
  disparate views of new modernism, 27–9
  from the Enlightenment, 23, 27
  idea of unity, 9
  inward turn of, 282–3
  Jameson, Fredric on, 22, 281–3
  literature, 9–10, 279
  modernist art as politically significant, 289–90
  multiplicity of new modernisms, 27
  postmodern rupture of, 23–4
  the problem of autonomy in, 280–4, 289–90
  relativity, 10
  return of, 22
  structures of feeling in literary contexts, 46
  universality in, 11
Moi, Toril, 259
Monáe, Janelle, 224
monism, 57
Moraru, Christian, 48
Moretti, Franco, 402, 403–5, 411
Morrall, Clare *see When the Floods Came* (Morrall)
Morton, Timothy, 175, 234

Muecke, Stephen, 216, 217
Mulgan, Tim, 326–7, 328
Munch, Edvard, *The Scream*, 45–6
Murphy, Timothy S., 47
myth-making, 225

Nadler, Steven, 416
Nancy, Jean-Luc, 66
narratives
  authors as narrators in autofiction, 49–51
  in climate crisis flood novels, 322, 326–33
  consolative role of narratives in crisis, 332
  contingency and realist narratives, 437–8, 439
  contingency's role in narrative worlding, 228
  metanarratives of postmodernism, 396–7
  micronarratives of postmodernism, 28, 34
  multiple drafts of the narrative self, 145–6
  narrative perspective and focalisation, 326
  neoliberalism and narrative realism, 430–1
  parochialism of in relation to climate change, 317–18
  proleptic narratives, 444–5
  recourse to grand narratives, 23, 26
narratology
  as creative and speculative, 226
  future-oriented second-personalism, 326–8
  of Latour's Gaia Project, 188–9, 191
Nealon, Jeffrey T., 26, 57
Negarestani, Reza, 373–4
neoliberalism
  as analytical category for contemporary US fiction, 429–30, 445
  as an assemblage of economic and security logics, 433–4
  and the finance novel, 430–1
  Foucault's concept of, 430
  geopolitics of in *The Stone Gods* (Winterson), 352, 353
  and the immunitary paradigm, 436
  impact on human activities, 340
  the logic of in *A Visit from the Good Squad* (Egan), 440–2
  as a plurality, 432
  in relation to risk, uncertainty and contingency, 431–5
  relation with contingency, 434–8, 446
  relation with security and risk, 433–4, 436–7
  and the self-reflexive risk society, 434
  speculative logic of, 436–7
  sustainability discourses of, 338–9
  under Trump's presidency, 446
New Historicism, 208
new materialisms
  the materiality of language, 218
  as new idealisms, 234

notion of matter, 176
overview of, 176
and a *reductio* of the academic field, 215–16
in relation to literary theory, 175
vital materialism, 176, 234, 239, 241
Nineteen Eighty-Four (Orwell)
Conant's reading of Rorty and Orwell, 263–4
concept of objective truth in, 262–3, 264, 265–6, 267, 268, 270–1
cruelty and violence in, 262, 263, 265–6
intellectual implication of totalitarianism, 266–7
Orwell's authorial intentions, 269–70
realist readings of, 262, 264, 268, 269
nonhuman others
affectivity in, 108
as agents of change, 193–4
human/nonhuman actants in actor-network theory, 179, 183
Latourian concept of nonhuman agency, 189
nonhuman agency, 180–2
nonhuman art objects, 200
in relation to the human for Emerson, Ralph, 239–40
sacrifice of in the Anthropocene, 318
Norris, Andrew, 284
Nussbaum, Martha, 4, 7

object-oriented ontology (OOO)
aesthetic formalism and, 199–200
aesthetic involvement, 209
artwork's environmental factors and experiences of, 202–3, 209, 211
autonomy within, 200
defence of sentimentality, 208, 210
duomining, 198, 205
formalism's holism, 201–2, 206, 211
formalism's separation of the human and the other, 200–1, 211
freedom, 206
the human in relation to the art-object, 201
overmining, 198, 205
protest novels as overmining, 205
the term 'object', 198
truth, 206
undermining, 198, 205
object-oriented philosophy
correlationism and, 124, 128
Harmanian objects, 176
nonrelational ontology, 176
overview of, 176
in relation to literary theory, 175
O'Brien, Flann, 226
Ockham's Razor, 147
'Oh dearism', 34
O'Malley, Pat, 432–3

ordinary language criticism (OLC)
authorial intentions, 268–70
Conant's reading of Rorty and Orwell, 263–4
concept of, 258–61
interaction between philosophy/theory and literature, 260–1, 263–5, 268–9, 270–2
interpretative conflict between Rorty and Conant, 258, 261–71, 273–4
risk of reading-in, 273
role of the literary critic, 274
similarities with close reading, 261
theorisation from inside the text, 265–6, 270
understanding of 'the ordinary', 264–5
the undoing of reading through philosophy, 263–4
ordinary language philosophy
concept of, 256, 259, 260
within literary criticism, 255–6
tradition of, 255
Orwell, George *see Nineteen Eighty-Four* (Orwell)
Oryx and Crake (Atwood)
Anthropocene narratives in, 350–1
Crake's teleologically sequential intelligence, 348–50
mass genetic engineering, 339, 350–1
more holistic forms of human subjectivity, 341
narrative loss embodied in, 332
security-driven intelligence, 349
social systems in, 347–8
O'Sullivan, Simon, 225

paradox, 205
paranoia
centrality of the individual in the novel, 414–15, 417–18
coefficient of collective paranoia, 413–14, 424
epistemological paranoia, 417–18
Freud's understanding of, 412
of the individual or group, 422
and individuation, 412–14, 424
Lacanian revisioning of, 413
ontological paranoia, 417–18
of possessive individualism, 417
and the post-Cartesian subject, 416
as projection, 412
of the reader, 418–19
responses to the transition of biopolitics, 424–6
and the rise of the modern, 411–13
paranoid reading
and changing biopolitical responses, 425–6
ecological view of, 426
hermeneutics of suspicion, 411, 425
influence on critical theory, 410
rigid temporality of, 423–4
Parisi, Luciana, 225
performatism, 59, 60
Perloff, Marjorie, 255

Pessoa, Fernando, 229
phallogocentrism, 59, 104, 105
philosophy
    everyday, the turn back to, 3
    and the predicament of theory, 10
    relationship with literature, 1, 3–4, 5–6, 8–9, 13–14, 103, 418
    separation of philosophy and literature, 4–5, 7–8, 12–13
Picasso, Pablo, 198, 202
Plato, 368, 369
poetry
    autonomy in Wallace Stevens's poetry, 291–5
    poetic language, 396–7, 398
    poetry/philosophy tension, 368–70
    as separate from philosophy, 5
    T. S. Eliot's conception of, 1
    see also romantic poets
Poirier, Richard, 235
the political
    in literature, 391–2
    non-political aesthetic ideology of modernism, 280
    politics of algorithmic control, 450, 457–8, 460–1
    theory of disciplinary control, 391, 419–22
    see also biopolitics
Pollock, Jackson
    art of in financial fiction, 450
    automatic art of, 458–9
    in *Kapitoil* (Wayne), 457–8
    left-wing politics of, 459–60
    in *The Map and the Territory* (Houellebecq), 457
    within the military-aesthetic complex, 460–1
    myth of, 461–2
    No. 5, 1948, 458–9
    technique of, 457, 458, 459
polymodernism
    aporias, 29
    cluelessness of, 28–34, 35, 36
    Dickens as polymodernist novelist, 36–7
    as post-truth epoch, 34–7
    term, 28
    transition from postmodernism to, 35–6
post-apocalyptic literature
    futurity in, 328, 330–1
    survival of humanity and humankind, 326
    techno-optimism and humanity's survival, 330
posthumanism
    critical posthumanism, 75, 79–82
    disembodiment of corporeal materiality, 79–82, 86–7
    emergence of, 74–5
    in relation to postmodernism, 75–6
    subjectivities, 87, 103–4

postmodernism
    the absent Thing, 64
    aporias, 29
    the body as linguistic construction, 80
    as cultural logic of late capitalism, 26
    debates over Western culture, 23–4
    demise of, 19, 22, 47, 48
    dislocation of language in, 395–7
    end of historicity, 44–5
    fragmentation of human subjectivity, 46–7
    impact of digital technologies on, 24, 25–6
    informational decontextualisation, 80–2
    Jameson, Fredric on, 28, 44–5, 452
    metanarratives of, 396–7
    micronarratives, 28, 34
    pattern/randomness binary, 80
    the 'real' of, 25–6
    recourse to grand narratives, 23, 26
    recursiveness, 49, 50–1, 67–8
    in relation to posthumanism, 75–6
    shift to metamodernism, 43
    societal victory of, 57–8, 59
    term, 22
    use of graphs and diagrams, 399–402
    as the vanquisher of modernism, 22–7
postmodernist fiction
    disembodiment in, 80
    fiction within the fiction, 49
    fragmented subjectivity in, 46–7
    metafictional strategies of, 58
    representation of the Real, 58–9
post-postmodernism
    aesthetic of, 59–60
    historioplastic metafiction, 61–2
    return to Hegel in, 60–2
poststructuralism
    human subjectivity and, 99
    the relation of 'literature' and 'philosophy', 103
Pozoga, Maciek, 221
pretence
    to counter against postmodernism, 59
    and the fictional object, 139–40
Price, Seth, 374, 375–6
protest novels, 204–5, 206
psychoanalysis, 105–6
Pulford, James, 51

Quine, Willard, 142–3

Rancière, Jacques, 358
realism
    agential realism, 219–20, 222
    The Bonfire of the Vanities (Wolfe), 452
    contingency and realist narratives, 437–8, 439
    in finance novels, 451–2, 455–7
    fusion with the ideal in romanticism, 234–5

realist readings of *Nineteen Eighty-Four* (Orwell), 262, 264, 268, 269
speculative realism, 234
reality
  aesthetic of the apparently real, 25, 60
  replacement with hyperreality, 45
reason
  inscription and, 10
  separation from lived practice, 6–8
  separation from the imagination, 8
  theoretical knowledge and, 6–7
remodernism, 25, 27, 28
Renner, Karen, 330
representation
  inferentionalist semantics as antidote to, 301–3
  of the Real in postmodernist fiction, 58–9
  removal of metaphor from the model of representation, 297, 303–4, 307–8
  representational aesthetics, 290, 297–8, 299, 300
  representational challenges of climate change, 318, 331–2
  representationalist theory of language, 298, 396
  in the Western philosophical imagination, 297, 301, 305
Robbins, Bruce, 444
Roden, David, 76
romantic poets
  Kant's influence on, 122, 125
  re-birth, theme of, 133–4
  strong correlationism in the work of, 125, 128
  weak correlationism in the work of, 126–8
  see also Shelley, Percy; Wordsworth, William
romanticism
  aisthetic vision, 236, 240, 241, 243
  art and literature and the aesthetic experience, 236–7, 241
  claim of the universal and, 10–11
  contemporary relevance of, 234
  of Emerson, Ralph, 236
  fusion of the ideal with the real, 234–5
  importance of intuition, 236
  neo-romantic metafiction, 65, 68
  neo-romantic values in metamodernism, 25, 27, 28, 62
  and the speculative turn, 234
  as a variant of German idealism, 134
Rorty, Richard
  distinction between literary and philosophical texts, 4, 7, 256
  on the metaphor of representation, 297, 303, 304
  reading of *Nineteen Eighty-Four* (Orwell), 262–71, 273–4
Rudrum, David, 273
Russell, Bertrand, 1, 143
Ryan, Marie-Laure, 327

Saldívar, Ramón, 438, 439
Samatar, Sofia, 223
Samuels, Robert, 24, 27, 28, 76, 86–7
Sanklecha, Pranay, 329
Saunders, Frances Stonor, 459–61
Saussure, Ferdinand de, 399
Savat, David, 421, 422, 423
Scheler, Max, 200–1, 202
Schelling, Friedrich Wilhelm Joseph, 237, 239, 241
Schönfeld, Martin, 323
science
  empirical investigation, 154
  inexplicable properties of intentional phenomena, 154–5
science fiction
  as the blurring of real life and fiction, 221
  Haraway's worlding and, 218–19, 221
science-fictioning, 225
scientific philosophy, 1–2
scopic human
  within the capitalist assemblage, 341
  concept of, 341
  as the individualised embodiment of the accident, 345
  in *Oryx and Crake* (Atwood), 348, 350
Searle, John, 8, 14
security imaginary
  biopolitical logic of security, 433
  conjuncture with economic neoliberalism, 433–4, 436–7
  in contemporary fiction, 431
  under Trump's presidency, 446
  in *A Visit from the Goon Squad* (Egan), 442–4
Sedgwick, Eve Kosofsky, 410, 423, 424, 425, 426
the self
  in Buddhist philosophy, 145
  causal relations and, 147–8
  centrality of the individual in the novel, 414–15, 417–18, 420, 422–3
  as a collection of perceptions, 146–7
  disciplinary control over, 420–2
  economic individualism, 419
  as fictional object, 145
  the illusion of, 148–9
  Kantian concept of, 147
  kenosis, 244
  the liberal individual, 416, 420, 423
  multiple drafts of the narrative self, 145–6
  paranoid individuation, 424
  possessive individualism, 416–17
  post-Cartesian subject, 415–16, 418
  projective identification, 412–13
  the sense of self, 145
  unitary experiences and, 147
  'You Are Not Your Browser History' (Thorp), 31–2
  see also human subjectivity

Sellars, Wilfrid, 298
semiotics, 60
   the material-semiotic, 218, 221, 224, 227, 228
   narrative semiotics in Latour's Gaia project, 176, 180, 183, 186, 188–9
   semiotic codes, 44–5
   semiotic explosions, 63
   semiotic squares, 399
sensibilism, 299
sentimental novels, 208
Serres, Michel, 317, 340
Seshagiri, Urmila, 48
Shaviro, Steven, 432, 451
Shawl, Nisi, 223–4
Shelley, Percy
   Defence of Poetry, 130–1
   'England in 1819', 133–4
   'Hymn to Intellectual Beauty', 128–9
   'The Mask of Anarchy', 134
   'Mont Blanc', 129–31
   'Mutability', 132
   new worlds, theme of, 133–4
   Prometheus Unbound, 134
   strong correlationism in the poetry of, 128–31
The Ship (Honeywell)
   first-person narrative perspective, 326–8
   future-oriented second-personalism, 327
   intergenerational issues, 328–9
   overpopulation's impact, 329
   privileged narrators of, 323–4
   role of book narratives, 332
   separation of the haves and the have-nots, 325, 326
   the value of those worth saving, 330–1
Shonkwiler, Alison, 430, 431, 451
Shteyngart, Gary *see Super Sad True Love Story* (Shteyngart)
Singh, Nikhil Pal, 446
Smith, Ali, *Autumn*, 35–7
Socrates, 205
Solar (McEwan)
   Beard's single-minded instrumental thinking, 338, 339, 341–2
   geoengineering solutions to climate change, 342–3
   more holistic forms of human subjectivity, 339, 341
   neoliberal sustainability discourses, 338–9
   normalised form of Anthropocene human subjectivity, 338
   technologically-enabled mass consumption, 344, 346
   teleological sequentiality in, 343–4
the soul, 152–3
speculation
   and German idealism, 234
   and romanticism, 234

speculative idealism, 234
speculative pragmatism, 235, 246
speculative realism, 234
speculative writing
   genre of, 217
   speculative fabulation, 226–7
   The Third Policeman (O'Brien), 226
steampunk, *Everfair* (Shawl), 223–4
Stevens, Wallace, 291–5
The Stone Gods (Winterson)
   the embedded subject in, 353–4
   geopolitics of neoliberalism, 352, 353
   holistic forms of human subjectivity, 339, 341
   the Holocene to Anthropocene transition, 338
   investment in artificial intelligence, 352–3
   narrative of, 351–2
   security technologies, 339
Stowe, Harriet Beecher, *The American Woman's Home*, 210; *see also Uncle Tom's Cabin* (Stowe)
subject *see* human subjectivity
Super Sad True Love Story (Shteyngart)
   acronyms in, 84–5
   digitally created social inequalities, 90–1
   digitisation of the body, 77, 83–4
   dis/embodiment, 82, 92–3
   as finance novel, 430
   informational decontextualisation, 82–3
   language as data, 82, 85, 91–2
   Lenny's ambivalent relationship with digital technology, 88–91
   narratives, 82
   overextended metaphoric embodiments, 85–6
symbolism, 216
Szalay, Michael, 441, 442

Taleb, Nassim Nicholas, 227–8
Tambling, Jeremy, 419–20
Taylor, Charles, 302
technology
   the accident thesis and, 344–5
   in the Anthropocene, 340–1, 344–5
   geoengineering solutions to climate change, 342–3
   geoengineering solutions to the Anthropocene, 351
   security technologies, 339
television
   corporate media ecology, 441–2
   reality TV, 25, 58, 60
theory
   and modern artwork, 12
   the predicament of, 10
   the problem of theory (Kantian), 6–7, 10, 11, 13–14
   separation of reason and, 8
   in the twentieth century, 12–13

Thirlwell, Adam, *Kapow!* 50–1
Thomson, Charles, 25, 27, 28
Thoreau, Henry David
    application of intimationist aesthetic to, 306, 309–10
    on sentences, 297
    sources of aesthetic value, 305–6, 307
    subject-object relationship, 306
    see also Walden, or Life in the Woods (Thoreau)
Thorp, Jer, 'You Are Not Your Browser History', 31–2
thought
    cogito ergo sum, 415–16
    correlate of thinking and being, 123
    effect of sensibilism on, 299
    role of language in, 299
Tompkins, Jane P., 204, 207–10, 211
transcendentalism
    art and access to the transcendental layer, 235, 241–2, 245–6
    Emersonian, 234, 235–6, 241–2, 245–6
    Kantian concept of, 122, 123
    in relation to historicity, 1–2, 10
    transcendental empiricism, 241
    transcendental subjectivity, 3
    use of aistheis, 241
Trump, Donald, 34, 35, 56, 60, 446
truth
    ability to remake one's own truth, 58, 59–60
    as belief or political affiliation, 56–7
    concept of objective truth in *Nineteen Eighty-Four* (Orwell), 262–3, 264, 265–6, 267, 268, 270–1
    idea of pure truth, 8
    knowledge in cyberspace, 74
    notion of truth in fiction, 144
    within object-oriented ontology (OOO), 206
    polymodernism as a post-truth epoch, 34–7
    relationship with myth, 368
    search for in the protest novel, 204
    separation from language, 5
Twain, Mark, 191–2

uchronia
    Afrofuturism as, 221–3
    Black Panther, 224
    and the fiction/reality boundary, 216–17
    steampunk as, 223–4
Uexküll, Jakob von, 357
Uncle Tom's Cabin (Stowe)
    defence of sentimentality in, 210
    importance of the context of, 203–4
    James Baldwin's critique of, 204–7, 211
    Jane P. Tompkins's critique of, 207–10, 211
    as a protest novel, 204–5, 206
    as a rethinking of the human world, 209–10
    sociopolitical effects of, 203
    as symbiosis, 211–12
    virtuous sentimentality of, 204, 206–7
ustopia, 220
utopia, 216–17, 220

Vermeulen, Pieter, 322, 331
Vermeulen, Timotheus, 25, 28–9, 50, 59, 60
Virilio, Paul, 340–1, 344–5, 358
virtual humanism
    autonomy within, 87–92
    concept of, 76
    paradoxical subject position of, 76, 87–8
    in *Super Sad True Love Story* (Shteyngart), 88–92
A Visit from the Goon Squad (Egan)
    acronyms in, 56
    contingency in, 442, 444–5
    corporate media ecology, 441–2
    intrusions of the authentic, 66–7, 68
    and the logic of neoliberalism, 440–2
    mimetic closure, 67–8
    narrative, 55–6
    postmodernist tropes in, 57
    proleptic narrative in, 444–5
    renewal in, 65
    security and risk concerns of, 442–4
    sublimation of the symbolic, 62–5, 68–70
    televisual quality of, 441
    temporal setting of, 440
    time in, 445
    T-ing and the symbolic form, 64–5
    T-ing communication, 62–4
    truth and meaning in, 56–7
vitalism
    new materialisms as, 176, 234, 239, 241
    strong correlationism as, 128

Walden, or Life in the Woods (Thoreau)
    application of intimationist aesthetic to, 306, 309–10
    Thoreau's aesthetic in, 307–8
    use of metaphor in, 306–7, 308
Walters, Jess, 431
Warhol, Andy, 45–6
Watt, Ian, 414–15
Waxman, Wayne, 299
Wayne, Teddy *see Kapitoil* (Wayne)
When the Floods Came (Morrall)
    first-person narrative perspective, 326–8
    future-oriented second-personalism, 327
    intergenerational issues, 328–9
    population control issues, 329–30
    privileged narrators of, 323–4
    role of book narratives, 332
    the value of those worth saving, 325–6, 330–1

Whitehead, Alfred North, 1, 219
Whitehead, Colson *see The Intuitionist* (Whitehead)
Wiener, Norbert, 80, 88
Williams, Raymond, 41, 44
Wintertson, Jeanette *see The Stone Gods* (Winterson)
Wittgenstein, Ludwig
   the experience of pain, 286, 287
   and ordinary language criticism, 255, 259, 260, 264
   and the problem of the present, 279
   representationalist theory of language, 298
   return to the everyday, 3
   the subject's relation to society, 282–3, 287–8
Wolfe, Tom, 452
women
   as authors and readers, 208
   as overly emotional, 207–8
Woolf, Virginia
   Between the Acts, 153
   Mrs Dalloway, 46
   and the turn back to everydayness, 2–3, 11
Wordsworth, William
   bond with nature, 125–6, 127–8
   'Lines Written a Few Miles above Tintern Abbey', 127
   'Lines Written in Early Spring', 125–7
   weak correlationism in the work of, 126–8
worlding
   active gerund of, 219
   Afrofuturism as an example of, 222–4
   in *Black Panther*, 224
   contingency's role in narrative worlding, 228
   fictioning, 225
   Heidegger's concept of, 217, 219
   heteronymy, 227–8, 229–30
   homonymy, 227–8, 229–30
   hyperstition, 224–5
   inappropriate/d others, 218–19
   literary texts as agents of, 180–2
   the material-semiotic, 218, 221, 224, 227, 228
   as matter(ing), 219–20
   myth-science, 225
   in science fiction, 218–19, 221
   speculative fabulation, 226–7
   world to worlding, 218, 219, 225
   the world-function of language, 217–18
Wright, Richard, 207, 209
writing
   as bodily practice (*écriture féminine*), 105, 107–8
   as individuate-ing, 107
   as a practice, 112

The Year of the Flood (Atwood)
   biocentric ethics in, 355–7
   critique of religion and social movements, 355
   ecologically embedded political movements, 339, 354
   God's Gardeners, 339, 354–5
   and the transition from the Holocene to the Anthropocene, 338
Young, Julian, 239

Žižek, Slavoj, 26, 59, 60

EU representative:
Easy Access System Europe
Mustamäe tee 50, 10621 Tallinn, Estonia
Gpsr.requests@easproject.com

www.ingramcontent.com/pod-product-compliance
Lightning Source LLC
Chambersburg PA
CBHW080922300426
44115CB00018B/2916